ROUTLEDGE HANDBOOK OF INTERNATIONAL SPORT BUSINESS

T0383945

Contemporary sport business is international. From global sport competitions and events, sponsorship deals and broadcasting rights to labour markets and lucrative flows of tourists, anybody working in sport business today has to have an international perspective. This book offers the broadest and most in-depth guide to the key themes in international sport business today, covering every core area from strategy and marketing to finance, media and the law.

Including authors from more than twenty countries spanning the Americas, Europe, Asia, Africa and Australia, this handbook addresses the most important issues in the world of sport business from a uniquely global perspective. Each chapter examines a particular cross-section of business and sport, encompassing all levels from grassroots to professional and elite. Divided into seven major subject areas, it offers insights from experts on:

- International Sport Business Strategy
- Sport Marketing
- Sport Economics and Finance
- International Sport Law
- Sport Media and Communication
- Sport Tourism
- Sport Development

The *Routledge Handbook of International Sport Business* is an essential resource for any course on sport business, sport management or international business.

Mark Dodds is a Professor of Sport Management at SUNY Cortland, USA. Mark earned a JD from Marquette University Law School and is a doctoral candidate at the University of Jyväskylä, Finland. His research interests include legal issues in sport business and sport corruption.

Kevin Heisey is an Associate Professor in the College of Business Administration at the American University in the Emirates, Dubai, UAE where he served as Associate Dean and director of the Sports Management and Master of Business Administration programmes. He currently serves as adjunct professor and subject matter expert in the "Economic & Financial

Management of Sport" component of the Master of Science in Sport Management at Liberty University, Lynchburg, Virginia, USA. Among his research interests are global sport business (finance, economics and marketing) and sport for development and peace.

Aila Ahonen is a Senior Lecturer at JAMK University of Applied Sciences, Finland. She teaches Sport Management and Sport Marketing, and her research areas are related to sport entrepreneurship and sport events. She is a board member of the European Association for Sport Management (EASM).

ROUTLEDGE HANDBOOK OF INTERNATIONAL SPORT BUSINESS

Edited by Mark Dodds,
Kevin Heisey and Aila Ahonen

LONDON AND NEW YORK

First published 2018 by Routledge

2 Park Square, Milton Park, Abingdon, Oxfordshire OX14 4RN
52 Vanderbilt Avenue, New York, NY 10017

Routledge is an imprint of the Taylor & Francis Group, an informa business

First issued in paperback 2020

British Library Cataloguing-in-Publication Data
A catalogue record for this book is available from the British Library

Library of Congress Cataloging-in-Publication Data
Names: Dodds, Mark, editor. | Heisey, Kevin editor. | Ahonen, Aila editor.
Title: Routledge handbook of international sport business / Edited by Mark Dodds,
Kevin Heisey and Aila Ahonen.
Description: Abingdon, Oxon ; New York, NY : Routledge, 2018. |
Series: Routledge international handbooks | Includes bibliographical references and index.
Identifiers: LCCN 2017015612 | ISBN 9781138891548 (hardback) |
ISBN 9781315709635 (ebook)
Subjects: LCSH: Sports—Economic aspects—Cross-cultural studies. |
Sports administration—Cross-cultural studies. | Sports—Marketing—
Cross-cultural studies.
Classification: LCC GV716 .R68 2018 | DDC 338.47796—dc23
LC record available at https://lccn.loc.gov/2017015612

ISBN: 978-1-138-89154-8 (hbk)
ISBN: 978-0-367-89687-4 (pbk)

Typeset in Bembo
by Keystroke, Neville Lodge, Tettenhall, Wolverhampton

CONTENTS

Contents

CONTRIBUTORS

Christina Aicher is a 2016 master's degree graduate from the Sports, Culture and Event Management Programme at the FH Kufstein, Austria.

Gerard A. Akindes is currently working for the Josoor Institute in Doha, Qatar. His roles with the Josoor Institute consist of organizing training and coordinating research projects in sport and events management. His research interests include sports broadcasting, elite athletes' migration and sports development and sports for development.

Emmanuel Bayle is Professor of Sport Management at the Institute of Sport Sciences, University of Lausanne (ISSUL), Switzerland. He has published several books and articles on Sports Management (*Great Leaders in Sport*, *Governance in Sport Organizations*, *CSR and Sport*) and also on the subjects of CSR and non-profit management. He is a specialist with regard to the governance, management and performance of Olympic sport organizations.

John Beech is an Honorary Research Fellow at Coventry University, UK. His main research interests are the (mis)management of football clubs as businesses and the net impact of sports mega-events. He lectures regularly at various European universities and is an International Professor at the Russian International Olympic University in Sochi, Russia.

Serkan Berber is a PhD Lecturer in the Sports Management Department at Anadolu University Faculty of Sports Sciences, Turkey. His research interests include sport events, sport tourism and sport management. He has published several articles in journals such as the *Journal of Human Kinetics*.

Louise Bielzer is Professor of International Event Management at Reinhold-Würth campus at the University of Heilbronn, Germany. Her research interests concentrate on corporate branded spaces, event venue development and management issues, although she often conducts comparative research in different sectors of the sport, cultural and business events industry.

Simon Boyes is Director of the Centre for Sports Law at Nottingham Law School, Nottingham Trent University, UK. Simon teaches, researches and publishes in a range of areas focusing on the interaction of the law with sport. He is co-author of the leading UK sports law student text.

Natasha T. Brison is an Assistant Professor at Texas A&M University in College Station, Texas, USA. Her research focuses on sport entity branding with an emphasis on value creation, management and protection through marketing and legal strategies. She has published several articles in journals such as the *Sport Marketing Quarterly* and the *Journal of Legal Aspects of Sport*.

Richard J. Buning is an Assistant Professor of Tourism, Conventions and Event Management in the School of Physical Education and Tourism Management at Indiana University–Purdue University Indianapolis, USA. His research focuses on sport tourism, event management and sport development.

Lauren M. Burch is an Assistant Professor of Marketing at Indiana University–Purdue University Columbus, USA. Her research interests include new media, framing, sport communication and marketing.

Kerri Cebula is an Assistant Professor of Sport Management and Leadership Studies at Kutztown University of Pennsylvania, USA. Her research interests include college athletics, motorsport and intellectual property law.

Sungho Cho is an Associate Professor of Sport Management at Bowling Green State University, Ohio, USA. His research interests include the use of social science methodology in legal research. He has published articles on the legal aspects of sport in journals such as the *Journal of Legal Aspects of Sport*.

Bogdan Ciomaga is a graduate student at Brock University, Canada, with an interest in organizational behaviour, sport policy and sport ethics. He has published in *European Sport Management Quarterly*, *Quest*, the *Journal of Sport Philosophy*, the *International Journal of Sport Policy and Politics* and *Sport, Ethics and Philosophy*.

Josephine Clausen is a PhD candidate at the Institute of Sports Studies at the University of Lausanne, Switzerland. Her research interests include management practices and organizational change in, and professionalization of, International Sport Federations. Before starting her PhD, she worked for three years at the Union Cycliste Internationale (International Cycling Union).

Pedro Guedes de Carvalho was the Dean of the Human and Social Sciences Faculty at the University of Beira Interior, Portugal, and PhD Professor of Economics. He has published around 30 articles in applied economics forums in sport, tourism and regional development. During his career he coordinated several university projects. He is currently a member of the ICSSPE Executive Board.

Heather L. Dichter is a Principal Lecturer in Sport Management at the Leicester Castle Business School and the International Centre for Sports History and Culture at De Montfort University, UK. Her research on sport and diplomacy has appeared in the *International Journal of the History of Sport* and in her co-edited book, *Diplomatic Games*.

Dan Drane is Chair for the Department of Physical Education, Sport and Human Performance at Winthrop University, USA. His research interests are related to sport management, marketing and youth sports.

Evan L. Frederick is currently an Assistant Professor of Sport Administration at the University of Louisville, USA. His research interests include fan–athlete interaction on social media platforms, as well as organizational communication through social media.

Matthew A. Gilbert, MBA, is an instructor of management and marketing at the American University in the Emirates. His research interests include educational technology and social media marketing. His first book, *edX E-Learning Course Development*, helps teachers and trainers design, develop and deploy a MOOC course for the edX platform.

Kyriaki (Kiki) Kaplanidou is an Associate Professor in the Department of Tourism, Recreation and Sport Management at the University of Florida, USA. Her research interests focus on the impacts and legacies that mega-sport events have on the quality of life of the residents of host cities.

Robert Kaspar is Assistant Professor of Sport Management at Seeburg Castle University (SCU) in Salzburg, Austria. His academic experiences in the field of sport and events management range from Austria to France and Russia. He is the co-editor of *The Business of Events Management*, published by Pearson Education in 2014.

Sara Keshkar is an Associate Professor of Sport Management at Allameh Tabataba'i University in Tehran, Iran. Her research interests include sport marketing and communications. She has published several articles and books on these subjects.

Lisa A. Kihl is an Associate Professor of Sport Management at the University of Minnesota, USA. Her research focuses on athletes' roles in sport governance, corruption in sport, corporate social responsibility and leadership. She has published her work in the *Journal of Sport Management,* the *Sport Management Review* and *Administration and Society.*

Kyoo Hong Kim is a Professor Emeritus of Economics at Bowling Green State University, Ohio, USA. His research interests include the application of game theory to sports economics. He has published articles on economic theory in journals such as the *Journal of Economic Theory*.

Carina Klein is a 2016 master's degree graduate from the Sports, Culture and Event Management Programme at the FH Kufstein, Austria.

Darlene A. Kluka is the Dean of the School of Human Performance and Leisure Sciences at Barry University, Florida, USA, and full Professor in Sport Management. Her research includes sport governance and women and sport. She has served as a member of the COSMA Board for two terms. She has published over 100 articles in the area of sport.

Brendon Knott is an Associate Professor in the Sport Management Department at the Cape Peninsula University of Technology in Cape Town, South Africa. He lectures and conducts research in applied areas of sport marketing, branding, sport tourism and sport mega-events, currently focusing on place branding through sport.

Brian D. Krohn is an Assistant Professor in the Department of Tourism, Conventions and Event Management at Indiana University–Purdue University Indianapolis, USA. His research is focused on consumer behaviour in the contexts of sport tourism, especially golf tourism, and includes the areas of motivation, satisfaction and decision-making.

Osmo Laitila is a sport management researcher at Haaga-Helia University of Applied Sciences, Finland, and part-time teacher at JAMK University of Applied Sciences, Finland. His research interests include sport business intelligence solutions, sport events and sport fans. He is a member of the EASM network and has presented his research at annual EASM conferences and contributed to several research papers and publications as co-author.

Dongfeng Liu is a Professor of Sport Management and Co-Dean of the Management School at the Shanghai University of Sport, China. He also holds an international professorship at INSEEC Business School. He has co-authored two books with Routledge and published over 30 articles on sport economics and management in peer-reviewed journals.

Tara Mahoney is an Associate Professor of Sport Management at SUNY Cortland, USA. Her research interests include participation sport, social media in sport and experiential learning in sport. She has published work in multiple international journals including the *International Journal of Sport Management and Marketing*, the *Nonprofit and Voluntary Sector Quarterly* and *Leisure Sciences*.

Vicky Martin is Chair of the Undergraduate Programme and Professor in Sport Management at Liberty University, Lynchburg, Virginia, USA. Her research interests include sport marketing, sociology of sport and sport ministry. She has published book chapters on sport management and also presented at sport management-related conferences.

Lauren McCoy is an Assistant Professor in Recreation and Sport Administration at Western Kentucky University, USA. She received her bachelor's degree from Stanford University and her law degree from Marquette University School of Law. Her research interests include legal issues associated with social media, athletes' rights and discrimination concerns.

Juthika Mehta is a marketing and communications professional at the Olympians Association of India and an Associate Faculty at the International Institute of Sports Management. Her research interests are organizational and governance structures in global sport. Her enthusiasm involves professionalizing sport management in India.

Ann Pegoraro is an Associate Professor in the School of Sports Administration at Laurentian University, Sudbury, Ontario, Canada. Her research primarily focuses on the intersection of sport and new media.

Risto Rasku is a Senior Lecturer at JAMK University of Applied Sciences/Sport Business School Finland, Jyväskylä. His research interests include business intelligence and sport marketing. He has edited books and published several articles on sport business in different journals.

Jim Reese is an Associate Professor at the American Public University System at Drexel University, Pennsylvania, USA. His research interests include ticket sales and ticket operations. He is the editor and author of multiple chapters in the sport management textbook, *Ticket Operations and Sales Management in Sport*.

Jonathan Robertson is a Lecturer in Sport Management at Deakin University, Melbourne, Australia. His research interests include social responsibility, entrepreneurship and organizations in the sport industry.

Sari Savolainen is a postdoctoral researcher in entrepreneurship, family business and cognitive science. She has worked as visiting researcher and professor in several universities in Europe. Before her academic career she worked as a specialist in entrepreneurship and business at her own company for more than 25 years.

Guido Schafmeister is Managing Partner at the Sport Management Academy of Bayreuth, Germany, and was a professor of media management. His research interests include sports and media as well as value creation. He has published articles in journals such as the *European Sport Management Quarterly* and the *International Journal of Event and Festival Management*.

Katie Schlenker is a Senior Lecturer in the Management Discipline Group at the UTS Business School, University of Technology Sydney, Australia. Her research interests and publications are in the areas of event evaluation, particularly the social impacts of events on host communities, sport event legacies, event leveraging strategies and the impacts of business events.

Nico Schulenkorf is Senior Lecturer for Sport Management at the University of Technology Sydney, Australia. His research focuses on the social, cultural and health-related outcomes of international sport-for-development and event management projects. He is co-founder and editor of the *Journal of Sport for Development*.

Susanne Schulz is a 2016 master's degree graduate from the Sports, Culture and Event Management Programme at the FH Kufstein, Austria.

Eric C. Schwarz is a Senior Lecturer in Sport Management, Chair of the Postgraduate Courses in Sport Business and Integrity and an Associate with the Institute of Sport, Exercise and Active Living (ISEAL) at Victoria University in Melbourne, Australia. His research interests include sport marketing, sport facility management and sport event management.

Valentina Starkova is a native of Almaty, Kazakhstan and currently a head tennis professional at Lakewood Country Club in Dallas, Texas, USA. Valentina obtained her master's degree in Sports Management and Administration at Liberty University, Virginia, while assisting the women's tennis team as a team manager.

Tim Ströbel is a Research Associate and Senior Lecturer at the Institute of Sport Science, University of Bern, Switzerland. His research interests include branding and sponsoring strategies in sport. He has presented several conference papers, book chapters and articles in journals such as the *European Sport Management Quarterly* and *Event Management*.

Rebecca Studin is a Chancellor's Academic Award recipient and Academic All-American from SUNY Cortland, USA. She is currently employed in the golf industry.

Claudia Stura is the Vice Director of Studies Sports, Culture and Event Management at Kufstein University of Applied Sciences in Austria. Her research interests are related to conflict management in sports teams and the use of sport as a tool in conflict reconciliation.

Kamilla Swart is a Professor and Masters in Sport Management Programme Director in the College of Business Administration, American University in the Emirates. Her research focus is on sport tourism and events, with a particular interest in policies, strategies and evaluation. She serves as Regional Editor (Africa) for the *Journal of Destination Marketing and Management*.

Lucie Thibault is a Professor at Brock University, Ontario, Canada. Her research interests include management, policy and governance of sport organizations. She serves on the editorial board of the *International Journal of Sport Policy and Politics* and the *European Sport Management Quarterly* and has published several scholarly articles, edited books and chapters in edited books.

Cem Tinaz is the Director of the School of Sport Sciences and Technology at Istanbul Bilgi University, Turkey. He has published in the areas of sport policy, sport event management and sport sponsorship. He has also participated as tournament coordinator, director and marketing manager at many international tennis events.

Douglas Michele Turco is a Senior Research Associate at the Sport Business School, Finland, and an expert in sport tourism and consumer behaviour.

Stefan Unterlechner is a 2016 master's degree graduate from the Sports, Culture and Event Management Programme at the FH Kufstein, Austria.

Noud van Herpen is a Senior Lecturer in Sport Management at The Hague University of Applied Sciences, the Netherlands. His research focuses on the evaluation of World and European championships, which can be used for sport business intelligence. He has published several articles related to this and has presented his work at many EASM conferences.

Derek Van Rheenen is an Associate Adjunct Professor and the Director of the Athletic Study Center at the University of California, Berkeley, USA. His research interests include cultural studies of sport, sport tourism and social sustainability. His publications have appeared in the *International Review for the Sociology of Sport* and the *Journal of Sport & Tourism*.

Herbert Woratschek is Professor and Head of Services Department at the University of Bayreuth, Germany. His research interests include value co-creation, service quality, and fan and sponsor engagement in sport. He has published over 140 articles in journals such as the *Journal of Service Research*, the *European Sport Management Quarterly*, the *Australasian Marketing Journal*, the *Journal of Strategic Marketing*, the *Marketing Journal of Research and Management*, the *Journal of Relationship Marketing*, the *Journal of Brand Management* and the *Journal of Retailing and Consumer Services*.

INTRODUCTION

Mark Dodds, Kevin Heisey and Aila Ahonen

The business of sport has become an international industry. Sport mega-events, sponsorships, teams and clubs, leagues, athletes, cities and countries, and just about every other type of sport organization that can be envisioned, are now competing in the global marketplace. These groups compete for revenue, viewers, fans and players. Because the industry has become international, the study of it also needs to be international.

This handbook began with that thought. It includes the work of authors from more than 20 different countries. These international scholars address sport business issues from almost every corner of the world. They examine the intersection of sport and international business with attention concentrated on the business decisions and outcomes from organizations engaged in the international sport business industry. Each individual topic reflects a relevant cross-section of business subjects and sport, and brings a unique and international perspective to the subject matter. These topics investigate professional, amateur and grassroots sport, mega and local events, global branding and third world sport development, tourism and media, gender issues and more.

The handbook is divided into seven subject areas, which allows grouping of the individual chapters based on common business-oriented themes. The subject areas are: international sport business strategy; sport marketing; sport economics and finance; legal aspects; sport media and communication; sport tourism; and sport development.

International sport business strategy

This section investigates the motivations, rationale and tactics used by sport organizations to expand operations into different cultures. International business strategy is considered from mega-event, International Sport Federation and educational perspectives.

Sport marketing

This section deals with the globalization of sport organizations and corporations reaching across borders. Sport sponsorship, sport consumer behaviour and branding decisions are influenced by cultural differences including gender and religious issues.

Sport economics and finance

This section surveys the economic issues in global sport. Among these issues are the economic impact of sport on a host nation or city, trade issues effecting sport merchandise and events, international taxation and ticket distribution issues.

Legal aspects

This section examines many legal issues associated with international sport business. Because sport crosses international boundaries, there are many conflicting laws and jurisdictions that need to be examined. These laws include intellectual property rights, corruption laws and governance concerns.

Sport media and communication

This section looks at the key aspects of sport media and the evolution of broadcasting in sport. The current generation has witnessed major technological innovations that have affected how fans consume and interact with sport. The topics range from sport sponsors using new media, sport organizations expanding into new cultures via media to sport media development in the Middle East and Africa.

Sport tourism

This section explores sport tourism and how it generates a significant flow of travellers worldwide. It includes discussion of both mega-events and grassroots events, active tourism, the use of facility and architecture and sustainability.

Sport development

This section considers sport as a catalyst for economic activity through entrepreneurism. The topics vary from developing an economically viable professional sport league, to the increased opportunity for female participation in sport and using sport to create change within a culture.

While there have been other international sport publications, this book is unique. The authors explore the international sport business industry through a focus on key issues to highlight the important business theory and concepts. The chosen areas provide current and topical information on the trends of sport business around the world.

The contributions in this book enhance the reputation of international sport business research. This is a growing area for examination. The editors expect that international studies, analysis, articles and reports will become more common at every sport-related academic proceeding. In fact, the authors within this book are the leaders of this movement, choosing to live, work, teach and lecture in different cultures.

Finally, the editors hope this book inspires other researchers, teachers and students to explore the sport world. It is important to challenge ourselves to "get out of our comfort areas" and investigate other societies.

Mark, Kevin and Aila

PART I

International sport business strategy

International sport business strategy involves positioning for the future which can involve developing corporate strategies in order to grow a sport organization, developing ways to expand into new geographic territories or developing strategies to build marketing, finance or human resource capacity. Strategy is part of the "big picture" planning process and a systematic approach includes assessing the environment, developing concepts and designing implementation plans. As the sport business has rapidly become a global one, many sport organizations have broadened their strategic focus to leverage and create international opportunities.

The chapters in Part I address international sport business strategy from different perspectives. The authors investigate mega-event bidding, the use of business analytics, the expansion of international sport into new geographic regions, new competitive formats and new educational practices.

1

EXPORT OF NATIONAL SPORT LEAGUES

Herbert Woratschek, Guido Schafmeister and Tim Ströbel

Introduction

The majority of elite sport leagues and clubs are organized as profit-oriented firms that must be managed in the same way as any other professional businesses. In European sport, football is the most advanced sport in this regard. The top five European clubs, Real Madrid CF, FC Barcelona, Manchester United FC, Paris Saint-Germain FC and FC Bayern Munich, generated €2.61 billion during the 2014/2015 season (Deloitte Sports Business Group, 2016). Sponsorship, media, and match day revenues from the largest 122 European football clubs reached €13.27 billion in 2014, which is equivalent to 67 per cent of the total revenues of the four major North American sports, the National Football League (NFL), Major League Basketball (MLB, the National Basketball Association (NBA) and the National Hockey League (NHL) (UEFA, 2015). European football leagues such as the English Premier League, the Spanish La Liga, the Italian Lega Serie A and the German Bundesliga are continuously seeking additional income.

Over the last years, most clubs and leagues focused on domestic markets to generate income. Even in sport management research, the analysis of match day revenues or gate receipts played an increasingly important role (e.g. Becker & Suls, 1983; Bird, 1982; Borland, 1987; Borland & Lye, 1992; Crains, Jennett, & Sloane, 1986; Czarnitzki & Stadtmann, 2002; Davies, Downward, & Jackson, 1995; Janssens & Késenne, 1987; Jennett, 1984; Peel & Thomas, 1988, 1992, 1996; Schofield, 1983; Siegfried & Eisenberg, 1980; Simmons, 1996; Wilson & Sim, 1995). The English Premier League was one of the first leagues to invest in marketing activities in foreign countries. This export of the national league enabled the Premier League to sell broadcasting rights as an opportunity to generate additional income in new markets outside Europe. Besides revenues of £5.14 billion from domestic broadcasting rights in the UK for the period 2016 to 2019, the Premier League is about to get £3.2 billion from international broadcasting rights for the same three years (*Daily Mail*, 2016).

The example of the Premier League shows that the focus in European football is on the export of national sport leagues. Of course, other opportunities to generate income such as merchandise, ticketing, sponsorships or naming rights still belong to the main income sources of leagues and clubs. Nevertheless, our focus is on the export of national sport leagues due to the large economic potential. Moreover, capacity restrictions do not exist. Stadium attendance has a natural boundary – the stadium capacity. The export of national leagues either via television or via internet broadcast does not possess any capacity restrictions.

Additional TV viewers all over the world do not compete for a limited amount of tickets. Furthermore, TV or internet broadcasts generate additional income but the additional costs for these broadcasts are rather low. Broadcasting signals usually exist for the domestic markets. Transmitting matches to foreign countries may create a need for foreign language commentaries but the infrastructure for transmitting signals already exists.

Due to the competitive advantage of the English Premier League over other European football leagues and the economic potential of the export of national sport leagues in general, we address the following research questions: How will international sales of European football leagues develop in future years? What are the opportunities and risks? What needs to be considered by the leagues' management to be attractive for international sales? Where are the most attractive target markets?

In order to answer these questions, this chapter first provides a theoretical background to sport broadcasting demand. A new theoretical demand model for the export of sport leagues is introduced. Second, the results of an empirical study with football managers in Europe involved in international sales activities of national sport leagues are presented. Third, based on the theoretical demand model and empirical insights, the opportunities and risks associated with the export of national sport leagues are discussed.

A demand model for the export of sport leagues

Export opportunities for national sport leagues only exist if there is a demand for broadcasts in foreign countries. Hence, the demand for sport broadcasts is the pivotal point. In general, the demand for sport broadcasts can be compared with the demand for stadium attendance. Relevant literature on stadium attendance is extensive, as is the list of possible influences on attendance. Among these are sport-specific influences such as the popularity of clubs and players (e.g. Baimbridge, Cameron & Dawson, 1995; Czarnitzki & Stadtmann, 2002; Janssens & Késenne, 1987) or the competitive balance in a league (e.g. Borland, 1987; Borland & Lye, 1992; Czarnitzki & Stadtmann, 2002; Dobson & Goddard, 1992; Hynds & Smith, 1994; Peel & Thomas, 1988, 1992, 1996; Szymanski, 2001). Furthermore, the relevance of each match in a championship competition has an impact on attendance (e.g. Borland & Lye, 1992; Czarnitzki & Stadtmann, 2002; Dobson & Goddard, 1992; Wilson & Sim, 1995) as do weather conditions, day of the week, or time of the day (e.g. Baimbridge, Cameron & Dawson, 1995, 1996; Czarnitzki & Stadtmann, 2002; Janssens & Késenne, 1987; Peel & Thomas, 1988; Schofield, 1983; Siegfried & Hinshaw, 1979). Last but not least, fan identification and motives influence sport spectators' behaviour (Borland, 1987; Borland & Lye, 1992; Campbell, Aiken & Kent, 2004; Czarnitzki & Stadtmann, 2002; Donavan, Carlson & Zimmermann, 2005; Funk, Mahony & Ridinger, 2002; Kahle, Kambara & Rose, 1996; LeAnne Spenner, Fenn & Crooker, 2004; Matsuoka, Chelladurai & Harada, 2003; Peel & Thomas, 1992; Robinson, Trail, Dick & Gillentine, 2005; Sutton, McDonald, Milne & Cimperman, 1997; Trail, Robinson, Dick & Gillentine, 2003; Trail, Fink & Anderson, 2003; Wann & Branscombe, 1993; Wann, Melnick, Russell & Pease, 2001; Woratschek, Durchholz, Maier & Ströbel, 2017). The influence factors listed affect both stadium attendance and TV audience ratings, although the strength of the influences might be different for stadium attendance and TV audiences. Nevertheless, these influence factors determine the demand for stadium attendance and TV broadcasts.

The majority of the existing literature focuses on the demand for certain matches on a certain day at a certain time. These analyses explain why the number of spectators fluctuates between different matches. Negotiations about broadcasting rights for the upcoming seasons are usually finalized well before the start of the next season. At that time, customers do not know anything about the weather conditions on certain days in the upcoming season. They do not even know which clubs will be part of the league. Relegation and promotion will cause changes. Furthermore, how will star players be involved? Do they still play successfully or might they even play at another club?

Consequently, we need a more general approach for the analysis of broadcasting rights. Information about the attractiveness of a particular national sport league is necessary. Information about the influence factors of average expected demand is more relevant than knowledge of the influence of rain or sunshine on the demand for a specific game. Therefore, the following paragraphs discuss a league's popularity, consumption capital and the buying power of the target market population as well as competition and TV market structure.

Popularity

The popularity of national sport leagues, clubs and players seems to determine the demand for broadcasting rights (Ferreira & Armstrong, 2004). Popularity makes a national sport league more attractive for foreign TV stations and the probability of international sales increases. The popularity of a national sport league often refers to a certain style of playing that is characteristic for the league, for example "kick and rush" was a long-time characteristic of English football clubs and "tiki-taka" was particularly associated with the style of playing of FC Barcelona. Of course, the uncertainty of the outcome of the league competitions as well as of single matches is also important. Popularity should usually increase with uncertainty and competitive balance (e.g. Rishe & Mondello, 2004; Schmidt & Berri, 2001).

Furthermore, the national monopoly of the sport leagues is a critical factor in their popularity. The monopoly is a credible signal for spectators that the nominated champion is without a doubt the best national club team. The monopoly is a unique selling proposition for the sale of broadcasting rights both domestically and internationally (Baimbridge, Cameron & Dawson, 1996).

The popularity of a national sport league will further increase if its clubs participate successfully in international competitions. International competitions such as the UEFA Champions League or the UEFA Europa League are important for the popularity of national leagues because clubs and players can present themselves to a broader audience. The better they perform at the international level the more likely the export of broadcasting rights seems to be since the interest of foreign spectators increases. In contrast, poor performance at the international level will reduce the popularity of a national league in the same manner as strong performance increases it. Hence, it is a key challenge for league managers to promote clubs and athletes to deliver their best performance.

Another critical factor for a league's popularity is having star players (Brandes, Franck & Nüesch, 2007). Appointing star players from other countries is an opportunity to boost the interest of foreign TV viewers. However, the focus on foreign star players can only have a short-term perspective. A league's popularity will suffer as soon as the foreign players leave for clubs in other countries. Hence, foreign players can be "useful" to boost the popularity in a short-term perspective, but long-term investments, such as continuous success in international competitions, are also necessary.

Consumption capital

Exporting national sport leagues will be difficult if the sport and its key characteristics are unknown in foreign markets. The target population should have at least some knowledge of the particular type of sport. In fact, this knowledge does not exist automatically as the intercultural context might lead to different preferences. For example, European football has been relatively unknown in North America for a long time, just as American football has in Europe. Consequently, European and American football teams have started to engage in the corresponding markets with invitation matches, official league matches played abroad or branch offices in order to build up knowledge of their sport. The theoretical background to this development refers to consumption capital theory. Stigler and Becker (1977) argue that consumers derive a higher utility from using products or services if they know more about the corresponding product or service. The same is true for sport marketing. If spectators know the rules, understand the style of playing and recognize star players, they will derive a higher utility from watching a game than spectators that do not have the same knowledge.

Knowledge in the sense of consumption capital is built up by using the product or service and learning more about it. Using and learning are investments in future consumption and lead to higher utility. In terms of European football, learning the rules would be an investment in future consumption for a North American spectator, for example. The same is true for knowledge of certain clubs and players.

In terms of sport in general, playing sport is another way to learn more about a certain type of sport. If a person plays football, watching the games of a national league provides a higher utility since players' moves will be understood with reference to his/her own practical experiences. European football is definitely a sport with a high consumption capital. In many countries around the world, children learn at a young age how to play football. Moreover, football is a topic of conversation in social life and in the news. Nevertheless, successful investment in consumption capital depends on the cultural context and society in general. Therefore, the analysis of consumption capital is a necessary requirement for the export of national sport leagues. An export will only be successful if a certain consumption capital is available or can be built up quickly. Of course, national leagues can support investments in consumption capital, but it seems to take a long time to increase consumption capital. That is why it seems useful to focus first on countries with an existing high level of consumption capital.

Buying power of the population in foreign countries

The main purpose of the export of national sport leagues is to generate income. In this sense, the buying power of the population in different foreign countries must be considered. Broadcasting fees depend, among other factors, on the buying power of the population (Woratschek & Schafmeister, 2005). This becomes obvious for pay TV since the TV viewers must pay for the broadcast. The amount of their payment will depend on their willingness and ability to pay. The latter is related to the buying power of a population. Private TV stations depend on advertising revenues. The advertisers' willingness to pay will increase with higher sales expectations. With regard to the export of national sport leagues, a primary focus should be on countries with a high buying power in the population, regardless of the sport league's broadcasting situation in the recipient country.

Competition

A football game in a stadium is a relatively unique experience. Similar experiences are only possible if similar clubs are close by. However, TV broadcasts are different. First, they are recordable. Second, they are in close competition to other broadcasts. Switching costs do not exist for TV viewers. They can easily switch to another channel. Leaving the stadium is usually more complicated and causes significant switching costs. Furthermore, TV viewers can switch to another channel to check the programme and easily return. The stadium visitor must leave the stadium and returning to the game is very unlikely. TV viewers remain more flexible concerning competing activities, which enforces the competition in the TV context. Therefore, competition is another critical factor for the export of national sport leagues. Besides other sport leagues, many competing cultural and leisure activities exist. If a certain weekday or a certain time of the day is already reserved for other activities, sport broadcasts can hardly succeed.

Moreover, time difference plays a role. Live broadcasts are usually more popular than recorded ones. For example, the NFL Super Bowl usually starts with the kick off at 6.30 pm Eastern US Time, which corresponds with 12.30 am Central European Time. Successful exports of sport events with such a time difference do not seem very likely. The national sport league has two opportunities to react – first, to focus on countries with smaller or no time difference and, second, to reschedule the kick-off to a more suitable time for the foreign country. However, the decision between national preferences and international export should depend on the expected revenues. If the export revenues are relatively small in comparison to revenues from the domestic market, the focus should remain on the traditional time slot, as in the case of the NFL Super Bowl on Sunday evening at 6.30 pm. Rescheduling seems to be an option particularly for those sports with a relatively small customer base in their domestic markets.

Structure of foreign TV markets

The attractiveness of foreign countries for the export of broadcasting rights also depends on the existence and structure of the pay TV sector. A country seems to be more attractive if the pay TV sector is well established and free-to-air television is rather weak. This assumption is supported by the observed amount paid for sport broadcasting rights in countries with a well-established pay TV sector. The broadcasting fees are usually higher in countries with a well-established and competitive pay TV sector (Solberg, 2002).

Interview study – Export of national sport leagues

Study design

This study consisted of interviews with nine sport managers who deal with the export of national sport leagues. The focus was on the German Bundesliga. Two managers are CEOs of Bundesliga clubs, one manager is responsible for the international relations of a Bundesliga club, four managers work for TV channels (one of them for a German TV channel and three for foreign TV stations respectively), one interviewee is manager of a league administration department and another is manager of an international broadcasting rights dealer.

An interview guideline based on the theoretical demand model for the export of sport leagues was developed for each interview. The interview questions covered the following topics:

1. The status quo of export.
2. The demand for sport broadcasts of domestic and foreign sport leagues.
3. Comparisons of the German Bundesliga and other European football leagues.

4. Market players.
5. Opportunities, threats and future goals.

All interviews were conducted between September and October 2005. At that time, the German Bundesliga was negotiating a new broadcasting rights deal. This contract was signed in December 2005. Furthermore, the Bundesliga management started to focus on internationalization and export of the Bundesliga to foreign markets. Comparing the results and insights from the 2005 interviews with current business reality is also very interesting: the theoretical model and most of the expected developments have been proved true.

Results[1]

The interviewed managers identified tremendous differences between the European leagues in terms of export. In particular, the German Bundesliga had a high backlog in terms of export: "*The Premier League earns 12 to 15 times more, the Italian and the Spanish leagues four to six times more than the German league*" (VI). The interviewed managers were sure that additional export opportunities did exist for the German Bundesliga, but they agreed as well that using the opportunities would take time. Taking this status quo into account, the main focus of the interview study was to explore reasons for the different situations of the European football leagues.

Last mover disadvantage

Looking at the German Bundesliga management, the interviewed managers claimed several mistakes. For example, nothing was done to sell the German Bundesliga internationally: "*At the moment the priority of sales efforts in Germany is on domestic sales*" (I); the other European leagues "*have ten years more of experience in international sales. They have an organizational structure and the organizational processes to sell internationally*" (V); "In England or Italy, there are many people working on international sales. They do not only have agencies working on this issue, but administrative staff in the league and the clubs" (II). The main reason for this inactivity was the high revenues from the domestic sales of broadcasting rights: "*Usually, the focus was on domestic sale*" (IV); "*Nobody thought of international sales. Unfortunately, that was the time when German football clubs were successful internationally. International sales came first to mind when the revenues went down*" (V).

Superstars

A national sport league has to belong to the top leagues of the world in order to sell internationally, but international star players did not play for the German Bundesliga: "*There is no German player who can make dreams come true*" (IX). All in all, there were not enough big names playing for the German Bundesliga: "*Foreign players in the Bundesliga draw attention in their home countries only but not internationally*" (VIII). Star players from foreign countries are another prerequisite for international sales: "*If tomorrow Wolfsburg hires three French players then the top club in France would be Wolfsburg*" (VIII). This statement gives an impression of the importance of star players for single clubs and the national sport leagues: "*Today the reality of the Bundesliga is very good, but you have to sell something more. You have to . . . create stories . . . week after week, day after day, you speak about it. You promote it*" (VIII). International star players were missing in the German Bundesliga: "*TV viewers are interested in stars and these stars play in other leagues, but not in the German Bundesliga. My point of view is that people watch foreign sport leagues to see stars*" (I). Star players create demand in foreign countries: "*For the Bundesliga, to be more attractive, there is for sure a need to attract some of the best players in the world. If you have . . . players like that than you have an interest all over the world*" (VIII). Additionally, players from foreign countries help to bridge cultural differences: "*But they have to play continuously. It is not enough if they are only waiting to replace other players on the field*" (IV). Furthermore, a lack of international well-known clubs has a negative impact on exports: "*They want to see stars. When I talk about stars, it is not only the players. The club is also a star. You can see it with Bayern Munich, Real Madrid, Juventus Turin, and Chelsea. You have stars inside the team, but the club itself is also a star*" (IX). Or to put in another way: "*There is one issue correlating with the international demand: How many good clubs belong to the national league? Are these clubs internationally known brands? England has at least four, Italy three to four, and Spain at least two international brands. Germany has only one*" (VII); "*Clubs that play continuously in the Champions League are by nature perceived as brands, even in Asia*" (VI); National sport leagues are better off in terms of export if two or three teams of the national leagues perform well on the international level (VI); "*It is important to have more clubs besides FC Bayern Munich that are also international brands*" (IV).

International sport competitions

German football clubs were not successful enough in the past to play an important role in international competitions. FC Bayern Munich is the only German club that belongs to the European Top Ten (V, VI). Having only one successful and internationally known club is a problem in the export market since there are no interesting derbies in the national league from a foreigners' perspective. "*Hertha or Stuttgart or Schalke are not international brands. They are just runner-up to the brand Bayern. . . . There are too few stories about the Bundesliga*" (VIII).

Market structure

Despite the relatively weak international representation of German football clubs, the attractiveness of foreign markets was given since "*the media landscape is still formable*" (III). This led to the discussion of the TV market structure: "*The size and the structure of the national TV market have to be taken into account*" (III). The interviewed managers saw a competitive pay TV sector as a promising characteristic of foreign TV markets: "*Free TV is nice to have but is not a revenue driver*" (III). Looking at the USA, some interviewed managers saw problems with other competing sport leagues, namely the US Major Leagues: "*The USA is a difficult market . . . with a highly competitive market structure which is dominated by successful national sport leagues*" (III). However, football can be an extension of the US sport landscape: "*If there are two or three Americans participating in the Bundesliga tomorrow . . . there would be, maybe not strong because football is not big there, but there would be more interest in following the Bundesliga*" (VIII). Besides the competition with other types of sport, competition with other leagues in the same sport is an issue. European premier leagues such as the British, the Spanish, the Italian and the German leagues are in competition with each other for the budgets of foreign TV stations.

Buying power

The interviewed managers looked at the economic prosperity of a country to evaluate its attractiveness for exports. Fast-growing economies were evaluated as more attractive than slow-moving ones. "*Boom countries*" with a high population are particularly interesting for international sales (IV). An advantage for the German Bundesliga in many of these "boom countries" is that the Bundesliga still has a positive reputation and that people are interested in football that is "*made in Germany*" (V). The discussion about "made in Germany" is more or less a discussion of popularity. However, the economic power of a nation is an additional criterion to evaluate export opportunities. Countries are attractive if : "*the buying power of the middle class is sufficient and people have spare time to watch the broadcasts*" (V). Foreign countries are only promising if the population has time to watch football broadcasts and if people are able and willing to pay for the broadcasts. Of course, advertisers can pay for the broadcast if they give money for transmitting their commercials, but their willingness and ability to pay for commercials also depends on the economic wealth of a nation. Commercials are useless if consumers cannot buy the advertised goods and services.

Profitability and reliability

A sport league has to be reliable and profitable to be successful in international sales. Reliability and profitability reduce the uncertainty of international partners. Risky operations and losses due to an ultimate focus on sporting success often put sport organizations in danger of bankruptcy. Hence, the profitability of clubs and leagues is a positive signal for international sales. Reliability is equally important since it ensures a timely execution of the matches without any complications: "*Matches are organized and scheduled*" (III); "*This is one of the assets of the Bundesliga and hopefully they will keep it*" (VII).

Atmosphere

Surprisingly enough, the interviewed managers evaluated facilities and spectators as important prerequisites for the export, although the export takes place via television. Facilities and spectators are responsible for the atmosphere, which is also transmitted via TV broadcasts into households around the world: "*Look around, wonderful stadiums, the best stadiums in the world, the best audiences in the world, the best atmosphere*" (IX); "*all the Bundesliga matches are very well covered, are taking place in . . . the best stadiums in Europe thanks to the World Cup*" (VIII).

Only a few interviewed managers saw competitive balance as a major prerequisite: "*we saw it in the last two seasons when Bremen was able to compete against Bayern Munich. The interest was definitely higher*" (VIII). Of course, competitive balance is desired, but it seems that international sales do not depend on competitive balance. According to the interviewed managers, football enthusiasm seemed to be more important:

> They were only thinking "German football, Kick and Rush, no interest". And my job was to tell them "Look, . . . this is real football passion, this is in Germany. You can compare the football in Germany and the football in England because the people are working in the same way, I mean, in terms of pure football" (IX)

or "*Many, many goals, it is very spectacular. . .* " (VIII). Although discussing competitive balance, these statements show that sport has to be full of passion and spectacle. In sport economics, competitive balance or uncertainty of results are used to measure the excitement and emotions that a sport league provokes. The interviews give us a hint that these measurements should be supplemented with atmosphere (e.g. Czarnitzki & Stadtmann, 2002; Peel & Thomas, 1992).

Cultural and historical background

"*Football enthusiasm*" (II) in the target markets makes it easier to export a national sport league. This enthusiasm is closely related to consumption capital as well as cultural and historical backgrounds. Target markets with a colonial history are more promising for international sales. In particular, England, Spain, and France are able to capitalize on their colonial history: "*If you think about the Premier League, the Liga, or even the French League, the history is the reason that even from abroad there is an interest in following one of these leagues*" (VIII). These historic linkages ease the export because language or cultural values are already known (VI).

TV technology

Finally, yet importantly, the technical quality of TV production is important for export activities. Foreign TV stations buy transmission signals and they are looking for good quality, of course: "*Germany is the most developed country in Europe . . . the organization, the stadiums, the TV production standard is very, very high*" (VIII).

Managerial implications for the export of national sport leagues

The above discussion of theoretical backgrounds and presented empirical findings allow us to draw some managerial implications for the export of national sport leagues. International popularity of both clubs and players seems to be the most important prerequisite for being successful on international markets. Therefore, leagues should invest in the popularity of their clubs and players. During the last few years, many clubs have started to organize promotion trips to foreign countries to play against local teams. Moreover, clubs can hire talented players from foreign countries to increase the awareness and popularity of the whole league. However, "*before the league does any kind of promotion in foreign countries they should give the money to clubs such as FC Bayern Munich to hire stars. That would help much more than promotion campaigns in foreign countries*" (VI).

Exporting will only be successful if the population in foreign countries is enthusiastic about the particular type of sport. Countries with a comparable national sport league might be appropriate to evaluate the enthusiasm – the consumption capital. For example, Asian or American countries have their own regional tournaments. European leagues are not necessarily that well known. Sport league-specific consumption capital needs to be built up, which makes selling broadcasting rights to these countries more difficult. However, a focus on countries with existing football leagues is also problematic. Well-established leagues, like the US Major Leagues, are strong competitors. Of course, other spare time activities and people's professional lives compete with sport broadcasts. Hence, the timing of TV broadcasts in foreign countries is important. The time difference can lead to unsuitable time slots such as during the night. Consequently, ideas to reschedule the kick-off to meet the prime time for sport broadcasts in foreign countries are often discussed. Nevertheless, TV viewers appreciate fan crowds and want to see and hear a great atmosphere in the stadium. If the kick-off time is switched, stadium attendance might decrease. This needs to be considered when decisions for or against rescheduling kick-off times are made.

Furthermore, the buying power in the target market must be evaluated. A high buying power will lead to more willingness to pay for media-related services such as sport broadcasts. Sales efforts should focus on target markets with a willingness to pay for media-related services.

Another implication deduced from the interview study refers to the TV market structure. The assumption of the interviewed managers is that selling to pay TV stations usually leads to higher revenues. Furthermore, broadcasting fees will be higher in countries with a competitive pay TV sector (Solberg, 2002). In general, free TV needs a huge number of spectators to be profitable, whereas pay TV can be profitable with a lower number of spectators.

Finally, yet importantly, the German Bundesliga has a last mover disadvantage in comparison with other leagues: "*If slots are blocked, it is difficult to get in*" (VII). Hence, an opportunity for the Bundesliga might be to search for countries where broadcasts of other national leagues are not yet popular.

Conclusion

Although the export of national sport leagues has become a major task for sport managers, theoretical models are missing. Based on theoretical considerations, factors such as popularity, consumption capital, competition, buying power, and structure of the foreign TV market determine export opportunities. Interviews with managers from different organizations support these theoretical considerations. The interviews confirmed the following influence factors for the export of national sport leagues:

- Popularity (superstars, international sport competitions)
- Buying power
- TV market structure
- Consumption capital (football enthusiasm)

Our theoretical arguments regarding competition do not seem to be decisive. Moreover, the interviews showed some additional aspects:

- First mover advantage/last mover disadvantage
- Cultural and historical background
- Profitability and reliability
- Atmosphere (in the stadium)
- TV technology

Furthermore, the interviews made clear that neither the league nor the clubs can successfully export a national sport league on their own. Players and clubs must be successful in international competitions. The league must support the clubs so that they can travel around the world as ambassadors. Furthermore, all clubs and leagues have to work together to hire international stars. In Germany, the club is responsible for covering transfer expenses although export revenues are entitled to all clubs. Nevertheless, league administration, clubs and players have to cooperate with each other to sell their national sport league successfully.

Notes

1 Quotations are in italic. The number at the end of each quotation is a reference to the interviewed managers, as names and organizations are treated confidentially due to the high-ranked positions of the interviewees.

References

Baimbridge, M., Cameron, S. & Dawson, P. (1995). Satellite broadcasting and match attendance: The case of rugby league. *Applied Economics Letters*, 2(10), 343–346.

Baimbridge, M., Cameron, S. & Dawson, P. (1996). Satellite television and the demand for football: A whole new ball game? *Scottish Journal of Political Economy, 43*(3), 317–333.

Becker, M. A. & Suls, J. (1983). Take me out to the ballgame: The effects of objective, social, and temporal performance information on the attendance at Major League baseball games. *Journal of Sport Psychology, 5*(3), 302–313.

Bird, P. H. W. N. (1982). The demand for league football. *Applied Economics, 14*(6), 637–649.

Borland, J. (1987). The demand for Australian Rules football. *The Economic Record, 63*(September), 220–230.

Borland, J. & Lye, J. (1992). Attendance at Australian Rules football: A panel study. *Applied Economics, 24*(9), 1053–1058.

Brandes, L., Franck, E. & Nüesch, S. (2007). Local heroes and superstars: An empirical analysis of star attraction in German soccer. *Journal of Sports Economics, 9*(3), 266–286.

Campbell, R. M., Aiken, D. & Kent, A. (2004). Beyond BIRGing and CORFing: Continuing the exploration of fan behavior. *Sport Marketing Quarterly, 13*(2), 151–157.

Crains, J., Jennett, N. & Sloane, P. J. (1986). The economics of professional team sports: A survey of theory and evidence. *Journal of Economic Studies, 13*(1), 3–80.

Czarnitzki, D. & Stadtmann, G. (2002). Uncertainty of outcome versus reputation: Empirical evidence for the first German football division. *Empirical Economics, 27*(1), 101–112.

Davies, B., Downward, P. & Jackson, I. (1995). The demand for rugby league: Evidence from causality test. *Applied Economics, 27*(10), 1003–1007.

Daily Mail (2016). "New year, new TV billions". Retrieved from <www.dailymail.co.uk/sport/football/article-3382281/New-year-new-TV-billions-Premier-League-rules-world-foreign-sales-games-set-hit-1billion-year-2016-deals.html>.

Deloitte Sports Business Group (2016). Top of the Table – Football Money League, Manchester, UK.

Dobson, S. M. & Goddard, J. A. (1992). The demand for standing and seated viewing accommodation in the English football league. *Applied Economics, 24*(10), 1155–1163.

Donavan, D. T., Carlson, B. D. & Zimmermann, M. (2005). The influence of personality traits on sports fan identification. *Sport Marketing Quarterly, 14*(1), 31–42.

Ferreira, M. & Armstrong, K. (2004). An exploratory examination of attributes influencing students' decision to attend college sport events. *Sport Marketing Quarterly, 13*(4), 194–208.

Funk, D., Mahony, D. & Ridinger, L. (2002). Characterizing consumer motivation as individual difference factors: Augmenting the sport interest inventory (SII) to explain level of spectator support. *Sport Marketing Quarterly, 11*(1), 33–43.

Hynds, M. & Smith, I. (1994). The demand for test match cricket. *Applied Economics Letters, 1*(7), 103–106.

Janssens, P. & Késenne, S. (1987). Belgian soccer attendances. *Tijdschrift voor Economie en Management, 32*(3), 305–315.

Jennett, N. (1984). Attendance, uncertainty of outcome and policy in Scottish League football. *Scottish Journal of Political Economy, 31*(2), 176–198.

Kahle, L. R., Kambara, K. M. & Rose, G. M. (1996). A functional model of fan attendance motivations for college football. *Sport Marketing Quarterly, 5*(4), 51–60.

LeAnne Spenner, E., Fenn, A. J. & Crooker, J. (2004). *The demand for NFL attendance: A rational addiction model.* [Working Paper]. Department of Economics and Business, Colorado College 2004–01, Colorado Springs, USA.

Matsuoka, H., Chelladurai, P. & Harada, M. (2003). Direct and interaction effects of team identification and satisfaction on intention to attend games. *Sport Marketing Quarterly, 12*(4), 244–253.

Peel, D. A. & Thomas, D. A. (1988). Outcome uncertainty and the demand for football: An analysis of match attendances in the English football league. *Scottish Journal of Political Economy, 35*(3), 242–249.

Peel, D. A. & Thomas, D. A. (1992). The demand for football: Some evidence on outcome uncertainty. *Empirical Economics, 17*(1), 323–331.

Peel, D. A. & Thomas, D. A. (1996). Attendance demand: An investigation of repeat fixtures. *Applied Economics Letters, 3*, 319–394.

Rishe, P. & Mondello, M. (2004). Ticket price determination in professional sports: An empirical analysis of the NBA, NFL, NHL, and Major League baseball. *Sport Marketing Quarterly, 13*(2), 104–112.

Robinson, M. J., Trail, G. T., Dick, R. J. & Gillentine, A. J. (2005). Fans vs. spectators: An analysis of those who attend intercollegiate football games. *Sport Marketing Quarterly, 14*(1), 43–53.

Schmidt, M. B. & Berri, D. J. (2001). Competitive balance and attendance – The case of Major League baseball. *Journal of Sports Economics*, *2*(2), 145–167.

Schofield, J. A. (1983). The demand for cricket: The case of the John Player League. *Applied Economics*, *15*(3), 283–296.

Siegfried, J. J. & Eisenberg, J. D. (1980). The demand for minor league baseball. *Atlantic Economic Journal*, *8*(2), 59–69.

Siegfried, J. J. & Hinshaw, C. E. (1979). The effect of lifting television blackouts on professional football no-shows. *Journal of Economics and Business*, *32*(1), 1–13.

Simmons, R. (1996). The demand for English league football: A club-level analysis. *Applied Economics*, *28*(2), 139–155.

Solberg, H. A. (2002). The economics of television sports rights: Europe and the US – A comparative analysis. *Norsk medietidsskrift*, *9*(2), 57–80.

Stigler, G. J. & Becker, G. S. (1977). De Gustibus Non Est Disputandum. *American Economic Review*, *67*(2), 76–90.

Sutton, W. A., McDonald, M. A., Milne, G. R. & Cimperman, J. (1997). Creating and fostering fan identification in professional sports. *Sport Marketing Quarterly*, *6*(1), 15–22.

Szymanski, S. (2001). Income inequality, competitive balance and the attractiveness of team sports: Some evidence and a natural experiment from English soccer. *Economic Journal*, *111*(469), F69–F84.

Trail, G. T., Fink, J. S. & Anderson, D. F. (2003). Sport spectator consumption behavior. *Sport Marketing Quarterly*, *12*(1), 8–17.

Trail, G., Robinson, M., Dick, R. & Gillentine, A. (2003). Motives and points of attachment: Fans versus spectators in intercollegiate athletics. *Sport Marketing Quarterly*, *12*(4), 217–227.

UEFA (2015). Club Licensing Benchmarking Report – Financial Year 2014.

Wann, D. L. & Branscombe, N. R. (1993). Sports fans: Measuring degree of identification with their team. *International Journal of Sport Psychology*, *24*(1), 1–17.

Wann, D. L., Melnick, M. J., Russell, G. W. & Pease, D. G. (2001). *Sport Fans – The Psychology and Social Impact of Spectators*. New York, London: Routledge.

Wilson, P., & Sim, B. (1995). The demand for semi-pro league football in Malaysia 1989–91: A panel data approach. *Applied Economics*, *27*(1), 131–138.

Woratschek, H., Durchholz, C., Maier, C. & Ströbel, T. (2017). Innovations in sport management: The role of motivations and value co-creation at public viewing events. *Event Management*, *21*(1), 1–12.

Woratschek, H. & Schafmeister, G. (2005). Assessing the determinants of broadcasting fees – Theoretical foundations and empirical evidence for the German soccer league. *Wirtschaftswissenschaftliche Diskussionspapiere Universität Bayreuth* [Economics Discussion Papers, University of Bayreuth] [11–05].

2

SPORT BUSINESS INTELLIGENCE AND THE WRC EVENT

Risto Rasku and Douglas Michele Turco

Introduction

Since 2011, Sport Business School (SBS) Finland has conducted more than 30 different research projects during the WRC Neste Rally Finland event in Jyväskylä. The WRC (World Rally Championship) is said to be the most challenging motorsport championship in the world (WRC.com). The races take place in approximately 15 different countries and Finland has hosted the event since 1973. Originally, the aim of the studies in this chapter was to collect in-depth information about the customer satisfaction experienced by different types of spectators and participating teams. During the past five years, the studies have also included the economic impact of the event for the host city, brand perceptions and personal value structures of the spectators, team members, volunteers and staff members, the expectations and satisfaction of event partners and sponsors as well as the views of non-spectators and the local citizens. In fact, the data collected from more than 10,000 interviews have been organized into a set of databases that can be considered an application of an ERP (Enterprise Resource Planning) system, and can be applied as a CRM (Customer Relationship Management) system for the event organizer.

The goal of this chapter is to illustrate the application of business intelligence (BI) in the context of a sport event and to introduce the core ideas of sport business intelligence (SBI). The chapter concentrates particularly on the specific needs and requirements of a sport event from BI and on the application of customer relationship management in this context, as well as the use of longitudinal data collection for the purposes of customer relationship management, SBI and legacy planning. As a result this case study illustrates the pragmatic application of this approach to the systematic development of the WRC Neste Rally Finland.

In order to succeed in the global sport marketplace, businesses must have insights of consumers' needs, wants, expectations and satisfactions. This chapter introduces SBI, and describes the SBI model devised for and applied to a world rally championship event and organization in the period 2011 to 2016, along with corresponding outcomes.

Business intelligence and sport

Business intelligence is a set of theories, methodologies, architectures and technologies that transform raw data into meaningful and useful information for business purposes. Large amounts of unstructured data are analysed to identify and develop new opportunities. Making use of new opportunities and implementing an effective strategy can provide a business with competitive market advantages and long-term stability (Rud, 2009). To be more pragmatic and to further understand the managerial meaning of BI, another definition by Williams and Williams is offered:

> BI combines products, technology, and methods to organize key information that management needs to improve profit and performance. More broadly, we think of BI as business information and business analyses within the context of key business processes that lead to decisions and actions and that result in improved business performance. In particular, BI means leveraging information assets within key business processes to achieve improved business performance.
>
> *Williams and Williams, 2006*

The core idea of BI is to provide historical, current and predictive views of business operations. In terms of functions, BI includes, for example, reporting, analytics, data mining, online processing, business performance management, benchmarking, text mining, and predictive and prescriptive analysis. Although BI is sometimes a synonym for competitive intelligence (because they both support decision-making) it uses technologies, processes and applications to analyse mostly internal, structured data and business processes while competitive intelligence gathers, analyses and disseminates information with a topical focus on company competitors. If understood broadly, BI can include the subset of competitive intelligence (Aho, 2011). According to Kobielus (2010): "business intelligence is a non-domain-specific catchall for all the types of analytic data that can be delivered to users in reports, dashboards, and the like".

Real-time business intelligence (RTBI) is the process of delivering information about business operations as they occur. Real time means "near to zero" latency and access to information whenever it is required (Rud, 2009). The speed of today's processing systems has moved classical data warehousing into the realm of real time. The result is RTBI. Business transactions as they occur are fed to a RTBI system that maintains the current state of the enterprise. The RTBI system not only supports the classic strategic functions of data warehousing for deriving information and knowledge from past enterprise activity, but it also provides real-time tactical support to drive enterprise actions that react immediately to events as they occur. As such, it replaces both the classic data warehouse and the enterprise application integration (EAI) functions. Such event-driven processing is a basic tenet of RTBI (Williams & Williams, 2006).

In this chapter SBI is defined as a rational and continuous development of sport events and organizations using advanced data collection and sophisticated analyses to support informed decision and quality improvement. In this respect the core idea of SBI is to apply the models of modern customer-oriented business to sport. This approach is merely an application of existing ways and means, even though it aims to take the specifics of this particular branch into account. In defining SBI, the unique nature of sport and its fans as not only customers but also service/experience contributors, athletes as performers, sport clubs as service providers and sport events as experiences are taken into account.

Sport business intelligence (SBI) applied to sport events

One way to consume sport as a service and experience is the sport event. Global sport organizations, including the IOC, FIFA, UEFA and NFL, are organizers of events and leagues and they capitalize on the customer value of their experiences either via spectatorship on scene, via media or through merchandise related to this experience. This format has been copied and applied by sport organizations and enterprises such as Champions League, KHL (Kontinental Hockey League), Premier League (UK), Bundesliga (Germany), and so forth, to model their business on a set of sport events (regular season matches plus championship playoffs) as a combination of product, service, and entertainment.

The production of an event as an experience has been studied and formatted by Pine and Gilmore who, as early as the late 1990s, introduced the concept of an experience economy (Pine & Gilmour, 1999). The notion of an experience-based economy generated several studies that aimed to analyse and improve the production, and increase the customer value of events as systematically produced experiences. Like amusement parks, well-organized sport events can (and have) become brands that are recognized, appreciated and evaluated by consumers (i.e. the FIFA World Cup, the NFL Super Bowl, etc.), not only during and after but also before the actual event. Because of this, the consumer experience creates expectations amongst the participants, but also amongst the ones who have not participated in the event but have been exposed to the brand. These expectations on their part create an expected value in the minds of these potential customers. The nature of this kind of sport event is always subjective, non-replicable, and produced and consumed simultaneously (Jago & Shaw, 1998). The entire timeline around the actual experience ultimately defines the customer satisfaction. Customer expectations can be considered "ground floor" for a satisfactory experience, and the time after the experience is the moment when the customer is able to analyse his/her satisfaction. Thus the data collection process in SBI applied to events should follow the event lifecycle: pre-, during, and post-event.

Figure 2.1 illustrates the different objectives for data collection along the three stages of the event production lifecycle. Before the event, it is possible, for example, to collect customer data about the expectations of customers and potential customers, about the personal values and perceptions of brand images of sponsors and partners, etc. At this time pen and paper might work as well as online questionnaires, and methodology can be chosen by the aims and objectives, access and availability of the subjects, etc. There is usually more time and more opportunity to answer survey questions. This phase is vital in terms of determining

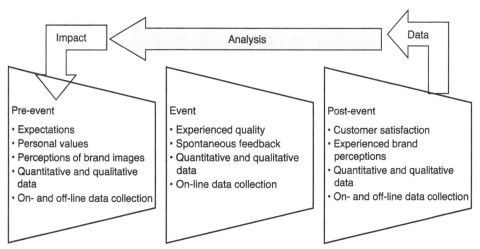

Figure 2.1 The process of sport business intelligence applied to a sport event (modified from Tynan & McKechnie, 2009)

(and possibly setting) expectations by the spectators, participants or viewers, but also other partners (i.e. sponsors) can articulate their expectations so that the event organizer can plan in advance to meet and even exceed these expectations. Social media networks offer an opportunity for data mining prior to the event. For example, Facebook or Twitter can be used to gain customer insights about events when studied systematically. These channels can generate spontaneous expressions of expectations, opinions and customer views worth monitoring.

During an event, customers with different cultural backgrounds and even nationalities are in the middle of their experiences and, at that moment, they usually do not wish to respond to enquiries but they should have the opportunity to give spontaneous feedback if they so desire. At best, this feedback should have instant impact on the ongoing experience and, therefore, sophisticated technology and methods that are online should be applied. For example, if the beer is warm and the sausages are cold, a customer will remember this as part of the experienced quality, but should the organizer get this message on time, he/she could fix the problem before the customer leaves and compensate the customer, thereby saving at least some of the experienced quality. At this critical moment online questionnaires and topics that relate directly to the services available are likely to prove the most useful and effective. In cases where the event lasts longer it is possible to enhance the experience during the event using the data collected. Should the organizer be aware of the best elements of the customer experience, it is of utmost importance to maintain this experienced quality, but when trying to exceed the expectations of the customer the organizer should also try to sharpen the good and fair parts to be excellent yet not forget the possible weaknesses either. This approach to development focuses on positively deviant performance – if the organization aims to be the best, it should concentrate its energy on its strengths and focus on opportunities instead of getting too tired trying to fix things that are not so good. Obvious problems must be solved instantly, but solving the problems should not be the main focus when aiming for the top.

Finally, after the event a customer is able to reflect upon the experiences and his/her satisfaction as a function between expectations and experience. At this phase, as before the event, respondents tend to have more time and opportunities to respond to questionnaires and interviews. After the event collecting customer data about the experience – the most memorable moments and perceptions of brand images of sponsors and partners, subsequent consumer behaviours, and so on – is possible, and also at this point these responses are valid and trustworthy. Again pen and paper might work as well as online questionnaires and methodology can be chosen more freely according to the aim and objective of the study.

The arrows (Figure 2.1) illustrate on one hand the continuity of the BI process and, on the other hand, the nature of event production. In many cases, the experienced event will be organized again at another place and moment in time: every four years for an Olympic Games or FIFA World Cup, annually for the IIHF Ice Hockey World Championships or monthly for the WRC rallies. Therefore, the post-event period can be considered also as the pre-game period of the following event. From a marketing perspective, constant communication with the client/customer is very important and if contact is lost with the consumer and his/her preferences, a competitor can distract the customer to a new purchase and new experience. The faithful customer is loyal to those who are interested in customers but also interesting and rewarding. Between purchases, brand loyalty requires constant brand communication and involvement. In order to be successful in this type of communication with modern consumers, both the event and the post-event period are vital for pre-game marketing.

Neste Rally Finland, AKK Sports Ltd and sport business intelligence by Webropol Ltd

The bases of SBI for Neste Rally Finland/AKK Sports Ltd resides in the collaboration of SBS Finland, Webropol Ltd and AKK Sports Ltd. Since 2011, SBS Finland has systematically collected data from the separate stakeholders of the event for the organizer AKK Sports Ltd using Webropol software and applications. This collaborative SBI process has enabled systematic data collection and prompt, accurate results for Finland's top rally event organization. Advanced data analyses were performed according to the specific needs and requirements of AKK Sports Ltd to aid their decision-making. Thus the event development process has been constant and based on empirical data and analyses instead of hunches and best guesses.

Philosophically, the application of SBI includes some very unique features. First, the main idea is to establish the most meaningful expectations for all the stakeholders (local people, spectators, drivers, teams, VIP guests from different countries and cultures, as well as sponsors and partners, etc.) and link them to the strategic planning of the event so that the experience created will most likely be positive in the minds of participants. This process uses the respondent's willingness to recommend the event experienced. Secondly, a clearly unique aspect is online surveying, which allows the organizer to improve the experienced quality during the event; the on-line data collection and constant real-time analysis makes it possible to monitor the experienced quality because all negative responses can be pinpointed and addressed when the respondent clicks the "send" button on a tablet. This option is also usable for staff motivation; exceptionally good feedback can generate appreciation of those who perform in an exceptionally good way!

Towards deeper understanding of the WRC experience

The starting line for Neste Rally Finland's SBI was established in 2011 and the first aim was to determine customer satisfaction (spectators and rally team members) with the event. As Woratscheck, Horbel & Popp (2014) state, the experience of a sport event is co-created by all participants and so the customer satisfaction of different stakeholders should be measured. A strategic view to customer satisfaction research was an essential part of all studies conducted. Theoretically this approach requires different structures of the survey instrument, as it is not only the absolute satisfaction evaluated by the respondent with, for example, the five-point Likert scale ranging from not satisfied at all to very satisfied, that reveals the satisfaction of the customer in a way that is meaningful for strategic planning. Instead, one should really know the validity and relational importance of different aspects of experienced service in order to maintain or improve the quality of the relevant satisfaction- or dissatisfaction-generating aspects in the mind of a customer.

To add insight to the above-mentioned challenge, Sport Business School Finland included a question in each questionnaire about willingness to recommend the event or experienced service. The customer's willingness to recommend the purchased service or product has been considered a new asset in operative marketing. In strategic brand management and marketing, the brand loyalty typologies often refer to customer activity in promoting the brand (Kapferer, 2012; Van den Brink, Odekerken-Schröder & Pauwels, 2006). By identifying the most important determinants of customer satisfaction correlating the respondent's willingness to recommend the event, development suggestions for marketing practices could be presented. Therefore, the determinants that have a stronger correlation to recommendation could be considered as the most important strategic strengths of the event in order to attract customers. This innovation prevailed in all subsequent satisfaction studies of the Neste Rally Finland.

The focus of the 2012 studies was to develop a deeper understanding of customers according to their values and their perceptions of the rally as a brand. This shift from 2011 was a logical next step, as when we are aware of the current situation of our customers according to their satisfactions, we should examine what kinds of customers we actually serve. The idea of developing a customer value profile combined with brand perceptions of an event experienced originated from a study of the FIFA World Cup 2010. The planning of the questionnaire for FIFA World Cup 2010 football fans and their social motives was based on the human value-structure introduced by Shalom Schwartz (1994). This questionnaire was then redesigned for the requirements of Neste Rally Finland event. The final questionnaire is a combination of the Portrait Values Questionnaire and Schwartz's Values Survey (Schwartz, 1994). The data were to be interpreted as the respondent's perception of football as a brand according to adjectives presenting certain values and a self-portrait reflecting these values in the respondent's personality. The questionnaire also had an open-ended question, where the respondent was asked to give the three most motivating reasons for his/her attendance. The main idea was to introduce the spectator population in a new light, not only to event organizers but also to the partners and sponsors of the event.

Findings from 2012 revealed interesting differences and similarities between rally spectators who followed the rally along the special stages and those who just visited the rally headquarters area and service park. These two segments overlapped only to some extent but, on the other hand, these findings led to another shift in focusing the data collection. In 2012 the customer satisfaction studies were primarily conducted online using web links on the official websites (www.nesterallyfinland.com). The idea was to automatize some data collection like the one monitoring the overall customer satisfaction during and after the event. As in the case of BI in more generic definition, this application was utilizing the idea of RTBI. In this particular case the RTBI system not only supported the classic strategic functions of data warehousing for deriving information and knowledge from customer activity, but also provided potential real-time tactical support to event organizers.

In 2013 the idea of the studies was to monitor both the expectations of sponsors and partners prior to the event, and the experienced quality after the event. The structure of the survey was designed to establish the most important factors of successful marketing co-operation using a two-staged interview of key personnel associated with event sponsorship and partnership. The main research aim was to determine the most relevant aspects of this sponsorship or partnership agreement through validation of all possible dimensions of marketing collaboration, and secondly, after the event, to evaluate the success in these dimensions. The analyses compared the relationships between expectations and experiences, indicating whether the organizer had been able to meet, exceed or had failed to meet the expectations of the partner/sponsor. This approach is a quality management tool and clearly points out the most important and valuable aspects of a successful sponsorship and partnership agreement.

Another focus of the studies in 2013 was on the values and brand perceptions of the spectators along the special stages. These studies revealed the differences between the two separate spectator segments in a new light. As expected, the viewers were a little different in terms of their personal values, their perception of rally as a brand was somewhat different and the motives for attending this event were not the same as for those who were interviewed in 2012 in the headquarters area.

The overall customer satisfaction was monitored in 2013 with an online web-based survey that was a slightly modified version of the study in 2012. Most of the findings made comparisons between 2012 and 2013 possible. From 2013 onwards, customer satisfaction has been studied in a similar way each year. It should be noted that these findings together can result in a pitfall for event organizers; when highly satisfied, loyal and experienced customers actively recommend the event, the expectations of first-timers can be extremely high and when they experience the event, these high expectations may not be met, and the new customers are disappointed. Some indications of this phenomenon can be found in longitudinal data.

One of the biggest efforts in terms of SBI applied to this rally event took place in 2013. SBS Finland was assigned by the rally organizer AKK Sports Ltd, together with the City of Jyväskylä, JYKES Ltd (Jyväskylä Regional Development Company) and the Regional Council of Central Finland, to study the economic and social impacts of Neste Rally Finland 2013 on the host city and the surrounding area. All studies were conducted between June and September 2013, before, during and after the event. The rally took place between 31 July and 3 August 2013. The aim and objective of this project was to determine the economic and social impacts and effects of the Neste Rally Finland event in the city of Jyväskylä and the surrounding region and also to monitor the attitudes of local people, local business, rally visitors, rally team members and media representatives to the event. The array of topics studied also included data about opinions and experiences of all these stakeholders in regards to the event (including open-ended pros and cons), respondents' willingness to recommend the event to other people (asked of rally visitors, rally teams and media representatives), the impact of the event on local residents and their quality of life, the impact of the event on the public image of the city of Jyväskylä and its surrounding region, the media coverage of the event (quality and quantity) and the earnings of NGOs and volunteers organizing special stages and other services for AKK Sports Ltd.

The research objectives for 2014 were set according to the findings and recommendations from all previous studies. Assessing quality management and continuous improvement were default research priorities, and required the inclusion of those who facilitated and produced specific facets of the event. One of the main objectives of the 2014 research was to find out what kind of people work in AKK Sports Ltd to organize the event, who volunteers for the rally and what kind of people are team members and drivers. Values and brand perceptions along with the main motives for attending were studied using the same questionnaire that had been previously used with spectators and team members. The value structures and brand perceptions of organizers and rally teams revealed interesting and useful data and findings. After generating a holistic picture of both the personal values of event participants and their perceptions of the core service, as well as the motivational factors for attendance, the rally organizer is now able to communicate more effectively with these stakeholders.

A new study in 2014 concentrated on the evaluation of special stages of the rally. The basic objective of this research was originally motivated by the Clerk of the Course of Neste Rally Finland. Being in charge of the rally route, he was interested practically in knowing how the spectators decide which special stages they participate in and spectate at. To get an idea of the most relevant arguments, this study first ranked the "best special stages" of the rally and then collected open-ended responses as to the motivation behind the choice made.

In 2015 Sport Business School Finland was collecting data not only during the Neste Rally Finland event, but also during the Finnish National Rally Championships. In practice, web-based surveys were conducted during five national rally events around Finland. The aim of this data collection was to monitor Finnish rally fans who were interested in rally as a form of motorsport and study whether these fans were the same as the spectators in Neste Rally Finland. In the same year a completely new innovation in the line of SBI was the study of non-spectators. These data are usually ignored as the organizers very typically focus on the existing customers and spectators. The logic of promotion via satisfied customers is old, useful and prevailing, but the fact is usually that the biggest potential of new consumers is amongst those who are currently not even aware and/or interested in your offer, in this case the rally event. In practice, the questions are addressed to respondents who are close to the event, have free time at that moment and can attend the event if they choose to do so. The results of this study indicated that almost all respondents were aware of the rally event, as 98 per cent of all respondents were able to name the event in the city. However, the most common reasons not to take part in this event were related to a lack of interest in rally and motorsports in general, and also a lack of time and interest in this kind of event. When asked about the possible willingness to attend the event, 68 per cent of the respondents would consider participation in the event. The terms of this participation were linked to social motives such as attendance with a group of friends, or similar.

While the study in 2014 concentrated on the evaluation of special stages of the rally, this study continued in 2015 in more detail. This time the respondents were asked to indicate how many special stages and other sites or events they planned to visit, rank the importance of certain factors when choosing the actual special stages, sites and events and also list the intended special stages, sites and events in which they would participate. The results of this study generated several clear and distinctive customer paths that were motivated by logical and correlating factors. For example, a very experienced spectator who had attended Neste Rally Finland more than ten times before as a spectator chose his special stages according to the suitable and possible timetable in three days and because of the spectating areas and specific jumps and curves, as well as because of the speed of the cars at those special stages. On the other hand, a first-timer wanted to see the start and the Harju special stage on the Friday because of its proximity to the city, the Service Park activities on the Saturday for easy access, as well as the music concerts for other kinds of festivities, as well as possibly attending the podium prize ceremonies on the Sunday.

In 2016 the focus of the study returned to the organizer, AKK Sports Ltd, and partly to the most loyal and engaged rally fans. The main idea was to start the implementation of BI on the operational processes of AKK Sports Ltd. The structure for customer data collection had been created, tested and systemized, and now the organization would prepare itself for data-driven planning and management. The ultimate aim and objective of the study on the staff of AKK Sports Ltd was to better understand the state of the organization and how it could further benefit from the data collected.

After reporting the 2016 study in the continuum and context of the studies and results from previous years, preparation for the 2017 study was launched. SBI has become essential to the advancement of Neste Rally Finland as a result of valid and reliable data management over time, proper analyses and sound decision-making by AKK Sports Ltd and SBS Finland. The years from 2017 to 2019 are planned to be the time during which AKK Sports Ltd, as the organizer of Neste Rally Finland, fully implements the SBI system.

Reflected in Gartner's BI maturity model (Rajterič, 2010), at this point BI and Performance Management become pervasive across all areas of the business and across part of the corporate culture. Here both BI and Performance Management systems become part of the business processes, and information is trustworthy and used at different levels of the organization. At this level of maturity the results are measureable and linked to specific goals and the usage of BI is available to suppliers, business partners and customers.

Sport business intelligence (SBI) in Neste Rally Finland as a process

The following figure illustrates how collected data accumulate annually. The idea is that the more valid and reliable data available, the more opportunities appear to improve their quality. When the quality and quantity of useful and relevant data increase, strategic planning can be based on knowledge instead of assumption. As in all businesses, strategies based on accurate market insight are the key to growth both in turnover and profit. Big data make big impact possible as the more data there are available, the deeper the data mining can reach and the more valuable findings and conclusions will be.

The starting line in August 2011 refers not only to the duration of the process but also to the idea of sequences within the process. As noted earlier, the SBI process is based on continuous data collection using advanced technology and sophisticated analysis at the moment when the service is offered and also before and after this "moment of truth". In other words, the 2011 studies were mostly conducted during the event and some additional data were collected after the event, but by 2012 the event planning process included some data collection that was based on the findings of 2011. When the impact studies were included in 2013, a substantial amount of data were collected from residents of the city of Jyväskylä months before the event. When referring to strategic planning for a successful business, the continuance of data collection linked to the redefinition of strategies and operations is a vital success factor. Important decisions should be made according to the best possible information available, and this approach ultimately merges the post-event phase with the pre-event phase resulting in a continuum that at best can be summarized as a "legacy planning process". In the context of an event the idea is, by data collection and management, to optimize the positive impacts and, at the same time, to minimize the negative impacts. The results from 2011 to 2016 and forthcoming years define our actions for tomorrow taking the long-term vision and mission into account as ultimate goals and objectives.

The amount of data available for data mining (illustrated in Figure 2.2 by the size of the dated boxes), refers concretely to the studies conducted and the data collected and available for analysis. Naturally, AKK Sports Ltd, as the rally organizer, has a substantial amount of data available from previous years, but those data were not systematically organized, easily usable or even accessible. When all the interviews of spectators in rally championship events, volunteers, sponsors, partners, non-spectators and all other spectators are added together, for the moment the database to be used for strategic planning and operative development totals 10,039 responses.

Conclusion

The previous pages describe the longitudinal logic of studies conducted and illustrate how the cumulative data combined with the application of BI can be used to improve the experienced value of rally events. This approach is an ongoing process rather than being project-based, and future studies are designed to deepen customer insights and assist strategic planning.

To date, the results of our SBI model applied to the Neste Rally Finland have led to improved strategic development and event operations. Starting with customer satisfaction amongst spectators and visitors in the Service Park and Rally Headquarters, as well as spectators along special stages, to the brand image of the city of Jyväskylä as the host city, and the impact of the rally event on local enterprises and companies, the focus of separate data collections changes according to the development process. For example, in the case of rally spectators the first survey concentrated on customer satisfaction, the second questionnaire aimed to reveal the perceptions of the rally as a brand amongst the spectators, and the third described personal features in term of values. This continuum offers an insight into rally spectators from the perspective of consumer behaviour and enables systematic long-term customer relationship management.

As our data reveal, the rally event is already offering participants and stakeholders good value for time and money, but the urge to enhance the experienced value remains. The next

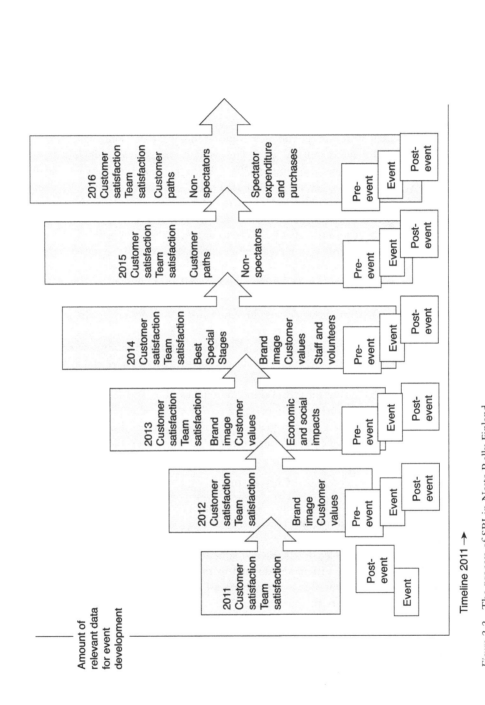

Figure 2.2 The process of SBI in Neste Rally Finland

phase in the process of implementing SBI aims to prepare AKK Sports Ltd, as the organizer of the Neste Rally Finland event, to plan, organize and implement the studies and data collection themselves. The idea is to transfer part of the expertise and tacit knowledge of SBS Finland staff and experts to the staff and experts of AKK Sports Ltd. The reason for this transfer is the assumption that when the organization starts to understand the benefits and opportunities of customer and partner data, it also becomes motivated in acquiring these data to support both operative and tactical planning and decision-making. Studies reveal different phases in the development of a company in its ability to produce and utilize data and information. These maturity models typically refer to the application of BI (Rajterič, 2010).

In addition to these new approaches, the collection of data with regard to overall customer satisfaction amongst spectators, rally drivers and teams, as well as sponsors and partners, is ongoing. The usefulness of data collected increases by accumulation and analysis, as the more data are available, the more new ideas for using them occur. The SBI application for AKK Sports Ltd and Neste Rally Finland is an ongoing process that requires trust between AKK Sports Ltd as event organizer and SBS Finland as the organization conducting the studies and processing the data. The first six years have been an excellent test drive for this developing relationship, as well as for the development of the event itself. As the first years together have shown, the importance and value of the SBI application is already realized to be extremely high, but the expectations of its usability and usefulness are also growing every year. It seems to be that knowing a lot makes you willing to know even more. That is why we are still seeking more event knowledge.

References

Aho, M. (2011). *A Construct for Performance Management Maturity Assessment.* Tampere University of Technology, Tampere, Finland: Faculty of Business and Technology Management.

Jago, L. K. & Shaw, R. N. (1998). Special events: A conceptual and definitional framework. *Festival Management and Event Tourism, 5*(1–1), 21–32.

Kapferer, J. N. (2012). *The New Strategic Brand Management: Advanced Insights and Strategic Thinking.* London and Philadelphia: Kogan Page.

Kobielus, J. (30 April 2010). What's Not BI? Oh, Don't Get Me Started. . . .Oops Too Late . . . Here Goes . . .. Available at <http://blogs.forrester.com/james_kobielus/10-04-30-what%E2%80%99s_not_bi_oh_don%E2%80%99t_get_me_startedoops_too_latehere_goes>. Accessed 10 April 2014.

Pine, J. B. & Gilmour, J. H. 1999. *Experience Economy, Work is Theatre and Every Business a Stage.* Aurora, OH, USA: Strategic Horizons LLP.

Rajterič, I. H. (2010). Overview of business intelligence maturity models. *Journal of Contemporary Management Issues, 15*(1), 47–67.

Rud, O. (2009). *Business Intelligence Success Factors: Tools for Aligning Your Business in the Global Economy.* Hoboken, NJ: Wiley & Sons.

Schwartz, S. H. (1994). Are there universal aspects in the structure and contents of human values? *Journal of Social Issues, 50*(4), 19–45.

Tynan, C. & McKechnie, S. (2009). Experience marketing: A review and reassessment. *Journal of Marketing Management, 25*, 501–517.

Van den Brink, D., Odekerken-Schröder, G. & Pauwels, P. (2006). The effect of strategic and tactical cause-related marketing on consumers' brand loyalty. *Journal of Consumer Marketing, 23*(1), 15–25.

Wrc.com. What is WRC? Available at <www.wrc.com/en/wrc/about-wrc/what-is-wrc/page/673—672-.html>. Accessed 9 January 2017.

Williams, S. & Williams, N. (2006). *Profit Impact of Business Intelligence.* Burlington, MA, USA: Morgan Kaufmann.

Woratschek, H., Horbel, C. & Popp, B. (2014). The sport value framework – a new fundamental logic for analyses in sport management. *European Sport Management Quarterly, 14*(1), 6–24.

3

THE UEFA EURO CHAMPIONSHIP 2020

A path to success or a mistake in the making?

Claudia Stura, Christina Aicher, Robert Kaspar,
Carina Klein, Susanne Schulz and Stefan Unterlechner

Introduction

The UEFA European Championship 2020 (UEFA EURO, 2020) is a pioneer project. For the first time, a mobile mega-event will take place over an entire continent. It will be hosted by 13 cities in 13 countries using mainly existing infrastructure, primarily football stadiums but also airports, railway stations and highways. The intent is that overall infrastructural costs should be much lower and, consequently, the pressure on each hosting city and country should be dramatically reduced (Böcking, 2012; UEFA.com, 2014; Weinreich, 2012a). In addition, it will become very difficult to host the Games from 2016 onwards, as 24 teams will then participate in the tournament. Other reasons given by UEFA refer to the 60th anniversary of the European championship, which will occur in 2020. UEFA has aimed, in this way, to bring the tournament to European fans' front doors (UEFA.com, 2014; UEFA.com, 2016). Finally, UEFA has stressed the opportunity for smaller countries to become part of this mega-event (Weinreich, 2012b; Winkler, 2014).

Newspaper reports highlight additional reasons, however. Since this new model offers the opportunity for smaller countries to become part of this mega-event, Michel Platini, UEFA president from 2007 to 2015, aimed to reward the small eastern European countries for electing him as president in 2007 (Weinreich, 2012b). Other sources argue that UEFA's decision was driven by the lack of bidding countries due to the increasing costs of hosting – in fact, Turkey was the only serious bidder. Since it had also bid for the 2020 Olympic Games, Turkish President Recep Tayyip Erdogan announced at the UEFA congress in Istanbul that it would withdraw its bid if the International Olympic Committee (IOC) granted it the Olympic Games. When Platini attempted to change UEFA's decision date for hosting EURO 2020 to a date prior to the IOC's decision date for the 2020 Games, IOC president Jacques Rogge intervened. Ever since, Platini has further pursued the idea of the European model (Weinreich, 2012a; Winkler, 2014).

While the reasons behind UEFA's decision may be multifaceted, the new model has received a great deal of attention. As well as UEFA, the IOC has discussed the idea of adapting the Olympic Games to this new format, in order to make bidding and hosting more attractive. With its Agenda 2020, it officially opened the door for the Olympic Games to be hosted over various countries (The *National*, 2014).

While international governing bodies seem to find the new model attractive, the new format may also suggest negative consequences, especially for tourism. While the traditional model, with one or two hosting countries, allowed the fan to fly into the country and then continue to travel from host city to host city by local transport, the distances at EURO 2020 make this nearly impossible. Distances such as those between Bilbao and Baku and between Rome and London require travelling by air in order to move between host cities. While UEFA claim that the format is intended to increase tourism and save costs by using existing facilities (Weinreich, 2012a; Winkler, 2014), the net tourism impact for any of the 13 host cities may be small. However, research on the actual implications of the new format is very limited. Consequently, this exploratory study aims to give initial insight into the potential positive and negative effects of this new event format for the hosts, as well as insight into the opportunities and limitations it may offer in being adapted to other sport mega-events, especially future editions of the Olympic Games.

This study is based on previous research in the context of sport mega-events. Since the literature in this field is somewhat limited, newspaper articles are also included. After a brief review of existing publications on reasons, opportunities, challenges and effects of sport mega-events, especially those previously hosted in two countries, the research design is then explained. This is followed by the major findings, a discussion of their implications and conclusions.

Why host sport mega-events? A brief review of the current literature

In bidding for sport mega-events, cities may be driven by a variety of motivations. While reasons are multifaceted, several studies refer especially to the strength of support from governments based on political motives for using sport events as arenas to construct and present national identities (Black & Van der Westhuizen, 2004; Maguire & Tuck, 2005; Xin, 2006) as well as to enhance their countries' image and soft power (Cornelissen, 2007; Marivoet, 2006; Roche, 2002). As a consequence, their cities receive more financial and political support than others. However, politicians justify their bids to host sport mega-events with claims that hosting the events supports or even boosts their national and local economies (Cornelissen, Bob & Swart, 2011; Cornelissen & Swart, 2006; Cornelissen, 2007; Solberg & Preuss, 2007), using economic impact studies done in advance that show economic gains (Baade & Matheson, 2016).

Economic effects – costs and benefits

However, *ex-post* economic impact studies show different results. In fact, many post-event studies have shown that costs were mostly underestimated and benefits overestimated (Horne & Manzenreiter, 2006; Preuss, 2004). For example, from 1968 to 2012 all Olympic Games cost more than estimated. On average, the costs were 150 per cent over the originally estimated budget, relating mainly to the general infrastructure, such as transportation and housing, and sport infrastructure, as well as operational costs, including administration, opening and closing ceremonies, and huge expenses on safety and security (Baade & Matheson, 2016).

In fact, safety and security measures have become major concerns in organizing sport mega-events. For example, Yu et al. (2009) highlighted three risks to a mega-sport event in the case of the Olympic Games in 2008 in Beijing: crime, such as kidnapping, petty theft, rape or internationally organized crime, socio-cultural sabotage and terrorism. The latter had already been especially addressed with regard to the Olympic Games; the IOC had already adapted their security standards against international terrorism (Coaffee, Fussey & Moore, 2011). For this reason, it is not surprising that the costs of security and safety have increased significantly. For example, security costs for Athens' Games in 2004 surpassed $1.6 billion, and they have remained nearly this high (Matheson, 2013). Similarly, in the case of EURO 2008, the host countries greatly increased their financial investments to secure these events, which led to the two countries making certain arrangements, for example visa agreements (Klauser, 2011). How the security standards would have to be adapted for polycentric events had to be uniquely addressed.

However, a positive effect of hosting mega-sport events was found to be an increase in tourists' overnight stays (Schmidt, 2012). Indeed, Szymanski (2002) pointed out that increased tourism is often the only economic benefit for the host countries in the years after the event is held. Similarly, Solberg and Preuss (2007) claimed that hosting major sport events can cause positive shifts in tourism demand on a long-term basis. Yet the researchers also pointed out that investments in the tourism sector seem to vary. For example, while the majority of Polish companies did not make specific investments in EURO 2012 (Wasilczuk & Zawadzki, 2013), China's private sector invested strongly in the tourism sector when preparing for Beijing 2008 (Sands, 2008). Nevertheless, even if expenditure in the tourism industries were to rise significantly due to a mega-event, additional revenues accrued might not counterbalance the host's investment costs (Solberg & Preuss, 2007) and, because of non-local capital owners, the money generated would be unlikely to re-circulate through the local economy (Matheson 2013).

Rütter et al. (2010) identified positive impacts of Euro 2008 on the job market in Austria and Switzerland but also pointed out that the number of new jobs provided due to the event was much lower than expected. Similarly, Baumann, Engelhardt and Matheson (2012) reported increased employment overall from the 2002 Olympics, but only within 12 months following the event. Overall, the economic impact appears to be limited. Preuss (2004) found that many mega-sport events only cover the operational costs but not the investment costs. For example, several stadiums have not been used in a profitable way after hosting mega-events (Schmidt, 2012). Since UEFA claimed that the format was intended to increase tourism and save costs by using existing facilities (Weinreich, 2012a; Winkler, 2014), these aspects were addressed in our study.

Social impacts

Research on the effects of sport mega-events on hosts has rarely focused on social aspects (Fredline, 2005), yet social impacts are often said to be another positive effect of hosting sport mega-events. Aside from an increase in soft power, sport mega-events often increase the number of members in sport associations (Schmidt, 2012) as well as increasing social capital and enhancing socialization (Baumann, Engelhardt, & Matheson, 2012). They may heighten the hosts' local and national citizens' feelings of shared experience and collective solidarity (Taks, 2013). Experiencing a euphoric atmosphere collectively creates a sense of community and meets the need for identification. For example, hosting the World Cup in 2006 contributed to strengthening the sense of community and national pride among German citizens and improved relationships between people of different ethnic origins (Ohmann, Jones & Wilkes, 2006).

However, events have also been found to have negative effects on their host citizens. For example, researchers have identified displacement or removal of local residents to clear space for the sporting venues, an exclusion of local resident participation due to high costs, or an increase in the crime rate (Fredline, 2005; Getz, 2005). News reports from recent sport mega-events, such as those in Brazil or China, have sadly confirmed these consequences. So it may be likely that those aspects may affect the sense of community identification as well as the atmosphere during the event. How different the atmosphere can be in two host countries during the same sport mega-event was demonstrated by Hellmann's (2012) report from the European Football Championship 2012 in Poland and Ukraine. While Poland's citizens and guests experienced a very positive atmosphere, this was not the case in the Ukraine. The author offered the explanation of Ukraine's domestic crisis at that time as well as difficulties with the coordination of the event between these two countries. However, it remains unclear how this spirit and sense of community could be preserved if the event were to be split between several countries (The *National*, 2014). Since Preuss et al. (2010) pointed out that the atmosphere is crucial in the success of a sport mega-event, and social impacts may vary due to the unique characteristics of the event (Fredline, 2005), the authors also considered this aspect in the present study.

Methodology

This exploratory study has aimed to answer the main research questions: what positive and negative effects may the EURO 2008 Championship imply? Which opportunities and limitations may it be suggested could be adapted to other sport mega-events, especially future Olympic Games? To gain an in-depth understanding of the problems and opportunities that can arise, a qualitative research rationale was chosen and purposive sampling was necessary. Since many different stakeholders are involved in organizing such an event, the authors interviewed experts from different fields. For example, individuals in leadership positions within sport organizations as well as within main sponsors of the European Championship in 2008 were included. Additionally, sport journalists were included who were involved in the European Championships in both 2008 and 2012 and various Olympic Games, together with experts from the safety and security sector, such as a safety representative for major events of a federal Ministry for the Interior who had hosted a previous EURO. Other interviewees included experts from umbrella organizations in organized sport who have worked with athletes, visitors or in venue management during past sport mega-events, such as EURO 2008. Finally, since fans are also affected by this future model of co-hosting, the authors also aimed to include the perspective of the spectators and interviewed Austrian fans who attended the European Football Championships in 2004, 2008 or 2012. In summary, 18 experts were interviewed to tackle the research questions from different perspectives and gain insights on various positive and negative consequences that might be offered by this new format.

The interview guide was developed based on findings from previous studies of mega-sport events with more than one host, such as the European Championships in 2008 and 2012, as well as on newspaper reports. Themes addressed included the following different categories: image, atmosphere and attractiveness for sport tourists, safety and security, economic benefits, especially tourism, and challenges and opportunities relating to marketing efforts. For example, Klauser (2012) reported on issues around the security concept at the UEFA European Football Championship 2008 in Austria and Switzerland. This led to the question: how can a security plan be developed for a multinational event? In addition, several questions concerning short-term and long-term effects on tourism or destination image of a host city were based on findings from Solberg and Preuss (2007). The interview questions were primarily open-ended.

The semi-structured interviews were conducted between March and December 2015. The interviews were conducted either face-to-face in a private and comfortable atmosphere, or via telephone or Skype, and lasted between 20 minutes and one hour. All interviews were recorded, transcribed and a thematic analysis was conducted with the most important facts highlighted. Primary codes were set up in accordance with findings from former studies. In addition, inductive coding was used to explore aspects that were not present in previous empirical research. In a second coding cycle, final codes were set up. To establish causal relationships, pattern matching was applied.

Internal validity was ensured through interviews using multiple sources of evidence, and a detailed research protocol ensured that the data collection procedure could be repeated and would provide similar results. The authors ensured inter-coder reliability by coding the same units of text, comparing their results and reconciling any discrepancies through discussion.

Results and discussion

This study's findings and discussions of the results are structured in accordance with the identified major themes. This section starts with the new event format offering new opportunities to host for smaller countries, followed by results on financial aspects, explaining the major findings in relation to the potential costs and benefits. Findings in relation to social aspects, in particular, the event spirit and the feeling of community are described next. Finally, findings relating to public screening and sponsoring are addressed.

Enabling the opportunity to host sport mega-events

Cities often have different resources available for bidding for the hosting of sport mega-events. Some cities get more support from their own government than others. This can be seen as the result of local political interests and the decision-making of international power networks in sport (Borgers, Vanreusel & Scheerder, 2013). Similarly, most interviewees stated that politicians have different interests in hosting sport mega-events according to their political intentions, and consequently support their cities' interest in bidding more or less financially and politically. In addition, smaller countries are sometimes simply not capable of hosting these events for financial reasons. However, in the case of the new format, as the majority of the interviewees perceived it, small countries may get the opportunity to bid, due to a smaller requirement for financial resources. Likewise, Winkler (2014) claimed that with this innovative polycentric concept, small cities like Copenhagen or Glasgow would get the opportunity to host these events, since the costs would be split between all hosts. Thus, the new concept offers new opportunities especially for small cities. However, as several interviewees pointed out that it may also imply that if a country only hosts one or two competitions of a multinational event, the support of its government would be marginal.

Financial costs and benefits

Major sport events often facilitate new investments. While the Olympic Games in 2008 in Beijing led to major investments in the private sector (Sands, 2008), such as the construction of additional hotels, the majority of the interviewees also stated that it is more likely that hotels and other businesses would not increase their investments if a multinational sport mega-event took place for only two or three days in their respective towns because the number of guests would be limited and the event would be short. However, all interviewees agreed upon the issue that major sport events also often require expensive investments in sport facilities as well as in non-sport, city-related infrastructure – regardless of how long the events take.

While UEFA chose the new format to enable the host cities to save costs (Weinreich, 2012a), many interviewees' perceptions were that using sport facilities and infrastructure that already existed would save some costs, but it would not be enough. The hosts would still have to modify existing facilities as well as construct new buildings. Indeed, the experts agreed that this new format would also require expensive investments in sport facilities as well as in non-sport, city-related infrastructure and emphasized that these investments would need to fit into the city's long-term plan in order to make the event economically successful for the host. Hence, using permanent locations, awarding two Euros in a row to the same host or applying a rotation would also reduce investment costs in sport facilities (Baade & Matheson, 2016).

In previous years, the costs of safety and security have increased significantly, especially due to the risk of terrorism (Yu, Klauser & Chan, 2009). Consequently, the interviewees emphasized an increase in complexity of the overall safety concept. An adapted security plan would have to be developed. The EURO 2020 security plan will need to be one common concept that all hosting countries agree on. However, due to the countries' different laws and regulations, it will most likely be a difficult process. In addition, as the interviewees perceived, the security concepts will have to meet the minimum security standards imposed by the umbrella organization, such as UEFA. It will most likely vary between the hosting countries, whether they implement the minimum standards or exceed them. Similarly, Klauser (2012) identified differences in the implementation of the security concept between Austria, an EU-member country, and Switzerland, a non-EU member, when they hosted the European Football Championship in 2008. For example, while the use of drones was allowed in Switzerland, it was not allowed in Austria. Furthermore, Switzerland used mobile fingerprint identification systems for better surveillance, while Austria did not. In addition, Switzerland's refusal to implement the EU Schengen agreement on European cross-border police cooperation increased the overall complexity of the safety operations.

One may argue that costs of security measures will be lower with the new format since the risks are diversified, but only a few interviewees predicted that this would be the case, with resulting lower security expenditures for the individual countries. On the contrary, most experts stressed that the risks could be higher at a multinational event because there would be more locations to attack. Hence, the costs of security and safety would still be high and could even exceed London 2012's costs of approximately €1billion or Sochi 2014's €2 billion (Spiller, 2015). In summary, the experts agreed that the security topic would be an important and sensitive issue in organizing a multinational event.

The IOC and other international sport confederations argue that this new format promotes sustainability (*Der Standard*, 2014). However, most interviewees had serious doubts about this reasoning. Aside from investments in facilities and infrastructure, the new format creates the need to transport athletes between venues in different countries, thus also losing the important athlete experience of a single Olympic village. In addition, while China demonstrated that the Olympic Games can be a reason for investing in environmental technology, these findings show that the investments would be divided among all hosting countries. Consequently, they would most likely be rather small in each hosting country and not comparable with China's long-term investment in transportation, urban renewal, high technology and sport facilities in Beijing, such as installing solid waste processing facilities

(Sands, 2008). Overall, the experts agreed that the hosting countries would most likely argue that their events were sustainable, for political or image reasons.

Benefits for destination branding and tourism

Overall, the interviewees agreed that the new model could mean a financial loss for the hosts. The only economic benefit would most likely be increased tourism in the host cities on a short-term basis. Similarly, Preuss et al. (2010) identified short-term positive impacts of the Euro 2008 for the tourism sector in Austria, such as an increased number of overnight stays the following year. While Solberg and Preuss (2007) suggested that hosting major sport events could also cause positive shifts in tourism demand on a long-term basis, several interviewees pointed out that an event lasting two or three days might not increase the destination brand significantly, even though global exposure would seem to contribute to tourism demand.

However, the polycentric model may offer several benefits – not only to reduce investment costs in sport facilities, but also to increase the destination brand and loyalty if any of the following ideas are considered: first, the usage of permanent locations; second, awarding two successive Games to the same host; or, third, designating a few venues that are used in rotation (Baade & Matheson, 2016; Kaplanidou, Jordan, Funk & Ridinger, 2012). In conjunction with a marketing strategy, the destination brand "Europe" with its cultural richness could be developed and, consequently, destination loyalty and tourism could be increased. That way, as the majority of the interviewees stated, the diversity of locations could increase the attractiveness of the tournament for the sport tourist. If the infrastructure, border control and customs are well coordinated, it may be possible that a multinational polycentric event can contribute to a stronger European identity. However, if organized poorly, the attractiveness could be reduced due to much greater logistical demands.

The spirit of one scattered community

Crucial to developing the destination brand "Europe", as well as the success of the mega-sport event, is the atmosphere at the venues and the feeling of "one community". While research has shown that many past mega-sport events created euphoria, national identification and pride as well as a sense of "we" and one community (Sands, 2008), most interviewees predicted that in the case of the new format, the spirit and flair might get lost. Additionally, the majority stated that the sense of community among the athletes would probably decrease and the existence of one Olympic village would become uncertain. Similarly, Simeoni (2014) raised the question whether the athletes might find themselves in Olympic isolation with the new format, situated in different countries without contact with other athletes from other disciplines.

Several interviewees further claimed that social media activities would not be able to reduce the feeling of distance between people. While social media may elicit emotions and link people to a certain degree, it might not replace the feeling of solidarity and community that emerges when people come together at major sport events. The IOC members had a similar debate during the Olympic Agenda 2020 meeting in September 2014. While they found no solution as to how the Olympic atmosphere could be preserved with the new format (The *National*, 2014), the majority of the interviewees' perception was that a common cultural programme by all hosts might help to create a sense of solidarity. The hosts could present themselves together to show cultural similarities and differences. However, most interviewees also claimed that even though the competitions would take place in different countries, all sport contests would be connected to each other due to the presence of the coherent marketing efforts. Hence, the consumer would perceive the tournament as a whole sport event with a consistent image.

New format, new issues – public screening and sponsoring

Alongside the key findings, the majority of the experts suggested that the new format would influence the popularity of public screenings and, to a certain degree, create new difficulties with regard to sponsoring. Since the competitions would take place in various locations, and people from several countries would most likely not travel between them, public screening events would not bring together as many different people as they have done with the current models of one or two hosts.

In addition, most interviewees pointed out that the new format would be less attractive for representing national or local sponsors, since only a few competitions would take place at one venue and, hence, fewer people could be reached. As a consequence, the official sponsors may limit their hospitality and other marketing activities to a few locations, such as those where the finals take place. Moreover, local and national businesses would most likely not be interested in advertising outside of their markets, where they are unknown. Even many international companies may not do business in these 13 countries. In such cases it would be more efficient to pick other events to address their specific target markets. However, the interviewees also stated that big international companies whose target markets are spread over these 13 countries could probably address a much larger audience with their marketing activities since viewer ratings (broadcasting) may increase. Finally, the interviewees referred to the importance of the spirit at international sport mega-events, which they usually use intentionally to reach their target audience. They stressed that the lack of community spirit and euphoric atmosphere could potentially hinder the marketing activities of any company.

Conclusions

Since the research to date on the prospective positive and negative impacts of polycentric events is very limited, this study gives some initial insights into the possibilities and limits of hosting sport mega-events in more than two countries. Contrary to the benefits that UEFA claims for this new event format, this study shows that the coordination of a major sport event in the new format may entail several potential difficulties, such as the highly complex creation and implementation of a safety and security concept. In addition, the new format might mean the potential loss of the euphoric atmosphere, spirit and sense of community. It would affect both athletes and spectators, hinder the marketing activities of the sponsors and, consequently, impair the overall success of the tournament. However, the interviewees also pointed out that under certain circumstances this format offers the opportunity to develop the destination brand "Europe" and, consequently, destination loyalty and tourism could be increased. In this case, organizers and hosts may have to think about new ways to create an unforgettable atmosphere and to promote positive social impacts that fit the unique characteristics of the new event format.

Finally, while UEFA stresses that a major advantage of the new format would be the use of existing sport venues and infrastructure, the interviewees stressed that expensive investment in sport facilities and infrastructure (UEFA.com, 2014) would be needed, since existing facilities would have to be modified and in some cities new venues would have to be constructed. Furthermore, contrary to the reasoning of UEFA, the experts stressed that it was a misconception that the new event format would be sustainable. Due to the challenges discussed, it is not surprising that several countries do not support the co-hosting idea. For example, the bidding committee for the Almaty 2022 Olympic Winter Games was not willing to split the sport event over a larger geographical area (Bisson, 2014).

Overall, while UEFA has praised the new event format as a path to success with multiple benefits, this study shows that the new event format might be neither a success nor a mistake in the making, but seems to retain several issues familiar to hosts of sport mega-events in the traditional format with one or two hosts. In addition, this format will cause several new challenges that need to be addressed in order to make the event successful. However, while this study has given an overview on the implications of the new format, the findings need to be addressed in more depth in future studies, relating them to particular events and their specific characteristics. Moreover, an evaluation of the UEFA European Championship 2020 would reveal further important insights into the opportunities and limitations of this new format and show whether a truly European feeling may develop as a result of hosting a tournament across an entire geographical area.

References

Baade, R. A. & Matheson, V. A. (2016). Going for the gold: The economics of the Olympics. *Journal of Economic Perspectives, 30*(2), 201–218.

Baumann, R., Engelhardt, B. & Matheson, V. A. (2012). Employment effects of the 2002 Winter Olympics in Salt Lake City, Utah. *Jahrbücher für Nationalökonomie und Statistik, 232*(3), 308–317.

Bisson, M. (2014). Almaty Rules Out Co-Hosting Plan for 2022 Winter Olympics. *Around the Rings.* Retrieved from <http://aroundtherings.com/site/A__49631/Title__Almaty-Rules-Out-Co-Hosting-Plan-for-2022-Winter-Olympics/292/Articles>. Accessed 15 February 2015.

Black, D. & Van der Westhuizen, J. (2004). The allure of global games for "semi-peripheral" polities and spaces: A research agenda. *Third World Quarterly, 25*(7), 1195–1214.

Böcking, D. (2012). "Der Ball rollt, der Rubel nicht". *Spiegel Online.* Retrieved from <http://www.spiegel.de/forum/wirtschaft/bilanz-von-sportereignissen-der-ball-rollt-der-rubel-nicht-thread-77484-1.html>. Accessed 4 February 2015.

Borgers, J. Vanreusel, B. & Scheerder, J. (2013). The diffusion of world sports events between 1891 and 2010: A study on globalisation. *Journal of Sports Management, 10*(2), 101–119.

Coaffee, J. Fussey, P. & Moore, C. (2011). Laminated security for London 2012: Enhancing security infrastructures to defend mega sporting events. *Urban Studies, 48*(15), 3311–3327.

Cornelissen, S. (2007). Crafting legacies: The changing political economy of global sport and the 2010 FIFA World Cup. *Politikon, 34*(3), 241–259.

Cornelissen, S., Bob, U. & Swart, K. (2011). Towards redefining the concept of legacy in relation to sport mega-events: Insights from the 2010 FIFA World Cup. *Development Southern Africa, 28*(3), 307–318.

Cornelissen, S. & Swart, K. (2006). The 2010 Football World Cup as a political construct: The challenge of making good on an African promise. In J. Horne & W. Manzenreiter (Eds), *Sports Mega Events: Social Scientific Analyses of a Global Phenomenon* (pp. 108–124). Malden, MA: Blackwell.

Der Standard. (2014). Olympia-Reformen: Dafürsein ist alles. Retrieved from <http://derstandard.at/2000009175790/Dafuersein-ist-alles>. Accessed 5 October 2015.

Fredline, E. (2005). Host and guest relations and sport tourism. *Sport in Society, 8*(2), 263–279.

Getz, D. (2005). *Festivals, Special Events and Tourism.* New York: Van Nostrand.

Hellmann, F. (2012). "EM-Gastgeber Polen und Ukraine – Turnier in zwei Welten". *Der Stern.* Retrieved from <www.stern.de/sport/fussball/em-2012/teams/em-gastgeber-polen-und-ukraine-turnier-in-zwei-welten-3675834.html>. Accessed 15 February 2015.

Horne, J. & Manzenreiter, W. (2006). An introduction to the sociology of sports mega-events. In J. Horne & W. Manzenreiter (Eds), *Sports Mega Events: Social Scientific Analyses of a Global Phenomenon* (pp. 1–24). Malden, MA: Blackwell.

Kaplanidou, K., Jordan, J., Funk, D. & Ridinger, L. (2012). Recurring sport events and destination image perceptions: Impact on active sport tourist behavioral intentions and place attachment. *Journal of Sport Management*, *26*(3), 237–248.

Klauser, F. (2011). Commonalities and specificities in mega-event securitization: The example of Euro 2008 in Austria and Switzerland. In C. Bennet & K. Haggerty (Eds), *Security Games*. London: Routledge.

Klauser, F. R. (2012). Interpretative flexibility of the event-city: Security, branding and urban entrepreneurialism at the European Football Championships 2008. *International Journal of Urban and Regional Research*, *36*(5), 1039–1052.

Krüger, M. (2001). Olympische Krisen – eine historische Analyse und pädagogische Folgerungen. In M. Krüger (Ed.), *Olympische Spiele: Bilanz und Perspektiven im 21. Jahrhundert*. Münster: LIT.

Maguire, J. & Tuck, J. (2005). A world in union? Rugby, globalization, and Irish identity. In J. Maguire (Ed.), *Power and Global Sport: Zones of Prestige, Emulation and Resistance* (pp. 109–129). London: Routledge.

Manzenreiter, W. (2004). Sportevents und makro-ökonomische Effekte: Theorie und Praxis am Beispiel der Fußball WM 2002. *Kurswechsel: Zeitschrift für gesellschafts-, wirtschafts-, und umweltpolitische Alternativen*, *2*, 67–79.

Marivoet, S. (2006). Uefa Euro 2004 Portugal: The social construction of a sports mega-event and spectacle. In J. Horne & W. Manzenreiter (Eds), *Sports Mega Events: Social Scientific Analyses of a Global Phenomenon* (pp. 127–143). Malden, MA: Blackwell.

Matheson, V. (2013). Assessing the Infrastructure Impact of Mega-Events in Emerging Economies. In G. K. Ingram & K. L. Brandt (Eds), *Infrastructure and Land Policies* (pp. 215–232). Cambridge, MA: Lincoln Land Institute.

National, The (2014). "More sports and co-hosting in Olympics could be a reality as IOC ring in reforms". Available at <www.thenational.ae/sport/other/more-sports-and-co-hosting-in-olympics-could-be-a-reality-as-ioc-ring-in-reforms>. Accessed 30 September 2016.

Ohmann, S., Jones, I., & Wilkes, K. (2006). The perceived social impacts of the 2006 Football World Cup on Munich residents. *Journal of Sport & Tourism*, *11*(2), 129–152.

Preuss, H. (2004). *The Economics of Staging the Olympics: A Comparison of the Games, 1972–2008*. Cheltenham, UK: Edward Elgar.

Preuss, H., Siller, H., Zehrer, A., Schütte, N. & Stickdorn, M. (2010). *Wirtschaftliche Wirkungen und Besucherzufriedenheit mit der UEFA EURO 2008: Eine empirische Analyse für Österreich*. Wiesbaden: Gabler.

Roche, M. (2002). The Olympics and "global citizenship". *Citizenship Studies*, *6*(2), 165–181.

Rütter, H., Popp, J., Holzhey, M. & Busin, C. (2010). *Wirtschaftliche Wirkungen der UEFA EURO 2008 TM in der Schweiz-Schlussbericht*. Rüschlikon, Switzerland: Rütter & Partner.

Sands, L. (2008). The 2008 Olympics' impact on China. *China Business Review*. Retrieved from <www.chinabusinessreview.com/the-2008-olympics-impact-on-china/>. Accessed 4 February 2015.

Schmidt, H. (2012). Fußballgroßveranstaltungen – sportpolitische Herausforderungen. In M.-P. Büch, W. Maennig & H.-J. Schulke (Eds), *Sport und Sportgroßveranstaltungen in Europa – zwischen Zentralstaat und Regionen*. Hamburg: University Press.

Simeoni, E. (2014). "Thomas Bachs, Agenda 2020: Das IOC im olympischen Reform-Rausch". *Die Frankfurter Allgemeine*. Available at <www.faz.net/aktuell/sport/sportpolitik/agenda-2020-das-ioc-im-olympischen-reform-rausch-13309819.html>. Accessed 4 February 2015.

Solberg, H. A. & Preuss, H. (2007). Major sport events and long-term tourism impacts. *Journal of Sport Management*, *21*(2), 213–234.

Spiller, C. (2015). "Olympische Spiele – Die Rechnung bitte". *Die Zeit Online*. Available at <www.zeit.de/sport/2015-03/olympia-kosten-berlin-hamburg>. Accessed 20 March 2015.

Szymanski, S. (2002). The economic impact of the World Cup. *World Economics*, *3*(1), 169–177.

Taks, M. (2013). Social sustainability of non-mega sport events in a global world. *European Journal for Sport and Society*, *10*(2), 121–141.

UEFA.com (2014). "UEFA-Präsident erwartet 2020 'großartige Momente'". Retrieved from <http://de.uefa.com/uefaeuro-2020/news/newsid=2151290.html>. Accessed 4 August 2016.

UEFA.com (2016). "Die wichtigsten Fakten zur UEFA EURO 2020". Retrieved from <http://de.uefa.com/uefaeuro-2020/news/newsid=2390029.html>. Accessed 28 September 2016.

Wasilczuk, J. & Zawadzki, K. (2013). Impact of Euro 2012 on the Pomeranian region and its small and medium enterprises in terms of competitiveness. *Journal of Business Strategy*, *10*(2), 22–37.

Weinreich, J. (2012a). "EM 2020: Platinis raffiniertes Fußballmanöver". *Spiegel Online*. Retrieved from <www.spiegel.de/sport/fussball/fussball-em-2020-platini-rettet-seine-endrunde-mit-24-teilnehmern-a-871600.html>. Accessed 4 February 2015.

Weinreich, J. (2012b). "Europaweite Fußball-EM 2020. Der Volltreffer". *Spiegel Online*. Retrieved from <www.spiegel.de/sport/fussball/em-2020-uefa-entscheidung-fuer-europaweites-turnier-ist-richtig-a-871492.html>. Accessed 4 February 2015.

Winkler, P. (2014). Trotz deutscher Nörgelei – Die Splitter-EM 2020 ist eine gute Uefa-Idee. *Focus Online*. Retrieved from <www.focus.de/sport/fussball/em_2020/trotz-deutscher-noergelei-warum-die-euro-2020-eine-gute-idee-ist_id_4146578.html>. Accessed 4 February 2015.

Xin, X. (2006). Modernizing China in the Olympic spotlight: China's national identity and the 2008 Bejing Olympiad. In J. Horne & W. Manzenreiter (Eds), *Sports Mega Events: Social Scientific Analyses of a Global Phenomenon*. Malden, MA: Blackwell.

Yu, Y., Klauser, F. & Chan, G. (2009). Governing security at the 2008 Beijing Olympics. *International Journal of the History of Sport*, *26*(3), 390–405.

4

MAJOR SPORT EVENTS AT THE CENTRE OF INTERNATIONAL SPORT FEDERATIONS' RESOURCE STRATEGY

Josephine Clausen and Emmanuel Bayle

Introduction – From regulating to commercializing sport events

> The stakes have moved up considerably, customers expect events to be international, to be bigger and better than previously and everything is geared towards achieving the bottom line.
>
> *Emery 2010, p. 166*

One hundred years ago, International Sport Federations (ISFs) came into existence for a practical reason – to organize and regulate international sports. The first modern Olympic Games (OG) in 1896 (Athens) made international rules indispensable and the growing success of the Games made major sport events more and more attractive. The historical function of ISFs can be compared to that of a government (Hoehn, 2006): they exert a legislative role by establishing rules, a judicial role by monitoring and enforcing these rules, and an executive role by organizing major sport events such as World Championships. Since their creation, ISFs have undergone important structural and functional evolution. Starting out as volunteer-run associations, IFs employ today up to 450 or more staff members at their headquarters (i.e. FIFA, UEFA). In literature, these evolutions are often categorized as organizational change. On one hand, they stem from internal needs for rationalization and efficiency (Chantelat, 2001; Dowling, Edwards & Washington, 2014) such as the hiring of paid managers, whose specialized background and expertise entails internal formalization and standardization procedures. On the other hand, they are the result of an adaption to external changes. ISFs have to adapt to an increasingly complex and competitive environment, including growing numbers of interest groups with varying and sometimes diverging expectations. In response to these pressures, ISFs invent different solutions. Looking at major sport events is one possible approach to investigating ISFs' strategic resource acquisition patterns. The findings reveal that observed patterns are either historically funded or emerge/have emerged as the result of changing environmental circumstances and organizations' internal response strategies to them.

For the analysis of ISFs' resource strategies, three aspects make international sport events an interesting starting point: (1) their constantly growing number and globalization, (2) their continuous commercialization, and (3) the lack of research on sport events from the perspective of ISFs. All three points are briefly outlined below:

1. The growing number and globalization of sport events: In 1975, the ISFs of the 25 sports represented at the OG counted 160 international events, these being World Championships, World Cups, Grand Prix, World Tours and so on. Within 38 years, this number rose to 2,162 events in 2013 (source: the Association of Summer Olympic International Federations (ASOIF)). Initially, the World Championships represented the sole and most important event of ISFs, crowning the best athletes of the sport. With the abolition of the Olympic amateur code in 1981, World Championships and their like became more attractive for top athletes (seeking prize money) which, in turn, lured spectators (seeking entertainment), broadcasters and sponsors (seeking a return on investment). Progressively, ISFs recognized their commercial value, began to define which rights had value (e.g. event hosting, event bidding, logo/naming rights, broadcasting and so on) and established ownership of these rights. Once event formats and rights had been established, many ISFs turned towards new countries in search of additional market opportunities and the global spread and development of their sport. Countries previously unknown for sport events entered the stage: in 2016, Qatar, a peninsula primarily covered with sand, hosted 85 major international sport events, and even Mongolia hosted 16 (e.g. Motocross World Championships, Sumo World Championships, international biathlon competition). Sport is no longer just a physical activity and social meeting point. It has become an economic product and an increasing number of actors from various levels try to leverage its financial potential.

2. The commercialization of sport events: Since the 1980s, the galloping commercialization of broadcasting and sponsorship rights linked to the sprouting economy around major sport events (e.g. Olympic Games), and increasing competition between top-level sports, have pushed ISFs to embrace strategic thinking and planning. For some ISFs, being on the Olympic Programme has become a financial comfort zone, but also a highly competitive affair. Through the first Olympic revenue distribution in 1992, totalling US$ 37.6 million, each of the 25 ISFs on the Olympic summer programme at that time received US$ 1.5 million. Over the years, the revenue share did not stop increasing, reaching a record high of US$ 526 million after the London 2012 Games (source: ASOIF). Although the financial windfall of the OG is uncontestably a blessing for ISFs, it can also result in a quandary. On the one hand, ISFs need to attract sponsors, investors and partners in order to finance a growing number of activities (strategic and operational) and defend their Olympic status (IOC evaluation criteria). Hence, ISFs have to be responsive to stakeholders' needs, wishes and expectations. On the other hand, ISFs need to stay true to their core values and missions and advocate their members' needs, wishes and expectations (Berrett & Slack, 2001). Navigating between these two poles, ISFs adopt different approaches to satisfy one side or the other. Strategic planning, including the setting of goals, an action plan to achieve these goals, and the mobilization and allocation of resources to execute the action plan, has become a valuable tool for sport federations, be it at the national (Shilbury & Ferkins, 2011) or international level (Nagel et al., 2015). Events appear to play a pivotal role in ISFs' strategy in terms of resource acquisition. Today, the success of an ISF's economic model largely depends on its capacity to commercialize its major events (e.g. broadcasting and sponsor rights, organizing fees).

3. Lack of research: Despite the exponential growth of international major sport events, little research exists on major sport events from the perspective of ISFs. Taking the perspective

of the organizing committee (e.g. Parent, 2008), previous studies primarily focus on event management (e.g. Leopkey & Parent, 2016; Parent & Smith-Swan 2013) and organization as well as commercialization (Lee & Taylor, 2005; Szymanski, 2003; Malfas, Theodoraki & Houlihan, 2004). In light of these evolutions, two central and so far unexplored questions emerge: which elements constitute ISFs' main sources of income and expenses? Which financial and strategic role do sport events occupy in ISFs' economic model?

This chapter starts with an overview of event types in international sport, followed by a general summary of ISFs' main sources of revenue. The main question of major sport events as a central element of ISFs' resource strategy is examined by applying a two-fold approach: first, observed commonalities across several ISFs are outlined; second, four cases exemplifying four different models of revenue generation are presented: FIFA as the international football federation, the FIH as the international hockey federation, FISA as the international rowing federation and the UCI as the international cycling federation. The evaluation of the four federations is based on an analytical model presented beforehand.

Federations' resource strategies through major sport events

Today, two major actors govern sport at a global level: the International Olympic Committee (IOC) organizing the OG every four years (Chappelet 2008) and ISFs regulating international sport and organizing World Championships and World Cups (Arcioni & Bayle, 2012). While the regulation, promotion and organization of their sport used to be ISFs' core mission and the reason for their emergence, sport events have taken centre stage, especially with regard to resource acquisition. This evolution results in a seemingly contradictory hybridity: established as associative non-profit structures, ISFs have developed a strong commercial orientation. Although these two rationales appear to be diametrically opposed, they are also complementary, as generating financial income is vital for the development and continuity of ISFs' activities (Bayle, 2000). ISFs partially or entirely delegate the organization of their events to an event organizer (for example, national federation, region, government). The delegation of organizing responsibilities, financial charges and profits depends on the type and appeal of the event. It is therefore important to first distinguish different types of events and event ownership.

Event types

Considering events as the central element of federations' sporting, economic, societal and organizational performance, Bayle distinguishes (2015) different types of sport events owned and/or organized by sport federations (international and national). Adapted to ISFs, four event types can be emphasized: World Championships, international circuits, promotional sport-for-all events and international multi-sport games. ISFs generally own the first three event types and are participants in the fourth type. Being the owners of the first three types empowers them to decide on the event allocation and to capitalize on commercial rights such as TV and sponsorship rights. ISFs usually concede ticketing and domestic sponsorship rights to the organizer, this being a national sport federation (NSF), region or private organizer. In this constellation, the ISF is in a position of power, especially if the event is very successful and attracts a number of potential organizers competing for the allocation.

1. *World Championships*: Often the flagship event of an ISF, these major one-off events may be held at differing periodicity depending on the ISF (e.g. the UCI and FISA every year,

FIFA and the FIH every four years). The ISF decides on the event allocation, often through a bidding process. Divided into men, women and, for some sports, mixed competitions (e.g. tennis, badminton), World Championships are organized for different age categories (e.g. Junior, Under 23, Elite, Masters).

2. *International circuits*: International circuits is a collective term for World Cups, World Tours, World Series, Grand Prix events and their like. ISFs generally own the circuit but not the events composing the circuit. Depending on the various aspects (e.g. the balance of power between the ISF and event organizers, historical reasons), events may be registered on the ISF calendar (e.g. Diamond League in athletics), constitute private professional circuits outside the full control of the ISF (e.g. ATP World Tour in tennis or PGA Championship in golf) or belong to a national sport federation (e.g. Australian Open, US Open) or a private organizer (e.g. Tour de France). In some sports, the international circuit, or even single events of it, are more powerful than the ISF's major event (e.g. tennis with Grand Slam, Tour de France in cycling).

3. *Promotional sport-for-all events*: Less focusing on competition, mass-participation events or international sport festivals are an opportunity for an ISF to promote its sport and reach out towards unexploited markets.

4. *International multi-sport games*: Although ISFs are only participants in these events (e.g. the Olympic Games, the Commonwealth Games, the Asian Games, university games, etc.), international multi-sport games can be of high sporting, strategic and economic importance as they convey visibility which, in turn, increases the attractiveness of a sport for sponsors, athletes and fans.

Although different event types may co-exist, ISFs' deliberate creation of an event portfolio that is tailored to their needs and strategy is a rather recent evolution. Event portfolio means in this case a deliberate pattern of events owned, organized and/or controlled by the ISF. The event portfolio has an impact not only on the federation's image, but also on its sporting, economic, societal and organizational performance. It is therefore hardly surprising that events occupy today a pivotal role in ISFs' strategy and resource acquisition. Within the event portfolio, events may be of different importance, creating a certain hierarchy. We assume that the economic value of events is determined by their importance.

Main sources of revenue

Unlike NSFs, ISFs are not dependent on government funding. Until the 1980s, ISFs functioned mainly thanks to the time and knowledge investment of a few passionate volunteers. At that time, ISFs' boards were almost entirely composed of individuals with a background in the respective sport (e.g. former athletes or presidents of a NSF). Especially in the early years of a federation, this prerequisite was inevitable as rules had to be established, requiring an extensive understanding of the sport. All functions within the ISF were then non-remunerated. Affiliation fees from NSFs and small sponsorship contracts were therefore sufficient to fund and maintain the ISFs' activities. This changed rapidly with the commercialization of major sport events and most of all the OG. Sponsors began to use sport events to showcase their products and ISFs began to compete for their financial resources. Two main sources of financial income arose from this situation for ISFs: (1) revenue from federations' own events and (2) the Olympic revenue.

Events

Looking at the last completed summer Olympic cycle (2012–2015), nine out of 18 summer Olympic ISFs for which information is available generated 50 per cent or more of their revenue through their events.

To a large extent, this situation is the result of a growing interest in televised sport and the rise of an international broadcasting industry. Television brought sport from the restricted reach of fields and stadiums into the living rooms of thousands of people. While the first FIFA World Cup (Uruguay, 1930) was attended by some 430,000 spectators in the stadiums, the 2014 FIFA World Cup (Brazil) counted 3.4 million spectators and another 26.3 billion TV viewers! The demand for televised sport has attracted not only media and sponsors, it has also increased the need for expert knowledge within federations in order to respond to stakeholders' expectations and produce attractive events. Profound organizational changes were needed to adapt to this new situation. The growth in size and number of events, a question of both the popularity of the sport and the ISFs' ability to capitalize on this popularity, is generally accompanied by a diversification and complexification of ISFs' activities. As a consequence, voluntary positions are no longer sufficient to carry out ISFs' administrative tasks and organize major sport events implying multiple stakeholders. Since the end of the 1980s and the beginning of the 1990s, ISFs have progressively hired paid Secretary Generals (e.g. FISA in 1989, the UCI in 1992), followed by a steadily increasing number of paid staff (especially in the ISFs with fast-growing events). FIFA has increased its staff from about 250 in 2003 to more than 450 in 2014, the UCI from three in 1991 to 79 in 2014 and even a smaller federation such as the FIH has more than doubled its staff within a relatively short time (2010–2015) from 14 to 35.

Table 4.1 Revenues from ISF events and Olympic revenue

Federation (IOC terminology)	Period analysed	Revenues from ISF events (% of overall revenue)	Olympic revenue (% of overall revenue)
BWF – Badminton Word Federation	2012–15	78%	21%
FEI – International Equestrian Federation	2012–15	78%	9%
FIE – International Fencing Federation	2012–13	3%	29%
FIFA – International Association Football Federation	2012–15	88%	0.4%
FIH – International Hockey Federation	2013–15	56%	32%
FINA – International Swimming Federation	2014–15	70%	21%
FISA – International Rowing Federation	2012–15	37%	52%
IJF – International Judo Federation	2012–14	64%	23%
ISAF – World Sailing	2012–13	13%	61%
ISSF – International Shooting Sport Federation	2012–15	2%	85%
ITF – International Tennis Federation	2012–15	75%	10%
ITTF – International Table Tennis Federation	2012–14	50%	31%
ITU – International Triathlon Union	2013–15	40%	56%
IWF – International Weightlifting Federation	2013–14	17%	56%
UCI – International Cycling Union	2012–15	70%	14%
UWW – United World Wrestling	2012–15	29%	40%
WA – World Archery	2012–14	31%	63%
WR – World Rugby	2012–15	97%	0%

Olympic revenue

The Olympic revenue share is closely related to the general evolution of broadcasting rights. For the 1960 Olympic Games (Rome), USA TV (today CBS) paid US$3.2 million (in today's dollars) for the broadcasting rights. Forty-eight years later, the broadcasting rights for the 2012 London Games were sold for nearly US$1.2 billion to NBC, a multiplication factor of more than 300! In a sense, the commercialization of and profit generated by the OG began with the 1984 Los Angeles Games. Under the direction of Peter Ueberroth (president and general manager of the Los Angeles Olympic Organizing Committee), the 1984 Games were the first to be privately organized and immediately generated a surplus of US$250 million. The following Games pursued the same strategy and with success. In 1992, the IOC distributed for the first time a part of the Games' proceeds to the ISFs: a total of US$37.6 million was equally divided between the 25 ISFs that figured on the Olympic Programme (US$1.5 million/ISF). Twenty years later, a total of US$526 million was divided between the 28 ISFs that were involved in the Olympic Programme of the 2012 London Games, this being US$19 million on average per ISF. Meanwhile, the IOC had introduced the *Evaluation Criteria for Sports and Disciplines* in 2004: based on the evaluation criteria, 30 per cent of the additional surplus of the OG dedicated to the ISFs is subsequently allocated, depending on the ISFs' contribution to the overall economic success of the Games (e.g. tickets sold, TV audience). After the 2012 London Games, the IAAF (athletics) was awarded the highest share – about US$47 million for a four-year period. The prospect of a higher share if outperforming other sports has entailed strong competition between Olympic ISFs as well as non-Olympic ISFs who seek to enter the Olympic Programme. The benefit of being an Olympic sport impacts at both the international and the national level: on the one hand, it contributes to the financing of ISFs' activities; on the other hand, governments tend to support NSFs of Olympic sports more generously with funds to increase their chances of beating other countries at OG, making sport a geopolitical tool.

In summary, ISFs' resource acquisition has changed drastically due to the explosion of broadcasting rights, the interest of sponsors in showcasing their products through televised sport events and the skyrocketing profitability of the Olympic Games. While affiliation from member fees and smaller sponsor contracts constituted the main source of income for many decades, the demand for televised sport spectacles has brought forth a new and more business-oriented rationality. Nevertheless, the spread between ISFs with high revenues and ISFs with low revenues is immense: while FIFA generated a comfortable US$2.096 billion in 2014, half of the non-Olympic, but recognized, ISFs function with less than €200,000 per year (source: Association of IOC-recognized International Sport Federations (ARISF)). The mission-based goal of ISFs is to finance the development of their sport, for example by cross-subsidizing unprofitable events (as is the case with 11 out of the 12 FIFA events), supporting national development programmes (e.g. FIH Targeted Assistance Programme) or helping to improve members' functioning (e.g. UCI Sharing Platform). In this context, federations' events and economic models should be a means to develop their sport. In order to understand and predict why some ISFs have more successful economic models than others, four Olympic ISFs of different sizes are analysed more closely. The main focus is on ISFs' events and their role in the federations' economic model.

International Sport Federations' economic model and the role of major sport events

It is very difficult to compare the functioning and economic models of ISFs for various reasons, such as accessibility to, as well as transparency and exhaustiveness of documents.

ISFs' organizational structure (e.g. bodies, departments, organizational complexity), functioning (e.g. organizational performance, behaviour and learning) and culture (traditions, values) play a significant role here. Initially, events such as World Championships were not created for financial reasons, but to determine the best athletes. This chapter does not claim to produce a comprehensive understanding of the development of ISFs' events over time. However, it tries to identify emerging commonalities regarding ISFs' economic models and the role of major sport events in it. Following this, the chapter proposes an analytical model and four exemplary cases to which this model has been applied.

Emerging commonalities

Despite limited comparability, a few emerging commonalities could be noticed between the federations in terms of event-related resource acquisition.

Event ownership and event rights

ISFs generally claim ownership over a minimum of one, often two, event types. These are World Championships (in some sports called World Cup) and international circuits (e.g. World Tour, World Cup, Grand Prix), both being major one-off competitions. ISFs also tend to sanction international events that are not their property. The ISF may register these events free of charge or against a calendar or organizer fee. In the case of the UCI, the calendar, licence and affiliation fees constitute 17 per cent of the federation's overall financial income (2012–2015: 40 per cent if the organizing fees are added). However, the claiming of property rights is only profitable if there are enough buyers. Then again, the more buyers that compete for the rights acquisition, the more the federation can raise the price. Risks inherent to this situation are excessive prices that stakeholders are not willing or able to pay, and unsatisfactory returns on investment for stakeholders.

Financial cycles around events

If one or several major events form the ISF's principal source of income, the federation has an interest in ensuring they function well. Financial cycles around ISFs' major events can be observed, meaning that important parts of the revenue from federations' flagship events are reinvested in the events. In the case of FIFA, the flagship event (the FIFA World Cup) is organized every four years. In 2014, FIFA generated 91 per cent of its overall income from the 2014 FIFA World Cup (e.g. 35 per cent from broadcasting rights, 23 per cent from ticketing and 22 per cent from marketing rights). In the same year, FIFA invested 42 per cent of all its expenses in the same event including, for instance, TV production (19 per cent) and prize money (18 per cent). On average, FIFA invested 53 per cent in events during 2012–2015, 41 per cent in the FIFA World Cup alone. In the case of the UCI, 25.5 per cent was invested in events during the same period.

Olympic revenue dependence

While the Olympic revenue share may be irrelevant in the budget of a very big federation such as FIFA (0.4 per cent), it is vital for many small federations such as ISSF (shooting) (85 per cent). Federations with high Olympic revenue dependence run the risk of not being self-sustainable without that money. For the last summer Olympic cycle (2012–2015), the average dependence of the 18 summer Olympic federations for which financial statements are available was about 33.5 per cent. It is of no surprise that Olympic sports, and especially those that are highly dependent on the Olympic revenue share, are making every effort to defend their place on the Olympic Programme.

Although the focus of this section is on ISFs' economic models, its impact on the wider system including continental and national federations is worth mentioning: ISFs generating important revenue through their own events are expected to invest larger parts of their expenses externally (i.e. primarily on events and development) and ISFs with average or low event profitability invest internally (i.e. primarily on operations, administration and governance). The following examples support this assumption: FIFA invested 71 per cent externally and 18 per cent internally (2012–2015), contrary to the FIH, which invested 37 per cent externally and 61 per cent internally (2013–2015) and FISA, which invested 31.5 per cent externally and 68 per cent internally (2012–2015).

Analytical model

For the purpose of illustration, data on event revenue were collected from 18 summer Olympic federations. In addition, four exemplary ISFs were selected for a more fine-grained analysis: FIFA, the UCI, the FIH and FISA. Data stem from externally audited financial statements and financial reports, event regulations, bidding documents, organizer guides, face-to-face interviews (n=15) with ISF officials and staff members from FIFA, the FIH, FISA and the UCI, as well as representatives of umbrella organizations, i.e. the Association of Summer Olympic International Federations (ASOIF), the Association of IOC Recognized International Sport Federations (ARISF), and SportAccord. We admit that data collection was complicated by the lack of available documents as well as by the varying exhaustiveness of documents (e.g. financial reports varied between seven and 156 pages). This undeniably impeded the data analysis and made direct comparability of ISFs more difficult. Findings should therefore be considered as approximate values rather than definite numbers.

Besides the described commonalities, ISFs' resource acquisitions through events are very difficult to classify for reasons already mentioned. A closer look at four Olympic summer federations of differing size illustrates the variety of income solutions adopted by them and the role that events play in these solutions. In an attempt to establish a replicable model of analysis, the authors selected several key variables. Some of these key variables are based on Chantelat's (2001) typology, which distinguishes between three kinds of expenditure in amateur sport clubs – sporting, social and economic expenditures. Chantelat calls the combination of the three kinds of expenditure the "production of sport clubs". Concluding from the analysis of 238 French amateur sport clubs, he determines six socio-economic patterns. These patterns emphasize the diversity of economic logics that characterizes amateur sport clubs. Adapted to ISFs, and in order to further our understanding of their financial flows and the part of their major sport events in them, a two-fold approach was adopted: first, by looking at ISFs' economic model (expenditures, sources of income) and, second, by establishing a basic event portfolio for each of the four ISFs analysed.

For the analysis of ISFs' economic model, six main variables were selected, three on the income side and three on the expenditure side. In the four models detailed on the following pages, the ISFs' main source of income and main expenditure are emphasized in bold letters.

While studies at club level mainly use the financial flow analysis to provide a tool capable of defining political subsidies to clubs (Chantelat, 2001), this chapter places ISFs' events at

Table 4.2 Main variables for analysing ISFs' economic model

Income	Expenditure
Events (e.g. TV and sponsor rights)	Events
Olympic revenue share	Administration (including governance and operations)
Fees (e.g. membership, licences, calendar)	Development

the centre of investigation. Following Bayle's (2015) perspective, which sees ISFs' major sport events at "the heart of their economic model", events are classified here as economic products. The main elements of event incomes are organizing rights, TV rights and sponsorship rights. A second variable is that of Olympic revenue share. The greater proportion of income is constituted by Olympic revenue share, the less the ISFs are self-sufficient. A final variable on the income side analyses fees of various natures (e.g. membership, licences, calendar). Historically, fees constituted ISFs' main source of income. With the increase and complexity of ISFs' activities and the hiring of paid staff to ensure and develop these activities, ISFs have needed to turn towards new sources of income. Today, the external financing of ISFs is common practice. However, in some federations the share of income from fees seems to remain relatively important.

On the expenditure side, expenses dedicated to events, administration and development are examined. Event expenses allow us to analyse whether the event balance sheet is even, whether events are profitable or whether they represent a costly activity for the ISF. A look at federations' administration expenses allows us to determine the remaining funds the ISF has at its disposal to finance activities other than administration. To complete the analysis of their economic model, their development expenses are examined. Development expenses should represent an important part. Using Chantelat's terms, the finality of ISFs as non-profit associations is, above all, supposed to be "extra-economic", meaning that the ISF is a corporate actor that should not seek financial gains for its headquarters as a priority, but redistribute a maximum of its gains to its members and the development of its sport. We expect ISFs with high income to redistribute larger parts into development than ISFs with lower income. We further assume that ISFs with high income from events, but low investment in development, follow an entrepreneurial logic rather than associative goals. Horch (2001) calls this process "auto-destruction", a process through which non-profit sport organizations lose their core values and identity.

With regard to ISFs' event portfolio, we base our analysis on four variables:

- Creation of the ISF (year)
- Size (number of paid staff)
- ISF events (number, periodicity)
- Flagship (event, discipline)

We assume that the age of an ISF might play a role in the presence of traditional (and sometimes mythical) events. Historically established events are not necessarily owned by the ISFs (e.g. the Tour de France in cycling, Wimbledon in tennis). To capitalize on these events, federations need to establish ownership rights. Depending on the power structures between the ISF and event organizers, strong negotiation skills are required. The second variable is that of size in terms of paid staff. Kikulis (2000), as well as Thibault, Slack and

Hinings (1991), equate the increased presence of paid staff with an increase in specialization as the workload can be divided more efficiently. The central variable here looks at ISF events, and notably the number of ISF events and their periodicity. These two elements are useful indicators for analysing whether an ISF is focusing rather on one or two events or whether it seeks to diversify its event portfolio even further. The focus on one event might signify that this event is particularly successful and therefore absorbs an important part of the federation's resources. At the same time, reliance on one event bears a major risk: the implosion of the financial system if the event does not attain the expected objectives (e.g. event cancellation, lack of/waning public interest). On the other hand, an event portfolio with many events bears the risk of image delusion which, in turn, is likely to impact the events' attractiveness for sponsors, TV broadcasters and fans. The fourth and final variable of the event portfolio examines the ISF's flagship, this being an event or a discipline. Indicators for this variable are the federations' own assessment, generally to be found on the ISF's website, and the income through this flagship.

Classification of economic models – a first attempt

The presentation of the following four cases constitutes an exploratory approach to the question of ISFs' economic model and the role of major sport events in it. This approach can be classified as a socio-economic rather than a managerial approach. In light of this relatively small sample, the validity of the analytical model and its variables discussed above, as well as findings presented hereafter, could be tested in the future by using a larger sample.

FIFA – One-mega-event model

The economic model of FIFA revolves around a single competition: the FIFA World Cup, a high profit mega-event generating 83 per cent of FIFA's overall revenue during the period 2012–2015. Compared to this, the remaining 11 FIFA World Cups are of insignificant economic impact. If we take a closer look at FIFA's income from 2014, about 91 per cent was generated through events, this being about US$1.9 billion. Of this 91 per cent, 90.4 per cent was generated through the FIFA World Cup alone. The detailed sources of income are as follows: broadcasting rights (35.4 per cent), ticketing (23 per cent), marketing rights (22.2 per cent), hospitality rights (5.3 per cent), licensing rights (2.5 per cent), other (2.6 per cent). The success of FIFA's economic model is grounded on two main elements. One is football's popularity. Football is probably one of the world's most popular sports. A large-scale FIFA survey from 2007 concluded that football counts 265 million players and 5 million referees worldwide, this being 4 per cent of the world's population at that time (source: Big Count, FIFA Magazine, July 2007). The other element is a close-knit strategy around the FIFA World Cup including commercial rights and limited risk-taking, as the following examples from the FIFA World Cup Regulations 2014 demonstrate:

Commercial rights: FIFA has established rights to the event's most profitable elements – "financial rights, audiovisual and radio recording, reproduction and broadcasting rights, multimedia rights, marketing and promotional rights" (Art. 15).

Limited risk-taking: FIFA takes no responsibility regarding damages relating to the organization and course of the FIFA World Cup, for either the preliminary or the final competition (Art. 2.3 and 27). Even though "[all] revenue from the exploitation of the commercial rights for the preliminary competition matches belongs to the host association" (Arts 24.1 and 24.4), the latter also has to cover expenses for insufficient financial outcomes of these matches.

Table 4.3 FIFA as an example of the one-mega-event model

Creation	1904
Size	Very big federation (>450 staff members in 2015)
FIFA events	1 major sport event format
	11 FIFA World Cups
	1 Confederations Cup
Flagship event/discipline	FIFA World Cup (since 1930; quadrennial)
	83% of FIFA's overall 2012–2015 revenue
Revenue (2012–2015)	US$5,826 billion of which
	Events: 88% of which
	FIFA World Cup: 83%
	TV and marketing rights: 68% (incl. FIFA World Cup)
	Other: 12% of which
	Financial income: 6.5%
	Olympic revenue: 0.4%
	Other operating income: 5.1%
Expenses (2012–2015)	US$5,757 billion of which
	Events: 53% of which
	FIFA World Cup: 41%
	Development: 18%
	Administration, operations and governance: 18% of which
	Administration: 7%
	Financial expenses: 6%
	Governance: 5%
	Other: 11%

The risk of the one-mega-event model consists of its high dependence on a single mega-event. FIFA's economic model around the FIFA World Cup functions as long as the federation finds buyers for its commercial rights, notably broadcasting and marketing rights, which represented together 68 per cent of FIFA's 2012–2015 income. Based on the FIFA example, we establish the hypothesis that ISFs with the characteristics of the one-mega-event model tend to be large in size, have a very profitable flagship event, high expenditure on their flagship events and moderate internal expenditure. Low administration costs in the case of FIFA (7 per cent) are notably related to a transfer of responsibility to the organizer.

UCI – The fee-collector model

The UCI model is built on two main pillars: (1) the UCI Road World Championships as the UCI's flagship event, and (2) calendar, licence and affiliation fees.

1. During the period 2012–2015, the UCI generated about 29 per cent through the UCI Road World Championships alone. The UCI establishes a contract with each World Championship and World Cup organizer individually. Depending on the organizer's capacity to commercialize marketing rights locally, the organizer buys between 30 and 60 per cent of the marketing rights from the UCI. Generally, these rights are negotiated in conjunction with the hosting fee of the event. However, the UCI WorldTour, with

Table 4.4 UCI as an example of the fee-collector model

Creation	1900
Size	Big federation (79 staff members in 2015)
UCI events	2 major sport event formats
	7 World Championships (annual)
	14 World Cups (annual)
Flagship event/discipline	Flagship discipline: Road cycling
	Flagship event: UCI Road World Championships (since 1921)
	42% of UCI's overall 2012–2015 revenue
Revenue (2012–2015)	CHF155.74 million of which
	Events: 54% of which
	UCI Road World Championships: approx. 29%
	Organizing fees: 23%
	Fees (calendar, licences, affiliation): 17%
	Olympic revenue: 14%
	Other: 15%
Expenses (2012–2015)	CHF132.427 million of which
	Administration, operations & governance: 52% of which
	Personnel expenses: 26%
	Governance: 20.5%
	Fees & Consultancy: 5.5%
	Events: 25.5%
	Development & training: 12.5%
	Other: 10%

cycling's most prestigious races (e.g. the Tour de France, the Giro d'Italia), escapes this rule. Besides communication rights, the UCI holds no commercial rights for these races. This explains the meagre income of CHF 240,000 for the UCI from the 2014 UCI WorldTour.

2. To counterbalance the historical arrangement of cycling's most prestigious races, the UCI, under the presidency of Hein Verbruggen (1991–2005), claimed control over the international cycling calendar, which used to be in the hands of the biggest cycling organizers. Today, calendar fees vary depending on the discipline and the race classification. The yearly registration of about 1,500 races on the UCI international calendar (all disciplines confounded) constitutes an important pillar in the UCI's economic model. They contributed 11% to the UCI's overall income in 2014. What is more, the official document labelled "Road – Calendar Fees" indicates that the UCI has increased the 2016 calendar fee by 31 per cent for UCI WorldTour races, from €24,369 for one-day races in 2015 to €31,923 in 2016). A similar strategy has been applied to teams with an increase of team licence fees in 2016. Team licence fees depend on the discipline and the tier that teams are in. The fee of €85,500 for the registration of a UCI WorldTour team in 2016 constitutes an increase of 11 per cent from 2015 to 2016. During the period from 2012 to 2015, organizer, affiliation, calendar and licence fees together represented 40 per cent of the UCI's overall revenue (23 per cent from organizer fees, 17 per cent from calendar, licence and affiliation fees).

The risk of this model lies in the need to keep the balance between the attractiveness of the ISF's main product and buyers' interest and financial capacity to pay the fixed fees. In the case of the UCI, the economic model is two-fold. On the one hand, it is based on the UCI Road World Championships as its flagship event. A successful financial return through this event requires a product sufficiently attractive for an organizer to pay the hosting fees in addition to the marketing rights owned by the UCI. On the other hand, the UCI's economic model is based on income from calendar and team licence fees. This supposes two things: first, that a stable number of cycling race organizers are able to produce profitable (or at least break-even) events; and, second, that sponsors behind cycling teams see a value big enough for them to financially support these, which, in turn, allows the team to register on the UCI calendar and participate in the races with a competitive set of riders. Currently, cycling teams suffer from the lack of sponsors willing to finance them on a long-term basis and at an amount that allows the team to cover increasing costs including UCI licence fees, travel costs or the team's entourage (e.g. sport director, medical and performance staff, etc.).

The main risks of the fee-collector model hence consist of a mismatch between the price level fixed by the ISF and the effective appeal of its product(s). Excessive pricing may entail precarious situations among the main fee payers. The strategy of the federation therefore needs to take into consideration not only its own financial needs, but also the capacity of its main actors to absorb higher fees while maintaining their activities. Based on the example of the UCI, we establish the hypothesis that the fee-collector model occurs perhaps more often in federations with very old event traditions. These traditional and historical events are sometimes more popular than the federation's events and financially independent of the latter. This makes it particularly difficult and delicate for the ISF to establish and impose ownership rights that allow them to capitalize on these prestigious events, which are outside the federation's property. Due to the important part of fees in the economic model and the need to administer these fees, administration expenses are assumed to be relatively high (e.g. the UCI: 52 per cent).

FIH – The mixed model

In the period from 2013 to 2014, the FIH's income was based on a resource mix including 32 per cent from Olympic revenue, 30 per cent from sponsors and 26 per cent from events, including TV rights and hosting fees. A majority of the FIH's expenses were spent internally (54 per cent), 22 per cent on events and 15 per cent on development. Although the FIH was previously "the sole owner of the media and marketing rights and all other commercial rights relating to the events that it organises" (FIH General Regulations, Art. 8.3.1), hosting fees were only introduced for the first time in 2015. Currently, the FIH splits commercial rights equally with the host organizations. According to the FIH business development director, this model "works if you have big events and big television", which is not the case for the FIH. In combination with a relatively high percentage of Olympic revenue, similarly structured ISFs, if they want to maintain and develop their activities, have to be creative and proactive. After the arrival of a new CEO in 2010, the FIH brought forward a number of potential solutions towards a more dynamic and sustainable model. The new action plan reposes on several pillars: a young and highly educated staff (in 2015, 74 per cent of the staff members held a university degree); the hiring of experts from inside and outside hockey/sport (marketing, communication, business); a long-term strategic plan (Hockey Revolution 2014–2024); and the creation of a new sporting format (Hockey5, a short-version form of hockey) capable of attracting new sponsors, spectators and athletes by showcasing field

Table 4.5 FIH as an example of the mixed model

Creation	1927
Size	Middle-sized federation (35 staff members in 2015)
FIH events	3 major sport event formats
	FIH World Cups (Junior, Indoor, Men/Women)
	Hockey World League
	Champions Trophy
Flagship event/discipline	FIH World Cup (since 1971; quadrennial)
Revenue (2013–2015)	CHF30.4 million of which
	Olympic revenue share: 32%
	Sponsors: 30%
	Events: 26% of which
	TV rights: 24%
	Hosting fees (since 2015): 2%
	Fees (licences, affiliations): 10%
	Other: 2%
Expenses (2013–2015)	CHF30.1 million of which
	Administration, operations and governance: 61% of which
	Administration & operations: 44%
	Marketing & communication: 10%
	Governance: 7%
	Events: 22% of which
	TV costs: 18%
	Development: 15%
	Other: 2%

hockey as an entertaining, young and urban sport while remaining true to its values of being a family and gender-equal sport.

The mixed model produces a fairly stable situation as it spreads ISFs' financial risks across several sources of income. However, in the specific case of the FIH, the relatively important Olympic revenue represents a risk as the federation has little influence on future redistribution modalities. An increase in TV rights (currently at 24 per cent) and the advent of hosting fees (currently at 2 per cent) might mitigate fluctuations in Olympic revenue. Based on the example of the FIH, we establish the hypothesis that ISFs with mixed-model characteristics tend to be dynamic organizational structures with a strong focus on strategic thinking and anticipation. Although the downfall of one source of income might not inevitably cause the collapse of the ISF's economic model, it requires a continuous analysis of the federation's environment, quick adaptation to change and a drive to explore new market opportunities as these diminish the risk of potential future shortcomings. Even in case of moderate incomes, we expect ISFs of the mixed model to invest a relatively significant share in development as successful member federations extend the ISFs' radius of action (e.g. events, athletes) and appeal (e.g. sponsors, broadcasting).

FISA – The Olympic-dependence model

During the period 2012–2015, FISA obtained 52 per cent of its funding from its Olympic revenue. For the most part, revenue was used to finance the federation's administration costs

Table 4.6 FISA as an example of the Olympic-dependence model

Creation	1892
Size	Small federation (about 19 staff members in 2015)
FISA events	5 major sport event formats
	World Rowing Championships (annual)
	European Rowing Championships (since 1893; annual)
	World Rowing Cups (annual)
	World Rowing Tour (annual)
	World Rowing Masters Regatta (annual)
Flagship event/discipline	World Rowing Championships (since 1962)
Revenue (2012–2015)	CHF30.2 million of which
	Olympic revenue share: 52%
	Events: 37%
	Other: 11%
Expenses (2012–2015)	CHF30.1 million of which
	Administration, operations and governance: 68% of which
	Marketing & communication: 19%
	Events: 22%
	Development: 9.5%
	Other: 0.5%

(68 per cent). There may be different reasons for this dependence, such as human resources (17 staff members in 2015) and low visibility. The higher an ISF's headcount, the more the organizational structure and functioning are likely to be specialized and coordinated, hence triggering higher performance. In the specific case of FISA, the promotion of rowing is difficult as it is an expensive sport in terms of equipment and facilities. In view of FISA's dependence, staying on the Olympic Programme is the federation's top priority: "[The] Olympic Games are a big machine. A lot of people, a lot of sports want to enter. [If FISA] doesn't move today, we are at risk. Because not being an Olympic sport destroys all the rest" (FISA President). The constantly growing prestige of the OG adds another pressure as desire to enter the Olympic Programme has increased competition between sports. In light of limited athlete capacity at the Games (around 10,500), the high number of rowing athletes raises some critics. With 550 athletes, rowing has the third highest number of athletes at the Games. Compared to this, triathlon only counts 96 athletes. Reducing the number of rowing athletes might allow other sports to enter the Games, but would weaken the position of FISA.

ISFs that function according to the Olympic-dependence model are under continuous pressure to defend their position on the Olympic Programme. The dependence makes them particularly vulnerable, as the slightest decrease in the attribution of the Olympic revenue share jeopardizes their economic model. Furthermore, dependence limits their scope of action. Aligning with IOC requirements and expectations ultimately becomes the safest pathway for them to ward off the discontent of the IOC and potential revenue reductions related herewith. However, IOC evaluation criteria and expectations can also be considered as a precious guide for federations in establishing a strategic plan that, ideally, results in more professionalization and organizational performance. Based on the example of FISA, we establish the hypothesis that ISFs with the characteristics of the Olympic-dependence model invest less in development as large parts of their revenue are consumed by administrative costs.

Conclusion and perspectives

In light of the small sample size, findings obviously cannot be generalized. The analysis is therefore limited to specific risks and challenges encountered by the four ISFs as well as some hypotheses. Nevertheless, it becomes evident that events are a necessary prerequisite for federations to attract sponsors and potential buyers of broadcasting and commercial rights. Without them, federations can no longer carry out either their historical mission or the activities they have developed over the years and the structures necessary for their maintenance (e.g. promotion and development of a sport at the grassroots level). This necessity is emphasized by the increase in major sport events and the evolution from volunteer-run structures towards more professionalized entities with an increasing business focus. The organization of attractive events requires sound expertise at various levels including sport, marketing, communication, administration (which can be summarized under the concept of specialization), written rules, policies and procedures (which can be summarized under the concept of formalization), strategic planning and performance evaluations (which can be summarized under the concept of rationalization), and an adapted decision-making structure (which can be centralized or decentralized).

In summary, the event portfolio has become a central part of ISFs' strategic and functional model. Whether this model follows a clearly defined strategy or whether it is the result of historical evolution and environmental circumstances depends on the federation itself. At the same time, each model can change rapidly and for various reasons. The arrival of a new key decision-maker (e.g. president, general director, etc.) may for instance influence the federation's strategy. Overall, federations have to face a number of new and complex challenges related to the growing importance of, and demand for, major sport events. One of them is the question of profit redistribution. Contributing considerably to the event profit, stakeholders (i.e. NSF, teams, clubs, athletes, organizers) might claim their part in profit redistribution. To avoid friction with main stakeholders, building compromises becomes indispensable for ISFs. Another challenge is that ISFs have to manage their dependence on events. Unforeseen elements such as event cancellation, security matters, the decreasing appeal of the event/sport, the concurrence of other sports, new events, and so on, may put their economic model at risk. Based on these observations, a couple of starting points for future research on the importance of major sport events in ISFs' strategic planning are proposed:

1. The question of ISFs' event portfolio as a strategic tool.
2. The question of ISFs' event ownership rights and organizing mode.
3. The question of ISFs' redistribution model of event profits.

References

Arcioni, S. & Bayle, E. (2012). La gouvernance des ONG: Le cas des fédérations sportives internationales. *La Gouvernance des Entreprises*, 175–212.

Bayle, E. (2000). La dynamique du processus de professionnalisation des sports collectifs: Les cas du football, du basket-ball et du rugby. *STAPS. Sciences et Techniques des Activités Physiques et Sportives*, *52*, 33–60.

Bayle, E. (2015). The sport federations' perspective. In M. M. Parent & J.-L. Chappelet (Eds), *Routledge Handbook of Sports Event Management* (pp. 109–122). London: Routledge.

Berrett, T. & Slack, T. (2001). A framework for the analysis of strategic approaches employed by non-profit sport organizations in seeking corporate sponsorship. *Sport Management Review*, *4*(1), 21–45.

Chantelat, P. (2001). *La professionnalisation des organisations sportives: Nouveaux enjeux, nouveaux débats.* France: L'Harmattan.

Chappelet, J.-L. (2008). *International Olympic Committee and the Olympic System: The Governance of World Sport*. London: Routledge.

Dowling, M. E. J. & Washington, M. (2014). Understanding the concept of professionalization in sport management research. *Sport Management Review, 17*(4), 520–529.

Emery, P. (2010). Past, present, future major sport event management practice: The practitioner perspective. *Sport Management Review, 13*(2), 158–170.

Hoehn, T. (2006). 21 Governance and governing bodies in sport. In W. Andreff & S. Szymanski (Eds), *Handbook on the Economics of Sport* (pp. 227–240). Cheltenham: Edward Elgar Publishing.

Horch, D. (2001). Le processus d'autodestruction des clubs sportifs en Allemagne. In P. Chantelat (Ed.), *La Professionnalisation des Organisations Sportives, Nouveaux Enjeux, Nouveaux Débats* (pp. 97–106). France: L'Harmattan.

Kikulis, L. M. (2000). Continuity and change in governance and decision making in national sport organizations: Institutional explanations. *Journal of Sport Management, 14*(4), 293–320.

Lee, C.-K. & Taylor, T. (2005). Critical reflections on the economic impact assessment of a mega-event: The case of 2002 FIFA World Cup. *Tourism Management, 26*(4), 595–603.

Leopkey, B. & Parent, M. (2016). The governance of Olympic legacy: Process, actors and mechanisms. *Leisure Studies, 36*(3), 438–451.

Malfas, M., Theodoraki, E. & Houlihan, B. (2004). Impacts of the Olympic Games as mega-events. *Municipal Engineer, 157*(3), 209–220.

Nagel, S., Schlesinger, T., Bayle, E. & Giauque, D. (2015). Professionalization of sport federations – a multi-level framework for analysing forms, causes and consequences. *European Sport Management Quarterly, 15*(4), 407–433.

Parent, M. (2008). Mega sporting events and sports development. In V. Girginov (Ed.), *Management of Sports Development* (pp. 147–163). London: Elsevier.

Parent, M. & Smith-Swan, S. (2013). *Managing Major Sports Events: Theory and Practice*. London: Routledge.

Parent, M. & Chappelet, J.-L. (2015). *Routledge Handbook of Sports Event Management*. London: Routledge.

Shilbury, D. & Ferkins, L. (2011). Professionalisation, sport governance and strategic capability. *Managing Leisure, 16*(2), 108–127.

Szymanski, S. (2003). The assessment: The economics of sport. *Oxford Review of Economic Policy, 19*(4), 467–477.

Thibault, L., Slack, T. & Hinings, B. (1991). Professionalism, structures and systems: The impact of professional staff on voluntary sport organizations. *International Review for the Sociology of Sport, 26*(2), 83–98.

5

HOSTING INTERNATIONAL SPORTING EVENTS

Heather L. Dichter

Introduction

Hosting international sport events, from world championships for a single sport to mega-events such as the Olympic Games or the FIFA World Cup, have become big business over the past few decades. These events have grown tremendously since their early incarnations in the late nineteenth and early twentieth centuries, when the competitors were over-whelmingly European and, in many cases, only male. In contrast, today the Summer Olympics have over 10,000 athletes competing, 45 per cent of whom were female at the London 2012 Olympics (Factsheet, 2016), are televised or live-streamed over the internet to every country in the world, and receive over $1 billion (€901 million) in sponsorship in the four-year period leading up to them. The popularity and appeal of sport make hosting sporting events desirable for both local politicians and national sport leaders who work together to convince the public and the international sport community that an event should be held in a specific location.

Following the financial and marketing success of the 1984 Los Angeles Olympics many cities sought to host this event, using increasingly corrupt tactics to secure enough support from Olympic members when they voted to select the host city. These actions culminated in the Salt Lake City, Utah bidding scandal. Since that time the International Olympic Committee (IOC) has passed two series of reforms, in December 1999 and again in December 2014, both of which have addressed the bidding process and the actions of potential and selected host cities of the Olympic Games.

Part of the appeal of hosting the Olympic Games is the legacy that the bid committee and local politicians promote as the lasting benefit to the local community for having spent money to organize the event. With events lasting several days or, in the case of the Euro or World Cup football tournaments, a full month, tourists spend multiple days in a foreign country, which provides a welcome injection of cash into a local economy. However, the truth of claims about the impact of a sporting event on a city or country can be difficult to measure and often legacies take several years to determine – and, in many cases, reveal quite the opposite effect of what had been promised in the bid documents.

Putting together a proposal to host a major international sporting event takes significant preparation and research to provide all of the required information to the international body. In addition to the athletic facilities themselves, bid committees must also address accommodation, transportation, health and medical services, media and broadcast services, security, marketing, ticketing, and legal issues that might arise. Organizers always want to provide an excellent venue for the athletic competition, which factors into the successful running of an event. Yet it is the aspects not directly related to the sporting contest that are even more important from the tourism perspective for a location to receive the public relations benefits and future legacies of having hosted a great event.

Since the 1990s potential host cities have faced growing opposition to hosting mega-events. A globally connected movement has been particularly effective in helping stop bids for the Olympic Games (Lenskyj, 2008). Public concern over costs for these mega-events surpassing any tourism or infrastructure gains has led to several potential host cities holding a referendum. Often these votes have demonstrated that the majority of residents do not want their city to host the Olympics, forcing the city to withdraw its candidature. Denver in Colorado, the only peacetime city to return the Olympic Games, did so after a statewide referendum to fund the Games failed (Coates and Wicker, 2015). Recent referenda have ended Olympic candidatures: Munich, Germany; Krakow, Poland; St. Moritz/Davos, Switzerland for the 2022 Winter Games; and Hannover, Germany for the 2024 Summer Games (Bird, 2015).

History

The IOC and international federations (IFs) each have a set process for determining the host city or country for their events. Interested locations compile the necessary information and inform the international body by a specified deadline of their desire to organize this event. The candidates present the benefits of their location to the international sport organization, which then votes in successive rounds until a location receives a clear majority. While this process has been straightforward for nearly a century, the perceived benefits of hosting these events has resulted in the proliferation of cities and countries trying to win the right to organize large-scale international sporting events, including world championships and the Olympic Games.

The early Olympic Games were not very large events, with barely more than 200 athletes competing in the first modern Olympic Games in Athens, Greece in 1896. It took until the 1912 Olympics in Stockholm, Sweden, for the Games to start adopting the aspects typically attributed to the modern event: the desire of athletes to compete in the Olympic Games, media coverage, the use of electronic timing devices and controversies regarding athletes' status to compete. The Great War forced the cancellation of the 1916 Olympic Games in Berlin, Germany, but the Olympics resumed in 1920 and continued to grow in the interwar period. The organizers of the 1924 Paris, France, Olympics arranged a winter sports week in Chamonix, France, three months before the Summer Games, and the IOC retroactively called these events the first Winter Olympics. With two events to oversee the IOC granted the right to organize the Winter Olympics to the country that won the Summer Games, and if that country refused they then opened the bidding for the Winter Games to other states. Thus, the Olympics in 1932 (USA) and 1936 (Germany) became the only instances when a country hosted both the Summer and Winter Games in the same year: 1932 in Los Angeles, California and Lake Placid, New York, and 1936 in Berlin and the Bavarian villages of Garmisch-Partenkirchen.

The success of the Olympics prompted FIFA, the world governing body of football, to establish its own international event. Football leaders saw the popularity of their matches at the Olympic Games and wanted to benefit from that demand themselves, prompting them to establish the FIFA World Cup, held first in 1930 in Uruguay and then in 1934 in Italy.

The FIFA World Cup quickly adopted the sponsorship and media strategies of the Olympic Games to become a popular and money-making event.

Europeans dominated the international sport organizations and also the location of these major international sporting events. Between 1896 and 1936, all but two years of the Olympic Games took place in Europe (the exceptions were all held in the USA: 1904 in St Louis, Missouri and 1932 in Los Angeles and Lake Placid), and the FIFA World Cup held two of its first three events in Europe, with France hosting the 1938 event. The Olympic movement had attempted to expand its global reach with Tokyo awarded the 1940 Olympic Games, but the Second World War forced the cancellation of those Games. While postwar decolonization accelerated the expansion of international sport participation as newly independent states joined IFs and the IOC, hosting major international sporting events remained largely entrenched in Europe. Japan did not host the Olympic Games until 1964 and Mexico City, Mexico, hosted the 1968 Olympic Games, but Rio de Janeiro, Brazil, was the first South American host of the Olympics in 2016, and no African city has yet hosted. FIFA's World Cup rotated between Europe and the Americas for decades, only going to Asia in 2002 (South Korea and Japan jointly hosting) and Africa in 2010 (South Africa).

The success of the 1984 Los Angeles Olympics, particularly the $225 million surplus, served as the model that other cities have wanted to replicate (Wilson, 2004; Wenn, 2015). Whereas the 1980 Summer Olympics had two cities bidding to host the Games (Moscow and Los Angeles) and Los Angeles faced no competitors to host the next Olympics, the success of the 1984 Games changed that landscape. The IOC immediately saw an increase in the number of cities vying to host the Olympics as the candidate cities hoped to reap the financial benefits of broadcast rights and the IOC's new sponsorship programme. Barcelona, Spain (1992) and Atlanta, Georgia (1996) emerged victorious from six-candidate competitions to host their Olympic Games, and the four subsequent contests each had a field of five candidate cities (Booth, 2011; Hong and Zhouxiang, 2012). Many of these cities' bid committees, however, engaged in unethical tactics in their efforts to win the Olympic Games. When a television station uncovered the corrupt actions of the Salt Lake City bid committee, global outrage prompted the IOC to implement reforms, including to the host city selection process. No longer could IOC members take all-expenses-paid trips to candidate cities. Instead, only members of the newly appointed Evaluation Commission inspected candidate cities, providing a report to IOC members (Report by the IOC 2000 Commission, 1999).

Even with these changes the process of bidding for the Olympic Games has not remained problem-free, prompting the IOC to pass a new set of reforms in December 2014. In an effort to reduce the high cost of bidding for the Olympic Games (even before a city wins the right to organize the Games), the IOC modified the process so that the organization would "invite potential candidate cities to present an Olympic project that best matches their sports, economic, social and environmental long-term planning needs" (Agenda 2020, 2014, p. 10). The IOC also added steps within the three-year invitation and candidature phases during the two reform processes in an attempt to minimize expenditure (see Table 5.1). Potential host cities spend significant time studying the possibility of bidding to host the Olympics, thus making the decision whether to host the Olympic Games more than a decade before the actual event begins.

The IOC has also broken the $250,000 (€225,000) fee to bid to host the Olympic Games into three payments spaced throughout the process so that cities that withdraw from the process or are not selected to continue do not spend as much money (Candidature Process, 2015). Chicago, Illinois, for instance, spent over $70 million (€50 million) in its losing effort to organize the 2016 Summer Olympics in the USA (Hula and Steinberg, 2010). The city received the fewest votes in the first round and was dropped from the running after the first

Table 5.1 2024 Olympic host city selection timeline following Agenda 2020 reforms (Candidature Process Olympic Games 2024, 2015)

Task	General date	2024 selection
Invitation Phase	9.5 years before Olympic Games	Mar–Sept 2015
Written confirmation of intention to bid for Olympic Games		16 Sept 2015
First part of Candidature File due		17 Feb 2016
Second part of Candidature File due		7 Oct 2016
Third part of Candidature File due		3 Feb 2017
Evaluation Commission report published		Jul 2017
Selection of host city	7 years before Olympic Games	Sept 2017

ballot. In the contest to host the 2018 Winter Olympics, Annecy, France, spent €30 million ($43 million) on a campaign which, from its inception, observers considered lagged behind its two rivals (Gold, 2011).

The costs associated with bidding to host the FIFA World Cup have been similarly astronomical. England's failed bid to host the 2018 edition of football's biggest tournament cost £21 million (nearly $35 million, €24 million), which netted them just two votes (FA reveals, 2011). Granted, the decision by FIFA to select the hosts of the 2018 and 2022 tournaments at the same time was later revealed to be extremely corrupt, leading to the downfall of longtime FIFA President Joseph "Sepp" Blatter. FIFA's reforms, in contrast to the IOC's reforms after the Salt Lake City scandal, did not include any changes to the bidding process for the World Cup (The Reform Process).

Whereas all members of the IOC vote to select the host city of the Olympic Games, some IFs have a smaller group within their membership which makes that decision, such as the Executive Committee of FIFA. In the case of the World Rowing Federation (FISA), the Council selects a location, the athlete's commission lends their support, and then the entirety of FISA's membership confirms that selection with a vote. This process to select the host of the World Rowing Championships takes more than a year from the opening of the invitation phase through to the selection at the FISA Congress. For other sports that can be contested in only a few locations around the world, such as bobsled, skeleton, and luge, venues submit bids each year to host world cup and lower circuit races, and to host the world championships, which the IF's Congress then approves (Kingston, 2015; Falloon, 2015).

The cost of hosting

Local governments use sport mega-events to implement new, or accelerate previously planned, urban infrastructure projects that should benefit the local population and tourists, and these costs are often not included in the official cost estimates that bid committees submit. Once a city or country is selected to organize a major sporting event, it forms an organizing committee – often including many of the individuals associated with the bid committee – and the proposals start to be turned into actual working plans. Although bid committees submit an estimated cost for organizing an event, the actual costs have long surpassed the earlier value (Flyvbjerg and Stewart, 2012). Many factors contribute to the rise in costs, and while security costs and urban infrastructure plans often relate directly to the playing of sport, they also facilitate the athlete and tourist experience.

Security costs have become a large portion of the costs of organizing mega-events. The massacre of Israeli athletes and coaches at the 1972 Olympic Games in Munich, Germany, prompted international sport to add security to its events. After the terrorist attacks of 11 September 2001 in the United States, security costs skyrocketed. The Winter Olympics in Salt Lake City was the first event following these attacks, with additional security procedures implemented on flights into the city as well as at venues. With the $200 million spent on security just five months after the terrorist attacks, Salt Lake City became, as Essex noted, "a new benchmark for the implementation of security plans and measures" (2011, p. 67). The costs associated with these efforts paled in comparison to the security costs for the next Summer Olympics in Athens, whose security bill totalled $1.5 billion. Four years later, in Beijing, China, the security costs reached $6.5 billion (Samatas, 2011).

Organizing committees must also ensure that transportation runs smoothly for athletes, officials and tourists, and failing to provide this component can cause logistical and public relations nightmares. As sporting events have grown in size, both in terms of athletes competing and spectators watching, transportation has become an important element of winning bids. Munich had already begun constructing its subway system in the 1960s, but the city's selection as host of the 1972 Olympics accelerated the pace of construction and prompted modifications so that one line now ended at the Olympic park and village (Schiller and Young, 2010). Poor transportation planning for Atlanta, and overreliance on personal cars, led to the 1996 Games being nicknamed "the chaos Games". Following Atlanta, the IOC added to its transportation requirements that media be provided with specially designated efficient transportation between venues and the press centre (and hopefully not write negative stories about the host city), and that an extensive mass transit system was essential (Kassens-Noor, 2012).

Recognizing this need to rely on mass transit, organizers are providing transportation to move spectators to the more remote locations or relying on existing public transportation. For the 2012 Olympics in London, tickets for each event came with an all-zones pass valid on the city's transportation network, which included buses, underground trains and light rail. Other sporting events have adopted this plan, with a ticket to the Four Hills ski jumping event in Innsbruck, Austria also allowing spectators to ride public transportation for free, to and from the venue. To reach the mountain venues at the 2006 Olympics in Turin, Italy, spectators caught a bus from one of the train stations to a central location in the mountains where they changed to a second bus to each specific venue. With the 2010 Winter Olympic events split between the Canadian cities of Vancouver and Whistler, organizers wanted to prevent congestion on the 120 kilometres (75 miles) of the Sea to Sky Highway which connects the two cities. The government widened the highway in the years preceding the Olympics, but the Vancouver organizers provided no public parking at any of the venues. Instead, ticket holders could purchase a ticket for the Olympic bus network from Vancouver to the mountain venues in Whistler.

Not all mega-event mass transit plans have been implemented as effectively. In January 2016, less than seven months before the Olympics began, the Rio de Janeiro mayor announced serious concerns that the vital metro line extension connecting the Athletes' Village and main Olympic Park with the central Olympic zone near Copacabana Beach would not be completed in time for the Games. Without this public transportation connection, driving this distance takes 30 minutes in good conditions but can take up to two hours during rush-hour conditions (Butler, 2016).

Similar problems have occurred with the creation of high speed railway lines designed to provide easy access to the host city from other metropolitan areas that are often included in bids. Delays in constructing major transportation components has frequently led to their not being completed in time for sport mega-events, resulting in less easy transportation options for tourists and, in some cases, bad publicity. The high-speed rail connection in Italy between Turin and Milan would have provided easier transportation for residents in Milan to attend the 2006 Games and also would have provided additional accommodation options. The portion of the line between Turin and Novara opened the same day as the Olympics began, but the remainder of the line to Milan was not completed until 2009. As plans to host sport mega-events have become more grandiose, the large-scale transportation plans have similarly expanded but without the capability to be ready for the sport event. In 2000 the provincial government of Gaueang in South Africa announced the Gautrain, the African continent's first rapid rail network, designed to connect Tschwane/Pretoria, Johannesburg and Johannesburg International Airport. Ostensibly to relieve commuters from road congestion, its supporters used the 2010 FIFA World Cup to try to overcome the delays in its construction. One month before the World Cup began only one section of the track opened; the entirety of the Gautrain's route was not finished until 2012 (Van der Westhuizen, 2007; Thomas, 2013).

The vision behind the Sochi, Russia, bid for the 2014 Winter Olympics was to build a winter sport resort inside the country as a vacation destination along with providing facilities at which national athletes could train domestically (Müller, 2014). These two aspects came to fruition, but construction costs for the highway and high-speed rail link that connected the coastal areas with the mountain resort area cost over $8 billion (€6 million), overrunning original cost projections by 90 per cent. Organizers touted the railway line connecting Sochi airport with the city as one of the most important legacies of the Olympic Games, yet a year after the Olympics ended, service to the airport had been suspended (Capps, 2015; Sonne, 2015).

Organizing committees and governments spend money on these aspects – especially security, urban infrastructure and venues – to ensure that the sport mega-event runs smoothly and that tourists and the media leave with a positive impression of the location. Although bid documents must state an estimated budget, the exorbitant costs of many of these transportation plans are not included because organizers claim governments plan to build these projects regardless of the bid outcome. Nonetheless, costs to organize mega-events continue to rise, even with reforms designed to reign in expenditure.

Legacies

Candidate cities emphasize the legacy that will remain long after the sporting event ends. Becca Leopkey and Milena M. Parent (2012) have traced the increasing use of the word 'legacy' within candidate city bid books and host city final reports. First used by Melbourne in Australia for the 1956 Summer Olympics and again by Mexico City for 1968, bid materials did not include the term with regularity until the 1980s. Cities promote the idea of long-term benefits to their public (Department for Culture, Media and Sport, 2012), even when the ability to measure these ideas is difficult. Nonetheless, both candidate cities and scholars continue to discuss the legacies of hosting the Olympic Games and other mega-events (Gratton and Preuss, 2008; Toohey, 2008; Dickson, Benson and Blackman, 2011; Billings and Holladay, 2012; Kassens-Noor, 2012; Grix, 2014).

Host cities and countries try to outdo their predecessors in terms of venues and the opening and closing ceremonies, leading to increased expenses. The Beijing organizers commissioned extraordinary venues for the 2008 Summer Olympics: the National Stadium (nicknamed the "Bird's Nest") and the National Aquatics Center (nicknamed the "Water Cube"). Gold and Gold have called these venues "two of the most iconic structures ever produced for an Olympic Games" (2011, p. 53). While these venues have become sites that foreign tourists visit when in Beijing, their post-Olympic use has been minimal but expensive. The Bird's Nest cost $480 million (€336 million) to build and its annual maintenance costs $11 million (€7.7 million) (Lim, 2012; Cook and Miles, 2011). The Bird's Nest will be reused for the opening and closing ceremonies for the 2022 Winter Olympics, which Beijing will also host, but that is just two days of official use for this venue, which has otherwise not done much except cost money to maintain (Beijing 2022 Applicant File).

Media have highlighted the demise of several Olympic facilities in the years after the Games, causing concern for the IOC and local populations who do not want to pay for these venues and events. For the Winter Olympics, the sliding track used for bobsleigh, skeleton and luge factors significantly into these costs. The organizers of the 1960 Winter Olympic Games in Squaw Valley, California decided against building a sliding track as a result of rising costs, leaving the 1960 Games as the only Winter Olympics not to contest any sliding sports (Ashwell, 2004). Since the 1976 Games many of the sliding tracks built for the Olympics remain in use for elite competition or for visitors to experience the sport. However, the sliding track built in Cesana, Italy for the 2006 Turin Olympics closed permanently in 2012 because of the high operating costs (Turin 2006 luge track, 2012).

Many of the 2004 Athens Olympic venues did not have pre-established long-term plans, which has left many of their facilities unused and abandoned. Some venues have continued as sport facilities, but others have been turned into shopping centres or businesses for commercial profit; several ideas for the post-Games use of venues did not come to fruition (Kissoudi, 2008). A decade after the conclusion of the Athens Games the *Guardian* (UK) published a photographic story revealing the extent of decay of the often graffiti-covered abandoned facilities (Bloor, 2014).

In an effort to reign in the costs to host the Olympic Games and the problem of "white elephant" facilities, the IOC included in its Agenda 2020 reforms the directive for the Evaluation Commission to place a "strong focus on sustainability and legacy" of the candidate cities. In contrast to their previous desire to have host cities build brand new venues, the IOC is now prioritizing "the maximum use of existing facilities and the use of temporary and demountable venues where no long-term venue legacy need exists or can be justified" (Agenda 2020, 2014, p. 10). These ideas prompted changes to the Almaty, Kazakhstan and Beijing bids for the 2022 Olympic Games. The IOC nonetheless selected Beijing to host the 2022 Winter Olympics even though the amounts of snow cover and interest in winter sports among the broader Chinese population are questionable, leading to speculation that the venues constructed for this mega-event will turn into white elephants similar to the Bird's Nest and Water Cube.

Whereas the Olympic Games require a variety of sport venues in a single city, major football tournaments such as the FIFA World Cup and UEFA's European Championship (often called the Euro) use several football stadiums across a country or two countries (e.g. the 2002 World Cup in Japan and South Korea, the 2008 Euro in Austria and Switzerland and the 2012 Euro in Poland and Ukraine). Germany, as host of the 2006 World Cup, had more venues that met the minimum requirement of 40,000 seats than the 12 stadiums used for the event. The next two hosts, South Africa and Brazil, however, have struggled to fill the large stadiums or even use them on a regular basis; a year after the World Cup the Brasilia stadium instead served as offices for city employees and a bus depot because the city lacks a professional team (Conn, 2013; Chaudhary, 2015). To prevent a similar result and, instead, trying to promote a more positive legacy from the vast construction happening in Qatar, the 2022 World Cup organizers plan to donate the modular upper levels from some of the twelve venues to African countries in need of football stadiums (Sannie, 2010).

Even with the Euro in two countries, the costs of hosting have been substantial. Limited interest in organizing the 2020 Euro tournament prompted UEFA to spread this event across 13 venues in Europe. UEFA's president noted that this decision would prevent any country with insufficient infrastructure from being burdened. Furthermore, regional grouping of venues could actually reduce travel for spectators compared to the great distances between the venues from the 2012 tournament (Riach, 2012). This new model for the 2020 Euro tournament has the potential to change the future of mega-events. Similarly, the IOC included in Agenda 2020 the possibility of having some events in another country to minimize costs, for example by reusing a nearby sliding track in the Winter Olympics (Agenda 2020, 2014).

Tourism

One of the most important aspects of hosting mega-events and other international sporting events is the influx of tourists to a city, both during the event and in the following years as a result of the lasting positive image of the city or country. Many people try to estimate the total revenue that a city or region will receive as a result of hosting an event, although these numbers are never precise. Furthermore, these estimates do not take into account the lost revenue that local residents choose not to spend by staying home or themselves travelling out of town to avoid the large crowds of tourists.

The hosting of mega-events is a significant source of sport tourism, as sporting events serve as the primary reason for spectators to travel to a location, although their ability to visit other sites within and nearby that location facilitates their decision to travel (Hinch and Higham, 2001). Local organizers hope that visitors leave with a more positive impression and the desire to return and that the global media audience is impressed enough to want to visit. However, as Black notes, "there is no obvious or easy translation of this sporting exposure to holiday plans and tourist arrivals" (2008, p. 472). Nonetheless, many cities continue to pursue this strategy. Halifax in Canada has used an events-based strategy of hosting international sport competitions to promote tourism to the city. While the increasing costs related to the bid for the 2014 Commonwealth Games, and the ballooning venue construction costs, led the city to withdraw its candidature, it has nonetheless hosted the World Junior Hockey Championships and the World Figure Skating Championships (Black, 2008). Unlike the costs associated with mega-events or second-order events such as the Commonwealth Games or Pan-American Games, hosting recurring major sporting events can contribute to greater marketing and tourism opportunities and the long-term viability of these events (McCartney, 2005). Events such as Wimbledon or the Macao Grand Prix attract first-time tourists as well as spectators who travel to the event annually.

Event organizers have also sought to attract the tourists and local population in a host city who do not have tickets to the sporting events by developing additional spaces secondary to the sporting venues. These areas, often called fan fests or live sites, provide additional branding opportunities for the event and its sponsors while simultaneously allowing for greater crowd control, a particular concern for major football tournaments because of the many "hooligans". Early attempts at fan fests in the 1990s were not very successful because of their location on the outskirts of cities (such as in Sweden at the 1992 Euro). The fan fests at the 2006 FIFA World Cup in Germany were located in the heart of each of the 12 host cities. Over 13 million people attended the fan fests, with 900,000 people flocking to the Fanmeile ("Fan mile") for Germany's games that began at the Brandenburg Gate in Berlin (Lauss and Szigetvari, 2010; Glass, 2014; McGillivray and Frew, 2015). Other cities across Germany also hosted public viewing areas, and the success of these fan fests in 2006 has since turned them into required components of football's World Cup and Euro events.

Conclusion

Cities or countries wanting to host an international sporting event will require tremendous amounts of time and money. The planning for mega-events such as the Olympic Games or the FIFA World Cup are exponentially greater, although all events have the same concerns: transportation, accommodation, selling tickets and merchandise, and security – all in addition to providing excellent venues for the athletes in order to have the best sport competition possible. These preparations necessitate close cooperation between sport and civic leaders which has, in the past, led to significant corruption in their efforts to bring mega-events to a city or country. Organizations such as the IOC have enacted a series of reforms to combat corruption in the bidding process and reduce the excessive cost overruns which host cities are guaranteed. Yet the popularity of sport and the rich television and sponsorship contracts and global recognition that go along with mega-events will continue to prompt civic boosters and sport leaders to attempt to host such international sport events.

References

Agenda 2020 (2014). *International Olympic Committee* [online]. Available at <www.olympic.org/ Documents/Olympic_Agenda_2020/Olympic_Agenda_2020-20-20_Recommendations-ENG. pdf>. Accessed 5 March 2016.

Ashwell, T. (2004). Squaw Valley 1960. In J. Findling and K. Pelle (Eds), *Encyclopedia of the Modern Olympic Movement* (pp. 337–343). Westport, CT: Greenwood Press.

Beijing 2022 Applicant File, vol. 1. (2014). Beijing 2022 Olympic Winter Games bid committee [online]. Available at <www.beijing-2022.cn/pdf/VOLUME1.pdf>. Accessed 8 March 2016.

Billings, S. and Holladay, J. S. (2012). Should cities go for the gold? The long-term impacts of hosting the Olympics. *Economic Inquiry*, *50*(3), 754–772.

Bird, H. (2015). The Olympic brand is in trouble. *BostInno* [online]. Available at <http://bostinno. streetwise.co/2015/12/01/upcoming-olympic-hosts-boston-2024-hamburg-referendum-history-shows-iocs-decline/>. Accessed 5 December 2015.

Black, D. (2008). Dreaming big: The pursuit of "second order" games as a strategic response to globalization. *Sport in Society*, *11*(4), 467–480.

Bloor, S. (2014). "Abandoned Athens Olympic 2004 venues, 10 years on – in pictures". The *Guardian* [online]. Available at <www.theguardian.com/sport/gallery/2014/aug/13/abandoned-athens-olympic-2004-venues-10-years-on-in-pictures>. Accessed 25 March 2016.

Booth, D. (2011). Olympic city bidding: An exegesis of power. *International Review for the Sociology of Sport*, *46*(4), 367–386.

Butler, N. (2016). Huge blow for Rio 2016 as Mayor admits vital Barra metro extension may not be ready in time. *Inside the Games* [online]. Available at <www.insidethegames.biz/articles/1034601/ huge-blow-for-rio-2016-as-mayor-admits-vital-barra-metro-extension-may-not-be-ready-in-time>. Accessed 8 March 2016.

Candidature Process Olympic Games 2024 (2015). *International Olympic Committee* [online]. Available at <www.olympic.org/Documents/Host_city_elections/Candidature_Process_Olympic_Games_ 2024.pdf>. Accessed 27 March 2016.

Capps, K. (2015). The Sochi Light Rail Is the Most Epic Failure in Olympic History. *CityLab* [online]. Available at <www.citylab.com/commute/2015/02/the-sochi-light-rail-is-the-most-epic-failure-in-olympic-history/385580/>. Accessed 6 March 2016.

Chaudhary, V. (2015). Brazil World Cup stadiums symbol of tournament's dubious legacy. *ESPN* [online]. Available at <www.espnfc.us/fifa-world-cup/4/blog/post/2492597/brazil-world-cup-stadiums-symbol-of-dubious-legacy>. Accessed 26 March 2016.

Coates, C. and Wicker, P. (2015). Why were voters against the 2022 Munich Winter Olympics in a referendum? *International Journal of Sport Finance*, 10(3), 267–283.

Conn, D. (2013). "South Africa plays host again but World Cup legacy still in question". The *Guardian* [online]. Available at <www.theguardian.com/football/blog/2013/jan/18/south-africa-africa-cup-of-nation>. Accessed 26 March 2016.

Cook, I. and Miles, S. (2011). Beijing 2008. In J. Gold and M. Gold (Eds), *Olympic Cities: City Agendas, Planning, and the World's Games, 1896–2016* (2nd edn) (pp. 340–358). London: Routledge.

Department for Culture, Media & Sport. (2012). Beyond 2012: The London 2012 legacy story. UK Government [online]. Available at <www.gov.uk/government/uploads/system/uploads/attachment_data/file/77993/DCMS_Beyond_2012_Legacy_Story.pdf>. Accessed 8 June 2015.

Dickson, T., Benson, A. and Blackman, D. (2011). Developing a framework for evaluating Olympic and Paralympic legacies. *Journal of Sport & Tourism*, 16(4), 285–302.

Essex, S. (2011). The Winter Olympics: Driving Urban Change, 1924–2014. In J. Gold and M. Gold (Eds), *Olympic Cities: City Agendas, Planning, and the World's Games, 1896–2016* (2nd edn) (pp. 56–69). London: Routledge.

"FA reveals true cost of England's failed 2018 World Cup bid". (2011). The *Guardian* [online]. Available at <www.theguardian.com/football/2011/oct/10/fa-cost-world-cup-bid>. Accessed 5 March 2016.

Factsheet: Women in the Olympic movement (2016). *International Olympic Committee*. [online]. Available at <www.olympic.org/Documents/Reference_documents_Factsheets/Women_in_Olympic_Movement.pdf>. Accessed 4 March 2016.

Falloon, D. (2015). "Sliding centre lands 2019 ISBF World Championships". *Pique Newsmagazine* [online]. Available at <www.piquenewsmagazine.com/whistler/sliding-centre-lands-2019-isbf-world-championships/Content?oid=2657235>. Accessed 1 April 2016.

Flyvbjerg, B. and Stewart, A. (2012). Olympic proportions: Cost and cost overrun at the Olympics 1960–1972. *Saïd Business School Working Papers* [online]. Available at <http://eureka.sbs.ox.ac.uk/4943/1/SSRN-id2382612_%282%29.pdf>. Accessed 5 March 2016.

Glass, N. (2014). Word of the Week: Fanmeile. [online] *German Missions in the United States*. Available at <www.germany.info/Vertretung/usa/en/__pr/GIC/TWIG__WoW/2014/24-Fanmeile.html>. Accessed 27 March 2016.

Gold, D. (2011). The citizens of Annecy have won, claim anti-Olympic body. *Inside the Games* [online]. Available at <www.insidethegames.biz/articles/13564/the-citizens-of-annecy-have-won-claim-anti-olympic-body>. Accessed 5 March 2016.

Gold, J. and Gold, M. (2011). From A to B: The Summer Olympics, 1896–2008. In J. Gold and M. Gold (Eds), *Olympic Cities: City Agendas, Planning, and the World's Games, 1896–2016* (2nd edn) (pp. 17–55). London: Routledge.

Gratton, C. and Preuss, H. (2008). Maximizing Olympic impacts by building up legacies. *International Journal of the History of Sport*, 25(14), pp. 1922–1938.

Grix, J. (Ed.) (2014). *Leveraging Legacies From Sports Mega-events: Concepts and Cases*. Basingstoke: Palgrave Macmillan.

Hinch, T. and Higham, J. (2001). Sport tourism: A framework for research. *International Journal of Tourism Research*, 3, 45–58.

Hong F. and Zhouxiang, L. (2012). Beijing's two bids for the Olympics: The political games. *International Journal of the History of Sport*, 29(1), 145–156.

Hula III, E. and Steinberg, S. (2010). Bidding for the Games – Chicago 2016 spent $70.8 million; Rome 2020. *Around the Rings* [online]. Available at <www.aroundtherings.com/site/A__34787/Title__Bidding-for-the-Games----Chicago-2016-Spent-%24708-Million-Rome-2020/292/Articles>. Accessed 5 March 2016.

Kassens-Noor, E. (2012). *Planning Olympic Legacies: Transport Dreams and Urban Realities*. London: Routledge.

Kingston, G. (2015). "Whistler launches bid for 2019 world bobsleigh and skeleton championships". *Vancouver Sun* [online]. Available at <www.vancouversun.com/sports/Whistler+launches+2019+world+bobsleigh+skeleton+championships/10912965/story.html>. Accessed 1 April 2016.

Kissoudi, P. (2008). The Athens Olympics: Optimistic legacies – post-Olympic assets and the struggle for their realization. *International Journal of the History of Sport*, 25(14), 1972–1990.

Lauss, G. and Szigetvari, A. (2010). Governing by fun: EURO 2008 and the appealing power of fan zones. *Soccer in Society*, *11*(6), 737–747.

Lenskyj, H. (2008). *Olympic Industry Resistance: Challenging Olympic Power and Propaganda*. Albany, NY: State University of New York Press.

Leopkey, B. and Parent, M. (2012). Olympic Games legacy: From general benefits to sustainable long-term legacy. *International Journal of the History of Sport*, *29*(6), 924–943.

Lim, L. (2012). China's post-Olympic woe: How to fill an empty nest. *NPR* [online]. Available at <www.npr.org/2012/07/10/156368611/chinas-post-olympic-woe-how-to-fill-an-empty-nest>. Accessed 8 March 2016.

McCartney, G. (2005). Hosting a recurring mega-event: Visitor raison d'être. *Journal of Sport Tourism*, *10*(2), 113–128.

McGillivray, D. and Frew, M. (2015). From fan parks to live sites: Mega events and the territorialization of urban space. *Urban Studies*, *52*(14), 2649–2663.

Müller, M. (2014). After Sochi 2014: costs and impacts of Russia's Olympic Games. *Eurasian Geography and Economics*, *55*(6), 628–655.

Report by the IOC 2000 Commission to the 110th IOC Session (1999). *International Olympic Committee* [online]. Available at <www.olympic.org/Documents/Reports/EN/en_report_588.pdf>. Accessed 3 January 2010.

Riach, J. (2012). "Euro 2020 to be hosted across Europe, Uefa announces". The *Guardian* [online]. Available at <www.theguardian.com/football/2012/dec/06/euro-2020-across-europe-uefa>. Accessed 26 March 2016.

Samatas, M. (2011). Surveillance in Athens 2004 and Beijing 2008: A comparison of the olympic surveillance modalities and legacies in two different Olympic host regimes. *Urban Studies*, *48*(15), 3347–3366.

Sannie, I. (2010). Africa to benefit from Qatar 2022 World Cup hosting. *BBC* [online]. Available at <http://news.bbc.co.uk/sport2/hi/football/africa/8690666.stm>. Accessed 26 March 2016.

Schiller, K. and Young, C. (2010). *The 1972 Munich Olympics and the Making of Modern Germany*. Berkeley: University of California Press.

Sonne, P. (2015). "One Year On, Sochi Suffers the Post-Olympic Blues". *Wall Street Journal* [online]. Available at <www.wsj.com/articles/one-year-on-sochi-suffers-the-post-olympic-blues-1423470558>. Accessed 6 March 2016.

The Reform Process. (n.d. [2016]). *FIFA* [online] Available at <www.fifa.com/governance/how-fifa-works/the-reform-process.html>. Accessed 5 March 2016.

Thomas, D. (2013). The Gautrain project in South Africa: A cautionary tale. *Journal of Contemporary African Studies*, *31*(1), 77–94.

Toohey, K. (2008). The Sydney Olympics: Striving for legacies – overcoming short-term disappointments and long-term deficiencies. *International Journal of the History of Sport*, *25*(14), 1,953–1,971.

Turin 2006 luge track closing due to high costs (2012). *ESPN* [online]. Available at <http://espn.go.com/espn/wire?id=8550523>. Accessed 8 March 2016.

Van der Westhuizen, J. (2007). Glitz, glamour and the Gautrain: Mega-projects as political symbols. *Politikon*, *34*(3), 333–351.

Wenn, S. (2015). Peter Ueberroth's legacy: How the 1984 Los Angeles Olympics changed the trajectory of the Olympic movement. *International Journal of the History of Sport*, *32*(1), 157–171.

Wilson, W. (2004). "Los Angeles 1984". In J. Findling and K. Pelle (Eds), *Encyclopedia of the Modern Olympic Movement* (pp. 207–215). Westport, CT: Greenwood Press.

6

GLOBALIZATION OF SPORT BUSINESS MANAGEMENT EDUCATION

Pedro Guedes de Carvalho and Darlene A. Kluka

Introduction

The potential of international business and the impact of sport globally are evident when analysing the profit line of sport events and corporations. In its 2005 report, "Global Entertainment and Media Outlook: 2005–2009", PricewaterhouseCooper (PwC) estimated that the global sport market would expand from US$82.8 billion in 2004 to US$168.9 billion in 2009 (PwC, 2005). In reality it reached US$145.34 billion in 2015 (Statista, 2016). In 2007 the NPD Group announced that worldwide sales in sport equipment, apparel and footwear increased 4 per cent to US$278.4 billion (AllBusiness, www.allbusiness.com). Despite a global economic downturn around 2007, the Beijing Summer Olympic Games showed a surplus of over £189.4 million. According to China's National Audit Office, the ¥1 billion surplus was more than double the most recent estimate of ¥4 million. The 2004 Athens Summer Olympic Games gained a surplus of approximately £95 million (Thibault, 2009).

The European Commission's group on Sport Economics estimated that sport business in a broader sense accounted for 3.7 per cent of EU Gross Domestic product (GDP) (European Commission, 2012) while Mel Young, CEO of the Homeless World Cup, claimed that some 2 per cent of global GDP was generated by sport-related business (EurActiv, 2009).

According to an European Commission study (2012), sport business has several important policy implications, as follows: (1) sport is an important economic sector with a share in national economies that is comparable to agriculture, forestry and fishing combined and expected to rise in the future; (2) sport represents a labour-intensive growth industry in the EU's 27 countries, which means that the expected growth in the sport industry is likely to lead to additional employment, with sport's share of total employment being higher than its share of value added; (3) sport can foster convergence across EU Member States because it is similar to a luxury good, with an income elasticity above one, meaning that sport production and services will grow faster in lower-income countries than in higher-income countries, helping to reduce economic imbalances; (4) sport has growth-enhancing specialization advantages because sport products and services can be found in many other sectors, such as tourism, insurance, legal consultancy and many more. This means that sport can help specific niche sectors develop, depending on the characteristics of sport demand and supply in a specific country. To quote from EU (2012):

> Examples of such specialization patterns can be observed in the UK (professional sports and betting), in Austria (tourism) and in Northern Europe (education). Further study and identification of these patterns may help to enhance the sector's contribution to the Europe 2020 Strategy.
>
> *European Commission, 2012*

Not only do mega sport events generate revenues, sport stars and champions do also. The financial sense of international sport at times of global financial crisis was questioned with the 2009 transfer of the Portuguese FIFA World Player of the Year, Cristiano Ronaldo, to the Spanish Football Club, Real Madrid. A world record fee of £80 million plus 25 per cent in additional fiscal benefits was attained when factoring in fiscal treatment between Spain and the UK. In fact, fiscal heterogeneity across countries will have a huge impact on sport actors' mobility as we can see from the choice some make for their fiscal residences (ex-tennis, -golf, -Formula One racers and so forth). Weber Shandwick Sport (2009), however, suggested that this international sport business decision might drive a sharp increase in shirt and merchandising sales, sponsorship revenue, match ticket sales and the global fan base. Ronaldo's appearance in the Real Madrid shirt also spawned opportunities for tour games to lucrative markets and revenues generated from these sport tourism visits (SportBusiness International, July, 2009) which presented new opportunities for sport managers as well.

International business opportunities in and through sport are evident on a global scale. These opportunities can easily move across national borders on all continents. Mega sport events and elite athletes benefit from the vast wealth of the Arabian Gulf. Athletes and coaches relocate to the Middle East with promises of new nationalities, impressive salaries and lifelong benefits. Middle East sponsors also cross national borders without difficulty when sport business opportunities are identified. Abu Dhabi-based Etihad Airways signed a multiple-year deal (from 2009 to 2012) of US$57 million to appear on the shirts of Manchester City and display the brand and logo on the City of Manchester Stadium, the club website, the match day programmes and other club merchandise. In the Far East, the Asian Tiger economies of China and Japan are becoming major players in the international sport business arena. The commercial power of China was evident during the aftermath of the 2008 Beijing Olympic Games. China is aiming for the world's soccer championship for 2050. It also wants to have foreign players and create new teams and competitions.

The ultimate success of sport globally depends upon the abilities of sport managers to include global mindsets and competencies, translation of threats, opportunities, trends, patterns and changes in the sport business environment (Goslin and Kluka, 2014). Are these global mindsets, competencies, dispositions and skill sets accessed and successfully mastered by individuals, allowing them to function and prosper in the sport business environment, through graduation from global sport business management programmes in higher education?

Sport business management education

Sport business management, as an academic discipline with a professional orientation, is one of the most rapidly growing globally (Skirstad & Trosien, 2013; Weese, 2002). One of the most significant drivers of this rapid growth appears to be globalization. At no other point in history have universities invested so much energy into seeking new means of expanding international networks, incorporating international perspectives into learning experiences and faculty research and establishing globally recognized brands (Deresky, 2017). The motives for this heightened initiative are numerous and include the pursuit of revenue, reputation, access, impact and influence. The costs and the risks to the higher education community globally are substantial. The complexities of globalization were amplified by the financial crisis that began in early 2007, the aftershocks of which are still being felt. Sport business, however, is increasing everywhere, generating money that can breed corruption. Large gaps remain in our knowledge about the globalization of sport business management education: the scale, scope, curriculum, modes of collaboration and impact. The concept of sport management business education reflects the need for effective management of sport beyond the for-profit environment. Presently, globalization has enlarged differences between rich and poor and also between extraordinary and ordinary. Non-profit sport will survive as a result of volunteers. It includes both non-profit and governmental agencies and any organization that requires effective management of sport in order to meet mission, goals and objectives. The journey from globalization to globalism will continue as long as people are driven to look across borders for resources, ideas, efficiencies and services. Examining the trends of globalization of sport business management programmes in higher education is important for several reasons, which are outlined below.

The sport business discipline served by professional orientation: The general mission of sport business management programmes in higher education is to educate and prepare talent to serve clients, organizations, communities and markets. As the field of sport business management evolves, the academy must evolve as well. The spectacular globalization of sport business management since the 1970s has created a significant demand for talent educated in the challenges and opportunities and singularities of globalization.

Globalization as a disruptive force for change in sport business management education: Globalization is changing former assumptions, practices and strategies. It appears to be motivated by strategic objectives related to many trends within the global business and economic environments as well as those related to globalization trends in higher education and in sport.

Quality of the learning experience for students: It appears that present efforts by sport business management programmes to globalize typically include a series of independent and fragmented activities. These activities are mostly focused on student and/or faculty diversity and the establishment of cross-border partnerships for student exchange. For example, several focus on collecting an array of activities (i.e. exchange programmes) with insufficient emphasis on learning experiences and intended outcomes. Accreditors of academic institutions need to set standards of excellence consistent with this new world. By these standards, sport business management programmes hold one another accountable for practices and policies that best serve their constituents. Expectations for the incorporation of global perspectives into the curriculum, the intellectual capital of faculty to keep pace with the evolution of sport business management practices in a global environment, cultural diversity, and programmes to ensure consistent quality across curricula and locations can provide a framework for this quality assurance. The methods through which programmes meet these expectations are likely to evolve substantially in the coming years.

The impact that sport business management programmes have on globalization itself: The role of sport business management programmes as drivers of globalization is a central enabler of increased prosperity around the sporting world. Those responsible for sport business management programmes must advocate the benefits of a globalization effort. These benefits extend to the business of higher education, which has the potential to increase access to, and increase the quality of, education gained worldwide. The globalization of sport business management education can facilitate the transfer of ideas and the collaborative development of innovations in fields that are related. These discoveries are fuelled by the same laws of physics, mathematical principles and biological systems that underlie basic research and innovation. Leaders in the field of sport business management will be influenced by contextual factors such as culture, social norms and national regulations or policy. They will create the organizational processes and settings that will enable the development of innovations to be implemented in a contextually complex society. Those who can lead in a global context are a critical resource for innovation and development, functioning as an efficiency tool applying globalization impacts in local specific environments (glocalization) while cooperating with different worldwide stakeholders and competitors (coopetition).

Inherent in higher education is the development of humans as contributors to societies. In the twenty-first century, the need for developing global citizens continues to be one of the important goals of colleges and universities throughout the world (Deresky, 2017). But what does being a global citizen mean? And how can sport business management education programmes contribute to this goal? These are questions that are being discussed on many campuses worldwide, particularly on those that use these questions to provide direction in shaping the nomenclature of their brands.

A global mindset for sport business management education

The Global Mindset Project (GMP), driven by the authoritative Thunderbird School of Global Management (2010), concluded that a global mindset is a vital characteristic of global citizenship. It is multi-dimensional and consists of a blend of intellectual capital, social capital and psychological capital. Specifically, intellectual capital reflects a global sport business manager's intellectual and cognitive capabilities and centres around knowledge of the global sport industry, understanding diverse value networks and organizations, understanding complex global issues in sport and possession of cultural intelligence. Social capital implies a sport business manager's ability to establish networks, relationships, norms and trust, and to maintain goodwill in social relationships across cultures and national boundaries. Psychological capital signifies a positive psychological profile toward contact with diverse cultures, an affinity for learning and exploring other cultures as well as personality traits of resiliency, curiosity, and a quest for adventure, extracting the best behaviour from each individual.

Competent people are the keys to managing complex strategies and organizations operating in the borderless, globalized world. A new framework of sport management competencies is required to direct the global flow of business activities and transactions. Levy *et al.* (2007) claimed that recent developments in multinational corporations have placed significant emphasis on the cognitive orientations of managers, giving rise to the construct of a global mindset that is presumed to be associated with the effective management of multinational corporations. In the highly complex environment of international sport business, managers cannot base their behaviour and decision-making on the narrow confines of a single cultural view. A global mindset is needed that combines an openness to, and diversity across, cultures and marketplaces with the ability to synthesize across this diversity. Two fundamental dimensions underlie a global mindset – cosmopolitan orientation and cognitive complexity. Managers demonstrating a global mindset are externally oriented and tend to operate across personal and national boundaries, as is required to function effectively in the international sport business arena. Cognitive complexity supplements the external orientation of the global mindset. The successful international sport business manager understands the complexity of the industry and can differentiate between numerous dimensions, paradoxes and challenges while at the same time identifying links between dimensions and synthesizing them into best practice. Managers demonstrating the crucial, yet often elusive, global mindset are labelled as high differentiators and high integrators by Gupta and Govindarajan (1991) and have a significant advantage in the globalized sport business environment (Boyasigiller, Beechler, Taylor and Levy, 2006).

Management theory analyses the context in which institutions conduct their business in detail. The intricacies, diversity and multi-dimensional layers of effective management are reflected in the dynamic internal and external management environment of business entities. Managing the macro-environment implies an understanding of economic forces, political systems, diverse infrastructures, legal requirements and dominant business cultures. At the same time, internal management environments have to be proactively in tune with and responsive to the dynamically changing external management environment through appropriate strategies, adaptive organizational structures and performance and control systems. Individual managers have to merge internal and external business environments into a meaningful composite through communication, negotiation, motivation and visionary leadership. The business of sport organizations operating only on a domestic level appears relatively simplistic as they deal with a given set of local variables and parameters. Sport as an industry is obviously not localized or restricted to one country. Sport as a product is extremely mobile and can go anywhere through competition and media coverage. Nearly every sport business management decision taken in the twenty-first century is influenced by variables in the international business context. The involvement of Kolpak cricket players in the English County Cricket League presents an example in this regard. Sport agents scout for cricket talent across national borders and offer contracts to deserving cricketers under the Kolpak legal agreement of the International Cricket Council. International Kolpak players 'sell' their sport talent to the highest bidder in the English Cricket League, and add value to English club cricket. The international business vision of Lalit Modi and Andrew Wildblood gave birth to the Indian Premier Cricket League (IPL) franchise. Modi, in an effort to enhance the Indian domestic cricket league by exposing it to global spectator audiences, auctioned eight cricket team franchises to the highest bidders for a total value of US$723.6 million in 2008. The IPL consists of eight cricket teams made up of international cricket players playing against each other in home and away matches. Franchisees bid for the services and skills of the world's top professional cricketers to strengthen their teams. Australia's Andrew Flintoff and England's Kevin Pietersen were each auctioned off for AU$1,550 million. A US$1.63 billion media deal was signed in 2008 with Multi Screen Media to broadcast matches on a global scale. Online video blogs by cricketers, live camera interaction, fantasy cricket and online betting took the action of the IPL beyond the borders of India and offered international business and sponsorship opportunities.

The globalization of sport business involves international management. International management rests on two basic premises that include the management tasks of planning, organizing, leading and controlling. These are needed to procure, allocate, utilize, coordinate and move human, financial, technological, physical and intellectual resources across borders and merge them into a unified new sport business event, product or service. International management further demands performing management tasks in a dynamic and heterogeneous business environment where parameters and variables change at different rates. Changes of government cause rapid political changes in the business environment; exchange rates fluctuate continuously, economic markets tumble unexpectedly and international trade and labour laws transform over time. Phatak *et al.* (2005) merge the concepts of international business and international management into a single definition that can be applied to a sport business context. They define international management as a process of achieving the global objectives of an organization by executing two core management activities: (1) effectively coordinating all resources across national borders to create new sport products and services;

and (2) charting strategies leading to desired business goals by skillfully and effectively navigating dynamic and often volatile international business parameters and variables.

In its basic form, international business can be defined as those business transactions and activities crossing national borders and involving two or more nations. International business has evolved to a level of sophistication and complexity that is characterized by networks of resources moving across national borders. When this definition is applied in an international sport business context, it reflects the movement of athletes, sport managers, board members, shareholders, fans, finished sporting goods, sport sponsorships, sport technology and sport events across national borders.

The technological dimension accelerates the migration across borders, not only of people, but also of information and sport equipment. Flows in the economic dimension are reflected by the movement of finances, sponsorships, prize money or endorsements. The media dimension entails the flow of information in digital or written format across national boundaries while the ideological dimension involves the flow of values, ideologies and social campaigns in the global sport arena.

Hill's (Hill & Kumar, 2012) two main components of globalization, namely globalization of markets and globalization of production, are also reflected in the sport industry. Sport satisfies universal needs the world over: competition, health and fitness, socialization, national and cultural pride, cooperation, power, control and structure. The uniformity and universality of sport activities have created global support and production markets while international sport events and leagues have demanded global operating and marketing strategies. Sport brand names like NIKE, Adidas or Gilbert are no longer national brands, but global brands. Globalization provides sport with new opportunities for expansion, growth, the flow of ideas and knowledge and new supporter bases. The traditional sports of Sumo wrestling and Taekwondo are no longer restricted to Asia, but have global participation and support bases. Elite athletes can train at high altitudes in one country while keeping in virtual contact with coaches in another country.

The sport industry has not escaped the issues of globalization of production. Globalization of production implies the sourcing of goods and services from global or decentralized locations to take advantage of competitive production inputs such as labour, materials and capital in order to lower cost structures and to compete more effectively. For example, NIKE outsources the production of footwear to the growing Asian business hub where favourable labour costs, tax treatment and trade regulations enhance their competitiveness in the global athletic shoe market. Major League Baseball (MLB) defines players from outside the USA as guest workers in the United States. Eastern Asia and Latin American countries have reputations as major baseball production nations and powerful MLB clubs are constantly scouting for cheaper players (products) they can import and exploit. The lure of financial gain accruing from a move to MLB offers a strong incentive for professional baseball players regarded as individual entrepreneurs and explains migration flows of cheaper human resources to MLB (Major League Baseball, 2005). Innovation in information and communication technology encourages and accelerates the basic components of globalization as it becomes easier and faster to move information, sport teams, sporting equipment and supporters around the world.

The movement of athletes, supporters, finances, sporting equipment and information requires a balance of global integration and local competitiveness. Strategic alliances and partnerships are essential ways to benefit from and manage globalization. Strategic alliances or partnerships involve agreements between one or more business entities for the purpose of serving a global market. Sport as a global product has eroded national boundaries and depends on partners and alliances to integrate resources, products and services. Interdependence as a response to globalization requires cooperation between organizations to minimize duplication of functions and to increase efficiency by positioning specific value-chain business activities in the most cost effective and suitable locations around the world.

Diverse governance structures, business driver values, business models, political ideologies, macro-economic policies and social systems collectively impact the dynamics of the international sport business environment. Ambiguous adherence to rules, procedures, principles, moral reasoning and regulations causes uncertainty that international managers have to grapple with. International management is characterized by diverse variables and these variables cannot easily be predicted. The magnitude and crippling effect of the 2009 global economic recession crisis was not totally foreseen. At the outset of the global economic crisis in 2008, the sport industry's expectations of weathering the volatile mixture of soaring oil prices, shrinking currencies and looming inflation were high. The collapse, however, of the American credit market and investment banking industry, followed by the steep decline in stock markets, forced a harsh reality on the sport industry. Corporate sponsors carefully rethought spending strategies. International venue managers kept a close check on events outside their national borders as to the impact on their bottom lines challenging them to ensure that events at their stadiums were part of the must-see happenings in uncertain economic times.

Globalization also refers to a business approach accepting that differences between national economic structures and markets are fading and that some products and services will become homogeneous. The business of international sport delivers products that are greatly homogeneous because of the governance structures of sport. Global sport governing bodies strictly regulate and standardize the nature of their product to enable comparisons (through setting and improving world records) and distribute their products in the form of leagues, World Cups, mega sport events and franchises to all corners of the world. Globalized marketing strategies in the international business of sport expose sport managers to heterogeneous social systems in different countries, forcing them to balance the principles of business models (i.e. profitability, return on investment, brand image) and the interests of all stakeholders, and the environment (i.e. human rights, health and safety, legal requirements, social stability, environmental footprint).

An inability to balance conflicting institutional demands may cause social risk to sport organizations operating across national borders. Social pressure groups challenge business decisions and actions carried out not only in one country but across national borders and can affect organizations' or events' reputations, sales or ticket volumes or legitimacy. Deresky (2017) skillfully applied Carrolls' Three-dimensional Conceptual Model of Corporate Performance to explain social responsibility in international business as ranging from the extreme of solely pursuing profit within the confines of the law to the opposite extreme of attempting to solve problems in society. In the domain of international social responsibility, sport managers must consider both the economic and social effects and the costs of business decisions on societies. Typical social issues addressed in sport business management endeavours include racial, gender, religious and sexual orientation discrimination, lack of equal access and opportunity, environmental sensitivity, consumer concerns and employee safety and welfare.

Curricular content and accreditation principles

The transformation of curricular content in sport business management education programmes seems to be an obvious response to the issue of globalization. The approaches that schools have begun to take in order to globalize curricula vary substantively across schools and, within schools, across educational levels (undergraduate, master's, executive master's and doctoral) as well as programmes. According to the Association to Advance Collegiate Schools of Business (AACSB, 2015) and the Commission on Sport Management Accreditation (COSMA, 2015), several points need to be considered when deciding upon curriculum content: (1) graduates need global mindsets and competencies in order to succeed in a global sport business environment; (2) students need international learning experiences that require a comprehensive approach to individual courses as well as overall programme design. Woven into the core curriculum of all sport business management programmes through goals, objectives and learning outcomes must be global perspectives as well as supplemental training in the field and experiential learning; (3) the content of sport management courses is delivered in a manner that is appropriate, effective and stimulates learning; (4) faculty in the programme must model ethical character and integrate ethical viewpoints and principles in their teaching; (5) faculty are effective teachers who are current in their fields and active in their professional contributions to their institution and discipline.

Accreditation principles continue to be used to evaluate the quality of degree programmes in several areas of the world and in several disciplines. Several principles have been devised by global and national accrediting bodies, summaries of which have been included below (e.g. AACSB; COSMA; Commission on Higher Education Accreditation (CHEA)). One of the most important principles relates to the outcomes assessment process (adapted from COSMA, 2015).

Principle: Outcomes assessment

A process is used to measure the effectiveness of an academic unit and the sport management programmes administered by that unit. A relevant mission and goals need to be clearly defined; a strategic plan needs to be in line with the mission and goals; an outcomes assessment process must be developed and implemented; sport management students must develop into well-educated, ethical, competent sport business management professionals. Other key principles are as follows.

Principle: Strategic planning

Strategic plans include an outcomes assessment plan for the sport business management programme and are linked to the budgeting and business processes. In addition to linkage to the mission and goals of the university and programme, the plan includes effective communication to current and prospective students. The university's organizational structure supports excellence in sport business management education.

Principle: Curriculum

The design of the curriculum must be relevant and current. It must ensure that students understand and are prepared to deal effectively with critical issues in a dynamic global environment. A common content core needs to be included. For example, six categories have been proposed by COSMA (2015): (1) foundations of sport (historical, sociological, psychological); (2) foundations of sport management (management concepts, governance and policy, international sport); (3) functions of sport management (operations, marketing, communications, infrastructure, events, finance and economics of sport); (4) sport management environment (organizational development); (5) legal and ethical aspects, diversity issues, technological advances; (6) integrative experiences and career planning (internship/practica/capstone experience; experiential learning).

Principle: Faculty

Sport business management programmes must be supported by qualified and competent faculty, have an effective method of recruiting faculty, evaluate faculty based on defined criteria, provide support for faculty development and scholarship and foster an academic climate conducive to excellence in teaching and learning.

Principle: Faculty scholarship/professional activities

Faculty members must be involved in scholarship and professional activities that enhance the depth and scope of their knowledge in areas they are teaching in. The scholarship of teaching, discovery, integration and application serve as basic tenets to the principle. Knowledge and application of ways in which students learn, faculty lines of research, interpretation and bringing new insights to bear on original research and application of knowledge gained from research comprise the above scholarship. Professional activities are related to a faculty member's recognized area of expertise to provide professionally related service to individuals or organizations in public and/or private sectors.

Principle: Resources

Resource support for the sport business management programme should be sufficient to sustain excellence in the areas of financial and physical facilities, learning and educational technology and support. This incorporates budgeting, libraries and equipment.

Principle: Internal and external relationships/oversight

Linkages must be evident internally (on campus) as well as externally (outside of campus and in the community). Admission to the institution requires policies and processes that are appropriate for sport business management degree programmes. Accountability to the public concerning student learning outcomes and achievement is also vital. There should also be experiential learning for students to work for sport organizations to gain useful, relevant experience for careers in the sport industry. The integration of theory and practice in skill development is essential for success. Accreditation of universities must also meet the standard of the degrees awarded at comparable institutions at the international university level.

Principle: Educational innovation

The continuous evaluation of pedagogical strategies that advance with technology utilization is important.

In order to acquire the elusive global mindset, educational institutions will be challenged to adapt programmes that facilitate the seamless movement of sport business managers in the borderless world of international sport business and equip the next generation of international sport business leaders. The following meta-competencies can form the foundation of global sport business management programmes aimed at developing a competent global mindset (Gooderham and Nordhaug, 2003).

- The competency to perform in a team setting
- The competency to manage change and transition
- The competency to manage workforce diversity

- The competency to communicate in various cultural settings
- The competency to develop global strategies and translate ideas into business transactions
- The competency to change personal ways of thinking from internal to external orientation
- The competency to be creative, learn and transfer knowledge across borders
- The competency to operate with a high degree of personal integrity and honesty
- The competency to be non-judgmental when confronted with confusing situations

Sport management is the study and practice involved in relation to all people, activities, organizations and businesses engaged in producing, facilitating, promoting or organizing any product that is sport, fitness and recreation related; and sport products, which can be goods, services, people, places or ideas (Parks, Zanger & Quarterman, 1998; Pitts, Fielding & Miller, 1994; Pitts and Stotlar, 2013).

Sport business management education in higher education began to be realized when universities in the United States of America created curricula and degree programmes in the 1970s to fill an increasing need for professional management of sport at many levels. The organization of sport itself has developed substantively over the past 160 years or so, with structures and functions that continue to evolve. These developments generally have been and continue to be necessary either in answering broad social, political and/or economic changes or in discussing specific issues within a sector (i.e. sport marketing, communication, finance, economics, history, development or law), theme (i.e. sport and women, ability, ethnicity, international comparison or religion) or level (i.e. professional, club, intercollegiate, high school or youth) of sport (Haag, Keskinen, and Talbot, 2013).

Professional and amateur sport teams, sporting goods manufacturers, sport tourism businesses, sport services organizations and sport science corporations continue to evolve into more sophisticated and professionally run businesses. Competition within and between each of these groups has become part of the environment for the future. This also includes more international and global perspectives. As this more sophisticated development occurs, sport business management becomes increasingly complex. Professional and ethical management skills are required to be successful in the sport industry.

Conclusion

The area of sport management is characterized by a very large number of people, most of whom are local in reach and orientation. Entry is relatively easy and recruitment primarily begins as a voluntary process. But the field of sport business management education is highly segmented along many dimensions including mission, organizational size, financial resources and reputation. Mobility across borders is relatively high for students, and low but growing for faculty, professionals and institutions. Institutions and professionals confront geographical mobility barriers from regulation, reputation, culture and capital. Institutions respond to globalization as a threat and as an opportunity. Globalization may summon new competitors for students, faculty or capital. At the same time, globalization may open opportunities to expand programmes, increase revenues and build brands. As a result, globalization has stimulated a new wave of competition among institutions as they jockey for position. Of particular interest are curriculum strategies and the use of strategic alliances, joint ventures, exchange programmes and operating agreements to leverage the reach of schools across borders. Sport business management educators and the networks they build are being called to collective action aimed at elevating the achievement of sport business management programme globalization efforts and, in turn, the ability of sport business management programmes to support positive economic and social change. The call to action includes roles for individuals within the bounds of their respective universities, as well as in concert with others across the world. The organizations that influence and support higher education, and sport business management education specifically, also have significant roles to play, namely fostering the qualified integration between scientific and tacit knowledge in sport. Excellence in sport managers will create new entrepreneurial opportunities, which will promote inclusive societies, increase sport-related jobs and better competitive behaviours in humanity. Sport, music and art will continue to be positioned in societies against possible isolation effects induced by new communication technologies.

The world needs new educational entrepreneurs able to tackle contemporary challenges in order to internalize the "good" of globalization with the "bad" of local short-sighted views. The new term to define this international movement is "glocalization". In economics literature, glocalization is a combination of the words, globalization and localization, which are used to describe a product or service that is developed and distributed globally, but it is also fashioned to accommodate the user or consumer in a local market. In the context of this chapter, this means that the product or service (sport management education) may be tailored to conform with local laws, customs or consumer preferences.

"Coopetition" is also a term in this chapter that frames the idea of sport management education. Institutions could compete under a "win-win-win" environment, meaning that two different institutions and their communities would benefit from consortium educational programmes. New international sport managers would then be able to provide values, concepts and experiences that would enable them to function professionally in the future. Products or services that are effectively "glocalized" are, by definition, going to be of much greater interest and need to the end user.

References

All Business. (2012). NPD releases global sports market estimate. Retrieved from <www.allbusiness.com/econoomy-economic-indicators/economic=-conditions-inflation/11404428-html>. Accessed 1 July 2016.

Association to Advance Collegiate Schools of Business Principles. (2015). Retrieved from <www.aacsb.org>. Accessed 1 July 2016.

Boyasigiller, N. A., Beechler, S., Taylor, S. & Levy, O. (2006). Leading with a global mindset. In M. Javidan, R. M. Steers & M. A. Hitt (Eds), *The Global Mindset: Advances in International Management* (pp. 131–149). Oxford: Elsevier.

Commission on Higher Education Accreditation Principles. (2015). Retrieved from <www.chea.org>. Accessed 1 July 2016.

Commission on Sport Management Accreditation Principles. (2015). Retrieved from <www.cosma.org>. Accessed 1 July 2016.

Danylchuk, K. (2012). The challenges of the internationalization of sport management academia. In A. Gillentine, R. Baker & J. Cuneen (Eds), *Paradigm shift: Critical Essays in Sport Management*. Scottsdale, AZ: Holcomb Hathaway.

Deresky, H. (2017). *International Management: Managing Across Borders and Cultures* (9th edn). Upper Saddle River, NJ: Pearson Prentice Hall.

EurActiv. (2009). Davos underline economic value of sport. Retrieved from <www.euractiv.com/en/sports/davos-underlines-economic-value-sport>. Accessed 1 July 2016.

European Commission. (2012). "Study on the Contribution of Sport to Economic Growth and Employment in the EU". Study commissioned by the Directorate-General Education and Culture. Final Report, November 2012. Retrieved from <www.google.pt/webhp?sourceid=chrome-instant&ion=1&espv=2&ie=UTF-8#q=Directorate-General+Education+and+Culture+Final+Report+November+2012>. Accessed 1 July 2016.

Gooderham, P. N. & Nordhaug, C. M. (2003). *International Management: Cross-boundary Challenges.* Malden, MA: Blackwell Publishing.

Goslin, A. E., & Kluka, D. A. (2014). Women and sport leadership: Perceptions of Malawi women educated in sport business leadership. *South African Journal for Research in Sport, Physical Education & Recreation, 36*(3), 93–108.

Gupta, V. & Govindarajan, V. (1991). Knowledge flows and the structure of control within multinational corporations. *Academy of Management Review, 16*(4), 768–792.

Haag, H., Keskinen, K. & Talbot, M. (Eds). (2013). *Directory of Sport Science.* Champaign, IL: Human Kinetics.

Hill, D. & Kumar, R. (Eds). (2012). *Global Neoliberalism and Education and its Consequences.* London: Routledge.

Levy, O., Beechler, S., Taylor, S. & Boyasigiller, N. A. (2007). What we talk about when we talk about "global mindset": Managerial cognition in multinational corporations. *Journal of International Business Studies, 38*, 231–258.

Major League Baseball. (2005). 29.2 percent of Major League Baseball players born outside the U.S. Retrieved from <www.mlb.mlb.com/NASAApp/mlb/news/press_releases>. Accessed 1 July 2016.

Parks, J. B., Zanger, B. R. K. & Quarterman, J. (1998). *Contemporary Sport Management.* Champaign, IL: Human Kinetics.

Parks, J., Quarterman, J. & Thibault, L. (2006). *Contemporary Sport Management* (3rd edn). Champaign, IL: Human Kinetics.

Phatak, A. V., Bhagat, R. S. & Kashlak, R. J. (2005). *Sport Business in the Global Marketplace.* New York: Palgrave MacMillan.

Pitts, B., Fielding, L. & Miller, L. (1994). *Introduction to Sport Management.* Champaign, IL: Human Kinetics.

Pitts, B. & Stotlar, D. (2013) *Foundations of Sport Marketing* (4th edn). Morgantown, WV: Fitness Information Technology.

PricewaterhouseCooper. (2005). Global entertainment and media outlook: 2005–2009 [report]. Retrieved from <https://kc3.pwc.es/local/es/kc3/publicaciones.nsf/V1/4D4DFD66E8BA6EEBC12 5714C00358861/$FILE/RE_gmeo.pdf>.

Skirstad, B. & Trosien, G. (2013). Sport management. In M. Talbot, H. Haag & K. Keskinen (Eds), *Directory of Sport Science* (6th edn). Berlin: International Council of Sport Science and Physical Education.

SportBusiness International. (July 2009). Is Ronaldo worth it? Issue 147, p. 8.

Statista 2016. Statistics Portal. Retrieved from <www.statista.com/statistics/194122/sporting-event-gate-revenue-worldwide-by-region-since-2004/>. Accessed 1 July 2016.

Thibault, L. (2009). Globalization of sport: An inconvenient truth. *Journal of Sport Management, 23*, 1–20.

Thunderbird School of Global Management (2010). Global leadership for global impact. Retrieved from <www.thunderbird.edu/about_thundement.htmerbird/inside_tbird/inside_tbird/mission_statement.htm>. Accessed 1 July 2016.

Weber Shandwick Sport (2009). Retrieved from <www.webershandwicksport.com>. Accessed 1 July 2016.

Weese, W. J. (2002). Opportunities and headaches: Dichotomous perspectives on the current and future hiring realities in sport management academy. *Journal of Sport Management, 16*(1), 1–17.

PART II

Sport marketing

Sport marketing developed through the fans' passionate support for sport. Typically, sport marketing is divided into two categories: marketing of sport, and marketing via sport. Both types apply to professional, amateur and grassroots sports. The marketing of sport refers to the promotion of an athlete, league, match or event. The sport can attract participants, spectators, investors, sponsors or other stakeholders. Sport has grown fast globally. There are international sport stars such as Michael Jordan, Lionel Messi and Usain Bolt. Mega-events such as the Olympics and FIFA World Cup are being hosted by emerging markets. Even local sporting events hope to attract international participants and spectators. Marketing via sport uses sport as a conduit for brands to connect to a sport fan. Sponsorship, endorsements and media buys are common techniques. Corporations are expanding into international markets. Sport can be an effective marketing channel to reach new consumers.

The following chapters investigate both topics of the marketing of sport and marketing via sport. The authors explore sport marketing through cultural perspectives including gender and religious concerns, and the expansion of sport into new geographic markets.

7

MARKETING IMPLICATIONS OF PLAYING REGULAR SEASON GAMES IN INTERNATIONAL MARKETS

Losing "home" domestic advantage or gaining "away" international advantage?

Eric C. Schwarz

Introduction

Over the past two decades, major league professional sports in the United States have been determined to play more games overseas (Koba, 2013). Reasons for this expansion into the international market include the desire to expand the brand awareness of teams and leagues to a broader audience, and ultimately seek out new revenue streams through gate revenues, sponsorships, media rights and merchandising (PricewaterhouseCoopers, 2011). However, there are some questions related to the effects on domestic fans and their continued support of teams that move home games overseas: will it alienate fans (Koba, 2013), or could it actually enhance the domestic brand and interest in the sport (McDonald, Karg & Lock, 2010)? There are also many questions about the unnecessary burdens being put on players as a result of international travel connected with the regular season – ranging from physical and emotional issues that may affect future performance (Longley, 2012) to the financial implications related to travel costs and additional taxation issues from other countries (MacDonald, 2014; Baker, 1990).

The purpose of this chapter is to analyse the marketing implications of playing regular season games in international markets. Starting with an analysis of the international efforts of four United States-based professional sports leagues – the National Basketball Association (NBA), the National Football League (NFL), the National Hockey League (NHL) and Major League Baseball (MLB) – over the past two decades, evidence is presented about the branding and financial reasons for moving beyond a US and Canadian market of nearly 350 million people to gain some of the global market of over seven billion. This is followed by an investigation about whether leagues and their teams are losing their "home" domestic marketing advantage by trying to gain an "away" international advantage, including a look into whether they are losing domestic fans as a result of these international efforts. Additional analysis examines the extra burdens being put on players, coaches and staff in terms of physical, emotional and financial considerations as a result of this travel.

Recent history – United States professional sports playing games overseas

Each of the four major professional sport leagues in the United States has been involved with playing games outside the domestic market, which is defined as the United States and Canada for the purposes of this chapter. In association with this expansion of playing games overseas, significant business operations have been maintained to support a multitude of functions beyond just the core product of the game experience.

The National Basketball Association has a history of international competition since 1978, when the Washington Bullets played an exhibition game in Israel, followed the next year by two exhibition games in China and one in the Philippines (NBA, 2014). Over the next five years there were numerous visits by international teams to the United States mainland, but in 1984 the Seattle SuperSonics played a series of six games in West Germany, Switzerland and Italy, while the Phoenix Suns and New Jersey Nets participated in the Italian Open. In July 1988 the Atlanta Hawks played a series of three exhibition games in the former Soviet Union. Soon after, in October 1988, the Boston Celtics beat Real Madrid in the inaugural McDonalds Championship – a tournament that ran for 11 seasons pitting NBA teams against various international league champions. Also during this period, the NBA started their regular season in Japan in 1990 – and did so a total of six times until 2003, as well as in Mexico City in 1997. Over the past 35 years, the NBA has held 128 preseason and exhibition games across Latin America (Mexico, Dominican Republic, Puerto Rico, Brazil), Asia (China, Japan, Philippines) and across Europe from England to Turkey. As far as regular season games, there have been 19 international games held between 1990 and 2014, with the majority (12) taking place in Japan between 1990 and 2003, and the NBA returning to overseas regular-season competition with four games in London since 2011, and one additional game in Mexico City in 2013.

The National Football League has sought to enter the international market in three distinct manners. First, from 1986 to 2005, the NFL promoted the American Bowl, a series of preseason games that sought to expand the brand awareness of American Football beyond United States borders. Games were played in Canada (Montreal, Toronto, Vancouver), Mexico (Mexico City, Monterrey), Europe (London, Berlin, Barcelona, Dublin), Japan (Tokyo, Osaka) and Australia (Sydney). The second effort was through the sponsoring of World League of American Football in 1991, where three teams from Europe (Frankfurt, Barcelona and London) participated with other spring-league teams from the United States and Canada. After two years, the league went on hiatus and reformed as NFL Europe with the original three Europeans teams, as well as new teams in Edinburgh, Dusseldorf and Amsterdam. The league struggled throughout its 11-year run with teams relocating and folding, and it eventually ceased operations in 2007. The end of the American Bowl and the folding of NFL Europe were replaced by the third and most current reach into the international market – playing regular season games outside the United States. The first experiment came in 2005 at Estadio Azteca in Mexico City. However, since 2007 and until 2016 the games have been exclusively played at Wembley Stadium in London. In 2016, the NFL played games at Wembley and Twickenham Stadiums in London, and it returned to Mexico City. In addition, the Buffalo Bills played one regular season game in Toronto from 2008 to 2013.

The National Hockey League has had the most significant international presence over the years, first playing a post-season exhibition tour in 1938 in England and France (nine games between the Detroit Red Wings and the Montreal Canadiens), and a longer 23-game tour by the Boston Bruins and New York Rangers in 1958 with games in England, France, Belgium, Switzerland and Austria). In 1976, the Washington Capitals played the Kansas City Scouts in a four-game series in Tokyo. While over time numerous European countries sent teams to the United States and Canada to play NHL teams in exhibitions – mainly from the Soviet Union – it was not until 1980 that NHL teams participated in pre-season hockey games against European opponents (NHL–Sweden tournament; represented by Washington Capitals and Minnesota North Stars). Since 1980 the NHL has played exhibitions in Finland, Sweden, Czechoslovakia/Czech Republic/Slovakia, the Soviet Union/Russia, Germany, Austria, England, Japan and Puerto Rico. In 2007, the NHL promoted "NHL Premiere", opening the regular season for the first time outside North America with two games in London between the Los Angeles Kings and the Anaheim Ducks. The NHL started their season in Europe every year through to 2012–2013.

Major League Baseball has had the longest involvement of barnstorming, exhibition and pre-season games in international markets – dating back as early as 1908 in Japan. Over the years, the most popular places for international exhibitions have been in Japan (the Japan All-Star Series, which took place at the end of the season every other year from 1986 to 2006) and Puerto Rico (the Roberto Clemente Series from 1976 to 1984 and 1987 to 1989). In 2006, MLB created the World Baseball Classic, a pre-season tournament of 16 baseball-playing nations vying for the title of World Champion. There have been three events to date (2006, 2009, 2013), with games being played in the United States, Japan, Puerto Rico, Taiwan, Canada and Mexico. With regard to pre-season games, since 1999 spring training, games have been played in various locations including Mexico, Venezuela, Puerto Rico, Japan, Cuba and China. In 1996, MLB played their first regular season outside the United States or Canada – a three-game series between the New York Mets and the San Diego Padres in Monterrey, Mexico. Since then, MLB has opened the regular season overseas six times – 1999 in Monterrey, three times in Tokyo (2000, 2004, 2008), once in Puerto Rico (2001) and most recently in Sydney, Australia (2014). Puerto Rico also hosted 22 regular season games of the Montreal Expos in 2004 prior to being sold and becoming the Washington Nationals (Major League Baseball, 2008).

Brand awareness and revenue generation

The curiosity and novelty of a new sport brand occupying a new location not only piques the interest of sport fans and builds consumer awareness, but also entices companies to create marketing partnerships to take advantage of engaging early adopters of the sport (Humphreys & Howard, 2008). As teams and leagues seek to attract a larger target market beyond domestic borders, the outlook of the global sport market changes in numerous ways including how sport and entertainment coverage is provided, the expansion of new and social media engagement, challenges related to the commercialization of the sport business, the continued rising costs of players as a result of additional opportunities, and the increase in broadcasting rights costs (PricewaterhouseCoopers, 2011). These challenges extend beyond league and teams to most sport governing bodies, who have "increasing pressure to grow their sports in international markets, while at the same time maintaining the local support base and the integrity of their competitions." (PricewaterhouseCoopers, 2011, p. 8)

The challenge is building brand equity, which includes ensuring that the perceived quality of the team or league is positive in the minds of the consumer so that they will want to build loyalty to the brand, become more deeply aware of the brand, and help expand the brand image. "Strong brand equity means that customers have high brand-name awareness, maintain a favorable brand image, perceive that the brand is of high quality, and are loyal to the brand" (Bodet & Chanavat, 2010, p. 57) in terms of the attributes and benefits of the brand, as well as customer attitudes toward the brand. Ultimately, building brand awareness requires teams and leagues to:

> refine marketing strategies to maintain a consistent level of engagement year-round or at least seasonally through the development of the sport through a low-level, consistent message of sports development at the grassroots level, which should increase market share and revenues as the sport's popularity grows.
>
> *Humphreys & Howard, 2008, p. 74*

Research shows the most successful United States league internationally thus far to be the NBA. According to the NBA's strategic plan, the league:

> has committed itself to become the world's most likeable, prominent, and respected professional sports organization – to accomplish that goal, the league and its teams have financed, organized, and implemented a number of basketball, educational, participative, and social events, programs, tours, and tournaments for years with several foreign companies.
>
> *Jozsa, 2011, p. 213*

Some of the global statistics for the NBA include: (1) events broadcast to 215 countries in over 40 languages; (2) licensed products being sold in over 100 countries; (3) a "Global Games" initiative – with over 125 international events taking place in 67 cities and 27 countries; (4) a new marketing campaign called "One Game One Love" – a series of television commercials, advertisements (print and online), and event integrations; and (5) NBA 3X – a global grassroots event – and "Basketball without Borders" – a developmental programme run in cooperation with the international federation of basketball (FIBA). Through their partnerships in China, last year the NBA viewership increased 30 per cent over the previous year, and resulting revenue has grown US$150 million (Horrow & Swatek, 2013). Overall, about 10 per cent of the NBA's revenue can be tracked to international operations (Koba, 2013). With the common knowledge that the number one goal of any business is to make a profit, new revenue generation needs to go hand-in-hand with any brand-building effort.

Other leagues are taking note of the international success of the NBA and trying to match the efforts. For MLB, the focus has been on building the global brand of baseball in conjunction with its population of players. Nearly 40 per cent of players in MLB are from outside the United States – coming from 22 countries (Baseball Almanac, 2013), not to mention the significant additional number of players under contract and playing in the minor leagues. According to the MLB International website (2014):

> Major League Baseball International (MLBI) focuses on the worldwide growth of baseball and the promotion of Major League Baseball and MLB Club trademarks and copyrights through special events, broadcasting, market development, licensing and sponsorship initiatives. MLBI is committed to showcasing the world's best baseball talent through international events around the globe. Broadcast in 233 countries and territories, Major League Baseball game telecasts are re-transmitted in

17 different languages. MLBI executes and supports game development programs targeting players and coaches from grassroots to elite levels. With an extensive list of marketing partners worldwide, MLBI continues to grow its position as a leader in the international marketplace.

It also works in partnership with the International Baseball Federation to develop and expand baseball leagues around the world and, as mentioned earlier in this article, to promote the World Baseball Classic. Overall less than 10 per cent of MLB revenue currently comes from international revenues (Koba, 2013), which is comparable to the NBA, so there is a great opportunity for growth.

The NHL, with its engrained brand equity internationally for over 75 years, and with a significant percentage of players coming from overseas (although the league is still heavily Canadian and American), "generates more than $1 billion US from NHL-licensed product sales worldwide" (Koba, 2013, p. 1), and additional media revenue with broadcasts to more than 160 countries (Koba, 2013). For the NFL, when it was announced that they were going to have their yearly "International Series" game in London each year starting in 2007, its website received more than one million applications for tickets (PricewaterhouseCoopers, 2011). With the success of the game, sold-out crowds, and increases in marketing and media revenue between 2007 and 2012, the NFL has expanded its footprint in London, playing two games there in 2013, and three games in 2014.

Regardless of the league, one thing is crucial for all to recognize – going forward globalization will be crucial to ongoing success. The United States and Canada only represent approximately 350 million of the seven-billion-person world market, or approximately 5 per cent of the world's population. While we are:

> in an era of economic uncertainty, what is clear is that the balance of global economic power is shifting east [towards Asia] and south [towards Latin America and in some cases Africa]. . . [and in order] to maintain the momentum of internationalization, sports must seek new revenues from the growing middle classes in emerging nations.
>
> *PricewaterhouseCoopers, 2011*

Effects on domestic fan base

As stated earlier, a significant "challenge for governing bodies is the increasing pressure to grow their sports in international markets, while at the same time maintaining the local support based and the integrity of their competitions" (PricewaterhouseCoopers, 2011, p. 8). So the question arises about whether moving home games overseas negatively affects domestic fans. For MLB, where there are 81 home games over a six-month period, and considering the limited number of games chosen to play overseas each year, the number of games overseas versus the number of games in a year makes it virtually insignificant for domestic fans.

On the other end of the spectrum is the NFL, where there are only eight regular season home games – to a maximum of approximately 13, including potential pre-season and play-off games. Interestingly enough, the majority of owners of NFL teams willing to give up home games to London from 2009 to 2016 have financial interests in England via the Barclays English Premier League. Tampa Bay had home games in 2009 and 2011 – the owner also owns Manchester United; St Louis in 2012 (ownership interest in Arsenal); and Jacksonville in 2013 – and contracted through 2016 (ownership of Fulham). Especially for the owners of Jacksonville and Tampa Bay, where there have been attendance struggles in recent years, the opportunity to play overseas has not affected their attendance numbers at other home games, and has given those owners an opportunity to make up for lost revenue.

In the middle are the NBA and NHL, each with 41 regular-season home games – far more than the NFL, but about half the games of an MLB season. Both leagues have had a significant presence in the international market for well over three decades, both leagues have significant numbers of international players, and the majority of games played overseas are either pre-season games, or early-season games where the loss of one home game would not be significantly missed by fans. In addition, with NBA and NHL players regularly participating in international competitions such as the Olympics (and with even the NHL shutting down the league for three weeks during Olympic years – and cancelling the All-Star Game in that year), there seems to be a better understanding of the place of each league in the global landscape.

Burdens on players, coaches and staff

But one area of concern not always considered is the burden of international competitions on players, coaches and staff. This includes the physical and emotional stresses created by travel and changes in sleep patterns, practice and training routines, and eating schedules – to name a few. For many players:

> these games are real love/hate experiences for the players . . . on the one hand they can be amazing trips to places you have never been, and on the other hand they can be "see the world in 48 hours" kinds of things . . . while a boon for the league and the marketing types, they can be rough to recover from – in some cases, teams can be jet-lagged for weeks and have it affect their regular season.
>
> *Schayes, 2013*

Overall, I believe most players see the excitement of playing overseas as trumping the physical and emotional burdens – or else the players' unions would block playing overseas.

The leagues do work with players and teams to attempt to reduce the burden as much as possible through adjustments to game schedules. For example, the NFL attempts to allow teams that play in London to be at home for a game the week before travelling to London, and allow the team's bye week after the trip to give them time to recover. MLB opened the 2014 season in Sydney, Australia with the Los Angeles Dodgers playing the Arizona Diamondbacks. To help lessen the burden, the teams chosen were from the west coast to lessen the travel impact, and games were played one week in advance of when other teams started the regular season. This gave the teams time to return to the United States to get re-acclimated – the teams had eight days off upon their return, and MLB kept the teams either at home (Arizona) or local (Los Angeles played in San Diego) for their first series. The NHL and NBA typically provide a one-week lead time prior to and after playing international games.

In addition to potential physical and emotional issues, there are also financial burdens that must be considered as a result of international competition. The already complex tax issues facing athletes earning incomes in various locations gets even more challenging when foreign tax issues must be considered. However, from an accounting standpoint, while more complex, the total financial implication on players, coaches and staff is no more significant than the tax implications in the United States when it comes to playing a small percentage of games overseas. The burden would be more significant if a team was permanently placed outside the United States in a country that does not have a tax treaty in place like as the United States–Canada tax treaty, which protects athletes from double-taxation (MacDonald, 2014; Internal Revenue Service, 1985). In addition, there would be more significant issues related to visa requirements and labour laws that could come into play.

However for a short-term event, the burden is minimal. Taking a NFL game in London for one game, game checks are subject to UK taxation, as well as a percentage of endorsement income for time in the UK (usually less than seven days) – with the rate being as high as 45 per cent, most of which can be received back via income tax filing at the US rate as a foreign tax credit – but an individual would still pay between 5 and 10 per cent of earnings through taxes for that period (Dosh, 2013; Baker, 1990), which is minimal in nature. In a more mathematical example, assume a player earns US$10 million per year in salary and endorsements. Dividing by 365 days, the athlete earns approximately US$27,400 per day. Assume the athlete is in London for a game for one week – he/she earns US$192,000 of his/her salary during the time in London. That figure is subject to a tax rate of 45 per cent, which equals US$86,300 that the athlete would need to pay to the United Kingdom. However, upon filing his/her tax return in the United States, the athlete would get a foreign tax credit on the tax return in the amount of the United States rate of 39.6 per cent. That would lower the tax liability of the athlete on the money earned for the game in London to 5.4 per cent, or US$10,368. Hence, playing the game in London cost the athlete approximately one-tenth of 1 per cent of their overall salary.

Conclusion

The evidence shows that each league will be involved with differing levels of international marketing and event operations, ranging from fully embracing global growth to dabbling in specific, targeted international efforts. Research also shows that there are divergent views on the effect of these efforts on the domestic fan base, and that the burdens placed on athletes, coaches, and staff are minimal in nature.

Cabral (2010) states that for a quality sport export strategy to be viable on the global stage: (1) team sports that are low maintenance are preferred; (2) the rules of the sport need to be less complex; (3) events need to be less than three hours in length; (4) exhibitions must be introduced to pique interest and increase demand; and (5) television coverage must supplement the efforts. In consideration of these factors, the league that seems to be poised to have the greatest global influence going forward – with the potential to grow to the scale of soccer around the world – is the sport of basketball . . . led by the NBA.

References

Baker, W. H. (1990). The tax significance of place of residence for professional athletes. *Marquette Sports Law Journal*, *1*(1), 1–39.

Baseball Almanac (2013). *Major League Baseball Players by Birthplace During the 2013 Season*. Retrieved from <www.baseball-almanac.com/players/birthplace.php?y=2013>. Accessed 13 March 2014.

Bodet, G. & Chanavat, N. (2010). Building global football brand equity – lessons from the Chinese market. *Asia Pacific Journal of Marketing & Logistics*, *22*(1), 55–66.

Cabral, L. (2010). *13 – Exporting Sport Entertainment: The NBA in China*. Retrieved from <http://luiscabral.org//economics/books/entertainment/13.nba.pdf>. Accessed 19 March 2014.

Dosh, K. (2013). *NFL in London Raises Legal Issues*. Retrieved from <http://espn.go.com/nfl/story /_/id/ 9716479/nfl-team-london-raises-legal-issues>. Accessed 26 February 2014.

Horrow, R. & Swatek, K. (2013). *NBA Tip Off 2013 – With Labor Peace, Tech Savvy, and a Big Global Footprint, is the Pro Basketball Business a Slam Dunk?* Retrieved from <www.bsports.com/ statsinsights/ nba/nba-tip-2013-labor-peace-tech-savvy-big-global-footprint-pro-basketball-business-slam-dunk>. Accessed 15 April 2015.

Humphreys, B. R. & Howard, D. R. (2008). *Business of Sports Volume 1: Perspectives on the Sports Industry*. Westport, CT: Greenwood Publishing.

Internal Revenue Service (1985). United States–Canada income tax convention. Retrieved from <www.irs.gov/pub/irs-trty/canada.pdf>. Accessed 15 March 2014.

Jozsa, F. P. (2011). *The National Basketball Association: Business, Organization, and Strategy*. Singapore: World Scientific Publishing Company.

Koba, M. (9 October 2013). *US Pro Teams Give "Away Game" a Whole New Meaning*. Retrieved from <www.cnbc.com/id/101095638>. Accessed 26 February 2014.

Longley, N. (2012). The impact of international competitions on competitive balance in domestic leagues: The case of the National Hockey League's participation in the Winter Olympics. *International Journal of Sport Finance*, 7(3), 249–261.

McDonald, H., Karg, A. J. & Lock, D. (2010). Leveraging fans' global football allegiances to build domestic league support. *Asia Pacific Journal of Marketing & Logistics*, 22(1), 67–89.

MacDonald, J. (2014). *Taxes: Cost of Being a Professional Athlete*. Retrieved from <www.bankrate.com/ finance/taxes/taxes-cost-professional-athlete.aspx>. Accessed 15 April 2014.

Major League Baseball (2008). *MLB Truly International*. Retrieved from <http://mlb.mlb.com/news/ print.jsp?ymd= 20080318&content_id=2443641&fext=.jsp&c_id=mlb>. Accessed 26 February 2014.

Major League Baseball International (2014). *MLB International*. Retrieved from <http://mlb.mlb.com/ mlb/international/mlbi_index.jsp>. Accessed 26 February 2014.

National Basketball Association (2014). *History of the NBA Global Games*. Retrieved from <www.nba. com/global/games2013/all-time-international-game-list.html>. Accessed 26 February 2014.

PricewaterhouseCoopers (2011). Changing the game: Outlook for the global sports market to 2015. Retrieved from <www.pwc.com/sportsoutlook>. Accessed 13 March 2014.

Schayes, D. (2013). *Why Preseason Trips, Near and Far, Can Be Onerous*. Retrieved from <www. sheridanhoops.com/2013/10/22/schayes-why-preseason-trips-near-and-far-can-be-onerous/>. Accessed 19 March 2014.

8

OLYMPIC GAMES' IMAGE PERCEPTIONS AMONG ONSITE SPECTATORS

The cases of Beijing, London and Sochi

Kyriaki (Kiki) Kaplanidou, Serkan Berber and Dan Drane

Introduction

The Olympic Games brand enjoys the highest brand recognition globally in the sport realm (Payne, 2006). Researchers have discussed the differences between the perceptions of consumers of the Olympic Games and manager perceptions of the Olympic Games' image in a number of areas (Seguin, Richelieu & Reilly, 2007). From the International Olympic Committee's (IOC) standpoint, there is always concern about how the Games are consumed and how the consumption process correlates with the IOC's image (Maguire, Barnard, Butler & Golding, 2008). This is why the IOC is conducting its own research regarding the Olympic brand globally (International Olympic Committee, 2013). The most recent research by the IOC regarding the Olympic brand suggests that it outperforms other global brands in the values of "Inspirational", "Heritage and Tradition", "Diversity", "Optimistic", "Excellence", "Global" and "Inclusive" (International Olympic Committee, 2013). In the latter research, consumer perceptions of the IOC were evaluated as well. The results revealed the highly positive consumers' attributions of the IOC as modern, transparent, dynamic, strict about doping, global and a leader (International Olympic Committee, 2013). Despite positive results in the IOC research, criticisms still remain about the Games being a capitalistic growth platform that often foists cultural products in each host city (Maguire, 2011) that can be reflected differently within different genders (Silk, 2011). Furthermore, non-IOC-sponsored research on Olympic Games' onsite spectator perceptions is lacking in the literature. Thus, a deeper understanding of images consumed by Olympic Games' spectators may shed light on the components of the Olympic Games' image given its potential to influence sport consumer behaviours and legacy outcomes such as tourism development (Kaplanidou, 2007; Kaplanidou, 2009, 2012). In addition, an exploration of the differences in the Olympic Games' image components between male and female Olympic spectators can shed light on the consumption process of the Olympic Games' brand. This chapter provides an overview of the current state of research on the Olympic Games' image as established by the IOC and field research. The chapter presents the importance of direct experience in the Olympic Games and discusses the formation of event image perceptions by spectators of the

Olympic Games. Three mega-events are explored in terms of their image: Beijing 2008, London 2012 and Sochi 2014. The chapter concludes with implications for Olympic marketing.

The IOC and the Olympic Games' image

The IOC is diligent about monitoring its Olympic brand and the Olympic Games' image worldwide. More specifically, the IOC hires private companies to monitor the image of the Games usually after each Olympic Games. For example, in 2014 the IOC conducted another private study that showed the positive image of the Olympic Games and the high recognition of the Olympic Summer and Winter Games globally (IOC, 2014). In addition, the IOC also monitors the marketing performance of each Olympic Games through its marketing reports.

According to the latest IOC marketing fact file (IOC, 2015a) the growth of the Olympic marketing revenue is impressive as during the 1993–1996 quadrennium the revenues were approximately $2.5 billion and during the 2009–2012 quadrennium they were approximately $8 billion. Marketing revenue is calculated from revenues found in broadcasting, the Olympic Partner Programme (TOP), the Organizing Committee for the Olympic Games (OCOG) domestic sponsorships, ticketing and licensing. Thus, the business viability of the Olympic brand is not in question despite recent challenges the IOC has faced with the low number of interested applicant cities for the Olympic Games. Therefore, dissecting the Olympic brand in order to understand what aspects form its dominant images is a necessary step for Olympic marketing. Nevertheless, the image of the Games as perceived from direct experience with the event is not found in the literature.

Direct experience and brand images

The notion of direct experience with a brand creates more salient beliefs and emotions relative to the brand itself. Direct experience with sport events has been found to boost various types of connections and meaning to an event (Kaplanidou & Vogt, 2010). The main idea of event brand perceptions is to understand the consumers' experience and connection with the event. For example, spectators of Olympic Games will place different weight on various Olympic Games' image elements. At the same time, athletes and delegates can perceive different dominant elements of the sport event and sport media can push different imagery for an Olympic Games according to what the media perceives to be important messages. Kaplanidou and Havitz (2010) found that situational involvement with the experience of attending the Olympic Games was higher than enduring and long-term involvement with the Games. In addition, the destination experience can add to the overall image perceptions of the event and create a stronger cognitive or affective position in the consumer's mind (Hallmann & Breuer, 2010; Hallmann, Kaplanidou & Breuer, 2010; Kaplanidou, 2010; Kaplanidou, Kerwin & Karadakis, 2013).

The images of the Olympic Games of Beijing, London and Sochi

The Olympic Games' host cities prepare carefully to host the Games. The host committee also creates a distinct message and image that is communicated to the global audience through the international media. For example, the spirit of the London 2012 Games aimed to be energetic, spirited, bright and youthful while their motto was "Inspire a Generation", reflecting the promise made when London bid for the Games (International Olympic Committee,

2012). For the Beijing Organizing Committee on the other hand, the goal was for the Games to be known as the "People's Games, Green Games and High-Tech Games" (International Olympic Committee, 2010). Sochi was promoted to be the athletes' Games as the athletes were in close proximity to the venues and the goal was to focus on their needs, so they used "Hot, Cool, Yours" as the Games' slogan (IOC, 2015b).

Is that, however, what the spectators perceive the image of the various Games to be? The lack of research with regards to this question is puzzling. Therefore, comparing and contrasting the spectators' perceptions about the Games with the Organizing Committees' positioning is important to explore. In addition, identifying if there are salient themes in the image of the Olympic Games can provide very useful marketing implications. Looking at the studies that examine the image of either destinations or sport events, it is clear that sport event images consist of cognitive and affective components that are identified through certain dimensions such as emotional, environmental and socio-cultural (Hallmann, Kaplanidou & Breuer, 2010; Kaplanidou, 2007; Kaplanidou, 2009, 2010). Also, as noted in the marketing report from the Torino 2006 Games:

> The essence of the Olympic Brand consists of three essential pillars. The first of these is Striving for Success, which is founded upon the ideals inherent in sport – such as striving, excellence, determination, being the best. Attributes that define the Olympic Games as a global festival – such as global, participation, celebration, unity, festive – constitute the second pillar, Celebration of Community. The third pillar, Positive Human Values, is composed of the attributes that fulfill our understanding of, and aspiration to, universal ideals: optimism, respectful, inspirational. These three pillars support a powerful, emotive brand that transcends sport and resonates strongly with the people of the world
>
> *International Olympic Committee, 2006, p. 25*

Brand image is an antecedent to brand equity and manifests through brand associations (knowledge structures) in memory (Keller, 2003). As Keller suggested, "two key areas of consumer research in branding revolve around the creation and representation of brand knowledge. The challenge and opportunity for consumer research in both of these areas is fully appreciating the broad scope and complexity involved" (p. 599). Thus, understanding the salience and strength of brand image components can contribute to an increase in the brand equity.

To understand the salience of the Olympic Games' brand image, data were collected from spectators and tourists of two consecutive summer Olympic Games – Beijing 2008 and London 2012 – and one Winter Olympic Games – the 2014 Sochi Winter Games. Presented first are the spectator perceptions of the 2008 and 2012 Summer Games' images, followed by the 2014 Sochi Winter Games, as the Sochi Games took place after the introduction of the IOC agenda 2020 that proposed changes for the Games' operations to increase its appeal.

Beijing and London

In order to examine the image perceptions of spectators who attended the Games, data were collected from people who were in the Olympic city. For Beijing, the number of respondents was 481, while for London it was 172. For Beijing there were 12 interviewers (all of whom were multi-lingual), working and collecting data every day during the Games, beginning one day before the event and finishing one day after the event concluded. The languages spoken by the interviewers included English, Spanish, Portuguese, Mandarin, Polish, Korean and

French. All the interviewers went through formal training before collecting data. Data were collected at various Olympic sites, tourist destinations, market districts and hotel districts using a three-page survey that included the questions in our study. For London 2012, the concentration of spectators was at the Olympic Park, thus the data were collected by one trained doctoral student during four days (29 July, 1, 4 and 12 August), both outside and inside the site. The question asked of the respondents was to list three words that came to mind when thinking about the Beijing/London Games. The words were then compiled into a master list and were coded following an open coding process that allowed the generation of concepts that could offer a foundation for theory building (Strauss & Corbin, 1990). For Beijing, there were 1,443 words and for London, 497. Two coders examined the data holistically, identified some common themes in the data and agreed on these categories. Then a word-by-word coding took place under the initial theme identification. For the majority of the word classification there were no differences in the coders' assignment of words. For the words where differences existed, final classification was resolved with discussion.

For the Beijing sample the demographics were as follows: the majority of the respondents (57.2 per cent) were female, with an average age of 32 years. The largest representations of spectators were from North America (28 per cent), Asia (20 per cent) and Europe (18 per cent). Regarding the image perceptions for Beijing, eight themes were identified: event prestige, commercial, organization/management, athletes, socio-cultural, host destination, sports competition and emotional. For London the same topics were revealed along with nationalism as a new theme for the London Games. For Beijing the most dominant theme was "athletes" while for London it was the "emotional" theme. The second most important theme for Beijing was the "sports competition" and the same was for London. The third most salient theme for Beijing was the "socio-cultural" theme while for London 2012, it was the "organization/management" aspect. The initial results from this comparison suggest that there seems to be some disconnect between the positioning of the Organizing Committee and the positioning of each Games in the consumers' mind.

For the London sample the demographics were as follows: the majority of the respondents (60 per cent) were male, with an average age of 38 years. The largest representations of spectators were from Britain (89.5 per cent). Regarding education, about 60 per cent of the sample had a college or advanced degree. Regarding the image perceptions for London 2012, the salience of the "emotional" theme for the London Games emerged given that creating inspiration drove the Organizing Committee's communication strategies. In addition, "sports competition" and "management/organization" emerged to reflect two themes that are connected with the direct experience of the spectators: the consumption of sports competition and the event's organization.

For Beijing, there was more disconnection with the positioning of the Organizing Committee as the respondents brought to mind mainly the athletes, the competition and socio-cultural aspects. The latter does align with the "Peoples' Games" positioning, but there was no connection to the "Green Games" and "Tech Games" themes. Rather, it seems the spectators regressed on the Olympic values of success, human values and inspiration as evident in some of the identified themes. Interestingly, the themes across the two Games differed in only one category – London's nationalism. But the sample generated in the London Games consisted primarily of British spectators, a limitation that has to be noted here. The sample from Beijing was more diverse as respondents came from all five continents. The commonality in the themes is encouraging the creation of a scale that measures the Olympic Games' image, which will benefit a number of stakeholders: the IOC, the Organizing Committee, the sponsors, to evaluate how the image of the Games influences outcomes such as loyalty and/or

Table 8.1 Three words that come to mind when thinking of the Olympic Games, coded in event image categories

Beijing	No. of words/ frequency	%	Word examples	London	No. of words/ frequency	%	Word examples
Emotional	86	5.96	amazing anxious apprehensive	Emotional	186	37.42	awesome amazing pride
Athletes	316	21.90	Bolt Phelps	Athletes	14	2.82	champions
Event prestige	191	13.24	extravagant elegant flashy	Event prestige	44	8.85	brilliant elite grand
Organization/ management	139	9.63	construction controlled overproduced	Organization/ management	67	13.48	busy expensive organized
Commercial	36	2.49	business advertisements profitable	Commercial	12	2.41	rings entertain- ment
Socio-cultural	226	15.66	Asia diverse conflict discrimination	Socio-cultural	10	2.01	inclusive culture
Host destination	131	9.08	Chinese circus Peking Great Wall	Host destination	51	10.26	rain tourists London
Sports competition	307	21.28	gymnasts gold marathon	Sports competition	85	17.10	dedication cycling victory
Unclassified	11	0.76	–	Nationalism	21	4.23	patriotic Great Britain
Total words	1443	100		Unclassified	7	1.41	–
				Total words	497	100	

satisfaction with Olympic Games' products and services. The results from Beijing and London are depicted in Table 8.1.

When the words of the London 2012 Olympic Games spectators were analysed through the qualitative software, Nvivo, the dominance of emotions was obvious and can be seen in Figure 8.1.

Similarly, for Beijing, when all the words provided by the Olympic Games' spectators were analysed by the Nvivo software a dominance of the athlete theme was revealed, as can be observed in Figure 8.2.

Sochi 2014

The understanding of Olympic Games' image perceptions has to be taken into consideration with policy changes put forth by the organization involved with the event. Introduced by the

Figure 8.1 Word cloud created from the London 2012 Olympic Games' spectators who offered three words to describe the image of the Games

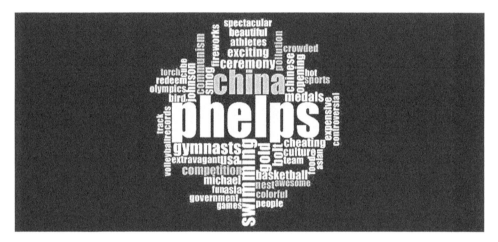

Figure 8.2 Word cloud created from the Beijing 2012 Olympic Games' spectators who offered three words to describe the image of the Games

IOC in February 2014, the Olympic Agenda 2020 aims to explore how to sustain Olympic values (excellence, friendship, respect) to ensure the long-term development of the Olympic movement (IOC, 2014). One of the key themes in that agenda is the topic of differentiation, which focuses on understanding the characteristics of each Olympic Games that are distinct to that particular Games. Within this mindset, this study explores the prominent thoughts among onsite spectators for the Sochi 2014 Games and how these relate to the Olympic brand since the introduction of the 2020 agenda. Data were collected by two trained interviewers between 9 and 17 February 2014 from 205 spectators who were primarily intercepted in restaurants within the Olympic Park in Sochi during the Games. A two-page self-administered survey was used. The majority of the respondents (62.4 per cent) were male, with an average age of 32 years (SD=7.51). The annual household income for 63 per cent of the respondents was between €20,000 and €40,000. The majority of the respondents were university graduates (84.4 per cent) and Caucasian (96.1 per cent). Two-thirds of respondents (66.8 per cent) were European, followed by American (12.7 per cent) and Canadian citizens (11.2 per cent). The majority of the respondents (85.4 per cent) said that the Sochi Olympics was their first Olympic experience while 14.6 per cent had visited one more Olympic Games previously. For most of the respondents, it was the first time visiting Sochi (92.2 per cent) and Russia (73.2 per cent).

The survey asked the respondents to write three words that came to mind when thinking about the 2014 Sochi Games. The results focused on the first word mentioned by the respondents to remove bias from further cognitive processing that could happen with the second and third word reference. A large percentage of the respondents offered words related to the Sochi Games tagline "Hot, Cool, Yours", followed by words related to the event management and organization, the host destination, emotional aspects and the sport competition, event prestige, socio-cultural aspects, commercial aspects, nationalism and athletes. These results are presented in Table 8.2.

Table 8.2 Three words that come to mind when thinking of the 2014 Sochi Olympic Games, coded in event image categories

	No. of words/ frequency	%	Word examples
Host destination	25	12.4	Black Sea sun snow hospitality, cheap
Organization/management	33	16.3	security construction transport crowd
Sochi brand	95	47.0	hot cool yours
Socio-cultural	4	2.0	friendly people international together nations
Emotional	16	7.9	amusement warmth energy passionate happy
Event prestige	6	3.0	big traditions excellence large
Sports competition	14	6.9	venues Olympic park facilities victory sports

(continued)

Table 8.2 Three words that come to mind when thinking of the 2014 Sochi Olympic Games, coded in event image categories *(continued)*

	No. of words/ frequency	%	Word examples
	2	1.0	athletes
			Olympians
Commercial	4	2.0	Bosco
			investment
Nationalism	3	1.5	nationalism
			patriotism
Total words	202	100	

Figure 8.3 Word cloud created from the Sochi 2014 Olympic Games spectators who offered three words to describe the image of the Games

Looking at Figure 8.3 depicting the word cloud from the spectators' input, it can be observed that the Games organization is at the centre of the word cloud and the event prestige is also evident from the words offered. The words "Hot, Cool, Yours" were not included in the analysis in order to create a more diverse visual stimulation for the rest of the themes.

Taken together the results suggest that the Olympic values permeate to some extent the perceived event image of the Games. These results, therefore, allow for a deeper understanding of the Olympic Games image that can aid the development and application of strategies related to each separate Games. These strategies can create a platform of differentiation for the Olympic Games' identity. Certainly, the results from Sochi suggest that the promotional efforts of the Sochi organizers were effective given that the Sochi tagline of "Hot, Cool, Yours" was mentioned the most by onsite spectators. Thus, promotions could have utilized more Olympic value content, which would have had a positive impact on increasing knowledge of the Olympic values among onsite Olympic Games spectators.

Synthesis of the findings

Looking at the freely elicited results of the image of the three Games it can be observed that similar image components emerged but that they held a different salience for each Games. Thus, the first observation of these results is that each Games creates a dynamic imagery and element interplay. It can be observed that the elements that spectators identified for the Olympic Games image relate to functional, symbolic and experiential components (Park, Jaworski & McInnis, 1986). In addition, some unique imagery aspects (Echtner & Ritchie, 1991), such as patriotism, emerged. As Keller (1993) notes, the brand associations structure that is based on direct experience seems to be a more complex structure where we can observe a dynamic interplay of attributes, benefits and attitudes. Direct experience empowers certain image themes related to the event delivery, which is not present in the Olympic brand image components in the research conducted by the IOC.

The most important aspect of this research relates to the implications these results have for Olympic marketing. Although the same themes emerged, there was a different dynamic of brand associations for each Games that was studied. Thus, there is potential for differential influence of each image component on sport consumption behaviours. Comparing back to the positioning of each Games, London seems to have achieved a large emotional engagement given the Games' positioning and efforts to connect people to "Inspiration". For Beijing, the athletes, the sport competition and socio-cultural aspects emerged, which connects to the People's Games aspect the Beijing Organizing Committee was aiming to promote, although despite the efforts no strong evidence toward the Green Games and Hi-Tech image was detected in the data. For Sochi, the results showed a similarity in the themes with the summer Games, which denoted that sport consumers process the direct experience of attending an event in similar "categories" that form the image of the event in their minds.

Implications for Olympic marketing

Given the similar categories that emerged among onsite Olympic Games sport spectators, it is quite significant for onsite Olympic marketing to be relevant mostly for onsite sponsorship activation and brand congruence of sponsors and the event. If the athletes are forming the dominant Olympic Games image theme, then onsite sponsors have the opportunity to leverage that connection for their products. As Kim and Kaplanidou (2014) found for the 2012 London Games, emotional connections to the brand along with interactivity enhanced spectators' attitudes toward onsite Olympic sponsor activation. For Sochi, there was a salience of onsite event brand promotion, which suggests that there was higher cognitive processing of the Olympic marketing elements that the Sochi organizers wanted to promote.

Based on the different saliency of the Olympic Games' image categories for each event, Olympic host destinations can create a point of differentiation for the Olympic image that leverages the salient image component with the destination's tourism experiences. In addition, Olympic values associated with the image, such as solidarity and socio-cultural aspects, can be used to create Olympic Values-diffused strategies to further build the brand "architecture" through brand associations (Anderson, 1981). This can be achieved through stronger social media activation and sponsor activation using onsite marketing, but also through TV commercials and community engagement.

References

Anderson, N. H. (1981). *Foundations of Information Integration Theory*. New York: Academic Press.

Echtner, C. M. & Ritchie, B. J. R. (1991). The meaning and measurement of destination image. *Journal of Tourism Studies*, *2*(2), 2–12.

Hallmann, K., & Breuer, C. (2010). The impact of image congruence between sport event and destination on behavioural intentions. *Tourism Review of AIEST – International Association of Scientific Experts in Tourism*, *65*(1), 66–74. <doi: http://dx.doi.org/10.1108/16605371011040915>.

Hallmann, K., Kaplanidou, K. & Breuer, C. (2010). Event image perceptions among active and passive sport tourists at marathon races: A qualitative and quantitative approach. *International Journal of Sports Marketing & Sponsorship*, *12*(1), 37–52.

International Olympic Committee (2006). *Marketing Report Torino 2006* (p. 132). Lausanne: International Olympic Committee.

International Olympic Committee (2010). *Factsheet: Legacies of the Games*. In I. O. Committee (Ed.) (pp. 1–9). Lausanne: International Olympic Committee.

International Olympic Committee (2012). *Marketing Report London 2012* (p. 85). Lausanne: International Olympic Commitee.

International Olympic Committee (2013). *The Olympic Brand Maintains its Global Strength and Recognition*. Retrieved from <www.olympic.org/news/the-olympic-brand-maintains-its-global-strength-and-recognition/190770>. Accessed 21 February 2013.

International Olympic Committee. (2014). "Post-Sochi research demonstrates appeal of Olympic Games and Olympic brand". *Olympic.org*. Retrieved from IOC latest news website <www.olympic.org/news/post-sochi-research-demonstrates-appeal-of-olympic-games-and-olympic-brand/234974>.

International Olympic Committee. (2015a). *Olympic Marketing Fact File 2015*. In I. O. Committee (Ed.) (p. 39). Lausanne: International Olympic Committee.

International Olympic Committee. (2015b). *Success of Sochi 2014 lives on*. IOC News. Retrieved from <www.olympic.org/news/success-of-sochi-2014-lives-on/243184>.

Kaplanidou, K. (2007). Affective event and destination image: Their influence on Olympic travelers' behavioral intentions. *Event Management*, *10*(2), 159–173.

Kaplanidou, K. (2009). Relationships among behavioral intentions, cognitive event and destination images among different geographic regions of Olympic Games spectators. *Journal of Sport & Tourism*, *14*(4), 249–272.

Kaplanidou, K. (2010). Active sport tourists: sport event image considerations. *Tourism Analysis*, *15*(3), 381–386.

Kaplanidou, K. (2012). The importance of legacy outcomes for Olympic Games four summer host cities residents' quality of life: 1996–2008. *European Sport Management Quarterly*, *12*(4), 397–433.

Kaplanidou, K. & Havitz, M. E. (2010). Exploring SI and EI of Olympic sports tourists: Does trip purpose matter? *International Journal of Sports Marketing & Sponsorship*, *11*(4), 74–89. <doi: 10.1108/IJSMS-11-04-2010-B006>.

Kaplanidou, K., Kerwin, S. & Karadakis, K. (2013). Understanding sport event success: exploring perceptions of sport event consumers and event providers. *Journal of Sport & Tourism*, *18*(3), 137–159. <doi: 10.1080/14775085.2013.861358>.

Kaplanidou, K. & Vogt, C. (2010). The meaning and measurement of a sport event experience among active sport tourists. *Journal of Sport Management*, *24*, 544–566.

Keller, K. L. (1993). Conceptualizing, measuring and managing customer-based brand equity. *Journal of Marketing*, *57*, 1–22.

Keller, K. L. (2003). Brand synthesis: The multidimensionality of brand knowledge. *Journal of Consumer Research*, *29*, 595–600.

Kim. A. & Kaplanidou, K. (2014). Consumer responses to on-site Olympic sponsorship activation: The impact of interactivity, emotions, and perceived image fit on brand attitude formation. *International Journal of Sport Management and Marketing (IJSMM)*, *15*(5/6), 279–300.

Maguire, J., Barnard, S., Butler, K. & Golding, P. (2008). "Celebrate humanity" or "consumers"? A critical evaluation of a brand in motion. *Social Identities*, *14*(1), 63–76. <doi: 10.1080/1350463 0701848598>.

Maguire, J. A. (2011). Branding and consumption in the IOC's "Celebrate Humanity" campaign. *Sport in Society*, *14*(7–8), 1056–1068. <doi: 10.1080/17430437.2011.603558>.

Park, C. W., Jaworski, B. J. & McInnis, D. (1986). Strategic brand concept-image management. *Journal of Marketing*, *50*(4), 135–145.

Payne, M. (2006). *Olympic Turnaround: How the Olympic Games Stepped Back from the Brink of Extinction to Become the World's Best Known Brand*. Westport, CT: Praeger Publishers, Greenwood Publishing.

Seguin, B., Richelieu, A. & Reilly, N. (2007). Leveraging the Olympic brand through the reconciliation of corporate and consumers brand perceptions. *International Journal of Sport Management and Marketing*, *3*(1–2), 3–22. <doi: 10.1504/ijsmm.2008.015958>.

Silk, M. (2011). Towards a sociological analysis of London 2012. *Sociology*, *45*(5), 733–748. <doi: 10.1177/0038038511413422>.

Strauss, A. & Corbin, J. (1990). *Basics of Qualitative Research*. Newbury Park, CA: Sage.

9

THE ROLE OF ENDORSEMENT IN INTERNATIONAL SPORT MARKETING

Sara Keshkar

Introduction

Endorsement is a form of support for, and approval of, a person, a product, an event or a company. Endorsements are one of the most important promotional activities used in sport. They have a special role in marketing products. Not only do sport celebrities make commercials for various sport products, but global brands also use them to market their non-sport-related products to the world.

Despite the importance of endorsements in sport marketing, how endorsements are used depends upon the culture of a target country. The manner in which cultures of the world differ can limit the way in which famous sport stars appear in advertisements and even limit the effects of marketing activities. The different attitudes of people in different cultures towards using human beings as advertising phenomena is an important factor to consider when choosing promotional strategies. On the other hand, the lifestyle of sport stars as "brands" themselves, or as endorsers of brands, is an important consideration when faced with such sociological attitudes. Sport stars' endorsement contracts can limit their lifestyle so that their behaviour differs from that of other people in many aspects. Their contracts can limit their behaviour and this is why some people consider endorsements to be "sports slavery". The characteristics of sport stars are another important factor that makes them effective endorsers. Although the favourite characteristics for "normal" celebrities can differ in different cultures, it seems that sport creates a set of favourite characteristics for its stars that transcend culture so that they can endorse products in any part of the world successfully.

What is endorsement?

As mentioned above, endorsement is a form of support for, and approval of, a person, a product, an event, or a company, and usually a celebrity has the main role in endorsement. Endorsement is sometimes called celebrity marketing. Celebrity marketing is a tactic featuring a famous person offering an endorsement of a product. This famous person might be an athlete, an actor, a musician, a scientist, a politician, a cartoon character, or anyone who is popular and well-known. Celebrity marketing is one of the fastest and easiest ways for companies to create brand associations in the minds of consumers. When a famous sport star endorses a product, that product may gain immediate credibility.

Endorsement can be presented in explicit or implicit form. When a sport star uses a product personally and enjoys it, it is an explicit form of endorsement; when sport stars get involved in the image of a brand without using it, it is the implicit form of endorsement. For example, when a sport celebrity attends a ceremony at which certain kinds of drinks are served, and the drink logos can be seen everywhere, he/she is partaking in implicit endorsement.

Endorsement can be used locally or globally. Sometimes endorsers are popular in a particular region, country or city. Companies then use the endorser for marketing products for the people who live in that area as a target market. Some celebrities who are popular throughout the world can be used in global marketing efforts – for example, when Nike uses sport celebrities to endorse new shoes to the world, the company uses global endorsement.

The importance of endorsement

Celebrity endorsement has been established as one of the most popular tools of advertising in modern times. It has become a trend and is perceived to be a winning formula for product marketing and brand building. Although some research findings show that there is no significant difference for all variables between those advertisements that have a celebrity endorser and those that do not, a celebrity endorsement has a special role in sport marketing.

The use of endorsers has become a common practice in the world of advertising. By some estimates, 14 per cent to 19 per cent of advertisements that aired in the United States up to 2008 featured celebrities that endorsed products and brands, and the number was over twice as high in certain foreign markets (Creswell, 2008). Celebrity and athlete endorsements, in particular, are big business: Nike, Adidas, Reebok and many other sport products companies in the world spend millions of dollars on athlete endorsement annually. Many companies outside the sport apparel industry are active participants as well. The use of celebrity endorsers as an advertising strategy is an important marketing effort. Any firm's decision to enlist an athlete endorser generally has a positive pay-off in brand-level sales both in an absolute sense and by market share (Elberse & Verleun, 2012).

Celebrity endorsement can be very important in different aspects of people's lives, so that celebrities can be an influence on people's important political decisions. For instance, in 2012, Scarborough examined "voters influenced by celebrity" in the United States of America. The results showed that voters influenced by celebrity account for 18 per cent of the population, or almost 34 million adults (Scarborough 2013).

Celebrity marketing has an impact on promoting good health practices. Organized health promotion and advocacy campaigns have long understood that by engaging a celebrity with a health issue or capitalizing on the interest generated by news of celebrity illnesses, coverage of the issue *de jour* can be increased to levels that would otherwise require stratospheric campaign budgets (Baker *et al.*, 1992; Chapman and Lupton, 1994). Basketball player Earvin "Magic" Johnson's HIV disclosure (Kalichman and Hunter, 1992; Kalichman *et al.*, 1993), Muhammad Ali's Parkinson's disease, Naser Hijazi's cancer, Marc-Vivien Foe's and Piermario Morosini's sudden death syndrome, Kareem Abdul-Jabbar's leukemia and Venus Williams' Sjögren's Syndrome, have not only made these people among the most famous sufferers of these conditions, but have immensely increased public awareness of these problems. Lou Gehrig, the great baseball player, was so loved and well-known that his disease, Amyotrophic Lateral Sclerosis (ALS), became known worldwide; the disease is now commonly referred to as "Lou Gehrig's disease".

Also the importance of celebrities in brand awareness among other markets, especially young people, is another role of celebrities in marketing. Statistics shows that 24 per cent of all internet users ages 16 to 24 years in 2014 discovered new brands through celebrity endorsements (Statista, 2014). The celebrity endorsement has a positive effect on corporate image, corporate credibility and corporate loyalty (Ghotbivayghan, Hoseinzadehshahri & Ebrahimi, 2015). Among famous celebrities, sport stars' endorsement has a special role in different aspects of an adolescent's life. Sport has become a popular and vital area in which young people find their heroes. Keshkar, Karegar & Biniaz (2013) showed that sport stars are the most important role models in adolescents' life in Iran. This is because sport remains one area where true greatness and superior beauty can be found (Goodman, 1993).

Advertisers use celebrity endorsement because of its greater benefits and the possibility of its immense influence. There are certain potential advantages of celebrity endorsement because celebrity-endorsed advertisements draw more attention when compared to non-celebrity-endorsed ones. This helps the company in repositioning its product/brand and finally empowers the company when it is new in the market or plans to go global (Erdogan, 1999).

Celebrity endorsement influence

Phang and Cyril de Run (2007) explored the issue of company image by assessing the reactions of respondents to advertising utilizing a celebrity endorser against that which does not. Interestingly they found no significant differences between various responses studied of two advertisement types. This indicates that the respondents viewed both advertisements similarly and reacted as such. At the same time, the data indicate that behavioural responses were consistently the lowest, followed by attitudinal responses towards the company and its image, and the highest was attitudinal responses towards the brand and the advertisement (Phang & Cyril de Run, 2007). Empirical studies have demonstrated that the use of celebrity endorsers is associated with positive effects (Atkin and Block, 1983; Freiden, 1984; Petty, Cacioppo & Schumann, 1983). Also, different studies have shown that the buying behaviour of a customer is strongly influenced by a company's efforts to use celebrities in order to build brand loyalty. Selecting a celebrity that is a good match to the product is a good way to sell products and services (Fathi & Kheiri, 2015).

Many celebrities are in the public eye not just for their work or social activities, but for the causes they support. Yet the strength of their influence has been called into question. According to a survey in the United States in 2008, 51 per cent of respondents said that celebrities make little or no positive difference to the issue they are promoting, while 44 per cent said they make a large or some difference. Opinion was further divided by age groups, with those in younger demographics believing celebrities make a positive impact (Public Relations Tactics, 2008).

In a study done in Iran, different aspects of athlete endorsement and its effects on customers' purchase intention were studied. For this study, Hossien Rezazadeh, an Iranian sport celebrity, was selected. Results showed that the most important factors of the Rezazadeh endorsement were physical power, a loveable personality, attractiveness and professional honesty. It was also revealed that all these aspects had a direct correlation with the customer's intention to purchase. Finally among different aspects of endorsement, only attractiveness and professional honesty could predict the customer's purchase intention (Rasooli, Saatchian & Elahi, 2014). Also in another study in Iran, results showed that sport stars' endorsements had an influence on customers' attentions, interest, desire and actual action in buying products (Khazayi, Yusefi & Sadeghi, 2015).

Researching the impact of national or international celebrity credibility on brand equity was the purpose of another Iranian study. The relationship between the endorser's credibility, brand credibility and brand equity was examined through a field experiment in Tehran. The results showed a positive and significant relationship between the endorser's credibility and brand credibility, and also between brand credibility and consumer-based brand equity that both depend on the celebrity's nationality (Mirabi & Lajevardi, 2016). A similar study in Taiwan investigated the influence of celebrity endorsements on online customer reviews on female shopping behaviour. Based on AIDMA (Attention Interest Desire Memory Action) and AISAS (Attention Interest Search Action Share) models, researchers designed an experiment to investigate consumer responses to a "search good" and an "experience good" respectively. According to the AIDMA Model, which is a psychological process model of consumers' purchasing activities, there are five key processes where a consumer notices a product, service or advertisement up to the purchase: Attention, in which the consumer first notices the product or advertisement, followed by Interest, Desire, Memory and Action. The AISAS Model as a consumption behaviour model emphasizes the key processes: Attention, Interest, Search, Action, Share (Sugiyama & Andree, 2011).

The results revealed that a "search good" (e.g. shoes) endorsed by a celebrity in an advertisement evoked significantly more attention, desire and action from the consumer than did one given only an online customer review. However, results showed that online customer reviews emerged higher than the celebrity endorsement on the scale of participants' memory, search and share attitudes toward the "experience good" (Wei & Lu, 2013).

Ace Metrix, a technology company that measures the impact of video advertising and provides the tools and insights to make better creative, analysed the impact of celebrities in TV advertising and found that they have little to none. Based on advertising data gathered from the beginning of January 2012 through to October 2013, Ace Metrix found that, in the aggregate, TV advertisements containing celebrities underperformed those without. However, there was a wide range in performance, leading the researchers to conclude that celebrity advertising is a "mixed bag" for the brands using them (Ace Metrix, 2014).

Research on celebrities' public influence (or lack thereof) in the United States showed that 45 per cent of US adults believe that celebrities can make either a large (11 per cent) or some (33 per cent) positive difference to issues they are promoting, but a greater proportion (51 per cent) feel that they make little to no difference. Interestingly, respondents were more convinced of celebrities' potential negative impact: 55 per cent believe that celebrities' negative publicity can have a somewhat (35 per cent) or very (20 per cent) damaging impact on the issue they are promoting (Harris Poll, 2013; Marketing Charts, 2014).

The study follows research suggesting that celebrities do not have much influence over consumers when it comes to marketing campaigns. In a study of global consumers' responses to advertising messages, Nielsen recently found that while humour resonated with a leading 47 per cent of respondents, celebrity endorsements only resonated with 12 per cent of them. Another study from Boston Consulting Group, reported by Media Post, indicates that celebrity endorsements garner less trust from consumers around the world than any other type of brand promotion (Marketing Charts, 2014).

In an earlier study examining why Americans engage with online advertisements (clicking on, watching, or paying attention to, an advertisement), Ipsos revealed that just one in ten respondents claimed to engage with advertisements because they like the spokesperson or celebrity, or because that person is someone they recognize. A more recent study commissioned by the Energy Saving Trust in the United Kingdom and conducted by Ipsos MORI, discovered that only 1 per cent of respondents would be swayed to buy a product by a celebrity endorsement.

Finally, while many celebrities have huge followings on social media, research from SocialToast suggests that its "Super Fans" (a collection of social media experts and professionals)

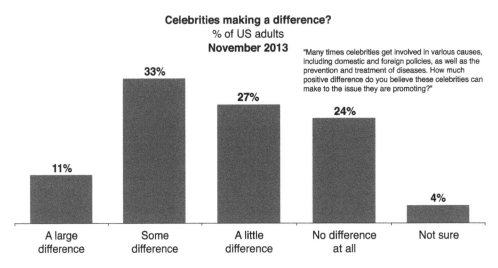

Figure 9.1 The role of celebrity marketing in creating positive effects on society (based on Harris Poll, 2013)

are more likely to be influenced on important issues by posts from their close friends, family members and even well-known bloggers (arguably celebrities of a sort) than politicians and athletes (Harris Poll, 2013).

In contrast, many studies show strong support for the use of celebrity endorsements, arguing that celebrities help to make brands recognizable and create a positive brand attitude (Petty, Cacioppo & Schumann, 1983), enhance the likelihood of purchase (Friedman & Friedman, 1979), foster brand loyalty, and positively impact word-of-mouth (Bush, Martin & Bush, 2004). Hoffner and Cantor (1991) also point out that people emulate the appearance and behaviour of the media celebrities that they admire.

Who can be an effective endorser?

According to Solomon (2013), a reference group is one whose attitudes or values are used by an individual as the basis for behaviour. Similarly, according to Mowen and Minor (2001), a reference group is one in which its values, norms, attitudes or beliefs are used as a guide to individual behaviour. An individual's reference groups are composed of all the groups that can influence his/her beliefs and behaviour, either directly or indirectly.

Reference groups can have three types of effect on people. They influence people through the norms, information and value-oriented demonstrative needs of consumers (Mowen & Minor, 2001). One instance of such groups is celebrities who are admired by the community because of their reputation, popularity, fame and other achievements, and firms use these individuals and organizations to encourage consumers to buy their goods (Abdolvand & Hoseinzadeh Emam, 2014).

In most cases, the source of a message can have a great impact on the likelihood of its adoption by the recipients. Credibility and attractiveness are two main characteristics of the source. There has to be a consistency between the needs of the recipient and the potential rewards provided by the source. For example, an attractive or beautiful source is more effective on those who are more sensitive to social approval and others' views. In contrast, a credible expert source, when associated with introverts, is more powerful (Solomon, 2013).

Credibility refers to the expertise, objectivity and reliability of a transmitter. Honesty and credibility is of particular significance especially when the company wants to advertise its corporate social responsibility activities in a way that benefits the community. A credible source is especially useful when encouraging consumers who still do not know much about the product or have not presented comment on it (Solomon, 2013).

Expertise can be defined as the extent to which the endorser (communicator) is perceived to be knowledgeable, skilful and experienced, and the statements it makes turn out to be valid. The benefit of using an expert endorser is that it enhances brand recall and positively affects the buying intentions of consumers (Erdogan, 1999; Mirabi & Lajevardi, 2016).

Trustworthiness can be defined as the extent to which the endorser is perceived to be believable, honest and dependable. The greater the proportion of these aspects, the higher the likelihood of the endorser being selected by the advertisers (Shimp, 2007; Rasooli, Saatchian & Elahi, 2014).

Source of attractiveness is a social value that recipients ascribe to a transmitter. This value is concerned with physical shape, personality, social status or similarity to the recipient. One study found that famous faces capture attention and are processed more efficiently by the brain than are "ordinary" faces (Solomon, 2013). When used properly, famous or expert spokespeople can be of great value in improving the fortunes of a product. A celebrity endorsement strategy can be an effective way to differentiate among similar products. One reason for this effectiveness is that consumers are better able to identify products that are associated with a spokesperson (Leeflang & Raaij, 1995). This is especially important when consumers do not perceive many actual differences among competitors, as often occurs when brands are in the mature stage of the product life cycle (Solomon, 2013).

Celebrities are considered to be an example of intellectual and opinion leaders and, in the form of a reference group, have the ability to direct the preferences of consumers toward a specific product or brand (Solomon & Assael, 1987; Solomon et al., 2002; Assael, 1984) Therefore, the interests and tastes of the customers can play an important role in the development of marketing and achieving success in this regard (Abdolvand & Hoseinzadeh Eman, 2014). It is quite evident that customers form positive and favourable perceptions about those endorsers who are physically attractive (Erdogan, 1999). Research findings show that attractive endorsers are good at influencing the beliefs of customers (Debevec & Kernan, 1984). That is why most advertisements depict attractive celebrities (Baker & Churchill Jr., 1977).

Attractiveness doesn't solely mean physical attractiveness; instead, it also encompasses the lifestyle of the endorser and his or her personality dimensions. According to McGuire (1968), three factors contribute to the effectiveness of message. These are: (1) familiarity of an endorser, (2) similarity of an endorser, and (3) liking an endorser. Similarity can be defined as the extent to which the receiver (customer) finds a resemblance between him/herself and the source (endorser). Familiarity refers to how much knowledge the receiver (customer) possesses about the source (endorser). Likeability is the affection the receiver (customer) develops towards the source (endorser) because of the physical attractiveness of the endorser (McGuire, 1968). Famous personalities take advantage of qualities and values that are cherished and respected by others. In other words, having different characteristics to social norms such as an unique lifestyle and individual charm, gives celebrities special skills to attract the attention of others in the category to which they are entering (Moukharji & Zhao, 2009; Abdolvand & Hosseinzadeh Emam, 2013).

Attractiveness refers to how physically attractive, elegant or likeable the source is to the audience. Therefore, endorsers who are perceived to be knowledgeable, reliable and attractive are considered credible and, in turn, induce consumers' positive attitudinal and behavioural responses to the brand and the product (Ohanian, 1991; Wei & Lu, 2013).

Advertisers try to hire such celebrities for endorsement who are not only attractive (Baker & Churchill Jr, 1977) but credible as well (Sternthal, Dholakia & Leavitt, 1978). Together these aspects cast a comprehensive impact upon the customers, as most of the customers prefer those celebrities who are credible and trustworthy, some like those who are attractive and possess charming physical features, and some look for and consider both of these dimensions (Ahmed, Azmat Mir & Farooq, 2012).

The characteristics of celebrities are a very important factor in turning them into favourite heroes within societies. The characteristics of what makes a favourite sport celebrity is not constant in every part of the world, and different cultures can present a different frame for characteristics of favourite sport celebrities. In Iran, Keshkar, Aramoon and Ghafouri (2014) studied sport celebrities' characteristics that can make sport stars effective endorsers. In their study, they used the Arai, Ko and Kaplanidou (2013) model, the Model of Athlete Brand Image (MABI), which consists of three dimensions that are crucial in developing consumer brand equity for athletes: athletic performance, attractive appearance and marketable lifestyle. Keshkar, Aramoon and Ghafouri (2014) showed that Iranians expect ethical, spiritual, religious and Persian cultural values in their superstars beside MABI Model items. Comparing a superstar's characteristics from the viewpoint of fans, athletes, coaches and sport management experts showed that Iranians believed that athletic performance was a more important factor for effective endorsement of their sport stars. After athletic performance, attractive appearance and the lifestyle of superstars were considered. However, there can be different viewpoints among people with different demographic characteristics. For example, people over 50 years old pay more attention to athletic expertise than people 20 to 30 years old, who consider physical attractiveness more important than other characteristics. Also, sport coaches did not like sport stars' endorsement just for physical fitness but preferred people to be impressed by their marketing activities because of expertise, performance, sportsmanship and cultural values and ethics. This is similar to results Hasaan (2016) achieved in his studies on sport fans in Pakistan. They showed that some fans try to tell their own narratives about sport stars that should be positive and culturally acceptable and other fans believe such stories and this can

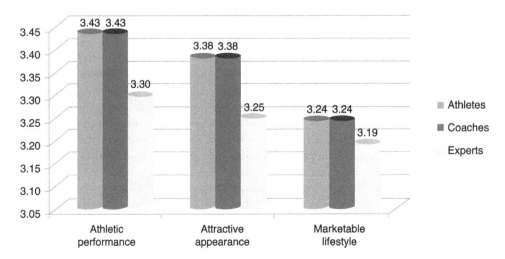

Figure 9.2 Effective celebrity characteristics (based on Keshkar, Aramoon & Ghafouri, 2014)

be an effective factor in successful marketing activities through sport celebrities' endorsement roles.

Celebrity endorsement includes different roles. Arora and Sahu (2014) have investigated four roles of customers (initiator, influencer, buyer and user). They showed that each of these roles is more affected by celebrity endorsement. Ahmed, Azmat Mir and Farooq (2012), in a study entitled "Effect of celebrity endorsement on customer buying behavior: A perspective from Pakistan", which was undertaken at the University of Pakistan, investigate the impact of celebrity endorsement on customer purchases and come to the conclusion that advertisements are always designed to attract the greater attention of the audience. For this study, marketers come up with different techniques. Celebrity endorsement is one of these. And as reported by previous studies, this study also affirms the importance of celebrity endorsement in advertisement campaigns by positively influencing the buying intention of the customers.

What products should be endorsed?

In a study in Iran, some pictures were prepared by Photoshop in which Iranian sport stars endorsed some products including sport equipment, drinks and foods, razors, cars, underwear, etc. These pictures were shown to different people (young and old, male and female, athlete and non-athlete). On all occasions, people laughed at the pictures of sport stars endorsing non-sport products such as drinks, foods and underwear. When asked for their reasons, they replied that they felt it was funny to see their sport heroes endorse non-sport and unimportant products. They did not like to see their heroes, whom they loved and put in a high position mentally, used for advertising worthless products. However, the endorsment of cars was not funny but was unexpected (Keshkar, Keshavarz, & Ghasemi 2016). In Iran, sport celebrities do not participate in advertising activities except on special occasions. This was why Iranian athletes endorsing cars was unexpected.

The personality of the endorser should be congruent with that of the product in such situations, and customers infer and assume such congruency more positively (Ahmed, Azmat Mir & Farooq, 2012). So if Iranian sport celebrities endorse sport facilities or equipment, or even products that relate to important industries with good positioning in society or are of high and strategic value in their country, then people can accept their endorsing activities and evaluate them positively. Automobile manufacturing in Iran is an important industry especially because of the different economic sanctions imposed against Iran, which made native manufacturers try to produce their own automobiles. Maybe it could be assumed that if Iranian athletes participate in endorsing important industries and/or products that are valuable to the economic situation of the country, then their efforts would not be evaluated negatively. These products could be related to important economic sectors including banking and finance, transportation, insurance and energy, in addition to sport-related industries. In this way, the importance and great position of Iranian sport celebrities could be related to the important strategic role of such products in the economy of Iran. Moreover, in addition to congruency between products and celebrities, it seems that social values are a very important factor in sport celebrity endorsement being effective among Iranians. It means that if celebrities endorse what is held dear in society then it can be both congruent and valuable. So this is why if Iranian sport stars endorse razors, it would be humourous but accepted, but if David Beckham endorsed Gillette razors it would not be funny because he does not belong to Iranian culture.

The key is to match the right celebrity with the right product and place them both in the right advertising campaign. If the combination is done well, it can lead to huge profits and an immediate change in the public perception of a company. If it is done poorly, it can ruin a brand overnight.

As described earlier, attractiveness and credibility are two important factors for effective celebrity endorsement. Now, the Product Match-Up, as the third source of endorsement efficiency, can be discussed. The Product Match-Up model states that there should be a perfect match between the celebrity personality characteristics and brand attributes. The extent to which a successful match-up happens can be determined by the degree of fitness between the brand and the celebrity (Erdogan, 1999). An advertisement in which the celebrity and the brand are highly congruent yields results that are more influential and believable (Michael, 1989). In Iran, the national football team includes many sport stars that Iranians, especially young boys and girls, respect and love. Most are enthusiastic fans and are very prejudiced about their stars. In 2008, the Iran Football Federation invited the Zar Macaroni Company to support the national football team as a sponsor. This annoyed fans and they began to oppose the pairing. They saw no match-up between Macaroni and their heroes. They said "while other teams in the world have sponsors like Nike, Benz, Mobile, why should our team and heroes be sponsored by a Macaroni company?" (Hamshahri, 2008; Fardanews, 2008). The negative public reaction forced the authorities of the football federation to change the sponsor. This example shows that considering the match-up between celebrities and the product can be an important factor for endorsement efficiency.

Today, companies are putting great emphasis on the importance of a proper match-up between the celebrity and the product. Whether it is a beverage company, or any other type, they are always looking eagerly for a fitting link between a celebrity's personality and their product attributes. This also happens on the part of customers who also expect congruity between celebrity and the product (Ohanian, 1991; Keshkar *et al.*, 2016). In 2012, the Iranian football star Javad Nekounam, who was team captain and widely regarded as one of Asia's greatest footballers, famous for being intelligent, fast and powerful, endorsed Caspian Iranian Motor Oil. Its motto was that it enabled intelligent, fast and powerful automobiles. So there was a good match-up and congruity between the star and the product.

The product/celebrity match-up does not rely solely on just ordinary congruency but on the physical attractiveness of the celebrity as well. Attractive celebrities are more persuasive, especially when endorsing products that enhance beauty, because customers assume that as the product enhances the beauty of the endorser, so it will in real life (Kamins, 1990). Nevertheless, in Iran, the physical beauty of sport stars is not an important factor in attracting people to the endorsed product. This is because none of the sport stars appear in advertisements showing their fit bodies – they all wear either sport uniforms or formal dress. This is despite the fact that most athlete endorsements in the world, including David Beckham, Ronaldo, Drogba and others, do show their beautiful and fit bodies in their advertising activities. Female athletic endorsement in Iran is much less prevalent than male endorsement and in their advertising activities they cover their bodies and their physical beauty more than men. So it is difficult for women's physical beauty and attractiveness in Iran to be a main factor in attracting people to the advertised product.

Endorsement and culture

Little is known about how celebrity endorsements correlate with cultural factors. McCracken (1989) explains that the success of celebrity-endorsed advertisements depends on whether the celebrity is meaningful to consumer values and norms within the culture. The main reason for the efficiency of celebrities' power is that this special group of people encompasses cultural meanings, and represents important categories such as status and social class and so on (Solomon, 2013).

Today, sport stars' endorsements are a standard marketing strategy in most countries. Different cultures in different countries have different attitudes towards celebrity marketing. For example, in Iran, a country with a legislation system and cultural values based on Islamic beliefs, using human beings as a marketing tool is not an acceptable action. After the Islamic Revolution in Iran, celebrities' presence in advertisements was limited by law because, according to Islamic beliefs, human beings have a respectful position and should not be used as marketing tool. But in 2013, Iran encountered serious economic sanctions so Iranians had to lean on their own economy and domestic introductions. For this reason, Iranian celebrities, especially sport stars, had an important role in persuading people to buy domestic products. As a result, instructions on how to use celebrity pictures in advertisements to support domestic industries were approved in order to emphasize the spirit of the overall economic policy of resistance, respect, trust and support of domestic industry.

Moreover, celebrities who are used in advertisements cannot live normal lives because their contracts limit their lifestyle. Most sport celebrities live under the most restrictive terms imaginable. Their careers are not their own. Trading companies own their names, their likenesses, their appearance and personal histories – this is what some call "sport slavery". Sport slavery, which refers to endorsement and sponsorship contracts that put serious limitations on the behaviour of sport stars and enforce tight supervision by sponsors, is not acceptable in some cultures including Iran and several other Islamic countries.

Sport as a global platform for introducing global celebrities

Some authors argue that celebrities and megastars with worldwide popularity transcend national boundaries and can help companies break through cultural barriers (Kaikati, 1987; Miciak & Shanklin, 1994). Still others point out the importance of understanding what celebrity endorsers mean to consumers across cultures (Paek, 2005). Today almost everyone in the world knows Cristiano Ronaldo, Roger Federer, Muhammad Ali, David Beckham and Diego Maradona. Different studies show that some sport stars have global fans and prove that sport and sport heroes are global properties. Maybe the behaviour of some sport megastars is not acceptable in some cultures but it is the nature of sport that makes it a global culture. People from different countries, including Iran, may have negative attitudes towards national celebrities in marketing but they can accept global sport megastar endorsement easily.

Conclusion

Sport celebrity marketing can be an effective marketing strategy only if the marketers consider credibility, attractiveness and match-up sources of endorsers. A credible and attractive sport celebrity can encourage customers to trust and think positively about products and companies. Also the Product Match-Up as a third source of endorsement efficiency should be emphasized in promotional activities of trading companies to encourage customers to buy products. Sport celebrity endorsement is a culturally dependent marketing strategy. Using human beings as a marketing tool is not an acceptable strategy in all cultures but sport has broken cultural boundaries and elite sport stars are global heroes. People of different cultures believe in them and the products they endorse.

Sara Keshkar

References

Abdolvand, M. A. & Hoseinzadeh Emam, A. (2014). Evaluating and prioritizing effective factors in selecting celebrity endorsements for advertising campaigns from the consumers' point of view. *Journal of Marketing Management*, 9(23), 19–40.

Ace Metrix (2014). Ace Metrix Study Confirms Celebrities Have Little to No Impact on Ad Effectiveness. Available at <www.acemetrix.com/about-us/company-news/press-releases/ace-metrix-study-confirms-celebrities-have-little-to-no-impact-on-ad-effectiveness>. Accessed 29 January 2014.

Ahmed, A., Azmat Mir, F. & Farooq, O. (2012). Effect of celebrity endorsement on customers' buying behavior: A perspective from Pakistan. *Interdisciplinary Journal of Contemporary Research in Business*, 4(5), 584–592.

Arai, A., Ko, Y. J. & Kaplanidou, K. (2013). Athlete brand image: Scale development and model test. *European Sport Management Quarterly*, 13(4), 383–403.

Arora, A. & Sahu, K. (2014). Celebrity endorsement and its effects on consumer behavior. *International Journal of Retailing and Rural Business Perspectives*, 3(2), 866–869.

Assael, H. (1984). *Behavior and Market Action*. Boston, Massachusetts: Kent Publishing Company.

Atkin, C. & Block, M. (1983). Effectiveness of celebrity endorsers. *Journal of Advertising Research*, 23(1), 57–61.

Baker, J. A., Lepley, C. J., Krishnan, S. & Victory, K. S. (1992). Celebrities as health educators: Media advocacy guidelines. *Journal of School Health*, 62, 433–435.

Baker, M. J. & Churchill Jr., G. A. (1977). The impact of physically attractive models on advertising evaluations. *Journal of Marketing Research (JMR)*, 14(4), 538–555.

Bush, A. J., Martin, G. A. & Bush, V. D. (2004). Sports celebrity influence on the behavioral intentions of Generation Y. *Journal of Advertising Research*, 44(1), 108–118.

Chapman, S. & Lupton, D. (1994). *The Fight for Public Health: Principles and Practice of Public Health Media Advocacy*. London: British Medical Journal Books.

Chapman, S. & Leask, J. A. (2001). Paid celebrity endorsement in health promotion: A case study from Australia. *Health Promotion International*, 16(4), 333–338.

Creswell, J. "Nothing Sells Like Celebrity". The *New York Times* (22 June 2008).

Debevec, K. & Kernan, J. B. (1984). More evidence on the effects of a presenter's attractiveness: Some cognitive, affective, and behavioral consequences. *Advances in Consumer Research*, 1, 127–132.

Elberse, A. & Verleun, J.(2012). The economic value of celebrity endorsements. *Journal of Advertising Research*, 52(2), 149–165.

Erdogan, Z. (1999). Celebrity endorsement: A literature review. *Journal of Marketing Management*, 15(4), 291–314.

Farda News Agency (2008). "Zar Makaron". [Persian article]. Available at <www.fardanews.com/fa/news/71862/>. Accessed 13 August 2016.

Fathi, F. & Kheiri, B. (2015). Celebrity endorsement and its effect on consumer behavior: A literature review. *International Journal of Review in Life Sciences*, 5(10), 619–626.

Friedman, H. H. & Friedman, L. (1979). Endorser effectiveness by product type. *Journal of Advertising Research*, 19(5), 63–71.

Freiden, J. (1984). Advertising spokesperson effects: An examination of endorser type and gender on two audiences. *Journal of Advertising Research*, 24(5), 33–41.

Ghotbivayghan, B., Hoseinzadehshahri, M. & Ebrahimi, M. (2015). Effect of celebrity endorsement on consumers, perception of corporate image, corporate credibility and corporate loyalty. *Case Studies in Business & Management Journal*, 2(1), 51–67.

Goodman, M. (1993). "Where have you gone, Joe DiMaggio?" *Utne Reader* [Quarterly American Magazine] 57, 103–104.

Hamshahri Newspaper (2008). "National football team advertising on the waves of criticism". [Persian article]. Available at <www.hamshahrionline.ir/details/72652>. Accessed 24 August 2016.

Harris Poll (2013). Half of Americans believe celebrities can make a positive difference when they support a cause. Available at <www.theharrispoll.com/health-and-life/Half_of_Americans_Believe_Celebrities_Can_Make_a_Positive_Difference_When_They_Support_a_Cause.html>. Accessed 29 July 2016.

Hasaan, A. (2016). Establishing athlete brand in cricket: Fans' perception about foreign cricketers in Pakistan Super League (PSL). *Pamukkale Journal of Sport Sciences*, 7(3), 23–39.

108

Hoffner, C. & Cantor, J. (1991). Perceiving and responding to mass media characters. In J. Bryant & D. Zillmann (Eds), *Responding to the Screen: Reception and Reaction Processes* (pp. 63–101). Hillsdale, NJ: Lawrence Erlbaum Associates.

Kaikati, J. G. (1987). Celebrity advertising: A review and synthesis. *International Journal of Advertising*, 2, 93–105.

Kalichman, S. C. & Hunter, T. L. (1992). The disclosure of celebrity HIV infection: Its effects on public attitudes. *American Journal of Public Health*, 82, 1374–1376.

Kalichman, S. C., Russell, R. L., Hunter, T. L. & Sarwer, D. B. (1993). Earvin "Magic" Johnson's HIV sero-status disclosure: Effects on men's perceptions of AIDS. *Journal of Consultation in Clinical Psychology*, 61, 887–891.

Kamins, M. A. (1990). An investigation into the "match-up" hypothesis in celebrity advertising: When beauty may be only skin deep. *Journal of Advertising*, 19(1), 4–13.

Keshkar, S., Aramoon, S. & Ghafouri, F. (2014). "The role of human branding and its features in sport from the viewpoint of academicians, coaches and student athletes in public universities of Tehran". [MA thesis]. Sport Sciences faculty, Allameh Tabataba'i University.

Keshkar, S., Karegar, G. & Biniaz. R. (2013). The role of television sport programs in transmitting moral values and role models among high school students of Islamabad Gharb City. *Journal of Sport Management*, 7(4), 601–619.

Keshkar, S., Keshavarz, B. & Ghasemi, H. (2016). "The role of domestic and international Sport Stars endorsement on attitude and behavior of Iranian people". [Research project]. Unpublished.

Khazayi, A. A., Yusefi, B. & Sadeghi, S. N. (2015). "Correlation between identification and sport celebrities endorsement on consumer behavior regarding to AIDA Model". [Sport Management MA thesis]. Sport Sciences faculty, Razi University.

Leeflang, P. S. H. & Van Raaij, W. F. (1995). The changing consumer in the European Union: A "meta-analysis". *International Journal of Research in Marketing*, 12(5), 373–387.

Marketing Charts (2014). "How influential are celebrities?" (Updated). Available at <www.marketingcharts.com/television/are-celebrities-that-influential-38018>. Accessed 23 July 2016.

McCracken, G. (1989). Who is the Celebrity Endorser? *Journal of Consumer Research*, 16(3), 310–321.

McGuire, W. J. (1968). Personality and susceptibility to social influence. In E. F. Borgatta & W. W. Lambert (Eds), *Handbook of Personality Theory and Research*. Chicago: Rand McNally [in press].

Michael, A. K. (1989). Celebrity and non-celebrity advertising in a two-sided context. *Journal of Advertising Research*, 6(7), 34–42.

Miciak, A. R. & Shanklin, W. L. (1994). Choosing celebrity endorsers. *Marketing Management*, 3(3), 87–94.

Mirabi, V. R. & Lajevardi, M. (2016). A conceptual model in marketing: Celebrity endorsement, brand credibility and brand equity. *Journal of Marketing & Consumer Research*, 22, 38–43.

Moukharji, A. & Zhao, L. (2009). Profit raising entry. *Journal of Industrial Economics*, 57/4, 870.

Mowen, J. C. & Minor, M. S. (2001). *Consumer Behavior: A Framework* (pp. 243–245). Upper Saddle River, NJ: Prentice-Hall.

Ohanian, R. (1991). The impact of celebrity spokespersons' perceived image on customers' intention to purchase. *Journal of Advertising Research*, 31(1), 46–54.

Paek, H. J. (2005). Understanding celebrity endorsers in cross-cultural contexts: A content analysis of South Korean and US newspaper advertising. *Asian Journal of Communication*, 15(2), 133–153.

Petty, R., Cacioppo J. & Schumann D. (1983). Central and peripheral routes to advertising effectiveness: The moderating role of involvement. *Journal of Consumer Research*, 10(2), 135–146.

Phang, G. & Cyril De Run, E. (2007). Celebrity endorsers and respondents' gender: Its impact on company, behavioral and attitudinal variables. *Jurnal Kemanusiaan*, 10, 38–55.

Public Relations Tactics (2008). "Public opinion divided about celebrity influence for causes they promote". Available at <www.prsa.org/Intelligence/Tactics/Articles/view/6C060835/101/Public_opinion_divided_about_celebrity_influence_f#.V34hh_l97IU>. Accessed 23 August 2016.

Rasooli , S. M., Saatchian, V. & Elahi, A. (2014). Prioritization of the aspects of athlete's endorsement on customers' purchase intention. *Sport Management Studies*, 6(24), 59–74.

Scarborough, N. (2013). Democrat voter base highly influenced by celebrity endorsements. Retrieved from <http://dialog.scarborough.com/index.php/democrat-voter-base-highly-influenced-by-celebrity-endorsements>. Accessed 29 July 2016.

Shimp, T. A. (2007). *Advertising, Promotion, and Other Aspects of Integrated Marketing Communications* (7th edn). Mason, OH: Thomson South-Western College Publishing.

Solomon, M. R. (2013). *Consumer Behavior: Buying, Having and Being* (10th edn). Harlow, UK: Pearson Education.

Solomon, M. R. & Assael, H. (1987). The forest or the trees? A gesalt approach to symbolic comsumption. In Umiker-Seboek, J. (Ed.), *Marketing and Semiotics: New Directions in the Study of Signs for Sale* (pp. 189–218). Berlin: Mounton de Gruyter.

Solomon, M., Bamossy, G., Askegaard, S. (2002). *Consumer Behaviour: A European Perspective* (2nd edn). NJ, USA: Prentice Hall Financial Times.

Statista (2014). Share of worldwide internet users who find brands through celebrity endorsements as of 4th quarter 2014, by age group. Retrieved from <www.statista.com/statistics/407838/celebrity-endorsement-brand-discovery-online-age>. Accessed 29 July 2016.

Sternthal, B., Dholakia, R. & Leavitt, C. (1978). The persuasive effect of source credibility: Tests of cognitive response. *Journal of Consumer Research*, 4(4), 252–260.

Sugiyama, K. & Andree, T. (2011). *The Dentsu Way: Secrets of Cross Switch Marketing from the World's Most Innovative Advertising Agency* (pp. 78–79). New York: McGraw-Hill.

Wei, P. & Lu, H. (2013). An examination of the celebrity endorsements and online customer reviews influence female consumers' shopping behavior. *Computers in Human Behavior, 29*, 193–201.

10

WOMEN'S TENNIS ASSOCIATION EFFORTS IN ASIAN MARKETS

Vicky Martin and Valentina Starkova

Introduction

The history of tennis is rich and goes back to ancient times, with its rapid development in England in the nineteenth century. Tennis used to be played on the grass lawns of England and was considered a luxurious way of passing the time for elite society. However, tennis has changed dramatically since its introduction globally as a competitive sport. It has spread to all continents and is played in many countries. The Women's Tennis Association (WTA) tour was created over the years and, as an international organization, its goal is to promote tennis throughout the world. In 2009, Stacey Allaster, the CEO of the WTA tour, decided to pursue the Asian market and created a "Road Map" to Asia, with the idea of bringing more top players to Asia after the US Open. Asia is a great place in which to develop tennis and attract new fans to the game. With the successes of Li Na, the fanbase grew, and more tournaments were added to the Asian calendar. The China Open became a mandatory event of the year. However, there are problems associated with the move of tennis into Asia as the number of top players' withdrawals has increased. Many players believe that the added tournaments add more pressure to the already tight schedule.

Formative years of tennis

Tennis has a rich history with multiple stages to its development. In order to grasp current strategies of the tennis business, it is beneficial to review the history of tennis and its origins. Dunning, Malcom and Waddington (2004) researched the history of modern lawn tennis from its origins to the latter part of the nineteenth century. They argue that the game of what we now know today as "tennis" originated during medieval times and had distinctively different features from the folk games played in ancient times (Dunning *et al.* 2004). There is some evidence showing that ball games were played in the Greek and Roman empires (Dunning *et al.*, 2004). However, "[the games] were held in low esteem and not deemed manly in these patriarchal societies . . . winning and losing seem to have been of minor importance" (Dunning *et al.*, 2004, p. 104).

Tennis became very popular in England, both as a recreational modern-day activity for elite society, and as a highly regulated and competitive sport (Dunning *et al.*, 2004, p. 104). The sport rapidly developed on a larger scale "within the context of wider social processes such as the development of a modern urban-industrial nation state and changing class and gender relations" (Dunning *et al.*, 2004, p. 104). Members of private clubs and respectable members of society had access to the game in the 1700s (Dunning *et al.*, 2004). They referred to it as "Field Tennis" and used any lawn surface they could find in their clubs or back yards (Dunning *et al.*, 2004). There were certain drawbacks to the ball that was used for the game of tennis, as it was not suitable for play on lawns (Dunning *et al.*, 2004). However, the game rapidly developed when Charles Goodyear discovered vulcanization as a treatment for the rubber ball (Dunning *et al.*, 2004). Vulcanization in essence increases the durability and elasticity of the ball (Dictionary.com). The ball had to be soft enough not to damage the grass, but at the same time bounce high enough for tennis players to be able to hit it back (Dunning *et al.*, 2004, p. 105).

In December 1873, Major Walter Clopton Wingfield observed the popularity of "tennis" in England, and published a set of rules (Dunning *et al.*, 2004). Wingfield named the game "Sphairstrike" (Dunning *et al.*, 2004). The game originally looked like a mix of croquet and cricket, but was more elegant in form, with the scoring based on 15-point games, and the net was borrowed from badminton and tennis (Dunning *et al.*, 2004). The game "Sphairstrike" was an immediate success and began to replace both badminton and croquet as a new favourite activity of the higher classes (Dunning *et al.*, 2004).

During the nineteenth century, most dominant pastimes in England were "manly", requiring physical fitness and considered unsuitable for women (Dunning *et al.*, 2004). However, tennis was one of the sports that gave social opportunity to all ages and both sexes, and was considered as an activity suitable for women because it offered mild exercise (Dunning *et al.*, 2004). Ladies played exclusively at the privately owned country clubs (Dunning *et al.*, 2004). Slowly, women's tennis became more competitive even though women's events were considered less important than men's at that time. The Men's Singles Championship at Wimbledon was introduced in 1881, whereas the Ladies' Singles Championship was not introduced until 1884, and female athletes received significantly smaller amounts of prize money than that of the men's events. The men's tennis championships were the first to be played and the women had to wait patiently for the men to complete their matches before they could begin their own (Dunning *et al.*, 2004).

Tennis became so popular that it spread out beyond the British Empire, mainly because the British army loved the sport and brought it to a new place every time it moved (Dunning *et al.*, 2004). Tennis was introduced to the United States in 1874 by Mary Ewing Outerbridge who played the sport while in Bermuda. Tennis was then introduced to Brazil and India in 1875, Germany in 1876, France in 1877 and Australia and Austria in 1878 (Dunning *et al.*, 2004). Unfortunately, there were many power struggles over who should be the main governing body of tennis. Finally, the matter was decided in October 1912, when the International Lawn Tennis Federation (ILTF) was founded in order to govern tennis throughout the world (Dunning *et al.*, 2004).

With the international growth of tennis, Yellis (n.d.) stated that tennis became more competitive and changed in many ways, such as being played with greater power, better equipment and more comfortable clothing. In addition, Yellis stated that tennis became more commercialized and evolved into an international sport business structure. Also, female athletes acquired a chance to be recognized internationally as gender barriers diminished significantly (Yellis, n.d.).

There has been a major shift with significant changes in the women's tennis professional tour, including an historic moment when women tennis players, for the first time in the history of the sport, were paid equal amounts in prize money as men at the Grand Slam tournaments. Equal pay occurred at the major four Grand Slam Tournaments: the US Open in 1973, the Australian Open in 2001, the French Open (Roland Garros) in 2006 and, finally, at Wimbledon in 2007 (Popovich, 2015).

The move of tennis into Asia

During the 1980s the growth in the sport of tennis continued its expansion around the world. According to Robson (2011), for the first time since computerized rankings were introduced in 1973, the entire top ten players in the WTA in 2011 hailed from different countries. Billie Jean King, former world number one tennis player, states:

> [J]ust like advancements on technology, science and business are now originating more frequently from markets around the globe, professional tennis players are coming not just from powerhouses in America and Australia as they did previously but from many, many different countries.
>
> *Cited in Robson, 2011*

Billie Jean King points out that "[i]n [her] era, [they] didn't have to play against the rest of the world, and now, tennis is truly global" (as cited in Robson, 2011). According to Robson, tennis was drifting away from the US, with the opening of new tennis centres all over the world providing more opportunities for potential players not needing to travel to the US to receive coaching and training. As a result of the shift from the US, Asia now recruits local talent and has developed new opportunities for bringing tennis into new markets for the Women's Tennis Tour (Robson, 2011).

Marshall (2011) analysed the data from the rankings of the top 100 players in the world in the 2000s, and "for the first time, the likes of China, Thailand and South Korea were now being represented in the game's elite". The first revolutionary female athlete from China was Yi Jing-Qian who, in 2000, participated in her second Olympic Games and fourth Federation Cup appearance, and rose to her career highest WTA ranking of 70 (Marshall, 2011). After Li Ting and Sun Tiantian won gold medals in doubles for China in the Athens Olympics in 2004, their coach mentioned in the press conference the need as a country to invest in tennis in order to produce more top players (Marshall, 2011). The Chinese Tennis Association responded to this request and decided to invest $725,000 in sending its women tennis players to compete abroad (Marshall, 2011). The efforts of the Chinese Tennis Association paid off when Li Na brought home the French Open Grand Slam title in 2011.

A former player and the ATP chairman, Chris Kermode, believes that "interest in the game in Asia, both on and off the court, is surging, with the emergence of Kei Nishikori as Japan's first-ever top 10 male player" (Thomas & Borg, 2014). Kermode believes that it is just the beginning of the colossal spur of interest in tennis in Asia (Thomas & Borg, 2014). The ATP chairman thinks that tennis, as a global sport business, should expand its boundaries "into new markets, new territories, new audiences . . . that may have never seen tennis before" (Thomas & Borg, 2014).

Marshall (2011) writes that tennis in China has been developing exponentially since the Olympic Games in Beijing. In 1988 China had one million recreational tennis players. The number grew to 14 million who can practice on 30,000 courts throughout the country. Moreover, the Chinese government is not going to stop the development at this point, but instead the goal is to have twice as many people playing tennis in the future (Marshall, 2011).

In addition, China is investing its money into tennis practice centres, providing training to 250 junior under-12 players, as well as to 100 junior coaches (Marshall, 2011). Furthermore, China has invented its own amateur tennis league, the Open Rating Tour, which launched in 2009, and created the Michael Chang Mission Hills Tennis Academy in Shenzhen (Marshall, 2011). The WTA has also opened its own offices in the country and introduced a new event to the calendar in October, the China Open (Marshall, 2011).

Growth within smaller markets such as Kazakhstan and Uzbekistan is gaining momentum. Kazakhstan and Uzbekistan have produced top-50 players in the last decade (Marshall, 2011). Marshall states that Kazakhstan introduced a new event to the professional circuit, the President's Cup, and its rapidly growing Davis Cup team is also becoming recognized internationally. These additions to tennis in Kazakhstan make the game more popular and increase the interest of the domestic fans. Therefore, Asia may be the future tennis destination due to multiple factors such as the globalization of tennis and investments made by Asian countries. China will continue to grow the most of all other Asia Pacific countries because its plan is to make more investments in tennis (Marshall, 2011).

Women's tennis expansion into Asia

Chinese tennis tournaments are rapidly developing. For instance, in 2008 there were only two WTA events in the region; however, 11 tennis events are scheduled to take place in 2015. The entire Asia Pacific had only seven tournaments in 2014, and 22 tournaments are scheduled for 2018 (Abulleil, 2014).

The first milestone that signified the development of the growth of women's tennis in Asia happened in 2009 when the former WTA's CEO, Stacey Allaster, represented the players and the tournaments of the Sony Ericsson WTA Tour for the first historical Beijing/China Open tournament (chinaopen.com, 2013). There are four mandatory premier events (Indian Wells, Key Biscayne, Madrid and Beijing) with prize money of $4.5 million (chinaopen.com, 2013). Allaster stated that the Beijing Open became the foundation for Chinese tennis and that it was her plan to stay focused on the fans to make tennis more popular in the region (chinaopen.com, 2013). She was determined that working with the China Tennis Association would help to educate and increase the fan base in China.

The move of women's tennis into Asia can be explained in terms of gross domestic product (GDP). Allaster explains that "[t]he WTA's growth strategy . . . is predicated on identifying markets that have 'the greatest propensity for GDP growth'" (SportsPro, 2015). She also explains that it is vital to implement the tennis business infrastructure within those markets "so that when the champion arrives, [the WTA is] ready and in a position to build her brand and the brand of the WTA" (SportsPro, 2015).

Another milestone occurred when Stacey Allaster made the most significant decision of deciding to bring the Women's Tennis Final Elite Eight Tournament to China (espnW, 2015). Similarly to Kermode's belief in the current development of Asian tennis, Allaster stated that having ten different countries represented by the top ten WTA players signifies the depth and globalization of women's tennis due to an increased number of tournaments in Asia Pacific (Marshall, 2011). Marshall argues that "[t]he last 30 years have seen the sport move into new markets . . . attracted wider audiences and encouraged young talent in a way that would have never seemed possible just a couple decades ago". In addition, with the popularity of the former world number two athlete Li Na, China will have more young tennis players who will make an impact on the tennis elite in the future (Marshall, 2011).

Li Na's "captivating personality and no-nonsense approach" also helped to bring people's attention to tennis in China (Marshall, 2011). Li Na's exceptional personality could play a significant role in the future. As an ambassador of tennis, she now potentially transforms tennis in China and beyond in the whole Asia-Pacific region. When she won the French

Open in 2011, Allaster named her win "the most important of the decade" because it boosted the interest of fans in the Asian region (Wilson, 2013). The WTA reported that the French Open final in 2011, when Li Na defeated Francesca Sciavone 6–4, 7–6, was watched by 116 million TV viewers in China (Wilson, 2013). Allaster points out that "[Li Na] will be an inspiration and create more Li Na's. But she transcends China, she is the first Asia-Pacific champion" (Wilson, 2013). Li Na, "who has influenced the continent like no other athlete had ever done" already contributed to the growth of tennis in the whole Asia-Pacific region (Abulleil, 2014). Allaster stated that:

> When I joined the WTA, my goal was to leave the organization on a stronger footing, and I feel a humble sense of pride in what we have all accomplished here. I have focused on what it means to be a champion and I have tried to be a strong role model for women to encourage success in the sports industry.
>
> *espnW, 2015*

In addition, Allaster is fond of China because she has seen pioneering work in the National Basketball Association (NBA) by the Commissioner and the international President, David Stern and Heidi Ueberroth, who were active in the Asian market 30 years ago. Allaster says "[Heidi] was out in those Asian markets, building before [the WTA] came along . . .. David is such a visionary" (SportsPro, 2015). Allaster is persuaded that with the global expansion of tennis, China should be the next strategic priority for the WTA to expand its operations into eastern Asia's culture. China is a huge strategic opportunity for growth and tennis development for the WTA tennis tour (Wilson, 2013).

Although Stacey Allaster retired in 2014, she left a footprint, and the WTA will build on this in the future (Abulleil, 2014). Allaster, who was named by *Forbes* magazine as one of the most powerful women in sports, had served as Chairman and CEO of the WTA since 2009 and stepped down on 2 October 2015 (Dunn, 2014). She was mainly focused on:

> global growth with Asia Pacific being the strategic priority, maximizing the fan experience through product innovations; securing a record number of new sponsors; ensuring the financial success of the sport; and enhancing the health and well-being of the athletes, while also fighting for gender equality.
>
> *Dunn, 2014*

Allaster says the women's tennis tour is becoming stronger especially with the prize money equality introduced in recent years (Wilson, 2013). The increase in popularity of the women's tour could mean that more sponsors may be interested in being associated with the WTA tour. For instance, the most renowned sponsors for the WTA include Dubai Duty Free, Oriflame, Jetstar and Western Union and the new "multiyear and multimillion dollar" sponsorship with Xerox. Allaster goes on to argue that "growth in sponsorship revenue has come about because of the needs of global brands to be more diverse" (Wilson, 2013). Moreover, "[T]he WTA . . . now has more events in Asia than it does in Europe" (Wilson, 2013).

During Allaster's tenure, she made immense changes in women's tennis. For example, "[t]he WTA and Perform Group signed a record setting, half-billion-dollar, 10-year live media rights deal in 2015" (espnW, 2015). In addition, prize money rose from $68.8 million in 2007 to $130 million in 2015 (espnW, 2015). In 2015, the contracted revenue the WTA generated was $1 billion (espnW, 2015). There was a 22.5 per cent increase in TV audiences in 2014 (espnW, 2015). Most importantly, Allaster achieved a goal of moving tennis into

Asia, creating 13 events scheduled for Asia-Pacific in 2015 (espnW, 2015). One of the events is the WTA Finals, which will be held in Singapore in 2018 (espnW, 2015).

Expansion of the WTA into Asia-Pacific regions

The WTA Finals are now being played in Singapore. According to SportsPro, the WTA will benefit with a 35 per cent increase in revenue after the event. In addition, Allaster admits, "The event . . . is the 'financial engine' that drives the WTA business . . . as well as the 'crown jewel of the organization that provides the halo for the brand'" (SpontsPro, 2015). The WTA will greatly benefit from moving tennis into the Asia-Pacific, and all the efforts of the WTA should pay off when tennis becomes a popular sport in the region (SportsPro, 2015). Since 2008 Allaster primarily focused on building a "solid Asian swing, post-US Open" schedule in the Asia-Pacific (SportsPro, 2015).

Furthermore, Allaster adds that the WTA's goal is to host six events in China in the 2015 season, with five of them to be a post-US Open series of tournaments. The ultimate goal is to focus the attention of the fans on Asia and China (Zhuhai Official Website, 2015). In the future the plan is "to build the event brand by virtue of resources of Hong Kong and Macao" (Zhuhai Official Website, 2015). There are six advantages that Zhuhai have outlined as being beneficial for the city and the event branding:

1. Top location – Hong Kong, Zhuhai and Macao international metropolitan area.
2. Top environment – Zhuhai is China's most liveable city, while Hengqin is an ecological island between urban scenery and natural landscape.
3. Top grade – it is China's third largest female tennis event.
4. Top players – each competition is between strong players.
5. Top venue – Zhuhai Hengqin International Tennis Centre is built according to top international standards.
6. Top partners – APG has the experience of operating 30 international tennis events and more than 30 international events (2015).

Furthermore, the WTA could have a very noticeable impact on the Asia-Pacific region culturally, as the working culture differs there from that of the West. For example, Allaster mentions that she felt inspired in Asia when she handed her business card to a young woman; she looked at it, and she looked at Allaster and said, "I have never received a business card from a woman with a CEO title" (SportsPro, 2015). Allaster felt respected in China and also thought that she would take "a lot of pride in that and responsibility to be successful and to inspire the youth and to set a good example and to share [her] experiences with them" (SportsPro, 2015).

The WTA will benefit from the partnership with Singapore in a variety of ways. First of all, the partnership with Singapore is the largest financial partnership ever completed in the history of the WTA (Dunn, 2014). The Women's Final event of the year was transformed from a six-day tennis event into a ten-sport entertainment spectacle, featuring many elements of entertainment, such as a Mariah Carey concert (Dunn, 2014). "The WTA is on top of the world" was the message that the former CEO of the WTA, delivered after the first time the season-ending showpiece was held in the Asia-Pacific region (Abulleil, 2014). In addition, the WTA implemented "a year-long campaign for the Road to Singapore that led to the WTA Finals, which for the first time brought past, current and future champions under one roof in a format designed to create a fan festival" (Abulleil, 2014).

Second, this partnership with Singapore is extremely beneficial for the WTA. The deal comprises five editions of the WTA Finals in Singapore from 2014 to 2018 (Abulleil, 2014). The women's year closing event started in Boca Raton in 1972 with prize money of $100,000 (Abulleil, 2014). Today, it has grown to $6.5 million, equal with the men's year-end event (Abulleil, 2014). Furthermore, successful partnership with Singapore has led to the opening of a new WTA office in the city, and one more office being opened in Beijing with the goal to develop tennis in China exclusively (Abulleil, 2014).

Currently, BNP Paribas is a title sponsor and SC Global is a presenting sponsor of the WTA Finals (formerly named the WTA Championships) (Abulleil, 2014). With 54 tournaments in 33 countries on the WTA calendar, the season-closing event is "the largest source of net revenue for the WTA" (Abulleil, 2014). Allaster pointed out that the net revenue "comes with the commercial relationship that [the WTA has] with the World Sport Group, Singapore Tourism Board and Sport Singapore" (Abulleil, 2014).

Another strategy to develop tennis in the Asia-Pacific region is the introduction of the WTA Elite Trophy Zhuhai. Allaster strongly believes that the growth strategy in Asia-Pacific works because there is "$5 trillion in GDP [in Asia-Pacific] within seven hours of Singapore" (Abulleil, 2014). One of Allaster's major plans is to establish an elite tournament in Zhuhai – "WTA Elite Trophy Zhuhai" (Zhuhai, 2015). The WTA's CEO met with Li Lingwei (Deputy Director of the General Administration of Sport of China's Tennis Administration Centre and Deputy Chairman of the Chinese Tennis Association), Long Guangyan (Deputy Director of the WTA Elite Trophy Zhuhai Preparatory Committee), and the Vice Mayor of Zhuhai attended the conference and delivered a speech (Zhuhai, 2015). It was reported that the newly established event "will be held in Zhuhai for five consecutive years from 2015 to 2019" (Zhuhai, 2015).

The organizers of the Zhuhai event strongly believe that in recent years "tennis has been developing rapidly and rising strongly in China" (Zhuhai, 2015). In addition, Chinese tennis players have achieved many successes internationally, thus captivating the interest of the domestic people who have become focused on the game (Zhuhai, 2015). Interestingly, the WTA Elite Trophy Zhuhai is one of the three top tennis events held in China (Zhuhai, 2015). According to Zhuhai, "[t]he event is a mandatory tournament [with] round robin system" and gives 700 points to the winner with a total prize money of $2.15 million.

Currently, the WTA has more than "2,500 players, representing 92 nations, competing at the WTA's 54 events and four Grand Slams in 33 countries, with total prize money this year being some $100m" (Wilson, 2013). Overall, there has been 70 per cent increase in women's prize money despite the world's economy (Wilson, 2013).

Problems associated with the move of tennis into Asian markets

The WTA's "Asian swing" begins right after the final Grand Slam, the US Open event in New York (AFP, 2015). However, some players are not able to handle the tight WTA schedule, and have to withdraw from the majority of the Asian tournaments. The WTA recently opened an office in Beijing as well as increasing the number of tournaments within China to eight. There are 23 tournaments in Asia, which is nearly 40 per cent of the tour (AFP, 2015). The Wuhan Open in China was inspired by the success of their own highly ranked tennis player Li Na, and was launched in 2014 (AFP, 2015). Unfortunately, Li Na was never able to participate, as she retired on the eve of the tournament, stating that her injuries would not let her compete (AFP, 2015). With the increase in the number of tournaments, there were unfortunately five retirements from the Wuhan Open in 2015, including in the tournament final (AFP, 2015). Garbine Muguruza retired in the final, passing the trophy to Venus Williams (AFP, 2015). Muguruza stated in her post-match interview: "I've played a lot of matches from Tokyo to here. So every time, you're like, I'm more tired. Next day, I'm more tired" (AFP, 2015).

Similarly to Muguruza, Caroline Wozniacki and Victoria Azarenka were excited on the third day of the tournament after their wins. However, they lost their matches on day four to lower-ranked opponents, stating that they were tired after a long year on the tour. World number two, Simona Halep, also lost to Britain's rising star, Johanna Konta. Halep stated: "It's very tough. Every day I'm thinking about the holiday. But I have to stay concentrated" (AFP, 2015). Konta, in turn, decided to withdraw from the next tournament, the China Open, stating that there was not enough time between tournaments allowing her to recover sufficiently to play at her best. Her match would have been played the next day at Beijing, after she lost to Williams at the Wuhan Open. Similarly, Belinda Bencic of Switzerland got to the final of the WTA Pan Pacific Open in Tokyo, where she lost to Agnieszka Radwanska. The following day, Bencic also made the decision to withdraw from her first match at the Wuhan Open, only 38 minutes into the match. She said that she still wanted to play the following week in Beijing, but "it is just end of the season and all the players are really tired" (AFP, 2015). Therefore, the Asian swing could face potential difficulties in the face of injuries and fatigue on the women's tour.

Furthermore, the new season begins in January in Australia, allowing only a few months of rest for the athletes and, as a result, many players withdraw from their first matches. For example, Serena Williams retired after 15 games into her match at the Hopman Cup exhibition match in 2015 due to her inflamed knee injury (Bodo, 2015). Sharapova and Halep followed Williams and withdrew from the Brisbane tournament, which indicated that the women pros might not have had enough time to recover during their post-season break (Bodo, 2015). These are some good examples of the "precautionary" withdrawals that upset tournament directors around the world (Bodo, 2015). In 2009, the WTA tour tried to prevent the frequent withdrawals from happening and created a "Road Map" for all the tournaments in a year.

In addition, the WTA calendar has expanded in the off-season since 2009. The length of the off-season is eight weeks. The new CEO of the WTA, Steve Simon, believes it to be difficult for many female athletes to get through the tight schedule and thus does not want to extend the schedule for the players (Clarey, 2015). Simon does not want to compress any tournaments and make the players play more in the shorter time frame, which could be unhealthy (Clarey, 2015). The two goals of the Road Map were to create a two-month break for the players and to make room for the Asian swing. However, it did not work and it transpired that the Asian market was hit the hardest with the number of the withdrawals.

Simon is aware of the Asian swing move and is opposed to the idea of ex-CEO Allaster's focus on the development of tennis in China. He states: "We need to make sure we respect the region and don't oversaturate it" (Clarey, 2015). Further, in his opinion, since tennis is such a global sport, it has to be developed globally in such regions as North America, Europe, India and South America and anywhere it makes sense (Clarey, 2015).

Conclusion

In conclusion, the history of tennis in its early stages, the globalization of the game in the last decades, the move of tennis into Asia and the current problems associated with that move have been explored. Tennis has become an extremely global sport, and people all over the world love the game. Tennis has changed dramatically since its first introduction in England in the nineteenth century. With the efforts of the WTA, and the tennis tour becoming more global in nature, the tour since 2009 has focused on Asia.

Stacey Allaster contributed enormously in developing a whole new Asian swing and the WTA Final in Singapore. However, the Asian swing has experienced problems with the withdrawals of top female tennis players due to the tight schedule. The WTA, like any global organization, is trying to expand while overcoming current obstacles in the process.

References

Abulleil, R. (2014). Why Asia holds key to long-term WTA health. *Sport 360* [online]. Available at <http://sport360.com/article/international/28046/why-asia-holds-key-long-term-wta-health>. Accessed 21 March 2016.

AFP (2015). Long season takes its toll on women's tennis players. *Yahoo! News* [online]. Available at <https://www.yahoo.com/news/long-season-takes-toll-wta-asia-swing-023210640.html?ref=gs>. Accessed 21 March 2016.

Bodo, P. (2015). Precautionary withdrawals creating more and more headaches on tour. *ESPN* [online]. Available at <http://espn.go.com/tennis/story/_/id/14508387/tennis-rash-early-wta-withdrawals-big-problem>. Accessed 21 March 2016.

China Open (13 October 2009). Stacey Allaster Press Conference [online]. Available at <www.chinaopen.com.cn/news/en/2009-10-13/1712207.shtml>. Accessed 21 March 2016.

Clarey, C. (2015). "WTA's new leader faces a host challenges". The *New York Times* [online]. Available at <www.nytimes.com/2015/10/26/sports/tennis/a-host-of-challenges-greet-wtas-new-leader.html>. Accessed 21 March 2016.

Dictionary.com. *Vulcanization defined*. (Accessed 21 March 2016).

Dunn, L. (2014). Women in business: Stacey Allaster, Chairman and CEO of the Women's Tennis Association. *Huffington Post* [online]. Available at <www.huffingtonpost.com/laura-dunn/women-in-business-stacey_b_6003734.html>. Accessed 21 March 2016.

Dunning, E., Malcolm, D. & Waddington, I. (2004). *Sport Histories: Figurational Studies in the Development of Modern Sports (1)*. Florence, US: Routledge. ProQuest ebrary [online]. Available at <http://site.ebrary.com.ezproxy.liberty.edu/lib/liberty/detail.action?docID=10098928>. Accessed 21 March 2016.

Emmet, J. (2014). The WTA in Singapore: How women's tennis measures parity in dollars. *SportsPro* [online]. Available at <www.sportspromedia.com/magazine_features/the_wta_in_singapore_how_womens_tennis_measures_parity_in_dollars>. Accessed 15 March 2017.

espnW (2015). By the numbers: Stacey Allaster's success at the WTA. *ESPN* [online]. Available at <http://espn.go.com/espnw/news-commentary/article/13729024/stacey-allaster-success-wta>. Accessed 21 March 2016.

Marshall, A. (7 February 2011). Tennis' global evolution is bringing the sport to new markets: An analysis. *Bleacher Report* [online]. Available at <http://bleacherreport.com/articles/594875-the-global-evolution-of-tennis-is-bringing-the-sport-to-new-markets-an-analysis>. Accessed 21 March 2016.

Popovich, N. (2015) "Battle of the sexes: Charting how women in tennis achieved equal pay". The *Guardian* [online]. Available at <www.theguardian.com/sport/2015/se[t11/how_women_achieved_equal_pay_usopen>. Accessed 15 March 2017.

Robson, D. (28 August 2011). Tennis stretches to every corner of the globe. *USA Today* [online]. Available at <http://usatoday30.usatoday.com/sports/tennis/2011-08-15-us-open-tennis-geographic-shift_n.htm>. Accessed 20 March 2016.

Thomas, A. & Borg, C. (26 November 2014). How tennis "conquered the world". CNN [online]. Available at <http://edition.cnn.com/2014/11/26/sport/tennis/chris-kermode-atp-tour-tennis/>. Accessed 21 March 2016.

Wilson, B. (2013). WTA serves up women's tennis for 40 years. BBC News [online]. Available at <www.bbc.com/news/business-22166977>. Accessed 21 March 2016.

Yellis, K. (n.d.). Guarding the Heritage of Tennis. International Tennis Hall of Fame Celebrating 50 Years [online]. Available at <www.researchgate.net/profile/Ken_Yellis/publication/297899552_Guarding_the_Heritage_of_Tennis/links/56e4134308ae65dd4cbe76ac.pdf>. Accessed 21 March 2016.

Zhuhai Official Website (2015). [Online]. Available at <www.wtaelitetrophy.com/Article.aspx?id=f7c2a596-7703-46ef-a0b0-0dbe7817e613>. Accessed 21 March 2016.

11

GLOBALIZING A BRAND THROUGH SPORT SPONSORSHIPS

The case of Turkish Airlines and its sport marketing efforts

Cem Tinaz

Introduction

Recently sponsorship has become an integral part of marketing communications. A significant number of not only international but also national companies have chosen to use sport sponsorships to reach their various marketing objectives, including increasing brand awareness and brand loyalty and creating or, in some cases, changing brand image. Sport sponsorship can create a unique emotional connection between the products and the consumers.

Globalization in sport, business and broadcasting/telecommunications require the sponsor brands to engage themselves in more integrated and sophisticated arrangements. Although significant research exists within the sponsorship sector that focuses on the effectiveness of sponsorships and the image fit between sport entities and sponsors, this chapter aims to analyse and conceptualize the strategic management of sport sponsorships. In order to do this, it uses the overall marketing strategy of Turkish Airlines, the national flag carrier airline of Turkey, as a good example.

The objectives of this study include: (1) defining sport sponsorship and explaining its unique features; (2) conceptualizing the strategic steps of sport sponsorship management; (3) examining the motives for sponsorship initiatives using the example of Turkish Airlines; (4) gaining an understanding of the decision-making process related to selection of sports properties; and (5) articulating the key insights of successful sponsorship management.

A definition of sponsorship

With its widely accepted definition, we can define sponsorship as an investment, in cash or in kind, in an activity, in return for access to the exploitable commercial potential associated with that activity (Meenaghan, 1991). Shank (1999) defined sports sponsorship as "investing in a sports entity (athlete, league, team or event) to support overall organizational objectives, marketing goals and/or promotional strategies". As Crompton (2004) has suggested, the sponsor can provide cash, goods or services and, in return, receives the opportunity to exploit the brand. Sponsorship could be considered as a mutual relationship between "the sponsored or sponsee" and "the sponsor". The sponsored entity is the owner of the rights and benefits, and it passes these on to the sponsor. It is widely accepted that to maintain a long-term relationship and deliver the expected results, sponsorship must deliver benefits to both parties. Sponsorship is described as an "activity that puts buyers and sellers together" (Sleight, 1989). As a result, both parties can benefit. Masterman defines sponsorship as:

> a mutually beneficial arrangement that consists of the provision of resources of funds, goods and/or services by an individual or body (the sponsor) to an individual or body (rights owner) in return for a set of rights that can be used in communications activity, for the achievement of objectives for commercial gain.
>
> *Masterman, 2007, p. 30*

Wang *et al.* (2011) stated that the credibility of the sponsor is influenced by the perceived congruence between the sponsored entity and the sponsor. Wang *et al.* continued that the credibility depends upon the sponsor's brand equity. There is a strong connection between high credibility and stronger brand equity. A sponsor has a high degree of credibility if it is considered believable and trustworthy by the consumers, whereas brand equity is defined as the combination of the image and the reputation of a brand (Wang *et al.*, 2011). Most sponsors are looking to create an emotional connection between their brand and the sport entity (sponsee). Through the sponsorship, the sponsor aims to reach its potential customers, often sport fans. As Madrigal (2001) has outlined, brands are using sponsorship as a part of their differentiation strategy.

Sponsorship is a combination of different communications tools. There are clear differences between advertising and sponsorships in terms of functions and effects. Consumers generally believe that the primary goal of advertising is to generate revenue for the brand; on the other hand, sponsorship places more emphasis on the benefits to society (Meenaghan, 2001). Indirectness is considered to be another distinguishing characteristic of sponsorship from other promotional methods. It means that the sponsorship is a secondary concern for the consumer, after the sport itself (Gwinner, 1997). The indirect objectives of sport sponsorships could be increasing sales, generating awareness or creating a desired image for the brand. Shank (2005) outlined that the indirect objectives of sponsorship can happen over the long term and can lead to increased sales. As Madrigal (2001) suggested, sponsorship acquisition mostly occurs in the relaxed environment of a social or sporting event. This environment allows the consumers to scan the communication message. On the other hand, the message communicated by advertising occurs in a persuasive environment where the consumer is pushed to purchase. Advertising effects can be seen within a short period, whereas sponsorship might need a much longer time to become effective. Research indicates that sponsorship should be considered as a long-term investment. Amis, Slack and Berrett (1999) suggested that sponsorship can provide a brand with a competitive advantage over its rivals over a long period of time.

Emergence of sponsorship as a strategic marketing tool

Although the ancient roots of sponsorship began almost 2000 years ago, the commercial history of sponsorship is quite short. In this chapter, we do not go back to the ancient and philanthropic beginnings of sponsorship. Our aim is to examine the modern usage of sponsorship, particularly its strategic management and implementation. Masterman (2007) indicated that the advent of television and television commercials offered new opportunities for advertisers to reach wider and larger audiences. Since sport was popular programming on television, advertisers saw sport as an attractive tool for brand promotions, and this, Masterman suggested, formed the roots of today's sponsorship industry. During the 1960s and 1970s, athlete endorsements were getting attention due to the increased popularity of athletes and, at the same time, televised events started to offer opportunities for brands to gain exposure without having to pay television advertising rates.

Sponsorship constitutes a marketing tool for brands that they can use to connect themselves with their potential customers through entertainment, arts or sport entities. Sponsorship is an integral and strategic investment for many industries that are seeking to reach sport consumers (Dees, 2004). Research indicates that, as of 30 years ago, sport continued to command the lion's share of the sponsorship market (IEG, 2008). No doubt the popularity of sport sponsorship depends not only on the reach of global sport events like the Olympic Games or World Cup but also on the popularity of sport stars such as Kobe Bryant and Lionel Messi. Madrigal (2001) suggested that the brands expect to transfer the positive feelings of sport consumers toward sport, and to its goods and/or services.

Despite the long history of sponsorship, until the 1980s sport sponsorship's primary aim was to place signage around the stadium or venue and to receive free tickets and/or hospitality services in return for the payment made to the sport entity (Masterman, 2007). The 1984 Summer Olympics, which were held in Los Angeles, USA, changed the perspective of the sponsors and the sport organizations. As Gratton and Taylor (2000) have outlined, the 1984 Summer Olympics were funded completely by the private sector. As such, this event is considered a milestone in event management and sponsorship implementation. After the Games, the International Olympic Committee (IOC) introduced the concept of categories of sponsorship (Meenaghan, 1998). Both the sponsors and the right holders saw the commercial potential of sport sponsorship, and they started to develop new ideas. As a result of these initiatives, sport sponsorship made a remarkable improvement and became one of the most effective marketing communication tools for brands as well as a valuable income source for right holders. In addition, new technological developments (the Internet, mobile communications, digital and high definition broadcasting and broadband) enabled both sides to expand their scope and reach a broader community of potential customers (Masterman, 2007). Compared to the cost of direct television advertising, sport sponsorships are mostly considered cost-effective because of high television coverage, which attracts millions of people across all ages, areas and lifestyles (Brassington & Pettit, 2000). Earlier perceptions of sponsorship arrangements, which were often regarded as donations, have radically changed into economic-based partnerships between mutually dependent organizations (Meenaghan 1998). Meenaghan (1998) also added that the clutter-free environment of sponsorship provides quality access to consumers at a reasonable cost and consequently has driven the initial development of the medium even further.

When we talk about sport sponsorships in the contemporary marketing world, we are not only talking about the relationship between the sponsors and right holders. Today's sport marketing operations occur in a system that involves different stakeholders such as the media, public opinion leaders, politicians and the community (Ferrand, Torrigiani & Povill, 2007). The globalization of sport has changed the media landscape and, specifically, how sport is broadcast. There is an increased acceptance of the commercialization of sport and the emergence of distinctive communication through sport. Lagae (2005) listed these as reasons for the increased interest in sport sponsorship. However, the increased popularity of sport sponsorships has created a highly cluttered communication environment in which attracting potential consumers is becoming more difficult. On the one hand, more brands are trying to exploit themselves through sponsorships and, on the other hand, sponsors are reporting declining recall rates from their sponsorship investments (Kraak & Olivier, 1997). The costs of sponsorship property rights are increasing because the sponsorship environment is becoming crowded. The result is reduced efficiency.

The number of marketing, public relations and sponsorship agencies has also increased during the last 30 years due to the popularity of using sponsorships as a communication tool. These agencies are offering sponsorship recruitment, management and consultancy services to rights owners (Masterman, 2007).

Without a doubt, sport sponsorship has become one of the most effective and popular marketing communication tools. According to IEG's annual year-end industry review (IEG, 2014), global sponsorship investments in sport have been showing steady growth. In 2014, sponsors from all parts of the world, excluding North America, spent US$34.7 billion on sponsorship. The share of sport sponsorship in the North American sponsorship market, where the American companies spent over US$14.7 billion on sport, is around 70 per cent. Some American professional sport leagues are receiving a tremendous amount of sponsorship income. According to another IEG study (2015), sponsorship spending on the National Basketball Association (NBA) and its 30 teams totalled US$739 million in the 2014–2015 season, showing a growth of 8.9 per cent on the previous year. These numbers are proof of brands' positive perception of sport sponsorship. Sponsorship is likely to continue to be one of the most popular marketing communications tools on a global scale.

Unique features of sponsorship

Today's companies are dealing with marketing-savvy consumers. Sport sponsorship constitutes an effective way to create product differentiation and is also a powerful way to create an emotional connection with the consumers. The emotional connection that sponsorship creates between the brand and the sport consumer leads to an increase in brand loyalty. This potential makes sport sponsorships valuable among the other elements of marketing. There is a consensus as sponsorship objectives are connected to the achievement of competitive advantage. As Rosen and Minsky (2011) outlined, "sponsorship can play a starring role in activating consumer behavior and motivating an entire system to do the same". But sponsorship is not a replacement for advertising, sales promotion or public relations (IEG, 2008). A sponsorship acquisition works best if it is used as part of integrated marketing communications, which include the use of all marketing methods. There are a variety of reasons that brands use sponsorship, each of which offers quite different benefits. As Masterman (2007) has indicated, these reasons could be corporate or product/brand related. There is another perspective where corporate, marketing or media-related objectives are listed. Research shows that brands are looking beyond the traditionally accepted benefits of sponsorship; they want to create partnerships that could provide a broader range of opportunities. One important aspect is that sponsorships enable brands to co-create their values. According to the conventional value creation perspective, the producer creates value. Valued products and services are exchanged between the producers and the consumers. However, according to the co-creation perspective, value is not only defined but also created both by the producers and consumers (Prahalad & Ramaswamy, 2004). Co-creation, which occurs during the sponsorship acquisition, can enable different parties like companies and customers to come together and jointly produce a mutually valued outcome.

Alexandris, Tsaousi and James (2007) suggested that an important objective of sponsorship is to create a better and more positive image for brands. Sponsorship can also constitute an effective platform for internal engagement. This feature allows brands to offer benefits for their staff and employees, and hence has a growing importance for brands. Building internal relations is widely regarded as a key corporate objective by many brands. According to Irwin, Sutton and McCarthy (2002) a sponsorship can lead to increased pride and loyalty in the employees of the company and this can lead to increased motivation and ultimately produc-tivity. Brands can also use the assets of their sponsorships to drive retail traffic and build sales.

Brands communicate through sponsorship, through the perceived attributes in the spon-sored object (Meenaghan & Shipley, 1999). The messages and experiences created through the sponsorships can lead to an enrichment of the consumers' own interpretation of the brand. Meenaghan and Shipley (1999) suggested that "a sponsor is buying in to the ready-made image of the rights owner's activity". Meenaghan (2001) has also outlined that "the communication effects of sponsorship vary according to the degree to which the individual consumer is involved with the sponsored activity". He concluded that the fans' awareness of the sponsor is higher if they are involved with the sport event (Meenaghan, 2001). Awareness is defined as the recall or recognition ability of the consumer about the sponsor communications input. He or she can recall or recognize the brand either only from memory, or with verbal or written cues (du Plessis, 1994). Another important factor that affects the attractiveness of the sponsorship is the fit between the sponsor and sponsored entity. Speed and Thompson (2000) concluded that the higher the fit, the higher the attractiveness will be. Achievement of a high level of fit between the sponsor and the sponsored entity can positively influence consumer attitudes towards the brand (Mazodier & Merunka, 2011).

Strategic sponsorship management

Gaining exposure and awareness through logo displays and branded signage was the original aim of the sponsor brand. However, while this approach could still be dominant for many sponsor brands, many brands aim to improve or maintain their relations with customers, suppliers and employees. Through this integrated approach, they can achieve multiple objectives. Dees (2004) has suggested that "a sponsorship activation must inform consumers what brand, product, or service is being promoted, create a positive emotion within the consumer, and then persuade them to display a specific behavior, such as intent to purchase" (p. 5).

The contemporary business world enables companies to use a variety of marketing tools. To produce effective results, the companies need to decide wisely which tool to use and which not to use. Meenaghan (1998) indicated that experience has increased management's understanding of sponsorship management and has led to increased sophistication in all aspects. This sophistication has enabled many brands to clearly state their objectives and select the most suitable avenue of sponsorship through personalized selection models. Additionally, brands have made the integration and exploitation of sponsorship essential components of their overall marketing plans. A return on investment evaluation also becomes a necessary process of successful sponsorship management.

The integrated structure of sport sponsorships provides a variety of competitive advantages, but it is still a complex choice, with important questions to consider. First, the brands should consider whether sport sponsorship is the most effective and efficient way of achieving their communications objectives. The second question about sponsorship is much more complex because the sport business involves different sport branches, organizations and events. What should be sponsored? Each decision involves both opportunities and risks. The third question determines how the sponsorship will be implemented. When developing a variety of communications, advertising, public relations, sponsorship and direct marketing should be seen as core components and used in synchronization. Sponsorship should be utilized with careful attention to public relations and advertising. Integrated communications management is critically important to achieving the desired goals. The sponsorship industry acknowledges that a figure at least equal to the direct costs of securing the property rights of a sponsorship is necessary for exploitation. However, many sponsors spend several times the property rights fee in order to maximize their return on investment (ROI) (Meenaghan, 1998).

According to Pitts and Stotlar (2007), the execution of sponsorship consists of four stages. The first stage is the decision to sponsor and the integration of the sponsorship into the companies' communication strategy. The second stage is the selection of the most suitable sponsorship vehicle. Sport offers a great variety of options for the brands, including sport competitions, athletes or teams, individual sport events or major multi-sport events. The third stage is the implementation and activation of the sponsorship, and the fourth stage is the evaluation of the sponsorship's effectiveness.

In their research, Rosen and Minsky outlined six strategic steps for successful sponsorship management (Rosen & Minsky, 2011). They suggested that the first step is to define objectives clearly. A brand should determine the objectives that could be achieved through sponsorships. The second step is to identify equity opportunities. Exclusivity is an important aspect of sponsorship acquisition as it is key to maximizing ROI. The brand should find a space, which it can actually "own", to maximize its marketing effects. In some regions and sport branches, the sponsorship market is very crowded; therefore, it is important to find a space where the brand can exhibit itself most prominently. The third step is to assess the fit between the brand and sport entity. As Crimmins and Horn (1996) also outlined, ensuring the fit between the marketing objectives of the brand and the sponsored asset is very important. The brand must know if the fans are in the company's target market and how many of the target members are in fact fans of the sport entity before finalizing their sponsorship decision. According to Rosen and Minsky, a brand should highlight its own value when negotiating the cost of sponsorship rights. The activation process of the sponsor could be very useful for the sport entity, in terms of creating public awareness and selling more tickets and/or merchandising products. To create value, meaning developing intimate relationships with potential customers and driving key behaviours in terms of sales, a sponsor should empower and utilize all relevant communication channels. The last step is measuring the sponsorship's effectiveness.

The case of Turkish Airlines

This part of the chapter aims to conceptualize the strategic steps of Turkish Airlines by explaining how it aimed to create a global brand using effective marketing communications, especially sport sponsorships. For conceptualization, official annual reports of Turkish Airlines published during the last decade, two in-depth interviews made with high-profile marketing officials and sponsorship literature were used simultaneously.

Turkish Airlines is the flag carrier of Turkey. Skytrax selected Turkish Airlines as Europe's Best Airline for five consecutive years between 2011 and 2015. Turkish Airlines has also been awarded the titles of World's Best Business Class Airline Lounge, and World's Best Business Class Lounge Dining at the 2015 Skytrax World Airline Awards. As of 2014, Turkish Airlines flew to 275 destinations worldwide, and this large number of destinations made them the fourth largest carrier in the world. Turkish Airlines has become a truly global brand over the last decade, thanks to its successful marketing efforts. Although it also uses traditional marketing tools, the success of Turkish Airlines, in terms of awareness and media coverage, depends significantly on its sport sponsorships. For Turkish Airlines, sports sponsorship is a vital component of any national or international marketing campaign. Currently Turkish Airlines has sponsoring partnerships in ten distinct sport branches, and these partnerships cover more than 35 countries. Before moving forward with the sponsorship-related communication strategies of Turkish Airlines and their effects, the overall tourism policy in Turkey during the last decade should be examined and understood. This is essential, since the success of Turkish Airlines is closely connected with the national tourism policy.

Turkey prepared a detailed master plan for tourism in 2008, aiming to achieve successful management and implementation of tourism efforts and boost the cooperation of the public and private sectors. The main objective of the plan was to ensure the healthy and sustainable development of the tourism sector, focusing on alternative tourism: coastal tourism, health and thermal tourism, winter sport, mountain climbing, adventure trips, plateau tourism and eco-tourism, conference and expo tourism, cruise ship and yacht tourism, and golf tourism. The master plan involved a planning approach that supported economic growth and was physically applicable and socially oriented. The planning reflected the principle of sustainable tourism, which aims to reach economic feasibility and viability. In regards to domestic tourism, the focus became to provide alternative tourism products with acceptable quality and afford-able prices to various groups in society. The master plan involved a route map to eliminate the transportation and infrastructure problems of densely populated and fast-growing cities. Another important aspect of the plan was to activate Total Quality Management in every aspect of the travel industry, developing a sense and awareness of quality and making quality measurable. The objectives to be achieved before 2023 are as follows:

- Increase the total accommodation capacity up to 1.5 million (from 850,000 in 2008)
- Increase the total number of golf courses by 50 (from 25 in 2008), marinas by 70 (from 40 in 2008)
- Double the number of congresses (159 congresses held in Turkey in 2011 (globally 23rd) – 114 of them in Istanbul (globally 9th))
- Increase the number of planes to 500 (from 317 in 2011)

The last of the above objectives is related to the growth strategy of Turkish Airlines. This strategy is still in progress, and Turkish Airlines is developing not only its products and services but also its distribution channels.

Competition in the aviation industry is very intense, and differentiation is crucial to gain an advantage. Turkish Airlines' differentiation strategy is based on sport sponsorship. A marketing executive from Turkish Airlines explains the meaning of sponsorships for Turkish Airlines as follows:

> Movie sponsorship as we did in Batman & Superman or sport sponsorships can be more effective and Turkish Airlines is well aware of that. These sponsorships support our brand in our new destinations. The movie trailer of Superman and Batman that was showed in halftime of Super Bowl is a good example to see how two things can be accomplished at once. You get coverage and create emotions. Of course, you may act as a standard advertiser who wants to promote his products but this is a very old fashioned way that every brand make use of.
>
> *Cevizcioglu, 2016*

He continued:

> I think that we can put advertising and sport sponsorships at the centre with regard to Turkish Airlines. For example, we manage our individual contracts through our advertising department. They are our brand ambassador. Messi, Drogba, Kobe Bryant, Caroline Wozniacki, Kevin Costner, Tiger Woods. In fact, they are all special contracts realized by our advertising department. We can say that sport sponsorship is the most important element together with advertising department.
>
> *Cevizcioglu, 2016*

Turkish Airlines began its professional sport sponsorship initiatives in 2006 when it became the official sponsor of the Turkish National Basketball Team (Annual Report, 2006). In 2006, as a result of a public offering, the share of the government's ownership in Turkish Airlines fell below 50 per cent. After this, the legal status of Turkish Airlines as a state corporation ended (Annual Report, 2006). As a result of the increased quality of various products and services (developed web-based services, partnerships with other airlines, new routes, technical improvements, quality certifications, focus on customer satisfaction, significantly upgraded in-flight catering, new and innovative in-flight offerings) and marketing efforts, Turkish Airlines grew by 20 per cent in just one year. The company increased its passenger numbers from 14 million to 17 million through both new aircraft additions and new routes. Net profit rose 28 per cent to US$132 million and operating income more than doubled to over US$404 million (Annual Report, 2007). In 2008, Turkish Airlines grew by 15.1 per cent and brought the total number of passengers to 22.6 million. The launch of Anadolu Jet, a partner brand for domestic flights, also triggered an expansion of the domestic flight network: the number of domestic passengers increased by 10.8 per cent from 2007 and reached 11.1 million (Annual Report, 2008). In the same year, Turkish Airlines started to put more emphasis on sponsorships and celebrity endorsements. For its endorsement choices, instead of featuring one-time appearances of stars on Turkish Airlines' advertisements, it positioned the stars to be its brand ambassadors. The marketing executive of Turkish Airlines explains the strategy as follows:

> What is intended to do is to create an image. Turkish Airlines was in a difficult situation in 2007 in terms of global awareness. First move to change this impression was using Kevin Costner as an ambassador. Kevin Costner was a milestone that allows us to qualify Turkish Airlines as a world brand. Barcelona and Manchester United make part of this too. The most effective factors that give support to the image are brand names and sport sponsorships. Extending the flight network between the years 2007–2008 and recognition of the brand anywhere in Europe and sponsorships activities have served to increase our recognition level and strengthen our brand image.
>
> *Cevizcioglu, 2016*

During 2009 and 2010, Turkish Airlines was the transportation sponsor of the leading soccer clubs of Turkey (Beşiktaş JK, Fenerbahçe SK, Trabzonspor, Galatasaray SK and Bursaspor) as well as for the Turkish national football team. In 2009, Turkish Airlines continued its growth in terms of economic indicators, but in 2010, it made huge attempts to become a global brand. First, it determined the sectors in which brand awareness needed to be raised. Then it started to use more appropriate forms of sports to better capture the attention of the chosen target groups. To reach the designated targets in selected locations, testimonials were solicited from the most prestigious individuals and teams (Annual Report, 2010). In 2010, Turkish Airlines became the third international sponsor of globally known FC Barcelona. In the same year, Turkish Airlines made a three-and-a-half-year sponsorship agreement with Manchester United. As the official airline sponsor of these teams, Turkish Airlines earned the exclusive rights to transport the teams to and from games and training camps. In the same year, Turkish Airlines also became the naming sponsor of Euroleague Basketball, the most important professional club basketball competition in Europe. In addition to the Euroleague naming rights, the Euroleague Final Four playoffs were conducted under the name "Turkish Airlines Euroleague Final Four". This partnership was one of the most effective as there was a perfect fit between the league participants' locations and Turkish Airlines' destinations. Turkish Airlines also secured the rights for the prime sponsor of the Turkish Basketball Federation for two and a half years. Through this deal, the brand successfully added the team members to its television advertisements. This "golden year of sponsorships" continued with other deals in basketball, tennis, golf, sailing and marathons. The marketing executive of Turkish Airlines explains the selection process as follows:

> We ask the amount of the budget that we are requested and the value of the advertisements that we can get for one year in exchange. Also, we ask ourselves that if we had not assumed this sponsorship but used the billboard that the club had allocated us in anywhere in the city, which amount would have the budget. We consider these issues and make an analysis to know the extent of the advantages that the club provides us. So the sponsorships have an important role at the moment of evaluating. For example, Marseille is very important for us by the history of the city and of the club so it is the most logical decision to compete with Emirates, which is the main sponsor of Paris, and to affirm our presence in France. For the flights headed to Los Angeles, it was contracted with Kobe and for those headed to Denmark, with Wozniacki. Rwanda is our new destination. By the moment we are challenging Air France and even we overtake it. For the flights headed to Rwanda we contracted a sponsorship agreement with bicycle team of Rwanda.
>
> *Cevizcioglu, 2016*

The strategies of the competitors are also a dominant factor for the selection process. The marketing executive of Turkish Airlines continues:

> If we want to make an agreement with a football team in France, we choose Marseille which is nine-time champion. Marseille is a unique French team that was champion of Champions League. Marseille is a very important city and has a great brand value and also is a football team with a very long-standing history. When they make a match, the Turkish Airlines' logo appears at the right upper corner of the shirts of the players at Le'Quipe. Turkish Airlines is actually a sponsor of Borussia Dortmund which is the second important team of Germany after Bayern. Bayern Munich has agreement with Lufthansa, which is logical because it is the airline company of that area. So, it is more reasonable for us to choose Borussia Dortmund. At the moment of making choice we take into account the most logical options in the market and the factors like image, reputation, feedback and yield which will serve us to accomplish our objectives.
>
> *Cevizcioglu, 2016*

Turkish Airlines' goal of becoming a global brand has a direct impact on the company's general strategies in the form of worldwide sponsorship activities. The success of Turkish Airlines' sport sponsorships as a marketing communication strategy depends on the following aspects:

* Strong image fit
* Correct customer segmentation
* Effective use of leveraging methods simultaneously – athlete endorsement, outdoor adverts, press releases, TV advertisements, stadium appearances, product placement, etc.
* High levels of media coverage and awareness through prominent and successful sport identities

Turkish Airlines seeks the balance between team, organization and brand ambassador to avoid reactions. It prefers global organizations like the Euro 2016, rugby, golf and basketball. Market research is a central element for strategic decisions.

In a highly competitive environment like sport sponsorships, making the right decision is critical for maximizing ROI. The marketing executive of Turkish Airlines explains the decision-making process as follows:

> Market prospections are based on the most popular cultural and sportive elements of a country. The preferences of the people in their daily life are very important for us. We realize studies according to the abundance ratio. For example, if we see a lack in Romania we conduct there a study. We ask whether that destination is attractive for the passengers or is a source that generates passengers. In fact, sport sponsorships and advertising department intervene as far as we receive requests from a determined destination and also when we are informed that that destination requires visibility. Market prospection is important but the most important things to do are to expand flight network or to increase the occupancy rate.
>
> *Cevizcioglu, 2016*

Since 2010, the Turkish Airlines marketing communication strategy has used various types of sport sponsorships. The Euroleague Basketball naming sponsorship was renewed in 2013 and, as a result, the company will hold the naming rights until 2020. In 2014, Turkish Airlines signed a three-year agreement to be one of the main sponsors of the European Rugby Champions Cup and the European Rugby Challenge Cup. Partnerships with various sport teams, events and professional athletes continue to grow and serve their corporate objectives. At the same time, the company recently announced a contract with Boeing for the largest purchase in aviation history by the end of 2021. In 2014, Turkish Airlines became the largest carrier worldwide with regard to the number of destinations, flying to 108 countries. Sport sponsorship provides good opportunities for a company striving to become a global brand and expand their reach. Turkish Airlines constitutes a good example for successful sport sponsorship management. The company seeks potential options in target markets, runs comprehensive research to select the most suitable alternative, activates the partnerships through different mediums and finally measures its ROI using a variety of methods.

References

Alexandris, K., Tsaousi, E. & James, J. (2007). Predicting sponsorship outcomes from attitudinal constructs: The case of a professional basketball event. *Sport Marketing Quarterly, 16*, 130–139.

Amis, J., Slack, T. & Berrett, T. (1999). Sport Sponsorship as Distinctive Competence. *European Journal of Marketing, 33/3,* 250–272.

Annual Report 2006 (2007) [online]. Istanbul. Available at <http://investor.turkishairlines.com/en/ financial-operational/annual-reports/1/2006>. Accessed 18 January 2016.

Annual Report 2007 (2008) [online]. Istanbul. Available at <http://investor.turkishairlines.com/en/ financialoperational/annualreports/1/2007>. Accessed 18 January 2016.

Annual Report 2008 (2009) [online]. Istanbul. Available at <http://investor.turkishairlines.com/en/ financial-operational/annual-reports/1/2008>. Accessed 18 January 2016.

Annual Report 2010 (2011) [online]. Istanbul. Available at <http://investor.turkishairlines.com/en/ financial-operational/annual-reports/1/2010>. Accessed 18 January 2016.

Brassington, F., & Pettitt, S. (2000). *Principles of Marketing.* Harlow, UK: Pearson Education.

Crimmins, J. & Horn, M. (1996). Sponsorship: From management ego trip to marketing success. *Journal of Advertising Research, 36*(4), 11–21.

Crompton, L. J. (2004). Conceptualization and alternate operationalization of the measurement of sponsorship effectiveness in sport. *Leisure Studies, 23*(3), 267–281.

Dees, W. (2004). "Measuring the Effectiveness of Commercial Sponsorships in Intercollegiate Athletics". [Unpublished PhD thesis]. University of Florida, Florida, USA.

du Plessis, E. (1994). Recognition versus recall. *Journal of Advertising Research, 34*(3), 75–91.

Ferrand, A., Torrigiani, L. & Povill, A. C. I. (2007). *Routledge Handbook of Sports Sponsorship: Successful Strategies.* Oxon: Routledge.

Gratton, C. & Taylor, P. (2000). *The Economics of Sport and Recreation: An Economic Analysis.* London: Spon Press.

Gwinner, K. (1997). A model of image creation and image transfer in event sponsorship. *International Marketing Review, 14*(3), 145–158.

IEG (2008). *IEG's Guide to Why Companies Sponsor* [online]. Available at <www.sponsorship.com/ Resources/What-CompaniesSponsor.aspx?print=printfriendly>. Accessed 7 March 2016.

IEG (2014). Sponsorship spending report: Where the dollars are going and trends for 2014 [online]. Available at <www.sponsorship.com/IEG/files/4e/4e525456-b2b1-4049-bd51-03d9c35ac507. pdf>. Accessed 6 March 2016.

IEG (2015). Sponsorship spending on the NBA totals $739 million in 2014–2015 season [online]. Available at <www.sponsorship.com/IEGSR/2015/09/28/Sponsorship-Spending-On-The-NBA-Totals-$739-Millio.aspx>. Accessed 6 March 2016.

Irwin, R., Sutton, W. & McCarthy, L. (2002). *Sport Promotion and Sales Management.* Champaign: Human Kinetics.

Kraak, E. & Olivier, A. (1997). Sponsorship effectiveness. [Paper presented at ESOMAR 1997 seminar "Advertising, sponsorship, promotions, new ways for optimizing integrated communication"]. Paris, France.

Lagae, W. (2005). *Sport Sponsorship and Marketing Communications: A European Perspective* (pp. 117–205). Edinburgh Gate: Prentice Hall.

Madrigal, R. (2001). Social identity effects in a belief-attitude-intentions hierarchy: Implications for corporate sponsorship. *Psychology & Marketing, 18*(2), 145– 165.

Masterman, G. (2007). *Sponsorship for a Return on Investment.* Burlington: Elsevier.

Mazodier, M. & Merunka, D. (2011). Achieving brand loyalty through sponsorship: The role of fit and self-congruity. *Journal of the Academy of Marketing Science, 40,* 807–820.

Meenaghan T. (1991). Role of sponsorship in marketing communication mix. *International Journal of Advertising, 10,* 35–47.

Meenaghan, T. (1998). Current developments and future directions in sponsorship. *International Journal of Advertising, 17*(1), 3–28.

Meenaghan, T. (2001). Understanding sponsorship effects. *Psychology and Marketing, 18*(2), 95–122.

Meenaghan, T. & Shipley, D. (1999). Media effect in commercial sponsorship. *European Journal of Marketing, 33,* Issue 3/4, 328.

Pitts, B. G. & Stotlar, D. K. (2007). *Fundamentals of Sport Marketing* (3rd edn). Morgantown, WV: Fitness Information Technology Publishers.

Prahalad, C. K. & Ramaswamy, V. (2004). Co-creating unique value with customers. *Strategy and Leadership, 32*(3), 4–9.

Rosen, W. & Minsky, L. (2011). Six steps to successful sponsorships. *Harvard Business Review* [online]. Available at <https://hbr.org/2011/07/six-steps-to-getting-sponsorsh>. Accessed 10 March 2016.

Shank, D. M. (1999). *Sports Marketing: A Strategic Perspective*. New Jersey: Prentice-Hall.

Shank, M. (2005). *Sports Marketing: A Strategic Perspective* (3rd edn). Upper Saddle River, NJ: Pearson Prentice Hall.

Sleight, S. (1989). *Sponsorship: What It Is and How to Use It*. Maidenhead, Berkshire: McGraw-Hill.

Speed, R. & Thompson, P. (2000). Determinants of sports sponsorship response, *Journal of the Academy of Marketing Science*, *28*(2), 226–238.

Wang, M. C. H., Cheng, J. M. S., Purwanto, B. M. & Erimurti, K. (2011). The determinants of the sports team sponsor's brand equity. *International Journal of Market Research*, *53*(6), 811–829.

PART III

Sport economics and finance

Sport has become increasingly commercialized. The trend knows no borders as it spreads across the globe bringing both growing revenues and costs to every corner of the sport business world. Much of the monetary growth can be attributed to improvements in broadcasting technology and innovations and advancements in the engagement and service of both spectators and participants. The international sport business serves more people and serves them better than ever before. As the global sport business grows, ideas and practices spread while constantly evolving to adapt to new contexts. The chapters in this section reflect the dynamic and innovative aspects of the international sport business.

First, we are reminded that it is still sport and the drive to win can eclipse all other concerns to the detriment of the financial bottom line as has often been the case with football. The subsequent chapters focus on the following topics: different approaches to sport-specific financial instruments, a fresh look beyond the economic impact of mega-events to examine the potential benefit of hosting small to mid-sized international events, innovative ticket revenue maximizing practices and China's efforts to become a global player in the export of professional sport.

12

FOOTBALL'S FAILING FINANCES

John Beech

Introduction

Sport as business has seen major changes in the last few decades. In a generic model, each sport has seen a progression from the early phases of foundation, codification and stratification, through a revolutionary phase of professionalization followed by an evolutionary phase of post-professionalization, to a more recent revolutionary phase of commercialization – the emergence of stakeholders external to the sport, such as sponsors and broadcasters – and, in some cases, on to a post commercialized phase. By "revolutionary", we can characterize the relevant phase as having high rates of change in a variety of dimensions, and operating with high levels of uncertainty for the owners of the sports clubs involved. Some sports have managed to reach a post-commercialized phase, which is characterized by reasonable levels of manageable change in a climate of reasonable certainty – examples are cycling, golf, snooker and tennis. Others, however, have struggled to cope adequately with commercialization, retaining high levels of change rate and uncertainty, a classic example being football (Beech, 2013).

With English football, commercialization began with the breakaway of the top 22 clubs from the Football League in 1992 to form the (English) Premier League. In the years leading up to this secession, the value of television rights for the then top tier in the English game, the old First Division, had grown rapidly. In 1986 a two-year contract had produced revenues of £6.3 million; the subsequent contract, for four years, raised £44 million. In 1992, BskyB paid £191.5 million for a five-year deal, and in 1997 it paid £670 million for the subsequent four-year deal.

For the top clubs in the late 1980s, how the revenues were distributed became a key issue. As the television company that bought the right to broadcast football games was really only interested in showing games played at the highest level, those clubs felt that they should receive more of the revenue. While this may seem not unreasonable, the necessary corollary was that lower-level clubs would receive less. In effect, the competitive balance began to become distorted, with rich clubs becoming even richer, and poor clubs struggling financially to keep up. This distortion, although initiated by the breakaway of the Premier League clubs, became, over time, even stronger because of rising television revenues from European competitions, which became the domain of a select few clubs in each country.

The growth of income from broadcasting continued to rise not only for domestic transmission, but across almost the whole globe. In South Korea for example, Kim (2010) noted that European football matches were broadcast live by several sports channels from various European leagues. MBC ESPN televised the English Premier League, English FA Cups, German Bundesliga, UEFA Champions League and the UEFA Cup. KBS N Sports had rights to telecast Italian Serie A and Spanish Premera Liga, while French Le Championnat and Dutch Eredivisie were broadcast by SBS Sports. Each of the channels broadcast live European football with two to six matches shown every weekend and one or two mid-week. This might also be considered a distortion of football finances – revenues from Korean broadcasters went to European clubs when they might have gone to domestic football clubs had the Korean television stations felt that Korean fans would want to see them on their screens.

The surge in revenue streams in the last two or three decades has not, of course, been confined to those from broadcasting. Two commercial sources have become increasingly significant: sponsorship and merchandising.

Sponsorship had historically been considered totally unacceptable by the (English) Football Association. The first attempt to introduce sponsorship, latterly in the form of what was in effect advertising on club shirts, had been made by Jimmy Hill as early as the 1970s. He tried to change the name of Coventry City FC to Coventry Talbot FC as part of a wider partnership with the local car manufacturer Talbot (subsequently acquired by Peugeot). When the FA prohibited this change he introduced the large "T", which was the Talbot logo, onto the players' shirts. The FA took a very dim view of this attempt to circumvent the ban on shirt advertising, and the club was specifically forbidden from using these shirts when games were broadcast. After a further attempt to introduce sponsored logos on club shirts by non-League Kettering Town, the FA progressively eased the ban – for non-televised games in 1977 and for televised games in 1983. By the 1982–1983 season, 17 of the then 22 top-tier clubs in English football wore sponsored shirts.

The growth in broadcasting, especially in countries in the Far East, extended the attractiveness of shirt sponsorship to commercial organizations. The sponsor's name is thus seen on television screens throughout China for example. This globalization of exposure drew in sponsors from North America, the Far East and the Middle East, creating considerably greater competition to sponsor a finite number of teams. Top teams such as Manchester United and Barcelona can sell shirt sponsorship rights for sums of up to £50 million per year. In a less direct way, sponsorship of a club's stadium, that is, the buying of the naming rights to the stadium, has become increasingly attractive.

The trend of increasing broadcasting revenues is not only likely to grow with respect to broadcasting on television. New revenue streams are emerging, derived from streaming or online broadcasting. North America's National Football League has an agreement with Twitter and, at the time of writing, both Facebook and Verizon are looking to move into the streaming of sports matches (McAlone, 2016).

In parallel with the development of sponsored shirts, an entirely new revenue stream has developed for clubs: the sale of replica shirts and other merchandising. It has become common practice to issue a home shirt, an away shirt and a third shirt (to avoid colour clashes with an opposing team), as well as the occasional "special edition". Frequently new shirts are issued each season for no obvious reason other than to exploit the need of fans to be seen in the latest version, and a change in sponsor automatically makes current shirts out of date. In England, shirts typically retail for around £50, and a club can expect to take, on each shirt (Rohlmann, reported in Hayward and Miller, 2016) a profit of approximately £21 (£18 as the retailer and £3 licensing fee).

The breakdown of revenue streams as percentages of total income varies very considerably. Top-tier clubs earn very strongly from broadcasting rights, and also from sponsorship deals (this, however, being not individualized but varying from deal to deal and hence season to season), and relatively little from match day receipts such as ticket sales and hospitality. Lower down in the football pyramid, television fees diminish quite rapidly (only top-flight football is wanted by broadcasters) and match day receipts rise in relative significance.

With revenue streams rising so strikingly in recent decades, and particularly since the formation of the Premier League, one might expect football clubs, at least those at the highest levels, to be highly profitable. This is, however, surprising as it might seem to someone unfamiliar with the football business, not generally the case.

Profitability in English football was at its worst from season 2001/2002 to season 2005/2006: the 92 clubs in the top four tiers managed a staggering aggregate loss of £1,014,000 (Beech, 2009). How was this possible? In the same period, 26 of the top 92 clubs suffered insolvency events, typically having to go into Administration. Even a Premier League club, Portsmouth, suffered the indignity of Administration in 2010. The broader pattern of insolvency events from season 1986/1987 to season 2008/2009 is shown in Figure 12.1 (Beech, Horsman & Magraw, 2008). Again the question needs to be asked, how was this possible?

Problems with debt are hardly confined to English clubs. Italy's Serie A clubs are reported to have aggregate debts of €365 million (Football Italia Staff, 2016). For Brazilian clubs, unsustainable tax debts have almost become a way of life (Young, 2015). Top Turkish club Fenerbahçe has been forced to issue equity in the face of an overall debt of TL1.1 billion (Özdabakoglu, 2016), one of a number of Turkish clubs in deep financial trouble (Reuters, 2016). In Romania, clubs struggle to pay players (Gornall, 2016) and Ukraine's Dnipro faces debts of $1.9 million (Associated Press, 2015). Even in Germany, where football clubs are generally run in a financially sustainable manner, Hamburg has reported a debt increase, to €90 million (ESPN Staff, 2016).

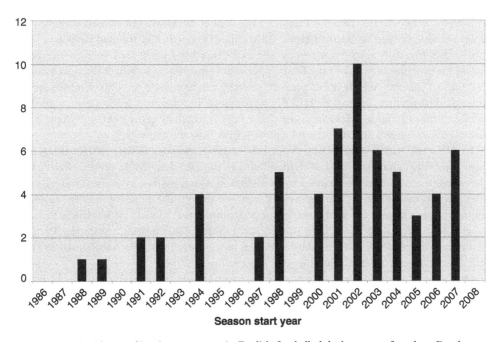

Season start year

Figure 12.1 Incidence of insolvency events in English football clubs by season (based on Beech, Horsman & Magraw, 2008)

Several factors, direct and indirect, can be identified as causes of this financial situation. These include the skewing of competitive balance, unsustainable financial doping, and the uncontrolled inflation of costs, together with combinations of these three factors. An over-arching theme to these factors is the absence of profit as a primary motivation of club owners.

The skewing of competitive balance

A club can gain competitive advantage in terms of raising high revenues either through its own efforts or through systems which inherently tip the scales, making rich clubs richer and, by definition, poor clubs poorer. Certainly some clubs are simply better than others in raising revenues. Manchester United has been one of the best clubs at exploiting sponsorship deals and developing the sale of merchandising. At the time of writing, the array of what the club euphemistically calls "partners" is surprisingly extensive and yet at times puzzling (Manchester United, 2016). It includes:

- Global partners: 22 partners, which mainly operate globally;
- Regional partners: 14 partners, mainly at national levels, strongly skewed towards the Far East;
- Media and telecommunications partners: 17 partners, at national levels, from throughout the world;
- Financial partners: 14 international partners.

The club's ability to leverage such a range of partnerships rests on its long-term good performance "on the pitch", and hence its ability to generate revenues to buy and pay the best players. Like the other major clubs in the Premier League, its revenues from broadcasting contracts reinforce its advantageous position, fuelling a virtuous spiral of revenue generation. This arises in two ways. First, the Premier League does not distribute all broadcasting revenues equally between its member clubs. Although 50 per cent *is* distributed equally, 25 per cent is distributed in a way that favours the clubs that have performed well on the pitch during the previous season, and the final 25 per cent is distributed to reflect the broadcaster's selection of matches which it has actually selected for broadcasting. This virtuous spiral, through qualification to play in UEFA's Champions League or Europa League, feeds a second virtuous spiral to reinforce a situation of the "rich clubs getting richer and the poor clubs getting poorer", and thus the receipt of UEFA broadcasting rights.

In a thorough analysis of income from broadcasting revenues, Harris (2015), using data from the UEFA Benchmarking Report, identifies the fact that, while revenues are ever-increasing, they are distributed in such a way that, not only within a country is there considerable distortion affecting competitive balance, but there is also a distortion of the financial clout between clubs in different countries. For example, the 20 clubs of England's Premier League now outstrip 597 top-flight sides across Europe. This, in turn, means the Premier League can afford to pay by far the highest wages in world football, which amounted to £1.9 million to club employees in the financial year ending in 2014.

How then are clubs in England's second tier to aim to join the Premier League, and how for that matter are weaker clubs in the Premier League to maintain that status? Until recently, as shown below, one obvious answer has been to find an owner who will act as a willing source of funds – the rich "benefactor". Such owners have been typical as owners of the clubs that have managed to rise up to the Premier League. Injections of capital have some-times been in the form of equity – shares purchased by the owner, leaving the club with no obligation to return the money to the owner at any time; the owner can only recover his money by selling the shares to another individual, a transaction that has no direct impact on the club's accounts. More typically, the "benefactor" lends the club money, thus loading the club with debt. Frequently this is described as "soft" debt, meaning that there is no pressure to repay capital and/or interest.

Unsustainable financial doping

This injecting of funds in order to "buy" success on the pitch by the purchase of better players (and the paying of their higher wages) has become known as "financial doping". As the term "doping" suggests, the process is addictive, and anti-social. It impacts on other clubs in that again competitive balance is distorted. While fans of the club may cheer their new-found success bought by the injections of capital, fans of other clubs competing in the same league may look on with envy and see it as very unfair, and unsporting, as the basis of success.

The phenomenon of financial doping is not confined to the higher tiers of football. The case of Eastwood Town FC, based in a small town in Nottinghamshire with a population of 18,000 people, provides a classic example of financial doping that not only proved to be unsustainable but also led to the demise of the club. In October 2007, a local businessman called Rob Yong bought the club, which was then playing in the Northern Premier League Premier Division (Tier 7 of England's football pyramid). In January 2010 Yong announced: "I personally pay the players' wages, and any other money that comes in from the fans through gate money and the like goes straight into the club". He also stated that: "My commitment was for five seasons, but I have now extended that to ten" (Anon., 2010). While the club initially achieved success and promotions, an obstacle to further promotion was reached with the need to upgrade the stadium to the standards required to play in the Conference North (Tier 6). The cost of upgrading was more than Yong was willing to finance, and in 2011 he and his fellow owner put the debt-free club up for sale for £1 (Anon., 2011). Although a new owner was found, any further club operation now required a continuing injection of funds as the club was no longer self-sustaining. Players departed, the club started to sink back down the pyramid and, by 2014, there was no other option than to wind it up.

Even more spectacular was the rise, fall and ultimate demise of Gretna FC. Gretna lies just within Scotland and has a population of under 3,000 people. Having initially played non-league football in England, the club switched to the Scottish league system. Bankrolled by millionaire Brooks Mileson it rapidly rose up the Scottish football pyramid, reaching the Scottish Premier League in 2007. Through illness (and rapidly his death) and the collapse of his personal fortune, Mileson was no longer willing and/or able to continue pouring money into the club. To no one's surprise, the club, totally incapable of surviving on conventional revenue streams, promptly collapsed and was wound up in 2008.

Other extreme examples of English clubs finding themselves operating financially unsustainable business models through the failure of "benefactor" owners to provide adequate funds for financial doping include Aldershot (Spencer Trethewy), Darlington (George Reynolds), Newport County (Jerry Sherman), Rushden and Diamonds (Max Griggs), Wrexham (Alex Hamilton) and York City (John Batchelor).

While these failures can be attributed to unsustainable financial doping, the general financial pressure on clubs to spend more and more to maintain their position within the football pyramid, let alone progress upwards through promotion, has grown ever more challenging because of inflation in the price of new players and the unrelenting rise in the market rate of players' wages.

John Beech

The uncontrolled inflation of costs

The major costs that face a football club are stadium redevelopment/replacement, the purchase of players and players' wages. The history of most major football clubs in the major European leagues stretches back at least a century. At some point in their history the owner will have realized that a late Victorian stadium does not best suit the needs of a modern club. For example, hospitality facilities (and hence revenues from them) are likely to be suboptimal. To maximize revenues, a club will want to generate revenues from its stadium on more than one day in 14 and will hence look to create facilities that will attract concerts and conferences, for example. While redevelopment may in itself cost less than building a new stadium to a more appropriate and modern design, there is often the possibility of selling the existing stadium at a city centre location with a high land value and building a new one on the city borders where land is cheaper. Certainly this can be successful, in particular if a benefactor owner is willing to pay the costs of this change in venue. However, there are a number of ways in which this can go badly wrong. Examples include if:

- the financial commitment of the new stadium results in the lack of funds for building a new team to play in the exalted status the club expects to achieve (Darlington);
- the club is relegated in the meantime and the new stadium is bigger than might have been desirable if the future could have been foreseen (Coventry). See also the case of planning a new stadium at Plymouth (Beech, 2010);
- changes in land prices impact negatively on financial projections (Arsenal);
- the club becomes homeless and is forced into "exile" (Worcester City);
- the process suffers multiple set-backs over a greatly extended timescale (Southend United, where a planned move from their current stadium at Roots Hall to a new ground at Fossetts Farm was announced in 2000 but still remains at a planning stage (Burbidge, 2015)).

"Caution" is clearly not a watchword among English clubs. Neither would it appear to be among other big clubs. Barcelona FC, for example, is planning a €600,000,000 new stadium at a time when the club's debt has risen from €287,000,000 to €328,000,000 (Cernensek, 2015). The club would argue that the debt is serviceable given the club's very high revenue streams, but the timing and scale of the new stadium seem questionable at least.

The decision regarding whether to press on with an existing stadium, redevelop it or build a new one is highly individual to a club, and is taken rarely. Other costs, regarding players and their wage levels, are however ever-present. They may be driven by the club's ambition and dependent on current success levels, but the ageing of players alone will inevitably drive a club into the recruitment market.

Driven by the increasing revenues and hence the ability to pay more, combined with the desire for success and the inherent competitiveness of clubs in a league structure, the price of players has suffered severe inflation over the years, and reflects an international marketplace, with arguably the top Spanish and Italian clubs as the drivers of inflation (see Table 12.1).

With wages there have been similarly high levels of inflation. As Figure 12.2 shows, by 2010 only basic salaries for Tier 4 players were similar to those received in the general population. Tier 3 players were comparatively well paid, receiving an average basic salary of £73,320, while Tier 2 players were earning a basic average of £211,068 per annum. Tier 1 (Premier League) players were earning a very handsome basic average of £1,162,350. To all these figures, bonuses need to be added. Again, there has been a very marked "vertical stretching"

140

Table 12.1 Selected significant transfer fee records

Year	Player	Fee (£)	From	To
1968	Pietro Anastasi	500,000	Varese (Italy)	Juventus (Italy)
1973	John Cruyff	933,000	Ajax (Netherlands)	Barcelona (Spain)
1982	Diego Maradona	3,000,000	Bocca Juniors (Argentina)	Barcelona (Spain)
1984	Diego Maradona	5,000,000	Barcelona (Spain)	Napoli (Italy)
1992	Jean-Pierre Papin	10,000,000	Marseille (France)	Milan (Italy)
1996	Alan Shearer	15,000,000	Blackburn Rovers (England)	Newcastle United (England)
1998	Denílson	21,500,000	São Paulo (Brazil)	Real Betis (Spain)
1999	Christian Vieri	21,100,000	Lazio (Italy)	Inter Milan (Italy)
2001	Zinedine Zidane	46,600,000	Juventus (Italy)	Real Madrid (Spain)
2009	Kaká	56,000,000	Milan (Italy)	Real Madrid (Spain)
2009	Cristiano Ronaldo	80,000,000	Manchester United (England)	Real Madrid (Spain)
2013	Gareth Bale	85,300,000	Tottenham Hotspur (England)	Real Madrid (Spain)

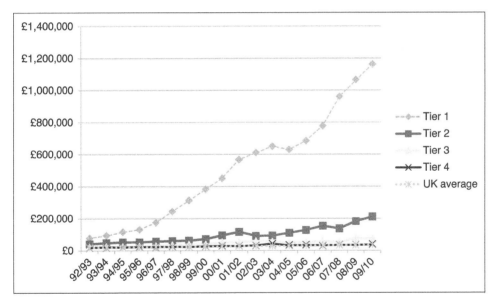

Figure 12.2 Average player salaries in the Premier League and the Football league (UK average provided for comparison) (based on Miller & Harris, 2011)

in the football pyramid – promotion inevitably involves significant increases in spending as well as increases in income. The temptation to overspend in a bid to gain promotion is understandable.

These trends show no signs of slowing down. More recent data (Harris, 2014) show that not only had Premier League salaries risen to an average of £2,300,000, but also that they were considerably higher than the averages in other major leagues around the world: German

Bundesliga (£1,460,000); Italy's Serie A (£1,300,000); Spain's La Liga (£1,200,000); France's La Ligue (£988,000); Russian Premier League (£902,000); and Brazil's Serie A (£583,000). Here, it is the top English clubs that are driving the inflation.

The ability of the Premier League to pay such high salaries derives from the very high broadcasting rights it earns. But this also results in increasing differentials with other European leagues:

> The English clubs' combined income of £3.3bn was a billion and a half pounds larger than the next-best league, Germany's Bundesliga (£1.8bn), and also way ahead of Spain's La Liga (£1.7bn), Italy's Serie A (£1.4bn) and France's Ligue 1 (£1.3bn).
>
> *Harris, 2015*

Non-English clubs are thus under strong (and arguably unreasonable) pressure to compete financially in a European market.

One further cause of the inflation in both transfer fees and salaries should be noted – the increase in use of players' agents. Not only does a club have to pay a higher fee in order to include any agent's fee, but it is also likely to have to pay a higher salary if the agent is worth his salt. In the 2014/2015 season, the 20 Premier League clubs together paid a rather surprising £129,857,560 to agents (Premier League, 2015), the Championship clubs £26,124,044, League 1 clubs £3,167,964, and League 2 clubs £1,007,920 (Football League, 2015), a total of just over £160 million for the 92 clubs. Of the 92, only one in League 1 and two in League 2 made no payments at all to agents.

The motivation of club owners

Why bother competing when the competitive balance has become increasingly skewed? The answer is not hard to find – unlike conventional businesses in the mainstream industries, owners are not necessarily motivated by seeking profits.

Success for a club is more typically measured in terms of utility maximization – successful performance on the pitch; achieving a high position in the table by the end of the season – than in terms of profit maximization. Unless an owner is cynically looking to extract a profit (and this is not unknown) from a club, his/her objective is likely to be reinvesting any operating profit in the form of better players – an owner is likely to have ambition for his/her club. With this type of owner, one might only expect the club to show a break-even in its accounts rather than a profit. With a severe outbreak of ambition, losses will not be a surprise!

How then might club owners be persuaded to reign in injudicious spending – spending that may help the club in the short term, but may jeopardize its existence in the mid- to long-term?

Attempts to reign in the worst financial excesses – Financial Fair Play (FFP) protocols

Given the lack of self-imposed restraint by clubs in financial dealings, it was perhaps inevitable that restraint would be imposed through regulation. Taking a leading stand has been UEFA with its Financial Fair Play protocols (UEFA, 2015, 2009).

The aim of FFP is to improve the overall financial health of European club football. Clubs are generally only allowed to spend up to €5million more than they earn per assessment period (three years), but no more. Similar FFP protocols have been introduced at governance levels where clubs would not be competing at European levels; for example, in England the Football League and the Conference have developed their own protocols.

FFP is problematic in a number of ways. First, it seeks to apply the same standards to clubs operating in 53 countries all in different circumstances. Second, it has faced legal challenges, notably by Manchester City and Paris Saint-Germaine, resulting in a relaxation of the rules (Ziegler, 2015).

These factors, together with its phased introduction, have made its usefulness in improving the financial health of European clubs questionable. Academic studies have tended to take theoretical perspectives when making assessments. An early paper (Grasso, 2011) highlights the problematic nature of selecting which forms of revenue generation are permissible, and the danger of reinforcing the strong position of the richer clubs. A study of the five major national leagues concludes that:

> Theoretically, the UEFA "financial fair-play" rules should yield more financial equality and rebalance European competitions even if differences in revenue will remain. However, the task is uneasy for UEFA as big and often highly indebted clubs are needed to insure Champions League and Europa League's appeal.
>
> *Drut & Raballand, 2012*

Another assessment is that "[FFP] does represent several remarkable steps, but that it probably requires amendments and enhancements in the future in reaction to the clubs' behaviour to accomplish its intended objectives" (Müller, Lammert & Hoveman, 2012). In a study of four major leagues, Peeters and Szymanski come to the conclusion that "the break-even constraint embedded in FFP could substantially reduce average payrolls and wage-to-turnover ratios, while strengthening the position of the traditional top teams" (Peeters & Szymanski, 2014). However, they further note that "since the benefits of the break-even rule to consumers remain unclear, we argue that these rent-shifting regulations might fall foul of European competition law" (Peeters & Szymanski, 2014). Writing alone in the same year, Szymanski makes an interesting case that "the objectives of FFP are not really fairness but financial efficiency" and that "the rules are unlikely to achieve efficiency". He further expresses concern that, "even from the perspective of fairness, the rules do little more than substitute one form of inequality for another" (Szymanski, 2014).

At the time of writing, few clubs had been sanctioned by UEFA for breaching the FFP protocol. The largest club punished so far has been Turkey's Galatasaray (UEFA, 2016), although a few smaller clubs have also been excluded from European competition, including Crvena Zvezda (Serbia), Malaga (Spain), FC Metalurh Donetsk (Ukraine) and Skonto FC (Latvia). Proceedings against others were withdrawn once the club had complied with FFP regulations.

The case of Portsmouth

The demise of Portsmouth provides the most spectacular collapse of an English football club. Historically the club had enjoyed considerable success in the immediate post-war years, but was relegated from the old First Division (Tier 1) in 1959. The club almost disappeared in 1976 but was saved by fans' donations of £25,000. In 1997, 51 per cent of the club's shares were sold for £1. The following year the club was placed into Administration.

In 1999, Milan Mandaric bought the club from the Administrators for £5 million. He subsequently injected some £20 million, and was able to sell the club for approximately

5 million in 2006, the club being a rather more attractive proposition by then as it was
playing in the Premier League.

There followed a series of benefactor owners who injected capital but who had varying
levels of commitment to the club – Alexandre Gaydamak, Sulaiman Al Fahim, Ali Al Faraj
and Balram Chainrai – and it sank into deeper financial crisis through the failure of the owners
to sustain the club's position by further injections of capital. As well as failing financially, it
became increasingly obvious that, left to the support of conventional revenue streams, the
club was totally incapable of supporting the kind of squad that had won the FA Cup in 2008.

In 2010 the club was once again in Administration, unable to meet its debts. It suffered
relegation in three consecutive seasons, and only survived through its purchase by Pompey
Supporters Trust, a fan-owned co-operative.

Conclusion

Self-restraint is not a feature of the financial dealings of football clubs. It is not likely to
become so, as owners will want to spend on better and more expensive players in order for
the club to perform better on the pitch.

In spite of increasing revenues, clubs all too easily fall into debt and operate unsustainable
business models. The best chance of avoiding wide-scale debts might be through imposed
regulation. Attempts to do this, notably by UEFA, have had only limited impact through
legal challenges by clubs that wish to continue "spending big". Financial sustainability across
the industry is not yet on the horizon.

References

Anon. (2010). "Eastwood drive for Conference Premier on course – Yong" [online]. *Nottingham: This is Nottingham.* Available at <www.nottinghampost.com/Eastwood-drive-Conference-Premier-course-8211-Yong/story-12239915-detail/story.html>. Accessed 10 March 2016.
Anon. (2011). "Shock as Badgers owner and chairman quit". *Eastwood and Kimberley Advertiser* (21 April).
Associated Press. (2015). "Ukrainian club Dnipro faces European ban over $1.9M debt" [online]. The *Times of India.* Available at <http://timesofindia.indiatimes.com/sports/football/top-stories/Ukrainian-club-Dnipro-faces-European-ban-over-1-9M-debt/articleshow/50221068.cms>. Accessed 14 March 2016.
Beech, J. (2009). "England". In S. Hamil & S. Chadwick (Eds), *Managing Football: An International Perspective.* Oxford: Elsevier.
Beech, J. (2010). "Are we going stark stadium bonkers?" [online]. *Football Management.* Available at <https://footballmanagement.wordpress.com/2010/04/02/are-we-going-stark-stadium-bonkers/>. Accessed 11 March 2016.
Beech, J. (2013). "Introduction: The commercialisation of sport". In J. Beech & S. Chadwick (Eds), *The Business of Sport Management* (2nd edn). Harlow: Pearson.
Beech, J., Horsman, S. & Magraw, J. (2008). "The circumstances in which English football clubs become insolvent". In J. Beech (Ed.), *The CIBS Working Paper Series.* Coventry University: Centre for the International Business of Sport Working Paper Series No.4.
Burbidge, I. (2015). "Southend United open their Fossetts Farm plans up to the public as they say work could start at the end of 2016". *Southend Echo* (26 October).
Cernensek, B. (2015). "FC Barcelona 2014–15 Financial Report Released" [online]. *Barca Blaugranes.* Available at <www.barcablaugranes.com/2015/7/17/8987367/fc-barcelona-2014-15-financial-report-released>. Accessed 12 March 2016.
Drut, B. & Raballand, G. (2012). "Why does financial regulation matter for European professional football clubs?" *International Journal of Sport Management and Marketing, 11*(1–2), 73–88.
ESPN Staff (2016). "Hamburg announce debts have increased to €90 million" [online]. *ESPNFC.* Available at <www.espnfc.com/german-bundesliga/story/2808080/hamburg-announce-debts-have-increased-to-%E2%82%AC90-million>. Accessed 14 March 2016.

Football Italia Staff (2016). "Serie A chokes on €365m loss" [online]. *Football Italia*. Available at <www. football-italia.net/80760/serie-chokes-%E2%82%AC365m-loss>. Accessed 14 March 2016.

Football League (2015). "Football League club payments to agents" [online]. *London: Football League*. Available at <www.football-league.co.uk/news/article/2015/football-league-club-payments-to-agents-2828445.aspx>. Accessed 12 March 2016.

Gornall, K. (2016). "Romanian football: Clubs in deep debts keep players as 'slaves'" [online]. London: BBC. Available at <http://www.bbc.co.uk/sport/football/35613249> Accessed 14 March 2016.

Grasso, G. (2011). *How Leveled is the Football Playing Field? A Study on Fair Play and Competition in the Football Sector*. Rome, Italy: BA, Universita Luiss Guido Carli.

Harris, N. (2014). "Premier League wages dwarf those around Europe with top-flight players in England earning an average of £2.3million a year . . . almost 60 per cent more than in Germany". *Daily Mail* (14 November).

Harris, N. (2015). "Premier League clubs earn more than Europe's 48 smallest leagues put together as TV money boosts England's elite" [online]. *Daily Mail*. Available at <www.dailymail.co.uk/sport/football/article-3281374/Premier-League-clubs-earn-Europe-s-48-smallest-leagues-TV-money-boosts-England-s-elite.html>. Accessed 10 March 2016.

Hayward, S. & Miller, A. (2016). "Replica football shirts rip-off as fans pay 1,000% mark-up on cost of manufacture". *Daily Mirror* (4 March).

Kim, C. (2010). "South Korea". In S. Hamil & S. Chadwick (Eds), *Managing Football: An International Perspective*. Oxford: Elsevier.

Manchester United (2016). "Official partners" [online]. *Manchester: Manchester United FC*. Available at <www.manutd.com/en/Partners.aspx>. Accessed 10 March 2016.

McAlone, N. (2016). "Facebook is bidding on the rights to stream big NFL games – and it wants to create a whole new experience" [online]. *Business Insider UK*. Available at <http://uk.businessinsider.com/facebook-confirms-its-bidding-on-nfl-streaming-rights-2016-3>. Accessed 8 March 2016.

Miller, A. & Harris, N. (2011). "REVEALED: Official English football wage figures for the past 25 years" [online]. *Sporting Intelligence*. Available at <www.sportingintelligence.com/2011/10/30/revealed-official-english-football-wage-figures-for-the-past-25-years-301002/>. Accessed 12 March 2016.

Müller, J. C., Lammert, J. & Hovemann, G. (2012). "The Financial Fair Play regulations of UEFA: An adequate concept to ensure the long-term viability and sustainability of European club football?" *International Journal of Sport Finance*, 7(2), 117–140.

Özdabakoglu, O. (2016). "Fenerbahçe issues equity to alleviate financial burden" [online]. *Istanbul: Daily Sabah*. Available at <www.dailysabah.com/money/2016/02/22/fenerbahce-issues-equity-to-alleviate-financial-burden>. Accessed 14 March 2016.

Peeters, T. & Szymanski, S. (2014). "Financial fair play in European football". *Economic Policy*, *29*(78), 343–390.

Premier League (2015). "Premier League releases agents' fees" [online]. *London: Premier League*. Available at <www.premierleague.com/en-gb/news/news/2015-16/nov/301115-premier-league-releases-agents-fees.html>. Accessed 12 March 2016.

Reuters (2016). "Debt-laden Turkish soccer clubs pay the price of ambition". *Daily Mail* (2 February).

Szymanski, S. (2014). "Fair is foul: A critical analysis of UEFA Financial Fair Play". *International Journal of Sport Finance*, *9*(3), 218–229.

UEFA (2009). "Financial Fair Play" [online]. Nyon: FIFA. Available at <www.uefa.com/uefa/footballfirst/protectingthegame/financialfairplay/index.html>. Accessed 23 May 2011.

UEFA (2015). "Financial fair play: all you need to know" [online]. *Nyon, Switzerland: UEFA*. Available at <www.uefa.com/community/news/newsid=2064391.html>. Accessed 12 March 2016.

UEFA (2016). "CFCB Adjudicatory Chamber renders Galatasaray decision" [online]. *Nyon: UEFA*. Available at <www.uefa.org/protecting-the-game/club-licensing-and-financial-fair-play/news/newsid=2338564.html>. Accessed 13 March 2016.

Young, J. (2015). "Brazilian football crippled by 'buy now pay later' ethos" [online]. *EPSNFC*. Available at <www.espnfc.co.uk/blog/espn-fc-united-blog/68/post/2234319/brazilian-football-crippled-by-buy-now-pay-later-ethos>. Accessed 14 March 2016.

Ziegler, M. (2015) "Uefa to relax FFP rules to allow more owner investment after Manchester City and PSG argue against unfairness". The *Independent* (18 May).

13

DEBENTURES IN THE UNITED KINGDOM AND SEAT LICENCES IN THE UNITED STATES

Assessing the similarities and differences

Kevin Heisey

Introduction

Game or match day revenue sources and facility design have evolved dramatically in recent decades. Seatless terraces, wooden grandstands, bleachers and seating mainly differentiated by the view of the action, have given way to stadiums and arenas offering a wide array of seating options and spectator amenities. Such features can include club lounge areas for food and drink service, specialized luxury suites, tables for couples and various other options that allow sport properties to customize the spectator experience and serve a wide variety of fans.

In addition to match day revenue, modern facilities are designed and constructed with non-match day revenue generation in mind as well. Daily uses of facility space can be as simple as being merchandise outlets for fans, club museums and for stadium tours, but many new facilities are also designed as commercial anchors with retail shops, office space and restaurants integrated as part of the facilities. The evolution of sports facilities finds sport properties becoming more engaged in the meetings, incentives, conferences and exhibition (MICE) industries (Leask & Digance, 2002). Connections with sport clubs and memorable events gives sport facilities attractive unique selling propositions compared to competitors (Lee, Parrish & Kim, 2015).

Creating and monetizing new facility-related revenue sources have played a role in transforming the financial nature of sport. The average value of a professional sport club or franchise has skyrocketed (Badenhausen, 2016) and one of the biggest factors in individual club increases in value is a new facility or a significant upgrade of existing facility features and amenities (Alexander & Kern, 2004).

When considering a new facility or significant upgrades to an existing facility, the core capital budgeting problem applies; significant capital expenditures are required upfront that lead to increased operating revenue in the future. Improved sport facility features and amenities and increases in the expected revenue they generate come with a higher price tag. New facilities and existing facility upgrades have become more and more expensive (Rieder, 2009) and result in the need for a variety of ways in which to raise the increasing initial capital expenditure. Whether the effort is entirely financed by a private sport property or through a public–private partnership, the initial capital funding burden on sport properties has been increasing.

The purpose of this chapter is to compare and contrast two different, but similar, instruments often used to meet the increasing capital demands – the debenture in the United Kingdom (UK) and seat licences in the United States (US) – in order to understand the contextual reasons why one instrument is preferred over the other, and to explore any potential benefit for those using debentures to use seat licences, and vice versa.

While the details and terms of both debentures and seat licences differ on a case-by-case basis, both instruments typically share similar attributes: a claim to event access through the right to buy a specific seat, or seats, at face value price for a defined time period, and the right to resell both the instrument (debenture or seat licence) and tickets at a market-based price. The primary differences between the two instruments are how the funds raised are treated for tax purposes and requirements to register as a financial security. Funds raised through debentures are treated as debt to be repaid and therefore not subject to income tax, while funds raised through seat licences are not repaid and are subject to taxation.

To explore the differences between the debentures used for UK sport facility financing and the seat licences used in the United States, the chapter starts with an expansion and overview of the recent development in sport facility commercial needs and facility financing trends in North America and Europe. Next, definitions, explanations and examples of, first, personal seat licences and, second, debentures as facility finance tools are discussed. The chapter concludes with a comparison and contrast of the benefits and drawbacks of each tool in its normal context and a determination of whether we should expect to see seat licences used in the UK or debentures used in the US.

Sport facility evolution and financing trends

From the end of the Second World War until the late 1980s and early 1990s, the major sport stadiums used and constructed were basic and utilitarian in both North America and Europe. Major sport stadiums in the US were typically multi-sport venues financed and owned by local municipalities. They were not ideal for either baseball or football, but they could host both sports, as well as concerts and other outdoor activities. During the period between 1970 and 1986, 45 stadiums were built in the US, 42 of them entirely publicly financed (Keating, 1999). Stadiums had a generic look and feel as well as generic names such as Fulton County Stadium (Atlanta), Riverfront Stadium (Cincinnati), Veterans Stadium (Philadelphia) and Three Rivers Stadium (Pittsburgh). At the same time in Europe, stadiums were also utilitarian, with many being older. They featured terraces where diehard fans stood for matches and events.

Starting in the late 1980s, a modern facility-building spree began and continues to this day (Brown *et al.*, 2010). The new facilities became less utilitarian and included an increasing number of features. In Europe, the new approach was partly in response to a series of tragic stadium disasters and an overall deteriorating environment at matches during the 1980s. New and stringent FIFA and UEFA requirements, and the desire for European countries to host major international football events, also played a role (Siebold & Klingmueller, 2004). On both continents spectator tastes and expectations were changing and sports were becoming more commercialized. All-seater stadiums became the norm. Fans began to attend, not just as spectators to the competition itself, but for the experience (Siebold & Klingmueller, 2004).

New stadiums come with more space per spectator and more seating options, with distinctions between each level of seating. Offerings of premium and luxury experiences are now the norm, whether it is access to a VIP club or other special food and beverage options, private catered suites or a range of other amenities. The inventory inside the modern stadium has been transformed to both serve customers and monetize space. Static advertisements and electronic scoreboards have been replaced by animated, high definition "ribbons" that circle the inside of many stadiums, as well as larger and more technologically capable animated video boards. Modern facilities are also designed with an eye towards monetizing non-match day use, through the provision of restaurants, retail outlets, museums and stadium tours. Many new facilities are built to be ideal sites for concerts and/or to compete in the MICE industry for meetings, events, banquets and other similar engagements.

The costs of the new features are reflected in significant increases in the amount spent on new sport facilities and upgrades. Crompton, Howard and Var (2003) show that the average cost of a new facility in the US rose from US$179 million in the 1960s to US$339 million for the period between 1995 and 2003 (in constant, 2003 dollars). Komisarchik and Fenn (2010) found similar increases, with the real cost of Major League Baseball (MLB) and National Football League (NFL) stadiums built between 1995 and 2010 being twice that of those built prior to 1995.

While public–private facility funding partnerships are usual in the US, they are a relatively recent and growing phenomenon in Europe, coinciding with the addition of amenities and the accompanying increased costs. On both continents, the dynamic between major professional sports and public subsidies is one characterized by conflict between public funds supporting the provision of the public good while not tipping the scales in favour of successful commercial enterprises. A public–private stadium financing partnership often consists of a patchwork of numerous funding sources coming from various levels of government, the primary tenants of the facility, and the tenant sport club's league. A sport club's private contribution often includes pledges of contractually obligated income (naming rights, concessionaire contracts, etc.), bank loans and bond issues. The sources of funds that come directly from fans, and the subject of this chapter, are seat licences and debentures.

Seat licences

Seat licences, commonly known as personal seat licences (PSLs), have become a popular source of funding used by NFL clubs and others in North American sports. Since 1995, 15 NFL clubs have issued some sort of seat licence in order to generate funds to build a new stadium or significantly upgrade an existing stadium. The basic characteristics of a seat licence are described as a "one-time purchase of the underlying rights to a particular seat (typically in a premium location) in the stadium" (Foster, Greyser & Walsh, 2009).

Texas Stadium in Irving, Texas, the long-time home of the Dallas Cowboys, is widely considered to be the first facility to use a PSL-type instrument for construction financing. In 1968 fans purchased 40-year "seat options", which helped finance the US$35 million stadium that opened in 1971 (Foster, Greyser & Walsh, 2009; Howard & Crompton, 2004). Despite the success in Texas, it wasn't until 25 years later, at the beginning of the late twentieth century's modern stadium boom, that the then expansion Carolina Panthers issued PSLs to finance their stadium. The Panthers' effort was a great success. They sold 62,000 seat licences, raising US$125 million (Howard & Crompton, 2004). The prices ranged from US$600 to US$5,400 for individual seats (Howard & Crompton, 2004) and the seat licence sales provided the biggest portion of the funding for the US$248 million stadium that opened in 1996.

Following the Panthers' example, the popularity of PSLs as part of facility financing grew in subsequent years. By 2011, 15 NFL clubs, five MLB clubs, two National Hockey League

(NHL) clubs and one National Basketball League (NBA) club had issued PSLs (Kraus, 2011). The licences are most popular in the NFL for two reasons. First, with the limited supply of games relative to the high demand for tickets (eight regular season home games per season), the benefit of locking in ownership of season ticket rights is more valuable to fans. It is not unusual for NFL teams to have waiting lists for prospective season ticket holders. Second, the NFL shares ticket revenue to a greater degree compared to other leagues. This gives more incentive for NFL owners to structure their offerings in a way that transfers revenues from ticket purchases, which must be shared, to PSL purchases, which are not.

MLB has a 162-game schedule, so it is easier for fans to get to games during the season and the commitment of a season ticket is much higher. These elements alone make PSLs less desirable for MLB fans. However, several teams have had success in raising funds for facility construction through PSL sales by restricting PSL offerings to the most desirable seats.

The San Francisco Giants issued "Charter Seat Licences" for 13,700 seats out of the 40,930 seats available. The licences sold for prices between US$1,500 and US$7,500 giving holders a "lifetime guarantee" of the right to purchase the seats assigned to the licence (Howard & Crompton, 2004), raising US$60 million towards the cost of the primarily privately financed stadium that opened in 2000 (Kraus, 2011). As part of a public–private financing scheme for the St Louis Cardinals' 46,861-seat Busch Stadium that opened in 2006, the team sold 10,500 PSLs and raised US$40 million (Kraus, 2011).

While the basic elements of a PSL hold for all issues (an upfront payment for the right to purchase tickets to a specified seat in the future and the obligation on the PSL holder to continue to purchase the associated tickets), there are several elements of the licence that vary depending on the terms of the agreement.

The most superficial variation is the actual name of the PSL. Here, we use the convention "personal" for the 'P' in PSL, however the terms "private", "preferred" and "permanent" have also been used. As noted above, the San Francisco Giants called their PSLs "Chartered Seat Licences". Some PSLs are called "Stadium Builder's Licences" to emphasize that the revenue generated from the sale will go directly towards building the new facility and not into the team owners' pockets.

The naming convention "Permanent Seat Licences" indicates that the owner has a permanent right to continue purchasing season tickets for the seat. The PSLs, called "Stadium Builder Licences", sold by the San Francisco 49ers to help fund Levi's Stadium are for the "life of the stadium" and give holders the "first option" to purchase similar rights for a new stadium with the licensor committed to making "reasonable efforts" to offer previous PSL holders the rights to comparable seats (Terms and Conditions of Levis Stadium SBLs, n.d.).

Terms may indicate that the licence is good for however long the team is playing in the facility or they may indicate a fixed time frame. The 40-year seat options sold by the Cowboys in 1968 for Texas Stadium are an effective example. The money raised from the options was used for the stadium that served as the home of the Cowboys from 1971 until 2008. While it didn't end up covering a full 40 years, the seat options sold by the Cowboys for the stadium that opened in 2009 are good until 1 January 2039 (Cowboys Stadium, n.d.).

PSL offerings include a varying degree of transferability with some being very liberal while others are more restrictive. It is common for sport clubs to host active resale markets for PSLs on their websites. Nearly US$20 million has been exchanged on the San Francisco Giants secondary market at an average price of US$5,214 per seat (San Francisco Giants, 2017), while the Dallas Cowboys, as of this writing, list 506 licences for sale at prices ranging from US$2,475 to US$275,000 per seat (Cowboys.strmarketplace.com, 2017). To sell a Dallas Cowboys seat option, the transaction must have the permission of the licensor and include a fee paid to the club. A transfer to an "immediate family member" can be done with no fee (Cowboys Stadium, n.d.). In addition to team-hosted secondary marketplaces, numerous independent PSL marketplaces exist as well, with some even giving investment and pricing advice and outlooks.

The option to resell a seat licence can be an attractive sales feature, and even serve as an investment incentive. Most of the NFL PSLs sold in the early 2000s have increased in value, some to a significant degree. *Forbes* magazine reports that the average value of a Pittsburgh Steelers PSL was eight times the initial value 11 years after the issue. PSLs for the Baltimore Ravens (243 per cent) and Chicago Bears (131 per cent) had increased significantly as well (Alexander, 2012). The early years of more recent PSL issues for the NFLs Dallas Cowboys, the New York Jets and the New York Giants have seen their values drop, perhaps indicating an adjustment in the initial pricing to more accurately reflect demand.

While PSLs come with the obligation to purchase the associated season tickets, there is typically no guarantee or protection against future increases in the ticket prices. Perhaps due to the incentive NFL owners have to shield revenue from the league's revenue sharing, some clubs do offer discounted season ticket pricing or loyalty pricing schemes associated with their PSL holders. Looking at the bigger picture, PSL-holding season ticket holders are key players in the financial success and stability of the club, so it is wise for clubs to do all they can to make sure there is high value associated with the PSL.

Debentures

A debenture is an unsecured bond, typically used as a financial instrument in raising capital through borrowing (Fried, DeSchriver & Mondello, 2013). A bond is similar to a long-term loan where an agreement specifies repayment of principal and interest over time (Fried, DeSchriver & Mondello, 2013). Bonds guaranteed by a local government tax base or by a specifically dedicated revenue source are often used in financing facilities in North America. Debentures are commonly used in Europe to support facility funding or facility upgrades. The All England Lawn Tennis Club (AELTC) has been using debentures since 1920 (Hunter, 2010). Other sport organizations who have used debentures as part of a facility financing package are Hampshire Cricket Club (Phillips, 2013), the Rugby Football Union (RFU), the Welsh Rugby Union and the Marylebone Cricket Club. Attempts by Barclay's Premier League Clubs, West Ham United and Arsenal to use debentures met supporter resistance and were ultimately scrapped (Wilson, 2016).

For a typical (non-sport) debenture issue, the core aspects of the security are the terms of repayment plus interest offered, with investors considering market for resale in their investment calculation. While sports debentures can be re-sold and offer a range of interest incentives, the primary benefits derived from the sport debenture are access to the right to purchase in-demand tickets and access to other amenities as part of sport attendance. Some include periodic interest payments, but others do not. As an example of terms of principal payback, the AELTC offers debentures covering fixed, five-year time periods, where the principal is repaid to the debenture holder at the end of the period, and presumably a new debenture issue takes place to cover the subsequent five-year period (The All England Lawn Tennis Ground, PLC). The RFU issued 75-year non-interest-bearing debentures, meaning the debenture holders get no interest and the principal is repaid in full in 75 years. The traditional returns on a bond simply do not exist for such an issue.

What debenture holders do get are specifically defined benefits over a specifically defined period. For the AELTC, the benefits period aligns with the length of the bond; for the RFU

75-year bond, the benefits period is for the ten years from 2017 to 2027 (England Rugby, 2017). The core benefits are some combination of either the right to a ticket or tickets, or the right to purchase a ticket or tickets at face value, parking at events, access to "debenture holders only" dining and concession areas and priority options regarding future debenture issues. Debenture holders often have the legal right to re-sell unused tickets, which is something the terms of normal ticketing agreements forbid in the UK.

Assessments of sports debentures as sound investments are mixed. Some see the underlying inflation of the price of, and demand for, tickets to certain events, such as Wimbledon, as far outpacing inflation in the underlying economy. While not as liquid as a traditional bond, tickets and/or the debentures can be re-sold at a potentially strong return (Hunter, 2010). Most say that debentures are only a good investment if one enjoys the sport and the intangible returns that come with attendance. The market for tickets is volatile and while tickets listing for well over face value on secondary markets draw attention, it is also possible that they go unsold or sell at a loss (Phillips, 2013).

US seat licences versus UK debentures

At the functional core, US seat licences and UK sport debentures are similar instruments. US textbook definitions of seat licences often cite debentures as being the "European version". In both cases, sport supporters pay upfront for tickets, or the right to purchase tickets, at face value and the funds are used for capital projects like facility construction or physical upgrades. The remaining aspects of the instruments could be considered fine details. However, there are two core differences that make the instruments distinctly different; how the funds raised are treated for tax purposes and if the instrument has to be registered as an official security or not. These two differences demonstrate important distinctions between the business structures, organization and practices of sport entities between the US and UK.

Funds raised through PSLs are considered club revenue and taxed as normal income or profit. Funds raised through a debenture issue are considered capital debt and not taxed. The tax benefit of debenture issues might appeal to US sport franchises as a means to decrease a tax burden associated with a PSL offering. Those issuing sport debentures in the UK would likely have increased tax burdens reducing the net capital raised if they shifted their debenture issues to PSL issues. While the favourable tax treatment of debenture funds compared to PSL funds is attractive in both the US and the UK, the US Internal Revenue System tax laws allow professional sports team owners to amortize and depreciate 100 per cent of the initial purchase price of the franchise over a 15-year period (Gardner, 2014). Because of this favourable tax treatment in the US, all things being equal, the tax benefit is less valuable.

The second key difference is whether or not the instrument has to be registered as a security. PSLs do not have to be registered as securities and the US Securities and Exchange Commission (SEC) treats them as outside of the investment realm. Levengood (2004) argues that PSLs could be treated as securities and thus be required to be registered with the SEC but that has not happened. Debentures sold to the public do require official registration under the United Kingdom Listing Authority and directive 2003/71/EC under European Union Law (Delgado & Morris, 2015) and would similarly require registration with the SEC in the US.

In practice, US PSL holders and UK sports debenture holders can gain financial benefits in the same ways; by re-selling their tickets and licences on the open market at a profit. While the term "investment", warnings of risk and recommendations to consult with a financial advisor are common in UK sport debenture documentation, the language of PSLs is clearly not investment oriented. PSL terms and conditions terminology is distinctly written in "consumer product" rather than "investment product" language. PSL holders get the right to buy seats and other amenities. Regarding re-sale and transferability, terms generally have provisions requiring club approval. If the club provides a re-sale platform for PSL holders, language indicates that it is provided as a service.

A requirement to register a debenture as a security is a significant detriment to professional sport franchise owners in the US. Nearly all clubs are privately owned and all major leagues require approval of the other league owners for a franchise sale to be completed. The impetus behind this is that the team owners see themselves as partners in closed leagues and see new owners as new partners. They are wary of public, corporate ownership of sports clubs and the potential of unwanted partners in ownership which that may bring.

The NFL has banned all corporate ownership for decades (Kaplan, 1998). One benefit of private ownership is that there are no requirements under US law for private entities to publicly disclose their financial details. With the closed league model in the US, owners find it beneficial to keep their overall finances private. It is easier for clubs to seek public assistance for facility funding, or to position ownership in collective bargaining negotiations with player unions, if the public is unaware of the financial conditions of the franchises.

In the UK and Europe, sport properties are typically public entities required to publicly report financial information. Ownership–athlete collective bargaining is not a prominent feature of the sport landscape and there is rarely a threat that a sports club or property will change locations in search of public funding support. When financial disclosure is already a required practice, it is removed as a disadvantage of issuing a debenture.

Conclusion

PSLs in the US and sport debentures in the UK share many functional similarities and the technicalities that make them different can seem superficial at first glance. However, on deeper examination, the differences between the two instruments are characteristic of the core differences in the business structure and organization in professional sport between the US and Europe. Debentures offer tax benefits that PSLs do not, but are debt and must be paid back (although payback dates can be so far into the future that the debt is irrelevant). While PSLs are widely used in the US, debentures are less popular in Europe as there have been instances of supporter resistance against the idea of paying money for the right to purchase tickets. Instances of PSLs being issued in Europe are rare or nonexistent.

Why are PSLs popular in the US? The legal treatment of PSLs as not being securities and not having to pay back debt makes them preferable to debentures. The reasons they are preferable are grounded in the core differences between the North American and European professional sport models. Keeping finances private gives US sports owners leverage in negotiations with both cities and professional athlete labour unions. The closed league model limits both the number of franchises available for cities, which creates competition among cities to host teams, and restricts the number of playing opportunities for athletes. This gives NFL owners an advantage over its players that Barclays Premier League clubs do not have. Public disclosure of finances would reduce the leverage US professional sports owners have in negotiations with cities and with players.

In the European open league model, the incentive to keep finances private does not exist to the extent that it does in the US. Cities already have clubs that can gain entry into the top leagues through performance on the pitch. There is no need to lure clubs away from another town, when it would be preferable to build up the club that is already there. The player–ownership relationship that exists in the US, where top players have few equivalent alternatives, does not exist in Europe to the same extent. Since those club–city and owner–athlete relationships exist on different terms in the European sport model, the motivation to keep finances private is lower than it is in the US. Ultimately, if this type of PSL/debenture capital fundraising tool gains more traction in Europe, it will be likely to continue in the formally registered debenture form, which gives issuers wide ranges of terms they can use to attract investors and delay repayment. In the US, PSLs are the well-established norm and the tax benefits of debentures seem to be overshadowed by the benefits of PSLs not being treated as a security. It is unlikely that debentures will replace PSLs, with the possible exception of publicly traded sport properties such as motorsport facility operators Dover Motorsports, Inc., the International Speedway Corporation and Speedway Motorsports, Inc. As publicly traded companies, they are already required to release financial information.

References

Alexander, D. (2012). "NFL PSLs have become very risky investments". *Forbes*. Retrieved from <www.forbes.com/sites/danalexander/2012/09/05/nfl-psls-have-become-very-risky-investments/#77becb333672>. Accessed 19 March 2017.

Alexander, D. & Kern, W. (2004). The economic determinants of professional sports franchise values. *Journal of Sports Economics*, 5(1), 51–66.

All England Lawn Tennis Ground, PLC, No. 1 Court Debenture Issue, 2017–2021. Available from <www.aeltc.com/debentures>.

Badenhausen, K. (2016). "Dallas Cowboys head the world's 50 most valuable sports teams of 2016". *Forbes*. Retrieved from <www.forbes.com/sites/kurtbadenhausen/2016/07/13/dallas-cowboys-head-the-worlds-50-most-valuable-sports-teams-of-2016/#3e2e186ff330>. Accessed 19 March 2017.

Brown, M., Rascher, D., Nagel, M. & McEvoy, C. (2010). *Financial Management in the Sport Industry* (1st edn). Scottsdale, Arizona: Holcomb Hathaway.

Cowboys Stadium (n.d.). *Cowboys Stadium Seat Option Agreement*.

Cowboys.strmarketplace.com (2017). Dallas Cowboys Seat Option Marketplace Buy & Sell Cowboys Seat Options. Retrieved from <https://cowboys.strmarketplace.com/> Accessed 28 February 2017.

Crompton, J., Howard, D. & Var, T. (2003). Financing major league facilities: Status, evolution and conflicting forces. *Journal of Sport Management*, 17(2), 156–184.

Delgado, A. & Morris, T. (2015). Debt capital markets in UK (England and Wales): Regulatory overview. Retrieved from <http://global.practicallaw.com/7-525-4130>. Accessed 20 March 2017.

England Rugby (2017). Rugby Football Union 75 year debentures. Retrieved from <www.englandrugby.com/mm/Document/General/General/01/31/99/80/DebentureTermsandConditions2017Series FINAL_English.pdf>. Accessed 19 March 2017.

Foster, G., Greyser, S. & Walsh, B. (2009). *The Business of Sports* (1st edn). Australia: South-Western Cengage Learning, p. 413.

Fried, G., DeSchriver, T. & Mondello, M. (2013). *Sport Finance* (1st edn). Leeds: Human Kinetics.

Gardner, M. (2014). Obscure law allows wealthy professional sports team owners to reap tax windfalls. *Tax Justice Blog*. Retrieved from <www.taxjusticeblog.org/archive/2014/10/how_overvaluing_professional_s.php#.WM8pEm996M9>. Accessed 20 March 2017.

Howard, D. & Crompton, J. (2004). *Financing Sport* (2nd edn). Morgantown, West Virginia: Fitness Information Technology, pp. 287–289.

Hunter, G. (2010). "Strike it rich with a sporting debenture?". The *Telegraph*. Retrieved from <www.telegraph.co.uk/finance/personalfinance/investing/7593251/Strike-it-rich-with-a-sporting-debenture.html>. Accessed 19 March 2017.

Kaplan, D. (1998). NFL ban on corporate owners likely to remain in place – for the time being. *Sports Business Journal*. Retrieved from <www.sportsbusinessdaily.com/Journal/Issues/1998/12/19981228/No-Topic-Name/NFL-Ban-On-Corporate-Owners-Likely-To-Remain-In-Place-151-For-The-Time-Being.aspx>. Accessed 20 March 2017.

Keating, R. (1999). Sports pork: The costly relationship between major league sports and government. *Policy Analysis* (339), 5–8. Retrieved from <https://object.cato.org/sites/cato.org/files/pubs/pdf/pa339.pdf?q=new-giants-stadium>. Accessed 19 March 2017.

Komisarchik, M. & Fenn, A. (2010). Trends in stadium and arena construction, 1995–2016. *SSRN Electronic Journal*. Retrieved from <https://papers.ssrn.com/sol3/papers.cfm?abstract_id=2844807>. Accessed 19 March 2017.

Kraus, J. (2011). Permanent Seat Licences. In *The Encyclopedia of Sport Management and Marketing* (1st edn). Thousand Oaks, California: Sage, pp. 1098–1099.

Leask, A. & Digance, J. (2002). Exploiting unused capacity. *Journal of Convention & Exhibition Management*, *3*(4), 17–35.

Lee, S., Parrish, C. & Kim, J. (2015). Sports stadiums as meeting and corporate/social event venues: A perspective from meeting/event planners and sport facility administrators. *Journal of Quality Assurance in Hospitality & Tourism*, *16*(2), 164–180.

Levengood, M. (2004). Unregistered securities in the National Football League: Can the Securities Act of 1933 protect season ticket holders and personal seat license holders. *Jeffrey S. Moorad Sports Law Journal*, *11*(2), 411–443.

Phillips, L. (2013). "Is investing in debentures a good idea?" The *Guardian*. Retrieved from <www.theguardian.com/money/2013/aug/15/investing-debentures-good-idea>. Accessed 19 March 2017.

Rieder, N. (2009). An analysis of sports facilities cost and development from 1989–2009. National Sports Law Institute of Marquette University Law School, pp. 1–16. Retrieved from <https://law.marquette.edu/assets/sports-law/pdf/sports-facility-reports/v10-sports-facility-costs.pdf>. Accessed 19 March 2017.

San Francisco Giants (2017). *Giants Seat Licence Marketplace – Sales Data*. Available from <sfgiants.seasonticketrights.com/Charter-Seat-Licenses-Sales-Data.aspx>.

Siebold, M. & Klingmueller, A. (2004). Sport facility financing development trends in Europe and Germany 2003. *Marquette Sports Law Review*, *15*(1), 76–77.

Terms and Conditions of Levis Stadium SBLs. (n.d.). Terms and Conditions of Levis Stadium SBLs. Retrieved from <http://levisstadium.strmarketplace.com/Images/library/Levis-Stadium/Terms_and_Conditions_Levis_Stadium_SBLs.pdf>. Accessed 19 March 2017.

Wilson, B. (2016). Paying to get the best seats in the sport stadium – BBC News. *BBC News*. Retrieved from <www.bbc.com/news/business-35763131>. Accessed 20 March 2017.

14

THE DIRECT ECONOMIC IMPACT OF INTERNATIONAL SPORT EVENTS FOR THE HOSTING CITY

Osmo Laitila and Noud van Herpen

Introduction

Cities and communities around the world are aware of the different possibilities and benefits that may stem from hosting an international sport event. Such events provide a platform for cities to pursue positive effects and financial growth despite history indicating that hosting sport events, especially mega and major sport events, does not generate only positive outcomes and impacts for communities. One common argument used to justify hosting and investing in sport events is the economic surplus and social welfare generated by the people and organizations that take part in the event in multiple different roles and forms.

Impacts generated by sport events appear in many ways, such as economic impacts, tourism and visitor impacts, social impacts, customer and visitor satisfaction, promotional value and brand image impacts, participation and cohesion, environmental impacts and effects on the lifestyle and vitality of the surrounding community. In this chapter, the direct economic impact generated by three international sport events organized in Finland and the Netherlands are assessed. The magnitude of the studied events can be estimated as medium-sized international sport events, with two of them being World Championships tournaments and the other a World Championships race.

Conducting event impact research is a complicated process which includes numerous phases and viewpoints. From policymakers' perspectives, surveying the benefits and disadvantages generated by sport events provides facts to endorse the very fundamental question in event bidding: to host or not to host. Presenting this question before the event, in time for bidding, requires projections and estimations of the possible event impact outcomes. The actual impact can be measured for the most part during and after the event, and its main purpose is to provide firsthand information for policymakers, organizers and partners, and the citizens, concerning the benefits of the event in perspective with the investments.

The basic rationale behind economic impact

The fundamental rationale behind economic impact is explained by Crompton, Lee and Shuster (2001), and illustrated in Figure 14.1. The rationale is based on a cycle where residents of the community pay funds to their city council in the form of taxes. The city council

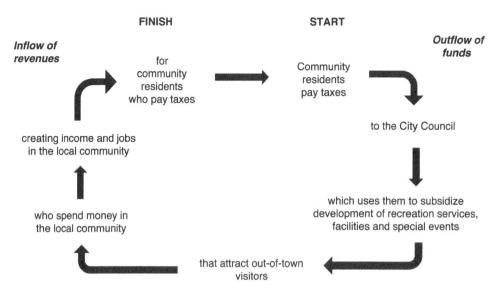

Figure 14.1 The conceptual rationale for undertaking economic impact studies (based on Crompton, Lee & Shuster, 2001)

uses a certain proportion of the citizens' funds to subsidize production of an event or to put towards the development of facilities and infrastructure. The event organized in the city or municipality attracts non-resident visitors to the area who spend money in the local community both inside and outside the event venue upon their visit. This new money from outside the community creates income and benefits for residents in the form of employment, new jobs and household income. The cycle is complete when the residents get a return on their investment through production of an event or development of a facility (Crompton, Lee & Shuster, 2001).

Crompton, Lee and Shuster (2001) add that the key purpose of economic impact studies is to measure the economic return to residents, and the main function of economic impact studies is to measure and estimate the magnitude of the return on the community.

The economic impact of sport events

The economic effects of sport events emerge in multiple different forms. Kasimati (2003) states that the economic effect occurs when hosting a sport event generates an inflow of funds to the local, regional and national economy which, most likely, would not have entered the economy without the hosting of the event. This stream of new money is spent by event stakeholders and participants such as broadcasters, sponsors, athletes and non-local event visitors and spectators who are referred to as tourists. Another definition, originally by Lieber and Alton (1983), states that the economic impact can be described as the net change in an economy that is a result of the sport event. The change within the economy is caused by the acquisition, operation, development and use of sport facilities and services (Crompton, 1995; Kasimati, 2003; Lee, 2008).

The evaluation of the total economic impact of sport events can be divided into three different levels. The first stage in studying the impact is to investigate the direct consumption generated by the non-local event visitors who visit the host region because of the event and inject a new inflow of money to the host economy services, such as accommodation, transportation and food. This is called direct economic impact. The second phase in total economic impact assessment includes the use of multipliers. Multipliers basically estimate how the initial direct economic impact generated, due to hosting the sport event, benefits the local economy after the direct consumption has stopped. The purpose of the indirect economic impact and induced economic impact is to investigate the value of post-event subsequent effects of the injected money (indirect economic impact) as well as the proportion of extra income consumed in businesses within the economy (induced effect) (Kasimati, 2003). The indirect and induced effects together are collectively referred to as secondary economic impact (Crompton, Lee & Schuster, 2001).

The three most often used economic impact multipliers are the sales or transactions multiplier, the household income multiplier and the employment multiplier (Kasimati, 2003). An analysis of the total economic impact can be easily exaggerated due to the use of inaccurate or false multipliers. In many cases, the reasons behind over-estimated secondary impact assessments are a lack of proper and reliable primary impact data, a lack of information concerning the local economy to create a valid multiplier, and the fact that multipliers are often borrowed from other industries or economies instead of being built according to the specific conditions of the economy under review (Gratton, Shibli & Coleman, 2006). Additionally, one problematic issue that comes from using multipliers is that it is almost impossible to make reliable fact-based estimations of how much of the primary inflow of money spent in the economy generated by the event participation is re-spent in the region by the businesses and households. In this chapter, research on economic impact focuses only on primary economic impact, and secondary economic impact is excluded from the results and conclusions.

Direct economic impact

In general, the challenge in comparing and estimating the validity of economic impact studies is that the research is often conducted applying different methodologies and data collection procedures. This leads to a situation where the study results are controversial. Preuss (2011) explains that one of the top challenges in economic impact studies is the insufficient knowledge and information about the consumption patterns of the event visitors and residents, and the absence of any reliable estimation of the number of people visiting the event. The economic impact caused by the events are short-term impulses that are mainly caused by consumption. An important factor in estimating the overall economic impact is to understand the number of event visitors and to take the crowding-out effect, the number of people avoiding the event, into account as a negative effect of the event. To study economic impact thoroughly, Preuss presents a bottom-up approach in studying the different event stake-holders. Defining individual consumption patterns, the number of nights' accommodation, visitors' motivation to visit the event as well as the gross number of visitors, are crucial aspects in economic impact evaluation (Preuss, 2007; 2011).

According to Preuss (2005) there are ten groups of event-affected persons to be recognized, as illustrated in Figure 14.2. The model identifies four groups that can be described as event-affected persons who do not stay in or enter the region due to the event. These groups are Runaways, Changers, and Avoiders (split into Cancellers and Pre/Post Switchers). Groups such as Home Stayers, Event Visitors, and Extentioners are the event-affected persons who contribute positively to the actual event impact by spending money on their visit to the event whereas the Runaways and Avoiders generate negative economic effects to the region

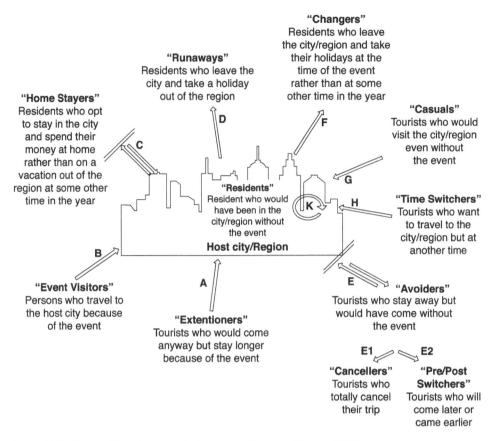

"Changers"
Residents who leave
the city/region and take
their holidays at the
time of the event
rather than at some
other time in the year

"Runaways"
Residents who leave the
city and take a holiday
out of the region

"Home Stayers"
Residents who opt
to stay in the city
and spend their
money at home
rather than on a
vacation out of the
region at some other
time in the year

"Casuals"
Tourists who would
visit the city/region
even without
the event

"Residents"
Resident who would
have been in the
city/region without
the event

Host city/Region

"Time Switchers"
Tourists who want
to travel to the
city/region but at
another time

"Event Visitors"
Persons who travel to
the host city because
of the event

"Extentioners"
Tourists who would come
anyway but stay longer
because of the event

"Avoiders"
Tourists who stay away but
would have come without
the event

"Cancellers"
Tourists who
totally cancel
their trip

**"Pre/Post
Switchers"**
Tourists who will
come later or
came earlier

Figure 14.2   Event-affected persons during events (based on Preuss, 2005)

(Preuss, 2005). Studying and measuring the negative economic impact of the Runaways and Avoiders is very challenging because it is difficult to estimate their numbers reliably.

The results in this chapter focus on direct economic impact – the crowding-out effect was not profoundly studied. The crowding-out in the Neste Oil Rally Finland 2013 was estimated to be similar to a normal weekend during the busiest summer holidays. In the Netherlands, crowding-out was estimated by comparing hotel accommodation availability and there was no reason to assume a significant crowding-out effect.

Economic impacts in sport in practice

Sport events are temporal by nature and can act as a trigger for multiple different short-term and long-term, positive or negative impacts. This chapter discusses internationally big events that are significantly smaller in size, scale, scope and reach than mega-events. However, non-mega sport events can be spectator and participant events, single-sport and multi-sport events, as well as one-day or multi-day events attracting local residents and visitors, and are hosted in different cities around the globe (Taks, Green, Misener & Chalip, 2014).

The three international sport events studied in this chapter are the Neste Oil Rally Finland World Rally Championship (WRC) race in 2013, hosted in the city of Jyväskylä, the Rabobank Hockey World Cup 2014, hosted in the city of The Hague and the Beach Volleyball World

Championships 2015, hosted partly in the city of The Hague. These events were chosen because they differ in the number of participants and spectators, the duration of the event and in terms of location (across the country, different cities, one city), the spectator profile (national and international, local and non-local) and in terms of whether the events are hosted annually or not. Regardless of the differences between these events, all could be described as medium-sized international sport events and their impact on the hosting city is of interest.

The studied international events

The Neste Oil Rally Finland is one of the World Rally Championship events driven around the world every year. It is one of the biggest annual sporting events in Finland. The history of the Neste Oil Rally Finland goes back to 1951 when the first edition of Rally Finland was organized. Officially, Neste Oil Rally Finland has been part of the World Rally Championships since 1973. Today the Neste Oil Rally Finland is a highly appreciated event among the drivers and rally fans, and is particularly famous for its fast gravel routes, impressive jumps and lake scenes in the middle of forests. The rally is extremely challenging for the drivers and co-drivers, as well as very attractive for spectators as huge crowds follow the action at the many special stages and at the rally Service Park located in the city of Jyväskylä. The Neste Oil Rally is driven annually at the end of July and lasts for three to four days.

The Rabobank Hockey World Cup is an international field hockey competition organized by the International Hockey Federation (FIH). The tournament began in 1971 and is held every four years, bridging the four years between the Summer Olympics. There is also a Women's Hockey World Cup, which has been held since 1974 and was organized by the International Federation of Women's Hockey Associations (IFWHA) until 1981, when the governing bodies merged into the current International Hockey Federation in 1982. The 2014 tournament was held in The Hague, Netherlands from 2 to 14 June.

The FIVB Beach Volleyball World Championships (senior men and women's tournaments) are the blue-ribbon FIVB-sanctioned events currently held every two (odd) years. The first was organized in Brazil in 1987 and was exported in 1997 to the USA (UCLA in Los Angeles), other tournaments were mainly held in Europe, and the 2015 Beach Volleyball World Championships were organized in the Netherlands from 26 June to 5 July. The tournament was held in four cities of which The Hague was the main venue, hosting the opening, the semi-finals and the finals. A temporary stadium, which had the city's parliament building as its backdrop, was constructed for the duration of the World Championships – a floating stadium on the "The Hofvijver" (Court Pond). The stadium seated 5,260 spectators and was the largest of the four World Championship venues (Amsterdam, Rotterdam, Apeldoorn and The Hague).

Methods

Research methodology used in the three studies presented in this chapter follows similar outlines and structures in each event. Preuss (2005) mentioned that Home Stayers, Event Visitors and Extentioners are the groups that contribute to the economic benefits. In the presented events, the direct economic impact is mainly generated by four different sub-groups of event visitors. First, the most essential group is spectators who come to visit the region outside the hosting city. Second, there are sports participants including athletes, coaches and team and/or athlete staff members. Third, there are the broadcasting personnel and media representatives such as journalists, producers and broadcasting staff. Finally, the fourth sub-group of event visitors are the persons who take part in the event as a part of the organizing committee, such as volunteers and event staff members. The first three groups were assessed by taking a survey and the fourth group, the event organizer, was interviewed for an insight concerning its expenditures.

Spectators were interviewed during the event using tablets and structured questionnaires. The time of the event, preferably after the initial few days, is the most convenient time to reach the target group for interview. Tablets were synchronized with the Webropol online survey or comparable software, which allows monitoring of the collected sample online and, if necessary, adjustment of the data collection according to the observations of the event population made at the time to fit the sample as well as possible. In addition to spectator interviews, VIP guests, sports participants and team members and, in case of the Rabobank Hockey World Cup and Beach Volleyball World Championships, the media representatives were also interviewed during the event. In the case of the Neste Oil Rally Finland, media representatives were surveyed shortly after the event since the event organizer could provide detailed email information about the accredited media.

Conducting event impact interviews onsite requires defining the exact data collection environment in order to ensure the validity of the data. In the cases here, the interviews were mostly completed in an area where interviewees were required to have a ticket or other equivalent access to the area. Respondents participating in the Neste Oil Rally Finland were interviewed at the closed special stages and inside the Rally Service Park. In the events held in the Netherlands, the spectators' data collection was conducted inside or around the venues. VIP guests were interviewed inside VIP areas.

Interviews were conducted by specially trained research fieldworkers. Respondents were randomly selected from the event population following the main principle that every tenth spectator was chosen to be approached for an interview. Field researchers were instructed to conduct interviews with persons who were at least 18 years old, participating in the event as a spectator and who could complete the questionnaire without difficulty. Questionnaires were available in English as well as in the native languages of Dutch and Finnish. Questions and survey metrics were developed based on the previous impact studies conducted, as well as a review of relevant literature. Especially important sources for designing this study concept were Preuss' (2005) study of the economic impact of visitors at major multi-sport events and Preuss' (2007) study of the conceptualization and measurement of legacies.

The data sample collected in the WRC Neste Oil Rally Finland was constructed from 1,121 responses, of which 115 were from athletes and rally team members, 968 were from spectators or VIP guests and 38 were from media representatives. The sample collected at the Rabobank Hockey World Cup consisted of 1,863 responses in total, and for the FIVB Beach Volleyball World Championships the number of completed surveys totalled 934. Deviation across different groups was comparable to the Rally event and corresponded well with actual numbers in each group.

The essential part of conducting economic impact studies is to understand the number of individuals participating in the event in different roles. The number of individuals is different from the number of event visits, and was estimated based on sold tickets and the collected data. The exact number of VIP guests, athletes and teams, as well as accredited media representatives, was given by the organizer, which improved the validity of the evaluation.

Results

The duration of the events ranged from three to 15 days and varied from venues with one-location city centre stadiums to special stages organized in multiple locations as far as

Table 14.1 Summary of the background information of the studied events

	WRC Rally	*WC Field Hockey*	*WC Beach Volleyball*
Number of competition days	3	15	10
Location	Headquarters in the city of Jyväskylä – 23 stages	Kyocera Stadium outside city centre	4 cities – stadium inside city centre
Number of individual visitors	Not published by the organizer	240,000	98,000 in total – 43,000 in The Hague
Male/Female	76–24%	56–44%	62–38%
Age (average)	35	42	39
Percentage of foreigners	8%	18%	7%
Percentage of locals	37% (central Finland)	11%	34%
Percentage from host country but not host city/region	55%	71%	59%

200 kilometres outside the organizing city. All three events can be considered as medium-sized when looking at the number of total event visits and the number of individual visitors. In all three events there were more men than women, with Rally being the event consisting of most males whereas in the Rabobank Hockey World Cup the distribution of men and women was close to even. The average age of the spectators varied from 35 to 42, but it must be considered that people under the age of 18 were not asked to fill out questionnaires, so the actual average age of the events population was lower. The Rabobank Hockey World Cup was the most international event with 18 per cent of all visitors coming from outside the Netherlands. In addition, the percentage of visits from people outside the host region, in this case the city of The Hague, was relatively high.

When the three events are compared, it is obvious that food and beverages were the main items on which people spent money. Furthermore, people who stayed overnight obviously spent a notable share of their total consumption on accommodation. Other expenses such as merchandise, public transport and shopping in the city were usually a smaller part of the total visitor expenditure. The organizing body should therefore focus on the possibility of the spectators buying food and beverages, as well as attracting people from long distances who are more likely to stay overnight – first, because they spent money on accommodation, but also because they spent more money on food and beverages. This is because they stay longer and therefore there is simply more demand for food and beverages. Overnight stayers also spent more money on souvenirs and official merchandise. Furthermore, it was clear that foreigners, on average, spent more money than national visitors. This makes foreign visitors a very important group of event participants from the economic impact leverage point of view.

Direct economic impact

In the Neste Oil Rally Finland 2013 the overall amount of consumption that survey participants spent on the host city and the surrounding region was €14.7 million, as shown in Table 14.2. Excluding the consumption generated by residents, the estimated surplus generated by event visitors outside the region was €13.7 million. Furthermore, the direct

Table 14.2 Direct economic impact on Jyväskylä region of the Neste Oil Rally Finland 2013

Group of participants	Consumption in the region (million Euros)
Spectators outside the region	€10.5
Spectators from the region (residents)	€0.8
VIP guests outside the region	€1.3
VIP guests from the region (residents)	€0.2
Teams	€0.7
Media	€0.2
Organizer	€1.0
Total expenditure	€14.7
Total direct economic impact (excluding residents)	€13.7

investments of the local municipality should be counted as a negative direct economic effect, which then sets the total direct net impact at €13.5 million. This is remarkable since the event is medium-sized, and the municipality is relatively small as there are slightly less than 140,000 inhabitants in the city area and 180,000 including the surrounding region. Total consumption, including ticket sales and rally merchandise, which were not counted as having direct economic impacts on the host region because the rally organizer was not based in Jyväskylä, was €17.0 million.

To compare, Table 14.3 illustrates an overview of the total economic impact of the Rabobank Hockey World Cup 2014. The total economic impact, after deducting the organizational costs, was approximately €12.0 million. Results also show that the event visitors made the most significant contribution to the economic impact. This is mainly explained by the spending they did during the day and the overnight stays. Event visitors provided a very notable positive contribution to the overall economic impact.

Table 14.3 Direct economic impact on The Hague of the Field Hockey World Cup 2014

	Group of participants	Consumption in the The Hague (million Euros)
Day expenditure	Event visitors	€6.3
	VIP guests	€0.2
	Participants	€1.5
	Media	€0.2
Accommodation costs	Event visitors	€3.5
	VIP guests	€0.1
	Participants	€0.4
Staying in the region after event	Event visitors	€2.0
	VIP guests	€0.03
Total		€14.23
Organizational costs		−€2.4
Total economic impact		€11.83

The direct economic impact generated by the visitors of the Beach Volleyball World Championships in 2015 in The Hague amounts to €0.6 million and is illustrated in Table 14.4.

Table 14.4 Direct economic impact on The Hague of the Beach Volleyball World Championships

Event visitors	Consumption in The Hague (million Euros)
Spectator day expenditure	€0.5
Accommodation costs	€0.1
Direct economic impact	€0.6

For additional visitors, this is the highest economic impact of the four host cities. Amsterdam follows with €0.5 million and Rotterdam and Apeldoorn gained €0.1 million.

In this particular case the organizing committee took care of the VIPs and media so their impact is accounted for in the economic impact of the organizing committee. Their net balance was negative for the city of The Hague with an amount of €0.4 million. The organizing committee received more money from inside the city boundaries than they spent in the city. The money that came from the city was mainly city council funding, proceeds from tickets bought by local residents and donations from a big city sponsor. This was €1.8 million in total, which means that the organizing committee spent €1.4 million, again within the city borders. If this €0.4 million is subtracted from the €0.6 million that was spent by the visitors, the direct economic impact accounted for €0.2 million.

Maximizing the economic benefits of hosting medium-sized international sport events

The differences in direct economic impact between the three events are remarkably high, ranging from €0.2 million at the Beach Volleyball World Championships to almost €14 million at the WRC Neste Oil Rally Finland. A key factor that plays an important role in generating direct economic impact is the number of non-local visitors attending the event but this alone does not explain the major differences in direct economic impacts between events. Explanations for differences can be found in visitor profiles, consumption patterns and event locations referring to the distances between event sites and city services.

Foreigners stay longer at the event and, in many cases, arrive well before the event starts. Foreign visitors stay overnight and spend more money per day and during their entire visit. Facilitating services for event visitors and understanding their motives for participation and needs for services during their stay is highly relevant for maximizing the consumption and the direct economic impact. With modern customer analytics and a customer relationship management mindset the desired service concepts and new business opportunities can be managed more efficiently and in a customer-oriented manner. Proper event visitor management requires cooperation between businesses and a broader strategic approach and planning to maximize the benefits for the event-affected persons, and for the community in return.

People staying overnight spend more money than day visitors even after subtracting the money spent on accommodation. Overnight visitors often create more demand for different services compared to the day visitors. Also, hosting an event in different cities will result in a behaviour where the locals may choose to visit the event in their own region instead of travelling to one single host city. In these cases, there are fewer non-local event visitors and more residents and people who would already have been in the area of interest. On the other hand, organizing an event in multiple locations may lower the threshold for taking part in the event as it may be more accessible due to the shorter geographical distance, and therefore add to the vitality and activity among locals.

The location of the event is one important aspect especially when talking about the possibilities for spending money. If a good event location is chosen, such as the city centre, it is possible to create more opportunities for consumption, such as restaurant services, especially for non-local event visitors. The number and quality of restaurants, bars and shops should be high and easily accessible as the event visitors' consumption patterns indicate that a significant amount of money is spent on food and beverages.

The region of interest (city versus region) of the event plays a notable role when calculating the direct economic impact. Increasing the region of interest leads to a situation where more money is spent inside the region but also the number of "residents" and "casuals" (see Figure 14.2) increases. The duration of the event also has a significant effect on the direct economic impact as the longer the event, the higher the economic impact. When comparing events, both factors should be accounted for.

Understanding the event population as well as collecting a valid sample of primary data, including the motives for event participation, is one of the most crucial aspects in successful event impact estimation. The population must be estimated more precisely than just by referring to the amount of tickets sold. Surveying the demographics of the population, such as the distribution of males, females and children, provides important facts to support the valid estimation of the population and also limits the risk of exaggeration in results.

The size of the event influences the positive and negative economic impacts. From the economic point of view, mega and major sport events generate more positive and yet more negative impacts compared to international medium-sized sport events. Smaller international sport events may benefit the local economy relatively more efficiently from the net benefit point of view since these events may rely more heavily on local resources (Taks *et al.*, 2014). Often the investments required to stage medium-sized sport events are significantly lower and the event organizer takes advantage of the existing infrastructure.

Maximizing the positive economic impact is always a result of excellent event management, where sports' rights holders, the event organizer, the hosting community and municipality, together with local businesses, fit together and create strategic goals to improve the event quality, and create value for event visitors starting from the point where a visitor leaves his/her home until the time he/she returns from the event. The success of the sport event is not measured just by the quality of the team or athletes' performance, but by a combination of the level of the sport and the quality of the value chain designed for visitors. Understanding the event visitors' motives for participation, satisfaction and experiences, consumption patterns, detailed visitor profiles and behaviour patterns in general, offers the tools and means for event stakeholders to plan activities that can potentially maximize the benefits of hosting sport events.

Conclusion

Measuring direct economic impact is an important tool in arguing for and against hosting international sport events. In this chapter, three different events have been evaluated and important elements of economic impact have been indicated. Results show that medium-sized international sport events can generate tremendous positive outcomes for the local economy if events are well managed and all the factors affecting the creation of economic impact are recognized. As mentioned earlier, the direct economic impact ranged from €0.2 million to €14 million for the host city and region. Even though the impact of the Beach Volleyball World Championships was significantly lower in comparison to the other events, the direct net impact was still positive. A factor that could explain this difference is the popularity of the sport in the host country. Beach Volleyball is a relatively new sport which became an Olympic sport in 1996 and is popular mainly in Brazil and the USA. In the Netherlands, there are around 40,000 active players. This is a fairly low number when compared to the Rabobank Hockey World Cup as the Royal Dutch Hockey Association has over 250,000 members.

Interestingly, in Finland rally drivers are amongst the most famous athletes. The parent organization AKK Motorsport, together with the regional motorsport organizations, has around 32,000 members in Finland, and compared to the population, motorsport with successful drivers is big sport in Finland. The rally event itself is one of the biggest international sporting events in Scandinavia. An event is likely to have a higher economic impact if the sport itself is more popular in the host country. Obviously, there are several reasons behind this rationale. The first argument is that the number of visitors is usually higher when the sport is widely supported. This of course increases the positive effect of the direct economic impact. Second, people are willing to travel longer distances when they are fans of a sport or a particular team. This increases the amount of money spent on travelling but, even more importantly, substantially more people from outside the region of interest come and visit the event. This has a positive effect on the economic impact. Fans are also investing more money on merchandise, for instance, when compared to first-time event visitors. The WRC Rally Finland is organized annually and the percentage of visitors who come to the event year after year is impressive as more than 80 per cent of spectators have participated in the event more than five times previously.

These hardcore fans are easy to recognize as they wear merchandise, carry flags and, in general, show their commitment to the event. The fans are followers of the sport and know everything there is to know about the drivers and the competition. At the Beach Volleyball World Championships this is totally different. For example, the rules of the game and tournament need to be explained by the event host several times. Besides spending money on merchandise, true fans are more likely to spend a longer time at an event. This can be seen by the percentage of *passe-partout* (multi-day or total event) tickets and by the average number of days/nights a visitor spends at the event. This can be partly explained by the travel distance. At the Beach Volleyball World Championships, there were three host cities. Therefore, people could choose to see the games closer to their homes and there was no need to stay overnight. As mentioned earlier, people who stayed overnight spent more money compared to day visitors.

The three events studied, and many examples shown in literature (see also Preuss, 2007, 2011; Taks *et al.*, 2014), show that international medium-sized sport events can be, if well managed, very beneficial to businesses in the host region. The benefits are particularly high because, in general, these non-mega events do not usually require big investment from the local community but generate a significant increase in consumption and direct economic impact.

References

Crompton, J. (1995). Economic impact analysis of sport facilities and events: Eleven sources of misapplication. *Journal of Sport Management, 9*(1), 14–35.

Crompton, J., Lee, S. & Shuster, T. (2001). A guide for undertaking economic impact studies: The Springfest example. *Journal of Travel Research, 40*(1), August 2001, 79–87.

Gratton, C., Shibli, S. & Coleman, R. (2006). The economic impact of major sport events: A review of ten events in the UK. *The Sociological Review, 54*(2), 41–58. Available at <http://onlinelibrary.wiley.com/doi/10.1111/j.1467-954X.2006.00652.x/abstract>. Accessed 23 February 2017.

Kasimati, E. (2003). Economic aspects and the Summer Olympics: A review of related research. *International Journal of Tourism Research*, *5*, 433–444. Available at <http://onlinelibrary.wiley.com/doi/10.1002/jtr.449/abstract>. Accessed 27 February 2017.

Lee, S. (2008). A review of economic impact studies on sporting events. *The Sport Journal*. February 2008.

Lieber, S. R. & Alton, D. J. (1983). Visitor expenditures and the economic impact of public recreation facilities in Illinois. In S. R. Lieber and D. R. Fesenmaier (Eds), *Recreation Planning & Management*, 36–54. London: E. & F. N. Spon.

Preuss, H. (2005). The economic impact of visitors at major multi-sport events. *European Sport Management Quarterly*, *5*(3), 281–301.

Preuss, H. (2007). The conceptualization and measurement of mega sport event legacies. *Journal of Sport & Tourism*, *12*(3–4), 207–227.

Preuss, H. (2011). A method for calculating the crowding-out effect in sport mega-event impact studies: The 2010 FIFA World Cup. *Development Southern Africa*, *28*(3), 367–385.

Taks, M., Green, B. C., Misener, L. & Chalip, L. (2014). Evaluating sport development outcomes: The case of a medium-sized international sport event. *European Sport Management Quarterly*, *14*(3), 213–237.

15

MAXIMIZING REVENUE THROUGH TICKETING TECHNOLOGY

Jim Reese

Introduction

Due to recent advances in technology, ticket offices now have an opportunity to better capture revenue streams and provide a wealth of services to enhance the fan experience. However, even though these technologies currently exist, technology controversies were created when a series of ticketing issues dominated the news internationally. First, some of the most loyal fans of the Republic of Ireland football team, including many season ticket holders who make a significant investment in the team (Seiferheld, 2012), were denied tickets to the Euro 2016 qualifier match versus Scotland (Ingham, 2014; McCauley, 2014; Smith, 2014). In addition, at the 2014 Glasgow Commonwealth Games available technology did not allow fans to resell or reprint tickets if they were lost, stolen, destroyed, or not received in the mail (Ingham, 2014). As if this was not enough, the ticket office at the 2014 Glasgow Commonwealth Games did not record seat locations for the tickets issued to the games. This meant that fans who lost their tickets, had them stolen, or who never received them in the mail were left out of pocket and unable to attend the events (Ingham, 2014).

This chapter discusses how current technology may be used to solve problems such as those experienced at the 2014 Commonwealth Games and the Euro 2016 qualifier match. Other state-of-the-art ticketing technologies to enhance fan experience, and maximize revenue, are also presented. This includes the use of automatic season ticket renewals (Lombardo, 2015), purchasing and upgrading tickets through text messages (Muret; 2012, 2015; Stone, 2013), the use of ticketless systems (Fisher & Muret, 2014; "Going Paperless", 2009; Kaplan, 2014), and several pricing strategies used to maximize ticket revenue (King, 2012; Koba, 2012; Leuty, 2015; Paul & Weinbach, 2013; Rascher, McEvoy, Nagel & Brown, 2007; Rishe, 2012; Shapiro & Drayer, 2012).

Season ticket holder priority systems

Whether season ticket holders, or just those who occasionally purchase tickets to individual games, many sport fans make significant investments in their favourite college or professional sport teams (Seiferheld, 2012). These investments come in a variety of forms such as time, financial commitment, emotional attachment, etc. They also range in level from die-hard fans to those who merely watch games on television. This level of attachment, or fan identification, has a significant impact on the consumption of the sport product (Wann, 1993; Wann & Branscombe, 1990, 1993; Wann, Roberts & Tindall, 1999). Predictably, the higher the level of fan identification, the higher sport product consumption will be (Wann, 1993; Wann & Branscombe, 1990, 1993; Wann, Roberts, & Tindall, 1999). For fans with the highest levels of fan identification, it is also predictable that they will demand the highest level of customer service from the sport organization (Seiferheld, 2012). Many of these fans consider their commitment of time, money and loyalty as an investment in the team. To satisfy this level of commitment, some teams have decided to communicate better with season ticket holders. For example, the Philadelphia Eagles created a 35-person season ticket holder advisory board to meet on a monthly basis (Seiferheld, 2012). This provides the team's most loyal fans with an opportunity to provide feedback to the organization with regard to policies and business practices (Seiferheld, 2012).

Such a mindset could significantly benefit the Football Association of Ireland (FAI) financially. By treating all fans at home games like season ticket holders, and providing premium technology and services that avoid the ticketing pitfalls experienced at the Euro qualifier and the Glasgow Commonwealth Games, the FAI could minimize empty seats and maximize all potential revenue streams including concessions, merchandise sales and parking revenue.

In order to avoid the situation that occurred at the 2014 Glasgow Commonwealth Games with some of the most loyal season ticket holders of the Republic of Ireland football team, a priority system should be established for ticket distribution. This can obviously be done for home games, but should also be done for away games in order to properly serve the team's most loyal fans. In order to understand how priority would work in distributing tickets, it would be helpful to understand how a priority system works in general.

There are several ways to set up a priority system for season ticket holders of sport organizations (Reese, 2004). In summary, a priority number, or the date of account creation, is used to represent the amount of time a season ticket holder account has been active. The season tickets holders, or club members, with the longest tenure are provided with first access to tickets, and other premium services. The Scottish Football Association (Scottish FA) appears to use a priority system when distributing tickets. For home games, fans must purchase tickets to multiple games in order to have ticket access (Home Matches, 2017). For away games, the Scottish FA requires that all fans purchase a membership of their Supporters Club before gaining access to tickets (Away Matches, 2017).

For the non-season ticket holders, a rewards system could be put in place to accomplish the same goal as a priority system. This has already been implemented with success by several rival football leagues such as the Scottish FA and the English Football Association (English FA) (McCauley, 2014). Simply stated, fans receive points based on a variety of preset consumption variables that may be tracked such as attendance, parking, concessions, merchandise and so on. Once season ticket holders have been serviced, any remaining tickets may be offered to non-season ticket holders with the highest rewards points. If such a system had been in place for the FAI at the Euro 2016 qualifier, they could have avoided an incredible amount of embarrassment and bad publicity (McCauley, 2014; Smith, 2014).

Priority is used for a number of functions within a ticket office. This includes such functions as seat relocation requests, ticket transfers, access to tickets to away games, access to tickets to post-season events when applicable and seating priority when relocating to a new facility (Reese, 2004).

Seat relocation requests are used when season ticket holders would like to change or improve the location of their seat(s). During the annual season ticket renewal process, seats not renewed are used for the seat relocation process. In theory, just a few seats not renewed in prime locations can trickle down to impact hundreds of fans interested in changing locations. In sport organizations with high season ticket renewal rates, seat relocations can be a slow process since few seats are turned back to the sport organization to use for seat upgrades. Most professional sport teams can expect 10 to 15 percent of their base of season ticket holders to request seat relocations each year (Spoelstra & DeLay, 2013).

Season ticket transfers occur when a season ticket holder permanently transfers the use of one or more seats to another person or business. Due to the financial impact of the secondary ticket market in areas with high ticket demand, many sport organizations only allow season tickets to be transferred to immediate family members such as children, grandchildren, spouses and siblings. The transfer process typically occurs for a designated period during off-season before season ticket invoices are generated. Issuing priority in transfer cases is simple if all seats in the account are transferred. When all seats are transferred the priority associated with the account goes to the new account holder on record. However, if all the seats are not transferred, the original priority stays with the remaining seats and the new account holder on record gets a new priority number assigned to the transferred seats. For example, imagine that a fan has six season tickets with the Denver Broncos of the National Football League (NFL). The team has 22,000 season ticket holders, each with their own priority number based on seniority, and the fan has had season tickets since 1960, which was the first year the team began playing. In this case, the best and oldest possible priority number would be #1, while the most recent would be approximately #22,000. The fan has a low priority number of 1,300, which is considered very desirable. If the fan wanted to transfer all six season tickets to his/her brother, his/her brother would receive the six seats as well as the priority number. However, what if the fan wanted to keep four seats for him/herself and transfer the remaining two seats in the account to his/her brother? In this case the priority number of 1,300 would remain with the four seats, and a new account would be created for his/her brother. The brother would receive the two seats with an account priority number of approximately 22,001. Handling transfers in this manner is the only way to ensure the integrity of the priority system.

The season ticket details in the previous paragraph can be used to see how priority would impact one's ability to secure tickets to an away game. Using an example from the NFL, but as with all policies that relate to priority, this example could easily be applied to the Republic of Ireland football team, or any other professional sport organization. Assume an individual is a Denver Broncos season ticket holder and has family in the San Diego, California area. The Broncos are playing an AFC West Division game away against the rival San Diego Chargers. The individual is interested in purchasing four tickets to the game. All NFL visiting teams receive an allocation of approximately 500 tickets for coaches, players and staff. Any unused tickets by the visiting team may be used to satisfy the needs of season ticket holders interested in tickets to away games. Requests for tickets to away games by season ticket holders are placed in order of priority. Based on demand, there may also be a limit on the number of tickets available to each season ticket holder. A limit of two to four tickets allows as many people as possible to have access to tickets. Tickets are distributed based on priority until the demand is satisfied or until tickets run out. If any tickets remain after taking care of Broncos season ticket requests they are returned to the San Diego Chargers to be made available to their own fans.

Post-season tickets to NFL games would be distributed in a similar way. For home games, season ticket holders have first right of refusal to purchase their existing seats for playoff games. Remaining tickets are made available to the general public on a first come, first served basis. However, for games at a neutral site, such as the Super Bowl, season ticket holder priority is again used since the demand for tickets far exceeds the available supply. According to the NFL, each of the two teams participating in the Super Bowl receives 17.5 percent of the tickets (Brown, 2014). A certain percentage of those tickets are allocated to season ticket holders of each respective team based on a lottery weighted by priority. The higher the season ticket holder's priority, the better chance they have to be selected to purchase a pair of Super Bowl tickets. Regardless of the number of season tickets a fan may have, each season ticket holder selected to receive tickets in the lottery may only purchase two Super Bowl tickets. As in the example used in the distribution of away game tickets, this ensures the maximum numbers of fans are able to receive tickets.

If this same logic is applied to the situation the FAI faced when distributing tickets for the 2016 Euro qualifier in Scotland, it is clear they could have handled the situation much better. From a demand perspective, the NFL post-season and the 2016 Euro qualifiers are very similar. The demand for tickets far exceeds the available supply. In such cases, the only fair way to distribute tickets fairly is to reward those who are most loyal to your organization first, the long-time season ticket holders. This did not happen with the FAI since no points or priority system was in place (McCauley, 2014). Although loyalty with sport fans runs deep, no sport organization wants to alienate their most passionate fans because every fan has their limit in regard to poor customer service. Sport organizations should be looking to build upon their fan base from generation to generation, not to alienate it. The FAI should have had a system in place to offer season ticket holders the first opportunity to purchase tickets for the 2016 Euro qualifier based on priority. Had this been done, most negative publicity could likely have been avoided.

The final example of the use of season ticket holder priority is in the relocation process of season ticket holders from an existing to a new facility. Relocating season ticket holders from one facility to another, in a location with strong season ticket demand, may be one of the most difficult tasks undertaken in ticket operations. For example, as previously stated, the Denver Broncos have approximately 22,000 season ticket holders. Those season ticket holders account for approximately 72,000 seats at Sports Authority Field in Denver, Colorado. Sports Authority Field has a total seating capacity of 75,125 seats (Welcome to Mile High, 2015), so season ticket holders utilize all but approximately 3,125 seats. Due to the number of differences between one facility and another it is almost impossible to make everyone happy during relocation. Variations in facilities can include such things as different seating capacities, fewer aisle seats, differences in the number of section and rows, less general seating due to the inclusion of premium seating and different sight lines, to name a few. Since an exact transfer from one facility to another is impossible, the goal of any ticketing staff is to relocate all fans to a "similar" seat location in the new facility, based on season ticket holder priority.

Although the relocation of season ticket holders to a new facility was not an issue for the FAI at the Euro 2016 qualifier match versus Scotland, this issue of priority will eventually present itself when a new stadium is constructed. Having a priority system in place will provide the ability to manage the relocation process efficiently and effectively.

Recording seat locations and ticket reprints

Using available technology to record the seat locations purchased by fans, as well as offering duplicate tickets, may significantly impact overall team revenues. Doing so minimizes the number of tickets that go unused. Unused tickets create a loss of revenue from ancillary areas such as concessions, licensed merchandise and parking.

In order to best serve fans, all tickets sold, even individual game tickets purchased with cash, should be recorded in an organization's ticketing system. This ensures that the person who purchased the tickets can receive duplicate tickets in the event that tickets are lost, stolen, destroyed or not received in the mail (Ingham, 2014; Reese, 2004). However, even today, many professional sport teams do not record contact information for fans during ticket sales transactions completed with cash. Recording sales information also guarantees that the tickets are authentic and that the purchaser of record will be the only person granted access to the seat locations at the event. In addition, the importance of printing bar codes on tickets and using scanners at stadium gates must be stressed. If bar codes and scanners are not utilized, there is no way to stop people with unauthorized tickets from entering the facility. This could cause hundreds of extra fans, without authentic seat locations, to improperly gain admission to an event (Ingham, 2014). When bar codes are printed on tickets, the most recent printed code is activated in the system. Whenever duplicate tickets are issued, the most recent code takes precedence at the gates. Previously printed bar codes are deactivated in the system so that they are not used for admission. This ensures that only one ticket for each seat location is used to enter a sport facility. In the case of tickets that are reported stolen, a police report is typically completed, making the falsification of the report punishable by law.

If the recording of seat locations had been done at the 2014 Glasgow Commonwealth Games, many of the problematic issues that were experienced by fans could have been avoided. Fans who had misplaced tickets or had tickets stolen could have had them reprinted, and would have had no need to repurchase them (Ingham, 2014). Similarly, fans who had never received tickets in the mail could have had them reprinted in advance of the event to be sure they would be granted admission (Ingham, 2014). According to officials at the 2014 Glasgow Commonwealth Games, the reason the ticketing technology was not implemented was due to the possibility of fraud (Ingham, 2014). However, based on how ticket barcodes can be created, activated and deactivated, depending on circumstances and the needs of a sport organization, fraud should be a non-issue (Ingham, 2014).

Current trends in ticketing technology

In addition to the benefits previously discussed, new trends in ticketing technology have not only enhanced the fan experience, but have provided an opportunity for sport organizations to manage fan data better, process payments in a more timely manner, generate incremental revenue through seat upgrades, virtually eliminate fraudulent tickets and maximize ticket revenue.

Ticketing technology has enhanced the fan experience in a number of ways. Automatic season ticket renewals eliminate the need for fans to worry whether they have remembered to renew their season tickets. Season ticket accounts can be set to be automatically renewed annually and billed to the preferred payment option of the fan. Long gone are the days of fans driving to the ticket office to make payments, mailing checks, or even needing to go online and pay with a credit card. Automatic season ticket renewals benefit sport organizations as well since renewal rates are increased, payments are received in a more timely and efficient manner, and fewer staff follow-ups are needed with season ticket holders (Lombardo, 2015). This benefits a sport organization financially in many ways. An increase in renewal rates allows the sport organization to capture a higher percentage of revenue earlier. Receiving revenue earlier provides organizations with the capital needed to compete for free agents and to negotiate player contracts. In addition, the earlier that revenue is received, the longer it can accrue interest at financial institutions. Fewer sales follow-ups by staff allow human resources to be managed more efficiently based on the staffing needs of the organization.

Current ticket technology also allows fans, specifically single seat purchasers, to conveniently upgrade seats after tickets have been purchased, and even after they have entered the stadium or arena (Muret, 2012). This allows fans who may not be happy with the location of their initial purchase, to pay the difference in price and relocate to a more desirable seat location as soon as possible. Although a great service for fans, the benefits are equally as great for sport organizations. Although there is a cost associated with investing in the technology, the service generates incremental revenue that may have never been captured. Once the initial investment is recouped, other than routine maintenance, all additional revenue is pure profit for the organization.

Some sport organizations communicate with fans through text messaging with opportunities to purchase seats through a company called ReplyBuy (Muret, 2015). ReplyBuy allows teams to send discounted ticket offers via text message several days in advance to fans registered for their program, which includes payment information. Then, if fans are interested in the offer, they can reply with the number of seats they want, their payment is processed, and they receive a digital ticket on their smartphone that can be used at the facility gate or printed at home in advance (Muret, 2015). Selling tickets through text messaging has been successful so far in the United States in several university athletic departments, the National Basketball Association (NBA) and the National Hockey League (NHL) (Muret, 2015).

Fraudulent or counterfeit tickets have been always been a serious issue for ticket offices (Dwyer, 2015; Weise, 2016). The use of ticketless ticketing systems, such as Flash Seats, has virtually eliminated the issue of fraudulent tickets. Flash Seats is currently used in the United States by several NBA teams such as the Cleveland Cavaliers, Utah Jazz, the Denver Nuggets, the Houston Rockets and the Minnesota Timberwolves. With Flash Seats, fans register on the Flash Seats website with a credit card or driver's license. Then, they are issued a bar code that may be used on a smartphone. When arriving at the facility, the fan can have either the bar code on the smartphone scanned at the gate, or swipe the form of identification they registered with on the Flash Seats website. A small piece of paper with the fan's seat location is then printed by the gate attendant and given to the fan as they enter the facility. If a fan has multiple seats on a season ticket account, they can simply assign a seat to each person for the entire season and each user can register with the same process on the Flash Seats website. If a regular ticket user is unable to attend one game, the substitute fan can register on the Flash Seats website, and have a ticket transferred to them for one game.

A ticketless system such as Flash Seats provides other benefits to sport organizations as well. First, security is enhanced because the names of people either attending, or scheduled to attend, an event at a facility are always known (Fisher & Muret, 2014). Second, this same enhanced data benefit of knowing the names of those in attendance provides a level of marketing that never existed with any previous types of ticketing systems. With some ticketing systems, tickets may be resold or passed from one person to the next to the point where sport organizations have no idea who ends up ultimately sitting in the seat at the event. It is hard to market to someone who can't be identified. With a ticketless system such as Flash Seats, the names and contact information for every person in attendance is known. From a marketing and sales perspective, this data is priceless. For example, if a person in attendance identified by Flash Seats is not a current customer, team officials can target that individual to be contacted about the possibility of attending future games (Fisher & Muret, 2014; Kaplan, 2014). In addition, if a casual fan has tickets transferred to them multiple times during a season, sales staff may identify that person as someone who could be a good candidate to purchase one of the team's mini-plans (Going Paperless, 2009). Third, ticketless systems provide a certain amount of control for sport organizations over the secondary ticket market. A "price floor" is an artificial price barrier used to ensure that prices on the secondary market do not fall below a certain level. These can be used to ensure that single game ticket prices do not fall below the price paid by the organization's season ticket holders, which can anger valued fans. Similarly, "price ceilings" may be used to place a limit on the amount that may be charged for single game tickets on the secondary market. In summary, both price floors and price ceilings may be used to set limits on the minimum and maximum amount for which tickets may be resold on the secondary market, thus regulating escalating prices for the average fan while protecting the investment of season ticket holders.

Finally, advances in ticketing technology now allow sport organizations to take advantage of pricing options that did not exist several years ago. The traditional fixed pricing model still exists at some levels of sport. However, at least in the United States, once the highest levels of Division I athletics and the professional level are reached, variable and dynamic pricing is the norm.

Unlike the traditional fixed pricing model, which charges the same price for every seat for the entire season, variable pricing charges different prices for seat locations based on a variety of factors such as opponent, month, special events, day of the week and time of the game (Rascher *et al.*, 2007). Similar to fixed pricing, variable prices are typically set and published before the start of the season. Fixed pricing allows sport organizations to take advantage of historical demand information to generate additional revenue. For example, fans may be willing to pay more to see a game against a rival opponent, or to attend a game on a weekend rather than on a weeknight (Rascher *et al.*, 2007). However, the weakness of variable pricing is that it does not allow pricing changes throughout the season. If prices are set too low with the variable pricing model, money is left on the table. If prices are set too high, demand may be impacted and revenue may be lost (Koba, 2012; Rascher *et al.*, 2007).

Dynamic pricing is the logical progression from the variable pricing model and was introduced into professional sport by the San Francisco Giants of Major League Baseball in 2009 (King, 2012; Paul and Weinbach, 2013; Shapiro & Drayer, 2012). In addition to the factors used in variable pricing, dynamic pricing uses sophisticated technology to incorporate a variety of additional ever-changing factors into the pricing of games such as starting pitcher, in-game promotions, weather, injuries, roster changes, win/loss records and even competing forms of entertainment in the local area (King, 2012). Like the airline and hotel industries, dynamic ticket pricing, with some exceptions, allows demand to set the final ticket prices (Koba, 2012; Paul & Weinbach, 2013).

Most dynamic ticket pricing systems in sport are not based on a true "free market" pricing model. In other words, there are floors and ceilings created in many cases in order to protect the organization from charging too little or too much for tickets (Koba, 2012). Price floors are common and were created to ensure that prices for individual games do not fall below those prices created per game for season ticket holders. This ensures that season ticket holders always get the best pricing. Price ceilings are less common but were created to limit the maximum amount that may be charged for an individual seat on the secondary market controlled by the team or league. The theory behind price ceilings is to keep ticket prices from escalating out of control so that the average fan can afford them. Many professional leagues, such as the NFL and the NBA, market and operate their own secondary market ticket exchanges. In addition, some specific teams, such as the NBA's Golden State Warriors, request that season ticket holders use the team's exchange for all secondary market transactions (Leuty, 2015).

The benefits of dynamic ticket pricing are that the available technology allows sport organizations to adjust ticket prices, in either direction, to account for any market conditions that may arise. In theory, this allows teams to maximize ticket revenue for all individual game tickets. It also encourages fans to purchase season tickets to lock in prices at the start of the season to avoid large fluctuations in demand (Rishe, 2012).

The limitation of dynamic ticket pricing is that the way in which fans are receiving the pricing model is still being evaluated. For example, on 29 November 2015, Kobe Bryant, long-time guard of the NBA's Los Angeles Lakers, announced that the 2015–2016 season would be his last (Keh, 2015). Bryant was scheduled to play a game against the Philadelphia 76ers in his hometown of Philadelphia just two days later. After the announcement of his pending retirement, the game sold out in less than 24 hours. The 76ers use tiered pricing, a form of dynamic ticket pricing, so that as soon as the retirement announcement was made, and demand for tickets increased, the 76ers moved tickets from their Tier B price point to Tier A pricing (Scott, 2015). The cheapest seats that normally sold for $24.00 began selling for $44.00, a 43 percent increase. This did not sit well with fans, especially since the 76ers had a record of 0–18 at the time. However, it is likely that the longer that dynamic ticket pricing is used, the more comfortable fans will become with the concept (Rishe, 2012).

Conclusion

In today's highly diverse global marketplace, competition for disposable income is fierce. The technology-driven millennial generation, typically referred to as those born between 1980 and 2000, has surpassed the baby boomers to become America's largest living generation (Andrews, 2016; Fisher, 2015). The preferred choice of millennials in regard to commerce is the smartphone; this also applies to the purchasing of tickets to sporting events (Andrews, 2016; Fisher, 2015). This trend is expected only to grow as the population relies more on technology to guide daily lives. It would be wise for sport organizations to utilize state-of-the-art technology to make it as easy as possible for customers to purchase and manage ticket accounts. Advanced technology in regard to ticketing systems will allow sport organizations to adequately reach all potential consumers and provide a superior level of customer service to retain season ticket holders.

References

Andrews, T. M. (2016). "It's official: Millennials have surpassed baby boomers to become America's largest living generation". The *Washington Post*. Available at <www.washingtonpost.com/news/morning-mix/wp/2016/04/26/its-official-millennials-have-surpassed-baby-boomers-to-become-americas-largest-living-generation/>. Accessed 1 May 2016.

Away Matches (2017). *Scottish Football Association*. Available at <http://tickets.scottishfa.co.uk/PagesPublic/ProductBrowse/ProductAway.aspx>. Accessed 25 February 2017.

Brown, J. (2014). "NFL is vague on fuzzy Super Bowl ticket math". *Denver Post*. Available at <www.denverpost.com/broncos/ci_25006344/nfl-is-vague-fuzzy-super-bowl-ticket-math>. Accessed 24 June 2015.

Dwyer, D. (2015). "Boston police warn sports fans of counterfeit tickets". *Boston Globe*. Available at <www.boston.com/news/untagged/2015/11/24/boston-police-warn-sports-fans-of-counterfeit-tickets>. Accessed 27 April 2016.

Fisher, E. (2015). Millennials put ticket strategies to test. *SportsBusiness Journal*. Available at <www.sportsbusinessdaily.com/Journal/Issues/2015/06/08/In-Depth/Ticketing-main.aspx>. Accessed 1 May 2016.

Fisher, E. & Muret, D. (2014). Teams make their case for mobile ticketing. *SportsBusiness Journal*, p. 1. Available at <www.sportsbusinessdaily.com/Journal/Issues/2014/04/28/In-Depth/Mobile-ticketing.aspx?hl=paperless%20ticketing&sc=0>. Accessed 13 March 2015.

Going Paperless (2009). *SportsBusiness Journal*. Available at <www.sportsbusinessdaily.com/Journal/Issues/2009/11/20091108/Technology-In-Sports/Ticketing.aspx?hl=flashseats&sc=0. Accessed 13 March 2015.

Home Matches (2017). *Scottish Football Association* [online]. Available at <tickets.scottishfa.co.uk/PagesPublic/ProductBrowse/ProductHome.aspx?soalready=xTbDJTnlJlxkGt/NTEYtNU6GR2PPeSvv1JuLYY+9gvE=>. Accessed 25 February 2017.

Ingham, A. (2014). Glasgow 2014 Commonwealth Games controversy over tickets. *Liberty Voice*. Available at <http://guardianlv.com/2014/07/glasgow-2014-commonwealth-games-controversy-over-tickets/>. Accessed 13 March 2015.

Kaplan, D. (2014). Almost half of NFL teams will use paperless ticketing. *SportsBusiness Journal*, p. 4, Available at <www.sportsbusinessdaily.com/Journal/Issues/2014/05/19/Leagues-and-Governing-Bodies/NFL-tickets.aspx?hl=paperless%20ticketing&sc=0>. Accessed 13 March 2015.

Keh, A. (2015). "Kobe Bryant announces retirement". The *New York Times*. Available at <www.nytimes.com/2015/11/30/sports/basketball/kobe-bryant-announces-retirement.html?_r=0>. Accessed 1 May 2016.

King, B. (2012). Ticket challenge: Getting the price right. *SportsBusiness Journal*, p. 1. Available at <www.sportsbusinessdaily.com/Journal/Issues/2012/03/19/In-Depth/Ticket-pricing.aspx?hl=Ticket%20challenge&sc=1>. Accessed 13 April 2015.

Koba, M. (2012). How dynamic pricing is changing sports ticketing. *CNBC*. Available at <www.cnbc.com/id/48194739>. Accessed 13 April 2015.

Leuty, R. (2015). "Warriors box out brokers in ticket resale play". *San Francisco Business Times*. Available at <www.bizjournals.com/sanfrancisco/blog/2015/03/golden-state-warriors-ticketmaster-stubhub-lyv.html?page=all>. Accessed 20 March 2015.

Lombardo, J. (2015). Cavaliers first in NBA to require automatic renewal. *SportsBusiness Journal*, p. 1. Available at <www.sportsbusinessdaily.com/Journal/Issues/2015/03/02/Franchises/Cavaliers-auto-renewal.aspx?hl=ticketing&sc=0>. Accessed 13 March 2015.

McCauley, C. (2014). "Why were the most loyal Irish fans denied tickets for the Scotland game?" The *Guardian*, Republic of Ireland Sportblog [blog] 31 October. Available at <www.theguardian.com/football/blog/2014/oct/31/republic-ireland-loyal-fans-denied-tickets-scotland-euro-2016-qualifier>. Accessed 13 March 2015.

Muret, D. (2012). Tech lets ticketed fans upgrade to better seats. *SportsBusiness Journal*, p. 6. Available at <www.sportsbusinessdaily.com/Journal/Issues/2012/10/08/Facilities/Seat-upgrades.aspx>. Accessed 8 April 2016.

Muret, D. (2015). Teams turn to text as quick, simple way to sell tickets. *SportsBusiness Journal*, p. 4. Available at <www.sportsbusinessdaily.com/Journal/Issues/2015/01/19/Facilities/ReplyBuy.aspx?hl=replybuy&sc=0>. Accessed 13 March 2015.

Paul, R. J. & Weinbach, A. P. (2013). Determinants of dynamic pricing premiums in Major League Baseball. *Sport Marketing Quarterly*, *22*(3), 152–165.

Rascher, D. A., McEvoy, C. D., Nagel, M. S. & Brown, M. T. (2007). Variable ticket pricing in Major League Baseball. *Journal of Sport Management*, *21*(3), July, 407–437.

Reese, J. T. (2004). Ticket operations in a professional sports team setting. In U. McMahon Beattie and I. Yeoman (Eds), *Sport and Leisure Operations Management* (pp. 167–179). London: Thomson Learning.

Rishe, P. (2012). Dynamic pricing: The future of ticket pricing in sports. *Forbes*. Available at <www.forbes.com/sites/prishe/2012/01/06/dynamic-pricing-the-future-of-ticket-pricing-in-sports/>. Accessed 1 March 2016.

Scott, K. (2015). It appears the Sixers raised Lakers game ticket prices at the last minute. *Crossing Broad*. Available at <www.crossingbroad.com/2015/12/it-appears-the-sixers-raised-lakers-game-ticket-prices-at-the-last-minute.html>. Accessed 1 May 2016.

Seiferheld, S. (2012). How teams can keep season-ticket holders committed. *SportsBusiness Journal*, p. 25, Available at <www.sportsbusinessdaily.com/Journal/Issues/2012/05/14/Opinion/Steve-Seiferheld.aspx?hl=eagles%20renewals&sc=0>. Accessed 13 March 2015.

Shapiro, S. L. & Drayer, J. (2012). A new age of demand-based pricing: An examination of dynamic ticket pricing and secondary market prices in Major League Baseball. *Journal of Sport Management*, *26*(6), November, 532–546.

Smith, A. (2014). "FAI accused of manhandling fans protesting about ticketing controversy". The *Guardian*, Republic of Ireland. Available at <www.theguardian.com/football/2014/nov/22/republic-of-ireland-fai-fans-protest-ticketing>. Accessed 13 March 2015.

Spoelstra, J. & DeLay, S. (2013). The ultimate toolkit to sell the last seat in the house. *Strategy & Tactics Playbook*, II, p. 188.

Stone, B. (2013). Don't like your seat? Baseball fans can now upgrade, mid-game. *Bloomberg*. Available at <www.bloomberg.com/news/articles/2013-03-13/dont-like-your-seat-baseball-fans-can-now-upgrade-mid-game>. Accessed 8 April 2016.

Wann, D. L. (1993). Aggression among highly identified spectators as a function of their need to maintain a positive social identity. *Journal of Sport & Social Issues*, *17*(2), 134–143.

Wann, D. L. & Branscombe, N. R. (1990). Die-hard and fair-weather fans: Effects of identification on BIRGing and CORFing tendencies. *Journal of Sport & Social Issues*, *14*(2), 103–117.

Wann, D. L. & Branscombe, N. R. (1993). Sports fans: Measuring degree of identification with their team. *International Journal of Sport Psychology*, *24*(1), 1–17.

Wann, D. L., Roberts, A. & Tindall, J. (1999). The role of team performance, team identification, and self-esteem in sport spectators' game preferences. *Perceptual & Motor Skills*, *89*(3), 945–950.

Weise, E. (2016). How StubHub fights counterfeit Super Bowl tickets. *USA Today*. Available at <www.usatoday.com/story/tech/news/2016/02/04/stubhub-counterfeit-super-bowl-50-tickets/79538428/>. Accessed 27 April 2016.

Welcome to Mile High (2015). "Sports Authority Field at Mile High". Available at <www.sportsauthorityfieldatmilehigh.com/stadium-information/about-us>. Accessed 23 June 2015.

16

SPORT INDUSTRY IN CHINA

Opportunities and challenges

Dongfeng Liu

Introduction

Since the adoption of the "reform and opening up" policy in 1978, China has experienced rapid economic and social development with growth rates averaging 10 per cent over 30 years – the fastest sustained expansion by a major economy in history (World Bank, 2016). China overtook Japan to become the world's second largest economy in 2010. Driven by economic growth and a rising awareness of health issues as a result of urbanization, the demand for sport products also grew fast. This is attributed to the growing popularity of sport participation and the increased number of sporting events of various types hosted in China (Liu, 2016). A sport market is emerging gradually.

In China, as in most other countries, the sport economy is not an independent industry reflected in a national account. As a result, no official figures regarding the economic importance of the sport industry were available until 2010 when China's General Administration of Sport released figures for the sport industry based on the first national sport industry survey (2008–2010). Based on a theoretic framework developed by a working group consisting of experts from Shanghai University of Sport and other leading sport institutions in China, this survey collected sport industry data for the years 2006 and 2007. The data were collected on a sample of nearly half of the 30 provinces on China's mainland. A second sport industry survey was conducted by China's National Statistics Bureau in conjunction with the General Administration of Sport with data collected from all 31 provinces of China's mainland (Taiwan, Hong Kong and Macau not included) in 2016, and the results were released at the end of 2016 (National Statistics Bureau, 2016). According to this survey, the gross value added (GVA) of the sport industry for 2015 in China was RMB 549.4 billion, which was 35.97 per cent higher than 2014 and accounted for 0.8 per cent of the national economy. The contribution of the sport industry to China's national economy is very low and still in its infancy compared to the West. In addition, the structure of the sport industry is imbalanced because it is still dominated by sporting goods. Manufacturing and sales of sporting goods accounted for 78.6 per cent of the sport economy in 2015. While China produces 65 per cent of the world's sport supplies, the domestic sporting goods businesses are at the low end of the value chain, and far behind global brands such as Nike or Adidas (Yunlong, 2008).

In addition, professional sports in China are also underdeveloped. Until the mid-1990s, sport in China remained the prerogative of the government. The situation began to change when a professional football championship was held in 1994. Initially confined to football but then extended to basketball, a professional sport market gradually emerged. Despite the initial rapid growth, the new financial stakes in football generated far-reaching corruption issues: match-fixing, illegal betting and the bribing of players or referees to influence the results of competitions (so-called "Black Whistles" scandals) quickly tarnished the image of the championship. The crackdown on corruption, which began in 2009, saw 58 current and former football officials, players and referees reprimanded for match-fixing and bribery (Kaiman, 2013). Both the level and reputation of professional sport in China reached new lows. In 2004, and at its corrupt worst, the top flight of the Chinese football league changed its name from "Chinese Serial A League" to "Chinese Super League", in the hope of a fresh start and image enhancement. In 2005, only one year after the name change, the average game attendance reached a record low of 10,000, down by almost 60 per cent from 24,000 in its heyday in 1996 (see Figure 16.1). Perhaps even more troublesome was the fact that the league went without a major sponsor after its title sponsor, Siemens, withdrew its investment owing to a lack of confidence in the league, and the league was mocked by the media and fans (Xu, 2005).

Corruption of the Chinese professional basketball industry seems less severe than that of football, but its quality and popularity has also remained limited. Disappointed by the domestic leagues, both Chinese fans and sponsors turned to international sports leagues such as the English Premier League or the National Basketball Association (NBA) from the US. For instance, one poll showed that about 85 per cent of China's mainland population were NBA fans, and six of the top ten favourite athletes in China were NBA athletes (Madden, 2005). The success of the NBA in China has also been recognized from its sponsorship deals with different Chinese companies, such as Li-Ning or Anta (famous domestic footwear

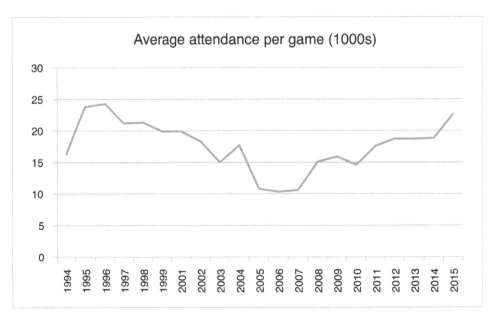

Figure 16.1 Attendance per game for Chinese top-flight football (1994–2015) (based on Wang (2003), and figures released by the Chinese Football Association)

brands), Homenice (a wood flooring brand), and Haier (a global home appliance company) (Marshall, 2006).

Despite these problems, based on the figures released by the General Administration of Sport, sport business in China has been growing rapidly over the past decade at an annual rate of around 18 per cent, which is much faster than the growth of the national economy at just below 10 per cent. In addition, although the sport economy in China is still dominated by sporting goods manufacturing, the structure is improving with the sport service sector now accounting for around 23 per cent of the total sports economy, an increase of 17 per cent in 2006. Thanks to a growing economy, urbanization and lifestyle change, sports consumption in China is gathering momentum.

Top-down reform in sport and soccer in China and the response from the society

On 20 October 2014, as part of its agenda for boosting employment, domestic consumption and other areas of the Chinese economy, China's Cabinet, the State Council, issued a national strategic policy titled "Opinions on Accelerating the Development of Sports Industry and Promoting Sports Consumption" (No. 46 Decree of 2014 by the State Council, named "the Guidelines" hereafter) to enhance the country's fast-growing sport industry (State Council of China, 2014). The Guidelines marked a milestone in the development of sport business. This was the first time the sport industry was singled out by the State Council as a new growth point of the economy with great business potential, and the promotion of sport participation was upgraded as a national strategy. Some of the ambitious targets to be reached by 2025 included:

- To promote national health and fitness through various sports and get more than 500 million citizens regularly participating in sports and physical activities.
- To generate a gross output of the sport industry worth RMB 5 trillion (equivalent to approximately US$815 billion) per annum.
- To create an average area of sport grounds in the country that is over two square metres per capita.

In addition, the Guidelines recommended measures that would be adopted by the government. Actually, the Guidelines also marked the beginning of the deregulation of tight control over sport development by the government, and thus the business market or private sector would play a leading role in meeting the growing demand for sport products and services. Among other things, the measures included the following:

- To promote the popularization of three types of ball sports (basketball, football and volleyball) the State Council will set up a long-term development plan for football, including construction of sports facilities and promotion of football on campuses.
- To professionalize more sport events, including improving the corporate governance structure of sport clubs and the establishment of a modern enterprise system in the sport sector.
- To provide financial support.
- To form a policy system that is conducive to the sport market's rapid growth by eliminating industrial, policy and regulatory barriers, such as complex administrative approval procedures.

- To lower the operational costs for the sport industry, the State Council has decided to lower business income tax to 15 per cent for those identified as high-tech sport enterprises. This rate is considerably lower than the approximately 25 per cent rate for other industries.
- To implement policies that introduce private capital into the sport sector via listing bond issuance by qualified enterprises.
- To encourage social capital to invest in the construction of sport facilities and the supply of sport-related products and services.
- To encourage foreign capital investment in the domestic sport industry.

Subsequently, the Guidelines were supplemented by another high profile strategic plan. The Overall Reform Plan to Boost the Development of Soccer in China ("the Soccer Plan" hereafter) was issued on 16 March 2015 (State Council of China, 2015). The Soccer Plan involves reform of almost every aspect of the sport, including the professional clubs, leagues, national teams, and youth and grassroots soccer, and was approved by China's central reform group and issued by the State Council. The significance of this Soccer Plan cannot be overstated. It shows the determination of the government to develop soccer in China because it comes from the highest level of China's government. It is also expected that the reform of soccer will serve as a pilot for other sports in China and thus mark the first concrete steps toward deregulation, and the further commercialization and professionalization of sport in general. Some of the highlights of this Soccer Plan included the following:

- The China Football Association should be delinked from its existing affiliation to the General Administration of Sport of China and work as a real non-governmental organization.
- A sports lottery will be used to increase investment in boosting soccer.
- The total number of elementary and middle schools featuring soccer will increase from approximately 5,000 to 20,000 in 2020 and to 50,000 in 2025.
- The long-term goals include bidding for the FIFA World Cup and bringing the national team to the top level in the world.

As a follow-up to the Soccer Plan, the "Mid-to-Long-Term Plan for Chinese Soccer Development" (2016–2050), a 35-year soccer development blueprint setting out short-, mid- and long-term objectives, was unveiled on 6 April 2016 by the National Development and Reform Commission, China's top planning body (National Development and Reform Commission, 2016). It set an ambitious goal for China to become a dominant soccer power in Asia by 2030 and a leading soccer power in the world by 2050.

Both the Guidelines and the Soccer Plan have been well received in China with positive reactions from both society and industry. The plans have significantly raised the profile of the sport business and put it into the spotlight in China. The most important and immediate impact of these policy documents can be seen from the huge unprecedented investment in the sport industry in general, and in the soccer business in particular, from the private sector, involving some of the richest businessmen in China (see Table 16.1). It is reported that Chinese mergers and acquisitions in the domestic and overseas sport markets have seen exponential growth since 2015, when the country spent almost ¥40 billion (around US$5.99 billion) in total investments with 33 deals valuing over ¥10 million (around US$1.50 million) (Guo, 2016). In 2015 alone, Wang Jianlin, the real estate tycoon topping China's rich list for years, made at least three major investments in the sport business, buying sport properties

Table 16.1 High profile sport deals by Chinese investors (based on news releases from major newspaper or Chinese websites such as China Daily, www.sina.com, www.sohu.com)

Date	Sport property	Contract value (US$)	Buyer	Owner of the buying company
Jan. 2015	20% of Spanish soccer team Club Atletico de Madrid	52 million	Wanda Group	Wang Jianlin
Feb. 2015	Swiss Infront Sports & Media (68.2% of the equity share holding)	1.2 billion	Wanda Group	Wang Jianlin
Aug. 2015	The World Triathlon Corporation (WTC)	650 million	Wanda Group	Wang Jianlin
Mar. 2016	FIFA Partner (up to 2030)	N/A	Wanda Group	Wang Jianlin
Jun. 2014	50% of Guangzhou Evergrande FC	192 million	Alibaba Group	Jack Ma
Sept. 2015	Establishment of Alibaba Sport Company	N/A	Alibaba Group	Jack Ma
Dec. 2015	8-year Presenting Partnership of Club World Cup	N/A	Alibaba Group	Jack Ma
Nov. 2015	100% of Jiangsu Football Club	80 million	Suning Group	Zhang Jindong
Jun. 2016	70% club Inter Milan	307 million	Suning Group	Zhang Jindong
Apr. 2017	99.9% club AC Milan	820 million	Chinese consortium	Yonghong Li
Oct. 2015	5-year (2016–2020) broadcasting rights of China's Super Football League	1.25 billion	Ti'ao Dongli	Li Ruigang

of almost US$2 billion (see Table 16.1). In October 2015, the Chinese top flight soccer league sold its five-year (2016–2020) broadcasting rights for a jaw-dropping record of ¥8 billion (about US$1.25 billion) with an average of ¥1.6 billion per season. This amount is 26 times higher than the previous 2015 season when the amount was only ¥60 million.

The massive crackdown on corruption in football has helped to clean up the sport and restore the image and credibility of the game. The fans are returning to the stadium to enjoy the game with stronger competition and better quality, partly due to the new investment drawn into the league. In 2015, the Chinese Super League (CSL) achieved an average live audience of 23,000 people per game, the highest in almost 20 years, and the highest attendance among all Asian football leagues (Zhou, 2015). The clubs in the top flight are now also spending huge sums of money buying big-name footballers from the international market. Jiangsu Suning spent a record high of €50 million to sign forward Brazilian midfielder Alex Teixeira on 5 February 2016. In total, during the January–February window of 2016, the Chinese football league's overall spending was worth a world-beating €334 million, outstripping the English Premier League's €253 million in January (CCTV, 2016).

Conclusion

Despite the huge investment from private sectors, it would be naive to think that those ambitious goals set by the policy documents will come easily or that the road ahead for sport business is a smooth one. The fact that the reform plan of a sport and its governing system has to come from the country's central government and be pushed by the nation's president implies the difficulties and potential resistance from the existing establishment. After all, any reform would involve redistribution of power and interests, and sport is no exception.

A major challenge regarding sport development in general and professional sport in particular has much to do with the centralized governmental sport administration system. Modelled on the former Soviet Union, one of the most fundamental functions of this centralized governing system is to win as many Olympic medals as possible to serve the national prestige, and anything else becomes secondary. Essentially, the Chinese sport governing system for elite sport consists of three subsystems: a highly centralized administrative system (providing governing, funding and support), a professional training system, and a sport events organizing system centring around the National Games every four years. As a result, all sport governing bodies in China, such as the China Football Association, are considered quasi-governmental organizations. Actually, the 70 national sport associations exist in parallel with 23 sport management centres (governmental departments) controlled and managed by the same group of people. In addition, most athletes who are trained at the provincial level or national team level are treated as full-time employees by the government. In other words, while a market economy has been largely established in China since the early 1990s, sport remains in a government-controlled and planned system. As a result, conflict between this planned system and market-based professional and commercial sport is unavoidable. It is actually believed that this centralized governing system itself has become one of the major obstacles that should be deregulated and reformed to release the huge market potential of the sport industry in China (Liu, 2008). On 24 February 2016, as a milestone in the reform of Chinese sport and football, the Chinese Football Management Centre was dissolved and the Chinese Football Association (CFA) was announced as formally detached from the government (i.e. the China Generational Administration of Sport or "GAS"). The fact that Mr Cai, the Deputy Minister of GAS, has remained to serve as the President of the newly restructured CFA seems to bring into question the autonomy the association can enjoy as an independent sport governing body.

In addition, there exists cultural challenge. The so-called modern sport, including football, is an imported culture for the Chinese. Over the past hundreds of years, through the dynasties in China, excellence in schoolwork and sitting for the competitive civil service examination to become a government official was the dream for every average Chinese person. As a result, anything else, including leisure activity, was considered a distraction from studying. While today a good degree does not necessarily guarantee a good job in China, schoolwork remains the paramount task for Chinese children. It is reported that increasing numbers of children in large cities across the country are experiencing joyless childhoods due to a lack of playtime (Xinhua, 2007). Unlike in the West where for many people sport has been a part of life since childhood, it is considered by many Chinese parents as a waste of time and a distraction from schoolwork. When some more open-minded parents do choose a hobby for their children, it is often learning a musical instrument, or painting, in preference to sport. When a parent decides that a child should play a sport seriously, more often than not, it is out of instrumental concern and either believing the child will become an elite athlete or study a sport-related degree in the future. The only time sport is considered important is when people get older and do exercises for health reasons. This is probably why the participation of senior citizens in sport is far higher in China than in the West (Liu, 2016b). Overall, participation in sport has to be improved to sustain a truly successful and prosperous sport business in China.

References

CCTV (2016). Chinese Super League on record spending. Retrieved from <http://english.cntv.cn/2016/02/29/VIDE69rPejl9GV5QYeDc7d9y160229.shtml>. Accessed 10 May 2016.

Guo, Y. (2016). Chinese buyers' 'shopping' spree for soccer clubs. *China.org.cn*. Retrieved from <www.china.org.cn/sports/2016-07/23/content_38943040.htm>. Accessed 2 July 2016.

Kaiman, J. (2013). "Match-fixing and bribery in Chinese football are endemic, sport insiders say". The *Guardian*. Retrieved from <www.theguardian.com/world/2013/feb/20/match-fixing-bribery-chinese-football>. Accessed 10 May 2016.

Liu, D. (2008). Review of national governing bodies' reform in China. *Academic Journal of Sport*, *9*, 21–25.

Liu, D. (2016). Social impact of major sports events perceived by host community. *International Journal of Sports Marketing & Sponsorship*, *17*(1), 78–91.

Liu. D. (2016b). Sport participation and measurement in developed countries in comparison with Shanghai. *Journal of Shanghai University of Sport*, *3*, 27–31.

Madden, N. (2005). NBA signs with China's Li-Ning. *Advertising Age*. Retrieved from <http://adage.com/article/the-world-ad-age-global-news-data/nba-signs-china-s-li-ning/101845/>. Accessed 10 May 2016.

Marshall, S. (2006). NBA scores big in China. *Crain's New York Business*. Retrieved from <www.crainsnewyork.com/article>. Accessed 10 May 2016.

National Development and Reform Commission (2016). Mid- to long-term plan for Chinese soccer development (2016–2050). [Published government document].

National Statics Bureau (2016). Economic importance of Chinese sport industry for 2015. [Published government document].

Plunkett Research (2014). Sports industry trends & statistics. Retrieved from <www.plunkettresearch.com/ sports-recreation-leisure-market-research/industry-statistics>. Accessed 10 May 2016.

State Council of China (2014). Opinions on accelerating the development of sports industry and promoting sports consumption. [Published government document].

State Council of China (2015). The overall reform plan to boost the development of soccer in China. [Published government document].

Wang, J. (2003). A study on the factors affecting the number of audience in China's Football League. *Shanghai Sport Science Research*, *24*(6), 27–29.

World Bank (2016). China overview. Retrieved from <www.worldbank.org/en/country/china/overview>. Accessed 6 April 2016.

Xinhua (2007). "China's children too busy for playtime". *China Daily*. Retrieved from <www.chinadaily.com.cn/china/2007-05/13/content_871182.htm>. Accessed 10 May 2016.

Xu, S. (2005). "Naked running of Chinese Super League in 2005". *South Urban Weekly*.

Yunlong, S. (2008). (August 3) China becomes major consumer in global sports supply market. *Xinhuanet*. Retrieved from <http://news.xinhuanet.com/english/2008-08/03/content_8917910.htm>. Accessed 8 May 2016.

Zhou. Z. (2015). Chinese Super League achieving record high attendance. Retrieved from <http://sports.cntv.cn/2015/11/04/ARTI1446598074168490.shtml>. Accessed 8 May 2016.

17

INTERNATIONAL TRADE IN SPORT PRODUCTS

Free trade agreements, sporting goods and playing talent

Sungho Cho and Kyoo Hong Kim

Introduction

After the Second World War, economic powers began to adopt the doctrine of non-discrimination and reciprocity in international trade. The commitment to free trade culminated in the formation of the General Agreement on Tariffs and Trade (GATT). By the 1980s, however, the evasion of GATT rules had become widespread due to various disputes between developed and developing nations. Such discord among the member countries resulted in voluntary export restraints and orderly marketing agreements which in turn seriously undermined the effectiveness of the GATT system that hinged on the idea of non-discrimination and reciprocity. In 1995, the World Trade Organization (WTO) replaced the GATT, and encompassed some areas not covered by its predecessor such as the international trade in intellectual property. With over 150 member countries within the new system, however, a multilateral consensus is still impractical and challenging.

Over the past decades, countries have tried to break away from the WTO system by establishing regional trade agreements, e.g. free trade agreements (FTAs). As of 2015, there are 262 regional trade agreements in force while the signatory countries of FTAs are still bound by the WTO. A notable example of an FTA is the North American Free Trade Agreement (NAFTA) signed in 1993 between the US, Mexico and Canada, which was designed to eliminate trade barriers in the region, increase investment opportunities and establish procedures for resolution in case of trade disputes. Another example is the one that the US signed with Korea in 2011, i.e. the US–South Korea Free Trade Agreement (KORUS FTA). Under the KORUS FTA, the trade surplus of the US service industry grew at an annual rate of 19 per cent in the region. Recently, the US Administration pursued a fast-track approval from the Republican side of the Congress to initiate another FTA negotiation, the Trans-Pacific Partnership (TPP). The TPP would link many of the large economies around the Pacific Rim, including the US, Japan, Australia and Canada, Chile and Mexico. According to the WTO, the worldwide trade volume has increased from $121 billion in 1948 to $36.7 trillion in 2013, which is an astonishing 303-fold growth.

In theory, the liberalization of international trade would be likely to provide key opportunities to tackle many issues in the global sport industry including restricted market access, the uniform protection of intellectual property rights and the reform of export restrictions. In fact, since a substantial number of sport products and services are still subject to high tariffs and other measures of protectionism, more multinational or multiregional coordination to establish free trade would be necessary for the continuing development of the $480–620 billion global sport industry (Collignon, Sultan & Santander, 2011). Given the significance, an exploration of FTAs and other trade agreements would be likely to provide insightful perspectives towards understanding various dynamics of the global sport industry. This chapter begins with economics theories and notions that may provide conceptual foundations to understanding international trade agreements. Legal aspects of FTAs and multilateral agreements are explored in terms of the constitutional grounds for ratification, the legal effectiveness of FTAs and relevant enforcement mechanisms. The international trade in sporting goods and athletic talent is then examined in terms of its unique market characteristics, production relocation strategy, relationship between economic integration and transnational trade in playing talent and equitable treatment of team franchises in multinational league operation under FTAs. A summary of the chapter is presented at the end.

Economics of trade

Although economists might have divergent views on many economic policies and phenomena, they almost unanimously support the benefits of free trade (Whaples, 2006). The economic argument for free trade dates back to Adam Smith's *The Wealth of Nations*, where the grandfather of modern economics challenged a then-prevalent notion, mercantilism. David Riccardo later advanced and refined Adam Smith's idea and conceptualized the famous theory of comparative advantages. The theory explains why countries need to engage in international trade even when one country's workers are more efficient at producing every single good than workers in other countries. He demonstrated that if two countries capable of producing two commodities are engaged in free trade, each country will increase its overall consumption by exporting one good for which it has comparative advantage while importing the other good, as far as there are differences among the countries in terms of the relative opportunity costs associated with the traded goods. Widely regarded as one of the most powerful and counter-intuitive insights in the history of economics, Ricardo's theory implies that comparative advantage rather than absolute advantage is responsible for much of international trade. It is also known that free trade enables more efficient resource allocation by exploiting the economies of scale from specialization because the average costs of production would be likely to decrease as the production scale increases. Specifically, in a sector that requires high fixed costs (called "natural monopoly industry" in economics), the efficiency obtained from the economies of scale would be significant. The benefits from the economies of scale would likely lead to lower consumer prices and efficient allocation of resources.

In fact, the North–South trading pattern that is frequently observed in the global sporting goods market supports the theory of comparative advantage and economies of scale. While developing countries generally export low-tech sporting goods, e.g. sneakers, developed countries produce high-tech goods such as wearable fitness devices with cutting-edge technology. Although a developed country may be able to produce high-tech as well as low-tech goods much more efficiently than a developing country, both countries would be better off when they focused on the goods with comparative advantage and traded with each other. Additionally, in terms of the economies of scale, the marginal cost of production would decrease when the countries specialize. For instance, a manufacturing process of athletic footwear requires long assembly lines with large inventories, i.e. high fixed costs. Thus, building one huge centralized manufacturing centre is better than running multiple small ones to lower the production costs. It is understandable why Nike concentrates footwear factories in China whereas Gymwatch StrenX still maintains its manufacturing units in Germany. This phenomenon is discussed in more detail later.

Theoretical rationale for regional trade agreements

While economists support free trade systems based on complete trade liberalization, generally, they do not accept regional trade agreements (RTAs), e.g. FTAs, as equally effective policies. It has been argued that FTAs are in fact threats to the carefully constructed postwar multilateral free trade system under the GATT and WTO (Bhagwati, 2008). During the last two decades, the world has witnessed a contrasted evolution of multilateral versus regional trade liberalization. While multilateral liberalization based on the ideas of non-discrimination and reciprocity has progressively slowed down, the number of free trade agreements has exponentially increased. A well-known economic problem with the bilateral and regional agreements is that, although they create trade among members, they also generate distortions through their inherently discriminatory mechanisms. Then the question is, if multilateral free trade is the best system, why are the number of regional trade agreements such as FTAs ever increasing? The following sections provide several theoretical explanations.

Free trade under a perfectly competitive market condition promotes economic efficiency. This is the first Fundamental Theorem of Welfare Economics envisioned by Adam Smith. Based on this premise, there is no need for regional trade agreements since governments' intent to maximize national welfare would avoid any deviation from the idea of free trade as a self-defeating choice. In spite of this well-established notion, unilateral trade policies that inefficiently restrict trade flows do occur, and trade agreements that aim to limit such unilateral actions have been put in place. One of the most fundamental reasons for this phenomenon is the fact that most international trade is conducted in imperfect markets. They are mostly oligopolistic. For instance, the European Champions League as a composite of different national leagues, e.g. Premier League, La Liga, Bundes Liga, Series A and suchlike, might be a good example of an oligopolistic market structure. The individual leagues maintain almost absolute market power over the respective national markets while also collectively controlling the interleague contests such as the Union of European Football Associations (UEFA) tournaments. Since the market is imperfectly competitive, there are inherent problems in the trade in playing talent within and among the leagues in terms of efficiency and fairness. This issue will be covered later in light of Bosman Ruling (*Union Royale Beige des Societes de Football Association* v. *Bosman* (1995)).

Economists have developed several theoretical notions to explain free trade agreements in terms of their systematic inefficiency. The first one is based on the concept of static terms of trade. The approach points out that a country would likely be tempted to manipulate static terms of trade (i.e. price of exports relative to imports) in order to increase its own national income at the expense of the other trading partners in the absence of a binding trade agreement. In essence, it is based on the fact that each country would get some considerable benefit by erecting trade barriers, at least in the short term. Particularly, countries with market power, usually developed countries, may not be able to resist the temptation to act in their own interests. Johnson (1954) analysed a situation where each country set restrictive trade policies for immediate benefits. The study demonstrated a "non-cooperative equilibrium" (known as the "Nash equilibrium") where the unilateral actions of the individual countries would

Table 17.1 Non-cooperative equilibrium: no multilateral agreement

	Rest of the world (ROW) pursue free trade	Rest of the world (ROW) sets restrictive trade policy
Country A pursues free trade	A's terms of trade (TOT) is at status quo, ROW 's terms of trade is at status quo	A's TOT worsens a lot, ROW's TOT improves a lot
Country A sets restrictive trade policy	A's TOT improves a lot, ROW's TOT worsens a lot	**A's TOT changes little but trade volume reduces, ROW's TOT changes little but trade volume reduces**

ultimately cancel out the overall gains as a whole in the world, i.e. systematic inefficiency. The restrictive trade policies established by all countries have little net effect on their static terms of trade, but lead to a significant contraction of the trade volume, which reduces total economic welfare (WTO, 2009).

Table 17.1 illustrates a simultaneous-move game between Country A and the rest of the world (ROW) with payoff matrices. Here, the Nash Equilibrium is the third row and third column (bold area), meaning that each player would probably choose the "dominant" strategy of restrictive trade policy (Nash Equilibrium), which leads to a less favourable outcome to virtually all the participants. While everyone could have been in a better position by choosing the "dominated" strategy, i.e. free trade without trade barriers, each player's self-interest in increasing their own benefits would make everyone worse off. The Nash Equilibrium here is Pareto-inefficient for all participants because they could have been in a better position by choosing the strategy of free trade, with the outcome in the second row and second column, but they would not. This payoff structure is caused by two factors: (1) if one country can cheat without getting caught, the cheater will attain more benefit; and (2) there is nothing to prevent the cheating by setting positive or negative inducement. Such a situation is often referred to as a "prisoner's dilemma". In the context of global trade, it can be avoided through a trade agreement between countries that may encourage them to cooperate rather than act unilaterally. By cooperating, they may be able to overcome this structural inefficiency (Mayer, 1981). Bagwell and Staiger (1999) theorized that reciprocity and non-discrimination are two simple solutions to the self-defeating prisoner's dilemma. Here it is important to note that in the absence of external punishment, the trade agreement needs to be self-enforcing because the signatories will not abide by the rules unless the observance of the agreement is in accordance with their own interests.

In sport, the above-mentioned prisoner's dilemma and Nash Equilibrium explain why maintaining competitive balance in a sport league might be a challenging issue. Competitive balance is crucial to sport leagues since it significantly affects the entertainment value of the athletic contests. Even though many stakeholders in the business are aware of the importance of parity on the playing field, every team possesses a self-interest in winning the contests. In particular, a big market team with a plenty of resources may not have the incentives to refrain from stockpiling playing talents in the roster. The prisoner's dilemma and Nash Equilibrium well explain the situation. While all teams in the league would be in a better position by avoiding wasteful arms races and maintaining competitive balance, each team's self-interest would probably drive everyone into the dominant strategy, i.e. arms races. Given the systematic problem, sport leagues usually implement several measures designed to maintain competitive balance, e.g. salary cap, reverse-order draft, restrictive free agency, and so on.

Another theoretical exposition is the dynamic perspective that takes into consideration a long-run and multi-dimensional relationship among trade partners. In reality, the simultaneous-move prisoner's dilemma game is likely to be repeated into a long-run situation. Thus the short-term gains from the evasion of the commitment to trade agreements would be balanced out by the long-term loss from possible retaliation. The multi-dimensional scope of dynamic perspective deals with some aspects not covered by the simultaneous game theory. For instance, when a government sets trade policies, some domestic sources of inefficiency might be unavoidable. First, a so-called time-inconsistency problem may occur. This happens when the government's decision to implement a certain trade policy for the future might not become effective when the future moment actually arrives. Several studies highlight that time-inconsistent trade policies may lead to systematic inefficiency (Amin, 2003; Matsuyama, 1990; Staiger & Tabellini, 1987). They indicate that while the government may wish to implement trade policies in order to increase social welfare, for example by providing temporary protection to an infant domestic industry, the policies would not bring their expected outcomes later because the market agents would already have responded and adjusted their behaviours in consideration of the known trade policies for the future. On the other hand, political pressures from lobbying groups may bring another type of inefficiency. Consider a country that does not have a comparative advantage in an economic sector. A set of import restrictions would reward the domestic producers and, at the same time, divert investments from other, presumably more efficient, activities. The cost of the intervention may become large in the long term. Lastly, according to Maggi and Rodriguez-Clare (1998), domestic pressures may force policy-makers to set high trade restrictions.

Given the structural problems involved with trade agreements, a government should undertake policy commitments that will bind its own future activity. That is, in addition to facilitating the cooperation between the trade partners, a trade agreement would need to reduce (or eliminate) the governments' own discretionary power in setting tariffs or returning to unilateral trade protectionism. Such provisions would improve the bargaining power of the country in the negotiation process and effectively deal with domestic pressures on the liberalized trade policy (WTO, 2009). As such, although the GATT and the WTO have been remarkable in terms of the promotion of free trade, the systems have also had a couple of critical shortcomings, i.e. the preferential arrangements among some groups of countries and an ineffective dispute settlement mechanism (DSM). Indeed, it is inherently difficult to arrange an effective multilateral free trade agreement among many sovereign entities due to unique domestic issues and collective dynamics among the member states.

Evolution from GATT/WTO to FTA

Given the variety of challenges associated with complete liberalization at the global level, countries have sought some limited liberalization within smaller groups, i.e. formation of discriminatory regional FTAs. The prevalence of this regionalism has been analysed in terms of systematic necessity under the game theory. Krugman (1991) was the first scholar who examined the question of all regional blocs of the world forming their own FTAs. The country proposing to form an FTA would, as the FTA was formed, (1) gain from trade creation and (2) also experience costs from trade diversion. In Krugman's model, for those countries in pursuit of FTAs, benefits from the trade creation would dominate the costs of trade diversion. In contrast, the rest of the world would lose from the trade diversion caused

Table 17.2 Non-cooperative equilibrium: WTO and FTA (based on an analysis conducted by Lewis, 2011)

	Member B cooperates under WTO	*Member B non-cooperates and focuses on FTA*
Member A cooperates under WTO	A wins some, B wins some	A loses more, B wins more
Member A non-cooperates and focuses on FTA	A wins more, B loses more	**A wins less, B wins less**

by the formation of the FTAs. Krugman's striking finding is that, when all countries form such local FTAs simultaneously, for every individual country the effects of the trade diversion imposed by all the other FTAs would outweigh the benefits of the trade creation generated from the particular FTA. The payoffs, as per Krugman, really make the situation like another prisoner's dilemma. Consider the following payoff matrices between WTO member countries, A and B.

As Table 17.2 illustrates, in a simultaneous move game between countries A and B, the Nash Equilibrium outcome results in the third row and third column (bold area). Because the WTO members focus on negotiating FTAs instead of the WTO multilateral liberalization, they are moving to a less favourable outcome than each would have achieved by adopting the "dominated" strategy, i.e. cooperating under the existing WTO system. The Nash Equilibrium is Pareto-inefficient for A and B because they could have been in a better position by choosing the strategy of focusing on the WTO system, which is the outcome in the first row and first column. It fits the pattern of another prisoner's dilemma because the choice of the dominant strategy will result in structural inefficiency. In fact, until the 1990s, the global sporting goods market had significantly relied upon the trade between highly compartmentalized FTAs such as NAFTA and the EU. Theoretically, such compartmentalized regionalization (Andreff, 2006b) might have been Pareto-inefficient. In brief, trade agreements may allow countries to cooperate in general but also bring trade war in cases of unilateral action. Second, countries may benefit from trade agreements as they would help governments commit to specific trade policies more consistently in the long term by enduring pressures from some domestic factions.

Legal aspects of free trade agreements

FTAs and other trade agreements are international treaties. When a treaty is agreed between delegates of signatory nations who have proper legal authority and is ratified through their respective domestic political regimes, it becomes a binding international contract between nations and within the domestic markets. The US Constitution delegates treaty-making power to the president and Senate. Article II § 2 of the Constitution states that the president "shall have power, by and with the advice and consent of the Senate, to make treaties, provided two thirds of the Senators present concur" (LexisNexis, 2016).

Although the constitutional provision expressly requires a super-majority vote within the Senate, some FTAs including NAFTA and the WTO have been approved by a simple majority vote by both houses under the doctrine of congressional–executive agreement. The doctrine reflects the long-standing congressional policy to support reciprocal trade relationships with other nations (Congressional Research Service, 2013). Basically, the doctrine allows the president to enter into a trade agreement with another country during a limited time frame, which becomes effective within the US only if the treaty is later approved by both houses' simple majority vote. This statutorily created temporary authority is called the Trade Promotion Authority of the President (Congressional Research Service, 2013). It intends to speed up trade negotiations. In *Made in the USA Foundation* v. *United States* (2001), the constitutionality of Trade Promotion Authority was challenged in a federal court. The 11th Circuit opined that such temporary authority is constitutional.

On the other hand, Article VI of the Constitution indicates the legal effectiveness of treaties within the US legal system: "[t]his Constitution . . . and all treaties . . . shall be the supreme law of the land; and the judges in every state shall be bound thereby, anything in the constitution or laws of any state to the contrary notwithstanding" (LexisNexis, 2016). Thus, FTAs supersede any conflicting state law (*Camphor Technologies, Inc.* v. *Biofer, S.P.A.* (2007)). In the federal system, since treaties are equivalent to federal statutes, FTAs are still subject to the scrutiny under the US Constitution (*Ex parte Medellin* (2008)). Finally, a treaty may not be inconsistent with so-called *jus cogens* norms that are the fundamental principles of international law that bind all nations in the world (*US* v. *Struckman* (2010)).

FTAs do not always provide a private cause of action to individual citizens to bring enforcement actions in domestic courts (*Cauthern* v. *State* (2004)). In general, it is presumed that a private citizen may not sue another individual citizen, corporation or foreign government for a violation of treaty unless the treaty is "self-executing" (*Katel Ltd Liability Co.* v. *AT & T Corp.* (2010)). Here "self-executing" means that the treaty expressly allows a private citizen to resort to private legal actions within the parameter of the treaty. The right to private litigation would not be recognized simply because the treaty provides substantive rules of conduct that may create significant benefits to individual citizens (*State* v. *Sanchez-Llamas* (2006)). A private citizen who intends to bring a legal action under a non-self-executing treaty must resort to other domestic law, e.g. statutes (*Renkel* v. *US* (2006)). In many cases, aggrieved private parties need to petition their governments to represent their interests through the process of renegotiation or international tribunals.

Different enforcement schemes have been devised and implemented to effectuate international treaties. Schneider (1999) proposed a conceptual framework that characterizes various enforcement regimes operated under different international treaties. The author identified particularities of enforcement systems in terms of: (1) individual rights and standing; (2) supremacy; (3) transparency; and (4) enforcement and punishment. The first variable of the analysis, individual rights and standing, is whether private citizens can bring legal actions against other individuals, companies or sovereign entities for violations. Second, supremacy means whether the decisions made from the dispute resolution system under the treaty would supersede other domestic law of the signatory nations. The third variable, transparency, is the extent to which the treaty's dispute resolution system discloses the information about the rationale of the decisions to maintain the transparency and predictability of the system. The last variable is enforcement and punishment, and examines whether the tribunal system has an effective enforcement mechanism including some punitive measures to create substantial deterrence effects. Based on this framework, the author evaluated the enforcement mechanisms of many treaties. The study categorized enforcement systems into four groups – negotiation regime, investor arbitration regime, international adjudication regime, and supernational court regime. Table 17.3 shows the categories and example treaties based on the proposed methodology.

Table 17.3 Classification of treaty enforcement system (Schneider, 1999)

Enforcement categories (example)	Variables of classification			
	Individual rights to sue	Supremacy over domestic law	Transparency and predictability	Enforcement system
Negotiation (GATT, NAFTA)	No	No	Not mandated	Voluntary compliance
Investor arbitration (New York Convention)	Only against government	No	No	Effective
International adjudication (WTO)	No	Yes	Yes	Questionable
Supernational court (European Court of Justice)	Yes	Yes	Yes	Very effective

International trade in sporting goods

Traditionally, the trade in sporting goods had been concentrated on the North–North trade among developed countries (Andreff, 2006b). One of the notable patterns in the global sporting goods market was so-called "regionalization" that happens within or between the continental trade blocs of developed countries (Andreff, 2006b). For instance, between 1974 and 1994, about two-thirds of NAFTA's sporting goods trade was within-the-bloc trade and with EU countries, whereas two-thirds of the EU's sporting goods trade was within-the-bloc trade and with the NAFTA countries (Andreff, 2006b). Recently, however, the sporting goods trade among newly industrialized Asian countries has exponentially increased. Consequently, the overall share of the NAFTA and EU blocs in the global trade has consistently declined (Andreff, 2006b).

The global sporting goods industry has several unique characteristics. Most of all, the industry is a highly segmented market (Andreff, 2006a). Since sport activities are diversified, especially in developed countries, one segment of sporting goods does not have a common utility value for another. For a recreational golfer living in Pennsylvania, his or her golf equipment becomes almost useless during the winter season when the same person enjoys skiing and snowboarding. A pair of tennis rackets does not have any utility value to tennis players when they ride mountain bikes. The size and growth of each sporting goods segment is likely to be determined by a function of various socioeconomic variables such as "fashion, the use value of sport good, its market price, households' professions and revenues, the population's use of equipment (equipment rate), and the sports good's life cycle" (Andreff, 2006a, p. 27). Indeed, sellers need to adjust to such a highly segmented market demand that may not grow at the same pace. In fact, the demand for sporting goods is extremely volatile in the long run (Andreff, 2006a).

The supply side of the industry is so-called "fringed global oligopoly" (Andreff, 2006a, p. 31). The global sporting goods market is basically dominated by a small number of multinational corporations competing at the international level. At the same time, such multinationals compete with a fringe of small local companies in domestic markets. Because a price war would not be prevalent in such an oligopolistic market structure, the main strategies for the dominating multinational firms to keep or increase their market share and profits are marketing efforts, research and development (R&D) and cost-saving tactics. As witnessed in any oligopoly, the multinationals usually establish a variety of entry barriers that may exclude new competitors, for example, a restrictive distribution system, unexploited patents, reliance on economies of scale, etc. (Andreff, 2006a). Since the 1990s, the growth rate of the global sporting goods industry has been much lower than in previous decades and the industry is deemed to enter into a consolidation phase (Lulof, 1998). Hence, there have been notable trans-border mergers and acquisitions since the 1990s, such as the Salomon and Reebok acquisition by Adidas, Converse by Nike, and so on. Indeed, the concentration of the industry is even more noticeable recently (Andreff, 2006b).

Sporting goods can be divided into two distinctive categories based on the degree of specialization and technology associated with product attributes, i.e. "equipment-intensive goods" and "trite goods" (Andreff, 2006b, p. 62). The equipment-intensive goods are those products with highly specialized unit values that are likely to require advanced R&D foundations and sophisticated manufacturing processes, such as ski, snowboard, golf, yacht and motor sport equipment, and so on. The trite goods category comprises those goods with relatively low unit values that could be used for a wider range of sport activities, for example footwear, sportswear, tracksuits and the like (Andreff, 2006b). An empirical investigation of the global trade in sporting goods (Andreff & Andreff, 2009) revealed that while a substantial number of developing countries are net exporters in the trite goods category, they are mostly net importers in the equipment-intensive goods category. In contrast, many net exporters in the equipment-intensive goods category are developed countries whereas most of them are net importers in the trite goods class. The study demonstrated the North–South trade pattern in the global sporting goods industry in terms of the relationship between technological diffusion and product attributes.

Another remarkable phenomenon in the industry is the production relocation strategy used by transnational sport branding firms such as Nike and Adidas. The production relocation in this context is a system of "outward-processing trade regulation" (Andreff, 2006b, p. 65). The process begins with the vertical disintegration between the manufacturing process and other business functions such as marketing, R&D and financing. It primarily intends to maintain a flexibly specialized production mechanism that can effectively respond to the highly volatile market demand in the global sporting goods industry. Under this system, all or almost all manufacturing is performed by subcontracting companies in developing countries with lower labour costs under so-called Original Equipment Manufacturer (OEM) contracts. The OEM practice is a production system in which a subcontractor firm makes a part or entire subsystem for another firm's end products. For instance, Nike's current business operation in the US does not have any production capacity at all (Andreff, 2006b), whereas all non-production units overseas are directly controlled by the Nike headquarters in Beaverton, Oregon. The Nike headquarters manages the entire process of product development, financing, marketing, governance and sales. It basically coordinates the input and output trade between the manufacturing centres located in developing countries, and consumer markets in developed countries (Donagu & Barff, 1990). This pattern of intra-firm North–South trade has become a predominant form of business operation in the global sporting goods industry. As a result, the majority of developed countries in NAFTA and the EU are currently net importers in the arena of the global sporting goods trade (Andreff, 2006b).

Normatively speaking, the international trade in sporting goods is conducted within the scope of this North–South trade pattern in conjunction with various FTAs and multilateral trade agreements. The production relocation mechanism, i.e. the outward-processing trade regulation based on the OEM production system, is fully subject to the trade flow of goods between the manufacturing centres in developing countries and the consumer markets in developed countries. Under the various forms of FTAs and other trade agreements, transnational sport branding firms seek the outward-trade benefits from the production strategy. Most of all, because FTAs and multilateral trade agreements presumably create socio-economic dynamics that would enhance the process of specialization, the North–South trade pattern in the global sporting goods industry, i.e. equipment-intensive goods exported from developed countries and trite goods exported from developing countries (Andreff & Andreff, 2009), would be continued and presumably enhanced.

International sporting goods trade and ancillary legal foundations

There are two ancillary legal foundations that would be crucial to the international trade in sporting goods along with FTAs and they are contract law and transnational protection of intellectual property rights. International trade agreements are an imperative means of private regulation in international goods transactions. A legally enforceable contract creates a private legal environment where a non-breaching party can ask a court of proper jurisdiction to provide a type of remedy in case of breach of contract. Here a remedy can be either a legal remedy (such as monetary compensation) or an equitable remedy (such as specific performance). The legal remedy is a type of compensation usually more favoured by courts in breach of contract cases. It is calculated from the economic loss that the non-breaching party should bear because of the breach at issue. On the other hand, the equitable remedy would be either specific performance or injunctive relief. A court order for specific performance mandates the breaching party to do something (e.g. tender of goods). The injunctive relief is provided from a court order not to do something (e.g. prohibit ownership transfer of traded goods in disputes).

In international goods transactions, parties may expressly agree upon which legal system governs the agreement, for example "contract law of State of New York including all statutory and common law". They may choose the venue and jurisdiction as far as the transaction has some impact on the jurisdiction. In the US, the Uniform Commercial Code (UCC) usually governs sales or lease of tangible goods. The UCC has eliminated many technicalities under the traditional common law of contracts in order to facilitate commercial transactions of tangible goods, particularly between merchants. UCC § 2–104 broadly defines a merchant as "a person that deals in goods of the kind or . . . having knowledge or skill peculiar to the practices or goods involved in the transaction" (LexisNexis, 2016). Thus, in many cases, if the contract parties choose US contract law as their controlling legal authority, the enforcement of the contract would probably be less complicated under the UCC.

Another important legal authority that may have profound impacts on international sporting goods trade is the Contracts for the International Sale of Goods (CISG). The CISG was adopted by the sixth special session of the General Assembly of the United Nations on the establishment of a New International Economic Order in 1980. The CISG Article 1(1) declares that the rule applies to contracts of sale of goods between parties whose places of business are in different states: (a) when the States are Contracting States or (b) when the rules of private international law lead to the application of the law of a Contracting State (LexisNexis, 2016). Here the Contracting States are those nations that have ratified the CISG as an effective legal authority in international transactions through the respective domestic political regimes. As of today, 84 nations have ratified the CISG to some degree. While the US has ratified most rules of the CISG, it has reserved the adoption of the Article 1(1)(b). This means that the CISG does not automatically supersede US contract law when an international transaction has a choice of law provision that expressly designates US contract law (e.g. State of New York contracts law) as the binding authority.

Since arbitration is more cost efficient and time-saving than formal judicial review, international trade contracts often include arbitration provisions. If a trade agreement indicates that all disputes related to the transaction will be resolved by the arbitrator's decision, the parties may not be able to resort to formal court proceedings as far as the contract formation was valid in the jurisdiction. An example arbitration clause would be:

> In the event a dispute shall arise between the parties to this contract, it is hereby agreed that the dispute shall be referred to (arbitrator or how to select arbitrator). For arbitration in accordance with the applicable United States Arbitration and Mediation Rules of Arbitration. The arbitrator's decision will be final and legally binding and judgment may be entered thereon.
>
> *United States Arbitration & Mediation, 2017*

A judicial review of the arbitrator's decision is extremely limited (*Major League Players Association* v. *Garvey* (2001)).

Because most sporting goods are inherently associated with various types of intellectual properties such as trademarks, patents and trade secrets, the protection of intellectual property rights might be another major concern in international trade. Trademark law mainly intends to protect general consumers from being confused as to the sources of goods or services. Under the law, an owner of a trademark may bring a lawsuit against another person who uses a deceptively similar mark in commerce if the plaintiff establishes three elements: (1) that the plaintiff's mark is legally protected; (2) that there was unauthorized use of the mark; and (3) that general consumers are likely to be confused by the defendant's use of the mark being deceptively similar to the plaintiff's mark. Interestingly, trademark law in general does not allow the general public's legal action against defendants even though they are in fact the parties harmed by the defendants' infractions of the law. Patent law provides an inventor of useful technology with a limited period (e.g. 20 years in the US) of exclusive rights to use and sell the technology. Both trademark and patent infringement are actionable under domestic intellectual property law as far as the enforcement system is in accordance with Article 41 of the Agreement on Trade-Related Aspects of Intellectual Property Rights promulgated by the World Trade Organization (World Trade Organization, 1994).

Spectating sport industry and RTAs/FTAs

In the context of international trade, the spectating sport industry has unique characteristics different from the global sporting goods market. Essentially, the spectating sport industry is an entertainment market that primarily relies on the playing talent of athletes. The labour market for such industry is a winner-take-all market where the market value of a small number of top-notch athletes' talent is extremely high (Frank & Bernanke, 2013). Recently, international trade in top-level athletic talents has become an important subject in the fields of sport law and economics (Ross, 2004). Even though nearly 20 per cent of global trade is the trade in services and labour (Cole & Guillin, 2015), most FTAs do not liberalize the trade in intangible services. Thus, the unrestricted trade in labour and services such as athletic talent requires some higher-level full-scale economic integration such as the European Union (EU), which is far more cohesive than typical FTAs (Cole & Guillin, 2015). As of this writing, a small fraction of international trade in athletic talent has been liberalized. Not only do public regulations such as immigration law constrain free trade in athletic talents, but also a range of transnational coordination among multiple domestic leagues also creates significant barriers to the trade in playing talent. For instance, a posting system between two or more sport leagues has significantly inhibitive effects on the international trade in athletes. Under a typical posting system, teams of foreign leagues interested in an athlete must participate in a bidding process to pay a transfer fee to the current employer to secure a new labour contract with the athlete. Usually, eligibility for such exogenous talent trade is even more restrictive than the free agency eligibility within the domestic league.

Once a high level of economic integration is established, however, restrictive measures such as an inhibitive posting system may not be allowed. The Bosman Ruling (*Union Royale Beige des Societes de Football Association* v. *Bosman* (1995)) demonstrates that labour constraints collusively set by sport leagues in the name of competitive balance and the protection of small domestic leagues might not be allowed under the full-scale economic integration such as the European Union. Bosman was a midfielder from the Belgian soccer team, RC Liege. In 1990, Bosman attempted to move to a French team, US Dunkerque. Pursuant to the transfer rule implemented by the Union of European Football Associations (UEFA), the current employer, RC Liege, demanded the French team, US Dunkerque, to pay a transfer fee. Additionally, UEFA limited the number of foreign players on a team roster under the so-called 3 + 2 rule. When the transfer was not executed, mainly due to those restrictive barriers, Bosman brought a legal action against RC Liege, the Belgian Football Association (URBSFA) and the UEFA. Bosman alleged that the UEFA's transfer rule and the 3 + 2 rule were in violation of Article 48 of the European Community Treaty that prohibited any unfair restriction on free movement of workers within the countries within the EU Community (Duffy, 2003).

In the trial, European soccer associations mainly argued that the disputed measures were necessary to maintain the competitive balance between big and small leagues. Nevertheless, the European Court of Justice decided in favour of Bosman. As a result, soccer players in European leagues now enjoy a great deal of professional mobility and higher salaries (Duffy, 2003). Relating to the Bosman Ruling, it is interesting to see that there is currently no legally certified labour union in European soccer in spite of the enormous economic pie at stake and sociocultural dynamics generally in favour of the unionization of labour. Presumably, following the ruling, soccer players may not have to resort to a strong labour union to protect their interest since the labour market is relatively open in the region. In contrast, all major professional sport leagues in the US have nationally certified labour unions probably due to the more restrictive market structure and the monopsony of the leagues (Ross, 2004).

In 2016, the United Kingdom opted to leave the European Union after a majority of voters in a national referendum supported the withdrawal. This so-called Brexit might have some impacts on British sport industry such as the English Premiere League (EPL). Since the Bosman Ruling affirmed the free movement of labour within the EU Community, the EPL could recruit talented young prospects within the EU bloc relatively easily. While players from non-EU countries entering the EPL had to obtain work permits pursuant to a set of qualifying criteria, players from EU countries did not undergo the same process. As a result, a number of young prospects from EU countries who might not have been qualified under the British work permit system began their careers in the league and had remarkable success, such as N'Golo Kante, Dimitri Payet and Riyad Mahrez. If Brexit significantly restricts such player development and the recruitment system around the EPL, the size of the talent pool may become smaller in the long run, which may have some negative impact on the entertainment value of the EPL contests. In addition, the declining value of the British pound after Brexit may influence the business operation of the league due to the devaluation of EPL franchises and broadcasting rights, higher retention costs for veteran players and so on.

Under an FTA, a transnational sport league encompassing more than one country might have to deal with an intriguing compliance issue because a treaty usually prohibits governments from treating domestic firms more favourably than foreign investments. For instance, because the NHL consists of team franchises located both in the US and Canada, the league might need to consider some implications of Article 1105 of the North American Free Trade Agreement (NAFTA). Article 1105 of NAFTA requires the signatory governments to provide "fair and equitable treatment and full protection and security" to investments of foreign companies (LexisNexis, 2016). On the other hand, Article 1116 allows firms in a NAFTA country to file a claim against governments of other member countries if the host countries' policies or laws harm their businesses (LexisNexis, 2016). The regulations would allow Canadian NHL teams to bring legal claims against US municipalities and state governments since many American NHL franchises have received various forms of government subsidies whereas Canadian NHL teams do not usually enjoy such government-induced advantages. Thus, Wu and Longley (2003) argue that a strict interpretation of the relevant NAFTA provisions would allow such legal action because Canadian-based NHL teams operating in the US could constitute an investment for the purpose of NAFTA. Nevertheless, the authors also raised a question as to whether the framers of NAFTA intended those enforcement provisions to be applied to the spectating sport industry where teams are more likely economic partners rather than genuine economic competitors.

Conclusion

Economic theories demonstrate that multilateral agreements to liberalize international trade would make all trade partners better off under the notion of specialization and comparative advantage. This chapter explored economics rationales explaining trade agreements in terms of non-cooperative equilibrium. While it is well known that liberalization of global trade would bring more benefits to everyone in perfectly competitive markets than otherwise, maintaining a multilateral trade agreement system is challenging in imperfectly competitive market conditions. Thus well-coordinated enforcement mechanisms are almost always necessary to establish sufficient deterrence effects on the deviant behaviour of participating trade partners.

In the United States, an FTA or multilateral trade agreement is deemed to be an international treaty. Therefore, the president negotiates on behalf of the country and the legislature needs ratifying accordingly. The legal authority of a treaty is equivalent to federal statutes enacted by the Congress. As a result, FTAs supersede any conflicting state law in the US. Many trade agreements do not provide private citizens with the right to bring legal actions. Usually, individual citizens of signatory member nations need to petition their own governments to represent their interests in the process of renegotiation or international tribunals. If an FTA is "self-executing", private individuals may bring legal claims against a host country's government and/or citizens. There is a wide variety of enforcement mechanisms in terms of the enforceability of treaties.

FTAs, multilateral trade agreements, and full-scale economic integration would have profound impacts on international transactions in sporting goods and athletic talents. The sporting goods industry is an oligopolistic industry where a small number of transnational firms compete in the global market by using non-pricing tactics such as R&D, marketing or production relocation strategy. The typical pattern of North–South trade has been predominant in the current global sporting goods industry. While most FTAs do not intend to liberalize the trade in labour or services, a full-scale economic integration such as the EU may remove measures of protectionism as evidenced in the Bosman Ruling (1995). A transnational sport league encompassing more than one country within an FTA might have to deal with the issue of equitable treatment when one of the governments provides subsidies to its domestic teams that are not available in another country.

References

Amin, M. (2003). *Time Inconsistency of Trade Policy and Multilateralism*. New York, NY: Columbia University Press.

Andreff, W. (2006a). "The sports goods industry". In W. Andreff & S. Szymanski (Eds), *Handbook on the Economics of Sport*. Northampton, MA: Edward Elgar Publishing (pp. 27–39).

Andreff, W. (2006b). "International trade in sports goods". In W. Andreff & S. Szymanski (Eds), *Handbook on the Economics of Sport*. Northampton, MA: Edward Elgar Publishing (pp. 59–67).

Andreff, M. & Andreff, W. (2009). Global trade in sports goods: International specialization of major trading countries. *European Sport Management Quarterly, 9*(3), 259–294.

Bagwell, K. & Staiger, R. (1999). An economic theory of GATT. *American Economic Review, 89*(1), 215–248.

Bhagwati, J. (2008). *Termites in the Trading System*. New York, NY: Oxford University Press.

Camphor Technologies, Inc. v. Biofer, S.P.A., 916 A.2d 142 (Super. Ct. 2007).

Cauthern v. State, 145 S.W.3d 571 (Tenn. Crim. App. 2004).

Cole, M. T. & Guillin, A. (2015). The determinants of trade agreements in services vs. goods. *International Economics, 144*, 66–82.

Collignon, H., Sultan, N. & Santander, C. (2011). *The Sports Market: Major Trends and Challenges in an Industry Full of Passion*. Available at <http://www.atkearney.com/documents/10192/6f46b880-f8d1-4909-9960-cc605bb1ff34>. Accessed 25 March 2016.

Congressional Research Service (2013). *Why certain trade agreements are approved as Congressional-Executive agreements rather than treaties*. Available at: <https://www.fas.org/sgp/crs/misc/97-896.pdf>. Accessed 10 March 2016.

Duffy, W. (2003). Football may be ill, but don't blame Bosman. *Sports Lawyers Journal, 10*, 295–315.

Donagu, M. T. & Barff, R. (1990). Nike just did it: International subcontracting and flexibility in athletic footwear production. *Journal of the Regional Studies Association, 24*, 537–551.

Ex parte Medellin, 552 US (491) 2008.

Frank, R. H. & Bernanke, B. S. (2013). *Principles of Economics (5th edition)*. New York, NY: McGraw-Hill.

Johnson, H. (1954). Optimum tariffs and retaliation. *Review of Economic Studies, 21*, 142–153.

Krugman, P. (1991). "Is bilateralism bad?" In E. Helpman and A. Razin (Eds), *International Trade and Trade Policy*, Cambridge, MA: MIT Press.

Lewis, M. K. (2011). The Prisoners' Dilemma posed by Free Trade Agreements: Can open access provisions provide an escape? *Chicago Journal of International Law, 11*, 631–661.

LexisNexis (2016). Contracts for International Sale of Goods (CISG), Art. 1(1).

LexisNexis (2016). North American Free Trade Agreement, Art. 1105, December 17, 1992, 32 I.L.M. 605.

LexisNexis (2016). North American Free Trade Agreement, Art. 1116, December 17, 1992, 32 I.L.M. 605.

LexisNexis (2016). Uniform Commercial Code § 2–104 (amended 2003).

LexisNexis (2016). United States Constitution, Art. II, § 2.

LexisNexis (2016). United States Constitution, Art. VI.

Katel Ltd Liability Co. v. AT & T Corp., 607 F.3d 60 (2d Cir. 2010).

Lulof, F. (1998). "Sporting goods business is show business". *WFSGI News Bulletin*, 26–27.

Made in the USA Foundation v. *United States*, 242 F.3d 1300 (11th Cir. 2001); 534 US 1039 (2001) (*certiorari* denied).

Maggi, G. & Rodriguez-Clare, A. (1998). The value of trade agreements in the presence of political pressures. *Journal of Political Economy, 106*, 574–601.

Major League Players Association v. *Garvey*, 532 US 504 (2001).

Matsuyama, K. (1990). Perfect equilibria in a trade liberalization game. *American Economic Review, 80*(3), 480–492.

Mayer, W. (1981). Theoretical considerations on negotiated tariff adjustments. *Oxford Economic Papers, 33*(1), 135–153.

Renkel v. *US,* 456 F.3d 640 (6th Cir. 2006).

Ross, S. F. (2004). Player restraints and competition law throughout the world. *Marquette Sport Law Review, 15,* 49–61.

Schneider, A. K. (1999). Getting along: The evolution of dispute resolution regimes in international trade organizations. *Michigan Journal of International Law, 20*(4), 697–773.

State v. *Sanchez-Llamas,* 548 US 331 (2006).

Staiger, R. W. & Tabellini, G. (1987). Discretionary trade policy and excessive protection. *American Economic Review,* 77(5), 823–837.

Union Royale Beige des Societes de Football Association v. *Bosman,* Case C-415/93, 1995 E.C.R. I-04921.

United States Arbitration & Mediation (2017). *Sample Arbitration Clause.* Available at <http://usam.com/sample-arbitration-clause/>. Accessed 9 March, 2017.

US v. *Struckman,* 611 F.3d 560 (9th Cir. 2010).

Whaples, R. (2006). "Do economists agree on anything? Yes!" *The Economists' Voice, 3*(9), 1–6.

World Trade Organization (1994). "Agreement on trade-related aspects of intellectual property rights". Available at <https://www.wto.org/english/tratop_e/trips_e/t_agm0_e.htm>. Accessed 15 March 2016.

World Trade Organization (2009). *The World Trade Report 2009.* [online] Available at <https://www.wto.org/english/res_e/publications_e/wtr15_e.htm>. Accessed 28 March 2016.

Wu, T. & Longley, N. (2003). The applicability of NAFTA to the subsidization of US-based NHL teams: Legal and economic perspectives. *Law and Business Review of the Americas, 9*(3), 571–592.

PART IV

Legal aspects

International sport brings together different nations with different legal systems under single sport governance structures. What is considered the norm in one country may be considered illegal in another. The major multinational sport organizations, FIFA and the IOC, often operate in their own legal system as they do not fall directly under the jurisdiction of any country while sport apparel brands known across the globe use chains of production and supply that span the globe. All of this results in new legal challenges regarding property rights, individual rights, sound governance and accountability. Well defined rights and a consistent legal framework that both transcends borders and honours the individual sovereignty of nations are necessary for international sport business to function at a high level. The authors in this Part address several pertinent issues.

The chapters in this section are particularly novel because their focus is directly linked to sport business. The authors investigate issues related to sport governance, corruption and bribery, intellectual property, image rights, athlete privacy concerns and trademark issues.

18

ATHLETE INVOLVEMENT IN THE GOVERNANCE OF SPORT ORGANIZATIONS

Bogdan Ciomaga, Lucie Thibault and Lisa A. Kihl

Introduction

Governance and democracy are important concepts for the effective operation of any organization. Bevir (2009) explained good governance as "a legitimate state with a democratic mandate, an efficient and open administration, and the use of competition and markets in the public and private sectors" (p. 26). In addition, Bevir (2009) acknowledged the quest of many international agencies to put in place checks and balances for executive powers to ensure appropriate representation, impartiality and equity. Accountability and responsible and transparent decision-making processes are also central elements of good governance. Although governance and democracy have been extensively featured in public organizations (i.e. governments), the concepts are relevant and important to private organizations (i.e. nonprofit and commercial organizations) operating in various sectors and industries.

In the context of sport, governance and democracy are essential particularly in light of the seemingly increasing number of incidents involving questionable behaviours and practices in sport. Based on these highly visible transgressions, it appears that numerous sport organizations are experiencing a crisis of governance (cf. Geeraert, 2015; Katwala, 2000). Questionable practices and behaviours in sport, in recent years have included corruption, bribery, cheating, doping, judging issues, betting and match fixing. As a result, many journalists, sport leaders and scholars have emphasized the need for good governance in sport (cf. Chaker, 2004; European Union, 2013; Forster, 2006; Geeraert, 2015; Geeraert, Alm & Groll, 2014; Hoye & Cuskelly, 2007; Jennings, 2007). Good governance in sport is defined as:

> the framework and culture within which a sports body sets policy, delivers its strategic objectives, engages with stakeholders, monitors performance, evaluates and manages risk and reports to its constituents on its activities and progress including the delivery of effective, sustainable and proportionate sports policy and regulation.
>
> *European Union, 2013, p. 5*

Along similar lines, the Commission of the European Communities (2007) identified common principles for good governance in sport, more specifically "transparency, democracy, accountability and representation of stakeholders (associations, federations, players, clubs, leagues, supporters, etc.)" (p. 12). The principle of transparency includes the development of clear procedures for organizational operations and decision making. Democracy refers to representation in the decision-making process by the stakeholders within the organization while accountability involves the act of being responsible with organizational resources and taking responsibility for one's actions (Henry & Lee, 2004). Representation of stakeholders is connected to democracy in that it ensures that the organization's stakeholders are represented in organizational operations and decision making (Henry & Lee, 2004).

On the topic of stakeholder representation, calls for athletes to be recognized as key stakeholders in sport organizations have been raised (cf. Katwala, 2000; Kihl, Kikulis & Thibault, 2007; Thibault, Kihl & Babiak, 2010). Spurred by the recommendation of the International Olympic Committee (IOC) 2000 Commission (1999) to establish athletes' commissions in national and international sport organizations, the idea of actively engaging athletes in organizations' governance appears to be gaining ground (cf. Katwala, 2000; Kihl *et al.*, 2007; Thibault *et al.*, 2010). In fact, the IOC Athletes' Commission (2014) published a *Guide to Developing an Effective Athletes' Commission* where the role and responsibilities of athletes in the governance of their sport organization were identified. Specifically, the IOC noted that Athletes' Commissions "are a platform where the views of athletes are represented and the voice of athletes can be heard" (p. 7). The IOC also underscored the fact that Athletes' Commissions are "an integral part of an organization's decision-making process" (p. 7). Furthermore, Thibault *et al.* (2010, p. 298) noted that:

> the establishment of athletes committees [or commissions] is one strategy to provide athletes with a voice in the organizations about issues that affect them, though it may not necessarily lead to a true athlete-centred approach. . . . Athletes should be asked about their perception of the most effective methods for their involvement in policies and decisions that affect them.

The purpose of this chapter is to present the various manifestations of athletes' participation in the governance of national sport organizations (NSOs) in four countries (Australia, Canada, the United Kingdom and the United States), focusing on the degree to which NSOs are athlete-centred, and on the challenges faced by the efforts to give athletes a voice, while at the same time evaluating the democratic character of each model of athletes' participation in governance.

Previous research on governance issues within international and national sport organizations have been featured (cf. Chaker 2004; Forster, 2006; Geeraert, 2015; Geeraert *et al.*, 2014; Katwala, 2000) as well as research focusing on the increasing role of athletes in the decision-making processes of international and national sport organizations (cf. Kihl *et al.*, 2007; Thibault *et al.*, 2010). In their discussion of deliberative democratic principles within athlete-centred sport, Kihl *et al.* (2007) noted that even if there is evidence of increased participation of athletes in decisions and policies of their sport organizations through deliberate and democratic processes, athletes' involvement may be limited and not yet "judged as a critical component to enhancing the quality and value of decisions or policies" (p. 24). In a survey of International Sport Federations' (ISFs) inclusion of Athletes' Committees (ACs) as part of their structure, Thibault *et al.* (2010) found that even though ACs were created and operational within most sport organizations, athletes' involvement in decisions and policies that directly affected them was not always evident. In fact, the authors noted that a small number of ISFs (seven out of 24) had ACs as part of their structure; however the membership of these committees did not include current or recently retired athletes. Thibault *et al.*'s (2010) findings supported previous work by Houlihan (2004) and Jackson and Ritchie (2007), confirming athletes' limited engagement in decision and policy making in sport organizations.

Based on our review of the literature on sport governance, there is no doubt that athletes are central stakeholders within sport organizations. What is questioned, however, is the role athletes play in the governance of their sport and their level of engagement in decision and policy making within their sport organization. By analysing and comparing athlete involvement in decision and policy making within NSOs in four countries, we can better understand how athletes contribute to the governance and democratic nature of their sport organizations as well as the challenges connected to athletes' involvement.

Methods

Data on governance of NSOs were collected from organizations from four countries (Australia (AU), Canada (CA), the United Kingdom (UK), and the United States (US)). Forty-seven non-Olympic and Olympic sports were chosen to provide a broader perspective. Information on governance practices was collected by accessing the websites of these NSOs and downloading documents such as constitutions and bylaws, organizational charts, ACs' descriptions, annual reports, and other documents deemed relevant. When the required information was not complete or was missing entirely, leaders of NSOs were contacted through electronic mail to obtain this information.

A total of 177 NSOs (CA=48, US=47, AU=43, UK=39) were identified. In the UK, in some sports, the governing NSOs covered the UK or Great Britain (e.g. athletics), while in other sports, there were only separate sport organizations for England, Scotland, Wales and Northern Ireland. Only the first type of organization was retained. Information on the existence of ACs was identified in 85 organizations (49.72 per cent of all organizations) – US=37 (78.72 per cent of US organizations), CA=21 (43.75 per cent of CA organizations), AU=20 (46.51 per cent of AU organizations), and UK=7 (17.95 per cent of UK organizations). Information on the presence of athletes' representatives on boards of directors or executive committees was identified in 115 organizations (67.23 per cent of all organizations) – US=46 (97.87 per cent of all US organizations), CA=36 (75.00 per cent of all Canadian organizations), AU=26 (60.47 per cent of all AU organizations), and UK=7 (17.95 per cent of all UK organizations). Information on the presence of athletes' representatives on committees was evident in 82 organizations (46.33 per cent of all organizations) – US=45 (95.74 per cent of all US organizations), CA=26 (54.17 per cent of all Canadian organizations), UK=8 (20.51 per cent of all UK organizations), and AU=3 (6.98 per cent of all AU organizations).

In order to determine the extent to which NSOs viewed athletes as central to their mission, a thematic qualitative analysis of the goals and objectives outlined by these organizations in their bylaws and constitutions was undertaken, under the assumption that these constitutive acts reflected the priorities guiding NSOs and defined the organizations' public image. The six stages described by Braun and Clarke (2006) (i.e. familiarizing with data, generalizing initial codes, searching for themes, reviewing themes, defining and naming themes and producing the report) were implemented to condense the data. The analysis was first carried out on CA organizations and then the themes obtained were deductively verified in the case of NSOs from the US, UK and AU. A similar thematic analysis was undertaken of goals and objectives for ACs in the NSOs studied, where such a committee existed.

In order to better understand athletes' roles in NSO governance and in an effort to avoid "one sidedness of the topic" (Patton, 2002, p. 109), a maximum variation approach was used, focusing on those NSOs that are outliers from the dominant governance patterns, highlighting the differences between various solutions to governance problems. These various solutions were then analysed from the point of view of the potential they offer athletes to participate in the administration of NSOs.

Athlete-centredness

A thematic qualitative analysis of the objectives presented in the constitutions/bylaws of NSOs in CA showed that organizations considered their primary responsibility to be sport-centred and administrative in nature, rather than athlete-centred. Thus, NSOs seemed primarily interested in a series of aspects pertaining to the good functioning of organizations, such as maintaining the status of the official governing body of a sport in CA, developing policy and programmes, organizing events and fielding national teams, as well as all operational aspects central to any organization (e.g. marketing, communication and financial management). The second main theme, the one revolving around fostering the growth of sport in CA, concerned development of expertise in athletes, coaches and officials, as well as increased performance and participation, awareness of the sport, management of rules, valuing the historical tradition of the sport and stimulating sport values such as fair play or amateurism.

While these two themes were found in all formulations of NSOs' objectives, athletes were not mentioned frequently. Of the 23 description of objectives, only seven mentioned athletes and a further ten mentioned members. However, most instances where "athletes" or "members" were included fell under the umbrella of administrative or sport-centric concerns. For example, when Boxing Canada identified as an objective to "arrange or assist in the arrangement of courses of instruction for coaches, athletes, officials or other interested persons in matters concerning the sport of amateur boxing" (Boxing Canada, 1992, p. 2), the interests of athletes were regarded as interlinked with those of sport. In this case, athletes were considered solely as athletes, rather than as potential participants in the governance. Similarly, when the Shooting Federation of Canada outlined the need to provide administrative support and service to members, these members were seen in an administrative sense, through their ability to implement the programmes of this sport organization. In these two examples, the interests of athletes were not guiding the actions of the organizations, but rather the athletes and members were supported only to the extent that they helped the growth of sport or the effective functioning of the organization.

Still, in the constitutions/bylaws of four Canadian sport organizations, athletes were regarded as having an influence over decision making. Some organizations included in their objectives forms of responsiveness to the interests of athletes. For example, Karate Canada identified the safety of athletes as a priority. Similarly, the Shooting Federation of Canada focused on protecting the interests of gun owners, but this objective seemed less a reflection of an athlete-centred approach and more about positioning this sport organization within the divisive political debate around gun ownership. It appears that the position the Shooting Federation of Canada took in this debate was necessary to maintain its legitimacy as an organization and as a sport.

Other organizations were more straightforward about their commitment to giving athletes a voice in policy and governance. The Canadian Tenpin Federation underlined the importance of being responsible to members, informing those engaged in sport, and reflecting their views in policy decisions, where individual athletes were considered members. The Canadian Amateur Wrestling Association identified an objective providing athletes with representation in the relevant international organization.

In other words, only in a limited number of cases did NSOs use language in their bylaws that construed these organizations as representing athletes. This language offered a background against which one could evaluate the degree to which governance frameworks promoting the participation of athletes in NSOs' governance were established. More precisely, if an NSO identified objectives that were sport- or administrative-centric, then the involvement of athletes in governance could be construed as an attempt to grow the sport and improve the functioning of the organization by connecting with the interest of athletes, in the same way a corporation might seek feedback from unions in order to improve organizational performance (Hall *et al.*, 2013). However, if an organization decided to select representing the interests and rights of athletes as an objective, then the involvement of athletes could be interpreted as an important part of an NSO's mission.

While this analysis applied to Canadian organizations, objectives in the bylaws/constitutions of NSOs of the other three countries followed similar patterns, with a dominant focus on sport- and administrative-related objectives and with limited interest in representing athletes' voices. Of the four Canadian NSOs with athlete-centric objectives, only in two cases were athlete-centric objectives found in the bylaws of organizations representing the same sports in different countries. First, one of the purposes of USA Shooting (2012a) was to keep athletes "informed of policy matters and reasonably reflect the views of such athletes in policy matters" (p. 5). Second, in the case of bowling, Tenpin Bowling Australia selected disseminating information to bowlers and representing their interests as one of their objectives, while the United States Bowling Congress stressed the need for the organization to be responsible to its members. Consequently, there was little commonality across sports, suggesting that international organizations had a limited influence on the degree to which a common athlete-centric vision of the objectives and purposes of NSOs was put in place.

Athlete-centredness in NSOs, outside these organizations' intentions as reflected in their declarations of purposes and objectives, took several forms. The most visible and concrete manifestations of an NSO's commitment to athletes' participation were organizational structures through which athletes were represented in decision making, of which three forms were examined: ACs, athletes' representatives on boards of directors or executive committees and athletes serving on other committees.

The prevalence of Athletes' Committees (ACs)

Of the 134 bylaws, 52 (38.8 per cent) made clear reference to an AC – US=30 (68.18 per cent of all US NSOs' bylaws), AU=14 (38.89 per cent of all AU NSOs' bylaws), CA=6 (15.38 per cent of all CA NSOs' bylaws) and UK=2 (13.33 per cent of all UK NSOs' bylaws). In spite of article 376 Membership (b)(2)(A) of the Ted Stevens Olympic and Amateur Sports Act (1978)[1] (US Senate, 1998), which clearly required that US organizations establish Athletes' Advisory Councils, at least three US sport organizations did not have such a structure. Furthermore, 11 organizations were identified in which the presence of ACs, although not mentioned in the bylaws, was mentioned in other sources (US=4, CA=4, AU=2, UK=1), which brought the total number of organizations with such a committee to 63 (US=34 (91.89 per cent of all US organizations for which information was identified)), AU=16 (80.0 per cent of all AU organizations), CA=10 (47.62 per cent of all CA organizations), and UK=3 (42.85 per cent of all UK organizations)).

It was important to understand that athletes' representation in NSOs could be traced to two sources. First, there was the international factor, represented by IOC, through its 1999 and 2001 recommendations to place athletes at the centre of the IOC, creating impetus for the establishment of ACs in National Olympic Committees (NOCs). For example, the 2001 recommendations by the IOC were published as a guide for ISFs and NOCs, suggesting the need to give athletes a voice in international and national sport organizations, under the form of ACs. Second, there was a national factor, with national governments and NSOs (e.g. Sport Canada) influencing athletes' participation in governance. For example, the Ted Stevens Act was a case of national contingent dynamics (i.e. the decision of the US Congress to give the US Olympic Committee authority over US amateur sport) directly and decisively influencing athletes' representation in NSOs. Also, Sport Canada's recommendation that NSOs establish ACs was an example of a national influence of a similar kind, although not using the coercive force of legislation.

The pattern of establishing ACs suggested that national dynamics play a very important role. The fact that the percentage of bylaws in which ACs were mentioned differed so widely between the four countries suggested that national factors played a more important role than international ones. While in the US, a very high percentage (68.18 per cent) of bylaws included ACs. In CA, a much lower percentage (15.38 per cent) of bylaws included ACs, and the same difference was maintained when the total number of NSOs with ACs was taken into consideration for the two countries. Furthermore, when NSOs representing the same sport across the four countries were compared, there was not one case in which all NSOs from the four countries representing one sport had established ACs. When the UK was eliminated from the comparison, due to the limited data retrieved, athletes from three sports were found to have ACs' representatives in their respective NSOs in AU, CA and the US: rugby sailing, and track and field. Of these two, Thibault *et al.* (2010) found that the ISFs representing sailing and track and field had ACs (with no data in the case of World Rugby, the ISF dedicated to rugby), suggesting that possibly in a limited number of cases ISFs could influence NSOs with regard to whether an AC was established. Still, the national factors seemed to play a central role, the Ted Stevens Act giving a clear indication of the effect of legislation on influencing NSOs. Although perfect compliance with the law was not achieved, this law had a significant impact on the degree to which ACs were established in US NSOs. It should be noted however that what this act did was to add coercive power to a decision made by USOC (and, ultimately, the IOC) to put in place ACs, so the Ted Stevens Act represented a combination of international and national influences.

Purposes and roles

ACs offered athletes a means of representation that was different in nature from that provided by athlete directors. While athlete directors had, for the most part, voting power on boards of directors or executive committees, they were limited in number (usually one or two directors). ACs, being composed of more athletes, were able to accommodate a diversity of interests, establishing a certain level of descriptive representation (i.e. a type of representation resulting from the leadership sharing relevant characteristics with its constituency, thus sharing similar experiences with this constituency). In fact, in many bylaws/constitutions ACs' composition was organized according to parity principles, which ensured that certain groups, defined on the basis of gender, sport speciality (e.g. alpine ski, cross-country ski, ski jumping or freestyle ski in ski federations), or geographical areas, were represented to a certain extent.

One approach to understanding how ACs helped athletes' voices be heard was to examine the reasons for which these committees were created. There were main categories of purposes associated with these committees: functional and representational. First, ACs were meant to improve the ability of organizations to achieve the two main objectives identified in the previous analysis: the growth of sport and administrative performance. Thus these committees were viewed as maintaining harmony between athletes, as well as improving communication in organizations by bridging the gap between athletes and leadership. Also, ACs promoted sport in the community, while at the same time facilitating ethical behaviour in athletes, which would help project a positive image of sport. This functional aspect of ACs was usually implied, but in the case of Taekwondo Australia (2013) it became explicit: "The purpose of the Athletes Commission is to provide a formal pathway and link between athletes, the Executive and relevant Committees to optimize the environment for Australian Taekwondo Athletes" (para. 2).

Second, ACs were regarded as fulfilling a representational function. Some formulations of this function were vague, referring to the responsibility of ACs to provide athletes with a voice in the development of organizational policy or to protect the interests and rights of athletes. Other ACs were more precise, like the capacity to nominate, elect or appoint representatives in decision-making positions on boards of directors and other committees, as well as participating in due process for athletes and raising athletes' awareness of their rights and obligations.

In essence, these purpose statements relating to ACs in NSOs painted a complex picture of the role these committees played: on the one hand, athletes' representation was conceived from a managerial perspective, while, on the other hand, it was seen as an expression of athletes' rights to participate in the decisions of NSOs. If athletes' representation in ACs was regarded from a managerial perspective, which was seen as furthering the organization's objectives, then athletes' participation in governance was justified only as long as the NSO drew a benefit from it. If athletes' representation in ACs was regarded as a right, then this representation needed to be ensured, regardless of the state or objectives of the organization. This latter type of purpose, which interpreted athletes' representation as a right, took two forms.

First, there were concrete responsibilities associated with ACs, which gave these committees a clear means of influencing NSOs' decisions. These responsibilities were nominating athletes' representatives (e.g. Triathlon Australia, US Sailing) and appointing or electing representatives (e.g. US Soccer), and establishing internal policy promoting the representation of athletes (e.g. US Soccer, US Diving). With regard to the first two responsibilities on the above list, in the US, ACs were granted responsibilities to enforce the Ted Stevens Act, especially those articles that mandated the participation of athletes' representatives on NSOs' boards and other committees.

Second, there were a number of vague purposes, like establishing communication and harmony among athletes and between athletes and the administration of NSOs, promoting sport and ethical behaviour, assisting in the development of policy, representing a forum where athletes' grievances could be expressed, and fostering awareness of athletes' rights. These purposes gave ACs an ancillary position in the organization, because they did not indicate means through which ACs could directly influence decisions made by NSOs, but rather ACs depended on decisional structures to bring about change. In the end, while ACs could communicate with boards of directors or managerial teams of NSOs, it was up to those boards and managers to use the information. If there was no clear commitment on the part of the organization for athletes' representation, then ACs could become empty structures, a danger magnified in the US NSOs, where ACs were mandated by the Ted Stevens Act. Still, even among these vague purposes, there were signs of deeper commitment to athlete governance. For example, one of the purposes of the US Shooting's AC was "to link the elite level athletes directly with the USOC without using the NGB [national governing body] as intermediary" (USA Shooting, 2012b, p. 1), increasing athletes' influence in sport and reducing NSO's control of athletes. Also, one of the purposes of Canada Tenpin Federation's AC was to ensure that international programmes and policies were athlete-focused, reflecting a commitment to athlete participation in governance that was visible in the bowling federations' documents.

For the most part, ACs were created as structures with limited influence in NSOs, providing input in the governance process, but with limited direct influence, which was usually manifested in the nomination and election of athletes' representatives. In the US, the priority given to the vague roles of ACs pertaining to communicating with boards of directors could be traced back to the Ted Stevens Act, which mandated the establishment of Athletes' Advisory Councils "to ensure communication between the corporation and such amateur athletes" (US Senate 1998, p. 13). The influence of this act was visible in the fact that a majority of ACs have "Advisory" in their name (17 out of 25 in the US). The convergence of the consultative nature of ACs in the other countries examined could be explained by referring to the influence of the IOC's report (made explicit in Australia Ice Racing's description of their AC), as the IOC's AC was regarded as having a consultative function (IOC, 2001).

The NSOs' commitment to the participation of athletes in governance could also be gleaned from the place that ACs occupied in the organizational structure of NSOs. There were several positions ACs occupied in NSOs, which was a result of the type of committee with which ACs were associated and the relationships between ACs and other committees or boards of directors. In certain NSOs (Badminton Canada, Australia Swimming), athletes were represented through committees, but these committees functioned only as members. From a certain perspective, this kind of arrangement seemed to be an indication that the organization was committed to athletes' engagement in NSO governance because, as members, athletes would have a direct role in the development of organizational policy and in the election of NSO leadership. From a different perspective, however, the influence of athletes' representatives in terms of voting privileges could be very limited. Thus, while in the case of Swimming Australia, the Swimmers' Association had one vote out of nine members' votes, in the case of Badminton Canada, the Players Association had only one vote out of 28 members' votes. Whether this kind of arrangement involving the representation of athletes through member associations was more conducive to athletes' participation in NSO governance than a committee within the organization is disputable. On the one hand, an outside member association would probably have had less access to relevant information than an NSO committee, a factor well documented in the governance literature (Hoye & Cuskelly, 2007), and would undermine the ability of athletes' representatives to pursue their interest within NSOs. On the other hand, member associations, through their right to vote on matters of policy and leadership, could influence NSOs in a very direct way.

For the most part, however, athletes were not represented through member associations, but rather through committees. As mentioned above, these committees could be differentiated based on the status they had in NSOs and on their relationship with other structures in these organizations. With regard to status, the importance of a committee within an organization could be determined by identifying where this committee stood relative to the distinction between standing (i.e. permanent) and *ad hoc* committees. Committees that functioned permanently had a more significant role in an organization, being needed continuously, while *ad hoc* committees were called upon only in certain contexts, when needed. While few NSOs clearly identified in their documents to what category their ACs belonged, the great majority of ACs designated as standing or permanent came from the US (e.g. US Boxing,

US Speedskating), while all the committees designated as *ad hoc* (i.e. ACs that may be established by boards of directors if the need was present) were part of Australian and Canadian NSOs (e.g. Australia Gymnastics, Bobsleigh Canada). One explanation for this pattern could be that in the US, ACs were mandated through the Ted Stevens Act, together with the representation of athletes on the committees of US NSOs, which gave these committees a larger degree of legitimacy, thus making it more likely that ACs were designated standing committees.

With regard to the position of ACs in the organizational structure of NSOs, ACs could be analysed on the basis of their relationship with other committees. In cases where athletes were not represented in standing committees, the interests of athletes were not voiced, leaving only boards of directors to take their needs into consideration. This kind of structure was widely encountered, with multiple NSOs (US=17, AU=5, CA=2 and UK=1) having ACs presented in their bylaws as separate from the other committees, reporting to boards of directors in a consultative position, but without any clear interaction with NSOs' standing committees.

Some challenges to the potential of ACs to represent athletes concerned the degree to which these committees represented the interests of athletes. First, the potential of ACs to represent athletes could be undercut by the composition of these committees (i.e. if non-athletes were appointed or elected to ACs). As argued in discourses defending gender quotas in employment, when representatives shared similar relevant characteristics with their constituency they were more likely to understand the experiences and interests of these constituencies (Rubio-Marin, 2012; Ruiz & Rubio-Marin, 2008). However, the data collected showed that the ACs identified were composed of athletes or recently retired athletes, so this was not a major concern.

Second, athletes' representation through ACs could be undermined if the members of these committees were not accountable to those whom they were supposed to represent, established through formal representation, which was achieved when a system for appointing representatives in organizational leadership was put in place (Pitkin, 1967). In the US, as a result of the Ted Stevens Act, in all NSOs for which data were identified the ACs (when they existed) were elected by athletes, thus creating a means of evaluating the performance of ACs. However, this process was only partially democratic, because for the overwhelming majority of ACs (29 out of 34), elite athletes were the only ones eligible to run for election or to elect the members of ACs. In the other countries, there were instances where members of ACs were selected either by boards of directors (e.g. Australia Canoe, Bobsleigh Canada) or by another committee (e.g. Gymnastics Canada). Besides those who elected or appointed the members of ACs, those who nominated these members were also important. While the candidates in elections for ACs were predominantly the athletes themselves, in the case of Australia Gymnastics, members of ACs were nominated by the members of this organization, then appointed by boards of directors.

Athletes' representatives on boards of directors

As mentioned above, the one function ACs had that gave them an effective way of directly influencing the decisions taken by NSOs was nominating and electing athlete directors or representatives on executive committees. Of all the bylaws identified, 100 per cent in the US, 71.79 per cent in CA, 33.33 per cent in AU, and 6.66 per cent in the UK made reference to an athletes' director. Predominantly, these directors had voting powers, but in certain UK NSOs (e.g. British Fencing Association, Great Britain Hockey) athletes' representatives on the board of directors could be invited to board meetings without the right to vote. As mentioned above, the concept of representation could be rather loose, with multiple meanings. Thus, representation could mean descriptive representation, when representatives and constituencies shared relevant characteristics (in this case, being an athlete or a recently retired athlete), as well as formal representation, which presupposed processes through which representatives were held accountable (Pitkin, 1967). In certain cases, athlete directors were not elected by athletes, but rather appointed by the board (e.g. Skate Canada), which undermined the conditions of formal representation, while still making descriptive representation possible. Even when athlete directors were elected, formal representation was not guaranteed. Thus athletes were elected from among members of the AC (e.g. USA Badminton), by all athletes who were eligible (e.g. USA Canoe/Kayak), or a mix of the two (e.g. US Field Hockey Association), as well as by all members (at large) of the organization (e.g. US Sailing). In this latter case, there was no mechanism for athletes to hold these representatives accountable. Just as in the case of ACs members, even when athlete directors were elected by athletes, it was usually elite athletes who were eligible to vote and run for this position, so formal representation was limited to elite athletes. In a small number of organizations (e.g. US Squash), all athletes had an opportunity to vote for athlete directors.

With regard to the percentage of board members who were representative of athletes, in the US, it was around 20 per cent, respecting the requirements laid out in the Ted Stevens Act, which required a representation of athletes at a level of at least 20 per cent of boards of directors and NSOs' committees. The highest percentage of athletes' representatives on the boards was 30 per cent, in US Canoe/Kayak. In the other three countries, the percentage of athlete directors varied between 5 per cent (UK Ski) and 25 per cent (Rugby Canada and Field Hockey Canada), with the majority at around 10 per cent. Consequently, while athletes' representatives could draw attention to athletes' interests when major decisions were made, their impact was limited. Still, having an athletes' director could function as a means of providing information regarding NSOs functioning to ACs, which could be especially useful when athletes were represented through a member association.

Athletes' representatives in other committees

As shown above, since ACs frequently functioned separately from NSOs committees, it was important for these committees to include athletes' representatives, in order to ensure that athletes' interests were taken into consideration throughout the decision-making process. In the US, the Ted Stevens Act mandated that all committees include at least 20 per cent athletes' representation, so the great majority of US NSOs' committees (45 out of 47) included athletes' representatives. With regard to the process through which these representatives were selected, ACs played an important role, either nominating or electing the representatives. In certain cases (e.g. US Diving, US Equestrian), representatives were elected by elite athletes, while in other cases, they were appointed by the board of directors (e.g. US Modern Pentathlon, US Racquetball), by the president (e.g. US Soccer), by the Chief Executive Officer (e.g. US Shooting) or by the members (e.g. US Rugby). As in the case of ACs, these representatives were elite athletes.

In CA, 25 NSOs included representatives on committees. In all cases where information was found, athletes had the power to elect representatives on committees. In AU, very few committees were found to have athletes' representatives on other committees (Australia Equestrian and Australia Fencing) and no bylaws included references to such a representative. In the UK, the bylaws of one NSO (e.g. UK Ski) included references to these representatives.

Seven UK NSOs where athletes were represented in committees were identified. It should be noted that unlike the US, where athletes' representatives were found on all committees, in the other three countries, these representatives were present only on certain committees, usually technical, nominating and judicial.

Conclusion

While a great deal of variability existed between NSOs of the four countries studied, there was also an important level of similarity, which could be attributed to the IOC model of governance, defined by the inclusion of an AC with a consultative role and of athlete directors elected by athletes. The Ted Stevens Olympic and Amateur Sports Act gave this model the coercive force of the law, which explained the overwhelming majority of US NSOs that shared a similar structure of athletes' representation. One of the advantages of this state of affairs was that it imposed a degree of athletes' representation on NSOs that otherwise might not be inclined to include athletes in their governance systems. However, this model of athletes' representation was problematic, because an NSO that was not committed to athletes' participation in governance could undermine it by minimizing the AC, by systematically ignoring the recommendations of this committee. Still, this model included athletes' representatives on boards and committees, so it provided athletes with the opportunity to influence decisions, although it was not clear how effective they could be, given that they had limited voting power. Unfortunately, athlete directors did not provide the same kind of representation as ACs. ACs' members were more numerous than athlete directors, so ACs could better reflect the diversity of all athletes. In fact, numerous NSOs included measures that were compatible with the idea of parity democracy, which referred to the effort of adopting mechanisms to overcome past underrepresentation (an idea that so far had been applied to gender alone) (Baudino, 2003; Praud & Dauphin, 2010). In the case of ACs, these measures included restrictions ensuring some balance in terms of gender, ability, sport speciality or geographical distribution. Consequently, a more effective model of athletes' representation would maintain the idea of an AC representing athletes, but give ACs a more effective means of influencing NSOs' decisions than simply the consultative roles that most ACs now include.

One solution that was uncovered during the analysis involved an AC that functioned as a member association, which gave it a series of powers such as electing leadership and setting general policy directions as a strategy of furthering the interests of athletes. This approach to athletes' representation would reflect the importance of athletes in sport and NSOs, something that statements of purposes in bylaws fail to recognize, as was demonstrated in our study. Enacting this change might require reconsidering the reasons NSOs exist and the place athletes occupy in these organizations, a change that would place athletes truly at the centre of NSOs. It would probably be naive to expect international and national sport organizations to transform themselves without any outside pressure. The best candidates for this outside force could be national governments and transnational organizations like the European Union (EU). These organizations are already based on democratic foundations and, as was shown in the EU's willingness to step in to protect the rights of individual athletes when these rights were threatened by anti-doping policies put forth by the World Anti-Doping Agency (Miah, 2002), it had both the power and willingness to intervene for ethical reasons. Unfortunately, it is also true that nations are interested in maximizing international sport performance, so the imperative of allowing athletes a greater power to defend their own interests might take a back seat to the race for Olympic medals.

Note

1 The Ted Stevens Olympic and Amateur Sports Act is a US law "appoint[ing] the USOC [United States Olympic Committee] as the coordinating body for all Olympic-related athletic activity in the United States. It specifically named the USOC coordinating body for athletic activity in the United States directly relating to international competition . . . The law also requires all governance councils of the USOC and NGBs [national sport governing bodies] to have at least 20 percent membership and voting power by 'recent and active' athletes" (Team USA, 2016, paras. 3 and 5).

References

Baudino, C. (2003). Parity reform in France: Promises and pitfalls. *Review of Policy Research, 20*(3), 385–400.

Bevir, M. (2009). *Key Concepts in Governance*. London: Sage.

Boxing Canada (1992). Constitution and by-laws. Available from <www.boxing.ca/documents/1-constitution-bylaws.pdf>. Accessed 25 July 2013.

Braun, V. & Clarke, V. (2006). Using thematic analytic in psychology. *Qualitative Research in Psychology, 3*(2), 77–101.

Chaker, A. N. (2004). *Good Governance in Sport: A European Survey*. Strasbourg, France: Council of Europe.

Commission of the European Communities (2007). *White Paper on Sport*. Brussels, Belgium. Available from <http://eur-lex.europa.eu/legalcontent/EN/TXT/PDF/?uri=CELEX:52007DC0391&from=EN>. Accessed 23 March 2016.

European Union (2013). Expert group "Good Governance" Deliverable 2. Principles of good governance in sport. Available from <http://ec.europa.eu/sport/library/policy_documents/xg-gg-201307-dlvrbl2-sept2013.pdf>. Accessed 23 March 2016.

Forster, J. (2006). Global sports organizations and their governance. *Corporate Governance, 6*(1), 72–83.

Geeraert, A. (2015). *Sports Governance Observer 2015. The Legitimacy Crisis in International Sports Governance*. Aarhus, DK: Play the Game. Available from <www.playthegame.org/media/4303278/SGO_report_final_2.pdf>. Accessed 23 March 2016.

Geeraert, A., Alm, J. & Groll, M. (2014). Good governance in international sport organisations: An analysis of the 35 Olympic sport governing bodies. *International Journal of Sport Policy and Politics, 6*(3), 281–306.

Hall, M., Huthinson, S., Purcell, J., Terry, M. & Parker, J. (2013). Promoting effective consultation? Assessing the impact of the ICE regulations. *British Journal of Industrial Relations, 51*(2), 355–381.

Henry, I. & Lee, P. C. (2004). Governance and ethics in sport. In J. Beech & S. Chadwick (Eds), *The Business of Sport Management* (pp. 25–42). Harlow, UK: Pearson Education.

Houlihan, B. (2004). Civil rights, doping control and the World Anti-Doping Code. *Sport in Society, 7*(3), 420–437.

Hoye, R. & Cuskelly, G. (2007). *Sport Governance*. Oxford: Elsevier Butterworth-Heinemann.

International Olympic Committee (1999). Report by the IOC 2000 Commission to the 110th IOC Session. Lausanne, CH: Author. Available from <www.olympic.org/Documents/Reports/EN/en_report_588.pdf>. Accessed 23 March 2016.

International Olympic Committee (2001). International Olympic Committee (IOC) Athletes' Commission terms of reference. Available from <www.olympic.org/Documents/Reports/EN/en_report_712.pdf>. Accessed 12 October, 2013.

International Olympic Committee Athletes' Commission (2014). Guide to developing an effective athletes' commission. Lausanne, CH: Author. Available from <www.olympic.org/Documents/Commissions_PDFfiles/Athletes/Guide_Reference_GB_DEF.PDF>. Accessed 23 March 2016.

Jackson, G. & Ritchie, I. (2007). Leave it to the experts: The politics of "athlete-centredness" in the Canadian sport system. *International Journal of Sport Management and Marketing, 2*(4), 396–411.

Jennings, A. (2007). *Foul! The Secret World of FIFA: Bribes, Vote Rigging and Ticket Scandals*. London: HarperSport.

Katwala, S. (2000). *Democratising Global Sport*. London: The Foreign Policy Centre.

Kihl, L. A., Kikulis, L. M. & Thibault, L. (2007). A deliberative democratic approach to athlete-centred sport: The dynamics of administrative and communicative power. *European Sport Management Quarterly, 7*(1), 1–30.

Miah, A. (2002). Governance, harmonisation, and genetics: The World Anti Doping Agency and its European connections. *European Sport Management Quarterly*, *2*(4), 350–369.

Patton, M. Q. (2002). *Qualitative Research and Evaluation Methods*. Thousand Oaks, California: Sage.

Pitkin, H. F. (1967). *The Concept of Representation*. Berkeley, California: University of California Press.

Praud, J. & Dauphin, S. (2010). *Parity Democracy: Women's Political Representation in Fifth Republic France*. Vancouver, British Columbia: University of British Columbia Press.

Rubio-Marin, R. (2012). Evolutions in antidiscrimination law in Europe and North America: A new European parity-democracy sex equality model and why it won't fly in the United States. *American Journal of Comparative Law*, *60*(1), 99–125.

Ruiz, B. R. & Rubio-Marin, R. (2008). The gender of representation: On democracy, equality, and parity. *International Journal of Constitutional Law*, *6*(2), 287–316.

Taekwondo Australia (2013). Athletes' Commission. Available from <www.taekwondoaustralia.com.au/athletes.php>. Accessed 23 July 2013.

Team USA (2016). History. Available from <www.teamusa.org/About-the-USOC/Inside-the-USOC/History>. Accessed 18 August 2016.

Thibault, L., Kihl, L. & Babiak, K. (2010). Democratization and governance in international sport: Addressing issues with athlete involvement in organizational policy. *International Journal of Sport Policy and Politics*, *2*(3), 275–302.

US Senate (1998). "Olympic and Amateur Sports Act Amendments of 1998". Report of the Committee on Commerce, Science and Transportation on S. 2119. Washington, DC: US Government Printing Office. Available from <www.congress.gov/105/crpt/srpt325/CRPT-105srpt325.pdf >. Accessed 3 May 2014.

USA Shooting (2012a). Bylaws of USA Shooting, Inc. Available from <www.usashooting.org/library/Policies_and_Procedures/2015_pdf/bylaws.pdf>. Accessed 10 December, 2014.

USA Shooting (2012b). USA Shooting policies and procedures. Athletes' Advisory Council Election Procedures. Available from <www.usashooting.org/library/Policies_and_Procedures/2015_pdf/XVII_AAC_Rep_Elect_3-19-12.pdf>. Accessed 10 December, 2014.

19

ATHLETE IMAGE RIGHTS IN THE US AND UK

Natasha T. Brison and Simon Boyes

Introduction

The commercial exploitation by high-profile athletes, of name, likeness, personality and goodwill, forms an important part of revenue creation within the sports industry. One of the most recognizable practices for athletes to benefit commercially from his/her image rights is acting as an endorser to help sell a company's products or services. Many professional athletes can earn as much as or more from endorsements than from their professional salaries. For example, in 2014 professional soccer player David Beckham received a $5.2 million annual salary and $42 million per year in endorsements from companies such as Adidas, Coty, H&M and Samsung (*Forbes*, 2015). The demand for athletes to endorse products and services is mostly due to an athlete's ability to transfer meanings and messages about a product or service to consumers (McCracken, 1989). These partnerships help companies to distinguish a product or service from those of its competitors and to influence consumer purchase decisions. In 2015, the top 100 highest-paid athletes in the world grossed over $917 million in endorsements (Weber, 2015). Although many companies follow the proper channels to create formal agreements with athletes for the use of their names, likeness and goodwill, there are those that choose not to do so and that proceed without the athlete's consent. Due to the substantial commercial advantages an athlete can provide, these unauthorized uses typically require the athletes to seek legal protection and enforcement. As such, the capacity of an athlete to engage meaningful legal protection for their interests in the commercial deployment of such image is of great significance.

There has been tremendous global expansion by professional sport leagues in the United States (US) to tap into fans in the United Kingdom (UK) and abroad. The National Basketball League (NBA) has played 158 games in 18 different countries and 45 international cities (NBA, 2015), and the National Football League (NFL) has had an International Series at Wembley Stadium in London since 2007 (NFL, 2015). Similarly, the Premier League (one of the most notable European football leagues) has expanded its global reach. In 2013 the Premier League negotiated a three-year broadcast rights agreement with the American network NBC for 380 matches a year through the 2015–2016 season, in hopes to grow the sport in the US along with its network audience (Levy, 2013). To capitalize also on the growth of the sport leagues, companies in each country may want to use an athlete's image to gain access to consumers, and the athletes themselves will undoubtedly wish to exploit the new commercial opportunities and markets available to them. These efforts may also give rise to unauthorized use in both the US and the UK.

This chapter serves as a general introduction to the evolution of athlete image rights in the US and the UK. First, an overview of how each country, under its respective laws, affords athletes protection of their image is discussed. Next, a comparative analysis of the similarities and differences within each country's legal system is examined. The chapter concludes with suggestions for safeguarding athlete image rights in the US, the UK, and abroad.

Protecting an athlete's right of publicity in the US

The right of publicity in the US originated in order to recognize that celebrities and non-celebrities have a right to control and profit from the use of their names, likenesses and any other characteristics that differentiate them from others in their particular trades, i.e. their market-able identity (Edwards, 1998). For an athlete, this right allows protection of his/her marketable identity from financial exploitation through unauthorized use. The right of publicity is rooted in the right of privacy, which began as a common law right to prevent "truthful but intrusive and embarrassing disclosures by the press" (Warren & Brandeis, 1890, p. 193). The concept evolved when William Prosser, a renowned Tort law scholar, characterized the right of publicity as the appropriation prong of the right of privacy (Prosser, 1960). Since then, courts have recognized publicity rights as a property right, and the damage to these rights as typically commercial in nature, causing injury to the "business value of [the] personal identity" (McCarthy, 1994, p. 134).

Enforcing an athlete's right of publicity

Protection of an athlete's marketable identity is enforced through either federal law, state statute or common law in the US. The Lanham Act (1946) provides athletes a federal civil cause of action for unauthorized use of their names, likeness or other distinguishable attributes that create "false designation of origin" or false descriptions (15 USC §1125(a)(2005)). Under Section 43(a) of the Lanham Act, a party is "prohibited [from using] . . . any symbol or device which is likely to deceive consumers as to the association, sponsorship, or approval of goods or services by another person". The burden of proof is on the plaintiff to show that consumers believe the unauthorized use implies an endorsement by the athlete. If this proof is not presented, the athlete's claims under federal law will be unsuccessful.

The elements for proving a state law claim are not as rigorous as a federal law claim. Claims to protect an athlete's interests under state law are based on common law, on statutes or on both. In the state of Missouri, the courts evaluate right of publicity claims by determining under common law whether: "(1) the defendant used the plaintiff's name as a symbol of his identity (2) without consent (3) and with the intent to attain a commercial advantage" (*Doe v. TCI Cablevision*, 2003, p. 365). Conversely, there is no common law right of publicity in the state of New York; the right of publicity is codified as part of the right of privacy statute (NY CLS Civ. R §50 (2000)). New York Civil Rights Law §50 provides protection for a person's name, portrait, picture, and voice. To establish a violation, the use of the person's identity must be: within the state of New York, used for advertising or trade purposes, and without written consent (NY CLS Civ. R §51 (2000)). In the state of California, however, courts use both common law and the enacted statute to protect against violations. To establish a *prima facie* case based on the common law right of publicity, the plaintiff must allege: "(1) the defendant's use of plaintiff's identity; (2) the appropriation of plaintiff's name or likeness to defendant's advantage, commercially or otherwise; (3) lack of consent; and (4) resulting injury" (*Abdul-Jabbar* v. *General Motors Corp.*, 1996, pp. 413–414).

Yet, to establish a *prima facie* case under California Civil Code §3344, a plaintiff must allege two additional elements: "(1) knowing use [by the defendant]; and (2) a direct connection . . . between the use and the commercial purpose". Although there are differences in pleading a claim under common law and California Civil Code §3344, courts have explained that section 3344 was ratified to supplement the common law cause of action for the right of publicity, not to supersede it (*Eastwood* v. *Superior Court for Los Angeles County*, 1983).

Evolution of the right of publicity

Professional athletes who recognize the commercial value of their images have been assertive in protecting their right of publicity. Several cases have been instrumental in demonstrating how an athlete's right of publicity may be protected in the US. This section highlights a few of these cases.

The earliest case to recognize an athlete's right of publicity was *Haelen Laboratories, Inc.* v. *Topps Chewing Gum, Inc.* ("*Haelen*") (1953). In *Haelen*, rival chewing gum manufacturers each claimed that the other party had persuaded athletes to breach their contracts permitting the use of their names and pictures for the marketing of chewing gum. It was during this court's decision that the right of publicity was recognized as a property right of "prominent persons . . . to receive compensation for authorizing advertisements", and was exclusive, assignable and descendible (*Haelen Laboratories, Inc.* v. *Topps Chewing Gum, Inc.*, 1953, p. 868).

In *Palmer* v. *Schonhorn Enterprises* (1967), several professional golfers, including Arnold Palmer, sought an injunction and damages for the unauthorized use of their names and profiles in a golf board game. The plaintiffs alleged that they had never consented to being included in the game, and the defendant's use of the golfers' names and biographies was deceitful misuse and commercialization of their names and reputations (*Palmer* v. *Schonhorn Enterprises*, 1967). Since the information contained in the profiles was readily available to the public through the news media, the defendants argued that they could reproduce this information without the consent of the golfers (*Palmer* v. *Schonhorn Enterprises*, 1967). The court rejected the argument and concluded that the facts and statistics were components of the golfers' marketable identities. Although the information was voluntarily disclosed in the news media, the court ruled it did not negate the golfers' right of publicity.

In 1996, former NBA player, Kareem Abdul-Jabbar (Abdul-Jabbar), asserted that the General Motor Corporation (GMC) and its advertising agency, Leo Burnett Company, violated his publicity rights by using his former name, Lew Alcindor, in a television commercial for an Oldsmobile Eighty-Eight without his consent (*Abdul-Jabbar* v. *General Motors Corp.*, 1996). GMC averred that Abdul-Jabbar had not used the name Lew Alcindor for commercial purposes in over ten years and therefore had abandoned the name, as well as any rights to protect the name. In its decision, the Ninth Circuit stated protection of the right of publicity is not limited to the appropriation of the athlete's name or likeness; it can also include the athlete's identity (*Abdul-Jabbar* v. *General Motors Corp.*, 1996). The court contended a person's birth name is an important part of their identity, and a birth name cannot be abandoned, even if the possessor does not use it commercially. The court further stated that the relevant point was not how the defendant had appropriated the athlete's identity, but whether the defendant had done so.

Former NBA player Michael Jordan (Jordan) filed a lawsuit in 2010 in the US District Court in the Northern District of Illinois against Dominick's Finer Foods, LLC (Dominick's) alleging that Dominick's used Jordan's identity in a nationally distributed advertisement for its Rancher's Reserve steaks without his consent (*Michael Jordan and Jump 23, Inc.* v. *Dominick's Finer Foods, LLC*, 2015). The advertisement in *Sports Illustrated* magazine's commemorative issue, entitled *Jordan: Celebrating a Hall of Fame Career*, depicted Jordan's name and the number 23 along with the phrase "You are a cut above" and a coupon for $2.00 off a Rancher's Reserve steak. Dominick's claimed that the full-page advertisement was to congratulate Jordan on his induction into the Basketball Hall of Fame. Jordan refuted their stance stating that the advertisement was more than a congratulatory gesture; it was designed to imply that Jordan had endorsed the product and to influence consumers to purchase a Rancher's Reserve steak. The District Court agreed with Jordan, and jurors awarded him $8.9 million in damages for the store's unauthorized use of this name (Associated Press, 2015).

Exception to the athlete's right of publicity

Although athletes have a right to protect their marketable identity from unauthorized use, it is not without limitations. Courts have held that athletes cannot restrict the use if it is protected by the First Amendment to the US Constitution, even if the use is commercial in nature. In these cases, courts have sought to balance the athlete's right of publicity against societal interest in freedom of expression. For example, in November 2011, professional wrestler Douglas "Pretty Boy" Somerson (Somerson) filed a right of publicity lawsuit against World Wrestling Entertainment, Inc. (WWE) in the Superior Court of Fulton County, Georgia (*Somerson* v. *World Wrestling Entertainment, Inc.*, 2013) for authorized use of his name, likeness and persona on the WWE websites. The WWE explained that Somerson's claim should fail because the references to Somerson were solely used "in the context of historical narratives of notable WWE performers and events" and "information such as this regarding the accomplishments of athletes . . . is [a] matter [of] public interest and therefore protected by the First Amendment" (*Somerson* v. *World Wrestling Entertainment, Inc.*, 2013, p. 1364). The Court agreed with the WWE, maintaining that the oration of factual data regarding an athlete's performance is a form of expression granted protection under the First Amendment.

Protecting athletes' image and personality rights in English law

In contrast with the position adopted in the US, in English law there exists no single free-standing right of publicity by which athletes are able to control and exploit the commercial use of their name, image and other factors particular to them. Instead such protection, where available, is acquired through the application of a range of general measures, none of which have as their specific objective the protection of image or personality. This is perhaps due to the historical absence of a privacy doctrine in English law, although privacy is exerting a growing influence as a consequence of the introduction of the Human Rights Act 1998 and the requirement to take account under Article 8 of the European Convention on Human Rights. Nonetheless, the law has had to address the issue in order to reflect the growing commodification and value of celebrity image in British society.

English law approaches to image and personality

Despite the lack of a single cause of action by which image and personality rights may be protected, licensing and assignment of such rights has now become commonplace. The English courts have recognized explicitly the economic significance of such rights and that they form an important part of the "assets" of high-profile athletes. In *Proactive Sports Management Ltd* v. *Rooney & Ors* (2011), the Manchester United and England footballer Wayne Rooney successfully challenged the contract under which the exploitation of his image – through sponsorship, merchandising, endorsement and branding – was undertaken by a sports management company. Although the case did not identify these interests as attracting specific legal protections it did, nonetheless, see the Court of Appeal recognize image and personality as tradeable commodities having the capacity to form the subject of a legally recognized contract.

In a much earlier case – *Tolley* v. *J. S. Fry & Sons Ltd* (1931) – the unauthorized use of a well-known amateur golfer's image on advertising for a chocolate bar was regarded by the House of Lords as being defamatory. The claimant was able to sue for libel on the basis of the suggestion that Fry was benefiting financially from the use of his image, which was a slur on his amateur status. Plainly, the applicability of this sort of approach is now much more limited, given that the status of the "gentleman amateur" has now disappeared and that high-profile athletes are, or seek to be, economically active. This may have application in a narrow range of circumstances in which image is deployed in association with a particular cause or group, but the likelihood of such a claim arising is slim.

Protection of image rights through actions in passing-off

The principal means by which image and personality have been protected in English law is by recourse through the common law tort of passing-off. The tort has general application; it protects the commercial goodwill and reputation of both legal and natural persons by preventing the unauthorized representation that services or goods emanate from a particular source when, in fact, no such connection exists. Though clearly useful when an athlete has commercial goodwill to protect, it does not extend to a general prohibition on the unauthorized commercial use of image or personality. This is principally as a consequence of the requirement that the athlete suffers damage to their goodwill because they operate in a "common field of activity" to the purported infringer (*McCulloch* v. *May*, 1947).

The utility of the tort of passing-off as a means to protect image or personality is also contingent on whether the alleged breach relates to merchandising or endorsement. The tort is used to protect either the production of goods bearing the likeness of, or otherwise associated with, the athlete, or where the image or personality is deployed in such a way to suggest an athlete's approval of a good or service, usually in the context of promotion or advertising.

In merchandising cases, actions have met with only limited success; the courts have generally taken the position that consumers are sufficiently sophisticated to understand that not all products bearing the name or likeness of an athlete, or any other well-known individual, emanate from them and, therefore, that the requirement for a "common field of activity" is not met. This reasoning is premised on the claim that purchasers of such goods are usually indifferent to their actual source, being interested only in the individual as their subject rather than their status as "official" or "authorized" (*Halliwell* v. *Panini*, 1997). There has been some indication that this position could be broadened, with the judgment of the High Court in *Mirage Studios* v. *Counter Feat Clothing* (1991). Here, the Court decided that where the claimant was involved in licensing the use of image for application to goods, even though they did not produce the goods themselves, the general public would understand and expect that this would be the case and, as a consequence, a "common field of activity" would exist. This case should be treated with a degree of caution as first, involving fictional rather than real characters and, second, a more limited approach having been deployed in subsequent cases.

A much more expansive approach has been adopted in relation to passing-off and endorsement. This is a relatively recent development, coming in the important case of *Irvine* v. *Talksport Ltd* (2002). The case was brought by Eddie Irvine, a former Formula One racing driver, against Talksport, a British radio station. Talksport had produced and distributed to potential advertisers a brochure containing an image of Irvine that had been manipulated to show him holding a portable radio bearing the words "TalkRadio". The judgment of the High Court, approved by the Court of Appeal, was that the law of passing-off should reflect the commercial reality of well-known persons exploiting their image by way of endorsement, within their own field of activity and more widely. According to the trial judge, unauthorized use of Irvine's image amounted to an unlawful appropriation of his goodwill in endorsing goods or services.

The Court of Appeal has affirmed the position developed in *Irvine* v. *Talksport Ltd* in the more recent case of *Fenty* v. *Arcadia Group Brands Ltd* (2015). This case also provides some evidence of a clearer link between the "merchandising" and "endorsement" cases. The case involved a claim for passing-off brought by the pop-star Rhianna against a fashion retailer that had, unauthorized by her, sold t-shirts bearing her image. Rhianna claimed that sales of the t-shirt damaged the goodwill in her own fashion activities. The retailer argued that, based on the position set out in the "merchandising" cases, Rhianna was effectively seeking the recognition of a free-standing image right. The trial judge determined that the fact that Rhianna had previously participated in the retailer's promotional activities, and that the image used on the t-shirt was strikingly similar to that used on one of her album covers, meant that purchasers would be deceived into believing she had authorized the product. Although this appears to develop the position established in *Irvine* v. *Talksport Ltd*, broadening it to include the application of an image to merchandise, as well as to endorsements, it appears that this case is quite distinctive on its facts, necessarily limiting its wider application.

Alternative approaches

More narrowly, it is possible to restrict deployment of an image – usually in relation to a specific, private event – when that image has been acquired in breach of the common law duty of confidence. In *Douglas* v. *Hello!* (2003), the claimants won a breach of confidence action in respect of the publication of illicit photographs taken at their wedding, the rights to which they had sold to a rival publication. The suggestion, based on the case of *Arsenal Football Club Plc* v. *Elite Sports Distribution* (2003), is that a similar position is likely to exist in relation to the taking and use of images in sport, where access to the stadium is subject to the acceptance of contractual terms regulating this. *Douglas* v. *Hello!* also involved the award of a nominal sum for the breach of data protection laws. However this remains an undeveloped aspect of this issue.

Quasi-legal avenues of redress also offer an alternative approach. In *Bedford* v. *The Number (118 118)* (2004), a retired athlete brought a successful action under the *UK Code of Broadcast Advertising* on the basis that a caricature based upon him effectively appropriated his likeness without his permission.

Other actions based on breach of confidence and human rights are open to athletes. However these relate to intrusions into private life, rather than the commercial exploitation of image and personality.

Comparative analysis of US and English law

There are subtle differences between the laws protecting athlete image rights in the US and those in the UK. In the US, it is clearly understood that athletes have a right to protect their identities from commercial exploitation by third parties without their consent. There are numerous cases where athletes have held companies accountable for misuse, and the damages awarded by the courts are reflective of the commercial value of the athlete's identity. Conversely, under English law, athletes have to develop the interest in their identity in order for it to be protected. Courts have required athletes and celebrities to establish that they have created goodwill regarding their identity that has been exploited without their consent. An example is the case of *Taverner Rutledge Ltd* v. *Trexpalm Ltd* (1975), in which the claimant marketed, without being licensed by the rights holders, lollipops as "Kojak Pops", named after the fictional television detective strongly associated with them. The claimant was nonetheless able to obtain an injunction against the defendant, even though their competing product was officially sanctioned. This was because the claimant had established goodwill in the market. Notably this case relates to a fictional character, but it does raise serious issues for professional athletes. Though the *Irvine* and *Fenty* cases have moved English law closer to recognizing rights in images, it remains the case that goodwill of some kind is required to act as a proxy for any interest in its protection.

In spite of the unique differences among the law in the US and the UK, there are strong similarities. In both the US and the UK, athletes have become as famous, if not more, as film and television stars. The images of these individuals are increasingly being used to promote companies' products and services, and both countries have recognized that there are rights associated with the use of an athlete's image. Specifically, these rights are based on property rights that have a commercial value which can be assigned to third parties. This is observed in the *Rooney* case as well as the *Haelen* case where the courts considered what rights could be protected as well as what rights could be transferred, or assigned, by the athlete.

When analysing cases of misuse, the test in both countries is based on athlete identifiability. It is not only that consumers were deceived into believing that the athlete had endorsed the product, but that they could identify the athlete solely by looking at the advertisement or product. Both countries acknowledge that the athlete's identity can involve the athlete's name, likeness, personality and goodwill, and this identity can be appropriated.

Athletes and celebrities in both countries have also had problems convincing judges about why individuals should aggressively protect this right. In the *Jordan* case previously mentioned, US District Court Judge Shadur believed Jordan's demand for damages was "greedy", and Jordan was creating a "legal mountain" from a "legal molehill" (Schmadeke & Sweeney, 2013, para. 5). A similar response was made in the *Fenty* case by Lord Justice Underhill, who regarded the case as "close to the borderline" and likely to be unique on its own facts.

In both countries, an athlete's claim for violation of his/her image rights is not absolute. An athlete's demand for damages in the US will not succeed if the alleged infringer has protection under the First Amendment of the US Constitution, i.e. the use was a form of expression. Under English law, the athlete must prove damage to their goodwill and the alleged breach must relate to endorsement, rather than to merchandising.

Suggestions for protecting the athlete's image rights

For an athlete, protecting one's image should be at the forefront of managing one's athlete brand. Since the lifespan of a professional athlete's career may be five years or less (Pavony & Thomas, 2012), it is important to capitalize on as many opportunities as possible in order to maximize revenue opportunities. For athletes who seek to protect the unauthorized use of their name, likeness or other aspects of their marketable identity, the following suggestions are presented. This involves the athlete: (1) determining the value of their image rights and the importance of protection; (2) obtaining a representative who is knowledgeable in trademark law in the US and in the UK; and (3) registering the aspects of their marketable identity that may be protected under trademark laws in each country.

First, the athlete should understand that they have a marketable identity that needs to be protected. An athlete's name, likeness and goodwill distinguish them from other athletes. Whether it is the use of the name, nickname, a photo, a gesture or a slogan, there are certain characteristics of an athlete that will set them apart from other athletes. Additionally, when a third party uses an athlete's name or likeness in conjunction with a good or service, it is there for the purposes of not only capitalizing on the strength of the athlete's reputation and goodwill but also to draw attention to the goods or service. The athlete should be steadfast in protecting the use of their marketable identity, as unauthorized use by a third party could imply endorsement for a product that the athlete does not support or approve of. Protecting the athlete's right of publicity may include seeking injunctive relief to prevent continuous infringement or pleading for damages. If the violation affects the future value of the athlete's marketable identity, courts may consider the amount of the benefit received by the infringer as well as how much the infringer has previously contracted for the use of similar rights (Margolies, 1994). Regardless of what remedies are sought, the athlete should take advantage of the protection afforded by the legal system.

Next, the athlete needs to obtain adequate representation by someone who specializes in trademark law and has familiarity with the laws in both countries. In the US, laws can vary from state to state. Some are based on common law, while others may rely on right of publicity statutes. There are also remedies under US federal law. Additionally, since an athlete's right of publicity is not recognized in the UK, the athlete may need to find an alternative solution under English law to protect the unauthorized use of his/her image or likeness. While passing-off is a common law tort, UK trademark law is inextricably interwoven with that of the European Union. Thus selecting the appropriate representation is essential for an athlete with global consumer appeal.

Lastly, once it is determined what aspects of the athlete's identity need to be protected, the athlete's trademarks should be registered with the appropriate entities in each country. In the US, athletes can register trademarks with the United States Patent and Trademark Office (USPTO). The USPTO allows submission of an application to register a mark based only on the applicant's bona fide intent to use the mark in interstate or international commerce as well as actual use of the mark (United States Patent and Trademark Office, 2016). Under English law, it is also possible that image and personality can be protected through registration under the Trade Marks Act 1994 at the Intellectual Property Office. A number of athletes have successfully registered their image, or aspects of it, as a Trade Mark; although the very well-known may be regarded as having become so high-profile as to render themselves generic and thus incapable of distinguishing between the sources of different goods and services – the function of the Trade Mark (*DIANA, PRINCESS OF WALES* Trade Mark, 2001). There is also registration under European and international application systems, such as the Madrid Protocol. Still, to apply for an international trademark, the athlete must already have a base application or registration in the US or the UK. In the English context, athletes would be well advised to seek to begin commercial exploitation of their image in all relevant markets as soon as possible, so that they begin to accrue vital goodwill.

Conclusion

Consumers are enthralled with an athlete's persona, and companies are eager to capitalize on the connection that consumers may have with a particular athlete. Athletes should take advantage of these opportunities. On the other hand, the use of the athlete's name, likeness or other aspects of their marketable identity should be protected. Athletes should seek adequate legal representation to aid in the protection and enforcement of their image rights. Although there are similarities in the US and the UK, there are unique differences in the terminology used and how best to protect an athlete's image. Failure to monitor violations of the athlete's right of publicity or unauthorized use of their image may damage the athlete's reputation and goodwill. This damage may result in the loss of future earnings. However, enforcement is not about the loss of financial payment; it is about ensuring that the athlete has control over who uses their likeness for commercial advantage.

References

Abdul-Jabbar v. *General Motors Corp.*, 85 F.3d 407 (9th Cir. 1996).

Arsenal Football Club Plc v. *Elite Sports Distribution* [2003] FSR 26 215.

Associated Press (2015). "Michael Jordan awarded $8.9M for grocery store's use of name" [online]. *NY Daily News*. Available at <www.nydailynews.com/sports/basketball/michael-jordan-awarded-8-9m-grocery-store-article-1.2333917>. Accessed 19 November 2015.

Bedford v. *The Number (118 118)* [2004] ISLR SLR-18.

California Civil Code, §3344 (West 2016).

Doe v. *TCI Cablevision*, 110 S.W.3d 363 (Mo. Sup. Ct. 2003).

Douglas v. *Hello!* No. 2 [2003] EWHC 786 (Ch).

Eastwood v. *Superior Court for Los Angeles County,* 149 Cal.App.3d 409 (1983).

Edwards, P. (1998). What's the score: Does the right of publicity protect professional sports leagues? *Albany Law Review, 62*(2), 579–622.

Fenty v. *Arcadia Group Brands Ltd* [2015] EWCA Civ 3.

Forbes (2015). David Beckham [online]. *Forbes*. Available at <www.forbes.com/profile/david-beckham/>. Accessed 17 November 2015.

Haelen Laboratories, Inc. v. *Topps Chewing Gum, Inc.*, 202 F.2d 866 (2nd Cir. 1953).

Halliwell v. *Panini* [1997] EMLR 94.

Irvine v. *Talksport Ltd* [2002] EWHC 367 (Ch).

Lanham Act, 15 USC. §1125(a) (2005).

Levy, D. (2013). EPL Coverage in US Rivals UK [online]. *Bleacher Report*. Available at <http://bleacherreport.com/articles/1739352-premier-league-coverage-in-america-should-suddenly-make-fans-in-uk-very-jealous>. Accessed 22 November 2013.

Margolies, A. (1994). Sports figures' right of publicity. *Sports Lawyers Journal, 1*, 359–376.

McCarthy, J. T. (1994). The human persona as commercial property: The right of publicity. *Columbia-VLA Journal of Law & the Arts, 19*, 129–148.

McCracken, G. (1989). Who is the celebrity endorser? Cultural foundations of the endorsement process. *Journal of Consumer Research, 16*(3), 310–321.

McCulloch v. *May* [1947] 2 All ER 845.

Michael Jordan and Jump 23, Inc. v. *Dominick's Finer Foods, LLC*, 115 F.Supp.3d 950 (N.D. Ill. 2015).

Mirage Studios v. *Counter Feat Clothing* [1991] F.S.R. 145.

NBA (2015). *NBA Global* [online]. NBA.com. Available at <www.nba.com/global/index.html>. Accessed 16 November 2015.

NFL (2015). *NFL International Series* [online]. NFL.com. Available at <www.nfl.com/kickoff>. Accessed 16 November 2015.

NY CLS Civ. R §50 (Consol. 2000).

NY CLS Civ. R §51 (Consol. 2000).

Palmer v. *Schonhorn Enterprises*, 232 A.2d 458 (N.J. Super. Ct. Ch. Div. 1967).

Pavony, B. H. and Thomas, J. (2012). For the love of the name: Professional athletes seek trademark protection. *Pace Intellectual Property, Sports & Entertainment Law Forum, 2*(1), 153–166.

Proactive Sports Management Ltd v. *Rooney & Ors* [2011] EWCA Civ. 1444.

Prosser, William L. (1960), Privacy, 48 Cal. L. Rev. 383.

Schmadeke, S. and Sweeney, A. (2013). Michael Jordan makes secret appearance in federal courthouse [online]. Tribunedigital-chicagotribune. Available at <http://articles.chicagotribune.com/

2013-06-14/news/ct-met-michael-jordan-dominicks-lawsuit-20130614_1_michael-jordan-fincr-foods-llc-frederick-sperling>. Accessed 16 March 2016.

Somerson v. *World Wrestling Entertainment, Inc.*, 956 F. Supp. 1360 (N.D. Georgia 2013).

Tolley v. *J. S. Fry & Sons Ltd* [1931] UKHL 1.

Taverner Rutledge Ltd v. *Trexpalm Ltd* [1975] FSR 479.

United States Patent and Trademark Office (2016). *Trademark Process* [online]. Available at <www.uspto.gov/trademarks-getting-started/trademark-process>. Accessed 30 March 2016.

Warren, S. D. and Brandeis, L. D. (1890). The right to privacy. *Harvard Law Review, 4*(5), 193–220.

Weber, S. (2015). *Top 100 highest-paid athlete endorsers of 2015* [online]. Available at <http://opendorse.com/blog/highest-paid-athlete-endorsers/>. Accessed 16 March 2016.

20

HOW CAN SPORT SPONSORS COMPLY WITH INTERNATIONAL CORRUPTION LAWS?

Mark Dodds

Introduction

Sport sponsorships can help a brand achieve commercial objectives such as direct sales or brand awareness. International sporting events are being hosted by nations with a "bribery-friendly" business culture. The nexus between anti-corruption laws and these "bribery-friendly" business cultures creates a tension for sport sponsors. Violations of applicable anti-corruption laws may lead to significant fines, criminal sanctions and negative publicity. It is imperative that sport sponsors know and comply with these laws. This chapter aims to discuss bribery law, identify potential red flags that may indicate violations and offer recommendations for legal compliance.

Corruption is the "misuse of entrusted power for private gain" (Transparency International, 2016). It tends to be a "hidden crime" (Joutsen & Keränen, 2009, p. 1). Often there are no witnesses to the offence but this crime harms the public by compensating actors for non-work, encouraging the abuse of power, decreasing market competition and misallocating resources. Corruption infects every business sector, including sport.

Maennig (2005) categorized the two types of sport corruption as "management corruption" and "competition corruption". Management corruption is decisions made by sporting officials away from the sporting arena (Maennig, 2005), and competition corruption is attempts to deliberately distort the outcome of a sporting contest (Gorse, 2014). However, corruption related to global sporting competitions is not limited to the actions of the governing body or to the event itself (Berg & Rojas, 2015). In fact, the United Nations Global Compact considers bribery connected to a sport sponsorship to be sport corruption as well.

However, the United Nations does not possess any legal authority over corruption. Individual nations define and criminalize corruption differently. There are some commonalities with many of these different laws. Generally, the laws typically make it illegal to bribe governmental officials in order to receive preferential treatment. This is known as active bribery. Passive bribery is asking for a bribe and is illegal in some countries but not all. The differences in the laws make compliance difficult for multinational companies, and especially for companies entering a new country for the first time. For instance, a company may reside in a jurisdiction where bribery is illegal but conduct business in a culture where corrupt behaviours such as bribery and kick-backs are expected.

In the business context, there are transactional bribes and outright purchase. A transactional bribe is a payment that is routinely and impersonally made to a public official to secure or accelerate the performance of his official function. This type of bribe is commonly known as a grease payment. An outright purchase is a payment made in order to secure the favour of a foreign employee who remains in place in an organization to which he appears to pay full loyalty while actually favouring the briber's interest.

While paying bribes (active bribery) is against the law for US and most European firms, it may be an accepted marketing activity for its competitors (Scott, Gilliard & Scott, 2002). In fact, Scott, Gilliard and Scott (2002) cite the National Export Strategy Report (1996) estimating that companies who are willing to bribe foreign officials win 80 per cent of all business contract decisions. Further, the companies that bribe are more likely to have home countries where bribery is either legal or accepted as an expected business practice (Scott, Gilliard & Scott, 2002). Even though the global economy is beginning to include companies from these bribery-friendly countries, their behaviour is not changing. In fact, increased competition from companies from bribery-friendly countries, as well as business competition within these bribery-friendly markets, may actually escalate the incentive for typically compliant companies to match the illegal behaviour.

Global sporting mega-events, such as the FIFA World Cup and the Olympic Games, are being hosted in countries that possess a bribery-friendly business culture, such as Brazil, China and Russia. In this type of business culture, the local business community officials may expect benefits that would violate bribery law. This culture may create a dilemma for an international company engaged in sport sponsorship, especially through the activation of this sponsorship. The company must comply with appropriate bribery laws but may be solicited by local officials to violate those laws in order to conduct business. Sport sponsors need to understand how anti-bribery laws work, what the law covers, how to comply with the law and whether the host location will increase legal scrutiny of the sponsorship activity.

Sponsorship and hospitality

Meenaghan (1983) defined sponsorship as the provision of assistance, either financial or in-kind, to activity by a commercial organization for the purpose of achieving commercial objectives. Sport sponsorship activation tactics may include hospitality. Hospitality is a unique experience that often includes entertainment such as sport event tickets, travel, accommodation, food and so on. The marketing world has thrived on hospitality and its gifts to create a better relationship with an existing or potential customer in expectation of future business (Feast, 2011).

Hospitality is a vital sport sponsorship component and the legal scrutiny for bribery activity related to this sales action is increasing (Dodds, 2015). Sponsors, especially in a corporate hospitality context, measure success by the number and level of decision makers entertained, and the business generated (Day, 2011). Programme elements that are highly desired by visitors are those that are not commonly experienced (Dodds & DeGaris, 2011). Tickets to a mega-event are highly desired. Thus providing a VIP experience with tickets to a sporting event creates a sought-after corporate hospitality programme, which can lead to a stronger relationship with the client.

Sponsorship corruption

Sponsors face many corruption-related risks (United Nations Global Compact, 2014, pp. 11–12). The risks include active bribery (the promise, offering or giving, directly or indirectly, of an undue advantage to become a sponsor), and passive bribery (the promise, offering or giving, directly or indirectly, of an undue advantage by the sport entity to obtain sponsorship). A sport sponsorship needs to be aware of potential conflicts of interest with event officials, government officials and third party agents. Finally, the misuse of a sport sponsorship to obtain an undue competitive advantage, and the misuse of sponsorship hospitality to obtain an undue advantage, may lead to corrupt behaviour.

Legal discussion

Many countries have created specific anti-corruption laws that regulate business conduct. These laws govern the bribery of their own officials as well as foreign officials of other sovereign nations.

In 1977, the United States' Foreign Corrupt Practices Act (FCPA) was the first law to criminalize the bribery of foreign officials. The foreign official requirement includes most employees of a state-owned business commonly utilized in China. This act does not require the corrupt payment to be cash but it can be gifts, entertainment, drinks, meals, transportation, lodging and other items that are common to a sport sponsorship's hospitality programme. Foreign companies listed on US stock exchanges or conducting significant business within the United States must comply with the FCPA. If there is a violation of the FCPA, the corporation is subject to a $2 million criminal fine and any individual (including corporate officers, directors or stockholders) who wilfully violates the provisions of the law is subject to a $250,000 fine and/or five years' imprisonment (Kaikati & Label, 1980). However, a payment that is a reasonable and bona fide expenditure directly related to the promotion of a product or service is allowed.

The United Kingdom's Bribery Act (2010) criminalizes any offer, promise or gift if any financial or other advantage is given to a foreign public official to obtain or retain business. This law specifically bans hospitality given with the intention to induce a person to perform a function improperly. Initially, this provision caused concern for sponsors of the 2012 Summer Olympic Games in London. However, enforcement of the Bribery Act has allowed reasonable hospitality expenses (Harrington, 2012).

In 2013, Brazil passed its anti-corruption law known as the Clean Companies Act. The enactment of this law helped to prepare Brazil for its hosting of the 2014 FIFA World Cup and the 2016 Rio Summer Olympic Games (Correia, Bartley & Freitas, 2013). This law forbids bribes to both domestic and foreign officials as well as related third parties for the purpose of gaining an unjust advantage. While the law is not limited to the bribing of foreign officials, it does not require proof of corrupt intent (Correia, Bartley & Freitas, 2013). Violations of the law may result in fines up to 20 per cent of the company's annual gross revenues (Correia, Bartley & Freitas, 2013) but no criminal penalties. A company may receive some leniency on its sanctions if it voluntarily discloses the violations and cooperates with any investigation (Latham & Watkins, 2014).

Illustrative cases

In 2013, Weatherford International faced bribery charges from improper hospitality expenses associated with the 2006 FIFA World Cup in Germany. Weatherford provided match tickets, travel and entertainment to officials of a state-owned company in Algeria to ensure the renewal of oil contracts (SEC.gov, 2013). Although Weatherford is a Swiss company and the activity was conducted in Germany, the FCPA applied because Weatherford had substantial operations in the US, including a headquarters in Houston, Texas (SEC.gov, 2013).

Weatherford was found to lack the internal controls needed to prevent corrupt behaviour. Although Weatherford paid almost $115 million on investigating the allegations (FCPAblog,com, 2013), it was fined more than $120 million including $1.875 million for its lack of cooperation with the government (SEC.gov, 2013).

As part of its 2008 Summer Olympic Games in Beijing, China, BHP Billiton Ltd, the Australian mining company whose stock trades on the New York Stock Exchange, supplied the gold, silver and bronze metal for the awards (Paul & Hornby, 2013). To activate this sponsorship, BHP Billiton Ltd provided hospitality for guests of China's state-owned steel-making firms. The hospitality included event tickets, luxury hotel accommodation and sight-seeing worth up to $16,000 per trip (SEC.gov, 2015). Although BHP Billiton Ltd had internal controls, it did not go far enough to prevent the bribery violations (Dodds, 2015). The corporate procedures required the expenses to be reviewed, but the expenses were never examined by anyone outside the business unit. BHP Billiton Ltd also failed to train its employees on bribery risks and prevention (SEC.gov, 2015). BHP Billiton Ltd self-reported these FCPA violations and cooperated with the government's investigation, which led to a settlement consisting of a $25 million fine (Dodds, 2015).

Sport sponsorship bribery activity may include infrastructure projects (Dodds and Palmero, 2016). A leading international engineering and services group, Bilfinger SE, faced allegations of corruption from its sponsorship of the 2014 FIFA World Cup in Brazil. The German company is accused of paying bribes related to orders to equip security command centres at 12 host cities (dw.com, 2015). The allegations focus on suspected payments to governmental officials who hired Bilfinger SE to supply 1,200 security monitors and software to run the police, fire and emergency services (dw.com, 2015). Bilfinger SE became the first international company to disclose to the Brazilian government that it may have paid bribes in order to seek leniency (Stauffer, 2015).

Identify risks

Sponsors using hospitality in connection with sporting events, especially in markets where business corruption is common, should be aware of potential risks (Rogers, 2014). Every sponsor needs to scrutinize the situation very closely in order to make certain that no corrupt behaviour is committed. Some red flags that may indicate corruptive behaviour include:

1. Using a third party agent, representative or distributor that has previously violated a local law, even if that law is not bribery. This act may indicate that the agent might create criminal liability for the sponsor via the agent's behaviour.
2. An unusual request for additional money such as a bonus or one-time payment. This payment may indicate a bribe, grease payment, or kickback to an official. The initial budget should cover all anticipated expenses. If there is a new expense, then the sponsor should investigate this expense with the vender or governmental agency directly.
3. An agent asking for additional money above the contracted amount.
4. Public or government officials (or family) who are stakeholders in the hosted organiza-tion. This might be commonplace in markets with state-owned companies (China), or developing nations with a bribery-friendly business culture. The bribery may include payments or benefits to close family members of the governmental official.
5. Additional travel requests (new location, additional persons, more luxurious accommo-dation, etc.) by the hospitality guests or third party agent.
6. Non-specific charges (training, appearance fee, publications, etc.) should be investigated directly. Bribery activity may be hidden within what appears to be a legitimate expense.

Recommendations

Sport sponsorship hospitality may be difficult to distinguish from a bribe. Both activities might include event tickets, transportation, lodging, food and entertainment. A sport sponsor needs to take steps in order to comply with bribery laws, especially in markets with bribery-friendly business cultures.

Every organization that engages in sport sponsorship should create a separate corporate compliance department overseeing all international marketing activity. The department must write a clear policy against the corruption of foreign officials. This policy needs to be endorsed by the highest levels of the organization (Day, 2011), with a clear commitment showing senior management obeying its procedures. The sport sponsor needs to establish a comprehensive training programme to review potential corrupt situations and red flags. This step reinforces proper behaviour. Finally, an internal enforcement department should review all hospitality contracts and expenses. All payments need to reflect reasonable and bona fide expenditure that is directly related to the promotion of a product or service. If potential violations are found, prompt disciplinary action needs to be taken (Kaikati & Label, 1980). This includes self-reporting the violations and cooperating with the government's investigation (Dodds, 2015). The Weatherford and BHP Billiton Ltd cases resulted in very different penalties that were due, in part, to the level of cooperation shown by the companies.

An organization that manages international sporting events should research all applicable laws to ensure its own compliance and that of its sponsors. Sporting events are being hosted by many developing nations. These markets may not regulate either active or passive bribery, or may not enforce any laws banning corrupt activity. Despite over 40 nations agreeing to the terms of the international Organization for Economic Co-operation and Development's [OECD] Anti-Bribery Convention agreement, Transparency International reports that only the US, Germany, the UK and Switzerland actively enforce it (Rising, 2013). Conversely, half of these countries showed little to no enforcement of their laws (Rising, 2013). Much of the limited enforcement is attributed to a lack of resources dedicated to its investigation and prosecution (Rising, 2013).

A sponsor should take additional care when hosting officials at corporate hospitality events. The sponsor should not select the particular official who will participate in the event, the selection should be made by the other organization, or using a predetermined, merit-based criteria. The company should investigate the list of attendees for relatives of governmental officials.

Finally, when contracting with a third party agent, a corporation should ensure that all expenditures are transparent, clearly documented and for the actual amount of any incurred expenses. This may prevent bribes that are hidden as legitimate expenses.

Conclusion

Anti-corruption law criminalizes bribery behaviour but does not change the corrupt culture that may exist where a sporting event is held (Dodds, 2016). Sport sponsors need to understand all applicable laws and create protocols that establish compliance. Sport sponsorships can be an effective tool to achieve commercial objectives. However, any corrupt actions may lead to a significant fine, criminal sanctions and negative publicity.

References

Berg, N. & Rojas, G. D. (2015). Shooting for effective anti-corruption compliance: A look at recent developments in Brazil. *Ropes and Gray*. Retrieved from <www.ropesgray.com/newsroom/alerts/2015/March/Shooting-for-Effective-Anti-Corruption-Compliance-A-Look-at-Recent-Developments-in-Brazil.aspx>. Accessed 26 March 2015.

Correia, M., Bartley, M. and Freitas, R. (2013). A comparison of the new Brazilian anticorruption law, the FCPA and the UK bribery act. *Association of Corporate Counsel*. Retrieved from <www.acc.com/legalresources/quickcounsel/cnbalfuba.cfm?makepdf=1>. Accessed 24 September 2013.

Day, H. (2011). How to avoid sponsorship and hospitality becoming forms of bribery. *Journal of Sponsorship*, 4(2), 100–104.

Dodds, M. & DeGaris, L. (2011). Using mobile marketing to engage NASCAR fans and increase sales. *Sports Management International Journal Choregia*, 7(1), 63–75.

Dodds, M. & Palmero, M. (2016). What can *Bilfinger* teach Olympic sponsors? *Sports Management International Journal Choregia*, 12(2), 43–54.

Dodds, M. (2016). Revisiting the Salt Lake City Olympic scandal: Would the outcome be different today? *Sports Management International Journal Choregia*, 12(1), 1–14.

Dodds, M. (2015). Foreign Corrupt Practices Act cases impact sport marketing strategies. *Sport Marketing Quarterly*, 24(4), 258–260.

dw.com (2015). "Germany's Bilfinger announces probe into possible Brazil 2014 World Cup bribes". *Reuters*. Retrieved from <www.dw.com/en/germanys-bilfinger-announces-probe-into-possible-brazil-2014-world-cup-bribes/a-18333176>. Accessed 22 March 2015.

FCPAblog.com (2013). Weatherford pays $152.6 million for FCPA violations, $100 million for trade sanctions. Retrieved from <www.fcpablog.com/blog/2013/11/26/weatherford-pays-1526-million-for-fcpa-violations-100-millio.html>. Accessed 26 November 2013.

Feast, S. (2011). There's no such thing as a free lunch. *Credit Management*, May 2011, 4.

Gorse, S. (2014). "Corruption in International Sport: Implications for Sponsorship Management". [Unpublished doctoral thesis]. Coventry University, UK.

Harrington, A. (2012). The Bribery Act – one year on. *Financial Management*, 41(3), 50–53.

Joutsen, M. & Keränen, J. (2009). Corruption and the prevention of corruption in Finland. Ministry of Justice: Finland.

Kaikati, J. & Label, W. (1980). American bribery legislation: An obstacle to international marketing. *Journal of Marketing*, 44(4), 38–43.

Latham & Watkins (2014). Brazilian anti-corruption law: 7 implications and challenges for companies doing business in Brazil. Retrieved from <www.lw.com/.../lw-brazil-anti-corruption-law>. Accessed 6 January 2014.

Maennig, W. (2005). Corruption in international sports and sport management: Forms, tendencies, extent and countermeasures. *European Sport Management Quarterly*, 5(2), 187–225.

Meenaghan, J. A. (1983). Commercial sponsorship. *European Journal of Marketing*, 17(7), 5–73.

Paul, S. and Hornby, L. (2013). "BHP Billiton faces corruption probe over Beijing Olympics". *Reuters*. Retrieved from <www.reuters.com/article/2013/03/13/us-bhp-investigation-olympics-idUS-BRE92C00G20130313>. Accessed 13 March 2013.

Rising, D. (2013). "Wathdog [sic]: Anti-bribery rules not being enforced". *Associated Press*. Retrieved from <http://abcnews.go.com/International/wireStory/wathdog- anti-bribery-rules-enforced-20502034>. Accessed 8 October 2013.

Rogers, H. L. (2014, May 30). Corporate hospitality is major risk area during World Cup. *Law360*. Retrieved from <www.law360.com/articles/542886/corporate-hospitality-is-major-risk-area-during-world-cup>. Accessed 30 May 2014.

Scott, J., Gilliard, D. & Scott, R. (2002). Eliminating bribery as a transactional marketing strategy. *International Journal of Commerce & Management*, 12(1), 1–17.

SEC.gov (2013). SEC charges Weatherford International with FCPA violations. Retrieved from <www.sec.gov/News/PressRelease/Detail/PressRelease/1370540415694#.VRAtTeHpx8t>. Accessed 26 November 2013.

SEC.gov (2015). SEC charges BHP Billiton with violating FCPA at Olympic Games. Retrieved from <www.sec.gov/news/pressrelease/2015-93.html>. Accessed 20 May 2015.

Stauffer, C. (2015). "Brazil comptroller says Germany's Bilfinger seeking leniency deal". *Reuters*. Retrieved from <www.reuters.com/article/2015/05/07/brazil-corruption-bilfinger-idUSLIN0XY1XY20150507>. Accessed 7 May 2015.

Transparency International (2016). What is corruption? Retrieved from <www.transparency.org/what-is-corruption/#define>. Accessed 13 July 2016.

United Nations Global Compact (2014). Fighting corruption in sport sponsorship and hospitality: A practical guide for companies. Retrieved from <www.unglobalcompact.org/docs/issues_doc/Anti-Corruption/SportsSponsorshipHospitalityGuide.pdf>. Accessed 13 July 2016.

21

TRADEMARK PROTECTION ACROSS BORDERS

Kerri Cebula

Introduction

The NFL Shield. "You'll never walk alone." Ferrari's prancing horse. All are examples of symbols or slogans used by international sport organizations to identify themselves to other organizations, and most importantly, to their fans. These symbols or slogans are trademarks. A trademark is defined by the Agreement on Trade-Related Aspects of Intellectual Property as "[a]ny sign, or combination of signs, capable of distinguishing the goods or services of one undertaking from those of other undertakings" (Agreement on Trade-Related Aspects of Intellectual Property Rights, 1994). This means that any symbol, such as the NFL's shield or Ferrari's prancing horse, or slogan such as "You'll never walk alone", that identifies a particular organization to consumers and fans can be protected by law to stop others from using those marks.

There are two general types of trademarks that are used in the sport industry: trademarks (also trade marks) and collective marks. Some countries distinguish between trademarks, which are reserved for goods, and service marks, which are reserved for services. Trademarks and service marks receive the same protection. Another type of mark is a collective marks, which is a trademark owned by an organization and is used by members of the organization to distinguish themselves as such.

Local registration

The first step sport organizations must take in protecting their trademarks (marks) is to either apply to register their mark or to complete the registration process in the organization's home country, depending on the system used to receive international registration. The organization will need to ensure that their marks are protectable under their country's laws. In general, a trademark will need to be distinctive, meaning a consumer will recognize the organization's mark as an indication that the good or service came from that organization. When a consumer sees goods with that mark on them, they know where the goods came from. Once local registration is applied for and/or registration is granted, there are two ways that an organization can protect their marks internationally. The first is to register their marks internationally through the Madrid System and the second is to rely on international treaties and individual registration to protect their marks.

International registration

The first way that an organization can protect its mark internationally is by registering it under the Madrid System. The Madrid System consists of what are commonly referred to as the Madrid Agreement and the Madrid Protocol. The Madrid Agreement Concerning the International Registration of Marks (Madrid Agreement or Agreement) was originally signed in April 1891 and was last revised in Stockholm in July 1967 (Madrid Agreement, 1967). It was last amended in September 1979 (Madrid Agreement, 1967). As of March 2016, there are 55 members of the Agreement. The Protocol Relating to the Madrid Agreement Concerning the International Registration of Marks (Madrid Protocol or Protocol) was adopted in June 1989 and last amended in November 2007. There are 97 members of the Protocol; as of October 2015, all members of the Agreement are members of the Protocol. If a country is a member of both the Agreement and the Protocol, the Protocol controls. The Agreement and the Protocol allow for central registration; an organization need only file one common application and choose which countries they would like to register in. Based on that common application, members of the Agreement and the Protocol will determine if the mark can be registered in their country. However, the Agreement and the Protocol also allow for a central attack, leading many organizations to forgo international registration.

Madrid Agreement Concerning the International Registration of Marks

Under Article 1(2) of the Agreement, a national of a member country can secure trademark registration in any other member country once they have received registration in their home country and filed their registration with the International Bureau of Intellectual Property, now known as the International Bureau of the World Intellectual Property Organization (International Bureau) (Madrid Agreement, 1967). The application does not come from the holder the way it does in local registration. Rather, it comes directly from the home registration office (Madrid Agreement, 1967). So, if a UK mark holder wishes to have international registration, the Intellectual Property Office files the application with the International Bureau. Article 3*bis* states that countries can choose to be included in the registration process automatically, meaning that every registration filed with the International Bureau will be protected in their country, or only included at the request of the mark holder (Madrid Agreement, 1967). Article 3*ter* requires the mark owner to include in the application any countries that have opted out of the automatic registration that they wish to receive protection from (Madrid Agreement, 1967). Under Article 4, a mark registered with the International Bureau will receive the same protection in all member countries as if the mark had been individually registered in each country (Madrid Agreement, 1967). Once a mark is registered at the International Bureau, it is registered for 20 years, with the possibility of renewal (Madrid Agreement, 1967). The mark can be renewed forever (Madrid Agreement, 1967).

Article 5 of the Agreement allows member countries to deny registration of a mark if the mark is un-protectable in that country within 12 months (Madrid Agreement, 1967). However, the grounds for refusal must be grounds that are in Article 6*quinquies* of the Paris Convention for the Protection of Industrial Property (Madrid Agreement, 1967). Article 6(3) states that if the mark's registration is cancelled but in its home country within the first five years of international registration, the mark's international registration is also cancelled (Madrid Agreement, 1967). This is known as the central attack. Once the International Bureau cancels the mark, it no longer receives protection under the Agreement (Madrid Agreement, 1967).

The Madrid Agreement does not specifically mention service marks and collective marks as marks that are protected. It does use the term "marks", which can be read to include service and collective marks.

The Protocol Relating to the Madrid Agreement Concerning the International Registration of Marks

The Madrid Protocol closely mirrors the Madrid Agreement, with some key differences. Under Article 2(1), a national of a member country can file for registration with the International Bureau once they receive registration, known as the Basic Registration, or once they have filed an application for protection in their home country, known as the Basic Application (Madrid Protocol, 1989). This allows an organization to protect its marks in other countries while waiting for final registration in its home country. It is the home registration office that will file the application (Madrid Protocol, 1989). As under the Agreement, Article 3*bis* states that the mark holder will receive registration only in the member states the holder specifically requests in their application (Madrid Protocol, 1989). Article 3*ter*(2) allows the holder to request additional countries, known as a territorial extension. Article 4(1)(a) requires that once a mark is registered with the International Bureau, it receives the same protection as if the mark has been individually registered in each country (Madrid Protocol, 1989). Once a mark is registered at the International Bureau, under the Protocol, it is registered for ten years and the mark is renewable (Madrid Protocol, 1989).

Article 5 allows member countries to deny registration to a mark if the mark is unprotectable in that country, but allows a member country up to 18 months to file the refusal (Madrid Protocol, 1989). Again, the grounds must be one of those listed in Article 6*quinquies* of the Paris Convention for the Protection of Intellectual Property (Madrid Protocol, 1989). As under the Madrid Agreement, the Protocol allows for central attack. If the Basic Registration has been cancelled or if the Basic Application has not been converted into a registration, the mark's international registration will be cancelled (Madrid Protocol, 1989). However, under the Protocol, a mark holder can transform the international registration into national registrations as long as it is done within three months of the cancellation and the holder follows all requirements of the country's laws and pays all applicable fees (Madrid Protocol, 1989). This can be expensive, possibly cost-prohibitive, but allows the holder to keep its priority date (Madrid Protocol, 1989). The Madrid Protocol also does not specifically mention service and collective marks, but also uses the generic term "marks", which can be read to include service and collective marks.

How does it work?

In practice, if a sport organization wishes to register its marks under the Madrid Agreement, it first has to ensure that it has received registration in its home country. Under the Protocol, the organization can file for protection either after it has filed for the mark or after it has received the registration. If a sport organization based in New Zealand wished to register its mark under the Agreement, it would first have to register it with the Intellectual Property Office of New Zealand (IPONZ). However, if it wished to file under the Protocol, it only has to file for registration of the mark with the IPONZ.

In order to receive protection under both the Agreement and the Protocol, the organization asks its home country to file its registration application with the International Bureau, making sure to state which countries it would like to receive protection in. In this scenario, the organization would ask the IPONZ to file. Once the application is filed, any member state may deny registration on one or more of the grounds listed in Article 6*quinquies* of the Paris Convention for the Protection of Industrial Property. An example of one such ground is if the mark the organization is trying to register infringes on the rights of a mark already held in that country. If there are no objections, the mark is protected in all member countries for a period of 20 years under the Agreement and ten years under the Protocol. However, if the home country, in this case IPONZ, were to cancel the organization's original registration within five years of the international application, the international registrations would also be cancelled. However, the organization would be permitted to change the international registration into national registrations, provided it does so within three months of the cancellation and pays all applicable fees in each country.

It is important to note that if a state is a member of both the Agreement and the Protocol, the Protocol controls and the organization will need to register under the Protocol. Germany is a member of both the Agreement and the Protocol; it will both request registration of marks, and register marks, under the Protocol. Registration under the Protocol is possible only if the member state is a member of the Protocol. For example, the US is a member of the Protocol only, and therefore, it will both request registration of marks and register marks under the Protocol. Registration under the Agreement is possible only if the member state is a member of the Agreement. As of March 2016, all members of the Agreement are also members of the Protocol and therefore there will be no registrations under the Agreement for the foreseeable future.

Several organizations prefer not to register their trademarks under the Madrid System because of the central attack provisions. They do not want to risk losing registration in all countries. While the transfer to national registration is nice and allows an organization to keep its priority date, the organization still has to spend the money on registering in each individual country; something they could have originally done. Also, only 97 countries are members of the system; if an organization were to expand to a country that is not part of the system, it would still need to individually register the marks.

International treaties

A second option a sport organization can choose to use to ensure international protection is to register its marks in each country individually and rely on international treaties to protect them. This is a time consuming and potentially expensive option, but it may be the only option if the country the organization is either based in, or the country it wishes to receive protection in, is not a signatory to either the Agreement or Protocol. There are two such treaties that deal specifically with trademarks: the Paris Convention for the Protection of Industrial Property, and the Agreement on Trade Related Aspects of Intellectual Property.

The Paris Convention for the Protection of Industrial Property

The Paris Convention for the Protection of Industrial Property (Paris Convention or Convention) was originally signed in March 1883 and was last revised at Stockholm in September 1967. It was last amended in 1979 (Paris Convention, 1979). As of January 2016, 176 countries are contracting states, that is, members of the Union, although ten of those countries have not accepted the Stockholm Revision. It is administered by the World Intellectual Property Organization.

Article 2 grants mark owners the same protection in other member countries as domestic marks receive in that country (Paris Convention, 1979). This means that Ferrari's prancing horses, registered marks in their home country of Italy, are to be treated in Australia as if Ferrari were an Australian company. Under Article 4, once a holder files an application for a trademark in a member country, it will enjoy a right of priority in other member countries as long as the holder files in other member countries within six months of receiving the right of priority (Paris Convention, 1979). This is particularly important in countries that are first to file. In a first-to-file country, trademark registration is based on who files a trademark application first, unlike a first-to-use country where registration is based on being the first to use the mark in trade or commerce. This right of priority protects the mark holder from others who may try to file first and block the organization from receiving registration.

Article 6 states that each country creates their own filing and registration procedures; mark owners must still register their mark in those countries in which they hope to receive protection (Paris Convention, 1979). It also states that the registration of marks is independent (Paris Convention, 1979). A member state cannot refuse an application or invalidate a registration if the mark has not been effected in its home country (Paris Convention for the Protection of Industrial Property, 1979). If a mark is cancelled in one country, it is not automatically cancelled in other countries (Paris Convention, 1979), which is very different from the Madrid Agreement and the Madrid Protocol.

Article 6*quinquies* of the Paris Convention requires that if a trademark is registered in the organization's home country, the mark "shall be accepted for filing and protected as is in the other countries of the Union." (Paris Convention, 1979). It also allows countries to deny registration if the mark seeking protection would infringe on the rights of a mark already held in that country (Paris Convention, 1979). For example, if the Indian Premier League, a professional Twenty20 cricket league in India, sought protection for its marks in the United Kingdom, the United Kingdom would be within its rights under the Convention to deny those marks protection as infringing on the Football Association's Premier League marks. It also allows for denial of a mark if it is "contrary to morality or public order" (Paris Convention, 1979). Also under the Convention, a country cannot deny a mark protection if it differs from the mark used in the home country "only in respect of elements that do not alter its distinctive character and do not affect its identity" (Paris Convention, 1979). For example, if the National Football League in the United States were to change the colours on its shield, it would not alter the distinctive character of the shield. Finally, in order to receive the benefits from Article 6*quinquies*, the mark needs to be registered in its country of origin (Paris Convention, 1979).

The Convention takes an extra step to protect what it calls well-known marks. Article 6*bis* requires member countries to either refuse to register, or to cancel the registration of, a mark that is likely to create confusion with a well-known mark (Paris Convention, 1979). This well-known mark does not have to be a registered mark to receive this protection. Either the country of registration or the country of use determines the definition of a well-known mark (Paris Convention, 1979). In the UK, Liverpool Football Club would be considered a well-known mark, but it would not necessarily be considered as such in the US. Under Article 6*bis*, the US has a duty to refuse to register or to cancel the registration of any mark in the US that would be likely to cause confusion with the Liverpool mark. It is important to note that the likelihood of confusion needs to be taken on a case-by-case basis. The holder of the mark has at least five years from the date of registration of the confusing mark to request cancellation (Paris Convention, 1979).

Under the Paris Convention, countries need to protect service marks, but are not required to register service marks (Paris Convention, 1979). Countries also need to protect collective marks and allow for registration of collective marks (Paris Convention, 1979). If the mark holder fails to use their mark in the country of registration, it can be cancelled after a reasonable amount of time unless the owner can show a valid reason why it was not used (Paris Convention, 1979).

The Agreement on Trade-Related Aspects of Intellectual Property Rights

The Agreement on Trade Related Aspects of Intellectual Property Rights (TRIPS) is administered by the World Treaty Organization (WTO) and is a party of the single undertaking, which means that TRIPS applies to all members of the WTO once they ascend to member status. As of November 2015, there are 162 members countries, with an additional 22 listed as observer governments. TRIPS incorporates the relevant articles of the Paris Convention stating in Article 2 that members of the WTO "shall comply with Articles 1 through 12 . . . of the Paris Convention" (TRIPS Agreement, 1994). Article 3 applies the national treatment requirements from the Paris Convention to the members of the WTO, and Article 4 states that all member nations must be treated equally, with certain exceptions (TRIPS Agreement, 1994).

Article 16(1) grants the owner of a registered mark:

> the exclusive right to prevent all third parties not having the owner's consent from using in the course of trade identical or similar signs for goods or services which are identical or similar in those in respect of which the trademark is registered where such a use would result in likelihood of confusion
>
> *TRIPS Agreement, 1994*

This prevents others from using the marks without the holder's consent and also protects the holder from marks that are likely to cause confusion.

Article 16(2) applies Article 6*bis* of the Paris Convention, but also gives guidelines to determine if a mark is well-known (TRIPS Agreement, 1994). Under TRIPS, a member has to look at the relevant sector of the public and the knowledge of the trademark (Agreement on Trade-Related Aspects of Intellectual Property Rights, 1994). To use the example from earlier, the US would have to look at the relevant sector of the public, which in the case of Liverpool would be soccer (or football) fans, and whether or not soccer (or football) fans in the US are familiar with Liverpool's marks. Article 16(3) prevents similar trademarks, even if the goods or services are not similar to the holder's registration, if there could be a connection between the two (TRIPS Agreement, 1994). TRIPS includes service marks in the definition of trademark, and therefore protects service marks. It does not mention collective marks (TRIPS Agreement, 1994). TRIPS states that trademark registration shall be no less than seven years and be renewable indefinitely (TRIPS Agreement, 1994).

Under Article 15(2), a country can make registration depend on using the mark. However, the country cannot require actual use of the mark to file the application for registration (TRIPS Agreement, 1994). A country can also require use of the mark to maintain registration (TRIPS Agreement, 1994). If it does, a country cannot cancel a mark until an uninterrupted period of at least three years has passed and the owner of the mark does not have a valid reason for not using the mark (TRIPS Agreement, 1994). Article 19(1) goes on to state that "[c]ircumstances arising independently of the will of the owner of the trademark which constitute an obstacle to the use . . . shall be recognized as valid reasons for non-use" (TRIPS Agreement, 1994).

The Paris Convention versus TRIPS

If a sport organization wishes to use the rights afforded to it under the Paris Convention, it is best to receive registration in its home country first. Once it does, the organization can choose which countries it would like to receive registration in, keeping in mind that it must file its subsequent applications within six months of receiving the right of priority, which is important in first-to-file countries. It also needs to keep in mind that it must use the registered mark in the subsequent country within a reasonable amount of time or the mark will be cancelled. While this is a time-consuming and possibly expensive process, more organizations choose to register their trademarks individually to prevent the central attack allowed under the Madrid Agreement and the Madrid Protocol.

TRIPS incorporates the relevant sections of the Paris Convention, so the registration procedures are the same. Under TRIPS, however, an organization does need to use its registered mark in the subsequent country within three years or the mark will be cancelled unless circumstances have prevented the organization from using the mark.

The Trademark Law Treaty

An organization that chooses to register its marks in each country individually and use its rights under international treaties needs to ensure that its mark is protectable and to follow the requirements in each country. The Trademark Law Treaty attempts to harmonize the registration process in signatory countries. The Trademark Law Treaty as signed in October 1994. As of January 2016, there are 53 countries that are parties to the treaty (Contracting Parties). There are two additional countries that have signed the treaty, but where it is not yet in force (Contracting Parties). Under Article 2, the Treaty applies to both trademarks and service marks, but not to collective marks (Trademark Law Treaty, 1994).

Community registration

There is one additional way in which to receive "international" protection and that is through a community trademark. These community trademarks are not truly international; rather the registration is for a specific set of countries. Three of the most well known communities are the European Union, the African Intellectual Property Organization and the African Regional Intellectual Property Organization.

The most well known of these communities is the European Union (EU). The EU consists of 28 member countries in Europe. The Council Regulation on the Community Trade Mark governs registration. A trademark issued in the EU is valid in all member countries and is managed by the European Intellectual Property Office. The EU is a member of the Madrid Protocol, which means that marks registered solely in the EU receive the same protection and benefits as if they were registered in a specific country.

The African Intellectual Property Organization (OAIP) consists of 17 member states, most of which are French-speaking countries. The OAIP is also a member of the Madrid Protocol. The African Regional Intellectual Property Organization (ARIPO) is made up of 19 member states, most of which are English-speaking countries. The Banjul Protocol on Marks governs trademark registration in the member states. As of March 2016, only nine of the 19 states are members of the Banjul Protocol on Marks. The ARIPO is not a member of the Madrid Protocol as of March 2016, which means that marks registered under the ARIPO must also be registered in a Protocol member country to receive the benefits of the Madrid Protocol.

Conclusion

In 2015, the total revenue generated, worldwide, from sports merchandise bearing those protected trademark symbols was forecast to be US$20.07 billion (Statista, 2016). What made this merchandise valuable was the presence of the sport organization's symbols. As the sport industry moves toward globalization, a sport organization needs to take steps to protect its marks, not just in its home country but internationally as well.

References

Agreement on Trade-Related Aspects of Intellectual Property Rights (15 April 1994), Marrakesh, Morocco.

Council Regulation (EC) 207/2009 on the Community trade mark [26 February 2009].

Madrid Agreement Concerning the International Registration of Marks (14 April 1891), as revised 14 July 1967.

Paris Convention for the Protection of Industrial Property (20 March 1883), as revised 14 July 1967.

Protocol Relating to the Madrid Agreement Concerning the International Registration of Marks (27 June 1989) [amended November 2007].

Statista (2016). Total Revenue Generated from Sports Merchandising Worldwide. Available at <www.statista.com/statistics/269797/worldwide-revenue-from-sports-merchandising/>. Accessed 28 March 2016.

Trademark Law Treaty (27 October 1994) Available at <www.wipo.int/treaties/en/ip/tlt/>. Accessed 1 July 2017.

22

PRIVACY AT WORK

Strategies for successful social media policies

Lauren McCoy

Introduction

The role of social media in sport business continues to grow and expand because of its use as a free marketing tool that provides a direct connection between the fan, the player and the organization. This tool, however, must be used with caution in sport business. The very "social" aspect of these websites makes it easy to blur the line between business and private information. Organizations are required to take social media missteps seriously because they can have a negative impact on the reputation of a player and on the team as a whole. In January 2016, Gerard Pique, central defender for FC Barcelona, came under scrutiny for comments that he made on Twitter about rival team, Real Madrid. La Liga's anti-violence committee reviewed his comments and sent them to Real Federacíon Española de Futbol's (RFEF) Sports Discipline Committee for further investigation (Corrigan, 2016). No fine or suspension related to this incident was made public; however, his actions have prompted the club to seek social media guidelines from La Liga to maintain privacy and limit social media use at certain times (ESPN, 2016).

FC Barcelona's reaction is a typical response as the impact of social media continues to grow. Instincts may lean towards strict monitoring to avoid the problems that occur when posts are submitted without thought towards the tone and intent of the message. But each organization must consider how its rules affect the privacy of athletes and respond with caution. If a monitoring policy is too restrictive or invasive, any accompanying punishment for social media misdeeds could be deemed invalid in a court of law.

Concern about privacy related to internet activity and the workplace is a recent legal development in both the United States and the European Union (EU). These laws seek to protect an internet user's right to privacy in the content posted or viewed online with a focus towards protecting against an employer's right to monitor or access an employee's internet activity (Poerio & Bain, 2012). The EU's privacy laws contain some of the strictest standards in the world, allowing for social media policies developed in consideration of EU law to be used universally (Ku, 2014). This chapter examines what international organizations can do in order to monitor and regulate the social media activity of employees under EU regulations by defining privacy laws, highlighting recent examples of those laws in practice and using this information to develop social media strategies for sport organizations to establish monitoring within the confines of the law.

Privacy law in the EU

Privacy is recognized as both a social practice and a legal right (Roagna, 2012). There is a long history in favour of protecting personal interests in Europe dating back to 1849 with *Prince Albert* v. *Strange*, a lawsuit from the United Kingdom. A publisher, William Strange, received access to a series of etchings reportedly drawn by Prince Albert and Queen Victoria. These etchings were meant to be private and all copies were in the hands of Prince Albert, his wife, Queen Victoria, or close friends of the couple. Mr Strange wished to publish the etchings in a catalogue and Prince Albert filed an injunction to prevent their release. Lord Cottingham, the adjudicator in this case, granted the injunction to stop the release of this material and recognized that common law establishes a right of property in confidence that allows materials meant to be private to stay that way (*Prince Albert* v. *Strange* (1849) 1 McN & G. 25). This case developed an extension to privacy beyond basic property rights to the "more general right of the individual to be let alone" (Warren & Brandeis, 1890).

Privacy rights are now codified into statutory law, including international declarations and directives. These directives establish the basic standards of privacy along with the more recent data specific protections (European Court of Human Rights, 2014). The modern era of technology has made private information readily available and continues the expansion or clarification of privacy rights. Going through the history and expansion of privacy rights granted in the EU can assist in highlighting privacy protection trends. These same trends can then be used to determine how teams and leagues may conduct social media monitoring of players without violating the law.

To start with, the right to protection against the intrusion of others was first established internationally with the United Nation's Universal Declaration of Human Rights (UDHR). This declaration, developed after the Second World War in 1948, established fundamental human rights to be universally protected by all member states, including privacy. Article 12 of the UDHR addresses privacy declaring that "[n]o one shall be subjected to arbitrary interference with his privacy, family, home or correspondence, nor to attacks upon his honour and reputation. Everyone has the right to the protection of the law against such interference or attacks" (United Nations, 2014, p. 4). While Article 12 makes a strong statement in favour of protecting interests, it is not legally binding. The UDHR is a declaration to be used as a guide for member states and common standards of achievement for people in all nations (Glendon, 2004), providing the motivation for codifying these fundamental rights into Europe.

In the EU, there are three legally binding statutory directives that include measures to govern privacy: Article 8 of the European Convention on Human Rights, the Council of Europe's Convention 108 and the EU's Data Protection Directive (European Court of Human Rights, 2014). An update to the Data Protection Directive supposed to develop a new perspective on data protection in the modern age, the General Data Protection Regulation, was voted into law in December 2015 with adoption expected in the spring of 2016 (European Commission, 2016). This chapter addresses the new regulations briefly, but with a focus on regulations existing at the time of publication.

The Council of Europe adopted the European Convention on Human Rights (ECHR) shortly after the UDHR in 1950. This document gave the Council of Europe member states an obligation to comply with fundamental rights recognized by the ECHR (European Court of Human Rights, 2014). Article 8 of the ECHR provides the specific information used to address the right of privacy for member states of the Council of Europe. It grants everyone the right to respect for private and family life, home and correspondence, similar to Article 12 of the UDHR. This right is not absolute. Exceptions are made for national security and public safety (Roagna, 2012).

Any direct complaint accusing violations of the ECHR must involve a member state being heard by the European Court of Human Rights in Strasbourg, France. The court, additionally, will only hear a complaint after all legal remedies on a state level have been exhausted. Typically, a complainant will have to take their claim to court, receive an opportunity for appeal, and then have a hearing before the highest court of the state (if applicable) before applying to the European Court of Human Rights (European Court of Human Rights, n.d). Even with these restrictions, private organizations must still abide by the established protections because the ECHR is codified into the national law of each member state (Myers, 2014).

There is no comprehensive definition of what Article 8 covers, but there is an established procedure used by courts to determine a potential violation. Violations are decided through a two-stage test that asks: Does the complaint fall within the remits of Article 8 and has there been interference with the rights established by Article 8? There are four possible dimensions to an Article 8 claim. It may either cover issues connected to private life, family life, home or correspondence (Roagna, 2012). Complaints related to social media policies could fit within the private life sphere because connection occurs on a case-by-case basis. Next, if interference is found, the court will examine the reasoning behind it. If the interference is found to be in accordance with the law, pursues a legitimate claim, or is necessary in a democratic society, then it will not violate Article 8 (Roagna, 2012). Examining the general application of this test in relation to social media policies is difficult because Article 8 considerations emphasize the responsibility of the member state instead of the requirements for a private individual or company.

The emergence of information technology led the Council of Europe to extend Article 8 to protect personal data and allow for more focus on individual organizations. In 1981, Convention 108 developed the only legally binding international instrument for data protection. This instrument applies to both the public and private sectors and seeks to protect the individual from any abuse occurring from the collection of their personal data. Convention 108, in Article 1, paragraph 2, defines personal data as any information that relates to an individual and the law applies to "information relating to groups of persons, associations, foundations, companies, corporations and any other bodies consisting directly or indirectly of individuals, whether or not such bodies possess legal personality" (Council of Europe, 1981). To avoid any violation of the Convention, organizations must ensure that data is obtained and processed fairly with a prohibition against the automatic collection of any data that reveals racial origin, political opinion, and religious or other beliefs (Council of Europe, 1981).

Fairness under the Convention focuses on transparency, declaring that the subject of the data search must know what information is being monitored and stored and be given the ability to correct the information if necessary (Council of Europe, 1981). Like Article 8 of the ECHR, this data protection under Convention 108 is not absolute. These rights may be restricted when overriding interests are at stake (European Court of Human Rights, 2014). The restrictions give organizations at least some latitude when it comes to social media policies because they provide an avenue to argue that restriction and monitoring are necessary to protect the rights of all instead of simply one individual. On the other hand, the focus of Convention 108 on transparency, and the history of privacy as a fundamental right, highlights the need to exercise caution in any attempt to monitor or punish employees for their social media activity without employee awareness of these policies.

When the EU was founded, the privacy protections previously established were incorporated into the Charter of Fundamental Rights and through a data protection law specific to the EU. Articles 7 and 8 of the Charter of Fundamental Rights cover respect for private and family life along with the right to data protection (Council of Europe, 2000). By covering these rights again in the Charter, they reached the status of being fundamental rights within the EU. These rights should not be considered as absolute, but must exist in relation to their function in society. This highlights that limitations will be accepted and imposed in some instances and that action must comply with the essence of those rights and the standards needed to protect the rights of others.

In 1995, data protection in the EU developed through Directive 95/46/EC (Fuster and Gellert, 2012). This law echoed the trends within member states to consider personal data as information worthy of legal protection for the sake of privacy with the purpose of creating uniformity (Council of Europe, 1995). Uniformity limits the freedom of member states to manoeuvre around the requirements of the directive while allowing for organizations to develop rules that can be used internationally. The Data Protection Directive was designed to give substance to the rights established within Convention 108 and expand them for modern times. Following Convention 108, the focus of the Data Protection Directive could address only EU member states. The addition of associated directives, the EU Institutions Data Protection Regulation and the e-Privacy Directive, developed protections against intrusions by institutions and data processed through publicly available electronic communications (European Court of Human Rights, 2014). These changes still left many with the feeling that the Data Protection Directive could be ineffective due to a lack of specificity or adaptability to modern electronic communication needs (Myers, 2014).

Created to replace the Data Protection Directive, the EU General Data Protection Regulation established a new perspective for privacy and electronic communications and extended coverage to all foreign companies processing the data of EU residents. One new perspective introduced in the 2012 draft allowed for the right to be forgotten, giving individuals the ability to erase personal data placed online unless the information is necessary for research purposes, for exercising freedom of expression and for information legally allowed to be obtained (Gilbert, 2015; Voss, 2014). The overall purpose of this change is to shift the focus of data protection to consider social media and create more protection for individual information. This shift should provide more analysis to determine the limits of social media regulation for organizations. However, since the EU General Data Protection Regulation only came into effect in the Spring of 2016, the impact of this change remains uncertain, with existing privacy laws providing the basis for any current analysis.

A common thread with each of these applicable privacy laws (other than the General Data Protection Regulation) is their incorporation into law prior to the widespread usage of social media sites. The law often has to catch up and adapt to technology changes as they occur in society. Article 29 of the Data Protection Directive provides for the creation of a working party tasked with defining the application of data protection rules and publishing opinions on related topics like social media (Massey, 2009). These opinions are not legally binding but do establish a working policy for how to comply with EU law.

The Article 29 Working Party published an opinion in June 2009 describing the connection between privacy and social media. This opinion established that personal data covered under the Data Protection Directive should include information posted on a social media website by individual users (Article 29 Data ProtectionWorking Party, 2009). With that protection come specific concerns for social media companies, even those with headquarters located in areas other than the EU, that include placing access to privacy settings on social media and warning individuals that their actions on social media may violate the privacy and data protection rights of others (Myers, 2014). What this opinion does is establish a direct connection between privacy and social media activity, meaning that any social media restriction must consider applicable privacy laws to be legal.

In addition to the Article 29 Working Party opinion, these three laws are still able to function successfully in the social media age because of the case-by-case nature of any appropriate analysis. Case law that directly addresses social media policies for the workplace does not currently exist, but there are a number of cases that have provided guidance as to how intrusions into social media can function or violate privacy rights. An examination of privacy for electronic communications in the workplace will shed light onto how organizations can proceed with any social media regulation.

Privacy in the workplace

The purpose of social media policies in sport is to regulate comments made by athletes and to make sure that this marketing resource does not lead to negative publicity for the organization. Since athletes are employees of the clubs and leagues they represent, any legal discussion involving social media policies must consider what constitutes privacy in the workplace. Defining privacy in the workplace is an interesting challenge. There are several privacy directives to explain the right of privacy in the EU, but none of these laws applies directly to regulating privacy in the workplace (Binder & Mansfield, 2013). Privacy is considered a fundamental right in the EU, which means that the rules meant to avoid state intrusion into private matters will apply to private organizations as well. To develop a comprehensive look into what is necessary to have a successful social media policy in the EU, existing case law can provide a focused analysis of privacy in the workplace.

Employment issues concerning privacy stem from two areas: recruiting and disciplinary action (Morrison Foerster, 2014). These two areas will be discussed and considered through a case study model. By using case studies, these scenarios provide examples of how individuals in sport business are using social media monitoring practices and how those practices impact, or potentially violate, privacy law in the EU.

Case study 1 – monitoring social media as a recruiting tool

It is commonplace for employers to use social media accounts to vet the personalities of potential employees (Broughton *et al.* 2013). Pat Connelly, Assistant General Manager for the Phoenix Suns, spoke about how teams use social media monitoring in preparation for the National Basketball Association's annual draft. He concluded that looking at social media has become part of the process, often not a large factor, but something that teams use to determine the character of a potential draftee (Esposito, 2015). This character representation is useful to highlight an individual's ability to represent the organization in a positive manner.

There is currently no existing case law determining the legality of monitoring programmes for the purpose of employee recruitment, but this information appears to be exactly what the Data Protection Directive is meant to protect (Macedo, 2015). The Directive identifies all data as personal unless made anonymous. This automatically includes information posted via social media under the Article 29 Working Party opinion discussed previously (Article 29 Data Protection Working Party, 2009).

The use of information found through social media in the recruiting process must give notice to the prospective employees that this type of monitoring will be completed. This notice must come with the consent of the prospective employee. Allowing employees to acknowledge the possibility of this type of monitoring and why it is being conducted goes a long way towards

---

establishing a transparency of action that will continue to protect privacy as required under the law. Further, an employer must highlight the purpose of the information that they are attempting to use, and have a legal reason for processing this type of personal data (Linklaters, 2014). This cannot simply be a general search for any information that can be gathered. The more information an employer can give to establish their reasoning for monitoring, the more their actions will be protected under privacy law and workplace standards in the EU.

Case study 2 – monitoring for negative comments and conduct on social media

Teams must also be concerned with social media comments that could reflect negatively upon an organization once a player joins a team. To promote the use of social media in a productive manner, teams may issue fines or suspensions related to negative conduct. In March 2016, Giuseppe Francone, a soccer player for Lanklaar VV in Belgium, was suspended for six games after insulting a referee on Facebook. The league believed this punishment was fitting to protect the privacy of the official who received a copy of the message from the player (Extra Mustard, 2016).

Belgium, as a member of the EU, must consider the fundamental right of privacy under Article 8 of the ECHR and the Data Protection Directive in establishing the legality of this punishment (European Court of Human Rights, 2014). The utilization of privacy law is not restricted to private life under EU law. The European Court of Human Rights ruled and confirmed in several cases that the privacy rights established under Article 8 of the ECHR extend to the workplace. This right, however, is not absolute. In *Benediktsdóttir* v. *Iceland*, a newspaper printed the email correspondence of Ms Benediktsdóttir without her permission. These emails were unlawfully obtained through the computer server connected to her former employer, Aktiverum ehf, and concerned personal communications related to workplace matters. It is unclear if any attempt to erase employee data was conducted after this company was sold. The court here focused on the balance between Ms Benediktsdóttir's Article 8 rights and the newspaper's right to freedom of expression. While Ms Benediktsdóttir was ultimately unsuccessful due to the criminal implications present in this case, her case establishes a precedent that workplace e-mail communications are entitled to privacy under Article 8 of the ECHR (*B* v. *Iceland* (2009) 38079/06).

With the established connection between privacy and workplace communications, the next consideration must focus on whether employers have the right to punish employees for their actions conducted on social media. Two similar, yet conflicting, cases from the United Kingdom (*Weeks* v. *Everything Everywhere Ltd* and *Smith* v. *Trafford Housing Trust*) provide guidance on this question. Neither of these cases directly challenges the Data Protection Act – the law developed for the purpose of complying with the EU's Data Protection Directive (Linklaters, 2014). Nevertheless, the Act highlights that privacy is a fundamental right in the United Kingdom and will be considered in connection to other applicable laws. The results of these cases could be compared to any other policies under question in the EU due to the connection to the Data Protection Directive.

Both *Weeks* v. *Everything Everywhere Ltd* and *Smith* v. *Trafford Housing Trust* involved employees posting comments on social media in their free time and both comments were considered by their employers to be negative and damaging to the workplace. In *Weeks*, Mr Weeks filed a lawsuit against his former employer, Everything Everywhere Ltd, after he was dismissed for gross misconduct related to his comments about the company on Facebook. Mr Weeks repeatedly described his workplace as "Dante's Inferno" on his Facebook account. Once his employer became aware of the disparaging remarks, Mr Weeks was asked to refrain from making any further disparaging remarks about the company. When he refused, he was dismissed from his position (*Weeks* v. *Everything Everywhere Ltd* [2012] ET 2503016).

Everything Everywhere Ltd based the dismissal decision on the company's social media policy that states that employees should not "criticize our brand, products, services, associated companies, suppliers, employees, other workers, contractors, shareholders, offices or customers in blogs or on other internet sites which allow you to post comments" (*Weeks* v. *Everything Everywhere Ltd* [2012] ET 2503016). This policy applied to employees' conduct at work and in their personal time. Mr Weeks was aware of this policy but still believed that his dismissal for personal comments was a violation of his right to private communications because his comments were reported to the company by a co-worker he had previously added as a friend on his Facebook account. Using the Employment Rights Act of 1996 to determine the fairness of Weeks' dismissal, the Employment Tribunal concluded that the employer's decision in this instance was reasonable and Mr Weeks had an opportunity to appreciate the impact of this policy (*Weeks* v. *Everything Everywhere Ltd* [2012] ET 2503016). The employer gave clear and explicit direction within the policy that it would apply at all times. Between this notice and an opportunity to improve his behaviour, the employer's actions were reasonable and not a violation of privacy.

Smith v. *Trafford Housing Trust* also involved an employee dismissed for comments made on Facebook. However, the social media policy at issue here did not contain any notification that comments made outside the working environment would be considered under the policy. Mr Smith, a practising Christian, posted a link to a BBC article to his Facebook page and expressed his opinions against gay marriage in churches. A co-worker, who was one of Smith's Facebook friends, responded to this post questioning his stance. Mr Smith responded and reiterated his position. Four days after posting these comments, Mr Smith was suspended with pay. His employer conducted an investigation into his conduct and recommended that Mr Smith's actions constituted gross misconduct deserving of dismissal, but instead demoted him and reduced his salary. Smith then filed a lawsuit alleging breach of his employment contract with Trafford Housing Trust (*Smith* v. *Trafford Housing Trust* [2012] EWHC 3221).

Trafford Housing Trust defined gross misconduct through their disciplinary procedures policy. Under this policy, gross misconduct includes "any deliberate act committed by a member of staff which is severely detrimental to the good conduct of the business or harmful to other members of staff" (*Smith* v. *Trafford Housing Trust* [2012] EWHC 3221). The organization further relied on the Code of Conduct that stated that employees were required to be non-judgmental, to respect the cultures and customs of any employee, and to not engage in any activity that may negatively impact the Trust either at work or outside work. The High Court interpreted the Code of Conduct as applying to work-related communications only because there was no express connection to personal communications outside the workplace. Employees may often have conflicting viewpoints, but an employer is required to respect those differences or risk violating the employee's freedom of speech. Ultimately, Mr Smith was successful and Trafford Housing Trust was declared in breach of contract (*Smith* v. *Trafford Housing Trust* [2012] EWHC 3221).

The different results here is predicated on the language of the Code of Conduct/social media policies at issue. The employer in *Weeks* was successful because it was clear and upfront about the implications of social media comments about the workplace and when these apply. However, the employer in *Smith* did not clearly apply its Code of Conduct to communication outside the workplace. It could be interpreted that transparency is a requirement for a successful policy regulating social media (Linklaters, 2014). Another focus is the content of the disciplined speech. While Weeks' comments were directly related to his employer and disparaging, Smith simply reflected his personal opinion in an arena viewable by his employer. The substance of the punishable comments plays a role in the effectiveness of a social media policy. Based on the results of these two cases, it could be inferred that a court will protect opinions that do not directly disparage others and punish those that impede on the rights of others. This means that harassing comments made to another in a public domain, i.e. comments criticizing a referee on Facebook, arguably can be punished because of the invasion of another's privacy.

Conclusion – lessons we can learn to monitor privacy within the law

Determining what is necessary to maintain a legal social media policy depends on the purpose of the policy. Using the examples discussed in the previous section (recruitment and preventing harassment/negative publicity), one can summarize strategies available to develop a successful social media policy that are mindful of privacy considerations within the EU. While these lessons focus on EU laws related to privacy, the stringent standards of privacy protection available under the EU will lead to policies that would be acceptable in any number of countries. Further, any sport organization conducting business in the EU, regardless of the business' home location, must abide by the fundamental right of privacy as written under EU law.

There are three focus areas for a successful social media policy and monitoring plan: transparency, focused language and protection of the fundamental rights of others. Transparency requires employers to inform any individual, either currently employed or seeking a job with that company, to be aware of any monitoring policy. Not only do they need to be aware that a policy exists, they must also understand the purpose of the policy and the information covered within the policy. Clear understanding of the policy in place protects privacy by alerting the employee to the potential intrusion and receiving their consent before a privacy violation can occur (Rotenberg, n.d.). It also highlights the reasoning behind monitoring and limits the employee's options for remedies if they are punished under the terms of the policy.

The second focus area of a successful social media policy is also related to transparency because specific language about the limits of the social media policy is necessary. In comparing *Weeks* v. *Everything Everywhere Ltd* and *Smith* v. *Trafford Housing Trust*, the differing result is linked to the clarity of the policy language and when that policy is applied to an employee's social media activity. If the employer has a reason to apply the social media policy to conduct both at work and away from the workplace, then it needs to be expressly addressed and explained to the employee (Linklaters, 2014). In sport business, the area of concern for teams and organizations would be those communications occurring during private time because that period is when negative commentary is most likely to occur without use of caution. Athletes and those associated with sport need to be aware of the constant presence of the public eye, especially in public forums like social media.

Finally, an effective social media policy must protect the fundamental rights of others, including the right of privacy and the employee's freedom of speech. Limiting monitoring or examination of social media accounts to instances where behaviour in violation of the policy is alleged goes a long way towards protecting these rights. With a limited focus for monitoring, the majority of employee communication would remain private and alleged violations would also provide probable cause for monitoring. That probable cause not only highlights the specific reason the employer instituted a monitoring policy but also protects the fundamental rights of others if the comments made in electronic communication are negative against others. As an example, the social media policy for the Football Association states that England players must "not publish (on Twitter or Facebook) anything that may cause or embarrass a member of the FA, the England squad and management" (Witherington, 2012). Criticism is prohibited at all times under the same policy (Witherington, 2012; Heyes, 2014).

Social media use in sport business provides many benefits for an organization; however, it must be used with caution. Maintaining a monitoring policy helps to remove some of the dangers or concerns associated with social media. These monitoring policies are legal and available to organizations as long as they are used with the same type of caution given to social media in general. Employers within any organization can protect their interests and the fundamental rights of their employees by instituting a policy of awareness. As long as an employee understands the limitations imposed on them and learns to consider the implications of their actions on others, these policies will not violate privacy laws under the EU.

References

Article 29. Data Protection Working Party (2009). Opinion 5/2009 on online social networking. Available from <http://ec.europa.eu/justice/data-protection/article-29/documentation/opinion-recommendation/files/2009/wp163_en.pdf>. Accessed 30 March 2016.

Benediktsdóttir v. *Iceland* (2009) 38079/06.

Binder, P. & Mansfield, N. R. (2013). Social networks and workplace risk: Classroom scenarios from a US and EU perspective. *Journal of Legal Studies Education, 30*(1), 1–44. Available from <EBSCOhost.com>. Accessed 15 January 2016.

Broughton, A., Foley, B., Ledermaier, S. & Cox, A. (2013). The use of social media in the recruitment process. Institute for Employment Studies. Available from <www.acas.org.uk/media/pdf/0/b/The-use-of-social-media-in-the-recruitment-process.pdf>. Accessed 27 March 2016.

Corrigan, D. (2016). Barcelona's Gerard Pique facing possible sanction over social media use [ESPNFC.com]. Available from <www.espnfc.us/barcelona/story/2787186/gerard-pique-facing-possible-sanction-over-social-media>. Accessed 8 March 2016.

Council of Europe (1981). *Convention for the protection of individuals with regard to automatic processing of personal data.* Available from <www.coe.int/en/web/conventions/full-list/-/conventions/treaty/108>. Accessed 3 March 2016.

Council of Europe (1995). *Directive 95/46/EC of the European Parliament and of the Council of 24 October 1995 on the protection of individuals with regard to the processing of personal data and on the free movement of such data.* Available from <http://eur-lex.europa.eu/legal-content/EN/TXT/?uri=uriserv:OJ.L_.1995.281.01.0031.01.ENG>. Accessed 3 March 2016.

Council of Europe (2000). Charter of fundamental rights of the European Union. *Official Journal of the European Union.* Available from <//eur-lex.europa.eu/legal-content/EN/TXT/?uri=CELEX:12012P/TXT>. Accessed 27 March 2016.

Council of Europe (n.d.). *Our member states.* Available from <www.coe.int/en/web/about-us/our-member-states>. Accessed 27 February 2016.

ESPN (2016). Barcelona may seek to limit Gerard Pique social media use – reports. [ESPNFC.com]. Available from <www.espnfc.us/barcelona/story/2824866/barcelona-may-limit-gerard-pique-social-media-use-reports>. Accessed 8 March 2016.

Esposito, G. (2015). Suns Retorter: Could Social Media Impact the NBA Draft? [NBA.com]. Available from <www.nba.com/suns/draft/suns-retorter-could-social-media-impact-nba-draft>. Accessed 17 March 2016.

European Commission (2016). *Reform of EU data protection rules.* Available from <http://ec.europa.eu/justice/data-protection/reform/index_en.htm>. Accessed 23 March 2016.

European Court of Human Rights (2014). *Handbook on European Data Protection Law*. Council of Europe. Available from <www.echr.coe.int/Documents/Handbook_data_protection_ENG.pdf>. Accessed 10 February 2016.

European Court of Human Rights (n.d.) *Questions and Answers*. Council of Europe. Available from <www.echr.coe.int/Documents/Questions_Answers_ENG.pdf>. Accessed 30 March 2016.

Extra Mustard (2016). Soccer player suspended six games for insulting ref on Facebook. *Sports Illustrated*. Available from <www.si.com/extra-mustard/2016/03/15/soccer-player-suspended-belgium-facebook-referee-insult#>. Accessed 17 March 2016.

Fuster, G. G. & Gellert, R. (2012). The fundamental right of data protection in the European Union: In search of an uncharted flight. *International Review of Law, Computers & Technology*, *26*(1), 73–82. Available from <EBSCOhost.com>. Accessed 15 January 2016.

Glendon, M. A. (2004). The Rule of Law in the Universal Declaration of Human Rights. *Northwestern Journal of International Human Rights*, *2*(1), 2–19. Available from <http://scholarlycommons.law. northwestern.edu/cgi/viewcontent.cgi?article=1008&context=njihr>. Accessed 3 March 2016.

Gilbert, F. (2015). The right of erasure or right to be forgotten: What the recent laws, cases, and guidelines mean for global companies. *Journal of Internet Law*, *18*(8), 13–20. Available from <EBSCOhost.com>. Accessed 3 March 2016.

Heyes, S. (2014). Social Media Governance in the English Premier League. Available from <www.8ms. com/2014/02/27/social-media-governance-english-premier-league/>. Accessed 27 March 2016.

Information Commissioner's Office (n.d.). The employment practices code. Available from <https:// ico.org.uk/media/for-organisations/documents/1064/the_employment_practices_code.pdf>. Accessed 26 March 2016.

Ku, R. S. R. (2014). Data privacy as a civil right: The EU gets it. *Kentucky Law Journal*, *103*, 391–404. Available from <www.kentuckylawjournal.org/wp-content/uploads/2015/02/103KyLJ391.pdf>. Accessed 27 March 2016.

Linklaters (2014). *Social Media and the Law: A Handbook for UK Companies*. Available from <www. linklaters.com/pdfs/mkt/. . ./tmt-social-media-report.pdf>. Accessed 27 March 2016.

Macedo, L. (2015). Monitoring of employees in the workplace: The very private parts of a job in the EU private sector. Available from <http://thepublicprivacy.com/2015/01/27/monitoring-employees-workplace-private-parts-job-eu-private-sector/>. Accessed 25 January 2016.

Massey, R. (2009). Privacy and Social Networks: A European Opinion. *Journal of Internet Law*, *13*(4), 13–17. Available from <EBSCOhost.com>. Accessed 3 March 2016.

Morrison Foerster (2014). Data protection masterclass: Spotlight on social media marketing and policies. [PowerPoint presentation]. MOFO Seminar Series, London. Available from <http://media.mofo. com/files/Uploads/Images/140121-Data-Protection-Masterclass-Spotlight-Social-Media.pdf>. Accessed 26 March 2016.

Myers, C. (2014). Digital immortality vs. "the right to be forgotten": A comparison of US and EU laws concerning social media privacy. *Romanian Journal of Communication & Public Relations*, *16*(3), 47–60. Available from Directory of Open Access Journals <http://journalofcommunication.ro/ oldsite/archive2/035/35/myers.pdf>. Accessed 3 March 2016.

Prince Albert v. *Strange* (1849) 1 McN. & G. 25.

Poerio, J. M. & Bain, L. (2012). Social media in the workplace: Employer protections versus employee privacy. *International Law News*. American Bar Association. Available from <www.americanbar.org/ publications/international_law_news/2012/fall/social_media_workplace_employer_protections_ versus_employee_privacy.html>. Accessed 22 September 2015.

Roagna, I. (2012). Protecting the right to respect for private and family life under the European Convention on Human Rights. Council of Europe. Available from <www.coe.int/t/dghl/cooperation/capacitybuilding/Source/documentation/hb11_privatelife_en.pdf>. Accessed 27 February 2016.

Rotenberg, M. (n.d.). Preserving Privacy in the Information Society. Available from <www.unesco. org/webworld/infoethics_2/eng/papers/paper_10.htm>. Accessed 3 March 2016.

Smith v. *Trafford Housing Trust* [2012] EWHC 3221.

United Nations (2014). The Universal Declaration of Human Rights. Available from <www.un.org/ en/universal-declaration-human-rights/>. Accessed 27 March 2016.

Voss, W. G. (2014). The right to be forgotten in the European Union: Enforcement in the Court of Justice and amendment to the proposed General Data Protection Regulation. *Journal of Internal Law*, *18*(1), 3–5. Available from <EBSCOhost.com>. Accessed 3 March 2016.

Warren, S. & Brandeis, L. (1890). The right to privacy. *Harvard Law Review*, *4*(5). Available from <http://faculty.uml.edu/sgallagher/Brandeisprivacy.htm/>. Accessed 3 March 2016.

Weeks v. *Everything Everywhere Ltd* [2012] ET 2503016.

Witherington, L. (2012). "England's FA Gives Players New Rules on Social Media". *Wall Street Journal* (17 October). Available from <www.wsj.com/articles/SB10000872396390444734804578062641765330554>. Accessed 26 March 2016.

PART V

Sport media and communication

Technology has influenced the media, perhaps more than any other aspect of sport. The printing press generated player stories and game statistics. The inventions of the radio in 1895 and television in 1927 certainly impacted modern sport. These machines allowed spectators to "watch" sporting events live without actually being there. Currently new media driven by the internet creates two-way mass communication where fans become engaged in the sport, its actors and the organization itself. The technology associated with sport media continues to attract a larger and more diverse audience.

The authors in this subject area focus on new media technology and its positive and potential negative effects on social media; the growth of broadcast technology in Africa; how sport organizations need to adjust its connections to fans and sponsors due to media expansion into new cultures and how new media can become a focal point for the growth of sports in new markets.

23

HIJACKING OF A HASHTAG

The case of #CheersToSochi

Lauren M. Burch, Ann Pegoraro and Evan L. Frederick

Introduction

Increased utilization of the internet and Web 2.0 platforms, such as social media sites, has shifted message control and branding initiatives to include the voice of the consumer. Consumers can engage in two-way communication with brands through posts and comments, which can impact the image and management of brands. As Bal, Campbell and Pitt (2012) acknowledged, "[m]oney and advertising are no longer the sole controllers of message dissemination. Stakeholder interaction is now key to brand and image management" (p. 204). While stakeholder engagement and interactivity now play an integral role in modern-day marketing, the digital media environment simultaneously increases the difficulty of branded initiatives staying on message.

In January 2014, McDonald's, an Olympic TOP sponsor of the 2014 Sochi Olympic Games, launched a social media campaign to activate its sponsorship. The overarching goal of this campaign was to encourage communication and connection between fans and Olympic athletes. Employing two main platforms, Twitter and an official webpage associated with the campaign, individuals could send personalized messages and good wishes to their favourite athletes and teams competing in Sochi through the hashtag #CheersToSochi, or by going to the website www.cheerstosochi.com (McDonald's, 2014). As part of the activation, six US and Canadian athletes agreed to five-figure endorsement deals with McDonald's to promote the #CheersToSochi campaign on Twitter and Facebook (Mickle, 2014).

Immediately following the launch of the campaign, Lesbian, Gay, Bisexual and Transgender (LGBT) and other activists "hijacked" the hashtag #CheersToSochi, using it in commentary to attack Russia's discriminatory policies regarding sexual orientation. In addition, the activists requested that the official Olympics sponsors (e.g. McDonald's and Coca-Cola) condemn Russia for these practices (Merevick, 2014). While sponsorship activation through social media provides a cost-effective alternative to traditional marketing channels, it also simultaneously allows consumers to influence messaging, and potentially reframe a campaign to promote an entirely different agenda. As such, the purpose of this chapter is to examine the hijacking of the #CheersToSochi social media sponsorship campaign through the lens of sponsorship activation and bottom-up framing, and discuss the potential impact on McDonald's brand image.

Sponsorship activation, the framing of messages and brand equity

Traditionally, sponsorship was viewed as a philanthropic effort of an organization (Ryan & Fahy, 2012). However, this focus shifted to a more market-based approach in the 1990s, placing the emphasis on brand awareness and image enhancement (Cornwell & Maignan, 1998; McDonald, 1991). As such, sponsorship was integrated as a promotional aspect of the marketing mix (Ryan & Fehy, 2012). Key to event sponsorship is activation, which creates an association with awareness, influencing attitude and purchase behaviour for the brand (Walliser, 2003).

From a sport perspective, it has been found that fans are three times more likely to purchase products when they are familiar with a brand (Horowitz, 2012) and, as such, sponsorship has emerged as a viable opportunity to create brand associations between events and sponsors. One sporting event that remains a popular avenue for sponsorship is the Olympic Games. The Olympic Partners (TOP) is a widely successful sponsorship programme, which generated more than $800 million in revenue for the International Olympic Committee (IOC) during the 2005–2008 Torino and Beijing Olympics cycle (Kang & Stotler, 2011), and warranted examination of the effectiveness and impact of Olympic sponsorship by various academics (e.g. Giannoulakis, Stotlar & Chatziefstathiou, 2008; Meng-Lewis, Thwaites & Pillai, 2014; Morgan & Frawley, 2011; Taylor, 2012).

Sponsorship without activation, however, provides little return on investment and, thus, requires additional resources to fully capitalize on the potential success of any sponsorship campaign (Cornwell & Maignan, 1998; DeGaris, West & Dodds, 2009; Papadimitriou & Apostolopoulou, 2009; Sylvestre & Moutinho, 2007). Cornwell, Weeks and Roy (2005) defined sponsorship activation through the term sponsorship-linked marketing, and framed it as marketing initiatives to communicate the link to a sponsorship. Further refinements of sponsorship differentiated between the types of communication utilized in sponsorship, specifically, activational communication and nonactivational communication (Weeks, Cornwell & Drennan, 2008). Nonactivational communication is passive and includes elements, such as on-site signage, which do not engage the audience. Elements such as event-related sweepstakes, contests or websites represent activational communication that focuses on interaction between the audience and the sponsor (Weeks *et al.*, 2008).

As sponsorship is a component of the promotional element of the marketing mix, it is traditionally activated in conjunction with all marketing efforts associated with a mega event (Ladousse, 2009; Papadimitriou & Apostolopoulou, 2009). Digital and mobile media that are now a part of marketing communication efforts have been utilized in sponsorship activation, as they enable activational communication and increased brand awareness (Santomier, 2008). Specifically, sponsorship-based websites and social media platforms such as Twitter and Facebook enable interaction and engagement between sponsors and audiences (Weeks *et al.*, 2008; O'Keefe, Titlebaum & Hill, 2009). While beneficial to sponsors in regard to activation, this two-way form of communication can also result in loss of message control through a process referred to as bottom-up framing.

Goffman (1974) defined frames as mental schemas that are employed to quickly categorize and process everyday information. In a communicating text or message, aspects or attributes are made more prominent to audiences through the selection and emphasis of certain features, at the exclusion of other features (Entman, 1993). This is known as traditional, or top-down framing. Conversely, the framing of content and messages produced by individuals in a digital environment is defined as bottom-up framing, which examines the content disseminated by individuals who are consistent producers of online media (Nisbet, 2010). Facilitating the rise to prominence of certain frames surrounding an issue is the concept of networked framing, which was defined by Meraz and Papacharissi (2013) to include crowdsourcing practices and reframing of content within an online environment. Networked framing contributes to the persistent usage of a term or hashtag, thus associating it with a specific meaning, and perhaps one different from that intended (Meraz & Papacharissi, 2013). While altering the meaning of messages could be viewed as a harmless endeavour, the reframing of messages could impact brand image, and overall brand equity.

In his definition of brand equity, Keller (1993) focused on the implications of marketing efforts that are specifically derived from the brand. As such, a brand has equity when marketing efforts result in outcomes that would not otherwise have been achieved had a brand not possessed a certain name. To achieve this outcome, an element of brand knowledge is required on the part of the consumer.

Brand knowledge consists of two components: brand awareness and brand image (Keller, 1993). Brand awareness is based upon brand recognition, which utilizes consumer associations with a brand to evoke past experiences (Yoo, 2014). Brand awareness is an integral part of the marketing process, as increased awareness of a brand has been associated with purchase considerations on the part of the consumer (Bettman & Park, 1980; Roselius, 1971).

The second component of brand knowledge is brand image, which also influences consumer purchase behaviour (Dobni & Zinkham, 1990). Brand image has been defined to include the attitudes or opinions associated with the brand in memory (Gardner & Levy, 1955; Herzog, 1963; Newman, 1957). According to Keller (1993), the perceptions of the brand stored in consumer memory are dependent upon the type, favourability, strength and uniqueness of brand associations. The framing of messages, while a communications-based concept has been found to influence the opinions of audiences (Andsager, 2000), thus the networked reframing of #CheersToSochi could impact the perceptions of consumers, and potentially influence the brand image and equity of McDonald's.

Results

In order to examine the nature of the hijacking of #CheersToSochi during sponsorship activation, the software tool Hashtracking, which scrapes Twitter data containing a specific hashtag, was used to collect the data. Data were collected between 31 January and 25 February 2014 resulting in a sample of 33,604 tweets that contained the #CheersToSochi hashtag. As this was a large sample size, thematic analysis of the data was first performed by another software tool, Leximancer, which was employed because it performs both thematic and semantic analysis on text (Bal, Campbell & Pitt, 2012), resulting in the determination of descriptors and dominant themes (Smith & Humphreys, 2006).

The total sample contained 9,254 (27.54 per cent) original tweets, 22,117 (65.82 per cent) retweets and 2,233 (6.65 per cent) replies. Tweets also contained other hashtags, with the most popular being #lgbt at 27.2 per cent (9,132), #sochi2014 at 19.8 per cent (6,663) and #russia at 11.7 per cent (3,931). McDonald's was mentioned in 2,112 tweets (6.28 per cent), Coca-Cola in 3,057 (9.10 per cent) and Visa in 1,192 (3.54 per cent).

Three key themes were identified in the #CheersToSochi content: LGBT, Gay and Sponsors. Seven peripheral themes were found and included: Principle 6, Putin, Athletes, send, Equality, #AmericaIsBeautiful and #CelebrateWithABite.

Results indicated a small amount of content related to sending cheers to Olympic athletes. Focusing on the themes of "athletes" and "send", a small number of tweets related to the intended purpose of the hashtag, such as "RT @lolojones: Send your cheers to your favorite athlete or team #Olympics #CheersToSochi". Conversely, a far greater number of tweets were focused on the LGBT issues surrounding Russian politics such as "#CheersToSochi: I don't think so. I don't send cheers to hateful places!". The peripheral themes of "Equality" and "Principle 6" were far more direct in their discussions of Russia, with tweets such as "NEWS #UN Chief calls for equality, non-discrimination at #Sochi @Olympics [link] @reuters #Russia #LGBT" indicative of content. The peripheral theme of "Putin" was predominately employed to directly comment on Russian President Vladimir Putin's role in human rights and the Olympic Games. For example, "#RUSSIA SisterCity Mayors of #Tallahassee #Orlando and #StPetersburg #FL urge #PUTIN to grow up #lgbt #CheersToSochi" highlighted such sentiments in tweet content.

The two peripheral themes, "#AmericaIsBeautiful" and "#CelebrateWithABite", were sponsor-related hashtags employed in unrelated marketing campaigns during the period of the Olympic Games. These hashtags were hijacked by Twitter users, in addition to #CheersToSochi, due to their association with the Olympic Games. The hashtag #AmericaIsBeautiful from a Coca Cola marketing campaign appeared in 1,105 Tweets in the sample, and was subsequently tied to the negative associations with Russian politics in tweets such as "#AmericaIsBeautiful because sponsorship of gay-bashing is really bad for your brand #CheersToSochi". The secondary McDonald's hashtag #CelebrateWithABite appeared in 890 tweets and was used in conjunction with the #CheersToSochi hashtag to reframe the messaging in both campaigns. For example, the tweets, "@McDonalds wants u 2 #CelebrateWithABite & by 'bite' they mean 'ignore blatant human rights violations'#CheersToSochi" and "#CelebrateWith ABite, @McDonalds? No thanks, I'm allergic to homophobia" were symbolic of this utilization. While the peripheral themes highlighted the trends in content associated with the #CheersToSochi hashtag, the three key themes of "LGBT", "Gay" and "Sponsors" provided greater context into the nature of the content specifically to McDonald's.

The key theme of "LGBT" was the top theme identified and it included the descriptors of: LGBT, Russia's, Sochi2014, Olympics, Sochi, rights, people, iocmedia, Twibbon, human, stand and message. The LGBT theme was present in 9,472 of the tweets. Tweet content such as "@ QueerNationNY: #CheersToSochi #LGBT RT @MelanieNathan1: Gays to protest Sochi Olympic opening at Russian Consulate" highlighted the utilization of the LGBT theme in relation to the #CheersToSochi hashtag. "Sochi 2014" and "Olympics" were also descriptors simultaneously present at a high rate with "LGBT", for example: "First they ignore you, then they ridicule you, then they fight you, and then you win. Gandhi #sochi2014 #Olympics #CheersToSochi #LGBT" and "absolutely disgusting – all American companies too [link] #buytheworldacoke *#Sochi2014* #LGBT #CheersToSochi #fail". To demonstrate their feelings towards a lack of action by the International Olympic Committee (IOC), users also incorporated the IOC into the discussion by tweeting content such as "#CheersToSochi #LGBT RT @dumpstoli: Sochi anti-gay stuff overblown, IOC's Dick Pound says", and reminding users of past IOC human rights transgressions: "Reminder: #IOC also thought the Nazis were no big deal. 'Anti-stuff overblown' #LGBT @iocmedia #CheersToSochi". Support for the LGBT community through #CheersToSochi was also generated by asking users to adopt a Twibbon, an application on Twitter used to promote various charities and causes by enabling supporters to customize their social network profile picture with a virtual badge (Chell & Mortimer, 2014). Tweets including the Twibbon included: "An effective method of supporting our #LGBT sisters & brothers in #Russia! [*Twibbon*] #CheersToSochi #homophobia #HumanRights", and "A synchronized call for #LGBT liberty and freedom worldwide just as the #Sochi2014 games begin. #CC14 #CheersToSochi".

The final set of descriptors associated with the LGBT theme involved human rights issues and requests for users to take a stand against discrimination. For example, content that focused on raising awareness of human rights included: "The #Olympic Charter states 'The practice of sport is a *#humanright*' and we tend to agree. #CheersToSochi #LGBT" and "#CheersToSochi grows. Find us on @facebook here: Not going away until the #LGBT people are *FREE WORLDWIDE*". Other users employed Twitter to admonish Russia for a lack of human rights in tweets such as: "Human rights reach low point! #LGBT #CheersToSochi RT @DChernyshenko: Olympic Flame reached Europe's highest point". The final descriptors associated with the LGBT theme included tweets asking users to take a stand on the issue of LGBT rights. Tweets such as: "We all have the right to #Love & #SpeakOut. Stand with #LGBT #Russia & basic #HumanRights #Sochi2014 #Cheers ToSochi #LoveIsLove", and "Beautiful commercial, @CocaCola. Now, how about decrying the abuse of LGBT in Russia. Take a stand", called for sponsors to take a stand, while other tweets focused on McDonald's not following other sponsors' leads: "@McDonalds @ CocaCola @Visa @samsung why does your marketing departments look to @ATT how to stand up for LGBT #CheersToSochi #speakout".

The second most prominent theme identified in the analysis was "gay" and included the following descriptors and names: gay, sponsors, Russians, arrests, activists, anti-gay, and laws. The gay theme was present in 3,526 tweets in the data sample. Content such as "RT @ avimat90210: #CheersToSochi: RT @Slate: Gay teens in Russia are beaten, humiliated & forced to drink urine. Gov't is OK with that" was indicative of this theme. Sub-topical categories present in this theme were messages that called out sponsors for their association with the Sochi Games. For example the tweet: "How would the ancient Greeks feel about Gay bashing at the Olympics? #CheersToSochi [link] Boycott all Olympic sponsors!" illustrated this behaviour. While many tweets called for action on the part of sponsors overall, others were directed at specific sponsors, such as: "@heidi_mcsista Found this on the internet why do you think gays are upset with @McDonalds???? #CheersToSochi" and "If @ CocaCola thinks including gay family in Super Bowl ad excuses sponsoring #Sochi they've been drinkin' too much cola #CheersToSochi". In tweet content that was indicative of the descriptor of "Russians" there were instances where individuals linked sponsors with violent events taking place in Sochi. For example, "#Homophobia u support @McDonaldsCorp #Russian men found guilty of murdering they believed was #gay", was a tweet that created an association between the sponsor and violent action. An obvious connection with the previously mentioned tweet was content mentioning "arrests". An example of such a tweet stated: "Beating gays, killing dogs, poisoned water, bad food, poor rooms, trash, construction, arrests . . . Not #CheersToSochi but JEERS to Sochi!". While calling attention to Russian policies, many of the "arrest" tweets were individuals reacting to gay individuals being arrested by Russian authorities, such as: "Russia makes first gay arrests of Sochi Olympics [link] via @gaystarnews #CheersToSochi".

The final two descriptors within this theme were "activists" and "laws", and reflected on the cultural and historical implications of the events taking place in Sochi. For example, "#LGBT activist defies Putin in #Russia with gay propaganda.'Berlin 1936 = Sochi 2014' #CheersToSochi" highlighted the historical references. Within this theme, individuals were again utilizing #CheersToSochi to tie the controversy taking place in Sochi back to the sponsors associated with the Games, thus reframing and redistributing content. Examples of these tweets included: "An LGBTQ activist set up a parody site of McDonald's #Cheers ToSochi website. And it's awesome" and "McDonald's #Sochi2014 website hijacked by gay activist to protest sponsorship #CheersToSochi". Tweets indicative of the "laws" descriptor focused primarily on the laws governing Russia and how they impacted both native citizens and those visiting for the Games. Examples of these tweets stated: "Olympians urge Russia to reconsider 'gay propaganda' laws [link] via @guardian #CheersToSochi" and "Editor, LGBT support group founder fined under Russia's 'gay propaganda' law via @CNN #Sochi2014".

The third most prominent theme identified within the analysis was "sponsors" and included the following descriptors and names: Coca Cola, McDonald's, hate, Visa and homophobia. Coca Cola was present in 3,057 tweets; McDonald's was present 2,112 tweets and Visa included in 1,192 tweets. The descriptors of "hate" and "homophobia" included content within the tweets that were highly critical and aggressive in nature towards the sponsors. For example, "#LGBTQ activists pushing back against @CocaCola & @McDonalds sponsorship of #Sochi's anti-gay thugs #CheersToSochi", "@stephenfry, I won't be eating @McDonalds or drinking @CocaCola today, failure to spk out 4 human rights in #russia #CheersTo Sochi", and "Olympic committee and sponsors like @McDonalds @Visa @CocaCola ignore #principle6 of Olympic charter #CheersToSochi" illustrated the negative valence associated with these descriptors. In addition to aggressive content, tweets to these sponsors were not passive or one-directional in their communication. In fact, many individuals engaged the sponsors directly in dialogue through the utilization of the sponsor's Twitter handle (e.g. @McDonalds). An example of this type of tweet content included "@CocaCola YOU don't condone 'intolerance of any kind anywhere in the world'! This proves otherwise". In addition to messages geared to attack official sponsors, many users also stated how the negative association with the Sochi Olympics affected consumers' brand loyalty. For example, "@pepsi over @CocaCola , @BurgerKing over @McDonalds, for everything else there is @MasterCard :)#CheersToSochi" highlighted the choices available to consumers. Additionally, individuals recognized the potential impact of these worldwide brands associating with this particular Olympic host country, which was highlighted in tweets such as the following: "Two of the biggest brands in the world sponsoring one of the biggest tragedies of this generation @McDonalds @CocaCola #CheersToSochi".

The final descriptors within the "sponsors" theme, "hate" and "homophobia", were also utilized in tweets that were highly critical of sponsors. Examples of these tweets included: "Who would have thought a monumental error of judgment would come back & bite @CocaCola (@CocaColaAU)? #CheersToSochi #hate #homophobia" and "@McDonalds So will you like some homophobia with that. #CheersToSochi". Regardless of the values and missions of the sponsoring organizations, various individuals perceived an association between the politics of Russia and the sponsors participating as part of the Sochi Olympics. For example, "Coke @CocaCola and @McDonalds supporting the most homophobic @Olympics ever. #CheersToSochi @iocmedia", "@McDonalds So will you like some homophobia with that. #CheersToSochi", and "@McDonalds, proud sponsor of homophobia. #CheersToSochi" illustrated these associations in content. Tweets within this theme were both one-directional and reciprocal in nature, with individuals using criticism or humour to attempt to engage the sponsors in dialogue.

Conclusion

As illustrated by the various themes and descriptors in commentary contained in tweet content, the two-way communication on Twitter enabled consumers to reframe the conversation surrounding #CheersToSochi. This was achieved by utilizing a tool that was originally designed to be the cornerstone of McDonald's digital marketing initiatives, the event-specific hashtag. The majority of individuals who participated as part of the #CheersToSochi conversation employed this hashtag as a point of origin to illustrate support for the LGBT community and contribute to online activism. Individuals used this hashtag to criticize sponsors for their affiliation with a country engaged in controversy for its discriminatory practices, and simultaneously encouraged protests by those who championed inequality. In addition, humour was also employed to poke fun or criticize Russia's political policies, and in turn to attack companies that were affiliated with the games through official sponsorships. The linkage or association created between the sponsor and the Sochi Olympic Games was negatively viewed as an endorsement of a country that was accepting of discrimination based on sexual orientation. Due to the association between the host of the event, Russia, and the sponsor, individuals were critical of sponsorship decisions regardless of whether the sponsoring organization's values were congruent with Russian political policy or not. Beyond creating an association between the host country's political beliefs and the sponsoring organization, #CheersToSochi also served the function of news dissemination, as individuals could follow the reframed conversation simply by searching for this hashtag.

The results of this study highlight interesting theoretical and practical implications in regard to brand equity, brand knowledge and its sub-component of brand image, and sponsorship activation. Due to organizational longevity, McDonald's and other official Olympic sponsors such as Coca-Cola probably possess high levels of brand awareness, brand recall and brand recognition. Employing Keller's (1993) brand equity model, the underlying sponsorship strategy may have been to positively reinforce a pre-existing brand image through the association with uplifting stories of Olympic athletes, which aligns with the market-based approach to sponsorship (Cornwell & Maignan, 1998; McDonald, 1991). The personal stories of Olympic athletes and their successes could have influenced the attitudes of consumers towards McDonald's as a brand through positive association, while simultaneously strengthening these associations to McDonald's through positive exposure.

Social media content has the potential to influence brand image (Bruhn, Schoenmueller & Schafer, 2012), and form brand associations through audience interaction (Yan, 2011). Prior to social media, promotional elements of the marketing mix, including sponsorship, all allowed for message control on the part of the organization. The one-way, mediated forms of communication utilized in organizational marketing communication efforts allowed for greater message control and positive valence in content, which subsequently influenced brand knowledge, awareness and particularly brand image. While the benefits of social media-based forms of sponsorship activation include increased brand awareness and engagement (Santomier, 2008; Yan, 2011), the same platforms also enable the potential for a loss of message control due to two-way communication. Social media enables consumers to act as content creators, and provides them with the ability to reframe content and influence brand image and brand equity. As such, in this instance the intended utilization of sponsorship activation and reinforcement of brand image was instead countered by the reframing of the #CheerToSochi hashtag by consumers who did not approve of the association between McDonald's and the Sochi Olympic Games.

Following the hijacking of #CheersToSochi, any potential benefits from the sponsorship activation, in terms of brand image, were negated as a result of networked framing. As indicated by the results, the context and tone of tweets containing #CheersToSochi were overwhelmingly negative. In addition, the hijacking may have also caused McDonald's to completely abandon any activation through the hashtag, as the results indicated that little content was focused on sending cheers to athletes. While this disassociation from the hashtag may have been a public relations tactic to reduce further negative impact, it also simultaneously prevented any attempt by McDonald's to regain message control. Further complicating the matter of activation was the reframing of these messages by individuals to create a negative association. As highlighted by Meraz and Papacharissi (2013), networked framing functions on crowdsourcing practices to build prominence, and the continued negative reframing of messaging found in the various descriptors in the "LGBT", "gay" and "sponsor" themes allowed the anti-Russia policies and sentiments to continue throughout the duration of the games. From a theoretical standpoint, not only does this illustrate the potential implications of networked framing on marketing concepts, but from a practical standpoint, the bottom-up, networked framing by individuals illustrates the potential pitfalls of social-media-based sponsorship activation.

Ultimately, the positive features associated with social media, such as two-way communication (Steyn, 2009) and networked collectivity (Yan, 2011), were used against sponsoring organizations. Organizations can benefit greatly from the engagement with audiences provided on social media. However, they must also be cognizant that the same medium can easily facilitate a loss of message control. In addition, the collectivity within a network that exists between individuals and fosters a sense of belonging also enables individuals to collectively form and rally around social causes.

From a sponsorship perspective, the loss of message control coupled with the networked reframing of content, and ability of individuals to collectively form around a cause (Pfeffer, Zorbach & Carley, 2014) created the perfect situation in which the negative associations of Russia's political policies were transferred through consumer associations to the various sponsoring organizations, and potentially negatively impacted brand image. Initial attacks by consumers on McDonald's through the utilization of #CheersToSochi were also transferred to any sponsor that had an association with the Sochi Olympic Games, and thus extended the negative associations to additional organizations and not exclusively to McDonald's, the sponsor that originated the campaign. Although potential damage could have been experienced by all sponsors associated with the Games, McDonald's brand image would have sustained the greatest impact, as it was its own hashtag (i.e. #CheersToSochi) that was specifically referenced in tweet content to attack and criticize sponsorship of the Olympic Games in Sochi. This hashtag served as the original starting point for online criticism, effectively acting as the base point for all crowdsourcing to determine the acceptance and reframing of the #CheersToSochi campaign on Twitter. The centralization of activism efforts, protests, outrage, cultural critiques and sponsor criticisms around #CheersToSochi only furthered the association of the brand in the minds of consumers worldwide.

The fact that McDonald's was only directly mentioned in 6.28 per cent of tweets also containing the hashtag #CheersToSochi perhaps helped to decrease the strength of the association in the mind of the consumer due to the reframing. In order to establish a brand association in the mind of the consumer, a direct public linking of the sponsor to the event must be present (McAlister, Kelly, Humphreys & Cornwell, 2012). As McDonald's was only directly linked with #CheersToSochi in 6.28 per cent of the tweet content, this level of exposure may not have been pervasive enough to fully establish a negative association in the minds of consumers, or change a pre-existing positive association. Perhaps more importantly, McDonald's possesses a significant amount of brand awareness, and consumers have more than likely already established brand recognition with the organization based upon past experiences. As such, previous consumer experiences with McDonald's and the brand may have mitigated the negative impact of the #CheersToSochi hijacking.

What remains to be determined is the impact of negative reframing on sponsorship campaigns that are activated through the social media platform. Marketing research initiatives should include consumer surveys that measure whether Twitter users have experienced a change in their perceptions, attitudes and behaviours toward a particular brand as a result of a failed marketing campaign. In addition to being a valuable source of information regarding consumer behaviour tendencies, this investigation would help to determine the potential impact of social media on the various brand constructs such as brand knowledge, brand awareness and brand image. The opportunity to engage in sponsorship activation and marketing efforts on social media provides numerous benefits. However, organizations must be aware that those same features can also result in the reframing of messaging that could negatively impact brand image, and ultimately influence the extent of the utilization of social media as part of the promotional mix and sponsorship activation campaign.

References

Andsager, J. L. (2000). How interest groups attempt to shape public opinion with competing news frames. *Journalism & Mass Communication Quarterly*, 77(3), 577–592.

Bal, A. S., Campbell, C. L. & Pitt, L. F. (2012). Viewer reactions to online political spoof videos and advertisements. In A. Close. (Ed.), *Online Consumer Behavior: Theory and Research in Social Media, Advertising, and E-tail* (pp. 185–208). New York: Routledge.

Bettman, J. R., & Park, C. W. (1990). Effects of prior knowledge and experience and phase of the choice process on consumer decision processes: A protocol analysis. *Journal of Consumer Research*, 7, 234–248.

Bruhn, M., Schoenmueller, V. & Schafer, D. B. (2012). Are social media replacing traditional media in terms of brand equity creation? *Management Research Review*, 35, 770–790.

Chell, K. and Mortimer, G. (2014). Investigating online recognition for blood donor retention: An experiential donor value approach. *International Journal of Nonprofit and Voluntary Sector Marketing*, 19, 143–163.

Cornwell, T. B. & Maignan, I. (1998). An international review of sponsorship research. *Journal of Advertising*, 27(1), 1–21.

Cornwell, T. B., Weeks, C. S. & Roy, D. P. (2005). Sponsorship-linked marketing: Opening the black box. *Journal of Advertising*, 34(2), 21–42.

DeGaris, L., West, C. & Dodds, M. (2009). Leveraging and activating NASCAR sponsorships with NASCAR-linked sales promotions. *Journal of Sponsorship*, 3(1), 88–97.

Dobni, D. & Zinkhan, G. M. (1990). In search of brand image: A foundational analysis. *Advances in Consumer Research*, 17, 110–119.

Entman, R. M. (1993). Framing: Toward clarification of a fractured paradigm. *Journal of Communication*, 43(4), 51–58.

Gardner, B. B. & Levy, S. J. (1955). The product and the brand. *Harvard Business Review*, 33, 33–39.

Giannoulakis, C., Stotlar, D. & Chatziefstathiou, D. (2008). Olympic sponsorship: Evolution, challenges, and impact on the Olympic Movement. *International Journal of Sports Marketing & Sponsorship*, 9(4), 256–270.

Goffman, E. (1974). *Frame Analysis: An Essay on the Organization of Experience*. New York: Harper & Row.

Herzog, H. (1963). Behavioral science concepts for analyzing the consumer. In P. Bliss (Ed.), *Marketing and the Behavioral Sciences* (pp. 76–86). Boston: Allyn and Bacon.

Horowitz, S. (2012). Sponsorship and branding: Practioners' articles how jersey sponsorship can be an effective marketing tool. *Journal of Brand Strategy*, 1(2), 180–184.

Kang, K. J. & Stotler, D. (2011). An investigation of factors influencing decision making for participation in The Olympic Partners Sponsorship: A case study of Samsung. *International Journal of Applied Sports Sciences*, 23(1), 225–250.

Keller, K. A. (1993). Conceptualizing, measuring, and managing customer-based brand equity. *Journal of Marketing*, 57, 1–22.

Ladousse, C. (2009). How Lenovo deploys powerful creative sponsorship activation techniques for a global brand. *Journal of Sponsorship*, 2(3), 199–205.

McAlister, A. R., Kelly, S. J., Humphreys, M. S. & Cornwell, T. B. (2012). Change in a sponsorship alliance and the communication implications of spontaneous recovery. *Journal of Advertising*, 41(1), 5–16.

McDonald, C. (1991). Sponsorship and image of the sponsor. *European Journal of Marketing*, 25(11), 31–39.

McDonald's (2014). McDonald's Invites Fans To Send #CheersToSochi During Sochi 2014 Olympic Winter Games. Retrieved from <http://news.mcdonalds.com/Corporate/manual-releases/2014/McDonald%E2%80%99s-Invites-Fans-to-Send-CheersToSochi-Duri>. Accessed 3 April 2014.

Meraz, S. & Papacharissi, Z. (2013). Networked gatekeeping and networked framing on #Egypt. *International Journal of Press/Politics*, *18*(2), 138–166.

Merevick, T. (5 February 2014). LGBT activists launch "cheers to Sochi" parody site after "hijacking" McDonald's hashtag. BuzzFeed. Retrieved from <www.buzzfeed.com/tonymerevick/lgbt-activists-launch-cheers-to-sochi-parody>. Accessed 1 April 2014.

Meng-Lewis, Y., Thwaites, D. & Pillai, K. G. (2014). Effectiveness of Olympic sponsorship by foreign and domestic companies: The influential role of consumer ethnocentrisim. *International Journal of Sports Marketing & Sponsorship*, *15*(2), 107–123.

Mickle, T. (10 February 2014). McDonald's adds athletes to #CheersToSochi campaign. *SportsBusiness Journal*. Retrieved from <www.sportsbusinessdaily.com/SB-Blogs/On-The-Ground/2014/02/SochiSiteMcDonaldssocial.aspx>. Accessed 3 April 2014.

Morgan, A. & Frawley, S. (2011). Sponsorship legacy and the hosting of an Olympic Games: The case of Sydney 2000. *Journal of Sponsorship*, *4*(3), 220–235.

Newman, J. W. (1957). New insights, new progress for marketing. *Harvard Business Review*, *35*, 95–102.

Nisbet, M. (2010). Knowledge into action: Framing the debates over climate change and poverty. In Paul D'Angelo & Jim Kuypers (Eds), *Doing Frame Analysis: Empirical and Theoretical Perspectives* (pp. 43–83). New York, NY: Routledge.

O'Keefe, R., Titlebaum, P. & Hill, C. (2009). Sponsorship activation: Turning money spent into money earned. *Journal of Sponsorship*, *3*(1), 43–53.

Papadimitriou, D. & Apostolopoulou, A. (2009). Olympic sponsorship activation and the creation of competitive advantage. *Journal of Promotion Management*, *15*(1), 90–117 <doi: 10.1080/10496490 902892754>.

Pfeffer, J. Zorbach, T. & Carley, K. M. (2014). Understanding online firestorms: Negative word-of-mouth dynamics in social media networks. *Journal of Marketing Communications*, *20*(1–2), 117–128.

Ryan, A. & Fahy, J. (2012). Evolving priorities in sponsorship: From management to network management. *Journal of Marketing Management*, *28*, 1132–1158.

Roselius, T. (1971). Consumer ranking of risk reduction methods. *Journal of Marketing*, *35*, 56–61.

Santomier, J. (2008). New media, branding and global sports sponsorship. *International Journal of Sports Marketing & Sponsorship*, *10*(1), 15–28.

Smith, A. E. & Humphreys, M. S. (2006). Evaluation of unsupervised semantic mapping of natural language with Leximancer concept mapping. *Behavior Research Methods*, *38*(2), 262–279.

Steyn, P. G. (2009). Online recommendation as the ultimate yardstick to measure sponsorship effectiveness. *Journal of Sponsorship*, *2*(4), 316–329.

Sylvestre, C. M. & Moutinho, L. (2007). Leveraging associations: The promotion of cultural sponsorships. *Journal of Promotion Management*, *13*(3), 281–303.

Taylor, C. R. (2012). The London Olympics: What advertisers should watch. *International Journal of Advertising*, *31*(3), 459–464.

Walliser, B. (2003). An international review of sponsorship research: Extension and update. *International Journal of Advertising*, *22*, 5–40.

Weeks, C. S., Cornwell, T. B. & Drennan, J. C. (2008). Leveraging sponsorships on the internet: Activation, congruence, and articulation. *Psychology & Marketing*, *25*(7), 637–654.

Yan, J. (2011). Social media in branding: Fulfilling a need. *Journal of Brand Management*, *18*, 688–696.

Yoo, C. Y. (2014). Branding potentials of keyword search ads: The effects of ad rankings on brand recognition and evaluations. *Journal of Advertising*, *43*(1), 85–99.

24

ARABIAN GULF GAME PLAN

The social media marketing strategy of the Emirates American Football League

Matthew A. Gilbert

Introduction

"Yusajel Hadaf!" This phrase can be heard among Arabic-speaking people in the United Arab Emirates (UAE) when their football (soccer) team scores a goal. However, the 2012 founding of the Emirates American Football League (EAFL) in the UAE, along with changes in athletic interests that include the National Football League (NFL) and American football, could change this. Nielsen Sports (2015) shares that "since 2011, the proportion of the UAE population . . . interested in the NFL has risen . . . by 0.7 percentage points. Whilst this looks to be a small increase, this . . . is equivalent to . . . 20,000 more NFL fans" (p. 4). The growth of this global market supports the overseas expansion initiatives of the NFL which "has made no secret of its desire to bring American football to a new international stage" (Gardiner, 2016, p. 1). There exists viable value in the NFL brand far beyond the borders of the United States; in fact there is potentially more outside of it than within it.

The opportunity for brands connected to American football includes organizations like the EAFL. While not part of the NFL, it benefits from an association with it. Notably, several individuals involved with the EAFL are former NFL and college players or coaches (Rees, 2015). The formula seems to be working. "The response from the community has been fantastic", said EAFL General Manager Dustin Cherniawski (Jones, 2015). A Canadian living in Dubai since 2008, he played defensive back with the Canadian Football League's Saskatchewan Roughriders from 2005 to 2007, winning the Grey Cup in his last year with the team. The visionary behind the EAFL, Cherniawski realized how social media could be used to tell a story, especially for football. As Cherniawski (2016) explains: "Social media is a key part of building this. American football is so socially media friendly; everything from the workout in the gym to the game-day product is about the mystery of the man behind the mask" (p. 1).

Although unique to the Gulf Cooperation Council (GCC) region, the EAFL is not alone in its mission to bring American football to a part of the world not typically associated with it, nor is its diversity of players unusual. Worldwide there is an impressive array of individuals playing American football in organized leagues. Supporting this, Seifert (2016) reports that "there are 80 countries with organized federations governing the game . . ., there are thousands of leagues and hundreds of thousands of boys, girls, men and women playing at levels ranging from high school to soccer-like club leagues" (p. 2).

Recognizing the global role and relevance of American football, this chapter explores the origins of the EAFL; shares the league's social media strategy as a means of marketing while creating a community of fans, players, and their families; and looks ahead to the future of the league and American football in the UAE.

Background

A non-profit, pay-to-play, full contact amateur American football league (Rees, 2015), the EAFL (which was legally established as EAFL Events, LLC) is unique to the UAE, where American football was previously, but less professionally, played. The league was founded in 2012 by Cherniawski with American expatriate Patrick Campos and German expatriate Kai Trompeter, who also coached the league's first team, the EAFL Falcons. Former minor league baseball pitcher Chris Wentzel merged the American football club he had started in 2010 with Cherniawski and Campos (Burton, 2013) to form the league.

Their local sponsor (a requirement for every expatriate business in the UAE) is Sheikh Khalid Saud Al Qasimi, a member of the royal family of Sharjah, one of the seven UAE Emirates. He first played American football while a student at the American University of Sharjah and played tight end for the Dubai Barracudas during the EAFL's first three seasons.

The EAFL initially started with one exhibition team, the EAFL Falcons, first branded as the UAE Falcons. Unfortunately, as Cherniawski (2016) explained: "whilst we thought it was a great idea, very quickly people said to be careful you don't represent yourself as though you were a national team because you're not made up of nationals".

The rebranded EAFL Falcons team includes all-star players from each EAFL team in five divisions: U13, U15, U17, U19, and Men. The teams play exhibitions abroad and in the UAE where they have hosted teams from Germany and Russia. The Falcons have also traveled to Holland, India, Kazakhstan, Lebanon, Serbia, Sri Lanka, Singapore, and the Netherlands. Every December the U13 and U15 teams travel to Orlando, Florida and compete in the Pop Warner Super Bowl; in 2016 the U13 team won the 2016 International Division title.

The function of the Falcons is promotional, yet also intended to be transformational about the development of American football internationally. As quoted in Read (2014), Campos, the EAFL Vice Chairman and Director of Youth Football, and EAFL Falcons coach, had this to say: "We are acting as leaders across international football . . .. We want to develop both youth and senior football in the country and raise awareness of the setup in the UAE, alongside developing the game internationally" (pp. 2, 3).

After launching with four teams in three UAE cities (Burton, 2013), the league expanded to seven teams in two Emirates: Abu Dhabi Capitals, Abu Dhabi Scorpions, Abu Dhabi Wild Cats, Al Ain Desert Foxes, Dubai Barracudas, Dubai Sand Vipers, and Dubai Stallions. The EAFL is organized into four youth divisions: PeeWee (eight to 11 years), Bantam (12 to 13 years), Jr Varsity (14 to 15 years) and Varsity (16 to 18 years); there is also an adult division, Men (19 years and older). The number of teams varies by year based on membership totals and locations of players. There is a development team, the Fujairah Bulls, in the eastern Emirate of Fujairah and a collection of future team names ready to go.

Demographically, the league is comprised almost entirely of expatriates from 53 nationalities (EAFL.com, 2016), consisting of 40 percent Western expatriates and the remaining 60 percent being Gulf Arabs, Egyptians, Japanese, Lebanese, Saudi, Sudanese, and Turks (Burton, 2013; Sands, 2013). The cost involved in playing varies; the Emirates American Football League (2016) outlines equipment fees ranging from 4,675 dirhams (US$1,273) to

6,425 dirhams (US$1,750), depending on a player's division and date of registration (Emirates American Football League, 2016).

The regular season starts with registration and pre-season strength and conditioning camp in September, followed by practice in October. Games, which are held on Fridays (the first day of the weekend in the UAE), commence in November and end in March with the Desert Bowl championship between the top two teams in each division (eafl.ae, 2017b). The 2016–2017 season concluded for all divisions with the Desert Bowl V game on Friday, 17 March 2017; the Men's Division Al Ain Desert Foxes beat the Abu Dhabi Wildcats 18 to 12, winning their first championship.

In attendance at the Junior Varsity and Men's Division games was NFL quarterback Robert Griffin III, who performed the coin toss for both games (Asser, 2017). Several former NFL and college football players have been involved with the EAFL, increasing the league's credibility, improving the level of performance, and attracting interest from abroad.

In April 2015, former University of Texas football coach Mack Brown visited Dubai to explore opportunities to expand the University of Texas brand in the Middle East (Asser, 2015). When asked about the EAFL, Brown shared the following:

> I think it's very unique because football isn't the common sport in this country. For these guys to have started with 12 players five or six years ago and now they're in the 100s and have great support, I think they're well on track.
>
> *Asser 2015, pp. 3, 4*

Given that the EAFL's vision is "to create EAFL programs in every Emirate, but also create an international hub in Dubai for youth American football outside North America" (eafl.ae, 2017a), it could be argued that the league is well on its way to realizing that idea.

Socializing

As noted by Borel (2014), "like any human endeavor, sports evolve over time. Science and technology fuel these changes" (p. 2). One technology that has fueled changes in sports is social media. By connecting players with their fans and bringing those fans together, social media creates online communities. According to Kemp (2017), there are 2.789 billion social media users worldwide; in the Middle East, there are 93 million people actively using social media. Additionally, 99 percent (9,200,000 people) in the UAE use social media.

Mobile devices play a big part in social media strategy in the Middle East. Radcliffe (2016) explains that "for many users, mobile is the only way that they interact with social networks" (p. 3). In the Middle East, there are more mobile phone subscriptions (312 million) than there are people (246 million); within that population, 83 million people actively use social media via mobile devices (Kemp, 2017).

Consumers in the UAE are very connected and accessible via social media, which bodes well for the EAFL. While traditional media remains relevant, social media is the primary driver of the EAFL's marketing strategy. As Cherniawski (2016) explains, "social media is just so much more accessible" (p. 13). To investigate the social media marketing strategy of the EAFL, four interviews were conducted with key league personnel. The first occurred in person with Cherniawski at EAFL headquarters in Sports City, Dubai in June 2016. The remaining three interviews occurred online in March 2017 using a questionnaire and a follow-up by email and Facebook Messenger. Two players, Louis McInnes and Simon Thurston, were interviewed, as well as Ross Crist, the EAFL's announcer.

Facebook

When the EAFL strategizes for social media they count on their franchise quarterback: Facebook. Explaining the role of Facebook, Cherniawski (2016, p. 4) elaborates as follows:

> I will talk about Facebook a lot because it's our number one platform. Here in the UAE 99 percent of the western expats, or western loving expats who are interested in western things, are on Facebook. We pay very little to reach a lot of people; and that gets people into our community because awareness is number one.

The first step into social media the EAFL took was to create a Facebook group; initially it served the organization's needs, but it limited their ability to communicate outside of that audience. Once the league decided to formalize its operations it proceeded to do the same with its social media strategy. Cherniawski (2016) shares how the EAFL proceeded, saying: "When we made that decision to formalize, we said we need a real Facebook page that represents the Emirates American Football League; we should have some team pages, so first thing I did was I snapped up all the handles" (p. 10).

The EAFL established https://www.facebook.com/emiratesamericanfootballleague/ as their main Facebook page and then reserved Facebook pages for each of the league's current and anticipated teams, each of which manages its own page with EAFL oversight. Cherniawski (2016) outlines his approach to maintaining brand standards while giving the teams creative freedom in the following passage: "You have to stay like a cheesecloth; you have to maintain the structural integrity of the fabric while letting things slip through, but it still generally maintains its form" (p. 2). On its Facebook page the EAFL shares events, photos and videos, as well as league information and updates; they also integrate their Instagram feed into the page to increase the exposure of that content. The Falcons page, at https://www.facebook.com/EAFLfalcons/, is similar. Both pages serve as a crossroads and virtual gathering place for league members.

The EAFL's investment in Facebook yielded measurable returns. Cherniawski (2016) notes that "Facebook is definitely where we have the most engagement. Our engagement is real . . . That's the easiest way to gauge engagement because there are actual metrics, likes, and shares, and views" (pp. 15, 26). Facebook figures prominently in the EAFL's future social media plans. Cherniawski (2016, p. 26) clarifies the league's strategic plan as being heavily focused on digital, especially Facebook:

> Our strategic plan for this year is to go heavily digital. We'll probably spend a good chunk of our marketing money on Facebook because we can do target advertising and a variety of different media formats. We can do video, giveaways, interviews, teasers, and events. There are so many different ways to market through Facebook.

However, since 93 percent of the region's 136 million monthly Facebook users access it via mobile device (Radcliffe, 2016), the EAFL must ensure that the content it shares on Facebook will display properly on such a device. Further, knowing that 52 percent of Arab youth share stories with their friends on Facebook (Radcliffe, 2016), continuing to create and curate content there is a sensible social media marketing strategy.

Website

After establishing an online presence with Facebook, the EAFL looked to solidify their social media strategy with a website. It was then that Cherniawski (2016) discovered the importance of controlling your brand when they found that EAFL.com was already taken and was being sold for US$27,000. Thinking creatively and practically the EAFL instead registered the country code top-level domain, EAFL.ae. Initially the website was a simple information page, but it has evolved into a robust Customer Relationship Management (CRM) system combined with a Content Management System (CMS). Players can register and create an account to personalize their online experience. Cherniawski said: "We only had 450 people in our league last year, but we've got 1200 signed up on our website. This is the next generation" (2016, p. 12).

Newspaper

The EAFL integrates traditional media with their social media marketing. Specifically, they pay for inclusion in the community pages in the back of the *Sport 360°* newspaper in Dubai. Cherniawski (2016) said that their paid inclusion in the newspaper entitles EAFL members to a free subscription of the paper. More importantly, however: "On Tuesdays, our guys can open the paper and see themselves, and then we can post that to social media. We will always do that because that connects print media, social media, and photography" (p. 26). The EAFL's arrangement with *Sport 360°* appears to be effective, but it is worth noting that, according to Radcliffe (2016), only 17 percent of Arab youths (aged 18 to 24) read newspapers daily for information; this is a significant drop from the 62 percent that did so in 2011.

Instagram

The EAFL started using Instagram in early 2014 for the league using the account @eafl_uae and, for the Falcons, @eafl_falcons. The Dubai Barracudas operate their own team account as well at @dubaibarracudas. On each of these accounts there are photos and videos from the games, team activities, and off-the-field events. Instagram content is cross-posted on the EAFL website and the EAFL Facebook page. With Instagram use in the UAE increasing from 38 percent of Internet users in 2014 to 60 percent in 2016 (Radcliffe, 2016), the EAFL would be wise to continue investing effort in this social media platform.

Twitter

The EAFL has a Twitter account, but uses it infrequently. Cherniawski (2016) sees it as more useful for news outlets and for distributing information to a wider audience. He says: "We're not really a news source; we could be, but our community is really not on Twitter" (p. 17). The EAFL uses Twitter to engage Dubai media outlets and provide them with game scores or other basic information. Although Thurston (2017) found the EAFL on Twitter, lately its influence in the Middle East has declined: Radcliffe (2016) shares that the number of active Twitter users in the region has dropped by 12 percent, a significant number.

Snapchat

The EAFL created a Snapchat account (@eafluae) in June 2016, but has not defined how it will be used. Cherniawski (2016) said: "I think Snapchat will work well for our Falcons trips because people actually want to follow along with what we're doing" (p. 14). They would be wise to start using it – Radcliffe (2016) reports that use of the app has tripled in two years.

Perspectives

Turning to the perspective of players in the league, Cherniawski (2016) shared how one of the league's Bantam Division players, was very active on social media: "He was a soccer kid and then he came over to football. He found his stride in football, so now he's all in. He's liking and commenting on absolutely everything we post" (p. 40). The 14-year-old boy from England, Louis McInnes, has played with the EAFL for four seasons on offense, defense, and special teams. He ended the 2016–2017 season winning the Bantam Division Desert Bowl V with his team, the Dubai Barracudas. Despite his preference for social media, he learned about the league from a friend through word-of-mouth. On a weekly basis, he visits the Facebook pages of the EAFL and Dubai Barracudas.

He regularly interacts with the EAFL's and the Barracudas' Instagram accounts, along with the EAFL's website and Twitter accounts (for the EAFL and Falcons). Typically, he looks at pictures and videos from the different divisions, but hopes to see more statistics and details about players. Interestingly, despite a heavy online orientation, he appreciates the offline activities that the league organizes: the EAFL creates a community of fans, players and their families through events within the community and by advertising the league at public events such as school fairs.

Players interact daily on Hudl (2016), a private, cloud-based system, where coaches and players review game film and practices. They also communicate in WhatsApp groups. Notably, with 93 percent of users daily, Radcliffe (2016) shows that WhatsApp is the most popular messaging service in the region.

Simon Thurston, a 44-year-old British citizen, played cornerback with the men's Dubai Barracudas during the 2015–2016 season and won the Desert Bowl V. Off the field he is the director of English content for a Dubai marketing agency and is the founder and host of the video podcast Sports Real. Evaluating EAFL's social strategy, Thurston (2017) believes that "what Dustin has done is incredible and it's what got me into playing. He's clearly made efforts to up their social media game this season and I hope this continues".

Drawn to the strategy, competitiveness, and camaraderie, Thurston (2017) enjoys playing football with other individuals from around the world. He is a regular visitor to the EAFL website and Instagram accounts where he "likes" and comments on posts. When asked why the EAFL has succeeded despite being in a culture that does not primarily embrace American football, Thurston (2017) shares the following insights:

> I believe it's due to the diversity of nationalities here. American Football isn't just popular stateside – Canada, South America and many European countries have organized leagues. The winter climate here is perfect for the game and some of the facilities across Dubai and Abu Dhabi are excellent.
>
> *Thurston, 2017*

Although not currently playing, Thurston (2017) still contributes to the EAFL's social media community, always looking for content to share with his social media circles. He asks: "Keep pushing out great content that people will share with friends and family" (Thurston, 2017).

Broadcasting

The EAFL uses both Android and Apple products to create, produce, and share their content on social media. Cherniawski personally uses an Android phone to post and upload material, but the EAFL film and edit all their post-game interviews on an iPad. With the iPad, they can attach a microphone or add lights with relative ease; they can then upload recordings to the cloud for storage or editing without needing to remove a storage card. Cherniawski (2016, p. 23) explains why they use this approach:

> The difference between this and, say, Final Cut Pro, is that you have to have a real specialized skill set; you kind of have to be in that industry to use Final Cut Pro. But to use Facebook, you can be seven years old; you can be an old granny. Everybody is using Facebook.

As the de facto "voice" of the EAFL, Ross Crist handles the league's broadcasting and game-announcing responsibilities. Crist (2017a) is an Instructor of Sport Studies with the Higher Colleges of Technology and is an American Sport Presenter on Dubai Eye 103.8 FM radio. Crist (2017a) relies on Twitter, Facebook, and Instagram to spread the word about games and other EAFL events. He also uploads post-game interviews on YouTube and uses his personal Snapchat account to promote the EAFL. Celebrating the completion of the fifth EAFL season Crist (2017b) shared the following observation on his Facebook page:

> I wrapped up my third season as the voice of the Emirates American Football League last night. Football has blossomed out in the UAE and a main reason for that is their founder and friend Dustin Cherniawski. Come check out a game next year!

Lessons

Using social media to create a community of fans, players, and their families while marketing their message to the population at large has been a learning experience for everyone involved at the EAFL. Cherniawski (2016) discussed experiencing funny moments and great successes as well as embarrassing incidents that were contained by better managing their channels. They have dealt with players tweeting personal thoughts about games using the team's social media accounts. They have also dealt with some unethical incidents involving the purchase of "likes", which added to their overall number but offered no real value beyond that. Cherniawski is astute about measuring engagement such as the number of comments or "likes" on a post compared with the number of "likes" for that page.

In the past the EAFL has spent 10,000 dirhams (US$2,723) for inclusion in a sport activity catalogue with a coupon. But, there was no way in which to track interest or discover if any leads came from it. Cherniawski (2016, p. 26) clarified that two coupons were redeemed, costing the league US$1,361.50 per person – a disproportionate acquisition cost versus the same investment on Facebook – saying:

> We could have reached 20 million people on Facebook for that kind of money. So, let's not do that again because we're not trying to explain to people what American football is. We're just trying to get them to know that American football is offered here.

Overall Cherniawski (2016, pp. 25–26) continues to see value in social media in general, but Facebook specifically, both through organic reach and paid promotion:

> We know that social media works, absolutely, and Facebook works to expand our reach. And doing the advertisements on the side of the page, promoting events, and promoting posts; that all works. We see a positive benefit there, and it's pretty cheap. So, for instance, Facebook, we might be able to promote a post for, let's call it $20 to get in front of upwards of five to ten thousand people.

Philosophically, Cherniawski realizes that there is a disconnect between the physical nature of the sport and the virtual nature of social media. But the EAFL connects those worlds while giving players a reason to put down their phones and engage with others, creating moments they can then share on social media. As he explains (pp. 12–13):

> Social media is great for updates and just generally keeping in touch, but you can't do our business through social media. We have a physical product, a physical service that they are going to come out and join; you can't do it from your couch. Once they join the league, then they can pump their chest on social media. Pictures of them wearing football equipment, running around all beat up on the field, is a real badge of pride for these guys. It lends itself very nicely to social media, and visually it's very appealing. If you go through our membership and you looked at all our Facebook profile pictures 30 percent is them wearing football equipment. So, that's a nice marketing opportunity.

It is also important to learn the laws and limitations that impact social media use in the Middle East. Radcliffe (2016) cautions "networks and services can be blocked . . . and issues around freedom of expression persist" (p. 3). UAE also bans virtual private networks (VPNs), which could limit the content that individuals can access during a social media campaign (Radcliffe, 2016). There are also laws prohibiting defamation or breaching the privacy of others, along with cultural concerns and governmental guidelines to follow.

Conclusion

In its five seasons of operation, the EAFL has sharpened its social media marketing strategy and continues to improve its efforts, focusing on reach and results. Managing their efforts with a small number of key individuals has been successful, yet challenging. Given its growth, the EAFL recognizes the need for a social media manager. The challenge is finding someone who understands American football, is in tune with the EAFL and who can create relevant content. Cherniawski (2016, p. 27) described an ideal candidate as follows:

> You need to be out there at practices, you need to be out there talking to the players, you need to be out there in the community, you need to be fair and balanced in how you represent the Stallions, the Barracudas, and the Sand Vipers, and Dubai versus Abu Dhabi. You need to have a nice mix of content. You produce that content, stay with that content, distribute that content.

Opportunities exist to improve the experiences of sports fans by focusing on their mobile phones. Mooney (2014) explains their increasing importance in the following passage:

"Mobile devices are popular as 'second screens' in home viewing of televised sports, but 70 percent of fans bring a mobile device to the stadium or arena and expect to use it during a game there as well" (p. 2).

Radcliffe (2016) indicates that 71 percent of UAE residents will consider advice from social media influencers prior to purchasing a product, so there is potential to leverage star players or NFL players with whom the league has been developing relationships. There also exists the possibility of a UAE national American football team. Quoted in Reedie (2014) Cherniawski anticipated such a team might exist within five years. Sheikh Khalid also shared that "an Emirati team . . . would be a huge achievement and something I believe we can do . . . we are on the right track in achieving such a feat" (Reedie, 2014).

After five successful seasons the EAFL has established its credibility within the UAE and far beyond its borders. Cherniawski's investment in the EAFL's social media marketing strategy as outlined in this chapter demonstrates the league's ability to capitalize on opportunities and manage limitations while avoiding risks.

References

Asser, J. (2017). NFL quarterback Robert Griffin III takes in Desert Bowl V at Dubai Sports City. *Sport 360°*. Retrieved from <http://sport360.com/article/other/eafl/226707/nfl-quarterback-robert-griffin-iii-takes-in-desert-bowl-v-at-dubai-sports-city/>. Accessed 19 March 2017.

Asser, J. (2015). A day with Mack Brown: A future for football in Middle East. *Sport 360°*. Retrieved from <http://sport360.com/article/eafl/41399/day-mack-brown-future-football-middle-east>. Accessed 19 March 2017.

Burton, N. (2013). American football breaks into the United Arab Emirates with the EAFL. In *Chat Sports*. Retrieved from <www.chatsports.com/nfl/a/American-football-breaks-into-the-United-Arab-Emirates-with-the-EAFL-19544>. Accessed 15 March 2017.

Borel, B. (2014). What will sports look like in the future? In *ideas.ted.com*. Retrieved from <http://ideas.ted.com/what-will-sports-look-like-in-the-future-three-ted-experts-discuss/>. Accessed 19 March 2017.

Cherniawski, D. (2016). [Interview with EAFL General Manager, Dustin Cherniawski].

Crist, R. (2017a). [Interview with EAFL Broadcaster, Ross Crist].

Crist, R. (2017b). I wrapped up my third season as the voice of the Emirates American Football League last night [Facebook]. Retrieved from <www.facebook.com/photo.php?fbid=10100844393817874&set=a.10100684948654324.2695473.12316266&type=3&theater>. Accessed 20 March 2017.

eafl.ae (2017a). EAFL | A message from the EAFL. Retrieved from <www.eafl.ae/page/about-us>. Accessed 15 March 2017.

eafl.ae (2017b). EAFL | Your frequently asked questions answered here. Retrieved from <www.eafl.ae/page/faq>. Accessed 15 March 2017.

Emirates American Football League (2016). *November Newsletter*. Dubai, United Arab Emirates: Emirates American Football League. Retrieved from <www.eafl.ae/assets/media/Newsletters/Newsletter%20-%20November%202016%20-%203-compressed.pdf>. Accessed 16 March 2017.

Gardiner, B. (2016). Inside the NFL's quest to build a truly global league. *Wired*. Retrieved from <www.wired.com/2016/01/inside-the-nfls-quest-to-build-a-truly-global-league/>. Accessed 15 March 2017.

Hudl (2016). About Hudl – Who We Are. Retrieved from <www.hudl.com/about>. Accessed 20 March 2017.

Jones, M. (2015). American football on the rise so why not join the EAFL boom. *Sport 360°*. Retrieved from <http://sport360.com/article/other/43363/going-out-american-football-rise-uae-so-why-not-join-eafl-boom>. Accessed 16 March 2017.

Kemp, S. (2017). Digital in 2017: Global Overview. In *We Are Social* [Blog]. Retrieved from <http://wearesocial.com/blog/2017/01/digital-in-2017-global-overview>. Accessed 20 March 2017.

Mooney, L. (2014). Five Key Trends That Are Driving the Business of Sports. In *Insights*. Retrieved from <www.gsb.stanford.edu/insights/five-key-trends-are-driving-business-sports>. Accessed 17 March 2017.

Nielsen Sports (2015). International Appeal: The Rise of the NFL. Retrieved from <http://nielsensports. com/international-appeal-rise-nfl/>. Accessed 15 March 2017.

Radcliffe, D. (2016). Social Media in the Middle East: The Story of 2016. *Social Media in the Middle East*. Eugene, Oregon: Damian Radcliffe. Retrieved from <https://damianradcliffe.wordpress. com/2016/12/07/report-social-media-in-the-middle-east-the-story-of-2016/>. Accessed 20 March 2017.

Read, B. (2014). The EAFL's mission to take American Football worldwide. *Sport 360°*. Retrieved from <http://sport360.com/article/other/eafl/24190/eafls-mission-take-american-football-worldwide/>. Accessed 19 March 2017.

Reedie, E. (2014). "An Emirati American football dream". *Gulf News*. Retrieved from <http:// gulfnews.com/sport/more-sport/an-emirati-american-football-dream-1.1396921>. Accessed 15 March 2017.

Rees, G. (2015). "Desert Ball: American football in the UAE". In *EDGARdaily.com*. Retrieved from <http://edgardaily.com/en/sport/2015/desert-ball-american-football-in-the-uae-29566>. Accessed 15 March 2017.

Sands, H. (2013). "Get into American football in Dubai". *Time Out Dubai*. Retrieved from <www. timeoutdubai.com/sportandoutdoor/features/37886-get-into-american-football-in-dubai>. Accessed 15 March 2017.

Seifert, K. (2016). How American football is becoming a worldwide sport. ESPN.com. Retrieved from <www.espn.com/nfl/story/_/id/15273529/how-american-football-becoming-worldwide-sport-europe-china-beyond>. Accessed 15 March 2017.

Thurston, S. (2017). [Interview with EAFL Men's Division Player, Simon Thurston].

25

INTERNATIONALIZATION AS A STRATEGY FOR SUCCESS IN THE LPGA

Tara Mahoney and Rebecca Studin

Introduction

Recently, the Ladies Professional Golf Association (LPGA) Tour had difficulty acquiring and retaining sponsors. Women's professional golf struggled to gain fan interest and obtain financial support in the United States, especially with the economic downturn. The lack of a large fan base led to decreased television ratings. This caused sponsors to cut their LPGA investment.

LPGA History

Contrary to public assumption, the United States Golf Association (USGA), the Professional Golf Association (PGA) of America and the LPGA are all separate entities. The USGA is the oldest organization and originated in 1894. The PGA was founded in 1916. In 1934, Helen Hicks became the first professional female golfer on a US tour (USGA history 2013). In 1950, 13 female golfers created the LPGA (LPGA history, 2013). Their mission was to develop a year-long tournament schedule for female golfers. Thus, the LPGA Tour is designed for female professional golfers to compete in golf.

The LPGA suffered significant drops in sponsorship between 2008 and 2011. During this time, the full schedule of 34 tournaments was cut to 23 tournaments ("Women in distress", 2009; Sirak, 2011). This cutting of tournaments is a direct result of a decrease in sponsor revenue. Originally, sport sponsorship was philanthropic. Then marketing objectives required sponsors to reevaluate their investments (Copeland, Frisby & McCarville, 1996).

Sport sponsorship

The increase of sponsorship as a tactic to meet corporate marketing objectives changed the relationship between sponsors and their properties. Sponsors look for methods to increase brand equity, staff relations, relations with other stakeholders and shareholder value (Walraven, Koning & Van Bottenburg, 2012). Properties depending on sponsorship revenue need to develop stronger relationships in order to fulfil the needs of all stakeholders. This approach demands communication integrating the sponsor's message within the property's marketing campaign, and incorporating the property in the sponsor's marketing strategy (Walraven, Koning & Van Bottenburg, 2012).

Integrated marketing communications is essential for success in the sport sponsorship industry, which is moving toward a more international audience (Farrelly, 2010). As sport organizations expand into different countries, the importance of sponsorship relationships increases. Unfortunately for the LPGA, many sponsorship directors resist contemporary methods of communication for global sponsorship, especially sponsorship of women's sport. Shaw and Amis (2001) suggest this is due to their being businessmen who started their careers without experience of international or women's sponsorship (Shaw & Amis, 2001).

Nowadays, sponsors expect their sponsorship of a sport organization to create favourable market conditions and generate a successful business endeavour (Walraven *et al.*, 2012). The LPGA has struggled to maintain a US fan base with the increased number of international players winning tournaments on its tour. US companies are less willing to sponsor a sport property when the probability of a less marketable player winning is highly likely (Dorman, 2008). The sponsors want to use winning players in their marketing campaigns (Dorman, 2008). This becomes difficult when the winning players are not identifiable in the sponsor's market.

International sport sponsorship

The international sport sponsorship industry has prospered from new technology in global communication. Companies, sponsors, organizations and fans are able to communicate easily on an international level (Amis & Cornwell, 2005). This immediate communication creates business opportunities. For example, broadcasting and new media technology gives fans from around the world the ability to watch their favourite athletes and matches. Also, integrated communications between sponsors and sport organizers makes it easy for companies to move towards national, international and global sport markets (Farrelly, 2010). Therefore, global sport sponsorship creates opportunities for athletes to become stars outside their native countries (Amis & Cornwell, 2005). This is how Tiger Woods created golf interest in countries such as Japan, Taiwan and China even though he is from the US (Capell, Lindorff, Moore & Takahashi, 1997).

Within the global sponsorship industry, the World Sponsorship Monitor ranks golf second in the list of top ten sponsored sports in terms of reported deals in 2007 (Fenton, 2009). In 2007, golf was ranked fifth in terms of dollar value for these sponsorship deals with a total of US$281 million (Fenton, 2009). These numbers reveal the high prevalence of international sponsorship in the golf industry.

LPGA sponsorship issues

The LPGA was caught in a difficult position. It began to lose fans, which led to struggles acquiring and maintaining sponsors. The strategy to gain new fans led to an increase in international tournaments. This initiative made it difficult for the LPGA to connect with its US sponsors. The LPGA needed to address its decreasing American fan base. The tour created an English-only policy to try to create marketable superstars. These celebrities would positively influence sponsorship campaigns and increase the overall success of the LPGA Tour.

The decreasing American fan base

Other US-based golf organizations like the PGA Tour and the SPGA (Senior Professional Golf Association) Tour have been able to maintain their US fan base, but the LPGA has not. The fan base is essential for sponsorships, television viewers and tournament attendance.

If sponsors want to promote their brand, the brand needs an audience. The LPGA's inability to foster a strong relationship with the US stems from the rising number of international golfers on the tour. Asian players are more competitive than ever. In 2012, only four of the 16 tournament winners were from the US (Voepel, 2012, para. 4). In fact, nine of the 12 international winners were from Asian countries (Statistics, 2013). Kristie Kerr said that only between five and six [Americans] could contend every week to win while there were 40 Asian competitors in the tournament (Rubenstein, 2010, para. 8). In 2013, only six Americans were among the top 20 money winners (Statistics, 2013). This low number has made it difficult to create a US fan base because the better golfers are international.

Americans like to support US athletes to win. Language barriers (especially with golfers from Asian countries) and a general indifference from American fans make it nearly impossible for the LPGA to create a relationship between American fans and international golfers (Rubenstein, 2010, para. 7). Further exacerbating the issue is the nature of the sport. Golf is an individual, rather than a team, sport. Team sports can offer a greater blend between international and US athletes within one team so a US fan can root for the team, including the international players. This desire to root for a team provides consumers with a sense of belonging and therefore creates a connection between the team and the consumer (Robinson, Trail & Kwon, 2004). The US teams give US fans the connection they need with international players. Unfortunately, US fans find it less appealing to root for international golfers when there is no connection.

The increase in Asian players affects the LPGA's sponsors. Typically, the best players in the sport offer the best sponsorship options. Alas, the best LPGA players are not marketable to the US fan base. The LPGA depends upon corporate sponsorship support for its financial survival (Dorman, 2008), and needs to feature competitive players in its promotions. Its financial viability is dependent upon corporate sponsorships (Dorman, 2008). If a less marketable Asian player is likely to win, a brand may be less likely to invest in sponsorship because the player does not connect with the US market. The language barrier between the Asian player and the US audience prevents this connection. Kwak Sang II from the Korea Ladies Professional Golf Association says that "when a player wins the championship, you want to expose her to the media, but if she can't speak English well, it limits the publicity efforts" of the sponsors (Dorman, 2008, p. 2).

In 2008, LPGA Commissioner Carolyn Bivens implemented an English-speaking only policy in order to improve the marketability of Asian golfers (Dorman, 2008). Although its aims were to help international players gain sponsorship, this policy actually damaged existing and potential sponsorship relationships (Wheaton, 2008). The policy required players to speak English during tournament Pro-Ams, media interviews and winner acceptance speeches (Stensvaag, 2009). The policy required only a basic level of communication in English rather than fluency or proficiency (Stensvaag, 2009). Players could be suspended if they did not pass an English oral exam within two years (Stensvaag, 2009).

The implementation of this policy was considered discriminatory towards the South Korean players. Although there were 121 international players from 26 different countries, Commissioner Carolyn Bivens met with the 45 South Korean players (Stensvaag, 2009) separately from the other 76 other international players.

The English-only rule was designed to increase the marketability of the international players. Unfortunately, the LPGA did not discuss its plans with its corporate sponsors who would have encouraged the LPGA not to implement the rule (Wheaton, 2008). This controversial rule drew complaints from lawmakers, sponsors and interest groups. Kip Diggs, State Farm media relations specialist, said the company would reconsider its sponsorship unless the LPGA removed the directive (Wheaton, 2008). The LPGA revoked the policy just two weeks after its proposal, but the damage had already been done (Stensvaag, 2009). The effects of the rule were lasting. State Farm did not renew its LPGA sponsorship in 2010 (Burke, 2012).

Strategic recommendations

Golf is a traditional and elitist sport (Leonard, 2013). The LPGA and the entire golf industry suffered from the 2008 financial crash because consumers had insufficient discretionary income to afford to play on luxury courses (Leonard, 2013). Once the financial environment improved, the golf industry needed to work to gain consumers.

Asian sponsorship opportunities

The influx of golf in Asia and Southeast Asia created new sponsorship markets. The LPGA must focus on Asian sponsors for the Asian markets. The golf markets in Asia continue to grow (Gammage, 2013). Korea and Japan established golf in the 1980s, and China is showing tremendous potential for growth (Gammage, 2013). Japan is a small country with very little room for expansive golf courses, yet people are willing to travel long distances just to get to a course to play a round of 18 holes (Gregory, 1995). Japan shows excellent potential for LPGA sponsorship because Japanese businessmen and company CEOs conduct business on the golf course (Gregory, 1995).

Asian markets provide significant media rights potential. The LPGA broadcast rights for South Korea grew from US$60,000 in 1994 to US$2.25 million in 2009, and then to over US$4.0 million in 2010 (Lee, Park, Kang & Lee, 2013). Unlike most of the world, South Korea supports its female golfers more than its male Korean golfers (Lim, 2009). South Korea has broadcast every LPGA tournament since 1998. Both Korean and foreign companies engaging in the Korean market should take advantage of this sport opportunity.

Golf in China has also shown significant growth. Since 2010, over 136 new golf courses have been constructed in China bringing the total to almost 600 (Gammage, 2013). There are more than 1.3 million golfers in China. The Chinese market watches golf on television. According to an HSBC study, "the TV audience for golf stands at 39.7 million [in China], greater than the total 31.1 million of the United States and the United Kingdom" (Gammage, 2013, para. 22). However, due to the buyer power of China's citizens, "the value of a Chinese viewer is only one-twentieth that of an American viewer" (Gammage, 2013, para. 22).

Marketing international players

In 1968, Sandra Post from Canada became the first international player to gain her LPGA tour card (Lim, 2009). In 1998, the LPGA had 122 international players from over 25 countries. International players like Annika Sorenstam of Sweden, Lorena Ochoa of Mexico and Se Ri Pak of Korea became stars on the LPGA tour (Lim, 2009). The success of these international players overshadowed that of American golfers. The LPGA needs to give fans a reason to watch and support both their American and international players (Fitch, Ozanian & Badenhausen, 2010). Spectators watch sporting events because they connect to sport organizations (Robinson *et al.*'s 2004) and to individual athletes like golfers. Robinson *et al.* (2004) described "Arnie's Army" as fans who followed their favourite golfer, Arnold Palmer.

Paharia, Keinan, Avery and Schor (2010) recommend using underdog narratives, delivering to consumers through a brand biography that presents the origins, life experiences and evolution over time, in order to connect to fans. Brand biographies could be commercials about athletes overcoming challenges, such as the one used to highlight the difficult upbringing experienced by the swimmer Michael Phelps (Paharia *et al.*, 2010, p. 776).

The LPGA can also feature its own players such as Stacey Lewis, an American who had childhood scoliosis and was required to wear a back brace for 18 hours a day, only removing it to play golf, until she eventually underwent a spinal fusion ("Stacey's story", 2009). Lewis found herself entering the final round of the 2008 US Women's Open with a one-stroke lead (Shefter, 2008). If she had won this tournament, she would have been the first LPGA golfer to win a major tournament at her professional debut (Shefter, 2008). These inspirational stories can connect the LPGA players with their fans and sponsors.

Conclusion

The LPGA has faced severe difficulties acquiring and retaining sponsors for its tournaments. This is because it lacked a strong US fan base, and the inexistence of a marketable, celebrity superstar made it difficult for the LPGA to connect with sponsors. The key to the LPGA's future success is Asian sponsorship revenue, specifically in South Korea, Japan and China. The LPGA must develop more in-depth profiles of their top players in order to create a connection between players and fans. This can be used to market American players to the United States, but also to depict the LPGA's Asian players in a more positive light. With rising numbers of South Koreans and other international players on tour, the LPGA can no longer try to ignore their existence. By showing American fans what these players are like off the course, international players could become more marketable in the US. There are millions of golf fans in the US, and the LPGA simply needs to create awareness about how exceptional their players are and ensure that future fans are exposed to these golfers.

References

Amis, J., & Cornwell, B. (2005). Sport sponsorship in a global age. *Global Sport Sponsorship*. New York, NY: Berg.

Burke, M. (2012, May 15). The LPGA's Michael Whan on the state of his tour, foreign players and Augusta's female problem. *Forbes*. Retrieved from <www.forbes.com/sites/monteburke/2012/05/15/the-lpgas-michael-whan-on-the-state-of-his-tour-foreign-players-and-augustas-female-problem/>. Accessed 15 June 2016.

Capell, K., Lindorff, D., Moore, J. & Takahashi, T. (1997). Tiger may drive Asia's golf nuts even wilder. *Businessweek* (3524), 37.

Copeland, R., Frisby, W. & McCarville, R. (1996). Understanding the sport sponsorship process from a corporate perspective. *Journal of Sport Management*, *10*(1), 32–48.

Dorman, L. (2008). "Fore! And it had better be in English". *International Herald Tribune* (28 August).

Farrelly, F. (2010). Not playing the game: Why sport sponsorship relationships break down. *Journal of Sport Management*, *24*(3), 319–337.

Fenton, W. (2009). The global sponsorship market. *Journal of Sponsorship*, *2*(2), 120–130.

Fitch, S., Ozanian, M. & Badenhausen, K. (2010). When big money doesn't play ball. *Forbes Asia*, *6*(1), 82–83.

Gammage, J. (2013) "China quickly evolving into a links-loving nation". The *Philadelphia Inquirer* (15 June). Retrieved from <http://articles.philly.com/2013-06-15/news/39994552_1_golf-legend-jack-nicklaus-east-asia-courses>. Accessed 17 June 2016.

Gregory, S. (1995). The secret to a successful business relationship is golf. *Asian Business Review*, 101.

Lee, Y. H., Park, I., Kang, J. & Lee, Y. (2013). An economic analysis of the sudden influx of Korean female golfers into the LPGA. In *Handbook on the Economics of Women in Sports* (pp. 388–410). Northampton, MA: Edward Elgar Publishing.

Leonard, T. (2013). "The evolution of the world of golf". The *San Diego Union Tribune* (19 October 2013). Retrieved from <www.utsandiego.com/news/2013/Oct/19/pga-country-club-golf-tiger-woods/>. Accessed 5 May 2015.

Lim, S. (2009). Racial and sexual discrimination occurring to Korean players on the LGPA Tour. *The University of Tennessee Research and Creative Exchange*. Retrieved from <http://trace.tennessee.edu/utk_graddiss/67>.

LPGA history (2013). *The LPGA* (15 November). Retrieved from <www.lpga.com/tcp/historytcp.aspx>. Accessed 21 June 2016.

Paharia, N., Keinan, A., Avery, J. & Schor, J. (2010). The underdog effect: The marketing of disadvantage and determination through brand biography. *Journal of Consumer Research*, *37*, 775–790.

Robinson, M., Trail, G. & Kwon, H. (2004). Motives and points of attachment of professional golf spectators. *Sport Management Review*, 7, 167–192.

Rubenstein, L. (2010), June 26. "LPGA looking for someone to fill the void". The *Globe and Mail* (26 June) (Canada). Retrieved from <www.theglobeandmail.com/sports/golf/someone-needs-to-fill-the-lpga-void/article1373918/>.

Shaw, S. & Amis, J. (2001). Image and investment: Sponsorship and women's sports. *Journal of Sport Management*, *15*(3), 219–246.

Shefter, D. (2008). Welcome to the show: Lewis leads in first pro event. *USGA U.S. Women's Open*. Retrieved from <www.uswomensopen.com/2008/news/sat_final.html>. Accessed 2 June 2016.

Sirak, R. (2011). LPGA loses State Farm as title sponsor. *Golf Digest* (25 February). Retrieved from <www.golfdigest.com/golf-tours-news/blog/localknowledge/2011/02/lpga-loses-state-farm-as-title-sponsor.html>. Accessed 2 July 2015.

Spain, S. (2012). LPGA lacks a connection with viewers. *ESPNW*. Retrieved from <http://espn.go.com/espnw/news-commentary/article/8390420/how-increase-lpga-tour-exposure>. Accessed 21 May 2016.

Stacy's Story. (2009). *Scoliosis Research Society*. Retrieved from <www.srs.org/stacy_lewis/about.php>. Accessed 21 May 2016.

Statistics (2013). *LPGA Tour*. Retrieved from <www.lpga.com/stats/golf-stats.aspx>. Accessed 24 July 2016.

Stensvaag, J. (2009). English-only rules: Title VII, Title II, and the Ladies Professional Golf Association's proposed English-only rule. *Journal of Gender, Race & Justice*, *13*, 241–273.

United States Golf Association [USGA] history. (2013). *USGA*. Retrieved from <www.usga.org/about_usga/history/USGA-History-1894-1910/>.

United States Golf Association [USGA] mission statement. (2013). *USGA*. Retrieved from <www.usga.org/about_usga/mission/Mission/>. Accessed 4 June 2014.

Voepel, M. (2012). How to increase LPGA's exposure: Parity a tough sell. *ESPNW*. Retrieved from <http://espn.go.com/espnw/news-commentary/article/8390420/how-increase-lpga-tour-exposure>. Accessed 30 December 2016.

Walraven, M., Koning, R. H. & Van Bottenburg, M. (2012). The effects of sports sponsorship: A review and research agenda. *Marketing Review*, *12*(1), 17–38.

Wheaton, K. (2008). Understand this, LPGA: Sponsors deserve better. *Advertising Age* (8 September).

Women in distress (2009). The *Wall Street Journal* (9 November). Retrieved from <http://online.wsj.com/article/SB10001424052748704888404574547943968191648.html>. Accessed 30 December 2016.

26

SPORTS MEDIA COMPLEX AND THE BUSINESS OF FOOTBALL IN AFRICA

Gerard A. Akindes

Introduction

The global sport broadcasting landscape has transformed substantially since the 1990s. These transformations have led to an increased competition for broadcasting rights acquisition. The capability for satellite broadcasting to reach a global market induces competition for a transnational audience. This competition by broadcasters has generated an exponential revenue growth for selected leagues, global sport governing bodies, clubs, franchises and players. With the global transformation of sport broadcasting, African competitions and sport audiences have become an integral part of the business of sport broadcasting. How have these transformations affected the business of sport in Africa?

This chapter analyses the impact that satellite TV has had on African football. The first part of the chapter outlines the history of television in Africa from its inception until the satellite transformation. The next part shows the implications of the media transformation for the key players of African football broadcasting. The chapter concludes with a discussion of the challenges that satellite TV broadcasting presents to the economic development of African football.

Television in Africa – a postcolonial media

In most South sub-Saharan African (SSA) countries, the availability of television has accompanied political decolonization, although British colonizers introduced it in Nigeria, Zimbabwe and Zambia (Bourgault, 1995). The first TV station in Africa started broadcasting in 1959 in Nigeria (Betiang, 2014, p. 1). In francophone SSA, television broadcasting began in 1962 in Congo Brazzaville with the assistance of a French company (Dioh, 2009). By the late 1980s, all SSA countries had television broadcasting.

North African television broadcasting is also a post-independence media phenomenon (Ziyati & Akindes, 2014). William Rugh (2004) indicates that all North African countries launched television broadcasting from 1960. Egypt was the first country to start television broadcasting, followed by the Maghreb.

In South Africa, the evolution of television broadcasting was defined more by the history of the apartheid regime. South African television broadcasting started in 1974 under apartheid

(Angelopulo & Potgieter, 2013a, p. 13; Leslie, 1995, p. 165) with the South Africa Broadcasting Corporation (SABC).

Although each country had a distinct history of television broadcasting, there are a few noticeable commonalities. Television broadcasting in all African countries was originally state-owned and controlled. The exception was North Africa, where Arabic is the official language, not French or English. Colonial languages rather than local languages dominated broadcasting (Ba, 1996; Mytton, Teer-Tomaselli & Tudesq, 2005). In SSA, production facilities were often under-developed; thus content depended on imported material (Ba, 1996; Mytton et al., 2005). These generalities remained valid until the late 1980s.

Democratization and privatization

Transnational television became possible in Africa for three basic reasons: new television technology, telecommunications and information technology and the deregulation of media (Mytton et al., 2005). By the 1980s, viewers with the appropriate receiver, decoder or satellite dish could access a wide range of satellite television channels. By 2016, numerous communication and telecommunication satellites provided free or pay-TV broadcasting across all political borders. Satellite television rendered state-owned television monopolies obsolete. Paterson (1998, p. 575) noted that satellite television added pressure to the already growing movements for democratization and economic liberalization in the early 1990s. Deregulation of media policies followed, coinciding with democratization, ending the monopoly of state-owned media in most African countries. Privately owned broadcasters emerged. New broadcasting technologies and satellite television had a revolutionary impact on the African mediascape and on Africans' consumption of televised content and sports programming.

Transnationalism and satellite broadcasting

The most important groups supplying the African audience through satellite were established outside the continent. From the late 1980s to the early 1990s, it became possible, with the right satellite dish and receiver, to watch content broadcast by the French Canal Horizons, Arab and South European broadcasters and, later, South African Multichoice. The dominant broadcasting languages of the transnational broadcasters were instrumental in defining their target audience and their preferences. The countries' official languages (French, Arabic and English) linguistically segmented the African audience. Figure 26.1 shows this relationship.

French transnational television in Africa

Satellite television technology facilitated access to French-speaking African viewers. By the early 1990s, three major francophone broadcasters were supplying programmes and sports broadcasting to several countries. France reformed its own government-owned media system in response to global, transnational broadcasting changes. Canal France International (CFI) was created in May 1989 to supply programmes to francophone television in Africa via satellite (Mytton et al., 2005). Until 2012, CFI provided selected European Champions Leagues' games free of charge to SSA television broadcasters.

TV5 is the second transnational French-speaking broadcaster, joining the air in francophone Africa in 1992. Initially, the broadcaster was termed TV5 Europe, providing material produced in France, French Belgium, Switzerland and Quebec-Canada. Viewers consider TV5 to be "francophonie television" more than CFI – not French television, but television

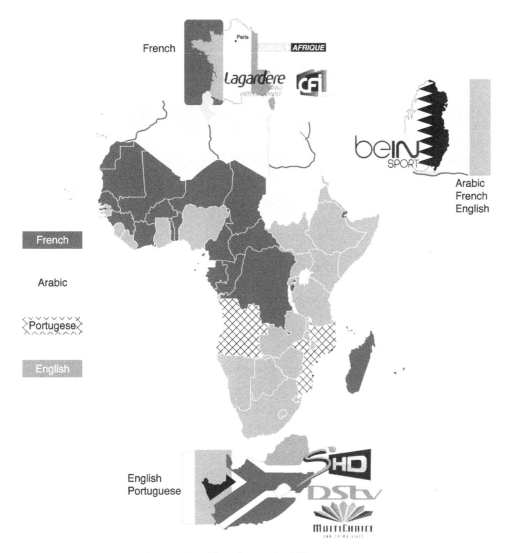

Figure 26.1   Language and transnational broadcasters in Africa

belonging to 51 French-speaking countries or regions. Sports programming with selected French football league and African competitions are broadcast by TV5.

Canal+ is the first privately owned television in France. Canal+ created Canal+ Horizons as its international affiliate in 1991 and launched Canal+ Sport in 2002. Canal+ Horizons was the first to provide pay-per-view television to francophone Africa and started broadcasting in 1991 in Senegal, Côte d'Ivoire, and Tunisia ("Historique – CANAL+ GROUPE", n.d.; MultiTV AFRIQUE, n.d.). Francophone SSA became, with time, the fastest growing pay-tv market for Canal+ Horizons African. A 2013 report by the Vivendi Group, the holding owner of Canal+, claims a strong growth, with 350,000 new African subscribers in 2013 (Vivandi Group, 2013).

CFI and TV5 continue to be part of the African mediascape as free-to-air television. Canal+ Horizons, in contrast, expanded and became the most significant French-speaking pay-TV supplier on the continent.

Gerard A. Akindes

South Africa in anglophone Africa

The trajectory of the mediascape transformation in English-speaking Africa was in different hands. South African conglomerate, Multichoice (owner of DStv, a multichannel satellite broadcaster) and Supersport were the main players in the anglophone arena. South Africa initiated media reform and liberalization under the apartheid regime, awarding the first license for pay-tv to Naspers, a consortium of newspaper publishers and media conglomerates, in 1986. They launched M-Net, an analog service, in 1992 (Multichoice, n.d.). M-Net then became Multichoice in 1993 and MIH Holdings in 1996 (Angelopulo & Potgieter, 2013b). Following the launch in 1995 of DStv, the digital satellite TV service across Africa, Multichoice became the main television satellite service provider in more than 20 African countries (Multichoice, n.d.). By the end of apartheid, Multichoice was established as a dominant satellite pay-TV provider in South Africa and across the continent (Alegi, 2010, p. 107). DStv is now available in more than 50 SSA countries ("MultiChoice Africa: Company History", n.d.).

By the early 2000s, Canal+ Horizons and Multichoice's DStv were in the leading position as pay-TV and satellite television providers in SSA. The early presence of sport broadcasting and, more specifically, football broadcasting with Canal+ Sport and Supersport shaped how Canal+ Horizons and Multichoice supplied television content to their subscribers in that part of Africa. In North Africa, because of the predominance of an Arabic-speaking audience and the geographic proximity to the Middle East and southern Europe, the dynamic of transnational television had a different trajectory.

The Arab transformation

North Africa was widely exposed to southern Europe and the far more influential Arabian Gulf free-to-air satellite television broadcasting. In 1985, the Arab league created the ambitious Arab Satellite Communications Organization (Arabsat) in Riyadh, Saudi Arabia, in order to enhance satellite communications in the Arab world. The launch of several communication satellites, such as Arabsat and Nilesat by Egypt and Orbit Communications in Saudi Arabia, led to a diversification of entertainment sources, particularly for football viewers (Chouikha, 2007). The emergence of television giants such as Arab Radio and Television (ART), Orbit and Al Jazeera Sports (now beIN SPORTS) radically transformed Middle Eastern and North African television broadcasting. In 2003, nearly 90 Arab satellite channels competed for over 71 million viewers in the region (Amara, 2007).

To summarize, by the early 1990s, the African mediascape was vastly altered for several reasons – democratization, media policy liberalization and new satellite broadcast technology. These factors pressured the government-owned content providers to change (Ba, 1996; Bourgault, 1995; Chalaby, 2005; Eribo & Jong-Ebot, 1997; Hydén, Leslie & Ogundimu, 2002). Media policies became more liberal as significant advancements in technology rendered state monopolies on television content obsolete (Mytton *et al.*, 2005). Thus transnational television broadcasters gained unprecedented transborder access to African audiences.

By the end of the 1990s, three main transnational television broadcasters were well established: the South African conglomerate Multichoice in 1993, French Canal+ Horizons in 1990, and Qatari Al Jazeera Sports in 2003. These international broadcasters recognized the important role of sport in capturing the pay-TV market share. Canal+ created its own sport channel, Canal+ Sport, in 2002. Multichoice created Supersport as a sport-exclusive content supplier in 1993. Al Jazeera Sports became beIN SPORTS in 2013. Canal+ Horizons was limited to five specialized sport channels, but Multichoice and Al Jazeera established

280

specialized sport entities with multiple sport channels. Miller *et al.* noted that Rupert Murdoch described sport as a "battering ram" into new television markets, and that executives at Telecommunication Corporation (TCI) called live matches "the universal glue for global content" (Miller, Lawrence, McKay & Rowe, 2004). In fact, to Canal Horizons, beIN SPORTS and Supersport, this was true: sport was definitely the "battering ram" mentioned by Rupert Murdoch. These companies used sport to grow their pay-TV market in Africa (Miller *et al.*, 2004, p. 90). Because football has been the most popular sport in terms of participation and viewership, football was consistently the king in supporting transnational broadcasters' expansion into pay-TV markets.

International football broadcasting and pay-TV

New technologies, deregulation and the liberalization of media across Africa have significantly increased audience access to football programming. Football broadcasting appeared initially as one of the best ways in which to capture viewers. In fact, from the early years of transnational broadcasting to African audiences, sport content represented 25 per cent of Canal Horizon programmes (Mytton *et al.*, 2005). Canal very early acquired the rights to the French football league, Ligue1, and became a key company in football broadcasting in France.

Canal+ Horizons – since its first broadcast in Africa – is the leading pay-TV company throughout French-speaking Africa. Canal+ Sport channels are available in Africa for US$20 per month and give access to all the sport programming supplied by Canal+ in France. Content such as live French Ligue1 games, selected European leagues' games and UEFA competitions are accessible to the African audience with no linguistic adaptation. Francophone audiences prefer to watch their games, when available, on French Canal+ because of the high production quality and the expertise of the pundits. Vidacs (1999) argues that for technical reasons, Cameroonians prefer games on French broadcasts, as is the case for the European Champions League games supplied. Canal+ Horizons subscriptions for public viewing in improvised "video theatres" across francophone cities (as discussed by Akindes, 2013) show how Canal+ Horizons' football programming contributes to the pay-tv penetration. Canal+ Horizons has dominated transnational sports broadcasting in francophone Africa since the early 1990s.

In English-speaking Africa, the dominant company supplying sport is the South African conglomerate Multichoice (with its satellite TV provider, DStv, and sport group, Supersport). A tour of the current website of Supersport shows 15 channels. There are 18 different sport competitions programmed (local, regional and global). The number of subscriptions to Supersport packages is not publicly known. However, in 2014, DStv announced more than five million subscribers in South Africa and more than three million household subscribers in the rest of Africa (Naspers – Integrated Report, 2014). Supersport offerings expanded with high-definition HD technology. After announcing its first HD channel in 2013 (Digital TV Europe, 2013), Supersport added seven more HD channels in 2014 (Digital TV Europe, 2014).

North Africa's proximity to Europe and the Middle East created a unique transnational crossroad. As described by Ziyati and Akindes (2014), the privately owned Saudi broadcaster, ART, attempted to control international football television by acquiring the right to show the FIFA World Cup in 2006. This attempt was not successful. Instead of paying a subscription fee to watch the World Cup, most viewers opted for alternative legal or illegal broadcasting from free-to-air European TV (e.g. German ZDF, French TF, Swiss TV and so forth). ART's experience as a pay-TV supplier has not been a success in North Africa. In 2010, ART TV Sports was acquired by Al Jazeera (Ziyati & Akindes, 2014). Al Jazeera Sports (now beIN SPORTS) became the main transnational supplier of international football competitions in North Africa. With the exception of local leagues broadcasting to a domestic audience, beIN SPORTS has a *de facto* monopoly in this region over international competitions such as the FIFA World Cup, the African Cup of Nations and the UEFA Champions League.

Satellite broadcasters Canal Horizons, beIN SPORTS and Supersport have transformed African access to football (a trend detailed in Akindes, 2013, 2014; Alegi, 2010; Owumelechili & Akindes, 2014). Thus access to satellite pay-TV from Canal Horizons and DStv with SuperSport and beIN SPORTS has boosted African audiences' accessibility to European football leagues and international football. African football fans can watch the most prestigious and globally popular leagues such as the English Premier League, the Spanish la Liga, the German Bundesliga, the French Ligue1 and the Italian Serie A. The major transnational broadcasters' capacity to acquire the most prestigious football competitions with high viewership made them the main suppliers of the top European leagues. Their respective programming of these competitions (live and replay) demonstrates their tacit geo-linguistic distribution of the African sport pay-TV viewership in situations where the role of the private or government-owned and controlled local television broadcaster is not significant.

The monopoly of Supersport, Canal+ Horizons and beIN SPORTS over international football content broadcasting in Africa has an important economic impact. Figure 26.2 shows broadcasting rights acquisition by broadcasters.

None of the competitions played in Africa and followed weekly by football fans in bars and special viewing spaces using satellite subscriptions (Akindes, 2013, 2014; Owumelechili & Akindes, 2014) generates any revenue to African football, clubs or leagues. The rights owners are European leagues, confederations and clubs, and they are the first beneficiaries of the broadcasting rights paid by the transnational broadcasters, regardless of the target audience. The broadcasting of European major football leagues and competitions with satellite and HD technology has digitized the viewing experience of African football fans with world-class broadcasting quality. Fan enthusiasm in Africa for European teams, however, does little for Africa's own local football. An analysis of the broadcasting-rights dynamic related to African football and competitions reveals different flows of revenue connecting African football governing bodies, leagues, national teams and clubs to the local and transnational broadcasters.

Broadcasting rights in sub-Saharan Africa

Technological advances and the liberalization of broadcasting laws led to the introduction of a new, global, private television media market. Since the 1980s, the television rights market has been a supply-side cartel facing the demand side, represented by various television channels (Andreff & Szymanski, 2006). With the increase in the number of television stations (both public and private) and transnational broadcasters, sports broadcasting rights acquisition became very competitive. Broadcasting rights revenues increased and continued to increase in the dominant European football and USA sport markets and for global events such as the FIFA World Cup and the Olympics.

The Confederation of African Football (CAF)

The Confederation of African Football is one of the most successful supplier-driven cases of the transnational television broadcasting rights economy in Africa. In 2000, the CAF signed a contract with French businessman and CEO of Sportfive, Jean-Claude Darmon, enabling it to broadcast four CAF competitions for US$50 million (Potet, 2002). In 2006, Sportfive was acquired by the French conglomerate, Lagardère Unlimited. Thus Sportfive had already

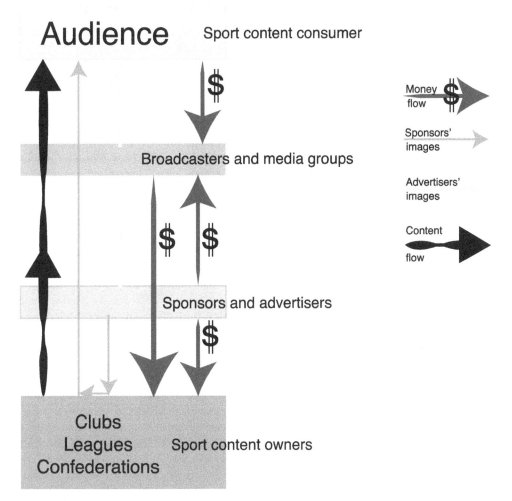

Figure 26.2 Content and money flow

monopolized the broadcasting of CAF competitions and then, as part of Lagardère Sports and Entertainment, renewed the contract with CAF until 2028 (Lagardère Sports and Entertainment, n.d.). This situation illustrates how satellite television broadcasting and media deregulation contributed to the privatization of Africa's elite football broadcasting economy.

Satellite television broadcasting and the transforming economics of football and media also gave CAF an opportunity to embrace the broadcasting rights economy and generate media and sponsorship revenues (Alegi, 2010, p. 110). Prior to the broadcasting rights opportunities, with Sportfive, CAF had limited opportunities for revenue generation beyond sponsorship and the early rights acquisition for Europe by Eurosport and by ART for the Arab world. Transnational broadcasting rights acquisition of African football competitions propelled CAF into the contemporary economic model of global sports where television broadcasting drives revenues. Besides the example of CAF's economic transformation, Supersport is another prominent illustration of how broadcasting rights have impacted the economic transformation of African football.

Supersport and broadcasting rights in sub-Saharan Africa

Since its inception, Supersport has aggressively acquired sports broadcasting rights for South African and international sports leagues and competitions. Rights acquisition evolved in three directions. The first priority was the early acquisition of international games, competitions and championships. The second focus was the South African sport market with local leagues, clubs and competitions. The third direction was the acquisition of local league games, championships and African competitions.

In the early 1990s, Supersport acquired the rights to broadcast international competitions such as the ICC Cricket World Cup in 1992. Supersport also acquired (in 1996) the television broadcasting rights for South Africa of the SANZAAR (South African, New Zealand, Australia and Argentina Rugby) Southern Hemisphere Rugby competition. This is often simply called "the Rugby championship". International competitions' broadcasting rights soon followed, such as the Olympics, various sport world championships and international tournaments. Since 2000, such offerings have been consistently available in Supersport's multiple channel programming. Supersport's programming brochure and website make it clear that very few popular international or continental competitions are not broadcast by that supplier.

In South Africa, their business strategy was extensive. Supersport rapidly pursued a national expansion of the most popular sports. As mentioned by Paul Smith (2016, p. 74), Multichoice's commercial strategy through Supersport for the past two decades was to provide wide television coverage of the popular sports in South Africa. By 2008, Smith argues, Multichoice controlled the coverage rights to virtually all South African broadcasts of domestic and international rugby and cricket (2016, p. 75). Around the same period, Multichoice added football to its sports broadcasting rights package.

The acquisition of the broadcasting rights of the Premier Soccer League (PSL) in 2007 was another significant moment that sealed Supersport's grip on South African domestic sport content. For example, Supersport outbid the government-owned SABC to acquire the rights to the PSL for more than US$114 million for a five-year deal, three times more than SABC's initial deal with the PSL (Cornelissen & Solberg, 2007, p. 306; Smith, 2016, p. 15). But part of the PSL's games remained free-to-air, due to several factors (Bob, Cornelissen, & Swart, n.d.; Cornelissen & Solberg, 2007; Smith, 2016) such as the racial history of South Africa, socioeconomic considerations and legal battles. After an agreement with SABC, the television rights of selected games of the PSL were sold to SABC for a free-to-air diffusion. Instead of an exclusive diffusion of PSL games, the broadcasting rights were shared between SABC and Supersport. Supersport renewed the deal with the PSL in 2011 for US$277.5 million over five years (Emmett, 2011).

The appetite of Supersport for domestic sport television rights acquisition was substantial in transforming the financial viability of South African football – now considered the richest sub-Saharan league and one of the continent's richest (Cornelissen & Solberg, 2007; Darby & Solberg, 2010). Multichoice's investment in South African football and television coverage of the PSL led to an increase in sponsorship and advertisement revenues for the South African PSL. The media nexus and the strong dependency of football on television rights are now built into the South African sport economy. Without any substantial competition from government or private local broadcasters, Supersport acquired far-ranging rights to the most popular South African leagues and competitions. The company continues to consolidate its quasi-monopoly on sports content on pay-TV in South Africa and beyond.

Multichoice's aggressive continental broadcasting rights acquisition evolved rapidly as well. In addition to acquiring the rights to the most popular international and continental competitions, such as the African Cup of Nations, Supersport localized its strategy by targeting football league rights in selected countries. For example, Multichoice acquired the broadcasting rights or engaged in a partnership with the Nigerian Football League in 2006 (allAfrica.com, 2006). Several African leagues signed with Supersport as well. In 2007, Zambia signed its first contract with Supersport. In 2008, the Kenyan Premier League (KPL) was broadcast live by Supersport. In 2013, Supersport signed with the Ghana Football Association (McPherson, 2013).

Since entering the SSA mediascape, Supersport has become the main player there. Gary Rathbone, a former executive of Supersport's division in Africa (outside South Africa), called the venture a success (Edwards, 2013). Rathbone believes that the business partnership of Supersport with the Kenyan Premier League (KPL) has brought football fans back into the stadium and attracted more sponsors. This claim was bolstered when the two most popular teams, Gor Mahhia FC and Leopards FC, had sold-out games (Akindes, 2014). Supersport does not disclose the amount paid for broadcasting rights to the KPL or the impact of their partnership on DStv subscriptions. The limited financial transparency of football governing bodies in Africa does not provide the necessary data to compare and correlate Supersport's involvement with the economic growth of KPL. It is therefore challenging to estimate how much this partnership has established an economic interdependency between a television broadcaster and a football league. Is it comparable to the interdependency in place in European leagues? It would seem logical to assume so. Despite the financial secrecy of broadcasting rights contracts between Supersport and various SSA FAs, a few observations can be made.

First, the news publicly announcing the deals does not mention any competition. So far, competition for acquiring local leagues' television broadcasting rights has not materialized in any African country. The technological and financial capacity of domestic broadcasters remains limited. These companies also seem uninterested in local sport teams and their events. In many countries, the government-owned broadcasters had often covered selected games, especially when a head of state was in the audience during a final. These practices, still in place, happened without formal commercial agreements between the league and the broadcaster.

Second, the countries selected are all English-speaking countries, with an already-established DStv subscription base and sizeable populations. During an interview, Rathbone posits that the business rationale of Supersport was primarily driven by subscription to DStv. He stated:

> For us, it is about where our audience is; we select areas where we have big sub-
> scriber bases. Even if you have the best football in the world and only ten people
> subscribe, you're wasting your money . . .. Zambia has a good league, but also a lot
> of Zambians live in Southern Africa and are a good audience for us. Our business is
> not sport, it's television. We leave sport to FIFA.
>
> *Rathbone, personal communication, 15 May 2015*

The last observation is to make note of the short length of the contracts. Comparable to broadcasting rights contracts in European football, Supersport agreements are for only three to five years. Several of the early contracts have been renewed without any major increase. In a non-competitive market, Supersport's business approach represents a limited risk for at least a decade. What are the chances for a new entrant? Without the emergence of a revolutionary broadcasting technology capable of bettering Multichoice's current production and broadcasting capacity, chances for a new entrant to compete with Supersport will depend more on structural changes in local broadcasting capacities and local football improvement (for example, upgrades in playing quality, infrastructure, management and the ability to consistently bring spectators to the games).

Multichoice grew as a result of successful broadcasting rights acquisition. Supersport's 24 sport channels (seven of which are HD) have made Supersport the dominant television sport content broadcaster in South Africa and in African English-speaking countries. Every English- or Portuguese-speaking African country has access to DStv and therefore SuperSport channels. Supersport even launched Supersport MaXimo in Portuguese in 2006 and subsequently extended its offerings to the lusophone audience to three separate channels.

In North Africa, the role of beIN SPORTS is comparable to the role of Canal+ Horizons and Supersport. Ziyati and Akindes (2014) consider that beIN SPORTS is now the only supplier of international sport to the North African audience. Although the local leagues' competitions are still controlled by the government or privately owned broadcasters, beIN SPORTS' acquisition of local leagues broadcasting rights with high audience potential is gradually happening. For instance, beIN SPORTS offered US$2.6 million to the Egyptian Football Association (EFA) (Ziyati & Akindes, 2014) to buy the broadcasting rights of the Egyptian Premier League in 2011. Otherwise, local football and competitions are not yet subject to broadcasters' demand in comparison to European football. BeIN SPORTS owns the broadcasting rights for the UEFA Champions League and the Europa Cup, CAF competitions and the most popular European leagues (the English Premier League, the Bundesliga, la Liga, the Serie A, and the Ligue1). As a transnational broadcaster with the financial backing of the State of Qatar, beIN SPORTS has a competitive advantage over any locally owned North African television broadcaster. With coverage in Arabic, English and French, beIN SPORTS' transnational programming captures all the official languages of North Africa.

The broadcasting rights' market and revenue capacity for African sports varies with the transnational broadcasters' strategies. Multichoice, Canal+ Horizons and beIN SPORTS owned the broadcasting rights of the most popular sports content such as European football, most of the CAF competitions and games and FIFA's main competitions including the World Cup. The transnational demand for such competitions creates an aggregate market, one that local leagues and competition cannot provide. In addition to their international sports broadcasting rights portfolio, Multichoice with Supersport are the most engaged with domestic leagues and competitions, and Canal+ Horizons is the least engaged. This distant engagement with African sport may transform as the current market growth slows down or welcomes new entrants. BeIN SPORTS already engaged with the Egyptian Football League and may extend their football monopoly in North Africa by acquiring local leagues' and competitions' broadcasting rights.

Conclusion

Rowe (2004), in discussing developed countries' sport and media relations, stated that sport and media supply each other with the capital, the audience and the content. The 1990s transformation of the African mediascape validates Rowe's argument to some extent. However, the main question is how capital, content and audience operate specifically in Africa. From a transnational perspective, African audiences, as viewers, are integral to a global transformation. The capital of the transnational broadcasters is invested in various international competitions' broadcasting rights. They also have capital in selected African football content to supply to the world (with Lagardère Sport and Media). But clearly, competitions such as the English Premier League have become the most popular televised sport content across Africa.

Africa has not been able to fully leverage the business potential of the sports broadcasting transformation initiated in the 1990s. Reasons for this include multiple factors related to the history of television, the financial and technological limitations of local broadcasters and the structural and managerial challenges of local leagues and clubs. Football and television in Africa have not been able to create an economic interdependency (as mentioned by Rowe). The exceptions are the Confederation of African Football competitions, South Africa and a few countries where Supersport is currently invested.

So television rights as a source of revenue for local leagues and clubs in Africa remain marginal. Figure 26.3 shows the commercial dimension of the relationship that inextricably binds media and sport. As explained by Nicholson (2007), the sport and media nexus is challenged in most African countries.

Nicholson's nexus has three main components: the flow of sport content, the flow of money and the consumers. These flows establish the "virtuous circle" of sport financing, illustrated in Figure 26.4. Starting the circle has prerequisites. Rathbone (2015) suggests that when television broadcasting is on board with a league, (1) games and competitions gain in visibility, (2) games attract more sponsors, and (3) with adequate marketing, TV brings spectators if the facility is comfortable and safe. It is important for television broadcasters to facilitate the content owners, the leagues or clubs to create the virtuous circle for African football's financial betterment. Leagues and clubs must currently work overtime on improving the quality of the content they supply to broadcasters and spectators. The virtuous circle could still gain the necessary momentum to sustain economically valuable leagues.

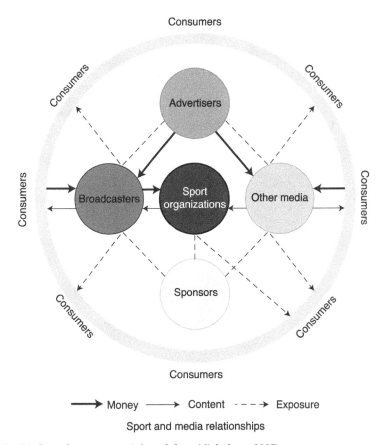

Figure 26.3 Media and sport nexus (adapted from Nicholson, 2007)

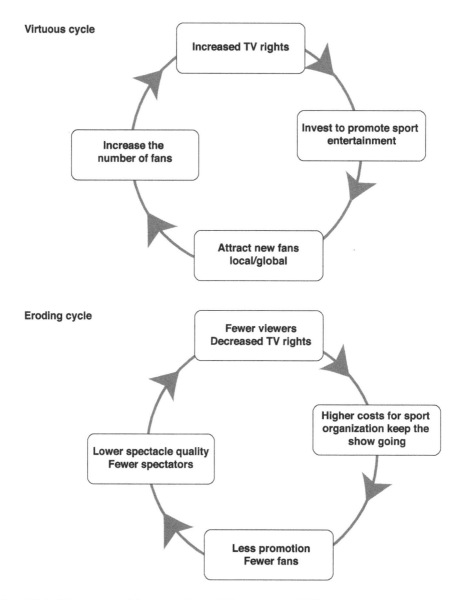

Figure 26.4 Virtuous and vicious cycle (adapted from Proctor, 1999)

Supersport's African–centred strategy demonstrates the viability of television broadcasters in financially engaging with local African football. However, the need for more competition across tacit linguistic barriers may lead to new entrants and more interest in local leagues and competitions.

Meanwhile, most leagues and clubs could increase their capacity to produce better games. Doing so helps avoid the vicious cycle that challenges the economic viability of most African football, especially the non-South African teams located in sub-Saharan Africa. An upheaval in broadcast technology could reshuffle the current monopolies and their priorities as radically as the popularization of satellite TV.

References

Akindes, G. (2013). Football bars: Urban sub-Saharan Africa's trans-local "stadiums". *International Journal of the History of Sport*, *28*(15), 2176–2190.

Akindes, G. (2014). From Stadium to Bars: Transnational Media and African Fan Identity. In *Identity and Nation in African Football: Fans, Community and Clubs* (p. 288). London: Palgrave Macmillan.

Alegi, P. (2010). *African Soccerscapes: How a Continent Changed the World's Game*. Athens: Ohio University Press.

allAfrica.com. (2006). Nigeria: As the League Goes Live. Retrieved from <http://allafrica.com/stories/200608250460.html>. Accessed 24 August 2016.

Amara, M. (2007). When the Arab world was Mobilized around the FIFA 2006 World Cup. *Journal of North African Studies*, *12*(4), 417–438.

Andreff, W. & Szymanski, S. (2006). *Handbook on the Economics of Sport*. Cheltenham, UK; Northampton, MA: Edward Elgar.

Angelopulo, G. & Potgieter, P. (2013). The economic specification of media ownership in South Africa communication. *South African Journal for Communication Theory and Research*, *39*(1), 1–19.

Ba, A. (1996). *Télévisions, paraboles et démocraties en Afrique noire*. Paris: L'Harmattan.

Betiang, L. (2014). Global drums and local masquerades: Fifty years of television broadcasting in Nigeria: 1959–2009. *SAGE Open*, *3*(4), 12.

Bob, U., Cornelissen, S. & Swart, K. (n.d.). South Africa. In *Managing Football: An International Perspective* (pp. 387–406). London: Elsevier.

Bourgault, L. M. (1995). *Mass Media in sub-Saharan Africa*. Bloomington: Indiana University Press.

Chalaby, J. K. (2005). *Transnational Television Worldwide: Towards a New Media Order*. London, New York: IB Tauris.

Chouikha, L. (2007). Satellite television in the Maghreb: Plural reception and interference of identities. *History and Anthropology*, *18*(3), 367–377.

Cornelissen, S. & Solberg, E. (2007). Sport mobility and circuits of power: The dynamics of football migration in Africa and the 2010 World Cup. *Politikon*, *34*(3), 295–314.

Darby, P. (1) & Solberg, E. (2). (2010). Differing trajectories: Football development and patterns of player migration in South Africa and Ghana. *Soccer and Society*, *11*(1–2), 118–130.

Digital TV Europe (2013). South Africa's SuperSport to launch new channels. Retrieved from <www.digitaltveurope.net/80312/south-africas-supersport-to-launch-new-channels/>. Accessed 18 July 2013.

Digital TV Europe (2014). SuperSport launches seventh HD channel on DStv. Retrieved from <www.digitaltveurope.net/171402/supersport-launches-seventh-hd-channel-on-dstv/>. Accessed 15 April 2014.

Dioh, T. (2009). *Histoire de la télévision en Afrique noire francophone, des origines à nos jours*. Paris: Khartala.

Edwards, P. (2013). Is satellite TV killing African football? Retrieved 9 October 2014, from <www.bbc.com/news/world-africa-21206500>. Accessed 10 September 2016.

Emmett, J. (2011). PSL renews agreement with Supersport. Retrieved from <www.sportspromedia.com/news/south_africas_renewed_psl_agreement_with_supersport>. Accessed 23 August 2016.

Eribo, F. & Jong-Ebot, W. (1997). *Press Freedom and Communication in Africa*. Trenton, NJ: Africa World Press.

Historique – CANAL+ GROUPE (n.d.). Retrieved from <www.canalplusgroupe.com/historique.html>. Accessed 23 August 2016.

Hydén, G., Leslie, M. & Ogundimu, F. F. (2003). *Media and Democracy in Africa*. New Brunswick, NJ: Transaction Publishers.

Lagardère Sports and Entertainment (n.d.). Lagardère Sports and Entertainment – Our history. Retrieved from <www.lagardere-se.com/about-us/our-history/#>. Accessed 23 October 2015.

Leslie, M. (1995). Television and capitalist hegemony in the "new" South Africa. *Howard Journal of Communications*, *6*(3), 164–172.

McPherson, I. (2013). SuperSport picks up Ghana Premier League rights. Retrieved from <www.sportspromedia.com/news/supersport_picks_up_ghana_premier_league_rights>. Accessed 24 August 2016.

Miller, T., Lawrence, G., McKay, J. & Rowe, D. (2004). Sports media sans frontières. In *Critical Readings: Sport, Culture and the Media* (pp. 84–98). Maidenhead, UK: Open University Press, McGraw-Hill.

Multichoice (n.d.). Company history. Retrieved from <www.multichoice.co.za/multichoice/content/en/page44122> Accessed 3 December 2016.

MultiChoice Africa (n.d.). Company history. Retrieved from <www.dstv.com/topic/multichoice-africa-company-history-20150721>. Accessed 22 August 2016.

MultiTV AFRIQUE (n.d.). Canal Plus Horizons (Tunisie) Télévision payante – Production (21 décembre 1991–17 octobre 2001). Retrieved from <www.africultures.com/php/index.php?nav=structure&no=2238>. Accessed 22 August 2016.

Mytton, G., Teer-Tomaselli, R. & Tudesq, A. J. (2005). *Transnational Television in Sub-Saharan Africa. Transnational Television Worldwide: Towards a New Media Order* (pp. 96–127). London: IB Tauris.

Naspers – Integrated Report (2014). Performance Review – Pay Television. Retrieved from <www.naspers-reports.com/2014/per-op-pay.php> Accessed 31 August 2016.

Nicholson, M. (2007). *Sport and the Media: Managing the Nexus*. Oxford; Burlington, MA: Elsevier.

Owumelechili, C. & Akindes, G. (2014). *Identity and Nation in African Football: Fans, Community and Clubs*. New York: Palgrave Macmillan.

Paterson, C. A. (1998). Reform or re-colonisation? The overhaul of African television. *Review of African Political Economy*, *25*(78), 571–583. Retrieved from <https://doi.org/10.1080/03056249808704344>.

Potet, F. (2002). Au bonheur des télévisions privées (Vol. 2002). Retrieved from <www.lemonde.fr/article/0,5987,3242--261143-VT,00.html>. Accessed 9 October 2016.

Proctor, K. (1999). Tendances et faits. *Diffusion UER Dossier Sports*, Hiver 1999–2000, 19–21.

Rathbone, G. (2015). [Personal communication], 15 May.

Rugh, W. A. (2004). *Arab Mass Media: Newspapers, Radio, and Television in Arab Politics*. Westport, CT: Greenwood Publishing Group.

Rowe, D. (2004). *Critical Readings: Sport, Culture and the Media*. Maidenhead, UK: Open University Press.

Smith, P. (2016). Television sports rights beyond the West: The cases of India and South Africa. *Global Media and Communication*, *12*(1), 67–83.

Vidacs, B. (1999). Football in Cameroon: A vehicle for the expansion and contraction of identity. *Sport in Society*, *2*(3), 100–117.

Vivandi Group (2013). Vivendi Group Annual Report [Annual Report] (p. 380). France. Retrieved from <www.vivendi.com/wp-content/uploads/2014/04/20140415_annual_report_doc_de_ref_2013_en.pdf>. Accessed 31 October 2014.

Ziyati, A. & Akindes, G. (2014). It's All About the Beautiful Game of Football, or Is It? On Television and Football in North Africa. In *Identity and Nation in African Football: Fans, Community and Clubs* (p. 36). New York: Palgrave Macmillan.

PART VI

Sport tourism

Although tourism has been vital to the economic development of many locations, sport tourism is a relatively new enterprise. Sport tourism includes three main categories: active or participatory sport tourism, event-based sport tourism, and sport facility/heritage tourism. Therefore, sport fans travel in order to play sport, watch sport or visit current and historical sport stadiums, arenas and other structures. The sport tourist travels to attend the FIFA World Cup, run the London Marathon, or visit the ancient ruins in Olympia, Greece. As more countries seek to develop their tourist sectors, their focus on sport in order to engage foreign visitors has grown.

The following chapters embrace sport tourism via different perspectives. However, the main theme connecting the chapters is that of serving the sport tourist. This tourist engages with sport via mega-events, small or local events and sport facilities. These chapters will help communities develop strategies to increase sport tourism.

27

GLOBAL SPORT TOURISM AND THE LURE OF MEGA-EVENTS

Brendon Knott and Kamilla Swart

Introduction

Despite the controversies surrounding FIFA, as well as the noted lack of public support for recent Olympic Games bids in Europe and North America, sport mega-events continue to be sought after and even considered as objects of policy among many developing nations. Within the broader business of sport tourism, this chapter highlights the role of mega-events and their associated legacies, particularly within the emerging nation context, using the case of South Africa as its reference.

The chapter discusses the role and significance of mega-events for the global tourism economy. It highlights how bidding for sport mega-events by nations has been promoted as an opportunity for generating a variety of legacies, from short-term tourism boosts, to longer-term tangible infrastructure and facility investments, and even to enhancing international reputation and brand image. From a theoretical perspective, the chapter clarifies the understanding of legacy and the types of legacies that can be expected from hosting sport mega-events, while it also sets out a number of practical recommendations for the sport tourism industry in order to leverage and sustain these legacies. The chapter uses many examples from the 2010 FIFA World Cup in South Africa. It also explores the experiences and lessons learnt by South African stakeholders from hosting the 2010 FIFA World Cup, based on empirical investigations conducted by the authors. While highlighting the value of mega-events, it questions the costs at which legacies are achieved and whether other event types could be successful in achieving the same benefits.

Mega-events and the business of sport tourism

Sport events have become an increasingly important component of global tourism economies (Cornelissen, 2007), becoming significant economic activities and making an important contribution to local and national economies in both the developed and the developing world. As a result, interest in hosting international sport events has continued to increase as destinations aim to reap the economic, socio-cultural and other benefits believed to derive from hosting such events.

Sport events occur on many different scales or levels, with the largest of these levels being the "mega-event". While definitions of mega-events are notoriously vague, it is useful to regard a mega-event as "distinctive, identified by the volume of visitors it attracts, economic revenue generated, and its psychological impact on attendees, that is, whether or not it is a 'must-see' event" (Hall & Hodges, 1997, p. 3). Mega-events usually require significant public funds to stage, and are thus unusual, or infrequent, in occurrence. They have significant economic and social impact, which is affected by the extent of the international dimension of the event. Getz (1997) further adds that mega-events are loaded with tradition, attract significant media attention at an international level and are often complemented by other smaller events that add to their greatness, such us parades and festivals.

Sports tourism is viewed as holding great potential for many of the emerging nation economies, particularly in the African continent. In South Africa, the industry is already fairly well established but still growing. Golf tourism, event tourism and adventure tourism are key drivers of the overall tourism market. South Africa has successfully hosted mega- and major sports events, such as the 1995 IRB Rugby World Cup, the 2003 ICC Cricket World Cup and the 2010 FIFA World Cup. Cape Town also bid for the 2004 Olympic Games, ultimately losing to Athens and continues to pursue bids for other sporting events. In many other African nations, there remain large untapped possibilities for the growth of this tourism niche market, particularly in the areas of adventure sports.

However, sport mega-events have received much criticism of late. The current global scandals surrounding FIFA, as well as other controversies linked with certain Olympic sports, combined with allegations of corruption and over-spending by recent FIFA and Olympic Games hosts, has resulted in a lack of popular support for recent bids for future mega-events from a number of cities. There is also a groundswell of opinion within the destination management literature that advocates a portfolio of events or the consideration of smaller, home-grown or non-sport events rather than continuing with a mega-event focus (e.g. Brown, Chalip, Jago & Mules, 2004; Chalip & Costa, 2005; Westerbeek & Linley, 2012).

Emerging nations and mega-events

Despite the criticism of mega-events within the developed world, sport mega-events have become increasingly important among emerging nations. So much so in fact, that they are now considered to be an object of policy for many nations. The powerful pursuit of the growing capital tied to the consumption of sport (Cornelissen, 2004) has made the quest for sport mega-events especially attractive to developing countries who are seeking heightened visibility and prestige within the context of globalization. Acquiring and hosting sport mega-events have become significant features in national and local development strategies (Nauright & Schimmel, 2005). Thus it is not surprising that BRICS (Brazil, Russia, India, China and South Africa) countries have been dominating the mega-event landscape in recent years, as illustrated in Table 27.1. Similarly, Japan will be hosting the 2019 Rugby World Cup, the first time in an Asian country, as well the 2020 Olympic Games, with Qatar hosting the FIFA World Cup for the first time in the Middle East. It is further evident from the global distribution of sport mega-events that second order mega-events such as the cricket and rugby World Cups have been hosted in emerging nations more regularly in comparison to first order mega-events such as the FIFA World Cup and Olympic Games.

Grix, Brannagan and Houlihan (2015) contend that Brazil's double host status (2014 FIFA World Cup and 2016 Olympic Games), provided that they both are hosted successfully, will in all likelihood be matched by political influence on the world stage as South Africa and China have shown as regular participants in multilateral summits such as the G20. However, there is much debate about the use of sport mega-events by emerging nations due to the opportunity

Table 27.1 BRICS emerging economies and sport mega-events

Country	Sport mega-events hosted (post-1990)
Brazil	2007 Pan-American Games
	2014 FIFA World Cup
	2016 Olympic Games
Russia	2014 Winter Olympic Games
	2018 FIFA World Cup
India	2010 Commonwealth Games
	2011 Cricket World Cup
China	2008 Olympic Games
	2015 IAAF World Athletics Championships
	2022 Winter Olympic Games
South Africa	1995 Rugby World Cup
	2003 Cricket World Cup
	2010 FIFA World Cup

costs being much higher as they have less money to fund basic needs of the population (Rocha, 2016). De Castro, Starepravo, Coakley and de Souza (2016, p. 383) argue that the proliferation of mega-events in emerging states results from business-based international non-government organizations such as the International Olympic Committee and FIFA moving their events to parts of the world where they are supported by "government officials seeking personal or state-based benefits combined with little resistance from the population that provides the labour and financial resources to host high-cost events" (de Castro *et al.*, 2016).

Mega-event legacies

The event impact literature is rather piecemeal, with mostly applied studies and economic analysis dominating (Dickinson & Shipway, 2007). While economic impact studies abound, there is growing recognition of the need to assess other impacts, such as the social, physical, environmental and tourism impacts of events and their interrelationships. Event impact studies have increased in importance, driven by the need to examine the positive and negative impacts of hosting events in order to justify public spending, and a need to leverage the best possible benefits for communities that host events. However, in the past decade, a longer-term impact approach has been advocated, with a focus on "legacy" (Cornelissen, Bob & Swart, 2011; Chappelet, 2012). The most recognized definition of event legacy is that it is considered as "all planned and unplanned, positive and negative, tangible and intangible structures created for and by a sport event that remains longer than the event itself" (Preuss 2007, p. 208).

Mega-events have differed in their approach to legacy planning. There have been more advances in formally establishing and passing on knowledge about event impacts of the Olympic Games than has been the case thus far with the FIFA World Cup. For example, the Olympic Games Global Impact (OGGI) project sets out to assess the economic and other impacts of the Games from their initial conceptualization, through to the bidding processes and their hosting, with the aim of evaluating the costs, legacies and yardsticks yielded by the experiences of Olympic host cities. However, a similar mechanism does not yet exist for the FIFA World Cup. Nevertheless, Cornelissen (2007, p. 248) maintains

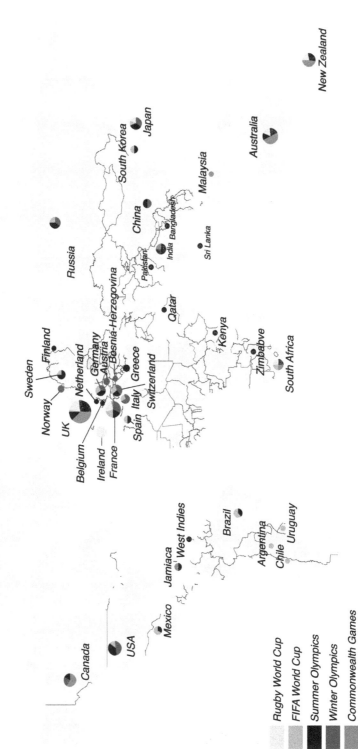

Figure 27.1 Global distribution of sport mega-events

Rugby World Cup
FIFA World Cup
Summer Olympics
Winter Olympics
Commonwealth Games
Cricket World Cup

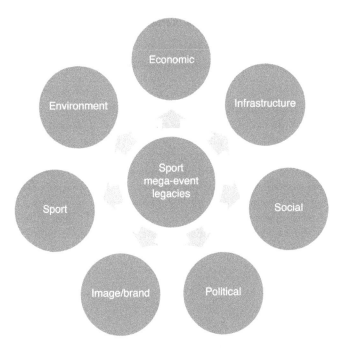

Figure 27.2 Sport mega-event legacies (adapted from Cornelissen *et al.* (2011), p. 311)

that "leaving appropriate long-term legacies has become a discourse which has left an indelible mark on the way in which planning for today's sport mega-events takes shape".

There are a variety of different types of legacies that can result from mega-events. These major areas/types of legacies are set out in Figure 27.2 and summarized below, with examples of legacies from the 2010 FIFA World Cup for the city of Cape Town given.

Infrastructure

This refers to the different types of networks, ranging from transport to telecommunications, which are renovated or developed for a mega-event and maintained after the event is complete. New access routes by air, water, road or rail are also part of the infrastructural legacy. For the 2010 FIFA World Cup, the South African government invested heavily in infrastructure upgrades, mainly on new stadiums, airport upgrades and public transport improvements. Examples of tourism infrastructure upgrades include the building of five new hotels in Cape Town alone, significant airport upgrades at Cape Town, Johannesburg and Port Elizabeth and a new airport in Durban and improved inner-city and airport transport links such as the "Gautrain" in Johannesburg. The infrastructure legacy also includes the buildings that were built for the mega-event but which serve no sporting function. These may also be changes that were made to the urban structure of the host city as well as the development of new urban districts and specialized areas. For example, the city of Cape Town developed a "fan walk" from the main train station in the city centre to the stadium. This included pedestrianization of roads, footbridges, city gentrification, improved security and general beautification of the area. There was also large-scale private investment in accommodation infrastructure, such as new hotels.

Economic

Usually this is the most frequently cited legacy area and is assessed by the changes in the number of permanent jobs created and in the unemployment rate of the host region, economic investment opportunities, foreign investment attraction and small business development/ entrepreneurship. The event creates opportunities for the host country/cities to engage in high-profile promotion of their products on a global scale. In South Africa, the hosting of the 2010 FIFA World Cup has highlighted the potential role that sport mega-events can play in promoting economic and developmental agendas. The total capital investment through public funds for the 2010 FIFA World Cup event was US$1.3 billion (Emmett, 2010a), while the total overall boost to the South African economy from the event was estimated to be US$13 billion over the six years preceding the event (Domingues, 2011). Sponsorship, television and hospitality revenues from the event were estimated at US$3.2 billion (Emmett, 2010a). The South African government expected to collect €1.1 billion in taxes and the direct tourism spend for the event was anticipated to be €1.4 billion (Emmett, 2010a), which translates into a net contribution to the country's annual GDP of 0.5 per cent for the 2010 period (Domingues, 2011).

Social

Social legacies could include nation building and contribution to national pride, changed perceptions of residents of the host city or region, education, racial harmony and environmental awareness. The 2010 event was expected to have a large social impact on the host nation, just as the 1995 Rugby World Cup had had for the new democratic nation. Football was largely viewed as the sport of choice for the majority black African population. Given South Africa's historic racial divisions and tensions, the event presented an opportunity for racial integration as fans of all race groups gathered in the stadiums, fan parks, and across the cities to support the national team. It also represented an opportunity for local residents to use the upgraded transport systems in many areas and to allay residents' fear of crime in the inner city areas.

Sport

The sport legacy includes the development of international standard sporting facilities and related infrastructure upgrades. These often become emblematic symbols for the host city and depict its link with sports (Swart & Bob, 2007). In South Africa, new stadiums were built in Cape Town, Port Elizabeth, Durban, Johannesburg, Nelspruit and Polokwane. Existing stadiums in Pretoria, Johannesburg, Rustenburg and Bloemfontein were upgraded for the event and also hosted the 2009 FIFA Confederations Cup. In total, ten stadiums across nine cities were used for the event. Besides facilities, a number of sport development initiatives resulted from the World Cup, such as the FIFA "Football for Hope" projects, amongst others. An increase in sport participation, support and sponsorship may also result as legacies of a mega-event. Sponsorship of the 2010 FIFA World Cup was mostly from large multinational companies. However, for the first time, an African company, MTN (a mobile telecommunications company), was a global sponsor of the event. The successful hosting of the 2010 event provided a head start for bidding for other major events after the World Cup, and lessons learned by governments, sporting bodies and business will play a major role in the further development of the sport tourism sector.

Environmental

The environmental impact of mega-events has demanded increasing attention. Key aspects of it include reducing the carbon footprint of an event and integrating greening principles, as well as climate-responsiveness. The 2010 FIFA World Cup Organizing Committee embarked on a public awareness and environmental education programme called "Green Goal". In Cape Town, the new stadium that was built consciously included environmental aspects such as a stadium roof that collected rain water for use in the neighbouring urban park. The Green Point urban park that was created alongside the new stadium also became a major tangible legacy of the event for the city.

Political

This includes the promotion of democracy and human rights and improved governance. New tasks for government actors may result in enhancement of capacity within the public sector, as well as the improvements in skills and human resource capital in public and private sectors. Communities may benefit from interventions by government or non-government organizations aimed at skills development. Cornelissen (2007) noted how governments have used mega-events to promote or redress their national image, especially as it relates to issues of governance and democracy. This can also overlap with the image/branding legacy.

Image/branding

The long-term image/branding benefits for a host nation, city or region include destination profiling, host-region exposure, setting or changing the image of a host destination, changes in tourist image and reputation and brand marketing for a host region. For developing countries, a mega-event may be a catalyst for destination development and provide a base for creating an international profile that will help attract visitors in the longer term (Cornelissen & Swart, 2006; Jago *et al.*, 2010). Within the tourism sector, the legacy could include a better known and understood destination brand and improved reputation for service delivery. The 2010 FIFA World Cup particularly aimed to change international perceptions of the African continent in general, and combat "Afro-pessimism" (Domingues, 2011, p. 42). As Africa's World Cup, the slogan for the event was "Ke Nako" (meaning "it's Africa's time") – "Celebrate Africa's humanity". Danny Jordaan (CEO of the 2010 Organizing Committee) claims that the enduring image of the South African people is now that of a "lively people ready to welcome the world" (Allen, Knott & Swart, 2013). The event will be remembered for its passionate football supporters and their unique style and dress, such as blowing a "vuvuzela" (plastic trumpet), wearing a "makarapa" (colourfully decorated headgear) and doing the "Diski" dance (a vibrant, energetic dance based on football movements).

Besides the broad categories named above, there has also been a greater acknowledgement of unintended consequences of mega-events (Spracklen, 2012). While the scope of legacy is extremely broad, there is also limited consensus on its definition, what it entails and how it should be conceptualized and measured (Van Wynsberghe, 2014). A more critical perspective has questioned the widely held assumption that there will in fact be a positive legacy from events (Dickinson & Shipway, 2007). Some scholars have questioned the positive benefits from events and the equity of their distribution. Post-event legacies of "white-elephants", overstatements of tourism gains, large financial burdens on host cities and destinations and the temporary nature of the "feel-good" effects on a host nation are examples of negative legacy impacts associated with sport mega-events. The inability to define legacy with any precision is a major reason why some are advocating a new focus emphasizing a more "systematic and purposeful" approach, called "leveraging" (Grix, 2012, p. 309). Chalip (2004, p. 228) defines leveraging as "the processes through which the benefits of investments are maximized". Leveraging can relate to short-term or "immediate" activities by event hosts or long-term activities before, and after, the event takes place (e.g. "to build the host community's image in order to enhance the quality of its brand or market position") (Chalip, 2004, p. 228).

Key considerations for mega-event hosts

The following section proposes a set of considerations for mega-event stakeholders based on empirical research conducted by the authors after the 2010 FIFA World Cup in South Africa (see Knott, 2015; Allen *et al.*, 2013). The experiences and lessons learnt by South African stakeholders from hosting the 2010 mega-event were elicited using in-depth interviews between two and three years post the event (n=27). Direct quotations from respondents are included for illustrative purposes in the sections below, with the names of the respondents omitted for the sake of confidentiality.

Mobilizing public support

The importance of gaining public support for a mega-event cannot be over-emphasized. Many recent failed bids are the result of a lack of popular support from residents and stakeholders. In Brazil, the lead-up to the 2014 FIFA World Cup as well as the event period was marred by public protests at the perceived corruption of organizers and the lack of perceived legacy for the host nation. A key strength of South Africa's success in 2010 was the fervent support, passion, unity and friendliness of the local population. This was especially significant given the nation's historically divided and isolated society. What transpired during the event was that the world saw "people celebrating in the street, people walking, people happy, people smiling" and "a fun, vibrant country that liked to party".

Importantly, this was not just by chance. Stakeholders had clearly designed leveraging campaigns to activate and mobilize support, enthusiasm and national pride among the residents. Campaigns such as "Fly the flag for South Africa" were directed at the local citizens, "to mobilize the nation to support the event". This leveraging campaign encouraged citizens to make the national flag prominent, to wear the national team colours, to learn the "Diski" special dance created for the event and to learn to sing the national anthem. Another campaign, "Football Friday", promoted the wearing of the national team shirt on Fridays in the year leading up to the event. Admittedly, South Africa's mega-event experience was prior to the FIFA corruption revelations. However, this just strengthens the need to mobilize public support for mega-events.

Plan for legacy and leveraging

The above-mentioned need to gain public support links to the imperative to plan for legacy. Legacy activities need to be planned for before, during and after the mega-event. A major obstacle to effecting legacy is that most event organizations do not exist after an event, or they are not able to dedicate budget and staff to the post-event period. While this emphasizes the importance of pre-event legacy planning, it also challenges event organizations to take a longer-term consideration of the impact of their events. A more demanding public and set of stakeholders are demanding legacy outcomes from events. In the South African case, stakeholders believed that many of the excellent legacy initiatives were not effectively communicated to the general public and relevant stakeholders. The public and the media were therefore not able to effectively assess the benefits from the event.

The more recent emphasis on leveraging advocates that a great number of stakeholders can utilize the pre-event, event and post-event period to achieve a number of related benefits. Outside of the event's operational effectiveness (which is particularly the focus of most emerging economy nations), there are a wide array of objectives that a mega-event can help to achieve for a diverse array of stakeholders. Once again, particularly the post-event period has been under-leveraged. It is up to the stakeholders to maintain the momentum of the benefits gained by hosting the event.

Importantly, all the respondents of the 2010 FIFA World Cup study noted the need for post-event leveraging, with some noting in the case of South Africa that there was "a missed opportunity to keep the momentum going" and that stakeholders were "not leveraging the benefits actively enough". They implored that "building on the momentum" that the World Cup provided was vital. A useful recommendation made by two of the South African respondents was to view the event planning process as three distinct parts, each of equal importance, namely, the pre-event, event and post-event periods. Each of these periods requires adequate planning, budgeting and staffing to ensure that the opportunities are leveraged most effectively. A further prominent recommendation by a number of respondents was for "a sustained pipeline of events" to follow the 2010 mega-event. Interestingly, however, these were not necessarily viewed as mega-events, but could also be non-sport, home-grown and annual events. Even mega-events in other nations could be targeted for communications that remind event visitors of the successes of their previous events.

Stakeholder inclusion and partnership

A mega-event requires the collaboration of a wide array of diverse stakeholders, many of whom may not have worked together before. A close association between the entities is required to achieve a set of common goals related to the opportunities created by the event. One of the South African respondents emphasized the importance of partnerships between different stakeholders, insisting that his organization looks for opportunities to partner with the rights holder, sponsors and the local organizers or host cities as they realize the potential of co-creating brand value: "Wherever there is opportunity for relationship we try build each other up". The South African stakeholders mentioned the improvement of relationships between private and public sectors, as well as the improved cooperation between different government levels and departments. In some instances, stakeholders noted difficulties and challenges working with different stakeholders, although these initial challenges were said to have improved over time, to a point where stakeholders expressed an intention for these partnerships to be sustained. In some instances, where there was initial conflict, a stakeholder needed to indicate how cooperation between the parties would result in benefits for both.

Conclusion

This chapter has discussed the context of mega-events and their contribution to the business of sport tourism. Despite much recent criticism of mega-events, this chapter has revealed that there are still many positive benefits associated with them. However, it argues that event managers and a multitude of stakeholders need to strategically plan for legacy and leveraging during the pre-event, event and post-event periods. Communication and inclusion or partnership with the public, as well as with stakeholders, is of vital importance to the long-term benefits to be gained from mega-events. These aspects are of particular importance to nations within the developing economies of the world. A more critical and informed populace is demanding attention to legacy for a mega-event host. This criticism is heightened in nations where resources may be scarce and social needs abound. With Brazil being a serial mega-event host nation and the likes of Russia (2018 FIFA World Cup), Qatar (2022 FIFA World Cup) and Dubai (2020 World Expo) hosting mega-events in the near future, the opportunities presented by mega-events are set to be tested in nations looking to establish themselves among the world's elite. While the South African example is promising in many respects, it is the ability of the nation to leverage the tangible and intangible legacies of the events in the longer term that will prove the real measure of the mega-event.

References

Allen, D., Knott, B., & Swart, K. (2013). "'Africa's tournament'? The branding legacy of the 2010 FIFA World Cup". *International Journal of the History of Sport*, *30*(16), 1994–2006.

Brown, G., Chalip, L., Jago, L. & Mules, T. (2004). Developing brand Australia: Examining the role of events. In N. Morgan, A. Pritchard & R. Pride (Eds), *Destination Branding: Creating the Unique Destination Proposition* (2nd edn) (pp. 279–305). Oxford: Butterworth-Heinemann.

Cape Town Tourism (2010). Tourism Industry Positive about the Impact of the World Cup on Future Tourism Growth for Cape Town. Cape Town Tourism official website (21 July 2010). Available from <www.capetown.travel/industry_blog/entry/tourism_industry_positive_about_the_impact_of_the_world_cup_on_future_touri>. Accessed 31 July 2010.

Chalip, L. (2004). Beyond impact: A general model for host community event leverage. In B. Ritchie & D. Adair (Eds), *Sport Tourism: Interrelationships, Impacts and Issues* (pp. 226–252). Clevedon: Channel View.

Chalip, L. & Costa, C. A. (2005). Sport event tourism and the destination brand: Towards a general theory. *Sport in Society: Cultures, Commerce, Media, Politics*, *8*(2), 218–237.

Chappelet, J. (2012). Mega sporting event legacies: A multifaceted concept. *Papeles de Europa*, *25*, 76–86.

Cornelissen, S. (2004). It's Africa's turn. The narratives and legitimations surrounding the Moroccan and South African bids for the 2006 and 2010 Finals. *Third World Quarterly*, *25*(7), 1293–1309.

Cornelissen, S. (2007). Crafting legacies: The changing political economy of global sport and the 2010 FIFA World Cup. *Politikon*, *34*(3), 241–259.

Cornelissen, S., Bob, U. & Swart, K. (2011). Towards redefining the concept of legacy in relation to sport mega-events: Insights from the 2010 FIFA World Cup. *Development Southern Africa*, *28*(3), 307–318.

Cornelissen, S. & Swart, K. (2006). The 2010 football World Cup as a political construct: The challenge of making good on an African promise. *Sociological Review*, *54*, 108–123.

De Castro, S. B., Starepravo, F. A. Coakley, J. & de Souza, D. L. (2016). Mega sporting events and public funding of sport in Brazil (2004–2011). *Leisure Studies*, *35*(3), 369–386.

Dickinson, J. & Shipway, R. (2007). Resource guide to the impact of events. Hospitality, Leisure, Sport and Tourism Network. The Higher Education Academy.

Domingues, B. (2011). A dream accomplished. *SportBusiness International*, *164*(1), 42–44.

Els, K. (2011). Arrivals show record increase in 2010. Southern African Tourism Update. Available from <www.tourismupdate.co.za/NewsDetails.aspx?newsId=58303>. Accessed 2 March 2016.

Emmett, J. (2010a). Africa arrives. *Sportspro*, *19*, 43–46.

Emmett, J. (2010b). The whole world in his hands. *Sportspro*, *19*, 48–56.

Getz, D. (1997). *Event Management and Event Tourism*. New York, NY: Cognizant Communication.

Grix, J. (2012). "Image" leveraging and sports mega-events: Germany and the 2006 FIFA World Cup. *Journal of Sport & Tourism*, *17*(4), 289–312.

Grix, J., Brannagan, P. M. & Houlihan, B. (2015). Interrogating state's soft power strategies: A case study of sports mega-events in Brazil and the UK. *Global Society*, *29*(3), 463–479.

Hall C. M. & Hodges J. (1997). The politics of place and identity in the Sydney 2000 Olympics: Sharing the spirit of corporatism. In M. Roche (Ed.), *Sport, Popular Culture & Identity* (pp. 95–112). Germany: Meyer & Meyer.

Jago, L., Dwyer, L., Lipman, G., Van Lill, D. & Vorster, S. (2010). Optimising the potential of mega-events: An overview. *International Journal of Event and Festival Management, 1*(3), 220–237.

Knott, B. (2015), "The strategic contribution of sport mega-events to nation branding: the case of South Africa and the 2010 FIFA World Cup". Unpublished PhD thesis, Bournemouth University, Bournemouth.

Nauright, J. & Schimmel, K. S. (2005). *The Political Economy of Sport*. Basingstoke: Palgrave Mcmillan.

Preuss, H. (2007). The conceptualisation and measurement of mega sport event legacies. *Journal of Sport & Tourism, 12*(3–4), 207–228.

Rocha, C. M. (2016). Support of politicians for the 2016 Olympic Games in Rio, *Leisure Studies, 35*(4), 487–504.

Spracklen, K. (2012). Special issue on the unintended policy consequences of the Olympics and Paralympics. *Journal of Policy Research in Tourism, Leisure and Events, 4*(2), 121–122.

Swart, K. & Bob, U. (2007). The eluding link: Toward developing a national sport tourism strategy in South Africa beyond 2010. *Politikon, 34*(3), 373–391.

Van Wynsberghe, R. (2014). Applying event leveraging using OGI data: A case study of Vancouver 2010. *Leisure Studies* (advance online publication) <doi: 10.1080/02614367.2014.986508>.

Westerbeek, H. M. & Linley, M. (2012). Building city brands through sport events: Theoretical and empirical perspectives. *Journal of Brand Strategy, 1*(2), 193–205.

28

SPORT FACILITIES TOURISM

Louise Bielzer

Introduction

Sport facilities tourism is located in a multi-dimensional reference frame of sport, architecture and tourism, but also has links to urban development, destination branding and marketing. Whereas sport tourism, "the active, passive or nostalgic engagement with sports and sports-related activities while travelling away from one's normal place of residence" (Smith, MacLeod & Robertson, 2010, p. 165), has been getting attention in literature for many years, the features of sport facilities tourism, with the aim of experiencing the architectural and symbolic dimension of those venues rather than the performative one, are not comprehensively explored in research and practice. However, various factors suggest the engagement with sport facilities tourism: more and more cities hosting major sport events select signature architects for the design of the sport infrastructure that has to be built for the events. The enormous investment into those structures urges us also to think about marketing the venues apart from sport events and sport use. Thanks to the spectacular architecture, target groups aside from sport participants and spectators may be attracted to "post-experience" the space during off-event times so that a new form of architectural tourism may evolve.

Sport facilities tourism is a phenomenon between sport tourism and architectural tourism, and provides manifold potential for the destination involved. This chapter aims to provide a comprehensive account of the various facets of this niche tourism and to link sport facilities in their various architectural and experiential dimensions with tourism.

Taking their different variations into consideration, sport facilities will be explored in their different dimensions and particularities first. They will further be introduced as icons or "third places" according to Oldenburg, and as part of the collective memory (Fairley, 2003, with further references) of people. Memory brings the reader to the next paragraphs dedicated to nostalgia and heritage sport tourism. In addition, architectural tourism is suggested as a point of reference. Following this, sport facilities tourism and destination marketing are explored.

Finally, the marketing mix is applied to sport facilities as product of a destination. The risks and opportunities that sport facilities tourism entails for the cities integrating it into their marketing strategy will be examined.

Sport facilities

Sport facilities can be defined as purpose-built facilities used for different types of physical exertion or athletic activity for entertainment or competition. A facility may be categorized as either a mono-sport facility (used for one specific type of sport only), or a multi-purpose sport facility.

Through exploring sport facilities as functional sites it can be seen that there are a wide range, from natural, outdoor sites to different types of indoor sport facilities including venues for "dry" sports, aquatics and ice sports. Generally, there are many ways to structure and classify sport facilities. They may be distinguished according to:

- Their government structures (ownership and management, e.g. public versus private), which might be an important factor when later discussing the potential of sport facilities as a product in destination marketing.
- Whether natural or man-made.
- Their use concept as mono- versus multi-sport facilities.
- Whether used for individual sport or team sport.
- Whether used for leisure sport or professional sport (Wadsack, 2011).

Although it varies to some extent, the classification may act as place for both active sport tourism and event sport tourism, and in some cases even as destination for heritage or nostalgia sport tourism, which will be discussed later. Figure 28.1 illustrates the variety of outdoor areas/facilities and indoor facilities, and their sub-categories.

The assignment of sport facilities may be to more than one category. It is obvious that every type of sport facility has a specific use concept depending on the purpose of the facility. Accordingly, requirements towards architecture, the room and functional layout also vary towards the design.

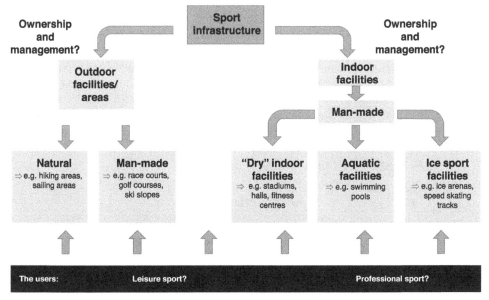

Figure 28.1 Sport infrastructure at a glance (based on Bielzer, 2014)

Governance structures range from fully publicly owned/managed facilities to fully privately owned/managed facilities. Specifically, for professional sport facilities, public–private partnerships have become a more popular model (Long, 2013) in which the responsibilities, costs and revenues are shared. Independently from governance structures and the respective type of facility, sport facilities have further characteristics in common:

- They require high initial investments, e.g. due to special requirements of sport associations or sport leagues.
- Sport facilities often record high operational costs due to their intensive use.
- The transfer for use to third parties is not easy due to the special building layouts and specific equipment for the respective type of sport.
- Sport facilities have many diverse stakeholders such as public entities and authorities, management companies, event organizers, the different users (active sportsmen, media, spectators, etc.), local residents and destination marketing organizations. This results in the need for a well-thought-out stakeholder communication strategy.
- Trends in sport are sometimes difficult to forecast.
- Costs for reinvestment might be high.
- Due to the above mentioned factors, sport facilities entail comparatively high uncertainties and risks for investors (Fried, 2010).

Generally, the design and concept of many forms of sport facilities are connected with the development of sport and society (Mandell, 1999). For example, some stadiums or arenas have a comparatively long history whereas others, such as some car race courses or extreme sport facilities, have been developed more recently but still show similar key building structures.

The design and architecture of sport facilities have become increasingly important. Many sport architectural firms such as HOK (Helmuth, Obata and Kassabaum) or gmp architects (Gerkan, Marg and Partners) do not focus on one specific famous or signature architect (the so-called "starchitect"). In these cases, the whole firm is known for its extensive expertise in sport facilities design and construction (Horne, 2011; Ponzini, 2014).

Thus sport facilities do not only have a functional architectural dimension. They represent an important element of the experience economy (Pine & Gilmore, 1998). Sport facilities both embody emotional and socio-cultural dimensions as part of people's collective memory and allow "escape" to those types of "third places" (Oldenburg, 1989) in order to experience sport or social activities.

Figure 28.2 indicates the multiple consumption patterns of sport facilities' tourists and shows that tourists are no longer classified according to one aspect of tourism consumption (Mazanec, 1997; Specht, 2015). This is an important understanding when it comes to developing an appropriate destination marketing strategy.

Sport facilities as icons

The perception of sport facilities, not only in their functional but also in their socio-cultural and emotional dimension, shows them as icons. Using spectacular architecture for sport facilities is no new phenomenon, examples being the Circus Maximus or the Colosseum in Rome, Italy. However, there is no comprehensive definition of what an iconic sport facility is. It is evident that iconic sport facilities are spectacular, architecturally unique spaces mainly used for professional sport (also providing space for other, non-sport purposes such as

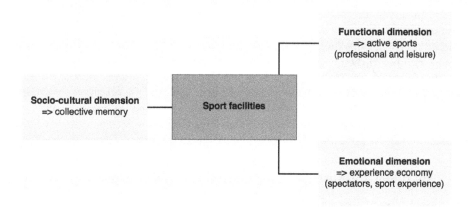

Figure 28.2 Multiple dimensions of sport facilities (based on Bielzer, 2016)

multifunctional sport arenas, for example), and are often built to host major sport events. By applying the Oxford Dictionary definition of "icon" (2016), iconic sport facilities become more symbolic of modern cities, artefacts and built representatives of sport experiences or worthy of veneration. Their development is often owed to major sport events as driving forces, as the Olympic Games or other sport championships illustrate (e.g. Chalkley & Essex, 1999; Essex & Chalkley, 2004).

Horne (2011) discusses the political and social impact that architects have on cities and elaborates on the relationship between sport, design and architecture in an urban context. According to Horne, further research should be carried out on the social role of sport architecture and architects. When looking back through history one might find historic icons of stadiums such as Wembley Stadium in the UK or the Maracanã Stadium in Rio de Janeiro, Brazil, or horse race courts such as Ascot Racecourse in Berkshire, UK. These might have a different geographic footprint (e.g. international or national). However, they are always built not only as functional spaces, but also as symbolic spaces. Following the concept of the spatial turn (e.g. Löw, 2008), the iconic nature of a sport facility also includes being an identification point for dedicated fans and for those sharing the same experiences, connotations, emotions and memorialization related to the respective facility. Sport facilities as artefacts are tangible as built environment, but at the same time intangible as symbolic spaces based on common emotional moments, experiences and social interaction. Hence, they embody meaning for people outside events due to their history, the lived emotions and experiences and the construction of social realities (Bielzer, 2014).

In addition to the above-mentioned historic icons there are contemporary architectural icons of sport facilities that have no specific cultural or social foundation based on the past. These facilities are designed by famous architects such as Zaha Hadid, Norman Foster or Jacques Herzog and Pierre de Meuron, often Pritzker Prize winners, and represent unique elements of urban development. The fact of engaging these signature architects is a comparatively recent phenomenon, observed in big cities that are bidding for major sport events such as the Olympic Games or other sporting World Championships. This development does not only relate to sport. Ponzini indicates that "this transnational circulation of architects, urban designers and planners" does not apply to spectacular, unique pieces of architecture only, "but also to outline the master plans for infrastructure hubs, corporation headquarters and institutional compounds, university campuses or museum complexes" (Ponzini, 2015, p. 2).

Nevertheless, in sport, there is the crucial question of sustainability respecting legacy and the long-term use of these facilities once the event is over to avoid the "White Elephants" syndrome (Alm *et al.*, 2016). The Football World Cup stadium in South Africa or the former Olympic Stadium in Athens from the 2004 Olympic Summer Games show that some of those venues, despite their spectacular architecture, might become "White Elephants" since they have been barely used since the events ended. Integrating these venues into a destination's marketing strategy is not only a big challenge but also an important economic issue.

Sport tourism, nostalgia sport tourism and heritage sport tourism

The concept of sport tourism as part of tourism studies has become more popular both in practice and in research since the 1990s (Gibson, 1998; 2002). It may be defined as "the active, passive or nostalgic engagement with sports and sports-related activities while travelling away from one's normal place of residence" (Smith, MacLeod & Robertson, 2010, p. 165). Active sport tourism includes people travelling for both professional sport and also for leisure sport activities.

A review of existing writing about sport tourism shows that many scholars refer to event sport tourism, meaning tourism generated in the host cities of sport events with an international or national scope (e.g. Gibson, 1998; Kulczycki & Hyatt, 2005). They focus mainly on visitor/spectator motivations to travel to those destinations and the impact this form of sport event-induced tourism has on the destinations (e.g. Fourie & Spronk, 2011; Funk & Bruun, 2007; Preuss, 2005; Roche, Spake & Joseph, 2013; Smith & Stewart, 2007; Solberg & Preuss, 2013). Only a few publications consider sport tourism at smaller events such as college sport events (Gibson, Willming & Holdnak, 2003) or by analysing small-scale sport event tourism such as events in Lake Kenyir, Malaysia (Yusof *et al.*, 2009).

Apart from the above, active sport tourism and adventure tourism – both reflecting active engagement with sport respectively, sport-related activities and the importance of experiences – gain more and more consideration in literature (e.g. Buckley, 2012; Hudson, 2008; Shephard and Evans, 2005). However, sport tourism research is said to be too often descriptive, examining what sport tourists do, rather than why they engage in sport or sport-related activities (Gibson, 2004).

Shipway and Kirkup explain the complexity of sport consumption experiences and sport tourism sites as "'third places' outside of the home and work environment" (Shipway and Kirkup, 2011, p. 127). Sport facilities as "third places" relate back to Oldenburg's concept of a "third place", that is, a place where people meet for social interaction away from the home ("first place") and from "second places" (such as work or school) (Oldenburg, 1989). Whereas some types of traditional third places, such as pubs or cafés, are said to be in decline, sport event locations represent alternative third places for people to meet and experience sportive and social interactions (Shipway & Kirkup, 2011).

With reference to "nostalgia", there is no common understanding of what nostalgia sport tourism is. In several publications it is described as visiting sport facilities, but also sport event destinations, sport museums or halls of fame (Kulczycki & Hyatt, 2005, with further references). Fairley and Gammon (2005) apply an even broader understanding of nostalgia sport tourism and, besides nostalgia for sport sites, places or artefacts, they consider social experiences as another important driver for nostalgia sport tourism. This might be the case when joining heritage sport events, sport theme vacations or relived social experiences when accompanying away games of a favourite sport team (Fairley & Gammon, 2005). Kulczycki and Hyatt analyse the motivations and experiences of nostalgia sport tourists who had travelled to have nostalgic experiences at live sport events. Furthermore, they explore the nostalgia of fans for a team after the team has relocated to a different market (Kulczycki & Hyatt, 2005) – a case that is not rare in closed sport leagues such as the American Big Four (the National Football League, Major League Baseball, the National Basketball Association and the National Hockey League) (Morris & Kraker, 2015).

Ramshow and Gammon (2005) distinguish four categories of sport heritage: tangible immobile heritage, tangible movable heritage, intangible heritage and goods and services. Whereas "retro sporting goods", such as jerseys from the past, represent a special form of merchandise, thus tangible objects remembering the past, intangible heritage includes chants, traditions or rituals. As tangible movable heritage the two authors define displays and artefacts shown in sport museums, expositions or halls of fame. Finally, tangible immovable heritage mainly consists of architecture, historic sporting venues, thus built structures for sport that cannot (easily) be relocated. Depending on the geographic scope, tangible immovable heritage may have local, regional, national or international significance (Ramshow & Gammon, 2005).

Some articles refer to heritage buildings and their impact on specific tourist destinations such as that by Willson and McIntosh for Hawke's Bay, New Zealand (Willson & McIntosh, 2007). Others explore heritage tourism in general as part of cultural tourism. One interesting example that has to be mentioned in the context of historical sport sites is Wimbledon. Undoubtedly being a heritage site and a historical sport icon, its power as a historic artefact is reflected, amongst others, in the fact that it hosts the only Grand Slam Tournament still played on grass and incorporates lots of traditions and rituals. Wimbledon is an interesting example of embodied cultural meanings connected with a historic sport site (English Heritage (the government's lead body for the historic environment), n.d.); Wagg, 2015).

In this context one might also think of examples of sport facilities that became famous due to tragic events. An example is the Hillsborough Stadium in Sheffield, UK, where 96 people died and more than 760 people were injured in a human crush during the FA Cup semi-final match between Liverpool FC and Nottingham Forest FC in 1989. From a tourism management point of view, this may be considered as a kind of dark tourism site (Smith *et al.*, 2010) and the question is how to eventually integrate such sites into a destination's marketing strategy.

Ramshow and Gammon emphasize that in nostalgia sport tourism, the focus lies on positivistic recollections and memorialization of the sporting past and nostalgia represents an intangible, glorious element of sport heritage. By contrast, sport heritage, as a broader concept, does not only include architecture and venues, objects and traditions, but also more negative memorialization of the sporting past. Thus, heritage sport tourism rather accentuates the supply side, the heritage elements of a place, object, attraction or sport destination, whereas nostalgia sport tourism mainly refers to the demand side, the motivations of the tourist (Ramshow & Gammon, 2005). However, there seems to be a lack of publications about sport tourism and modern iconic sport facilities as vehicles to increase sport tourism from a destination marketing point of view.

Architectural tourism

Studies on architectural tourism are still at a comparatively early stage and there is no common definition of architectural tourism (Specht, 2015). Publications related to architecture as a key factor in tourism mainly approach the topic in the sense of historic monuments or buildings as part of cultural heritage. Accordingly, architectural tourism is viewed as part of cultural, nostalgia or heritage tourism (Smith *et al.*, 2010). Specht questions if the concept of classifying tourists into categories such as business tourists, leisure tourists or another type is still useful when discussing urban tourism and architectural tourism. In fact, he argues that the categorization of tourists should rather depend on the tourist's individual perceptions (Specht, 2015).

One of the early publications specifically dedicated to architectural tourism was the dissertation written by Shaw. In the "analysis of architectural tourism and its influence on urban design from 1997 to 2007" he discussed signature architecture as an element of urban redevelopment (Shaw, 2008). Later, Craggs *et al.* developed the concept of "architectural enthusiasm" when examining the participation in architectural tours of the Twentieth Century Society, a UK architectural conservation group. Apart from "seeing" historical monuments or buildings, the authors highlighted the role of shared emotions and experiences when tourists visited built environment. However, they did not specifically consider contemporary architecture (Craggs, Geoghegan & Neate, 2013).

On the contrary, Specht puts a strong focus on the architectural tourist who is interested in contemporary architecture. He discusses architectural tourism from a destination's management perspective as well as in the context of urban development and space. Architecture is usually classified based on style or the date of completion of the buildings, whereas most tourists perceive it just as 'historic' or 'modern', not considering specific styles. According to Specht, contemporary architectural tourists may be classified based on their levels of interest in contemporary architecture and their intent to visit contemporary architecture (Specht, 2011; 2014; 2015).

Ponzini provides a good overview of current research into architectural design and "starchitecture" in urban development and as part of inter-urban competition. He points out the lack of comprehensive research beyond the economic dimension of starchitecture (Ponzini 2014). For office buildings, Ponzini indicates that signature architecture contributes to higher rental fees for the buildings that are therefore more attractive for investors. However, it seems that there are no similar studies for sport facilities available, even though reality indicates the increasing involvement of famous architects, specifically in cities hosting international sport hallmark events such as the Olympic Games or the Soccer World Championships. Generally, it has to be stated that architecture itself is not likely to be the only reason that tourists are interested in visiting a destination. In fact, architecture might be the initial spark in planning a trip to a destination but, ultimately, it is more about experiencing the different attractions at a destination during a trip (Schwarzer, 2005; Specht, 2015).

Sport facilities tourism and destination marketing

Current research on destination marketing, destination branding and sport tourism is copious and manifold. Due to the increasing and international competition, and the fear of being considered "substitutable", destinations aim to differentiate themselves from competitors by transforming into distinctive brands or at least developing and maintaining unique selling propositions such as specific place brands (Ashworth & Kavaratzis, 2010). Destination branding, therefore, constitutes an important frame of reference for destination marketing and image management (Baker & Cameron, 2008; Kavaratzis, 2004; Lucarelli & Brorström, 2013). Basically and by tradition, architecture might serve as a means of differentiation. Professional sport or major sporting event facilities are subjects of extensive media coverage, which contributes to the distinctiveness of a destination. However, publications specifically referring to sport facilities tourism are rare and often focus on the role and potential of stadiums in tourism (e.g. Stevens & Williams, 2001; John, 2002; Gammon, 2011). Brown *et al.* conducted an empirical study examining the interdependencies between sport involvement, place attachment, event satisfaction and spectator intentions in the case of the London Summer Olympic Games. They concluded that spectators' experiences and place attachment had an effect on event satisfaction. However, it did not have an effect on the intention to revisit the host city (Brown, Smith & Assaker, 2016).

Considering the performative dimension, sport facilities tourism in many cases equals heritage sport tourism since the visit of the site or place is motivated by the wish to experience a team's past success, past events, rituals or traditions. However, the architectural dimension of sport facility tourism goes beyond heritage sport tourism. The integration of contemporary iconic sport facilities overlaps with architectural tourism that seeks to experience architecture with the performative dimension in second rank only. In this case, contemporary sport facilities built by signature architects form a destination category of their own, which is attractive not only to sport tourists, but also to architectural tourists. Hence, the potential to market these venues is manifold although the product is difficult to conceive.

As already stated above, sport facilities as artefacts, as built but also as symbolic spaces, may provide a big potential for destinations to market themselves. First, besides the positive effects of active sport tourists for a destination, the media attention given to sport facilities for professional sport teams or major sport events implies good opportunities for destinations for the hosting of more events. Second, because of the specific use of the buildings for leisure purposes such as seeing a favourite team playing or visiting multi-sport events, various target groups might be interested in "post-experiencing" the space once the event is over. This is one of the connecting points for heritage or nostalgia sport tourism. Third, more big cities select famous architects – "starchitects" – to design newly built sport infrastructure for major sport events or professional sport. On the one hand, this results in a certain additional media attention due to the architect as a brand. On the other hand, the spectacular architecture allows the destination to reach additional target groups such as architectural tourists.

SPORT FACILITIES TOURISM

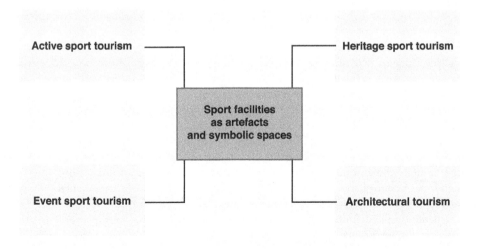

Figure 28.3 Links of sport facilities to forms of tourism (based on Bielzer, 2016)

It is enormously challenging to adapt historic sports facilities, including former Olympic Stadiums that are still in use today, for use in league sport or other sport events (e.g. the Olympic Stadium Berlin in Germany, which is still used for the regular league games of Hertha BSC). Bainer analyses the "legacy of memory", exploring the role of the Olympic stadiums of Helsinki and Stockholm as "living memorials" (Bainer, 2015).

On the one hand, these venues are part of the collective memory of people. They may be a destination for heritage tourism, a place to memorize sporting history. On the other hand, for the current use they have to keep up with the requirements of their tenants and other stakeholders such as sponsors and media, and be attractive for active and passive sport tourists, too. This means that they not only have to be well maintained – sometimes even under special conditions as listed buildings – but they also have to be state-of-the-art in terms of technical and design requirements formulated by, for example, the sport leagues or sport associations responsible for the games taking place in the venue. Consequently, this causes high costs and a sensitive handling of the sporting past and the diverse stakeholders and target groups of the facility.

However, the spectacular architecture of professional sport facilities implies a certain "automatic" media attention and therefore already has the advantage for a destination of being present in the minds of potential tourists due to sport media coverage without specific marketing communication.

The marketing of a sport facility usually refers to active and passive sport consumers, in other words to sport event participants such as players, trainers or team managers and sport spectators in the facility. On the b2b level, sport facility marketing may be directed towards business partners such as service providers (catering companies, technology providers, etc.), media or sponsors (Schwarz, Hall & Shibli, 2010). However, considering sport facilities as both tangible built places but also intangible symbolic spaces requires a more comprehensive understanding of the sport consumer, including for example heritage sport tourists experiencing the facility outside events. Furthermore, architectural tourists interested in contemporary architectural icons have to be taken into account as a target group of an icon sport facility, too. For them, the functional sport dimension of the facility might be of secondary importance. As already noted, it is important no longer to classify tourists according to only one aspect of tourism consumption. For sport facilities' tourists, this means being aware of the tourist's multiple motivations for visiting a facility and his/her diverse tourism consumption patterns (seeing a game, being emotionally involved in winning or losing in sport, experiencing the venue as a historic site and part of nostalgia or heritage tourism, etc.). On the one hand, this approach makes it more difficult for a destination to develop a target group-oriented marketing strategy. On the other hand, it also provides the opportunity to reach broader target groups with the same tourism product, but different allocations of meaning and, accordingly, a distinct target audience communication.

Applying the classical marketing mix to a destination, respectively a sport facility, as a place, it has to be stated that there is a certain variance in the "product". Besides the above elaborated dimensions of a sport facility as a built and, at the same time, symbolic space, the venue may be perceived as an own product, but also as part of a destination's product. Due to the multiple dimensions and the various impacting factors on a sport facility, there is a certain lack of control about the product, too. The development of supplementary products as well as of the price, the place and the promotion dimension of a sport facility's marketing mix depends on the definition of the core product first. Figure 28.4 exemplarily shows these dimensions in dependence of the product definition.

The variety of manifestations of sport facilities and their stakeholder requirements is important to consider when discussing the pros and cons of integrating sport facilities into a

Sport facilities tourists and their diverse consumption patterns?

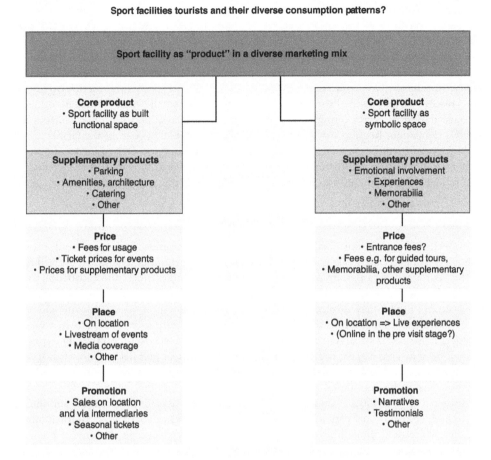

Figure 28.4 Sport facilities as products of the marketing mix (based on Bielzer, 2016)

destination's marketing strategy. In many cases, architecture itself contributes to the perception of the facility as a place brand, but this is not the only factor. Even more, long-term use, a positive image creation and cultivation and good building conditions are crucial for a sport facility as product or product element of destination marketing.

Independently of the respective governance structures (fully private, fully public or PPP), it is important that the marketing of a sport facility is consistent with other marketing activities of the destination. For this, the close cooperation of all stakeholders is needed.

When discussing positive factors for a destination, a sport facility as artefact, in combination with a special performative element such as a major sport event or a permanent tenant playing in the facility, is hard to copy for competing destinations. Furthermore, unlike temporary events, sport facilities are permanent elements in a destination's branding and marketing mix. Due to their cultural, social and symbolic meaning the facilities may be positioned in the market for the long term and must not be positioned afresh for the sake of such events. Lastly, if the sport facility is designed by a signature architect, the destination might also target specific touristic groups such as architectural tourists.

On the other hand, sport facilities also entail risks for a destination. First, the above-mentioned factor of "permanence" might turn into a risk in case of the negative outcomes of a sport event such as "White Elephants". As place brands in general, sport facilities may neither easily be changed, nor withdrawn from the market if not successful any more (Fay, 2005). In addition, the comparatively high operating expenses and maintenance costs might be a challenge for the destination, at least in the case of a publicly owned and operated facility. Specifically, for contemporary architectural icons in sport infrastructure there are more risks to be discussed. First, iconic architecture is often the focus of negative media coverage due to its skyrocketing costs and construction delays. This not only damages the facility's reputation, but also that of the destination as a whole. Second, if the facility is not used by a permanent home team it might fall into oblivion due to a lack of media attention. Finally, contemporary architectural icons in sport might suffer from a lack of acceptance by local residents due to the eventual cultural detachedness of the architecture.

Conclusion

It has been shown that sport facilities as, on the one side, tangible, built spaces and, on the other side, intangible symbolic spaces provide manifold opportunities to attract sport facilities' tourists. For a destination, they might be a suitable tool to differentiate the destination from its competitors. Destination marketers must know the different consumption patterns and expectations of the different tourists to be able to manage the sportscape as product element of the destination's marketing strategy. Considering the sport facility as an own tourism product, it is crucial to design suitable encounter experiences for the different types of tourists, be they active sport tourists, heritage sport tourists or architectural tourists. In the course of this, not only the functional, but also the cultural, cognitive and emotional dimension has to be considered as frame of reference.

However, sport facilities as tourism destinations also entail risks for a destination, specifically due to high costs and only partial "control" of the product. Since architecture is not autotelic and the architectural dimension without performative and/or heritage elements as complementary does not attract masses of sport facilities' tourists, a long-term-oriented, consistent use concept for the facility is vital. If it is about iconic sport facilities, the type of "iconicness" has to be examined carefully before identifying specific target groups of tourists and developing an aligned marketing strategy. Further study, specifically of contemporary architectural sport icons, would be of interest. In this context, an interdisciplinary approach is desirable.

References

Alm, J., Solberg H. A., Storm R. K. & Jacobsen, T. G. (2016). Hosting major sports events: The challenge of taming white elephants. *Leisure Studies, 35*(5), 564–582.

Ashworth, G. & Kavaratzis, M. (2010) (Eds). *Towards Effective Place Brand Management: Branding European Cities and Regions*. Cheltenham: Edward Elgar Publishing.

Bainer, A. (2015). The legacy of memory: The Stockholm and Helsinki Olympic stadia as living memorials. In R. Holt, & D. Ruta (Eds), *Routledge Handbook of Sport and Legacy: Meeting the Challenge of Major Sports Events*. Oxon: Routledge.

Baker, M. J. & Cameron, E. (2008). Critical success factors in destination marketing. *Tourism & Hospitality Research, 8*(2), 79–97.

Bielzer, L. (2014). Iconic sports facilities as part of a destination's tourism potential? In A. Hebbel-Seer, T. Horky & H. J. Schulke (Eds), *Sport und Stadtmarketing*. Munich: BoD Books on Demand.

Brown, G., Smith, A. & Assaker, G. (2016). Revisiting the host city: An empirical examination of sport involvement, place attachment, event satisfaction and spectator intentions at the London Olympics. *Tourism Management, 55*, 160–172.

Buckley, R. (2012). Rush as a key motivation in skilled adventure tourism: Resolving the risk recreation paradox. *Tourism Management, 33*(4), 961–970.

Chalkley, B. & Essex, S. (1999). Urban development through hosting international events: A history of the Olympic Games. *Planning Perspectives, 14*(4), 369–394.

Craggs, R., Geoghegan, H. & Neate, H. (2013). Architectural enthusiasm: Visiting buildings with The Twentieth Century Society. *Environment and Planning D. Society & Space, 31*(5), 879–896.

English Heritage. Available from <https://content.historicengland.org.uk/images-books/publications/conservation-bulletin-68/cb-68.pdf/>.

Essex, S. & Chalkley, B. (2004). Mega-sporting events in urban and regional policy: A history of the Winter Olympics. *Planning Perspectives, 19*(2), 201–204.

Fairley, S. (2003). In search of relived social experience: Group-based nostalgia sport tourism. *Journal of Sport Management, 17*(3), 284–304.

Fairley, S. & Gammon, S. (2005). Something lived, something learned: Nostalgia's expanding role in sport tourism. *Sport in Society: Cultures, Commerce, Media, Politics, 8*(2), 182–197.

Fay, Y. (2005). Branding the nation: What is being branded? *Journal of Vacation Marketing, 12*(1), 5–14.

Fourie, J. & Spronk, K. (2011). South African mega-sport events and their impact on tourism. *Journal of Sport & Tourism, 16*(1), 75–97.

Fried, G. (2010). *Managing Sport Facilities* (2nd edn). Champaign, IL: Human Kinetics.

Funk, D. C. & Bruun, T. J. (2007). The role of socio-psychological and culture-education motives in marketing international sport tourism: A cross-cultural perspective. *Tourism management, 28*(3), 806–819.

Gammon, S. J. (2011). "Sporting" new attractions? The commodification of the sleeping stadium. In R. Sharpley & P. R. Stone (Eds), *Tourist Experience: Contemporary Perspectives* (pp. 115–126). Oxon: Routledge.

Gammon, S. & Fear, V. (2005). Stadia tours and the power of backstage. *Journal of Sport Tourism, 10*(4), 243–252.

Gibson, H. J. (1998): Sport tourism: A critical analysis of research. *Sport Management Review, 1*(1), 45–76.

Gibson, H. J. (2002). Sport tourism at a crossroad? Considerations for the future. In S. Gammon & J. Kurtzman (Eds), *Sports Tourism: Principles and Practice* (pp. 111–128). Eastbourne: Leisure Studies Association.

Gibson, H. J. (2004). Moving beyond the "what is and who" of sport tourism to understanding "why". *Journal of Sport & Tourism, 9*(3), 247–265.

Gibson, H. J., Willming, C. & Holdnak, A. (2003). Small-scale event sport tourism: Fans as tourists. *Tourism Management, 24*(2), 181–190.

Horne, J. (2011). Architects, stadia and sport spectacles: Notes on the role of architects in the building of sport stadia and making of world-class cities. *International Review for the Sociology of Sport, 46*(2), 205–227.

Hudson, S. (2008). *Sport and Adventure Tourism*. New York: Haworth Press.

John, G. (2002). Stadia and tourism. In S. Gammon & J. Kutzman (Eds), *Sports Tourism: Principles and Practice* (pp. 53–60). Eastbourne: Leisure Studies Association.

Kavaratzis, M. (2004). From city marketing to city branding: Towards a theoretical framework for developing city brands. *Place Branding, 1*(1), 58–73.

Kulczycki, C. & Hyatt, C. (2005). Expanding the conceptualization of nostalgia sport tourism: Lessons learned from fans left behind after sport franchise relocation. *Journal of Tourism, 10*(4), 273–293.

Löw, M. (2008). The constitution of space: The structuration of spaces through the simultaneity of effect and perception. *European Journal of Social Theory, 11*(1), 25–49.

Lucarelli, A. & Berg, P.-O. (2011). City branding: A state-of-the-art review of the research domain. *Journal of Place Management and Development, 4*(1), 9–27.

Lucarelli, A. & Brorström, S. (2013). Problematizing place branding research: A meta-theoretical analysis of the literature. *The Marketing Review, 13*(1), 65–81.

Long, J. G. (2013). *Public/Private Partnerships for Major League Sport Facilities*. New York: Routledge.

Mandell, R. D. (1999). *Sport: A Cultural History*. Lincoln, Nebraska: iUniverse.

Mazanec, J. A. (1997). Segmenting city tourists into vacation styles. In J. A. Mazanec (Ed.) *International City Tourism: Analysis and Strategy* (pp. 114–128). London: Pinter.

Morris, D. & Kraker, D. (2015). Rooting the home team: Why the Packers won't leave – and why the Browns did. In K. David & R. E. Washington (Eds), *Sociological Perspectives on Sport. The Games Outside the Games* (pp. 220–226). New York: Routledge.

Ockman, J. & Frausto, S. (2005) (Eds). *Architourism: Authentic, Escapist, Exotic, Spectacular*. Munich: Prestel Publishing.

Oldenburg, R. (1989). *The Great Good Place: Café, Coffee Shops, Community Centers, Beauty Parlors, General Stores, Bars, Hangouts, and How They Get You Through the Day*. New York: Paragon House Publishers.

Pine II, J. and Gilmore, J. H. (1998). Welcome to the experience economy. *Harvard Business Review*, *76*(4), 97–105.

Ponzini, D. (2014). The values of starchitecture: Commodification of architectural design in contemporary cities. *Organizational Aesthetics*, *3*(1), 10–18.

Ponzini, D. (2015). "The transnational circulation of master plans and urban megaprojects: Shortcomings and challenges for local planners and designers". Paper presented at the RC21 International Conference on "The ideal city: Between myth and reality. Representations, policies, contradictions and challenges for tomorrow's urban life" in Urbino, Italy, 25–27 August 2015. <http://www.rc21.org/en/conferences/urbino2015/>.

Preuss, H. (2005). The economic impact of visitors at major multi-sport events. *European Sport Management Quarterly*, *5*(3), 281–301.

Ramshow, G. & Gammon, S. (2005). More than just Nostalgia? Exploring the heritage/sport tourism Nexus. *Journal of Sport & Tourism*, *10*, 229–241.

Roche, S., Spake, D. F. & Joseph, M. (2013). A model of sporting event tourism as economic development. *Sport, Business and Management: An International Journal*, *3*(2), 147–157.

Schwarz, E. C., Hall, S. & Shibli, S. (2010). *Sport Facility Operations Management. A Global Perspective*. London: Routledge.

Schwarzer, M. (2005). Architecture and mass tourism. In J. Ockman & S. Frausto (Eds), *Architourism: Authentic, Escapist, Exotic, Spectacular* (pp. 12–31). Munich: Prestel Publishing.

Shaw, G. "Tourism by design: An analysis of architectural tourism and its influence on urban design from 1997 to 2007". [Thesis], University of Caliornia, Davis, 2008.

Shephard, G. & Evans, S. (2005). Adventure tourism – hard decisions, soft options and home for tea: Adventures on the hoof. In M. Novelli (Ed.), *Niche Tourism: Contemporary Issues, Trends and Cases* (pp. 201–209). Oxford: Butterworth-Heinemann.

Shipway, R. & Kirkup, N. (2011). Understanding sport tourism experiences: Exploring the participant – spectator nexus. In R. Sharpley & P. R. Stone (Eds), *Tourist Experience, Contemporary perspectives* (pp. 127–139). Oxon: Routledge.

Smith, M., MacLeod, N. & Robertson, M. H. (2010). *Key Concepts in Tourist Studies*. London: Sage.

Smith, A. C. & Stewart, B. (2007). The travelling fan: Understanding the mechanisms of sport fan consumption in a sport tourism setting. *Journal of Sport & Tourism*, *12*(3–4), 155–181.

Solberg, H. A. & Preuss, H. (2013). Major sport events and long-term tourism impacts. In M. Weed (Ed.), *Sport & Leisure Management* (pp. 359–381). London: Sage Publications.

Specht, J. (2011). Architecture and the destination image: Something familiar, something new, something virtual, something true. In S. Sonnenburg & L. Baker (Eds), *Branded Spaces. Experience Enactments and Entanglements* (pp. 43–61). Wiesbaden: Springer.

Specht, J. (2014). *Architectural Tourism. Building for Urban Travel Destinations*. Wiesbaden: Springer.

Specht, J. (2015). Towards a new role model of the contemporary architectural tourist. In S. Sonnenburg & D. Wee (Eds), *Touring Consumption* (pp. 303–318). Wiesbaden: Springer VS.

Stevens, T. & Williams, C. (2001). Stadia and tourism-related facilities. *Travel & Tourism Analyst*, *2*, 59–73.

Wadsack, R. (2011). Sportanlagen – Vielfalt und Systematisierungsansätze. In L. Bielzer & R. Wadsack (Eds), *Betrieb von Sport- und Veranstaltungsimmobilien. Managementherausforderungen und Handlungsoptionen* (pp. 35–50). Frankfurt: Peter Lang.

Wagg, S. (2015). Sacred turf: The Wimbledon tennis championships and the changing politics of Englishness. *Sport in Society, Cultures, Commerce, Media, Politics*, Special Issue, 1–15.

Willson, G. B. & McIntosh, A. J. (2007). Heritage buildings and tourism: An experiential view. *Journal of Heritage Tourism*, *2*(2), 75–93.

Yusof, A., Omar-Fauzee, M. S., Shah, P. M. & Geok, S. K. (2009). Exploring small-scale sport event tourism in Malaysia. *Research Journal of International Studies*, *9*, 47–58.

29

PROMOTING RESPONSIBLE SUSTAINABILITY IN SPORT TOURISM

A logic model approach

Derek Van Rheenen

Introduction

Seasoned travellers and culturally sensitive tourists seek to blend in as citizens of the world, following a cultural code of conduct that is both respectful and responsible. Responsible travel or tourism is based on three interrelated principles when visiting a foreign land: (1) a genuine attempt to understand the host culture; (2) a respect for the people who live there; and (3) a commitment to tread lightly on the local environment (Lea, 1993; Scheyvens, 2002; Leslie, 2012). Seasoned travellers understand these qualities as an openness and opportunity to learn, embracing a position of culturally sensitive inquiry and humility.

Like individual tourists who follow their own responsible code of conduct when travelling in a foreign land, companies, organizations and government agencies sponsoring tourism activities and events are increasingly held responsible for ethical behaviours. The term responsible tourism (RT) emerged in the 1980s "as a way of doing tourism planning, policy and development to ensure that benefits are optimally distributed among impacted populations, governments, tourists and investors" (Husbands and Harrison, 1996, p. 1). In addition to seeking an equitable distribution of benefits or rewards, responsible tourism likewise seeks to limit the deleterious costs associated with these positive outcomes.

A focus on social and corporate responsibility has led scholars and practitioners to acknowledge a triple bottom line, focusing not only on economic, but also on environmental and social factors. The triple bottom line (TBL) approach has been described as a framework for measuring and reporting performance against economic, social and environmental parameters, or as a philosophy in which companies, governments and public or voluntary organizations must comprehensively evaluate their impacts and account for their actions (Elkington, 1997; Getz, 2009, p. 71) The primary goal of a TBL approach is to leverage positive outcomes while mitigating negative impacts.

Despite a general recognition of the need for responsible tourism – a need purportedly recognized by most stakeholders today – economic priorities often prevail at a significant cost in social and environmental repercussions. A limited regard for responsible sustainability exists at all levels of government – local, regional, national, international – and across numerous markets and sectors of the tourism industry. The challenge crosses geographic borders and boundaries, and persists despite findings that show companies who measure, manage and disclose more in their reporting of sustainability indicators enjoy considerable advantage when compared to their non-reporting peers (Governance and Accountability Institute, 2012).

While this assessment of the tourism industry today may prompt an ethical conviction on the part of informed stakeholders, there remains limited consensus on how to measure both good and bad performance relative to the triple bottom line. An efficient and accessible method of measurement promises to create blueprints for successful local, regional and global efforts. While there exist reporting tools to evaluate responsible sustainability, such as the Global Reporting Initiative (GRI), ISO26000 and Dow Jones Sustainability Index North America, these measurement tools are primarily summative judgements, rather than tools that provide strategies for improvement. These tools are likewise sophisticated and cumbersome to use, requiring significant resources to utilize them effectively. As such, the accounting instruments have been used primarily by large companies and organizations in developed nations, far less in developing countries.

This chapter offers a modest attempt to address this current issue and the corresponding opportunity associated with this widespread problem. Specifically, this chapter proposes the use of an evaluative tool, or logic model, to strategically plan, implement and evaluate tourism activities and events. This proposal is in line with recent trends within the evaluation literature to focus greater attention on equity and sustainability rather than simply on accounting and reporting (Donaldson and Picciotto, 2016; Patton, 2011; Shulha, Caruthers & Hopson, 2010). The underlying premise of a logic model is that an evaluation tool must also be a strategic and iterative planning instrument with a specific set of desired outcomes central to the model. If we begin with an understanding that (1) responsible sustainability remains relatively elusive within the global economy, particularly among certain sectors such as the tourism/leisure industry; and (2) responsible sustainability is a desired and viable goal internationally; then (3) we are able to build a logic model with this positive impact in mind, focusing on the process of achieving these outcomes in the short, medium and long term.

This chapter begins to outline the construction of a logic model, recognizing the need to move beyond Fortune Global 500 companies to include small and medium-sized organizations and activities worldwide. The chapter focuses on one business sector in particular, the high-profile sport tourism industry, to demonstrate both the challenges and opportunities in building a logic model focused on responsible sustainability.

Refining the field – sport tourism and responsible sustainability

The principle of sustainability received widespread attention within the Brundtland Report, a report written for the United Nations World Commission on Environment and Development (WCED, 1987). The report highlighted the need for countries and multinational corporations to pay closer attention to the social and environmental impacts of economic growth and development, "to meet the needs of the present without compromising the needs of future generations" (p. 1). A general call to action has been prompted by the liberalization of international markets and the evolution of global capitalism, characterized by worldwide wealth disparities, climate change and international human rights violations.

As one of the fastest growing sectors in the world today, the global tourism industry must confront the ethical and legal mandates regarding sustainability. Certain sectors of tourism, such as sport tourism, are particularly scrutinized concerning responsible sustainability, given the high-profile nature of international mega events, such as the Olympics or the Fédération Internationale de Football Association (FIFA) World Cup.

Residents of host cities and nations often argue that resources utilized during the preparation and staging process of major sporting events might have been better spent on socially sustainable programmes for local citizens and communities who have significant needs (Gibson & Watts, 2013). These needs are often undervalued in the planning process, while tangible and intangible benefits, such as economic gains and the "psychic reward" of community pride, are often exaggerated (Coates & Humphreys, 2003; Gelan, 2003; Gibson, Willming & Holdnak, 2003).

In preparation for hosting the 2014 World Cup, for example, Brazil spent nearly $15 billion, with $11.3 billion in public works spending alone. Of this infrastructure spending, $3.66 billion was used for new and refurbished stadiums, 90 per cent of which came from public money, despite promises by former President Luiz Inacio Lula da Silva that all stadiums would be privately funded (Matheson, 2014). Many of these publicly financed stadiums now sit vacant (Garcia-Navarro, 2015; Manfred, 2015). The Brazilian case is not unique. Scholars have long argued how sports subsidies cannot be justified on the grounds of local economic development, job creation and income growth (Baade & Dye, 1990; Coates & Humphreys, 2003; Hunter, 1988; Mules, 1998). In response to criticisms levelled at FIFA in the build-up to the 2014 World Cup in Brazil, the sport federation stated:

> FIFA believes that its social responsibility is a crucial element of the sustainable success of its events, but the World Cup can only be used as a tool or as a catalyst for change in a country if everyone involved pulls in the same direction as part of a global strategy.
>
> *FIFA, 2014a*

Both Russia and Qatar have likewise received negative attention concerning their commitment to human rights during their efforts to enhance their global prestige through the 2014 Winter Olympics and the 2022 World Cup, respectively. In Russia, attention was focused on what critics have called state-sponsored homophobia (Dorf, 2013; Fierstein, 2013; Higgins, 2013; Van Rheenen, 2014), while scholars and human rights organizations have compared the Qatari government's treatment of migrant workers to slave labour (Amnesty International, 2016; Kamrava & Babar, 2012; Pessoa, Harkness & Gardner, 2014; International Trade Union Confederation, 2014). Both FIFA and the IOC have been harshly criticized for their lacklustre efforts at supporting social sustainability in these host nations (Crary and Leff, 2013; Erfani, 2015; Kidd, 2010; Kidd & Donnelly, 2000; Ngonyama, 2010; Wong, 2013).

Although mega sporting events receive international attention, countries and companies sponsoring small and medium-sized sport tourism activities and events must also address the need to balance economic, environmental and social dimensions. There is a particular need to provide an accessible model for stakeholders to plan, implement and evaluate the impact of these activities and events. This need continues despite the historical gains made in response to a TBL approach.

A TBL approach to sport tourism activities and events

While Elkington (1997) describes the TBL as both a measurement tool and a philosophical approach, it has been most effective in proposing a more ethical vision that runs counter to a strict *laissez-faire* faith in free-market forces. As a result of global demographic and ecological changes, according to Elkington, capitalism will have to evolve and focus on sustainability in order to balance the needs of people, the planet and the economic motivation for profit (the 3Ps).

A TBL approach takes into consideration the social and environmental impacts of a business venture in addition to the traditional measure of profit generation, such as return on investment or shareholder value. The concept of TBL shifts a company's responsibility to "stakeholders" rather than "shareholders", fundamentally altering the decision-making process (Adams & Zutshi, 2004; Dwyer, 2015; Robins, 2006). In large companies, primary stakeholders are those who "bear some form of risk as a result of having invested some form of capital, human or financial, something of value, in a firm" (Clarkson, 1994, p. 5). They generally comprise employees, shareholders (capital suppliers), suppliers, customers, community residents and the natural environment (Clarkson, 1995; Hillman & Keim, 2001; Starik, 1995).

Because few sport tourism events would occur without public support and subsidies (Burgan & Mules, 2001; Mules & Dwyer, 2005), local leaders, organizing sponsors, government agencies and domestic and International Sport Federations become primary stakeholders and therefore have a moral obligation to promote responsible sustainability and to protect the quality of life of local residents (Fredline, 2005). This moral obligation led Getz (2009) to call for a new paradigm that includes a TBL evaluation both in selecting and evaluating events.

As a result of these paradigm shifts globally, small and large companies alike seek ways to engage a wider group of stakeholders and to better understand the social and environmental impact of their business practices. A consciousness of conscience, framed as corporate social responsibility (CSR) or holistic corporate responsibility (HCR), now factors into boardroom discussions and sponsorship decisions. Ideally, hosting rights would be determined based on a nation's track record regarding responsible sustainability.

The challenge of a TBL approach is not its ethical orientation to do the right thing but its practical application as a reporting tool. While Elkington noted that sustainable auditing will become essential for making business decisions transparent in the twenty-first century, there has been little agreement on the steps needed to achieve a TBL balance sheet. The process of measuring sustainable development is tremendously complex, as it requires a universally accepted accounting method. TBL offers no common unit of measurement. As such, Getz (2009, p. 64) argues that "there are substantial challenges involved in implementing the TBL approach, notably the difficulty of comparing tangibles and intangibles, and the current underdevelopment and under-utilization of non-economic measures of value and impact that can be applied to events". While this problem persists, sport tourism scholars have begun to make the intangible more tangible through developing comprehensive impact studies that provide measurements for intangibles such as event excitement, civic pride and enhanced community attachment (Crompton, 2004; Fredline, Jago & Deery, 2002, 2003; Kim & Walker, 2012; Müller, 2012).

Similar to Getz (2009), Brown, Marshall and Dillard (2006) have found fault in the premise of the TBL as a reporting tool. They argue that the "bottom line" is a metaphor applied to business accounting, whereby a common metric sums a vast array of costs and benefits to ascertain net income or earnings on corporate financial statements. On page 22 they write:

> The concept of triple bottom line, in fact, often turns out to be a "good old fashioned single bottom line plus vague commitments to social and environmental

concerns" (Norman & MacDonald, 2004). The economic bottom line, as the dominant bottom line frame, can project attributes of measurability and aggregation onto those systems that they do not possess. In this case, implying that the attributes are similar conveys an illusion of compensatory precision and validity.

Thus, the "triple bottom line" applies a singular bottom line metaphor to include the social and environmental aspects of a business organization, assuming that the application of these additional aspects conforms to a singular accounting methodology.

Despite widespread concern from scholars and practitioners regarding the TBL as a reliable reporting tool (Dwyer, 2015; Stoddard, Pollard & Evans, 2012; Krajinovic, 2015; Porter & Kramer, 2006), several large-scale efforts have been made to measure responsible sustainability, including the GRI, Dow Jones and ISO 26000. The GRI has received the greatest attention in providing a reliable reporting framework for non-financial or sustainability indicators. Both FIFA and the International Olympic Committee (IOC), for example, have publicly pledged their commitment to sustainability and the use of the GRI as a reporting tool (IOC, 2012; FIFA, 2014b).

Developed in 1997 as a joint initiative by the Coalition of Environmentally Responsible Economies and the United Nations Environment Programme, the GRI offers a comprehensive sustainability reporting framework for organizations to measure and disclose their activities, products and services to internal and external stakeholders. Specifically, the GRI suggests five broad categories of sustainability: (1) the organization's economic performance; (2) its environmental performance; (3) its social performance; (4) its labour practices; and (5) its public policies and implementation (GRI, 2012).

The number of companies following the GRI guidelines to report sustainability data has increased dramatically since the establishment of the reporting tool. These increases in sustainable reporting have been most prevalent among large multinational companies. For example, 79 per cent of Fortune Global 500 companies produce sustainability reports; more than three out of four of these reports are based on the GRI Guidelines (Governance and Accountability Institute, 2015).

While the framework is designed to provide universal standards to all organizations, regardless of size, scope and whether public or private, the use of GRI guidelines is less common a practice among smaller to medium-sized firms and among companies in developing nations. As Yadava and Sinha report:

> In India, out of 721,719 registered companies, only 68 companies have developed sustainability reports and a total of 104 reports have been submitted to GRI in the last decade. It is noted that out of the total report submitted from India to GRI, only 20 reports were comprehensive in nature and only 11 reports were based on 2011 guidelines (Global Reporting Initiative Resource Library, 2012).
>
> *Yadava & Sinha, 2015, pp. 2–3*

The GRI (2015) acknowledges these shortcomings, noting that "awareness of sustainability reporting is still low, particularly in developing countries where other safety nets might not be in place for communities and workers affected by private sector actions" (GRI, 2015, p. 29).

Researchers have likewise found that reporting social aspects of corporate responsibility lags well behind reporting on environmental factors (Adams, 2002; Kolk, 2003). Brown,

Marshall and Dillard (2006, p. 9), argue that "the road to social sustainability reflects more of a meandering and awkward afterthought . . ., an objectification through mechanistic management (e.g. social capital), and a subordinated and imprecise objective within an enhanced reporting initiative (e.g. triple bottom line)".

Finally, there are discrepancies in GRI usage by the industrial sector. As Stoddard, Pollard and Evans (2012, p. 237) report,

> only 14 of the nearly 1300 GRI reporting organizations internationally (about 1per cent) were reported to be in the tourism/leisure industry sector . . . . These statistics suggest that the reporting framework may be too cumbersome for many (smaller) tourism organizations to follow, indicating a need for more practical evaluation tools.

One way to address this need is to look to current trends in the evaluation literature and the use of logic models to remedy this need.

A proposed logic model for responsible sustainability in sport tourism

The transdiscipline of evaluation has historically been focused on donor or customer satisfaction and accounting concerns. More recently, the field of evaluation has become interested in facilitating social justice by helping to develop more equitable organizations and governments (Donaldson & Picciotto, 2016; Hopson, 2009; Patton, 2011; Stake, 2003). Evaluation efforts to promote responsible sustainability at both the micro- and macro-levels fall well within this agenda as does the modest effort of constructing an accessible logic model for sustainability.

Logic models evolved out of evaluation research and have been used in numerous settings and across a number of programmes and organizations (Donaldson and Lipsey, 2006; Gargani, 2013; Jordan & Mortensen, 1997; Jordan, Reed & Mortensen, 1997; Shakman & Rodriguez, 2015; Scheirer, 1994; Wells and Arthur-Banning, 2008; W. K. Kellogg Foundation, 2004; Wholey, 2004).

As depicted in Figure 29.1, a logic model is a graphic representation of the relationship among an activity's inputs or resources (what is invested in the activity), the activities or strategies, the outputs (what is done with those resources/investments) and the resulting outcomes. While logic models can have structural flexibility, traditional logic models are often presented as linear, implying causality from one action to the next. The theory or logic underlying a logic model proposes a series of if–then relationships central to a potential activity or event (Jones, 2012; McLaughlin & Jordan, 1999, 2004). Hypothesized linkages from one column to the next illustrate these if–then propositions. If the model includes x input, for example, then the model might predict y output based upon a corresponding strategy. A y output, in turn, will predict a z outcome. As a simple example, the input of two aspirin results in reduced tension or headache, with the desired outcome of allowing an employee to return to work.

Figure 29.1 Logic model relationships

Logic models have built in assumptions agreed upon by stakeholders. A successful logic model makes explicit underlying beliefs or assumptions. In order to address the criticism of the TBL approach previously discussed, the construction of a logic model for sustainable responsibility can effectively utilize the TBL as its conceptual framework. This effort recognizes the TBL as a philosophical orientation rather than as a reliable reporting tool.

Inputs are the financial, human and natural resources that combine to develop a proposed activity or event. Strategies are the game plan, a series of steps or activities taken to achieve a set of desired outcomes. Outputs represent what is done with the inputs or resources, how they are used to achieve a set of outcomes. These may include goods and services, communication plans, reports, promotional information, meetings and events. In other words, the output is the "data" that prove that the activity or strategy occurred (Shakman, 2014).

Outcomes are the short-, medium- and long-term results of the model's implementation. These outcomes represent both costs and benefits, with the summation of these results producing potential positive and negative impacts. Summative evaluation is an important part of the model but is preceded by a formative, iterative and multi-step process. The evaluation draws on the design and implementation phases previously conducted, assessing short-, medium- and long-term outcomes. These outcomes will define impact. This approach to performance measurement requires more than keeping score *post hoc*.

Logic models are effective tools for programme or policy design and planning when implemented within an iterative process. The process of designing and utilizing a logic model is more iterative than strictly linear, beginning with the desired impacts and working backwards and then forwards, stopping at times and regrouping to begin anew with the long-term goal always in mind. In this regard, logic models should be seen as living documents to be referred to throughout the life of the activity and altered as needed (Shakman & Rodriquez, 2015). As a strategic planning process rather than a product, logic models allow stakeholders to work together towards a common goal or set of goals, such as the promotion of financial and non-financial sustainability. Logic models are well suited to be applied to sport tourism activities and events as they afford greater inclusion of stakeholders and a more participatory method of performance measurement.

The proposed logic model for responsible sustainability in sport tourism draws on existing literature, particularly the scholarship focused on impact and legacy studies. Although sometimes used interchangeably, Preuss (2007) distinguishes between "impact" and "legacy", where impacts are caused by shorter-term activities, while legacies represent longer-term effects. Many of these studies have specifically addressed economic impacts and legacies (Baade, Baumann and Matheson, 2008; Coates and Humphreys, 2003; Crompton, 1995; Hagn and Maennig, 2007; Hudson, 2001; Ritchie, 1996), while others have focused on the social and environmental impacts (Burns & Mules, 1986; Collins, Jones & Munday, 2009; Crompton, 2006; Fredline & Faulkner, 2000; Fredline, Jago & Deery, 2002, 2003; Jones, 2001; Misener & Mason, 2006; Wheeler & Nauright, 2006) of sport tourism activities and events. Several researchers have taken a more holistic approach to responsible sustainability framed within a TBL approach (Fredline, 2005; Fredline *et al.*, 2004, 2005; Getz, 2009; Stoddard, Pollard & Evans, 2012).

But, like accounting tools that measure the positive and negative impacts once an activity or event has already taken place, impact and legacy studies often focus on *ex post* summative performance evaluations without including the formative component of how to achieve the desired goals of sustainability. Graphically, the focus has been on the far right of the proposed logic model rather than on the critical steps needed to strategically achieve specific outcomes (e.g. left to right).

Table 29.1 The logic model framework

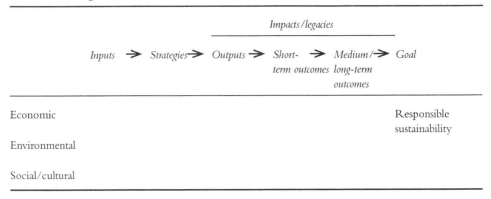

			Impacts/legacies		
Inputs →	Strategies→	Outputs →	Short-term outcomes →	Medium/long-term outcomes →	Goal
Economic					Responsible sustainability
Environmental					
Social/cultural					

Thus, drawing on extant literature, as well as existing reporting tools such as the GRI, a logic model for responsible sustainability in sport tourism provides an accessible and iterative tool for the strategic planning, implementation and evaluation of a given activity or event. The model seeks to provide stakeholders with a dynamic (working) document or template. As depicted in Table 29.1, the logic model utilizes the TBL as a guiding assumption, such that financial and non-financial sustainability may be promoted and pursued simultaneously. Assuming that the desired goal and ultimate impact is responsible or ethical sustainability, stakeholders work backwards (and then forwards) to design and develop an effective activity or event.

In order to be sure, stakeholders will have varying commitments to the economic, environmental and social dimensions of the model, but genuine inclusion and participation presupposes a social and cultural etiquette among stakeholders, much as seasoned travellers follow a cultural code of conduct that is both respectful and responsive. For responsible sustainability to be achieved within the sport tourism industry, all parties or perspectives must be valued without any one party presuming priority or ignoring other perspectives. A shared vision and commitment to collaboration will help to ensure the effectiveness of any sport tourism coalition.

There are numerous manuals that provide a useful blueprint for how best to build an effective logic model (Jones, 2012; Knowlton & Phillips, 2012; McLaughlin & Jordan, 1999, 2004; Shakman, 2014; Shakman & Rodriguez, 2015; Scheirer, 1994; W. K. Kellogg, 2004). As depicted in Figure 29.2, the model proposed here is a relatively simple heuristic intended to be accessible to the broadest range of stakeholders possible. The initial step in this process, then, is for the organizing body or event manager to determine which groups comprise the key stakeholders. For example, the GRI defines "affected stakeholders . . . as those individuals, communities, or causes that may intentionally or unintentionally be impacted positively or negatively by the work of the organization, and to whom specific accountability duties arise" (2015, p. 65).

These stakeholders can then be invited to participate in the planning, implementation and evaluation of the activity or event. A consultant or facilitator might be utilized to initiate the process, train stakeholders in the use of logic models, and provide guidelines as how best to proceed collectively. Once stakeholders have been assembled, this coalition can collect all relevant information necessary to engage the process fully. This information includes key contextual factors needed for the successful implementation of an activity or event.

The second step of this process is to define assumptions and potential problems inherent to the logic model. Based on the logic model proposed within this chapter, responsible sustainability

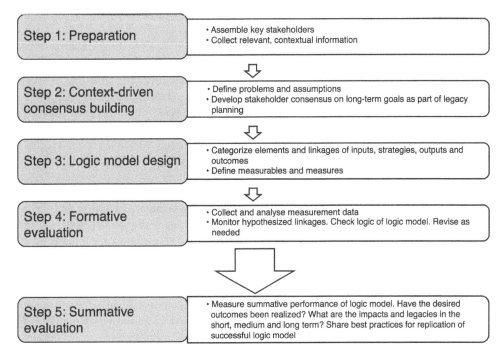

Figure 29.2   A five-step logic model for responsible sustainability in sport tourism

is needed within the larger tourism industry, and specifically within the sport tourism sector. The belief that financial and non-financial sustainability is possible serves as the underlying assumption of this model. The planning, design and implementation process is then initiated based on the articulated problem statement, corresponding assumption and desired goal.

The initial step of determining, inviting and engaging stakeholders to assemble information becomes a strategy of how best to utilize critical inputs or resources within the project. Specific stakeholders, such as local government agencies, sponsors and local community groups, may be spelled out within the model.

It is useful for stakeholders to review the range of performance indicators articulated in existing accounting instruments and scholarship in advance of planning an activity or event. For example, the Olympic Games Global Impact (OGGI) programme utilizes several indicators (Furrer, 2002; IOC, 2006) specific to mega-sporting events, while impact and legacy studies of small- to medium-sized activities or events often focus on more localized indicators specific to a given site and/or sport tourism activity. These indicators can then be assembled as a list or inventory.

Depending on the scope and size of a given activity, not all indicators will apply equally. This evaluative process allows stakeholders to prioritize resources and evaluate potential limitations to the model. For example, a coalition will probably ask about the financial and natural resources required for a successful project to take place. Who is, or will be, responsible for these resources? Control traditionally rests in the hands of those purportedly paying the bill and/or who hold positions of power, particularly those in the private sector. As we have noted throughout this chapter, however, results represent more than a single bottom line. Public monies and protection of the public good may not be monitored well by stakeholders focused primarily on revenue generation. The public is a diverse array of constituents, demonstrating the need for key stakeholders to be identified and included within this process. Among these stakeholders, a more equitable oversight of costs and benefits will help realize a logic model for financial and nonfinancial sustainability.

The third step of the logic model involves defining measurables by categorizing the information collected and cataloguing it into the relative columns of the table. This process seeks to identify inputs, strategies and outputs relative to the desired outcomes.

The use of the logic model's if–then propositions are useful building blocks to think through how particular actions might produce more or less desired results. These propositions may be projected for short-, medium- and long-range outcomes, building on one another.

For example, as illustrated in Table 29.2, the strategic planning of appropriate infrastructure spending seeks to maximize venue efficiency to result in both reduced costs and revenue generation. Economic efficiency need not be environmentally insensitive. The promotion of green technologies throughout the planning and implementation phase of sport tourism activities and events will minimize CO_2 emissions and pressures on sensitive ecology, leading to the reduction of pollution. Simultaneously, community forums and meetings seek to include key stakeholders in order to foster social integration and community cohesiveness. The long-term benefit of such social sustainability will create increased social equity and quality of life for local residents and communities.

The next phase of the process focuses on the formative summation of the logic model through the collection and analysis of measurement data. Activities can then be monitored, analysing the proposed linkages and short-term outcomes. Adjustments can be made as needed. When the projected results are not realized in the short-term and/or unintended costs are incurred as a result, the plan may need to change to correct faulty hypotheses. This is one of the primary benefits of an iterative logic model flexible enough to adjust as an activity or event develops. A coalition of stakeholders consistently checks the underlying logic of the logic model for optimal results.

The fifth and final step of the process is the summative evaluation of measurement performance. How has the logic model worked? Have the projected outcomes been realized? Because evaluation has been ongoing throughout as an iterative process, reporting is far more predictable than is the case with *ex post facto* tools such as the GRI or impact studies that measure outcomes after an event. If the design and planning phases have clearly articulated sustainable indicators inherent to the logic model, the final evaluation phase simply tests a series of proposed hypotheses. A successful logic model will not only become an accessible tool for multiple stakeholders; the model will also be empirically grounded and therefore reliable.

Conclusion

There remains a persistent need for governments and industry leaders to help promote responsible sustainability. A consciousness of conscience underlies the TBL philosophy, whereby public and private organizations and agencies seek ways to understand better the social and environmental impact of their business practices. In theory, greater awareness breeds more responsible behaviour.

While there has been increased utilization of accounting tools such as the GRI, it has been primarily large, well-resourced (e.g. Fortune Global 500) companies who use these reporting tools. Certain sectors of the global economy, such as the tourism industry, lag well behind other sectors. In particular, the high-profile sport tourism industry highlights the need to balance the economic promotion of sport tourism activities and events with a similar commitment to social and environmental health and well-being. While well-meaning in

Table 29.2 A general logic model for sport tourism

	Inputs →	Strategies →	Outputs →	Short-term outcomes →	Medium/long-term outcomes →	Goal
				Impacts/legacies		
Economic	Stakeholders: • Participants (e.g. athletes, coaches, spectators, support staff)	• Promote and market event and site location • Maximize venue efficiency	• Promotional materials produced • Targeted infrastructure spending and development	• Local image enhanced • Profit on investment • Unnecessary infrastructure spending and opportunity costs minimized	• Future tourism promotion • Positive economic development	
Environmental	Agencies • Governments • NGOs Resources • Investment • Natural resources • Infrastructure	• Develop and enforce comprehensive environmental standards • Leverage events for environmental education such as greater awareness of recycling, energy efficiency, and pollution control • Infrastructure development for the public good • Promote and incentivize greater use of green technologies	• Evaluation reports produced • Marketing materials promoting environmental sustainability • Community infrastructure and health needs (i.e. water, sewage, transportation) improved • Environmentally responsible technologies used at venues and local environment (e.g. stadiums)	• Minimized CO_2, noise, traffic, congestion, temporary crowding, and pressure on sensitive ecology • Enhanced awareness and enforcement of existing laws and regulations • Improvements made to local water and forestry systems • Impact on water and air quality minimized	• Positive or neutral environmental impact • Urban and ecological regeneration • Environmentally conscious strategies utilized in ongoing tourism sector • Greater use of alternative energy sources	Responsible Sustainability
	Laws/rights • Land use					
Social/cultural	• Fair labour • Disability • Gender/racial equity	• Include key stakeholders in a meaningful and consistent manner throughout planning • Leverage events to improve community health and wellness • Create and enforce rules around historic architecture/artefacts/culturally significant locations • Develop and enforce comprehensive fair labour and equity standards	• Community forums and meetings held • Public transportation infrastructure improved • Social problems at local site combatted (i.e. homelessness, crime, unemployment) • Natural resource use evaluated • Labour practices monitored	• Social integration, community development, and community pride fostered • Enhanced accessibility for local community • Unjust displacement of local community minimized • Enhanced awareness and enforcement of fair labour and equity standards	• Enhanced quality of life • Maintenance of historic and culturally significant landmarks • Increased social equity and fair labour practices • Greater awareness and protection of all human rights	

their approach, instruments such as the GRI primarily provide *ex post* evaluations of sustainability indicators. Most impact and legacy studies have similarly focused on outcomes rather than on the planning and implementation required to achieve these desired results. Logic models represent efforts in the current evaluation scholarship to create additional tools for organizations to promote social justice and equity.

Within the current context, then, this chapter has proposed a logic model for responsible sustainability in sport tourism. The proposed model attempts to provide a more accessible method for stakeholders to communicate within an iterative decision-making process. It provides a universal graphic language for the articulation of inputs, outputs and desired outcomes that can be localized to the context of small- and medium-sized organizations. Logic models allow for the strategic planning, implementation and evaluation of these desired outcomes, thereby complementing existing reporting tools, such as the GRI. If stakeholders begin with a shared vision of realizing responsible sustainability, participants can plan and then build models to meet this goal. Successful logic models can then be replicated and empirically tested in other locales and across different types of sport tourism activities and events. It is my hope that the five-step process outlined in this chapter may be a useful tool for stakeholders interested in promoting responsible sustainability within the sport tourism industry.

References

Adams, C.A. (2002). Internal organisational factors influencing corporate social and ethical reporting: Beyond current theorising. *Accounting, Auditing & Accountability Journal, 15*(2), 223–250.

Adams, C. and Zutshi, A. (2004). Corporate social responsibility: Why business should act responsibly and be accountable. *Australian Accounting Review, 14*(34), 31–39.

Amnesty International (2016). *Qatar: World Cup of shame* [online]. Available at <www.amnesty.org/en/latest/campaigns/2016/03/qatar-world-cup-of-shame/>. Accessed 7 March 2016.

Baade, R. A. and Dye, R. F. (1990). The impact of stadium and professional sports on metropolitan area development. *Growth & Change, 21*(2), 1–14.

Baade, R. A. Baumann, R. & Matheson, V. A. (2008). Selling the game: Estimating the economic impact of professional sports through taxable sales. *Southern Economic Journal, 47*(3), 794–810.

Burns, J. P. A. & Mules, T. J. (1986). *The Adelaide Grand Prix: The Impact of a Special Event.* Adelaide, Australia: Centre for South Australian Economic Studies.

Brown, D., Marshall, R. S. & Dillard, J. F. (2006). *Triple bottom line: A business metaphor for a social construct* [online]. Barcelona: Departament d'Economia de l'Empresa, Universitat Autònoma de Barcelona. Available at <www.recercat.cat/bitstream/handle/2072/2223/UABDT06-2.pdf?sequence=1>. Accessed 20 July 2016.

Burgan, B. & Mules, T. (2001). Reconciling cost-benefit and economic impact assessment for event tourism. *Tourism Economics, 7*(4), 321–330.

Coates, D. & Humphreys, B. R. (2003). Professional sports facilities, franchises and urban economic development. *Public Finance and Management, 3*(3), 335–357.

Collins, A., Jones, C. & Munday, M. (2009). Assessing the environmental impacts of mega sporting events: Two options? *Tourism Management, 30*(6), 828–837.

Clarkson, M. (1994). A risk-based model of stakeholder theory. In *Proceedings of the Second Toronto Conference on Stakeholder Theory* (pp. 18–19). Toronto: Centre for Corporate Social Performance & Ethics, University of Toronto.

Clarkson, M. E. (1995). A stakeholder framework for analysing and evaluating corporate social performance. *Academy of Management Review, 20*(1), 92–117.

Crary, D. & Leff, L. "Russia's anti-gay laws impact Olympics, vodka sales". The *Huffington Post* [online] (29 July 2013). Available at <www.yahoo.com/news/russian-anti-gay-laws-impact-olympics-vodka-sales-202546428.html?ref=gs>. Accessed 22 February 2016.

Crompton, J. L. (1995). Economic impact analysis of sports facilities and events: Eleven sources of misapplication. *Journal of Sport Management, 9*(1), 14–35.

Crompton, J. L. (2004). Conceptualization and alternate operationalizations of the measurement of sponsorship effectiveness in sport. *Leisure Studies, 23*(3), 267–281.

Crompton, J. L. (2006). Economic impact studies: Instruments for political shenanigans? *Journal of Travel Research*, *45*(1), 67–82.

Donaldson, S. I., & Picciotto, R. (Eds) (2016). *Evaluation for an Equitable Society*. Charlotte, NC: Information Age Publishing.

Donaldson, S. I. & Lipsey, M. W. (2006). Roles for theory in contemporary evaluation practice: Developing practical knowledge. In I. Shaw, J. C. Greene & M. M. Mark (Eds) *Handbook of Evaluation: Policies, Programs and Practices* (pp. 56–75). London: Sage.

Dorf, J. "Homophobia in Russia: A bigger fight". The *Huffington Post* [online] (10 October 2013). Available at <www.huffingtonpost.com/julie-dorf/homophobia-in-russia-a-bi_b_4073509.html>. Accessed 6 June 2016.

Dwyer, L. (2015). Triple bottom line reporting as a basis for sustainable tourism: Opportunities and challenges. *Acta Turistica*, *27*(1), 33–62.

Elkington, J. (1997). *Cannibals with Forks. The Triple Bottom Line of 21st Century Business*. Oxford: Capstone.

Erfani, A. (2015). Kicking away responsibility: FIFA's role in response to migrant worker abuses in Qatar's 2022 World Cup. *Jeffrey S. Moorad Sports Law Journal*, *22*(2), 623–662.

Fédération Internationale de Football Association (FIFA) (2014a). *FAQ: Setting the record straight* [pdf]. FIFA.com. Available at <www.fifa.com/mm/document/tournament/competition/02/36/32/63/faq_en_neutral.pdf>. Accessed 15 June 2016.

Fédération Internationale de Football Association (FIFA) (2014b). *Sustainability report of the 2014 FIFA World Cup Brazil* [pdf]. Zurich, Switzerland: Fédération Internationale de Football Association (FIFA) and the 2014 FIFA World Cup Local Organizing Committee (LOC). Available at: <www.fifa.com/mm/document/afsocial/general/02/50/92/69/sustainabilityreportofthe2020fwc_neutral.pdf>. Accessed 15 June 2016.

Fierstein, H. "Russia's anti-gay crackdown". The *New York Times* [online] (21 July 2013). Available at <www.nytimes.com/2013/07/22/opinion/russias-anti-gay-crackdown.html>. Accessed 5 July 2016.

Fredline, E. (2005). Host and guest relations and sport tourism. *Sport in Society*, *8*(2), 263–279.

Fredline, E. & Faulkner, B. (2000). Host community reactions: A cluster analysis. *Annals of Tourism Research*, *27*(3), 763–784.

Fredline, L., Jago, L. K. & Deery, M. (2002). Assessing the social impacts of events: Scale development. In L. Jago, M. Deery, R. Harris, A. M. Hede & J. Allen (Eds), *Events and Place Making* (pp. 760–787). Sydney, Australia: Australian Centre for Event Management, University of Technology. Available at <www.uts.edu.au/sites/default/files/Events%20and%20Place%20Making%20-%20Conference%20Proceedings.pdf>. Accessed 5 March 2016.

Fredline, L., Jago, L. & Deery, M. (2003). The development of a generic scale to measure the social impacts of events. *Event management*, *8*(1), 23–37.

Fredline, L., Raybould, R., Jago, L.K. & Deery, M. (2004). Triple bottom line event evaluation: Progress toward a technique to assist in planning and managing events in a sustainable manner. In *The Scottish Hotel School, Tourism: State of the Art II Conference*. Glasgow, Scotland (27–30 June 2004). Glasgow: University of Strathclyde.

Fredline, L., Raybould, M., Jago, L. & Deery, M. (2005, July). Triple bottom line event evaluation: A proposed framework for holistic event evaluation. In Allen, J. (Ed.) *The Impacts of Events: Proceedings of the International Event Research Conference* (pp. 2–15). Sydney: Australian Centre for Event Management University of Technology.

Furrer, P. (2002). Sustainable Olympic Games: A dream or a reality? *Bollettino della Società Geografica Italiana*, *7*(4).

Garcia-Navarro, L. (2015). Brazil's World Cup Legacy Includes $550M Stadium-Turned-Parking Lot. *NPR* [online] (11 May). Available at <www.npr.org/sections/parallels/2015/05/11/405955547/brazils-world-cup-legacy-includes-550m-stadium-turned-parking-lot>. Accessed 10 July 2016.

Gargani, J. (2013). What can practitioners learn from theorists' logic models? *Evaluation and Program Planning*, *38*, 81–88.

Gelan, A. (2003). Local economic impacts: The British open. *Annals of Tourism Research*, *30*(2), 406–425.

Getz, D. (2009). Policy for sustainable and responsible festivals and events: Institutionalization of a new paradigm. *Journal of Policy Research in Tourism, Leisure & Events*, *1*(1), 61–78.

Gibson, O. & Watts, J. "World cup: Rio favelas being 'socially cleansed in run up to sporting events'". The *Guardian* [online] (5 December 2013). Available at <www.theguardian.com/world/2013/dec/05/world-cup-favelas-socially-cleansed-olympics>. Accessed 23 June 2016.

Gibson, H. J., Willming, C. & Holdnak, A. (2003). Small-scale event sport tourism: Fans as tourists. *Tourism Management*, *24*(2), 181–190.

Governance and Accountability Institute (2012). *2012 corporate ESG/sustainability/responsibility reporting. Does it matter?* [pdf] New York: Governance & Accountability Institute. Available at <www.ga-institute.com/fileadmin/user_upload/Reports/SP500_-_Final_12-15-12.pdf>. Accessed 8 June 2016.

Governance and Accountability Institute (2015). *Flash report: Seventy-five per cent of the S&P index published corporate sustainability reports in 2014* [online]. Available at <www.ga-institute.com/nc/issue-master-system/news-details/npage/1/article/flash-report-seventy-five-percent-75-of-the-sp-index-published-corporate-sustainability-rep.html>. Accessed 14 July 2016.

Global Reporting Initiative (2012). *GRI annual report 2011–2012* [pdf]. Amsterdam: Global Reporting Initiative. Available at <www.globalreporting.org/resourcelibrary/GRI-Annual-Report-2011-2012.pdf>. Accessed 26 May 2016.

Global Reporting Initiative (2015). *GRI annual report 2014–2015* [pdf]. Amsterdam: Global Reporting Initiative. Available at <www.globalreporting.org/resourcelibrary/GRIs%20Combined%20Report%202014-2015.pdf>. Accessed 26 May 2016.

Hagn, F. & Maennig, W. (2007). Labour market effects of the 2006 Soccer World Cup in Germany. *Hamburg Contemporary Economic Discussions* (8). Available at <SSRN:http://ssrn.com/abstract=1541950> or <http://dx.doi.org/10.2139/ssrn.1541950>. Accessed 10 July 2016.

Higgins, A. "Facing fury over antigay law, Stoli says 'Russian? Not really'". The *New York Times* [online] (7 September 2013). Available at <www.nytimes.com/2013/09/08/world/europe/facing-fury-over-antigay-law-stoli-says-russian-not-really.html?_r=0>. Accessed 29 June 2016.

Hillman, A. J. & Keim, G. D. (2001). Shareholder value, stakeholder management, and social issues: What's the bottom line? *Strategic Management Journal*, *22*, 125–139.

Hopson, R. (2009). Reclaiming knowledge at the margins: Culturally responsive evaluation in the current evaluation moment. In K. Ryan & J. B. Cousins (Eds), *Sage International Handbook of Educational Evaluation* (pp. 429–446). Thousand Oaks, CA: Sage.

Hudson, I. (2001). The use and misuse of economic impact analysis the case of professional sports. *Journal of Sport & Social Issues*, *25*(1), 20–39.

Hunter, W. J. (1988). *Economic Impact Studies: Inaccurate, Misleading, and Unnecessary*. Chicago: Heartland Institute.

Husbands, W. & Harrison, L. C. (1996). Practicing responsible tourism: Understanding tourism today to prepare for tomorrow. In L.C. Harrison & W. Husbands (Eds), *Practicing Responsible Tourism: International Case Studies in Tourism Planning, Policy, and Development* (pp. 1–15). New York: John Wiley & Sons.

International Olympic Committee (2006). Focus: Olympic Games global impact. *Olympic Review* [online] (June). Available at <https://stillmed.olympic.org/Documents/Reports/EN/en_report_1077.pdf>. Accessed 10 June 2016.

International Olympic Committee (2012). New reporting framework underlies IOC's commitment to sustainability. *Olympic.org* [online] (25 January). Available at <www.olympic.org/news/new-reporting-framework-underlines-ioc-s-commitment-to-sustainability>. Accessed 10 June 2016.

International Trade Union Confederation (2014). *The case against Qatar*. Brussels: ITUC. Available at <www.ituc-csi.org/IMG/pdf/the_case_against_qatar_en_web170314.pdf>. Accessed 16 July 2016.

Jones, R. N. (2001). An environmental risk assessment/management framework for climate change impact assessments. *Natural Hazards*, *23*(2–3), 197–230.

Jones, P. (2012). *Inputs, Outputs, Outcomes: Using a Misunderstood Approach, Successfully: An Excitant White Paper* [online]. Wansford, UK: Excitant Ltd. Available at <http://excitant.co.uk/wp-content/uploads/2012/08/Understanding-Inputs-Outputs-Outcomes-Excitant-white-paper.pdf>. Accessed 7 March 2016.

Jordan, G. B. & Mortensen, J. C. (1997). Measuring the performance of research and technology programs: A balanced scorecard approach. *Journal of Technology Transfer*, *22*(2), 13–20.

Jordan, G. B., Reed, J. H. & Mortensen, J. C. (1997, June). Measuring and managing the performance of energy programs: An in-depth Case study. In *Eighth Annual National Energy Services Conference*, Washington, DC.

Kamrava, M. & Babar, Z. (Eds) (2012). *Migrant Labor in the Persian Gulf*. London: Hurst.

Kidd, B. (2010). Human rights and the Olympic Movement after Beijing. *Sport in Society*, *13*(5), 901–910.

Kidd, B., & Donnelly, P. (2000). Human rights in sports. *International Review for the Sociology of Sport*, *35*(2), 131–148.

Kim, W. & Walker, M. (2012). Measuring the social impacts associated with Super Bowl XLIII: Preliminary development of a psychic income scale. *Sport Management Review*, 15(1), 91–108.

Knowlton, L. W. & Phillips, C. C. (2012). *The Logic Model Guidebook: Better Strategies for Great Results.* (2nd edn). London: Sage.

Kolk, A. (2003). Trends in sustainability reporting by the Fortune Global 250. *Business Strategy and the Environment*, 12(5), 279–291.

Krajinovic, V. (2015). Challenging the key issues in measuring sustainable tourism development. *Acta Turistica*, 27(1), 63–91.

Lea, J. P. (1993). Tourism development ethics in the Third World. *Annals of Tourism Research*, 20(4), 701–715.

Leslie, D. (Ed.) (2012). *Responsible Tourism: Concepts, Theory and Practice.* Cambridge, MA: CABI.

Manfred, T. (2015). Brazil's $3 billion World Cup stadiums are becoming white elephants a year later. *Business Insider* [online] (May 13). Available at <www.businessinsider.com/brazil-world-cup-stadiums-one-year-later-2015-5>. Accessed 15 July 2016.

Matheson, V. (2014). Were the billions Brazil spent on World Cup stadiums worth it? *FiveThirtyEight* [online] (June 28). Available at <http://fivethirtyeight.com/features/were-the-billions-brazil-spent-on-world-cup-stadiums-worth-it/>. Accessed 15 July 2016.

McLaughlin, J. A. & Jordan, G. B. (1999). Logic models: A tool for telling your programs performance story. *Evaluation & Program Planning*, 22(1), 65–72.

McLaughlin, J. A. & Jordan, G. B. (2004). Using logic models. In K. E. Newcomer, H. P. Hatry & J. S. Wholey (Eds), *Handbook of Practical Program Evaluation* (pp. 7–32). (4th edn). Hoboken, NJ: Jossey-Bass.

Misener, L. & Mason, D. S. (2006). Creating community networks: Can sporting events offer meaningful sources of social capital? *Managing Leisure*, 11(1), 39–56.

Mules, T. (1998). Taxpayer subsidies for major sporting events. *Sport Management Review*, 1(1), 25–43.

Mules, T. & Dwyer, L. (2005). Public sector support for sport tourism events: The role of cost-benefit analysis. *Sport in Society*, 8(2), 338–355.

Müller, M. (2012). Popular perception of urban transformation through mega-events: Understanding support for the 2014 Winter Olympics in Sochi. *Environment and Planning C: Government and Policy*, 30(4), 693–711.

Norman, W. & MacDonald, C. (2004). Getting to the bottom of "triple bottom line". *Business Ethics Quarterly*, 14(2), 243–262.

Ngonyama, P. (2010). The 2010 FIFA World Cup: Critical voices from below. *Soccer & Society*, 11(1–2), 168–180.

Patton, M. Q. (2011). *Essentials of Utilization-focused Evaluation.* Thousand Oaks, CA: Sage.

Pessoa, S., Harkness, L. & Gardner, A. (2014). Ethiopian labor migrants and the "free visa" system in Qatar. *Human Organization*, 73(3), 205–213.

Porter, M. E. & Kramer, M. R. (2006). Strategy and society: The link between corporate social responsibility and competitive advantage. *Harvard Business Review*, 84(12), 78–92.

Preuss, H. (2007). The conceptualization and measurement of mega sport event legacies. *Journal of Sport & Tourism*, 12(3–4), 207–228.

Ritchie, B. W. (1996). How special are special events? The economic impact and strategic development of the New Zealand Masters Games. *Festival Management & Event Tourism*, 4(3–1), 117–126.

Robins, F. (2006). The challenge of TBL: A responsibility to whom? *Business and Society Review*, 111(1), 1–14.

Scheyvens, R. (2002). *Tourism for Development: Empowering Communities.* London: Prentice Hall.

Shakman, K. (2014). *Logic Models to support program design, implementation and evaluation: A workbook created by the regional educational laboratory – Northeast and Islands* [online]. Waltham, MA: Education Development Center. Available at <www.sedl.org/afterschool/iqa/events/webinars/LogicModel_Workbook_2014.pdf>. Accessed 1 March 2016.

Shakman, K. & Rodriguez, S. M. (2015). "Logic models for program design, implementation, and evaluation: Workshop toolkit (REL 2015-057)". Washington, DC: US Department of Education, Institute of Education Sciences, National Center for Education Evaluation and Regional Assistance, Regional Educational Laboratory Northeast & Islands. Available at <http://ies.ed.gov/ncee/edlabs>. Accessed 27 February 2016.

Scheirer, M. A. (1994). Designing and using process evaluation. In J. S. Wholey, H. P. Hatry & K. E. Newcomer (Eds), *Handbook of Practical Program Evaluation* (pp. 40–60). San Francisco, CA: John Wiley & Sons.

Shulha, L. M., Caruthers, F. A. & Hopson, R. K. (2010). *The Program Evaluation Standards: A Guide for Evaluators and Evaluation Users.* Thousand Oaks, CA: Sage.

Stake, R. (2003). Responsive evaluation. In T. Kellaghan & D. L. Stufflebeam (Eds), *International Handbook of Educational Evaluation* (pp. 63–68). Dordrecht, Netherlands: Springer Science+Business Media.

Starik, M. (1995). Should trees have managerial standing? Toward stakeholder status for non-human nature. *Journal of Business Ethics, 14*(3), 207–217.

Stoddard, J. E., Pollard, C. E. & Evans, M. R. (2012). The triple bottom line: A framework for sustainable tourism development. *International Journal of Hospitality & Tourism Administration, 13*(3), 233–258.

Van Rheenen, D. (2014). A skunk at the garden party: The Sochi Olympics, state-sponsored homophobia and prospects for human rights through mega sporting events. *Journal of Sport & Tourism, 19*(2), 127–144.

W. K. Kellogg Foundation (2004). *Logic Model Development Guide* [online]. Battle Creek, MI: WK Kellogg Foundation. Available at <www.smartgivers.org/uploads/logicmodelguidepdf.pdf>. Accessed 1 March 2016.

Wells, M. S. & Arthur-Banning, S. G. (2008). The logic of youth development: Constructing a logic model of youth development through sport. *Journal of Park & Recreation Administration, 26*(2), 189–202.

Wheeler, K. & Nauright, J. (2006). A global perspective on the environmental impact of golf. *Sport in Society, 9*(3), 427–443.

Wholey, J. S. (2004). Exploratory evaluation. In J. S. Wholey, H. P. Hatry & K. E. Newcomer (Eds), *Handbook of Practical Program Evaluation* (pp. 81–99). (3rd edn). San Francisco, CA: Jossey-Bass.

Wong, C. M. "Russia's anti-gay law will impact foreign tourists, possible Olympic athletes: report". The *Huffington Post* [online] (11 July 2013). Available at <www.huffingtonpost.com/2013/07/11/russia-gay-law-tourists-_n_3581217.html>. Accessed 7 July 2016.

World Commission on Environment and Development (1987). *Our Common Future.* Oxford: Oxford University Press.

Yadava, R. N. & Sinha, B. (2015). Scoring sustainability reports using GRI 2011 guidelines for assessing environmental, economic, and social dimensions of leading public and private Indian companies. *Journal of Business Ethics*, pp. 1–10 [online]. Available at <http://dx.doi.org/10.1007/s10551-015-2597-1>. Accessed 10 July 2016.

Yarbrough, D. B., Shulha, L. M., Hopson, R. K. & Caruthers, F. A. (2010). *The Program Evaluation Standards: A Guide for Evaluators and Evaluation Users.* (3rd edn). Los Angeles, CA: Sage.

30

SMALL-SCALE ACTIVE SPORT TOURISM IS INTERNATIONAL BUSINESS

Richard J. Buning and Brian D. Krohn

Introduction

Sport tourism is a driver of community and tourism development through visitor expenditure. Research suggests that sport tourism provides social (e.g. cultural identity, lower crime) environmental (e.g. increased parks, restoration) and economic (e.g. job creation, small business) benefits to a host community (e.g. Hirtz & Ross, 2010; Taks, Chalip & Green, 2015). As a result, the process of organizing, bidding and hosting events such as the Olympics, the FIFA World Cup and other major international sport events is a complex but highly sought after endeavour for destinations seeking to leverage sport event tourism for community development. Many of the destinations involved in these bids are interested in drawing spectator interest not only for onsite visits, but also for television broadcasts, media reports, other word-of-mouth discussions and destination image enhancement. These events, however, focus mostly on passive sport participants, that is, those that either attend the event to watch in person or those that watch, read and hear about the event away from the event site. Conversely, the role of physically active sport events and activities in creating positive impacts for communities and destinations is often overlooked. Perhaps the perceived relative community impact of active sport events is thought to be smaller and less prestigious than large-scale spectator-focused events. However small-scale events provide positive community impacts that are created at a fraction of the cost.

Travelling to actively participate in a sport of interest is a distinct segment of the sport tourism industry (Gibson, 1998a). Often this style of travel is provoked or stimulated through events as individuals seek opportunities to celebrate their sport participation and surround themselves with the related subculture (Green & Chalip, 1998). This segment of sport tourism has been denoted as "event active sport tourism" (Kaplanidou & Gibson, 2010), which encompasses sport participants travelling to actively participate in a sport event. Although active sport tourism tends to be relatively small-scale compared to spectator-based sport tourism, it has the ability to attract people from around the world and compete within the international tourism market. Thus, this chapter provides a definitional effort, an overview of the community and individual benefits of small-scale active sport events (e.g. local running races, golf tournaments, cycling competitions), an overview of the prevailing conceptual framework and examples of destinations that have developed tourism strategies around small-scale active sport tourism.

A definitional effort

Although numerous chapters, articles and reports have been published on sport tourism and sport events, no universal definition exists to characterize small-scale active sport tourism. Although scholars have suggested several categorizations of sport tourism over the years, participation and non-participation (i.e. spectator) have been distinguished as distinct (see Weed (2009) or Van Rheenen, Cernaiano and Sobry (2016) for a greater discussion). The definition provided by Gibson (1998b) is the most widely accepted as she explains active sport tourism as "leisure based travel that takes individuals temporarily outside of their home communities to participate in physical activities". Still, this definition does not consider that active sport tourism can occur within the context of events (e.g. marathons, triathlons, bike tours) or without an event, which is often the case with sports like golf and winter sports. Thus, in the context of events, Kaplanidou and Gibson (2010) provide the term "active event sport tourists" to describe "participatory sports-related travel associated with event participation". Another issue that arises in definitional discussions related to sport and tourism is whether the activity (i.e. active event participation) is the primary purpose of the travel (e.g. Gammon & Robinson, 1997; Standeven & DeKnop, 1999). In his textbook on event tourism, Getz (2013) addresses this issue as he describes the term as a "destination event". These types of events are created for the specific purpose of attracting tourists from regional to international markets primarily based on the attractiveness of the event (Getz, 2013, p. 166). Thus the tourism, event and sport aspects of the term seem to be relatively well known. However, what is meant by "small-scale" leaves much to interpretation. There seems to be a consensus on what constitutes a mega-event or at least what events are considered mega (e.g. the Olympics, the FIFA World Cup, the Pan American Games), but specific parameters that distinguish small-scale events from larger events are missing. Since the bulk of research on small-scale events seems to focus around sustainability, Higham's (1999) discussion of the scale of sport tourism can be drawn upon.

Community benefits

Sustainability

Small-scale sport tourism is often considered a viable and sustainable alternative to hosting large-scale or mega-events (Gibson, Kaplanidou & Kang, 2012). Large-scale sport tourism has been widely criticized for its failure to use facilities post-event, its large financial burdens and its negative environmental impacts among other issues (e.g. Collins, Jones & Munday, 2009; Hiller, 2006; Lee & Taylor, 2005). However, sport tourism on a small scale as described by Higham (1999) creates a regular flow of visitors, needs little to no public funding, uses existing infrastructure and is of an appropriate size for a community to handle. The draw for communities to host large-scale sport events is the assumed positive economic, tourism and community impact, but if communities adopt an approach that creates a portfolio of small-scale events, a variety of synergistic benefits will arise without the negative consequences of large-scale strategies (Ziakas & Costa, 2011a; 2011b). Specifically, if destinations adopt a small-scale event portfolio strategy overall tourism will improve as destinations develop a stronger image/brand, a wider variety of tourist interests will be attracted, seasonality issues will decline and multiple purposes will be served (Ziakas, 2014).

This portfolio approach allows communities to realize many of the non-economic benefits that are often associated with large-scale events. For example, events that are multi-cultural in nature bring the opportunity for social and cultural interaction (Roche, 1992). These interactions including the sharing of ideas, customs, history and beliefs become a significant key to the globalization of culture and understanding/appreciation of our differences. Sport events that attract participants and spectators from multiple regions/countries, such as the Olympics or the FIFA World Cup, are perfect examples of the coming together of multiple cultures in one place (Parry, 2006). Smaller, but equally multi-cultural, sport events that have a much lower proportion of passive participants also create opportunities for cultural exchange, perhaps even more so than mega-events. However, the benefits of social and cultural exchange are much less known (Müller, Zoonen & Roode, 2008), and event organizers are generally less aware of the extent of these benefits.

Social impact

Chalip (2006) discusses the possibilities and advantages of leveraging sport events for positive social impact. These social impacts are not limited to the tourist who visits a destination for the sake of competing, or to those associated with the event, but are also felt by the host community. The gathering of individuals with varying cultural perspectives, backgrounds and/or histories creates an environment in which to address significant social issues either directly or indirectly. When these gatherings result in an alteration of the communal effect, these experiences are considered *liminoid*. Liminality can create a safe environment in which to explore difficult social issues or find comfort, such that these social issues are secondary to the focus of the event, which in this case is sport participation. Sport also has the ability to bring people together, through their commonality in sport, who otherwise would not have come together. This feeling of social connectedness creates an enhanced social bond and lowers the perceived cultural barriers that otherwise exist. The building and enhancement of a sense of community are referred to as *communitas*.

Perhaps developing these feelings of social exploration and celebration is easier when the destination takes an active portfolio perspective. For example, O'Brien (2007) discusses how a surf festival in Australia was leveraged to extend visitors' stays, find ways to retain event expenditures, enhance business relationships and, perhaps most importantly, further the notion that a sport subculture (in this case, longboarding) provides significant value to the destination. The sport subculture was found to be a recurring theme impacting the success of leveraging. The long-term success of leveraging was found in how the destination builds its reputation as a "surf town" built around a core subculture of "longboarding".

Individual benefits

Although destinations and events are motivated towards hosting events to drive tourism and ultimately stimulate positive economic and social impacts, benefits also arise for the individuals who participate in this style of travel and event participation. Specifically, positive individual outcomes related to physical activity, the creation and maintenance of a healthy lifestyle, social connection, identity and sense of community have been explored in previous research. For example, a fundamental reason that event active sport tourism exists as a tourism market is based on the desire that sport participants have to create and share identities related to the sport (i.e. Green & Chalip, 1998). As explained by Green and Jones (2005), sport tourism allows the participant to construct or confirm an identity, a time and place to interact with others who share the subculture, an opportunity to celebrate his/her sport identity, a means to advance his/her leisure career (i.e. advance from local to international events) and to demonstrate his/her status and experience in the sport. Similarly, social connection to other participants is a primary driver and motivator of sport event participation and travel. Often people seek out active sport events as a way to meet people and make new friends. If they continue to pursue event participation, eventually friendships will develop with other participants. Many researchers have explored social motivation in this context (e.g. Aicher, Karadakis & Eddosary, 2015; Funk, Toohey & Bruun, 2007; Patterson, Getz & Gubb, 2016), but Buning and Gibson (2015) explain that social connections evolve to create lasting and enduring friendships, which motivate individuals to continue their event participation. Often this leads to an advanced stage when the participants become immersed in the social world surrounding the sport, the events and the related travel.

Several projects have explored the idea that participant sport events can serve as an intervention for physical activity for inactive, or minimally active, adults. Bowles, Rissel and Bauman (2006) investigated a large Australian cycling event and found that first time and novice participants increased their time spent cycling in the month after the event. Similarly, Funk, Jordan, Ridinger and Kaplanidou (2011), through a study of marathon participants in Philadelphia, Pennsylvania, explored intentions and attitudes three months after the event. The authors found that the event sustained positive attitudes and intentions towards physically active leisure for those who had a relatively high amount of previous event participation. Further, Funk *et al.* (2011) found positive attitudes towards exercise and future intentions improved amongst the least active participants. Subsequent work by Lane, Murphy, Bauman and Chey (2010; 2012) suggests that events can stimulate the inactive to increase their physical activity leading up to an event and afterwards, but some participants will relapse to low levels of activity within three months of the event. However, despite general concerns of physical inactivity many individuals create and maintain lifestyles based upon active event travel. Buning and Gibson (2015) explain that some participants may initially be motivated by health concerns, but the majority begin to appreciate and realize the health benefits related to event participation later in their careers and this often motivates them to maintain their participation and travel. Further, these health benefits are not purely physical and many individuals involved in active event participation and travel report mental health benefits typically related to being able to escape daily life and cope with stress (e.g. Buning & Gibson, 2015; Hodeck & Hoveman, 2016; Shipway & Holloway, 2010).

Active-sport-event travel career

An emerging effort to organize the conceptual understanding of active sport travel related to events was proposed by Getz (2008) as the "event travel career", which combined the underlying ideas of "serious leisure" (Stebbins, 1992) and "travel careers" (Pearce, 2005). Later, Getz and McConnell (2011) argued that individuals engaged in event travel can create a potentially life-long career of travel to sport events which is shaped by changing motives, travel style, temporal patterns, geographic preferences and patterns, event type and destination criteria. Building on this work, Buning and Gibson (2015; 2016) developed the Active-Sport-Event Travel Career concept (ASETC), defined as "a career-like pattern of involvement and commitment to event-related travel and participation in physically active sport events, which leads to progression through time with regard to motivations, preferences, and modified behavior". As individuals progressively experience active sport travel they move along a trajectory that is demarcated by six stages (Figure 30.1).

First, the initiation stage occurs as an individual experiences his/her first event-specific trip, which is spurred by a variety of motivational factors such as friends being already engaged

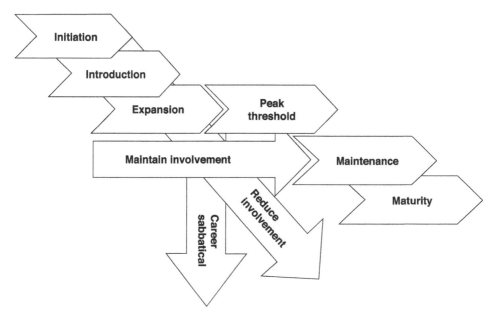

Figure 30.1   Active-sport-event travel career trajectory

in the activity or the desire to become physically fit. At this point, the participant has minimal knowledge of the activity and the related travel until the second stage (introduction) occurs as he/she travels to more events and becomes progressively more knowledgeable and skilled in the activity. During the introduction stage, the participant probably has little to no social connection to other participants in the activity and uses a minimalistic travel style. Progressing further, the expansion stage occurs as the individual begins to connect with other participants, develops preferences towards event, travel and destination characteristics and possibly branches out into other types of events. Next, the peak threshold stage occurs as the participant hits a point where he/she is unable to increase participation frequency any further due to constraints. At this pivotal moment, the participant might choose to take a break from the activity (i.e. a career sabbatical), reduce his/her involvement or maintain his/her involvement. Fifth, progressing forward the maintenance stage occurs as the participant maintains his/her involvement/frequency, is strongly motivated to continue to maintain social connections and a healthy lifestyle, which may lead to a disconnect with people outside the activity. Lastly, the maturity stage occurs, often leading to reduced travel frequency and linked to an advanced stage of life. Individuals at the final stage become quite critical of event, destination and travel characteristics and are likely to mentor new participants and volunteer as a way to give back to the activity.

International examples of small-scale active sport tourism

Cycling in Bend/Oakridge, Oregon, USA

Cycling-related tourism is an established and rising market as communities, cities, states and countries seek to attract cyclists through events, trails, paths, networks and organized bike tours. A landmark study commissioned by the European Parliament found that 2.2 billion cycling tourism trips occur annually in Europe producing more than €44 billion in value (Weston, Davies, Lumsdon, McGrath, Peeters, Eijgelaar & Piket, 2012). Also, research into cycling tourism has become quite popular with scholars investigating locations and contexts ranging from a South African bike tour (Kruger, Myburgh, & Saayman, 2016) and a large Australian road cycling event (i.e. Lamont & Jenkins, 2013) to infrastructure and destination development in Ireland and Belgium (i.e. Deenihan & Caulfield, 2014; Cox, 2012). Recently, a study published by Buning, Cole, and McNamee (2016) investigated a portfolio of mountain bike events around Oakridge and Bend Oregon located in the Pacific Northwest US. Over the years Bend has become an international destination for mountain biking due to a comprehensive approach implemented by local destination marketing organizations (e.g. Visit Bend, Central Oregon Visitors Association), event organizers and local stakeholders (e.g. mountain bike clubs, local businesses). In 2016, Visit Bend reported that 4 per cent of the approximately 3 million visitor trips to Bend consisted of international visitors (RRC Associates, 2016). Buning *et al.* (2016) found that the visitors to a single event located in the area travelled more than 1,000 miles on average, spending $169.21 per day per person in the host community. Further, the mountain bike visitors travelled in groups averaging between three and four people per travel party and staying for three to four nights. According to Freeman and Thomlinson (2014) mountain biking offers a sustainable tourism product to destinations, but requires a coherent and collective effort implemented by public and private stakeholders working towards common goals.

Using Freeman and Thomlinson's (2014) framework for community-based mountain bike tourism, the international success of the Bend/Oakridge area can be explained through contingent (e.g. community champions, legislation, physical geography, funding) and non-contingent factors (e.g. mountain bike clubs, supportive services, destination marketing, mountain bike event/culture/lifestyle). For example, mountain biking in Bend/Oakridge primarily occurs in the Deschutes National Forest. In order for tourist awareness and access to occur several factors must work in unison including the availability of conducive physical geography, legislation/regulations to allow land access, clubs to build and maintain trails, local bike shop support through bike rentals and trail information, local funding for trail projects and effective destination marketing. Although the success of a portfolio of relatively small mountain bike events seems to be due to the event promoters, these events are being organized in a truly supportive environment, from local volunteers to federal regulations allowing land access. Similar cycling tourism success is occurring around the world in a variety of cycling disciplines both in the context of events (e.g. Buning, Cole & McNamee, 2016) or without events, such as trail networks (e.g. Downward, Lumsdon & Weston, 2009). Indeed, through a meta-analysis of cycling studies worldwide, Weed *et al.* (2014) found that leisure and tourism cyclists spend on average €43.33 per day per person when staying overnight to cycle, whether it be in an event context or a trail/path network.

Golf in Myrtle Beach, South Carolina, USA

While there are examples of local business owners/managers not accepting and supporting destination development and marketing strategies, there are examples of sport-focused destinations where support can be both direct and indirect. Take, for example, the development of Myrtle Beach, South Carolina, which began as a fairly remote beachfront destination on the Atlantic coast of the USA. As golf courses in the area became known for high quality and superior natural designs, the number of golf courses grew to over 100 while golf visitors topped 3.4 million annually in 2015, all within a 60-mile stretch of coastline known as the Grand Strand (Myrtle Beach Area Convention and Visitors Bureau, 2016). Tourism promoters develop travel packages that include rounds of golf at multiple golf courses, lodging and transportation paired with food and beverage. These packages are sold to visitors from many regions in the USA as well as many countries throughout the world. Visit Myrtle Beach, which acts as the local tax-subsidized destination management organization (DMO), leverages Myrtle Beach's worldwide reputation as a golf destination to promote other forms of tourism as well (e.g. beach activities, shopping, gastronomy, outdoor activities).

While Visit Myrtle Beach employs several tactics to grow tourism in the region, including promoting attractions such as shopping, natural environmental features and a wide variety of events, many of the gains in tourism objects started with private business. Significant increases in length of stay, levels of participation (measured in number of rounds played) and retaining visitor spending can be attributed to two actions (see Krohn, 2007; 2008; 2014). First, the concept of a stay-and-play package was developed and grew out of the desire to increase golf participation. Partnerships between lodging, food service providers and golf facilities resulted in better control of where sport tourists spent tourism dollars. However, some limitations were discovered when these "package golfers" desired to extend their stay and engage in further sport participation, but felt that the end of the package signalled the end of the stay. The second action, which started with partnerships between golf facility owners and hospitality providers, was engaging in coopetition. Golf tourists in the region prefer to play early in the morning which affords the opportunity to play a second round in the afternoon. Golf course managers learned to adjust the booking and starting procedures to increase morning capacity, but also built partnerships to provide a mechanism for afternoon play. Previously, a manager who was focused primarily on developing additional business would encourage the golfer to play the same course a second time. Managers are now more likely to engage in coopetition by calling other local courses and arranging afternoon tee-times, and in some cases assisting with transportation to these other "competitor" sites. As a result, local managers have noticed that golfers are more likely to return the following year if provided with the opportunity to experience other local courses.

Myrtle Beach, and other similar golf destinations, promote the "portfolio" of assets from individual businesses to create a specific active-sport experience. Destinations with a location of unique trails can leverage not just the assets for hikers, mountain bikers or off-road automobile activities, but also include other destination activities to provide a reputation as a multi-faceted destination built around a leverageable theme. These themes, such as a golf sub-culture in Myrtle Beach or longboard subculture as discussed by O'Brien (2007), can also provide opportunities for liminoid experiences. One of roles of the local DMO might be to help develop/provide opportunities for these active-sport tourists to engage in extended social interaction. For example, golf tourists to Myrtle Beach tend to spend the entire stay with the original four to 12 people with whom they travelled. However, are there opportunities to develop social interactions between travel parties that might focus on developing communities? Feelings of celebration need not be limited to events designed exclusively for that purpose. DMOs can develop opportunities for informal non-event or small-event interactions that increase feelings of connectedness with other participants and thus increase overall feelings of satisfaction and intentions to revisit the destination.

Nautically themed portfolio, Portimao, Portugal

Destinations seeking to differentiate from nearby cities can take an event portfolio approach to create an identity and brand. Leveraging local subculture can facilitate participation from community and governmental players/partners. An example of this approach undertaken in

Portugal is described in a study on leveraging conducted by Pereira, Mascarenhas, Flores and Pires (2015). According to Portugal's statistic institute (INE, 2016), 2015 saw 10.18 million visitors, with 3.7 international visitors to the Algarve region. The city of Portimao is a classic coastal/beach resort in Portugal's Algarve region, but has deliberately attempted to break away from the "sun and sand" image of neighbouring cities by developing a portfolio of nautically themed events. The work by Pereira *et al.* (2015) explored six nautical events organized around four strategic goals adapted from Chalip's work on the leveraging benefits of sport events (Chalip, 2004; 2006). These goals were as follows: (1) to optimize total trade and revenue, (2) to enhance host destination image, (3) to foster social interaction, and (4) to foster a feeling of celebration.

The results of the study by Pereira *et al.* (2015) demonstrated that a portfolio of events enabled the construction of a nautically themed destination brand. The successful creation of the new destination was built by leveraging local assets and existing events developed and hosted by individual private organizations described as external event organization committees (EEOC). Pereira *et al.* (2015) found that the local actors (decision-makers and involved partners) consistently supported the goals to "enhance the host destination image" and to "optimize total trade and revenue". However, much of the actions undertaken by the EEOCs towards leveraging were discovered to be accidental or incidental rather than a component of a deliberate shared strategic plan by the events. Thus, the overall process was quite inefficient as unclear goals, lack of coordination amongst events, siloed working styles and disorganized leverage led to failed and missed opportunities. Overall, the authors found that the economically focused actions were implemented more often than the social leverage actions and the benefits of leveraging a themed portfolio of events were directly connected to coordinating local actions as well as the EEOCs.

Four sports in active sport tourism, Messinia, Greece

Active sport tourism development is frequently examined through the lens of either a single sport (such as cycling, golf or winter sports and mentioned previously) or as a portfolio of commonly themed active sport tourism events (such as longboarding or nautical events). An alternative method of evaluating the impact of active sport tourism is to consider the collection of activities in a region. For example, Drakakis and Papadaskalopoulos (2014) conducted a study of four largely unconnected sports that did not engage in portfolio-type promotional activities in Messinia, Greece. A report for the Hellenic Statistical Authority (2016) indicated 23.6 million international tourists, of which just under 10 per cent visit the region surrounding Messinia. This largely rural region is located on the southwestern tip of Greece and has a strong agricultural economy that is boosted by tourism. Geographical features make this a favourable area for active sport tourism, which includes the primary activities of golf and windsurfing, but also horseback riding and scuba diving. The primary purpose of this study was to report the economic impact of these four activities in order to determine their relative contribution to the local economy.

An insightful component of this research is to consider the importance of specific activities that bring visitors to the region. The "propulsive activity" is described as the activity that serves as the primary catalyst of development in the surrounding region. These activities create positive impact in the local economy through revenue, income, employment and business development and aid in the development of economies of scale. Tourism can serve as the propulsive activity for a region looking to develop and/or expand business and other economic activity. Previous research has developed and supported the idea that propulsive activities are developed through, and around, as tourism can serve to develop and increase economic activity to both urban and non-urban areas. Drakakis and Papadaskalopoulos (2014) found that golf is a propulsive activity within Messinia that has important implications not only to the local economy, but to the larger industry of international sport tourism. Significant impacts on the region within Greece include additional flights from more European countries and beyond (with planned promotion and development). As a result, this creates increased exposure and visitation for other activities, such as "secondary" active sport tourism opportunities like wind surfing or scuba diving, which then increases lodging, food service and attraction expenditures.

Destinations seeking to create and develop an internationally focused active sport tourism reputation do not necessarily need to have a single sport such as those at Bend, Oregon or Myrtle Beach, South Carolina, or themed events like those at Portimao, Portugal. Rather, a destination can start with a significant propulsive activity that can serve as a central branding theme. This activity can serve as a framework to develop future effective development and growth in related businesses, and to support businesses, infrastructure and the overall economy. Drakakis and Papadaskalopoulos (2014) also suggest that this framework can become a blueprint to assist policymakers in beginning to promote a destination as a collection of activities, rather than only a single propulsive activity. While destinations that have a history of cooperation and perhaps have the advantage of a funded promotional organization (e.g. Visit Myrtle Beach, Visit Bend) may already have a successful framework in place, destinations that lack such cooperation can benefit from the focus on propulsive sport tourism activities.

Many destinations throughout the world have openly accepted the development of golf-centred resorts and even stand-alone golf facilities to serve as the central focus for tourism. However, where these destinations struggle is in understanding that the golf developer is creating the focus and is often seen as a competitor, rather than a partner in creating an active sport tourism network in which all players will benefit from the central "propulsive active sport tourism activity" of golf. Drakakis and Papadaskalopoulos (2014) point out that in places where the golf developer becomes the only, or significantly largest, motivator for development, the network collapses due to the collapse of equality, trust and reliability. Long-term sustainability and viability require all components of the destination economy to participate, and thus benefit in the long run. Studies of expenditures, length of stay and travel distance are necessary for destinations seeking to identify the most important, and perhaps a central propulsive activity, on which to build a network of active sport tourism. Once a destination develops the support structure and buy-in from local business and governmental players, then planning toward themed or portfolio reputations are possible.

Conclusion

Most of the media exposure and previous research in sport tourism have been focused on the passive activities of viewing sport in hallmark or mega-sport event settings. Events such as the FIFA World Cup, or the Olympics make it easy to see the connections to international perspectives of sport business. However, the media exposure and research on active sport tourism are much less clear, albeit gaining exposure rapidly. Research has shown that significant positive outcomes can come from active sport tourism, and this chapter describes how even "small-scale" activities and events can be a catalyst for economic growth, social progress, personal development and destination image/branding.

The primary concept to consider when looking to leverage small-scale active sport tourism for international exposure is to understand the various components involved. First, the active sport tourist needs be a primary consideration, as seen from the perspective of the active-sport-event travel career, in settings where event reputation, level of competition and/or ancillary support structure would attract a specific type of tourist at a specific level of competitive skill. However, the active sport tourist need not only be attending events, but also participating for recreational and leisure benefits to allow economic and development value to occur. Second, with knowledge about what types of sport tourists might be attracted, small-scale active sport tourism events can be developed to create a portfolio in which to build a reputation and powerful destination image. Third, destinations can look to leverage existing infrastructure to promote the destination. This could be structured around a specific sport, such as cycling or golf, a collection of sports requiring the same natural features, such as winter sports or coastal/beach recreation, or a reputation developed over time at a destination, such as longboarding. Understanding the attributes and strengths of the destination or region allows for effective international exposure through promotion. Finally, if a review of the tourist, events and infrastructure does not readily suggest a central theme, then a focus on a "propulsive activity" can become the central point of destination planning, development and promotional efforts. While the desirability of large-scale sport tourism can be quite attractive to a destination, there are multiple ways that a destination can leverage existing features for tourism development. As described here, small-scale sport tourism can operate on an international level while requiring a fraction of the resources.

References

Aicher, T. J., Karadakis, K. & Eddosary, M. M. (2015). Comparison of sport tourists' and locals' motivation to participate in a running event. *International Journal of Event and Festival Management*, 6(3), 215–234.

Bowles, H. R. Rissel, C. & Bauman, A. (2006). Mass community cycling events: Who participates and is their behavior influenced by participation? *International Journal of Behavioral Nutrition and Physical Activity*, 3(39), 1–7.

Buning, R. J., Cole, Z. & McNamee, J. (2016). Visitor expenditure within a mountain bike event portfolio: Determinants, outcomes, and variations. *Journal of Sport & Tourism*, 20(2), 103–122.

Buning, R. J. & Gibson, H. J. (2015). The evolution of active-sport-event travel careers. *Journal of Sport Management*, 29, 555–569.

Buning, R. J. & Gibson, H. J. (2016). The trajectory of active-sport-event travel careers: A social worlds' perspective. *Journal of Sport Management*, 30, 265–281.

Chalip, L. (2004). Beyond impact: A general model for sport event leverage. In B. Ritchie & D. Adair (Eds), *Sport Tourism: Interrelationships, Impacts and Issues* (pp. 226–252). Clevedon: Channel View.

Chalip, L. (2006). Towards social leverage of sport events. *Journal of Sport & Tourism*, 11(2), 109–127.

Collins, A., Jones, C. & Munday, M. (2009). Assessing the environmental impacts of mega sporting events: Two options? *Tourism Management*, 30, 828–837.

Cox, P. (2012). Strategies promoting cycle tourism in Belgium: Practices and implications. *Tourism Planning & Development*, 9(1), 25–39.

Deenihan, G. & Caulfield, B. (2014). Do tourists value different levels of cycling infrastructure? *Tourism Management*, 46, 92–101.

Downward, P., Lumsdon, L. & Weston. R. (2009). Visitor expenditure: The case of cycle recreation and tourism. *Journal of Sport & Tourism*, 14(1), 25–42.

Drakakis, P. & Papadaskalopoulos, A. (2014) Economic contribution of active sport tourism: The case of four sport activities in Messinia, Greece. *Journal of Sport & Tourism*, 19(3–4), 199–231.

Freeman, R. & Thomlinson, E. (2014). Mountain bike tourism and community development in British Columbia: Critical success factors for the future. *Tourism Review International*, 18(1/2), 9–22.

Funk, D., Jordan, J., Ridinger, L. & Kaplanidou, K. (2011). Capacity of mass participant sport events for the development of activity commitment and future exercise intention. *Leisure Sciences*, 33(3), 250–268.

Funk, D., Toohey, K. & Bruun, T. (2007). International sport event participation: Prior sport involvement; destination image; and travel motives. *European Sport Management Quarterly*, 7(3), 227–248.

Gammon, S. & Robinson, T. (1997). Sport and tourism: A conceptual framework. *Journal of Sport & Tourism*, 4(3), 11–18.

Getz, D. (2008). Event tourism: Definition, evolution, and research. *Tourism Management*, 29(3), 403–428.

Getz, D. (2013). *Event Tourism: Concepts, International Case Studies, and Research*. Putnam Valley, NY: Cognizant Communication.

Getz, D. & McConnell, A. (2011). Serious sport tourism and event travel careers. *Journal of Sport Management*, 25, 326–338.

Gibson, H. J. (1998a). Active sport tourism: Who participates? *Leisure Studies*, 17(2), 155–170.

Gibson, H. J. (1998b). Sport tourism: A critical analysis of research. *Sport Management Review*, 1, 45–76.

Gibson, H. J., Kaplanidou, K. & Kang, S. J. (2012). Small-scale event sport tourism: A case study in sustainable tourism. *Sport Management Review*, 15(2), 160–170.

Green, B. C. & Chalip, L. (1998). Sport tourism as the celebration of subculture. *Annals of Tourism Research*, 25(2), 275–291.

Green, B. C. & Jones, I. (2005). Serious leisure, social identity, and sport tourism. *Sport in Society*, 8(2), 164–181.

Hellenic Statistical Authority. (2016). *Arrivals of non-residents in Greece*. Retrieved from the Hellenistic Statistical Authority website <www.statistics.gr/en/statistics/-/publication/STO04/->. Accessed 1 March 2017.

Higham, J. (1999). Commentary-Sport as an avenue for tourism development: An analysis of the positive and negative impacts of sport tourism. *Current Issues in Tourism*, 2(1), 82–90.

Hiller, H. H. (2006). Post-event outcomes and the post-modern turn: The Olympics and urban transformations. *European Sport Marketing Quarterly*, 6(4), 317–332.

Hirtz, N. & Ross, C. (2010). The perceived impacts of sport tourism: An urban host community perspective. *Journal of Sport Management*, 24, 119–138.

Hodeck, A. & Hoveman, G. (2016). Motivation of active sport tourists in a German highland destination – a cross-seasonal comparison. *Journal of Sport & Tourism*, <doi: 10.1080/14775085.2016. 1235988>.

INE. (2016). *Entrances of non-resident tourists by place of residence*. Retrieved from INE, Portugal's Statistic Institute website <www.ine.pt/xportal/xmain?xpgid=ine_main&xpid=INE>.

Kaplanidou, K. & Gibson, H. (2010). Predicting behavioral intentions of active event sport tourists: The case of a small-scale recurring sports event. *Journal of Sport & Tourism*, 15, 163–179.

Krohn, B. D. (2007). "Growth of golf tourism in South Myrtle Beach". [Unpublished report]. Visit Myrtle Beach. Myrtle Beach, SC.

Krohn, B. D. (2008). "The influence of attribute performance appraisal, emotion and time on the satisfaction response of golf travelers". [Doctoral dissertation]. Clemson University, SC, USA.

Krohn, B. D. (2014). A case study review of golf tourism and its conjunction with a destination. *Proceedings of the 2014 Annual Leisure Studies Association Conference*. Paisley, Scotland.

Kruger, M., Myburgh, E. & Saayman, M. (2016). A motivation-based typology of road cyclists in the Cape Town Cycle Tour, South Africa. *Journal of Travel & Tourism Marketing*, 33(3), 83–403.

Lamont, M. & Jenkins, J. (2013). Segmentation of cycling event participants: A two-step cluster method utilizing recreation specialization. *Event Management*, 17(4), 391–407.

Lane, A., Murphy, N., Bauman, A. & Chey, T. (2010). Randomized controlled trial to increase physical activity among insufficiently active women following their participation in a mass event. *Health Education Journal*, 69(3), 287–296.

Lane, A., Murphy, N., Bauman, A. & Chey, T. (2012). Active for a day: Predictors of relapse among physically active mass event participants. *Journal of Physical Activity and Health*, 9, 48–52.

Lee, C. & Taylor, T. (2005). Critical reflections on the economic impact assessment of a mega-event: The case of 2002 FIFA World Cup. *Tourism Management*, 26, 565–603.

Müller, F., Zoonen, L. V. & Roode, L. D. (2008). The integrative power of sport: Imagined and real effects of sport events on multicultural integration. *Sociology of Sport Journal*, 25(3), 387–401.

Myrtle Beach Area Convention and Visitors Bureau (2016). *Myrtle Beach Golf Courses*. Retrieved from <www.visitmyrtlebeach.com/things-to-do/golf/courses/>. Accessed 1 March 2017.

O'Brien, D. (2007). Points of leverage: Maximizing host community benefit from a regional surfing festival. *European Sport Management Quarterly*, 7(2), 141–165.

Parry, J. (2006). Sport and Olympism: Universals and multiculturalism. *Journal of the Philosophy of Sport*, *33*(2), 188–204.

Patterson, I., Getz, D. & Gubb, K. (2016). The social world and event travel career of the serious yoga devotee. *Leisure Studies*, *35*(3), 293–313.

Pearce, P. L. (2005). *Tourist Behaviour: Themes and Conceptual Schemes.* Buffalo, NY: Channel View Publications.

Pereira, E. C., Mascarenhas, M. V., Flores, A. J. & Pires, G. M. (2015). Nautical small-scale sports events portfolio: A strategic leveraging approach. *European Sport Management Quarterly*, *15*(1), 27–47.

Roche, M. (1992). Mega-events and micro-modernization: On the sociology of the new urban tourism. *British Journal of Sociology*, *43*(4), 563–600.

RRC Associates, Inc. (2016). *Bend Area Visitor Survey.* Retrieved from the Visit Bend website <www.visitbend.com/About-Us/summer-survey-2008/>.

Standeven, J. & DeKnop, P. (1999). *Sport Tourism.* Champaign, IL: Human Kinetics.

Stebbins, R. A. (1992). *Amateurs, Professionals, and Serious Leisure.* Buffalo, NY: McGill-Queen's University Press.

Shipway, R. & Holloway, I. (2010). Running free: Embracing a healthy lifestyle through distance running. *Perspectives in Public Health*, *130*(5), 270–276.

Taks, M., Chalip, L. & Green, B. C. (2015). Impacts and strategic outcomes form non-mega sport events for local communities. *European Sport Management Quarterly*, *15*(1), 1–6.

Van Rheenen, D., Cernaiani, S. & Sobry, C. (2016). Defining sport tourism: A content analysis of an evolving epistemology. *Journal of Sport & Tourism* <doi: 10.1080/14775085.2016.1229212>.

Weed, M. (2009). Progress in sport tourism research? A meta-review and exploration of futures. *Tourism Management*, *30*(5), 615–628.

Weed, M., Bull, C., Brown, M., Dowse, S., Lovell, J., Mansfield, L. & Wellard, I. (2014). A systematic review and meta-analyses of the potential local economic impact of tourism and leisure cycling and the development of an evidence-based market segmentation. *Tourism Review International*, *18*(1/2), 37–55.

Weston, R., Davies, N., Lumsdon, L., McGrath, P., Peeters, P., Eijgelaar, E. & Piket, P. (2012). The European cycle route network EuroVelo: Challenges and opportunities for sustainable tourism. Retrieved from the European Parliament website <www.europarl.europa.eu/RegData/etudes/etudes/join/2012/474569/IPOL-TRAN_ET(2012)474569_EN.pdf>. Accessed 10 October 2016.

Ziakas, V. (2014). Planning and leveraging event portfolios: Toward a holistic theory. *Journal of Hospitality Marketing & Management*, *23*, 327–356.

Ziakas, V. & Costa, C. A. (2011a). The use of an event portfolio in regional community and tourism development: Creating synergy between sport and cultural events. *Journal of Sport & Tourism*, *16*(2), 149–175.

Ziakas, V. & Costa, C. A. (2011b). Event portfolio and multi-purpose development: Establishing the conceptual grounds. *Sport Management Review*, *14*(4), 409–423.

PART VII

Sport development

The United Nations and the International Olympic Committee are the most prominent of the many multinational organizations, governments and communities who have embraced the idea that sport can play a key role in economic, educational, and social development. Here we take the term "development" in the broad sense of both sport as a tool for achieving broad development objectives and the sport business as something to be developed itself.

The chapters in this section explore a variety of approaches starting with the development of professional cricket into an international phenomenon in India, the effectiveness and role of one-off, special events in supporting long-term development aims, followed by a development approach firmly rooted in sport business that pairs business-oriented practices to achieve social goals. Throughout the world, small and medium-sized sport clubs are transitioning from public funding to financial self-sufficiency as illustrated by a small ice hockey club's entrepreneurial approach to developing success both on the ice and in the marketplace. The final chapter highlights a case where intractable problems in a challenging environment are being tackled through cooperation and collaboration among globally and socially diverse organizations.

31

INDIA

From a cricketing nation to a business industry

Juthika Mehta

Introduction

The sphere and history of cricket in India are vast and filled with diverse perspectives. It was the first sport adopted from the British rulers and India is now one of the international powers of the game. This chapter examines the journey of how cricket in India evolved into a monetized sport for the benefit of all stakeholders involved.

Cricket and India are synonymous to any sporting enthusiast. However, this was not always the case. Cricket was brought to India in the 1700s by the British and initially played only by the elite. There was not much grandeur around the sport until the late 1900s. This era saw the beginning of role models within the sport of cricket. Thus having good performers, and a youthful team, was a big deal. It began the journey towards cricket's financial success.

The sport leveraging easily relatable heroes and consistent performances suddenly garnered fan interest. The 1983 World Cup began with high hopes, and more interest in the sport from India as a nation than any time previously (International Cricket Council, 2016). With India winning the title, the economics of the game began to change. But this event only scratched the surface of the true potential of India on its journey towards becoming a cricketing nation. The 1983 World Cup win ignited a revolution, among players and fans alike.

The International Cricketing Council (ICC), the international governing body of the sport, currently has 123 member countries (*Daily Sun*, 2016). The Board of Control for Cricket in India (BCCI), India's national governing body, has been a part of the ICC since 1929. This period was characterized by dramatic changes in the development and governance of the sport. Internationally, throughout the 1900s, sport was being commoditized to match the needs of technology, commerce and viewership, which had a significant impact on the development of the sport.

When all of these factors came together, the success rate grew to a phenomenal extent. The commodification implied playing sport within television-friendly timeframes, with teams that were media friendly, and that had larger fan followings, etc. Therefore, the more popular teams received more media attention and appeared in more televised matches.

With the 2000 era setting in, the BCCI had, for the first time ever, appointed a foreign coach, John Wright, to lead its national team (Kitchin, 2009). Sahara had bagged the sponsorship for the Indian cricket team for Rs 400 Crore for a four-year period ending in December 2009, and had agreed to continue for six additional months, as BCCI could not find any replacement sponsors (Press Trust of India, 2010). The Sahara group was the only major sponsor and its logos were prominent on all jerseys for the Indian National Team.

This period marked the rise of star players such as Anil Kumble, Saurav Ganguly, Sachin Tendulkar, Rahul Dravid and V. V. S. Laxman, commonly known as the Big Five. As pillars of Team India, the Big Five took the sport ahead in the late 1990s. The international sporting industry was changing through globalization and sport in India was following the pattern. "The fact was that we could stand up shoulder to shoulder with any country in the world in this sport" (Mehta & Raman, 2016).

Despite great success and popular role models, cricket began to lose some of its popular appeal. A cricket game lasted longer than most other competitive sports. The English cricket authorities came up with a T20 format originally as filler to the test cricket just to gain some audience excitement and a new following. It was much more television-friendly than the one-day version – and almost unrecognizable from traditional five-day test matches (Angikaar, 2015). With the ICC seeking to promote credible international cricket across a wide range of nations (Rumford & Wagg, 2010), cricket was finding it difficult to package itself around a television format that could help it increase its media success. The T20 format, as an answer to media-packaging challenges, became a huge success, and the ICC acknowledged the same.

With consistent performances came more commercial interest, thus more financial success within the sport. Until the introduction of the T20 format, Indian cricket survived financially solely on its international matches. The local governing bodies struggled because of a major lack of finances. Rather than earning money from broadcast rights, the Doordarshan Channel (DD) was known to have charged the BCCI for telecasting matches at this time.

T20 format

The globalization of cricket in its truest sense happened with the introduction of the Indian Premier League (IPL) (Press Trust of India, 2008). This new T20 format was media friendly, brought in immense commercial gains and encouraged players from across the globe to participate. However these players had to be from countries under the ICC umbrella. This requirement increased the international platform for auctioning players, led international stars being invited to play for local Indian teams and garnered immense interest amongst fans due to the celebrities involved (Mustafa, 2013). The bigger commercial brands combined with bigger names playing cricket created something revolutionary. The inclusion of the world's best players created more competition and excitement for viewers. The BCCI had now developed more sophisticated marketing and more avenues to monetize the sport.

In 2007, the ICC organized an international Twenty20 World Cup that was played in South Africa and won by India (Gemmell & Majumdar, 2007). Soon after, the International Cricket League (ICL) was started by a local brand called Zee Network. The ICL lacked backing from the BCCI or ICC and had to disband two years later in 2009 (Gupta, 2009).

The ICL tournaments were between four international teams: World XI, India, Pakistan and Bangladesh. Each team was coached by a former international cricketer and comprised four international players, two established Indian players and eight budding domestic talents. It had prize money of US$1 million. In contrast, the IPL was designed to grow to being the highest money-making system in Indian sport. Statistics show that the second highest-paid league in the world on a pro-rata basis is the Indian Premier League (Sawer, 2010). The IPL had city-based franchises. As of today there are nine franchises that participate in the league.

A few franchisees have undergone financial trouble and have changed owners, cities, etc. but the league appears to be on a sustainable path (TNN, 2013).

Commercialization of cricket

The money involved in cricket was increasing rapidly and nearly quadrupling. The second season of the league saw almost US$4,108,000 in revenue accrued before the first ball was even bowled. This revenue came from individual auctioning of players, broadcasting/media rights, mobile and internet rights, gate receipts and other smaller opportunities that helped brands enhance their returns on investment. The IPL revenues created financial security for the board, the players and the individuals involved in management of this new form of cricket (Sayani, 2016). The BCCI also formatted the league to enable individual team owners to further sell various sponsorships to recover their investment through the season making it a profitable revenue model for all involved in the league (Press Trust of India, 2010).

The tournament winner earns a cash prize of US$3 million, with additional cash prizes for the best pitcher and outfielder and a variety of other special awards (Kohli, 2009). The figures for winning an IPL season, however, are US$1.5 million for second position in the tournament and US$900,000 for third and fourth place alike (Wharton University of Pennsylvania, 2007). It created opportunities for more crowd participation with activities such as the Vodafone fan army, Pepsi VIP box, and a seat upgrade for contest winners that were all real-time fan interactions offered to sponsor companies (Chennai, 2016).

A closer look at this era reveals progress in the sport of cricket in India played between 2006 and 2010. The BCCI successfully sold its media rights for over US$612 million, accounting for the richest governing council in the Asian sector. Then, the league sold its television marketing rights in 2010 to Nimbus Communications for 2000 Crore INR for a period of four years, and 31.5 Crore INR per international match. The bigger revenue led to higher salaries for players. In comparison to any other sport in India, cricket was breaking all rules – monetarily, visually on how the game was perceived and psychologically in the mindsets of those governing the sport. However, as a truly global sport, cricket did not compare to football, tennis, golf or auto racing. To cope with difficulties and to catch up with other sports, cricket made some revolutionary changes. A comparison of the 1983 World Cup and the 2007 ICC World T20 Cup (BCCI – Cricket/History) illustrates this growth. In 1983 it was difficult for the ICC to pay each player 100,000 INR but in 2007 the players earned 8,000,000 INR each. These changes not only helped the sport sustain itself but also reflected strong governance, helping to successfully create a monopoly of revenue generation in India within the sport.

The IPL also involved other national cricket boards and helped them generate higher incomes in turn for their players (TenSports Desk, 2016). The ICC schemed a better retirement plan for players who were not young, fit and part of the Indian team, but were legends in themselves, to play alongside their younger counterparts in these matches.

In 2005, the Indian national team kit rights were sold to Nike. The deal was sealed for a handsome US$27.2 million (Sharma & Raol, 2011). India continued with the same kit sponsor (TotalSportek2, 2015), however the title sponsor changed to Star India from the Sahara Group who signed in 2006 for US$596,000 for four years. Star India signed a deal of approximately US$315,000 per match for a bilateral series and almost US$100,000 for the title sponsorship, broadcast, internet and mobile rights through 2018. The BCCI was clear about the division of the huge sums of revenue to the grass roots and redevelopment of the weaker sections of the sport, such as women's cricket, and to development in states that lacked a stronger grass-roots foothold in the game. While there was one format and one league gaining all the attention, the BCCI decided to build stronger foundations and strengthen the other existing formats.

Survival of the fittest

The other surviving formats/leagues of cricket include the following: amongst domestic matches, many are named after players, such as the Duleep Trophy, the Ranji Trophy and the Iranian Trophy, and used for the selection of national teams, the NKP Salve Challenger Trophy (the most popular after the IPL), the Vijay Hazare Trophy and the Deodhar Trophy, the highest awards for one-day fixtures and the Vinoo Mankad Trophy and the Yagnik Trophy for the under 19s and university tournaments to help select other Ranji teams.

The IPL replaced the Inter-State T20 Championship. There is also the Karnataka and Maharashtra and, now, the Tamil Nadu Premier League which is played within the state or regional clubs. There is also a women's Interstate T20 championship held every year. BCCI also facilitates a corporate event for a cricket-crazy country called the BCCI Corporate Trophy, which allows corporations to register and participate to win a cup.

In attempts to replicate the success of cricket and mimic the structure of the league, tennis and badminton have successfully started their own leagues. Kabbadi, a traditional sport, has replicated the cricket format and found its way to revival and survival (Indo-Asian News Service for Cricket Country, 2014).

The IPL garnered more global opportunities for matches, players, teams, cricket bodies and sponsors. It hired IMG on a ten-year contract to undertake operations of an international standard for the entire tournament. The IPL created a fantastic opportunity through reciprocal interdependence for other industries, such as the sporting goods industry, that led to massive economic growth in those markets. There was also sports infrastructure development as a post tournament legacy. Additionally, the IPL utilized international cheerleaders for matches and created demand for foreign employment. This ideation of the IPL put BCCI on the map, making it the richest cricketing board in the entire cricket industry.

In addition to the evolutionary journey of cricket there were some revolutionary changes: the play of the game was bigger, better and bolder than ever. Most of this growth happened with revenue changes within the IPL. For example, event bids were announced and companies were invited to put in tenders, and potential franchisees submitted bids for the city they wished to represent. Player auctions require that a bid amount needs to be specified by the organizing organization. Teams are required have a minimum 16-player squad, with a maximum of four compulsory international players and four players from the under-21 BCCI pool of players. This ensures a fair, competitive balance amongst the teams and an opportunity for all international, seasoned and fresher players, to play alongside each other.

The sponsorship rights for the IPL title sponsorship is valued at a phenomenal US$2.5 billion for five years and secured by PepsiCo India. There are many other opportunities to create value or a return on investment for sponsorships offered by BCCI. These sponsorships attract global brands looking to enter or impact Indian markets such as Vivo and Toshiba. However, the IPL also offers other sponsorship categories enabling smaller companies to become official partners such as Kingfisher Airlines, Hero Honda and Vodafone. There has been close to US$5 billion generated just through sponsorship rights, which become part of the pool shared with the franchisees (Gupta, 2009).

The IPL is a property owned by BCCI hence it earns money from broadcasters, sponsors and franchisees who pay franchise fees to participate in the league (Nendick & Balsara n.d.). However, the revenue earned from media, broadcasting and sponsorship now becomes a

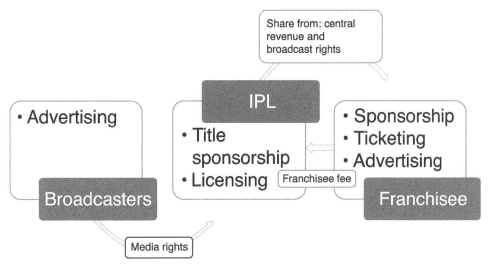

Figure 31.1 Financial division support to uplift cricket (based on TotalSportek2, 2016)

pool of central revenue that is divided amongst the BCCI, prize money for the league and the franchisees.

In the first year, the BCCI sold eight franchisees for a combined total of US$723.59 million and currently in 2017 there are eight teams that play, each of them worth millions of dollars. The franchise fee is paid at an annual 10 per cent over ten years to the BCCI (Sathosh, 2013). The franchisees have also been given the liberty to sign their own individual sponsorship deals to recoup the monetary gains to sustain their teams. These sponsorships include kit sponsors, title sponsors for their teams and so on. However this is strictly monitored by the BCCI within specific sponsorship guidelines, which ensures the visual integrity of the sport.

Additionally, each team is allowed to control 80 per cent of its home ground match hospitality and ticket revenue, and the remaining 20 per cent is distributed amongst IPL/BCCI governing body members. This model of revenue distribution has not been very effective. The franchisees find it difficult to make a profit and only just break even every year. However, the owners of these franchisees were carefully chosen ensuring that the teams/owners are not looking for short-term profits but rather long-term investments. This creates a priority for opportunities to market parent companies through advertising and sponsorship.

The franchisee has several individual costs that it incurs in order to participate in the league. It must pay the yearly franchise fee. The franchisee incurs costs of players, which can be between US$4 and US$6 million per year. Each player is bound by a three-year contract with the team and can be traded at the team's will. However, not all players can be traded because the franchisee has a requirement to retain a minimum of four players every season. The team's costs also include coaches, support staff and managers, administrative costs, and its individually chosen stadiums, which are seven-match contracts per an amount set by the BCCI. This cost can vary from stadium to stadium but, on average, works out to approximately US$2.5 million per match, enabling regional stadiums to earn some income. Finally, an additional marketing cost that each franchisee pays to promote its teams can be close to between US$3 million and US$4 million per year.

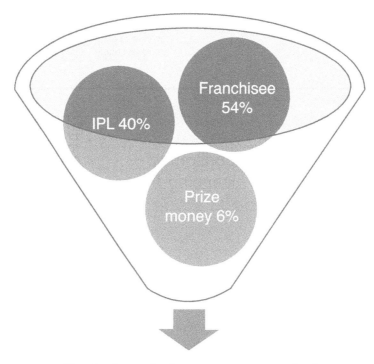

Central pool of revenue generated

Figure 31.2 Central pool of revenue generated

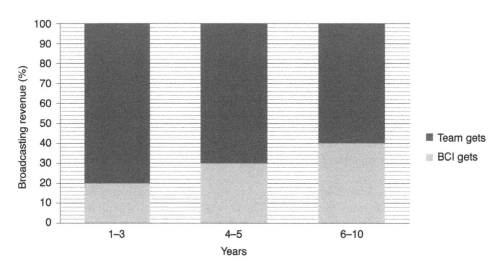

Figure 31.3 Broadcasting revenue distribution (based on TotalSportek2, 2016)

Broadcasting is the game changer

The television and media rights are divided between the BCCI and the franchisees. The division is 20:80 for the first three years and then set to 40:60 thereafter. This tests the market for fan interest and puts a higher risk on the BCCI instead of the individual franchisees. The BCCI generates its highest income from broadcasting rights. For example, Sony pays US$1.02 billion for a ten-year contract. This revenue is shared with about US$60 million distributed amongst franchisee teams and US$40 million to the BCCI or IPL.

There has been a revolution in marketing and branding with cricketers. Sachin Tendulkar became the first athlete associated with brands like Pepsi, MRF, Adidas, Britannia, Fiat Palio, Canon, Airtel, Philips, Visa, Castrol, Coca-Cola, Colgate and ESPN Star Sports. He was the first to show Indian athletes what kind of money celebrities could earn for themselves beyond cricket like their international counterparts.

In 2016, Sachin Tendulkar and Shane Warne further globalized the sport with the Cricket All-Star event (Rediff.com, 2015). This event plays exhibition matches in the United States and other countries to enhance the global reach and popularity of the sport.

Conclusion

Cricket dominates the sports industry in India. But football, badminton and kabbadi are not far behind on the league survival scale. There is now a popular Pro kabbadi League, a three-year-old tournament called the Indian Soccer League (ISL) working in a similar format to the IPL with franchisees in local cities and similar revenue peaks involved. Overall, sport is growing in India. The 2016 Summer Olympics at Rio de Janeiro attracted the largest contingent of 124 athletes in various disciplines to qualify for Team India.

Amidst all this growth is the revolutionizing of the game of cricket (Crick, 2007) with the creation of the IPL, its revenue model, the growth of international interest and conversion into a business industry (KPMG, 2014). This growth has created a popular global sport business (Kaufman & Patterson, 2005). Cricket has evolved from a strictly amateur game into a multibillion-dollar industry that is starting to grow exponentially as the developing world embraces the sport (Glover, 2013).

In a single decade cricket has become commercially successful in an economically developing country, doing something not many sports could have done. The BCCI changed a cricketing nation into a successful global industry. This sport model can be replicated to grow other sports and rapidly develop the Indian sports industry. Cricket is popular but has not yet reached its full potential; cricket is far from having consolidated its position as a global sport (Mehta & Raman, 2016).

References

Angikaar, C. (2015). How Lalit Modi methodically created Indian cricket's biggest brand. [E-journal]. Available from <thefield.scroll.in/734476/how-lalit-modi-methodically-created-indian-crickets-biggest-brand>. Accessed March 2017.

Chennai (2016). "Star India wins 'Team Sponsorship' rights". The *Hindu* [online]. Available from <www.thehindu.com/sport/cricket/star-india-wins-team-sponsorship-rights/article5440512.ece>. Accessed 24 March 2017.

Crick, E. (2007). Cricket and Indian National Consciousness for the Institute of Peace and Conflict Studies [online]. Available from <www.ipcs.org/pdf_file/issue/560458831IPCS-ResearchPaper9-EmilyCrick.pdf>. Accessed October 2016.

Daily Sun (2016). Globalization of Cricket [online]. Available from <www.daily-sun.com/printversion/details/122061/Globalisation-of-Cricket>. Accessed 18 August 2016.

Gemmell, J. & Majumdar, B. (2007). Cricket, Race and the 2007 World Cup. *Sport in Society: Cultures, Commerce, Media, Politics*, *10*(1), 1–10.

Glover, T. (2013). Cricket now more than just a sport; it is big business [online]. The *National*. Available from <www.thenational.ae/business/economy/cricket-now-more-than-just-a-sport-it-is-big-business>. Accessed September 2016.

Gupta, A. (2009). India and the IPL: Cricket's Globalized Empire [E-Journal]. The Round Table. *Commonwealth Journal of International Affairs*, *98*(401), 201–211. Available from <www.tandfonline.com/doi/abs/10.1080/00358530902757875>. Accessed June 2016.

Indo-Asian News Service for Cricket Country (2014). IPL success embodies emergence of sports as global industry, says India's representative at UN [online]. Available from <www.cricketcountry.com/news/ipl-success-embodies-emergence-of-sports-as-global-industry-says-indias-representative-at-un-201044>. Accessed October 2016.

International Cricket Council (2016). Board of Controlling Cricket in India [online]. Available from <www.icc-cricket.com/about/71/icc-members/full-members/india>. Accessed 18 August 2016.

Kaufman, J. & Patterson, O. (2005). Cross-national cultural diffusion: The global spread of cricket. *American Sociological Review* [Online], *70*(1), 82–110. Available from <http://scholar.harvard.edu/files/patterson/files/cricket_asr_final.pdf>. Accessed September 2016.

Kitchin, P. (2009). Sponsorship management in cricket: A case study of the Stanford Super Series. The West Indian Cricket Board and Digicel. *Sport Business Centre Case Study Paper Series*, *1*(1), 8. Available from <https://www.researchgate.net/publication/275947123_Sponsorship_Management_in_Cricket_A_Case_Study_of_the_Stanford_Super_Series_the_West_Indian_Cricket_Board_and_Digicel>. Accessed September 2016.

Kohli, R. (2009). The Launch of the Indian Premier League. *Columbia CaseWorks* [online]. Available from <www.columbia.edu/~rk35/IPL.pdf>. Accessed July 2016.

KPMG Report (2014). Business of sports: Shaping a successful innings for the Indian sports industry [online]. Available from <www.smri.in/wp-content/uploads/2015/02/Business-of-Sports-KPMG.pdf>. Accessed September 2016.

Mehta, J. & Raman, S. (2016). *Personal Interview*.

Mustafa, F. (2013). Cricket and globalization: Global processes and the imperial game. *Journal of Global History*, *8*, 318–341 [online]. Available from <http://journals.cambridge.org/abstract_S1740022813000247>. Accessed August 2016.

Nendick, J. & Balsara, F. (n.d). Spotlight on India's entertainment economy: Seizing new growth opportunities. *Ernst & Young* [online]. Available from <www.academia.edu/8356661/Spotlight_on_Indias_entertainment_economy_Seizing_new_growth_opportunities>. Accessed September 2016.

Sawer, P. (2010). "Premiership stars are 'poor men' of sport". The *Telegraph* [online]. Available from <www.telegraph.co.uk/sport/football/news/7530789/Premiership-stars-are-poor-men-of-sport.html>. Accessed 2 January 2017.

Press Trust of India (2008). IPL has globalized cricket: Tendulkar [online]. Available from <http://indiatoday.intoday.in/story/IPL has globalized cricket: Tendulkar/1/9128.html>. Accessed 18 September 2016.

Press Trust of India (2010). BCCI invites tender for team sponsorship [online]. Available from <http://sports.ndtv.com/cricket/news/141982-bcci-invites-tender-for-team-sponsorship>. Accessed 21 August 2016.

Rediff.com (2015). Globalization of Cricket [online]. Available from <www.rediff.com/cricket/report/if-we-dont-take-steps-globalization-of-cricket-will-never-happen-sachin-tendulkar-warne/20151103.htm>. Accessed October 2016.

Rumford, C. & Wagg, S. (2010). Cricket and Globalization [online]. Newcastle upon Tyne, UK: Cambridge Scholars Publishing. Available from <www.cambridgescholars.com/download/sample/58377>. Accessed August 2016.

Sathosh, S. R. (2013). Cup that changed the face of Indian cricket. *Khelnama* [online]. Available from <www.khelnama.com/130625/cricket/features/cup-changed-face-indian-cricket/10158>. Accessed October 2016.

Sayani (2016). "From entertainment to emergence of new talents: IPL has done a lot of good to cricket". *Indian Sports News* [online]. Available from <www.indiansportsnews.com/cricket-news/39249-from-entertainment-to-emergence-of-new-talents-ipl-has-done-a-lot-of-good-to-cricket>. Accessed January 2017.

Sharma, S. & Raol, K. S. (2011). "Nike to remain sponsor of Team India kit". The *Times of India* [online]. Available from <http://timesofindia.indiatimes.com/business/india-business/Nike-to-remain-sponsor-of-Team-India-kit/articleshow/8085543.cms>. Accessed June 2016.

TenSports Desk (2016). Various cricket boards around US$1.05 million to release players for IPL [e-journal]. Available from <www.tensports.com/news/bcci-pays-various-cricket-boards-around-us-105-million-release-players-ipl>. Accessed July 2016.

TNN (2013). "Indian Premier League: How it all started". The *Times of India* [online]. Available from <http://timesofindia.indiatimes.com/ipl-history/Indian-Premier-League-How-it-all-started/articleshow/19337875.cms>. Accessed August 2016.

TotalSportek2 (2015). Nike 5 year kit deal with Indian cricket worth $60 million [online]. Available from <www.totalsportek.com/money/nike-5-year-kit-deal-india-cricket-worth-60-million/>. Accessed September 2016.

TotalSportek2 (2016). Broadcasting Revenue Distribution [image]. Available from <www.totalsportek.com/money/indian-premier-league-revenue-distribution/>. Accessed 26 September 2016.

TotalSportek2 (2016). Financial division & support to uplift cricket [image]. Available from <www.totalsportek.com/money/indian-premier-league-revenue-distribution/>. Accessed 26 September 2016.

Wharton University of Pennsylvania (2007). Cricket in India: It's big business but not businesslike [online]. Available from <http://knowledge.wharton.upenn.edu/article/cricket-in-india-its-big-business-but-not-businesslike/>. Accessed December 2016.

32

THE ROLE OF HIGHLIGHT EVENTS IN SPORT-FOR-DEVELOPMENT

Nico Schulenkorf and Katie Schlenker

Introduction

In contrast to traditional forms of sport development that focus on improving skill and talent, sport-for-development (SFD) programs are being designed to go beyond the delivery of sport itself to make important contributions to improvements in people's health, livelihood and overall wellbeing (Sherry, Schulenkorf & Phillips, 2016). Designed correctly, SFD programs can also play a pivotal role in fostering social inclusion, education and gender equity in disadvantaged communities (Levermore & Beacom, 2009; Schulenkorf & Adair, 2014). As such, the concept of SFD is receiving increased attention from both practitioners and academics around the world as an innovative, active and engaging approach to socio-cultural, economic and health-related development. While recognizing the important role that sport *can* play in local and international development, current research suggests that the use of sport for development purposes is neither simple nor inherently successful, and the achievement of "success" depends heavily on the design and management of SFD projects (Coalter, 2010; Darnell & Black, 2011; Coalter, 2013).

Nexus between sport-for-development and highlight events

Within the context of SFD programs around the world, there is evidence of special events designed as part of the overall program portfolio, used as a means of engaging communities and contributing to wider development outcomes (Sugden, 2006; Schulenkorf & Edwards, 2012; Schulenkorf & Schlenker, 2017; Welty Peachey, Borland, Lobpries & Cohen, 2015). This is hardly surprising given the proven ability of special events to generate positive economic, socio-cultural participation and health-related impacts.

From an economic perspective, events are attractive to communities and destinations given the contributions they can make to local, state and national economies. Events generate economic benefits by attracting new money into a destination in the form of investment and tourist spending; through stimulating business activity; and through creating income and employment opportunities (Carlsen, 2004; Getz, 2007; Dwyer & Jago, 2012). Through increased media coverage associated with an event, destinations can also benefit economically in the longer term through destination awareness and increased tourist visitation (Carlsen, 2004; Dwyer, Forsyth & Spurr, 2005).

In addition to their potential economic benefits, events can provide a wide range of positive social impacts on both participants and the wider host community, including opportunities for celebration and entertainment as well as social interaction with other members of the community or with visitors to the community (Delamere, Wankel & Hinch, 2001; Dimmock & Tiyce, 2001; Small, Edwards & Sheridan, 2005; Schlenker, Foley & Getz, 2010). Moreover, special events may contribute to the celebration and enhancement of cultural traditions, the opportunity to develop community spirit and pride and the acquisition of new (management) skills (Chalip & McGuirty, 2004; Misener & Mason, 2006; Kellett, Hede & Chalip, 2008; O'Brien & Chalip, 2008). In short, special events are often a welcome attraction to members of the community, as they engender feelings of camaraderie that allow for engagement and learning to occur.

Special events are also recognized as having the potential to generate positive participation and health-related impacts. Increased participation can be in the form of more regular involvement in sport clubs or physical activity groups (Weed, Coren, Fiore, Wellard, Mansfield, Chatziefstathiou & Dowse, 2012; Craig & Bauman, 2014), or ideally, encouraging inactive members of the community to become "more active more often" (Brown & Massey, 2001; Shipway, 2007). Aside from participation in sports or physical activity, special events also have the potential to encourage greater community participation in activities associated with the event theme, for example music, culture or the arts (Getz, 1997; Dwyer, Mellor, Mistilis & Mules, 2000). Participation as active volunteers presents another important aspect of community life.

Despite the increased awareness and knowledge of the role that special events can play in community development efforts, there are very few studies that investigate the specific contribution of special events to SFD endeavors in the extant literature. This lack of research attention may be explained by the general belief that regularly conducted SFD programs offer a greater likelihood of long-term success than one-off, transitory events. In fact, much of the SFD literature argues that regular and ongoing programs are much more likely to have sustained impacts on a community than the "helicopter approach" whereby, for example, a famous sport personality is brought in for a fleeting visit with community members, in the hope of inspiring them to become active and motivated (Coalter, 2010; 2013).

Schulenkorf and Adair (2013) argue, however, that one-off special events may well have the ability to play a key role within the context of ongoing, regularized SFD programs. They suggest that as an out-of-the-ordinary peak moment within the SFD calendar, a "highlight event" may, for example, renew interest among local participants, but also arouse interest among those who have yet to engage in sport, physical activity or community programs. Participatory special events may thus have the potential to lead to what Weed, Coren and Fiore (2008) have described as the "festival effect". While the authors use this term in the context of mega-events, it is applicable at other scales, describing the effect of the positive emotions surrounding a special event that may result in people from the wider community becoming incidentally active and "drawn from their sofas" to either take part in, or witness, the show. Furthermore, if managed and marketed accordingly, a special event can showcase and promote the wider SFD program to local, regional and even national politicians, as well as to sport associations, potential sponsors and the media. This, in turn, may facilitate additional business activities that may benefit sport participants, organizers and the wider community.

Two noteworthy studies that investigate the specific contribution of special events to SFD endeavors were conducted by Schulenkorf and Edwards (2012) and Welty Peachey, Borland, Lobpries and Cohen (2015). First, Schulenkorf and Edwards investigated SFD event projects in the ethnically divided Sri Lanka and highlighted that social and cultural benefits can best be achieved if event organizers and host communities focus strategically on children as catalysts for change; provide event-related sociocultural opportunities; engage in social, cultural, political and educational event leverage activities; and combine large-scale events with regular SFD programs. Importantly, Schulenkorf and Edwards suggest that while regular SFD programs create opportunities for a "deepening and intensification of contacts and friendships" (p. 385), highlight events are often capable of extending these relationships to others in the wider community.

More recently, Welty Peachey and colleagues (2015) conducted research on the social impacts and growth potential of SFD events, confirming that such events are able to cultivate liminality and a sense of community for those involved. In line with earlier research, they suggest that SFD event organizers design both formal and informal opportunities for social interactions through a variety of sport and ancillary events to build *communitas* and to create additional opportunities for social leverage. Their findings highlight the contributions to broader community development endeavors made by a special event, through cultivating a sense of community, creating opportunities for relationship building and the development of social capital.

The theoretical concept that encapsulates the previously discussed opportunities is referred to as "event leveraging". Chalip (2004) introduced the term into the sport and event management spheres, arguing that in order to achieve event leverage, event organizers must move beyond the planning of direct event impacts and, instead, focus on creating strategic opportunities that will achieve lasting outcomes for host communities. The concept thus provides the theoretical underpinning for this chapter as it engages with the opportunity of one-off events to contribute to wider and more lasting development outcomes in communities (Chalip, 2004; 2006; O'Brien & Chalip, 2008).

Event contributions

Having established the theoretical backdrop and a clear argument for increased research into highlight events as a part of SFD programs, the remainder of this chapter focuses on discussing the opportunities and challenges of using highlight events to deliver benefits to participants and wider community stakeholders. In particular, we draw from previous conceptual and empirical research into SFD programs conducted in Australia and the Pacific Islands, which have incorporated cultural festivals, inter-school competitions or carnivals as highlight events. Importantly, these highlight events were part of a holistic SFD portfolio and therefore had a strategic place as "nested" elements in wider community development work. This is in contrast to stand-alone events that have been widely criticized for their limited impact and lack of sustainability, given the absence of follow-up activities that maintain or grow newly generated impacts (see, for example, Schulenkorf, 2012).

In short, the discussion that follows overviews the important contributions made by highlight sport events within the context of ongoing, regularized SFD programs. These contributions are in the areas of: creating new excitement; re-engaging stakeholders; building local management capacity; and leveraging partnerships.

Creating new excitement

Previous research conducted on SFD projects (Misener & Schulenkorf, 2016; Schulenkorf, 2016) identifies an important contribution made by highlight events in creating new excitement and additional interest among students, parents and the wider community. In fact, many people look forward to a day of sport and culture where they can watch performances, showcase newly learned skills and engage in non-sporting activities. Moreover, many young sportspeople are motivated to play and perform in front of a larger audience, while members of the wider community can be drawn into the event in various roles, participating as supporters, as volunteers, or by cheering on their children during sport and cultural performances. In line with the theoretical idea of leveraging events for social purposes (Chalip, 2006; O'Brien, 2007; O'Brien & Chalip, 2008), it is suggested that in the context of ongoing SFD programs, special events have the ability to create additional liminoid spaces for participants and the local community.

One-off special events can also create excitement for other event stakeholders, including commercial partners and sponsors, who are excited about the extra visibility of sport activities – and related sponsorship campaigns – around highlight events. While the financial engagement by local partners and sponsors in a developing country context often remains marginal, the connections and networks established with the business community may provide opportunities and benefits for future programming and in-kind support. Arguably, increased business support and new sponsorship deals are more likely if SFD events are to grow into larger event projects that open their doors for international teams and tourists (O'Brien, 2007; O'Brien & Chalip, 2008; Misener & Schulenkorf, 2016). This area presents an interesting opportunity for future research and empirical studies into the nexus of sport, events and tourism development.

Re-engaging stakeholders

When viewed as a strategic tool forming part of an SFD program, a special event can bring to life what might be a largely concealed, ongoing SFD program. A one-off or highlight event, by its very nature, brings a burst of attention to the ongoing SFD program, which can contribute to engaging or re-engaging various event stakeholders. First, a one-off event can engage new participants who have not previously been aware of, or involved with, the SFD program. The special event provides the initial opportunity to engage newcomers, who may, in turn, be encouraged to engage with other elements of the ongoing SFD program. Second, special events can also present an opportunity to renew the interest of those participants who were previously part of a SFD program, but whose interest and active participation could not be sustained by the regular program of activities. The highlight event may be the stimulus they need to re-engage with the program. Third, previous research suggests that SFD organizers may leverage highlight events to secure additional funding and/or community support for the goals of the SFD program (O'Brien & Chalip, 2008; Schulenkorf & Edwards, 2012; Welty Peachey *et al.*, 2015). And finally, stakeholder re-engagement may go beyond participants themselves as highlight events can be leveraged for the purpose of business stakeholder (re)activation, including sponsors and government departments (see e.g. Taks, Misener, Chalip & Green, 2013, Craig & Bauman, 2014).

Building local management capacity

Highlight sport events can be viewed as an opportunity to contribute to building the skills and management capabilities of participants and the wider community. While the majority of international SFD programs are coordinated and often also managed by international development staff (Schulenkorf, Sherry & Rowe, 2016), the inclusion of a "highlight event" such as a sports tournament or festival into an SFD program can provide an opportunity for local community engagement in the design and delivery of projects. Previous research supports that when local staff and community members are given the freedom to experiment around specific elements of the event design and day-to-day management, this increase in responsibility can develop their professional skills and leadership capability (see e.g. Schulenkorf, Sugden & Burdsey, 2014; Sherry & Schulenkorf, 2016). However, SFD organizers should not expect "too much, too quickly" from the local contributors. It is suggested that if too much organizational control is handed over in a short period of time then local communities and their sporting clubs could feel overwhelmed by the magnitude of managerial and sport-specific tasks assigned to them. As previously argued by Schulenkorf (2010), a full transfer of management power – which includes independent organizing of programs and activities – can and should only be achieved progressively over time, and with the background support of experienced SFD managers or change agents.

Leveraging partnerships

To achieve the wider aim of awareness building around pressing community issues, organizers often use SFD events as a social vehicle through which they engage partners in joint communication of messages. In other words, partnerships with key stakeholders are leveraged to increase the SFD initiative's reach and impact. From a theoretical perspective, the activation of key stakeholders links with the leverage strategy of cooperating with the media to showcase social issues (see O'Brien & Chalip, 2008). Moreover, it extends the focus beyond the media to include additional partners in an attempt to publicize social and health-related development issues. Especially in small communities or island states, relevant partnerships with potent organizations such as the Red Cross, the Ministry of Health, the police force or army personnel provide an effective opportunity to grow social messages to a wider audience.

Beyond local partnerships on the micro- and meso-levels, special events may also be an attractive vehicle to engage in strategic cooperation on the macro-level. In other words, if an SFD program becomes more visible – one of the benefits that special events such as festivals can provide – large development organizations may come on board as strategic partners in an attempt to further grow and leverage core messages. Schulenkorf and Adair (2013) have previously argued for strategic engagements between sport and non-sport organizations to allow for a deepening and widening of relationships through SFD. As testimony to this proposal, a recent cooperation agreement between the SFD program of the Oceania Football Confederation (Just Play) and the United Nations Children's Fund (2014) highlights the potential for sport organizations to connect with large development agencies – a strategic move that may lead to a multiplier effect in terms of generating additional awareness, interest, financial resources and commitment (Schulenkorf & Schlenker, 2017).

Caveats

This chapter suggests that highlight sport events are capable of making important contributions to broader community development efforts within the context of ongoing, regularized SFD programs. However, it should be acknowledged that there are challenges and limitations to one-off events. In particular, a "highlight event" that is not integrated into wider, more concerted efforts at community development runs the risk of being isolated and unsustainable. This reinforces the importance of integrating special events within an overarching SFD program if they are to achieve success as a means of community engagement (Sugden, 2006,

Schulenkorf & Edwards, 2012, Welty Peachey *et al.*, 2015). At the same time, it is possible that even a well-integrated special event can create negative impacts and unintended consequences for (at least part of) the community and/or participants (Balduck, Maes & Buelens, 2011; Jeanes & Magee, 2014). For example, communities are often faced with extra financial and social burdens, while participants must deal with additional sporting commitments and psychological pressure to perform in front of a large audience (Holt, Kingsley, Tink & Scherer, 2011). Negative consequences can influence media portrayal of the event, which can in turn contribute to an unfavourable public perception of it. Moreover, any damage to the event's reputation can also damage the reputation of the wider SFD program and its organizers and host community. This can have serious implications for the continued social and financial commitment of event participants, wider communities and business stakeholders.

Conclusion

As a vehicle for the creation of social, cultural, political, economic and health-related benefits, sport events have become an increasingly popular instrument at the local, regional, national and international level. In line with this trend, SFD programs have started to integrate special events as strategic elements in their development portfolios. This chapter reported on the specific contributions that sport events may add to regular, ongoing and participatory SFD program activities. In short, it is suggested that highlight events can create new interest and excitement for SFD activities, re-engage stakeholders to the wider SFD program, provide opportunities to build and shape local management capacity and leverage social and business partnerships.

Overall, special events provide a multitude of opportunities for SFD programs; hence, SFD organizers and local communities should take the contributions of special events into account when designing new development portfolios. While the focus of regular and ongoing SFD activities will always remain on the *deepening* of existing relationships and networks, special events allow for the *widening* of participation and the *proliferation* of program scope. In fact – as discussed in this chapter – the inclusion of highlight events allows for a vital showcasing of SFD projects and their goals to a wider cross-section of a host community, including potentially new participants, family members, sponsors, government bodies and sport associations. This stimulus seems particularly important where project organizers are looking to maximize social and business-related benefits through a process of sustained engagement and empowerment of locals in the management of community development projects.

References

Balduck, A.-L., Maes, M. & Buelens, M. (2011). The social impact of the Tour de France: Comparisons of residents' pre- and post-event perceptions. *European Sport Management Quarterly*, *11*(2), 91–113.

Brown, A. & Massey, J. (2001). *Literature Review: The Impact of Major Sporting Events*. [Report published by Manchester Institute for Popular Culture, Manchester Metropolitan University].

Carlsen, J. (2004). The economics and evaluation of festivals and events. In I. Yeoman, M. Robertson, J. Ali-Knight, S. Drummond & U. Mcmahon-Beattie (Eds), *Festival and Events Management: An International Arts and Culture Perspective* (pp. 246–259). Oxford, UK: Elsevier,.

Chalip, L. (2004). Beyond impact: A general model for host community event leverage. In B. Ritchie & D. Adair (Eds), *Sport Tourism: Interrelationships, Impacts and Issues* (pp. 226–252). Clevedon: Channel View.

Chalip, L. (2006). Towards social leverage of sport events. *Journal of Sport & Tourism*, *11*(2), 109–127.

Chalip, L. & Mcguirty, J. (2004). Bundling sport events with the host destination. *Journal of Sport Tourism, 9*(3), 267–282.

Coalter, F. (2010). The politics of sport-for-development: Limited focus programmes and broad gauge problems? *International Review for the Sociology of Sport, 45*(3), 295–314.

Coalter, F. (2013). *Sport for Development: What Game Are We Playing?* Abingdon, United Kingdom: Routledge.

Craig, C. L. & Bauman, A. (2014). The impact of the Vancouver Winter Olympics on population level physical activity and sport participation among Canadian children and adolescents: Population-based study. *International Journal of Behavioral Nutrition and Physical Activity, 11*(107), 1–9.

Darnell, S. C. & Black, D. R. (2011). Mainstreaming sport into international development studies. *Third World Quarterly, 32*(3), 367–378.

Delamere, T. A., Wankel, L. M. & Hinch, T. D. (2001). Development of a scale to measure resident attitudes toward the social impacts of community festivals, Part I: Item generation and purification of the measure. *Event Management, 7*(1), 11–24.

Dimmock, K. & Tiyce, M. (2001). Festivals and events: Celebrating special interest tourism. In N. Douglas & R. Derrett (Eds), *Special Interest Tourism* (pp. 355–383). Milton, Queensland: John Wiley & Sons.

Dwyer, L., Forsyth, P. & Spurr, R. (2005). Estimating the impacts of special events on an economy. *Journal of Travel Research, 43*(4), 351–359.

Dwyer, L. & Jago, L. (2012). The economic contribution of special events. In S. J. Page & J. Connell (Eds), *The Routledge Handbook of Events* (pp. 129–147). Abingdon: Routledge.

Dwyer, L., Mellor, R., Mistilis, N. & Mules, T. (2000). A framework for assessing "tangible" and "intangible" impacts of events and conventions. *Event Management, 6*(3), 175–189.

Getz, D. (1997). *Event Management and Event Tourism.* New York: Cognizant Communication Corp.

Getz, D. (2007). *Event Studies: Theory, Research and Policy for Planned Events.* Oxford: Butterworth-Heinemann.

Holt, N. L., Kingsley, B. C., Tink, L. N. & Scherer, J. (2011). Benefits and challenges associated with sport participation by children and parents from low-income families. *Psychology of Sport and Exercise, 12*(5), 490–499.

Jeanes, R. & Magee, J. (2014). Promoting gender empowerment through sport? Exploring the experiences of Zambian footballers. In N. Schulenkorf & D. Adair (Eds), *Global Sport-for-Development: Critical Perspectives* (pp. 134–154). Basingstoke: Palgrave Macmillan.

Kellett, P., Hede, A.-M. & Chalip, L. (2008). Social policy for sport events: Leveraging (relationships with) teams from other nations for community benefit. *European Sport Management Quarterly, 8*(2), 101–121.

Levermore, R. & Beacom, A. (Eds) (2009) *Sport and International Development.* Basingstoke, United Kingdom: Palgrave Macmillan.

Misener, L. & Mason, D. S. (2006). Creating community networks: Can sporting events offer meaningful sources of social capital? *Managing Leisure, 11*(1), 39–56.

Misener, L. & Schulenkorf, N. (2016). Rethinking the social value of sport events through an asset-based community development (ABCD) perspective. *Journal of Sport Management, 30*(3), 329–340. <doi:http://dx.doi.org/10.1123/jsm.2015-0203>.

O'Brien, D. (2007). Points of Leverage: Maximizing Host Community Benefit from a Regional Surfing Festival. *European Sport Management Quarterly, 7*(2), 141–165.

O'Brien, D. & Chalip, L. (2008). Sport events and strategic leveraging: Pushing towards the triple bottom line. In A. Woodside & D. Martin (Eds), *Tourism Management: Analysis, Behaviour and Strategy* (pp. 318–338). Wallingford, UK; Cambridge, MA: CABI.

Schlenker, K., Foley, C. & Getz, D. (2010). *ENCORE Festival and event evaluation kit: Review and redevelopment.* Gold Coast, Australia: S. T. C. R. Centre.

Schulenkorf, N. (2010). The roles and responsibilities of a change agent in sport event development projects. *Sport Management Review, 13*(2), 118–128.

Schulenkorf, N. (2012). Sustainable community development through sport and events: A conceptual framework for Sport-for-Development projects. *Sport Management Review, 15*(1), 1–12.

Schulenkorf, N. (2016). The contributions of special events to sport-for-development programs. *Journal of Sport Management, 30*(6), 629–642. <doi:10.1123/JSM.2016-0066>.

Schulenkorf, N. & Adair, D. (2013). Temporality, transience and regularity in sport-for-development: Synchronizing programs with events. *Journal of Policy Research in Tourism, Leisure and Events, 5*(1), 99–104.

Schulenkorf, N. & Adair, D. (Eds) (2014). *Global Sport-for-Development: Critical Perspectives*. Basingstoke, United Kingdom: Palgrave Macmillan.

Schulenkorf, N. & Edwards, D. (2012). Maximizing positive social impacts: Strategies for sustaining and leveraging the benefits of intercommunity sport events in divided societies. *Journal of Sport Management, 26*(5), 379–390.

Schulenkorf, N. & Schlenker, K. (2017). Leveraging Sport Events to Maximize Community Benefits in Low- and Middle-Income Countries. *Event Management, 21*(2), 217–231. <doi:10.3727/152599 517X14878772869766>.

Schulenkorf, N., Sherry, E. & Rowe, K. (2016). Sport-for-Development: An Integrated Literature Review. *Journal of Sport Management, 30*(1), 22–39.

Schulenkorf, N., Sugden, J. & Burdsey, D. (2014). Sport for development and peace as contested terrain: Place, community, ownership. *International Journal of Sport Policy, 6*(3), 371–378.

Sherry, E. & Schulenkorf, N. (2016). League Bilong Laif: Rugby, education and sport-for-development partnerships in Papua New Guinea. *Sport, Education and Society, 21*(4), 513–530.

Sherry, E., Schulenkorf, N. & Phillips, P. (Eds) (2016) *Managing Sport Development: An International Approach*. Abingdon: Routledge.

Shipway, R. (2007). Sustainable legacies for the 2012 Olympic Games. *Journal of the Royal Society for the Promotion of Health, 127*(3), 119–124.

Small, K., Edwards, D. & Sheridan, L. (2005). A flexible framework for socio-cultural impact evaluation of a festival. *International Journal of Event Management Research, 1*(1), 66–77.

Sugden, J. (2006). Teaching and playing sport for conflict resolution and co-existence in Israel. *International Review for the Sociology of Sport, 41*(2), 221–240.

Taks, M., Misener, L., Chalip, L. & Green, B.C. (2013). Leveraging sport events for participation. *Canadian Journal of Social Research, 3*(1), 12–23.

United Nations Children's Fund (2014). *UNICEF and OFC join hands to move Just Play Programme forward* [online]. UNICEF South Pacific. Available from <www.unicef.org/pacificislands/1852_22232.html>. Accessed 15 February 2016.

Weed, M., Coren, E. & Fiore, J. (2008). A systematic review of the evidence base for developing a physical activity, sport and health legacy from the London 2012 Olympic and Paralympic Games: Report to funders. Canterbury, United Kingdom.

Weed, M., Coren, E., Fiore, J., Wellard, I., Mansfield, L., Chatziefstathiou, D. & Dowse, S. (2012). Developing a physical activity legacy from the London 2012 Olympic and Paralympic Games: A policy-led systematic review. *Perspectives in Public Health, 132*(2), 75–80.

Welty Peachey, J., Borland, J., Lobpries, J. & Cohen, A. (2015). Managing impact: Leveraging sacred spaces and community celebration to maximize social capital at a sport-for-development event. *Sport Management Review, 18*(1), 86–98.

33

SOCIAL ENTREPRENEURSHIP AND SPORT

Jonathan Robertson

Introduction

This chapter explores the emerging organizational paradigm of social entrepreneurship and how it may be applicable within the sport industry. Over the past two decades, sport organizations have incrementally shifted towards forms of organizing that meet multiple requirements from diverse stakeholder groups. Profit-seeking organizations increasingly deliver social and economic outcomes based on perceived social responsibilities, such as Nike's "Girl Effect", which focuses on empowering young women in developing countries. Nonprofit organizations now use commercial terminology such as (social) return on investment to evaluate and legitimize their work within an increasingly competitive funding environment. Entrepreneurs are able to assess existing competitive environments and select a particular location and form of incorporation that best fits the multiple demands of a particular competitive landscape. An emerging organizational paradigm within entrepreneurship is social enterprises, which exist to "leverage economic activity to pursue a social objective and implement social change" (Mair, Battilana & Cardenas, 2012, p. 356). Social entrepreneurship – conceptually – addresses several shortcomings of current sport development approaches. First, at the heart of the concept is the idea that market-based (business) solutions can (in)directly address social problems (Yunus and Weber, 2010). Second, social enterprises are able to become financially autonomous and independent from external funders. Financial autonomy removes continual reliance on third parties for economic resources, simultaneously enabling long-term decision making independent of funding cycles and allowing senior management to be directed toward mission-critical activities. Third, social justice is central to social enterprises. The centrality of principles of social justice ensures that social enterprises provide better than minimal working conditions within the organization and its supply chain, prior to the pursuit of overt actions to benefit society. Social enterprises can therefore be characterized as market orientated, financially autonomous and socially just forms of organizing that exist to address a social problem. Social entrepreneurship (the concept), social enterprise (the organizational form) and social entrepreneur (the individual) are used interchangeably throughout this chapter to explain different aspects of the developing field of social entrepreneurship. Social sport business is one type of social enterprise and is utilized as a tool for explaining aspects of the broader concept of social entrepreneurship (Westerbeek, 2010; Yunus & Weber, 2010).

Broad representation and description of the social entrepreneurship concept in its entirety are not the aim of this chapter. Rather, the aim is to emphasize central tenants of social enterprise (i.e. market-based solutions to social problems; financial autonomy and scalability; and, a socially just workplace) as a potential mechanism for a more (social) value-adding sport industry.

In its broadest definition, social enterprise has existed since the industrial revolution with several social institutions using a portion of commercial exchanges or altruistic donations to fund social development activities (e.g. the Church, the state, philanthropists) (Battilana & Lee, 2014). Despite this, relatively few organizations have been designed to solely generate revenue from the market for the sole purpose of alleviating a social ill. Over the past century, the way society views the responsibility of – and uses for – incorporated "corporate" organizations has fundamentally changed (Bowen, 1953; Carroll, 1979; Freeman, 1984; Friedman,1970; Prahalad, 2006; Yunus & Weber, 2010). One-time profit-maximizing organizations are now required to demonstrate a responsibility to society whilst maintaining the fiduciary responsibilities to owners/shareholders (McWilliams & Siegel, 2000; Schwartz & Carroll, 2008). Traditionally altruistic nonprofit organizations were progressively influenced by market-based competition for access to funding and donations whilst trying to remain true to their social mission (Weerawardena, McDonald & Sullivan Mort, 2010). Simultaneously, across the organizational landscape, the public sector has increasingly been required to achieve more, with less, in a complex and interconnected environment. Existing organizations have not been equipped to deal with this changing landscape. From the perspective of maximizing a single goal, this change has resulted in paradoxical organizational forms such as highly socially responsible public companies and commercially orientated charities. Environmental pressure to produce competing social and economic goals has given rise to the field of social entrepreneurship (Drayton, 2002).

Building on this perspective, social enterprises/social sport businesses are not organizational forms but rather an approach to alleviating social problems via the most appropriate market-based mechanisms – and consequently organizational forms – that are available to the social entrepreneur within a given legislative and regulative environment. The framework selected herein is based on Mohummad Yunus' concept of social business that is fundamentally a company with specifically designed constitutional articles to limit profit-maximizing behaviour and promote the attainment of social objectives. Yunus won the Nobel Peace Prize in 2006 for his social business, the Grameen Bank. The bank was a traditional bank, however its founding documents and subsequent objectives and behaviour were designed specifically to achieve a social development objective. Grameen greatly impacted social and economic development by offering micro-loans with good terms and community support to help lift people out of poverty. At the end of this chapter a case study of Jinta Sport is provided (pp. 370–371), which demonstrates how these principles can be translated into the sport industry. The case study investigates one of the first FairTrade®-certified sporting goods manufacturers in the world, and exemplifies the challenges and opportunities for social sport business to generate social change within a competitive marketplace.

Social entrepreneurship and social sport business

Environmental pressures to deliver dual social and economic goals are affecting the organizational form of established and new enterprises alike (Murphy & Coombes, 2009). Although not all new organizations are entrepreneurial or socially orientated (Drucker, 1998), the focus of this chapter is on organizations that meet both criteria. The formation of such organizations has been driven through social entrepreneurship (Dees, 1998). Davis

(2002, p. 7) argues that "social entrepreneurship extends the definition of entrepreneurship by its emphasis on ethical integrity and maximizing social value rather than private value or profit". The surplus generated from market-based activities is used as a resource for delivering social value to society rather than amassing private wealth generation.

By definition, there are several forms that social enterprises can take, from corporations that are highly social responsible to charities that have extensive commercial operations and marketing departments. In countries, such as the United States (low-profit limited liability companies (L3C)) and the United Kingdom (community interest companies (CIC)) there are legal forms of incorporation available to social entrepreneurs looking to start a social enterprise. Furthermore, in countries lacking such legislation there exist third-party nongovernmental organizations (NGOs) that legitimize organizations as social enterprises based on their operations (e.g. BCorp). Social entrepreneurship broadly considers the ways in which aspects of nonprofit and for profit organizations can come together to create a hybrid form of organizing aimed at realizing social change. Dees (1998, p. 1) describes social entrepreneurship as:

> important in that it implies a blurring of sector boundaries. In addition to innovative not-for-profit ventures, social entrepreneurship can include social purpose business ventures . . . and hybrid organizations mixing not-for-profit and for-profit elements . . . Social entrepreneurs look for the most effective methods of serving their social missions.

In that sense, attempts to define the term "social entrepreneurship" have parallels with early attempts to define the term "social responsibility" 40 years ago, to which Votaw (1972, p. 25) argued, "the term is a brilliant one; it means something, but not always the same thing, to everybody". Much of the last decade of research on social entrepreneurship has focused on descriptive efforts to identify what social entrepreneurship actually is.

The extent to which economic and social objectives are central and commercialized (Peredo & McLean, 2006), and replicable and direct (Martin & Osberg, 2007), is often not explicitly defined within the term "social entrepreneurship". As such, social entrepreneurship often lacks a degree of specificity in regard to real world application (e.g. issues such as tax, profit distribution and constitution are variable). In reviewing the term, Peredo and McLean (2006) suggested that the organizational categorization of social enterprises depends on (1) the centrality of social goals to the organization and (2) the extent to which social goals play a role in commercial exchanges. A central social mission that plays a role in commercial exchanges distinguishes "social" from standard "commercial" entrepreneurship (Austin, Stevenson & Wei-Skillern, 2006). The commercial view of entrepreneurship positions entre-preneurs as primarily economic actors who operate within areas that may produce unintended positive social outcomes in the pursuit of economic goals (Austin, Stevenson & Wei-Skillern, 2006; Schumpeter, 1947). In contrast, social entrepreneurship positions the social mission as "explicit and central" to the purpose of the social entrepreneur (Dees, 1998). The central importance of social goals as the primary organizational objective ensures that surplus eco-nomic resources are viewed as a means for social betterment, rather than an ends for private wealth. Commercial exchanges can support social objective achievement directly (e.g. the employment of disadvantaged groups to produce a football) or indirectly (e.g. the sale of sport services to cross-subsidize a development programme).

This chapter explores the increasingly popular business paradigm of social business and how it may be applicable as a tool of social development within the international sport industry (Yunus & Weber, 2010). The purpose of this selection – as opposed to the existing legislated forms of organizing outlined above – enables the discussion to proceed based on a broad set of guidelines that can conceptually fit a variety of contexts. Simultaneously it does not exclude areas based on a specific state's legislative framework (e.g. as L3Cs and CICs do). In their seminal work *Building Social Business: The New Kind of Capitalism That Serves Humanity's Most Pressing Needs*, Yunus and Weber make the case that:

> in contrast with social entrepreneurship, social business is a very specific type of business – a non-loss, non-dividend company with a social objective. A social business may pursue goals similar to those sought by some social entrepreneurs, but the specific business structure of social business makes it distinctive and unique.
>
> *Yunus & Weber, 2010, p. 4*

Yunus and Weber outline two types of business they think can sustainably address "social and environmental ills. Type 1 social businesses are non-loss, non-dividend companies that return all initial investment back to investors. Type 2 social businesses are profit-maximizing companies operated by people from low socioeconomic backgrounds, the profits of which go towards improving their socioeconomic status and position. The Type 1 social business is chosen as the initial framework in which to explore social entrepreneurship in sport for development, as Type 1 does not exclude anyone from operating the business on the basis of socioeconomic status and is specifically designed to address social problems. The selection of this organizational approach is designed to exemplify one type of social sport business for the purpose of exploring the concept within the sport industry. In practice, variations are likely to exist in a number of areas, including but not limited to:

- constitution and ownership structure (e.g. nonprofit, for-profit, cooperatives)
- returns to shareholders ranging from none (e.g. nonprofit), to moderated or constrained (e.g. Community Interest Company or social business), to unrestricted (e.g. linked solely to social objectives or commercial success)
- centrality of social mission (e.g. central social mission or commercial business unit that cross-subsidizes social actions)

The use of social sport business therefore enables a discussion around the relative utility of social entrepreneurship to the area of sport for development. In the sporting context, Westerbeek argues that the application of social sport business can have the following benefits within the sport industry:

> [Sport business and sport development organizations] will not deliver maximum output regarding social outcomes – the first not because it seeks a profit as a primary outcome and the second not because it depends on third-party contributions in the process of generating sufficient resources.
>
> *Westerbeek, 2010, p. 1415*

Maximizing in this context is paradoxically counterproductive to optimal social value creation. Social value in sport development cannot be maximized sufficiently without independence from third party funders and the operational autonomy that financial independence brings with it. Profit maximization for a private minority cannot be maximized if the public good is taken into material consideration by the organization. Hence, a hybrid form of organizing is required to optimize, in contrast to maximizing, social and economic outcomes within a multidimensional environment (Battilana & Dorado, 2010). Central to the idea of social and economic value optimization are three tenets of social sport business: market-based solutions to social problems; financial autonomy and scalability; and a socially just workplace.

Market-based solutions to social problems

Commercially viable solutions to social problems challenge the foundation of altruistic approaches to sport development. Although the central social objective from which organizational performance is measured remains the primary organizational objective, the mechanism to achieve this objective is in the form of an incorporated company organizational structure. Economic resources are gained from revenue earned from the free market sale of products and services that have value to consumers. External financial capital is conceptualized as investment requiring repayment, rather than funding that requires continuous sourcing from government or funders. Investors will have the principal investment repaid; however dividend payment, if any at all, is made on the premise of quantifiable progress against a predetermined social goal. As a company, the social sport business pays taxes. Unlike non-profit organizational forms, social sport business does not avoid company tax rates and therefore contributes to state funding via tax payment on monies earned (the relative merits of government expenditure is beyond the scope of this chapter). As a form of incorporated business, social sport businesses are required to comply with a higher level of company regulation and reporting requirements than many nonprofit organizations, ensuring a higher level of public transparency.

Concurrently, the organization exists to achieve a social goal ensuring profit-maximizing behaviour is tempered by articles or replaceable rules in its constitution. To avoid the risk of mission drift, and to maintain dual social and economic goals, stakeholder provisions such as constitutional articles and governance structures need to be made explicit in hybrid forms of organizing (Ebrahim, Battilana & Mair, 2014). The effect of such articles tempers investor expectations of immediate financial returns (Friedman, 1970) and simultaneously writes forms of social contracts into the founding constitution of the company (Donaldson & Dunfee, 1999). This allows the social sport business to be owned by shareholders that are afforded limited liability via the process of incorporating the company. Via the sale of ownership shares, the social sport business is able to raise and generate funds from the public which it can use for expanding the enterprise in its infancy (Yunus & Weber, 2010). Conversely, as investors are entering into the ownership of the social sport business with pre-existing knowledge of moderated financial returns, the explicit requirement for organizational behaviour to be directed toward profit-maximizing behaviour does not become an issue. Different investor logics and investor rationalities drive investment in social sport businesses (Nicholls, 2010). For social investors, the paradigm shifts from traditional one-way altruistic investment towards philanthropic activities in which no financial return is sought, to the return of that initial investment and redirection into another social enterprise. This process or social (re)investment multiplies the financial and social impact of a single monetary amount several times. The microfinance nonprofit organization, Kiva, is an example of this process in action. Traditional "donors" are repositioned as "investors" and lend (not donate) $25 sums to social enterprises around the world; the organization has a repayment rate of over 98 per cent to investors (Kiva, 2016). Each sum multiplies once repaid and reinvested in another social enterprise.

Social sport businesses redirect the economic capital that an entrepreneur may strive for to a social end. Lessons from successful business entrepreneurship in the sport industry are thus valuable for understanding the conceptual utility of social sport business. Recent examples of business entrepreneurship creating economic value within the sport industry include the Indian Premier League (a cricket competition in India), Zuffa LLC (which manages the Ultimate Fighting Championship), Under Armour (sporting goods manufacturer) and the YES Network (which owns the television rights to several of New York's sports teams) (Foster, 2013). Over the past two decades these companies have demonstrated that multi-billion dollar businesses can be formed and scaled quickly. However, as in the broader corporate sector the financial wealth of these companies accrues often to a few private individuals and such companies arguably produce minimal demonstrable social benefit relative to their economic size and position in society. Whilst the scale of the above enterprises are clearly outliers, and therefore difficult to replicate, such examples provide insight into the potential of the concept to redirect innovative and entrepreneurial activities from private wealth generation to the long-term alleviation of social problems. On the micro scale, such social sport businesses are beginning to develop (see the Jinta Sport case study near the end of this chapter). The utility of social sport business is the redirection of financial capital generated from market-based sources to fund financially autonomous and scalable solutions to social problems.

Financial autonomy and scalable solutions

Financial autonomy and scalable solutions differentiate social sport businesses from other social service providers in the sport development space (e.g. nonprofits, charities and other non-governmental organizations). While an explicit and central social purpose is crucial, it is also shared with ventures such as social activism and social service providers. Martin and Osberg (2007) distinguish social entrepreneurship from social activism in that social entrepreneurship involves direct action, rather than indirect action that would more commonly be associated with awareness-raising activism. Furthermore, social sport business is differentiated from social service organizations on the basis that it is self-replicable to a point where a new equilibrium is created and sustained within the targeted area of disadvantage. Social sport business does not rely on continuous funding and generally views any financial capital put into the organization as a form of investment that is to be repaid. Once initial capital is repaid, any further shareholder returns (if any at all) are premised on the attainment of the organization's stated social objective. Social enterprises are more able to scale their operations due to generating their own resources from the market. As commercially viable businesses, social enterprises are thus freed from funding constraints and reliance on third parties. Financial independence enables strategic timelines to be lengthened, managerial focus on the mission rather than on funding, and long-term decisions made in the best interest of the organization rather than on the basis of short-term funding needs.

In the corporate setting, social sport business has the potential to advance the corporate social responsibility paradigm. Traditionally, the social and economic responsibilities of the corporate organizational form have been viewed as opposing, giving rise to a field of research that investigates the influence of social responsibility on financial performance (Margolis and Walsh, 2003). Applying the social entrepreneurship concept to corporate social responsibility minimizes the tension between the social and financial performance of an organization. Corporations may choose to invest in social enterprises as financially autonomous sub-units that utilize market-based solutions to pursue social missions. Once operational and commercially viable, the social sport business sub-unit repays the initial capital to the parent company for reinvestment in another social enterprise, whilst simultaneously and quantifiably addressing a social issue. This process both enables the first social sport business to scale (because it generates its funds from the market), provides startup capital for a second social sport business sub-unit (from the repaid capital of the first social sport business) and does not violate the maximization of shareholder returns beyond the opportunity cost of the initial financial capital investment. Furthermore, the opportunity cost of the initial capital investment may be offset by the increasing scale social returns and the brand benefits these can bring to an organization.

A socially just workplace

Social justice is at the core of social sport business. Social justice, particularly in the explicit avoidance of exploitation, is a reminder that a highly commercial approach to social problems is the means and not the ends of the organization. In broad definitions of social enterprise the market-based solution to achieving social change is vigorously put forth. However, if the means by which economic resources are gained are not ethical (e.g. via the exploitation of workers or the environment), then the ends and identification as a social sport business are unjustifiable. Doing no harm to the organization's stakeholders (workforce, supply chain, community and the environment) is a key aspect of social sport business. In the sport development context it is incongruent with the aims of social sport business to be running sport development programmes in one country using sport equipment manufactured by exploitative child labour in run-down factories in another country. The achievement of development goals in the former is offset by the exploitation of children in latter.

The final and most powerful point put forth by Yunus and Weber (2010) is that social sport business should be "done with joy". The aspect of enjoying what one does and finding passion in helping people is central to the implicit attraction of social enterprise. Social sport business should provide at least average wages to employees with considerations for better-than-average working arrangements. These may include childcare provisions, flexible working hours and locations and creating a good organizational culture. In summary, the means by which a social problem is alleviated are just as important as the socially beneficial ends.

The case study of Jinta Sport, a FairTrade®-certified social sport business

Jinta Sport is part of Etiko Pty Ltd, an Australian company that has produced sport equipment since 2007. The mission of the company is to "not only offer consumers high quality, well priced sports gear, but also to help create a positive change in the world" (Jinta Sport – About Us, n.d.). In addition to apparel, Jinta Sport sells a range of football, futsal, Australian Rules football, netball and rugby balls globally. The word "Jinta" comes from the Warlpiri word for "one" or "winner". The Warlpiri are an Aboriginal people located in a remote part of the Northern Territory of Australia. As part of the organization's commitment to community development, 2.5 per cent of each sale goes to the Warlpiri Youth Development Aboriginal Corporation, which assists Aboriginal youth in remote communities.

Jinta Sport is a FairTrade®-certified company. FairTrade® is a global certification and verification body that has existed since the 1940s. FairTrade® Australia was established in 2003. The FairTrade® movement's focus is on ensuring decent working conditions in developing countries for workers in the supply chain of major commodities such as cocoa, cotton, coffee and a

---

growing number of other products. FairTrade® is based on ten principles (World Fair Trade Organization, 2013):

- creating opportunities for economically disadvantaged producers
- transparency and accountability
- fair trading practices
- payment of a fair price
- ensuring no child labour and forced labour
- commitment to nondiscrimination, gender equity and women's economic empowerment, and freedom of association
- ensuring good working conditions
- providing capacity building
- promoting fair trade
- respect for the environment

In order to receive certification, organizations must demonstrate compliance with the above criteria. Jinta Sport manufactures sporting goods in India and Pakistan. As part of FairTrade® certification the organization must pay a FairTrade® minimum price to manufacturers that ensures that a minimum price is set and that prices cannot fall below a pre-defined level. In turn, this ensures minimum wages are paid by the producer organizations. Additionally, a FairTrade® premium of 15 per cent of a product's wholesale price goes towards community investment in social, environmental and economic development projects. In Pakistan, these premiums have been used to buy and instal water filters in remote villages that have no access to clean drinking water and are consequently at greater risk of waterborne diseases. In the factories that produce Jinta Sport products, FairTrade® premiums have also allowed workers to start a cooperative to purchase food staples such as legumes, rice and ghee (a common type of butter in Pakistan) at wholesale prices. The cooperative covers operational expenses by adding 5 per cent to the wholesale price and then on selling the food to workers. This method has significantly reduced the cost of everyday food items for workers.

The structural features of FairTrade® that are embedded into Jinta Sport are complemented by actively engaging with NGOs and charities. World Vision partnered with Jinta Sport to produce footballs for the "One Goal Campaign" throughout Asia. The campaign aims to bring awareness of child malnutrition in Asia by increasing the number of children who are well-nourished (from birth up to the age of five); increasing the adoption of healthy lifestyles for children aged between six and 18; and, increasing grass-roots football activities in Asia (World Vision International, 2015). Jinta Sport supplied 300 balls for World Vision to use in its programmes.

Jinta Sport operates in the highly competitive sport manufacturing and retail industries. Revenue is generated via market-based competition in the retail space to sell products that offer consumers value. From the revenue generated, the company pays company taxes to the Australian government as well as incorporating additional overheads (FairTrade® premiums and accreditation costs; Warlpiri community development contribution and charity contributions) into the retail price. Despite these additional overheads that other competitors do not carry, the organization manages to compete and succeed in this market via efficient and innovate products and operations. Furthermore, it sells its products in a variety of countries and is able to scale its operations, generating more social change as the organization grows. Jinta Sport can be considered a social sport business prototype.

Conclusion

The term "social sport business" is premised on the assumption that there may be sustainable business solutions to social problems that public, private and nonprofit organizations are increasingly looking to answer using sport as a medium. Established organizational entities are unlikely to become social sport businesses due to a historical legacy of institutionalized behaviour and organizational structures, such as fiduciary responsibilities to shareholders or nonprofit clauses. Future research should consider the motivators and constraints for established private entities to enter into agreements to create, or partner with, social sport businesses as a method of discharging their social responsibilities. Joint ventures between private (profit-seeking) entities and social sport businesses may be a potential way to increase social outcomes at a low or neutral cost, within a company's corporate social responsibility portfolio. For sport development in established sport markets, social entrepreneurship holds the potential to assist sport in the delivery of solutions that address complex and often resource-intensive problems outside the traditional scope of operations. Moreover, future research may further investigate the increasing commercial nature of nonprofit organizations and shifts towards social entrepreneurship as a possible answer to resource constraints. In particular, future research could focus on market-based solutions to endemic social problems within the nonprofit sport sector.

In the 1950s "social responsibility" was an abstract business concept. At the turn of the millennium billion-dollar sport assets such as the Indian Premier League and the Yes Network did not exist. Despite its obvious appeal and hybrid approach to social problems, social entrepreneurship is not an abstract debate for welfare states and philanthropists. Social sport businesses could pave the way for similar initiatives across the sport industry. Social sport business as a new form of organization may well lead to more effective delivery of economic and social outcomes in society at large. The current approach to sport development is not insufficient – rather, we argue, it is incomplete. The time period required to achieve sustained social change rarely aligns with funding cycles. Corporate and nonprofit approaches are viewed as mutually exclusive rather than on a continuum, and lacking continual funding or market-based solutions, the economies of scale required for scalable social change remain elusive. In spite of these constraints, sport development NGOs, government funders and corporate philanthropists have realized extensive social change in many areas. Social sport business could be the next step in the generation of social value within the international sport industry.

References

Austin, J. Stevenson, H. & Wei-Skillern, J. (2006). Social and commercial entrepreneurship: Same, different or both? *Entrepreneurship: Theory and Practice*, *30*(1), 1–22.

Battilana, J. & Dorado, S. (2010). Building sustainable hybrid organizations: The case of commercial microfinance organizations. *Academy of Management Journal*, *53*(6), 1419–1440.

Battilana, J. & Lee, M. (2014). Advancing research on hybrid organizing – insights from the study of social enterprises. *Academy of Management Annals*, *8*(1), 397–441.

Bowen, H. R. (1953). *Social Responsibilities of the Businessman*. New York: Harper & Row.

Carroll, A. B. (1979). A three-dimensional conceptual model of corporate performance. *Academy of Management Review*, *4*(4), 497–505.

Davis, S. (2002). Social Entrepreneurship: Towards an entrepreneurial culture for social and economic development. Paper presented to the Youth Employment Summit, Alexandria, Egypt.

Dees, J. G. (1998). *The Meaning of "Social Entrepreneurship"*. Comments and suggestions contributed from the Social Entrepreneurship Founders Working Group. Durham, NC: Center for the Advancement of Social Entrepreneurship, Fuqua School of Business, Duke University. Available at <http://faculty.fuqua.duke.edu/centers/case/files/dees-SE.pdf>.

Donaldson, T. & Dunfee, T. W. (1999). *Ties That Bind: A Social Contract Approach to Business Ethics*. Boston: Harvard Business Press.

Drayton, W. (2002). The citizen sector: Becoming as entrepreneurial and competitive as business. *California Management Review, 44*(3), 120–132.

Drucker, P. F. (1998). The discipline of innovation. *Harvard Business Review* (November–December), 149–157.

Ebrahim, A., Battilana, J. & Mair, J. (2014). The governance of social enterprises: Mission drift and accountability challenges in hybrid organizations. *Research in Organizational Behavior, 34*, 81–100.

Foster, G. (2013). George Foster: Entrepreneurship in Sports. Stanford Graduate School of Business. Retrieved from <www.youtube.com/watch?v=fu7uU7L2sRw>. Accessed 15 January 2016.

Freeman, R. E. (1984). *Strategic Management: A Stakeholder Approach*. Boston: Pittman.

Friedman, M. (1970). "The social responsibility of business is to increase its profits". *New York Times Magazine*.

Jinta Sport – About Us (n.d.). Jinta Sport. Retrieved from <http://jintasport.com.au/about-us/>. Accessed 26 February 2016.

Kiva (2016). Kiva Statistics. Retrieved from <www.kiva.org/about/stats/>/>. Accessed 26 February 2016.

Mair, J., Battilana, J. & Cardenas, J. (2012). Social entrepreneurship in theory and practice. *Journal of Business Ethics, 111*(3), 353–373.

Margolis, J. D. & Walsh, J. P. (2003). Misery loves companies: Rethinking social initiatives by business. *Administrative Science Quarterly, 48*(2), 268–305.

Martin, R. L. & Osberg, S. (2007). Social entrepreneurship: The case for definition, *Stanford Social Innovation Review* (Spring), 28–39.

McWilliams, A. & Siegel, D. (2000). Corporate social responsibility: A theory of the firm perspective. *Academy of Management Review, 26*(1), 117–127.

Murphy, P. J. & Coombes, S. M. (2009). A model of social entrepreneurial discovery. *Journal of Business Ethics, 87*(3), 325–336.

Nicholls, A. (2010). The institutionalization of social investment: The interplay of investment logics and investor rationalities. *Journal of Social Entrepreneurship, 1*(1), 70–100.

Peredo, A. M. & McLean, M. (2006). Social entrepreneurship: A critical review of the concept. *Journal of World Business, 41*(1), 56–65.

Prahalad, C. K. (2006). *The Fortune at the Bottom of the Pyramid: Eradicating Poverty Through Profits*. Pennsylvania: Wharton School Publishing.

Schumpeter, J. (1947). *Capitalism, Socialism, and Democracy* (2nd edn). New York: Free Press.

Schwartz, M. S. & Carroll, A. B. (2008). Integrating and unifying competing and complementary frameworks: The search for a common core in the business and society field. *Business Society, 47*(2), 148–186.

Votaw, D. (1972). Genius becomes rare: A comment on the doctrine of social responsibility. *California Management Review, 15*(2), 25–31.

Weerawardena, J., McDonald, R. E. & Sullivan Mort, G. (2010). Sustainability of nonprofit organizations: An empirical investigation, *Journal of World Business: Special Edition – Sustainable Business, 45*(4), 346–356.

Westerbeek, H. (2010). Commercial sport and local communities: A market niche for social sport business? *Sport in Society, 13*(9), 1411–1415.

World Fair Trade Organization (2013). 10 Principles of Fair Trade. World Fair Trade Organization. Retrieved from <www.wfto.com/fair-trade/10-principles-fair-trade>. Accessed 27 February 2016.

World Vision International (2015). One Goal Campaign: Nutrition for Every Child. World Vision International. Retrieved from <www.wvi.org/health/one-goal-campaign-nutrition-every-child>. Accessed 27 February 2016.

Yunus, M. & Weber, K. (2010). *Building Social Business – The New Kind of Capitalism that Serves Humanity's Most Pressing Needs*. New York: Public Affairs.

34

THE IMPORTANCE OF ENTREPRENEURSHIP IN SMALL AND MEDIUM-SIZED SPORT ENTERPRISES

Aila Ahonen and Sari Savolainen

Introduction

Entrepreneurship is an interesting area of research in the field of sport management since sport has been studied from various business viewpoints, such as marketing, management and leadership, whereas sport entrepreneurship has gained much less attention. Sport is a complex phenomenon; the commercial aspirations growing together with non-profit goals makes it difficult to identify whether sport enterprises are profit-seeking businesses or more social enterprises. Although the sport industry is growing rapidly in both the non-profit and profit-seeking sectors, sport organizations in Europe are still mainly non-profit and often run, at least partly, by volunteers. However, during the past couple of decades, more sport organizations have been transferred to privately owned enterprises and sport has become highly commercialized business. In Finland, where the case example is from, the change has happened, especially at the highest level of sport, since the public sector pulled out from funding professional or semi-professional sport. Sport entrepreneurship is rather a new phenomenon in Finland, existing since the 1990s, while in the US, sport has been commercialized for much longer. Although sport entrepreneurship has been most noticeable at the highest level, it exists on all levels from elite sport to grassroots sport (Gilmore, Gallagher & O'Dwyer, 2011; Ratten, 2011).

Sport entrepreneurship has been defined as sport-related organizations acting innovatively in a business context (Ratten, 2010; Cilletti & Chadwick, 2012). The role of entrepreneurship, and especially the role of an entrepreneur, has become important in small and medium-sized sport enterprises (SME) due to commercialization. Business, in general, targets profit maximization whereas, in sport business, the target could be utility maximization (Spender, 1989). This does not mean that profit is not important in sport entrepreneurship but entrepreneurs and business managers of sport-related enterprises can enhance their economic performance by harnessing the power of sport to deliver community and social objectives (Smith & Westerbeek, 2007). Entrepreneurs in SMEs are often motivated by something other than financial returns and have a strong passion for their sport.

The aim of this chapter is to identify the importance of entrepreneurship in small and medium-sized sport enterprises. The chapter introduces some basic definitions of "entrepreneur" and "entrepreneurship" and presents some of the common features of sport and entrepreneurship that are discussed in the literature. A short case example of the importance of entrepreneurial orientation in an ice hockey SME from Finland further illustrates the phenomenon introduced in this chapter.

Entrepreneurship and entrepreneur

Entrepreneurship researchers have provided several different definitions of entrepreneurship as a phenomenon. The first definitions of entrepreneurship can be found in Richard Cantillion's writings (1680–1743) (Landström, 2006). The first modern definition of entrepreneurship is Schumpeter's (1934). He defined entrepreneurship and entrepreneurs as follows: "the carrying out of new combinations can be called enterprise and the individuals whose function it is to carry out them can be called entrepreneurs" (Schumpeter, 1934). Schumpeter sees that the entrepreneur is his own technical expert, professional specialist, buying and selling agent, head of his office, his own personal manager and legal adviser. Schumpeter's definition shows the differences between our way of thinking and the way of thinking in the 1930s but it is still applicable today. Nowadays the entrepreneur usually has a large business network with support functions rather than doing everything himself. Entrepreneurship is a combination of innovativeness (Schumpeter, 1934), effectiveness (Kirzner, 1982) and opportunity recognition (Shane, 2003). Entrepreneurship is a mixture of risk-taking, investing and potential growth-seeking (Holt, Rutherford & Clohessy, 2007). The same characteristics can be identified as crucial for a sport organization's leadership.

Shane (2003) defined entrepreneurship as an activity that involves the discovery, evaluation and exploitation of opportunities to introduce new goods and services, ways of organizing, markets, processes and raw materials through organizing efforts that previously had not existed (see also, Venkataraman, 1997; Shane & Venkataraman, 2000). This entrepreneurship definition includes explanations of why, when and how entrepreneurial opportunities exist; the sources of those opportunities and the forms that they take; the processes of opportunity discovery and evaluation; the acquisition of resources for the exploitation of these opportunities; the act of opportunity exploitation; why, when and how some individuals and not others discover, evaluate, gather resources for and exploit opportunities; the strategies used to pursue opportunities; and the organizing efforts to exploit them (Shane, 2003; Shane & Venkataraman, 2000). Some people see more opportunities than others and are therefore more likely to become entrepreneurs. Resourcefulness is often connected to entrepreneurship and entrepreneurial resourcefulness has been defined as the ability to identify opportunities in the environment and regulate behaviour to successfully manage an organization in order to pursue the opportunity (Misra & Kumar, 2000). In general, resourcefulness means the ability to self-regulate and direct one's behaviour successfully in order to cope with stressful and challenging situations (Meichenbaum, 1977). Correspondingly, Welter and Xheneti (2013) see resourcefulness as a dynamic concept encompassing multiple practices that change over time. These are results from a close interplay of multiple contexts with entrepreneurial behaviour. The sport business environment is a constantly changing one that requires resourceful management and leadership skills from entrepreneurs.

Cole (1959) has defined an entrepreneur as an individual who is primarily responsible for gathering the necessary resources to initiate a business. Pickle and Abrahamson (1990) define an entrepreneur as a person who organizes and manages a business by undertaking and assuming the risks for the sake of profit. On the other hand, entrepreneurs are individuals who implement entrepreneurship by discovery, evaluation and exploitation of opportunities (Shane & Venkataraman, 2000). They see that an entrepreneur evaluates perceived opportunities and strives to make the decisions that will enable the firm to realize sustainable growth. This opportunity exploitation often involves high risks. In sport business, for example, risks include hiring expensive players without any guarantee of their performance. Entrepreneurs' abilities to bear these risks influence a firm's performance and its potential to develop and grow. Entrepreneurs are often seen as individuals, usually founder-owners, who perceive entrepreneurial opportunities, exploit those opportunities, establish ventures by certain means and purposes and manage their ventures in a certain way (Gibb, 2002).

The individual characteristics of an entrepreneur have frequently been a topic of investigation in various studies (Leibenstein, 1968; Brockhaus,1982; Kuratko & Hodgetts, 1995; Giannetti & Simonov, 2004; Timmons & Spinelli, 2009). Different writers define different personal characteristics as important for an entrepreneur. An example of an earlier conceptualization is presented by Leibenstein (1968), who defines the entrepreneur as an individual or group of individuals with four major characteristics: (1) the entrepreneur connects different markets, (2) he can make up for market deficiencies, (3) he is an input-completer, and (4) he creates or expands time-binding, input-transforming entities (i.e. firms) (Leibenstein, 1968). Leibenstein thus concentrates more on the task of an entrepreneur than the individual or psychological characteristics.

Schumpeter defines entrepreneurs as a special type, their behaviour as a special problem, and their motivating power as drawn from several significant phenomena (Schumpeter, 1934). Entrepreneurial characteristics include, for example, the desire for responsibility, entrepreneurial family background, confidence, entrepreneurial freedom, ambition, competitiveness, future orientation and value for money (Mariotti & Glackin, 2012, pp. 6–10; Scarborough, 2011, pp. 20–24). Timmons and Spinelli (2009) divide entrepreneurial characteristics into three different categories: core characteristics, achievable characteristics and non-entrepreneurial characteristics. The most important core characteristics are commitment and determination, which can help to overcome some possible obstacles. They see successful entrepreneurs as good leaders and supportive managers, who do not try to achieve excessive independence from the surrounding environment. They are opportunity-seeking, ready to act in a fast-changing, turbulent environment. They are creative, self-confident and able to cope with a reasonable amount of risk and uncertainty (Timmons & Spinelli, 2009, pp. 249–262). Entrepreneurs enjoy the freedom of owning their own business but do not prefer the often long working hours, and non-monetary aspects are great motivators in venturing into business (Alstete, 2008).

Ownership, and especially psychological ownership, is an interesting context in which to explain entrepreneurship in sport, even though it is not commonly connected to theories of entrepreneurship. In practice, every entrepreneur is a business owner, which brings along entrepreneurial responsibilities, duties, rights and even risks of losing the target of ownership. Legal ownership is defined by the owner being able to exercise his natural powers over the subject-matter without interference, and more or less excludes other people from such interference (Holmes [1881] 1946, p. 246). The owner answers only to himself. Psychological ownership is defined as a cognitive-affective construct that is based on individuals' feelings of possessiveness and of being psychologically tied or attached to objects that are material and immaterial in nature (Pierce, Kostova & Dirks, 2001). Understanding ownership and psychological ownership in sport entrepreneurship is important since sport business activities are often strongly connected to sport itself and the feelings it causes. Furthermore, sport entrepreneurs are often emotionally connected to the sport, and these kinds of emotions in business activities cannot be found in many other fields of business.

Entrepreneurship in entrepreneurially-driven sport organizations

Professional sport has undergone major structural and operational changes over the past decade and it is both similar to and different from a traditional business. However, all business ventures, including sport, aim to widen their market share, build a strong brand and make profit (Smith and Stewart, 2010). Sport contains many features similar to entrepreneurship; in both, the aim is to win and to be a forerunner compared to competitors. The traditional aim of on-field success is still important in sport but there is a growing awareness that revenue and profits, together with sporting success, are the key to overall successful performance (Smith & Stewart, 2010). In sport SMEs, sporting success does not guarantee success in business, and therefore it is essential that the business knowledge of the entrepreneur is of a high standard. One fast-growing form of sport entrepreneurship is event organization. The growing number of sport events have also become an important economic and social driver for regional development around the world. According to Hall (2006), sport events, and especially sport mega-events, are very important forms of urban sport entrepreneurship.

Sport entrepreneurship in SMEs is very heterogenic in nature; it contains different businesses from several sectors. Sport entrepreneurship and entrepreneurial actions in SMEs can be divided into four main categories: (1) sport events and participation activities, (2) sport supplies and services, (3) sport facilities and arenas, and (4) sport investors and owners (see Figure 34.1). Entrepreneurial activities and business actions can happen while simultaneously overlapping in different categories.

Very often SMEs act in all the areas of sport entrepreneurship described in Figure 34.1. Entrepreneurs' social networks between sport organizations and external business providers give them opportunities to access knowledge, information and other resources (Ratten & Ferreira, 2016). Wide stakeholder networks are essential for sport entrepreneurs to create value for their customers.

Successful sport entrepreneurship requires innovation, creativity, proactivity and the ability to take risks (Ratten, 2011; Cilletti, 2012). In the sport industry, there is a growing amount of entrepreneurial opportunity, and individuals who can recognize and exploit these opportunities are needed (Cilletti & Chadwick, 2012). Entrepreneurship in sport can be based on earlier activity in the same field of sport. An athlete might have seen an opportunity for entrepreneurial activities connected to sport during his/her active sport career, and utilized this opportunity later. Sometimes entrepreneurship can be built on the earlier non-profit organization's actions around sport. Very often non-profit voluntary work has dried up or public funding has decreased, and the organization has changed into a profit-seeking business.

Ratten (2011) introduces a theory of sport-based entrepreneurship, arguing that "sport is an entrepreneurial process as innovation and change are key elements of sport". Sport-based entrepreneurship exists when sport-related entrepreneurial opportunities are exploited by creating value. Sport entrepreneurship comprises individual entrepreneurs who combine

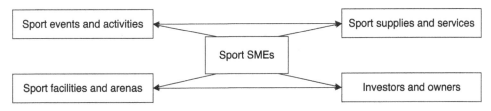

Figure 34.1 Main forms of small and medium-sized sport entrepreneurship

opportunities that arise from their networks, and optimize resources where they are effective (Ratten, 2011). Moore and Levermore (2012) argue that resource constraints, informality, an authoritarian management style and short-termism in decision making are characteristics in SMEs in sport business. These are characteristics that are connected to entrepreneurial orientation as well. Lumpkin and Dess (1996) and Covin and Slevin (1991) identify autonomy, innovativeness, risk-taking and competitive aggressiveness to be dimensions of entrepreneurial orientation, while Kreiser and Davis (2010) add innovation and proactiveness to these characteristics to exploit entrepreneurial behaviour. An entrepreneurial orientation together with a favourable environment and the right organizational structure is needed to achieve profitable firm performance or growth (Kreiser & Davis, 2010).

Innovativeness, proactiveness and risk-taking are identified as key concepts of sport entrepreneurship by Cilletti (2012). Technological innovations and new media solutions have provided opportunities for sport enterprises to expand their businesses. The sport sector's uniqueness in terms of uncertainty of outcome and fast changes requires proactive actions from sport entrepreneurs. Risk taking in terms of financial risks such as athlete contracts, licences and market-related risk, together with social risks of serving change agents or breaking down traditional barriers, are characteristics of sport entrepreneurship (Cilletti, 2012).

The case of entrepreneurial development in JYP Ice Hockey Club

Ice hockey is the most popular sport in Finland in terms of spectators and broadcasting. Finland has also been very successful in ice hockey in international competitions, such as the Olympics or World Championships, by winning several medals over the years. Jyväskylä Ice Hockey Club (JYP) is a small-town ice hockey team that has played in the Finnish national league since 1985. JYP is also one of the most successful businesses within the national ice hockey league companies in Finland with several national championships and a European Trophy league win in 2013. JYP operated as a non-profit organization until it was corporatized at the turn of the century (Ruuska, 2013). Today, JYP operates as an SME and a majority of its shares are owned by the entrepreneur, who also acts as a chairman of the board. The first push for the corporatization was that player contracts were seen as employment contracts by the taxation authorities, and profit-seeking ice hockey clubs could no longer identify themselves as non-profit organizations. The benefits of the corporatization were that decision-making processes became streamlined and entrepreneur-centred risk taking increased, access to financial capital became easier and competitiveness grew substantially. The owner-entrepreneur invested heavily in the club at the beginning and took big risks in terms of player recruitment and team building (Ahonen, 2017).

JYP has gained on-ice success and managed to develop that into a business success even though the facilities and environment have provided some challenges. JYP operates in the smallest ice hockey arena in the national league and its home market in a mid-sized city with multiple sport offerings is rather small (Ahonen, 2017). In 2004, JYP published a strategy called "Mission 2007" and defined a clear growth strategy in terms of sporting success and revenues. It succeeded in terms of marketing and finances but not in terms of sporting success. The success in sport followed a couple of years later in 2009 when it won the Finnish National Championship title for the first time (JYP, 2017). Behind this success was its owner-entrepreneur's entrepreneurial orientation, innovativeness and willingness to take risks (Ahonen, 2017).

JYP's entrepreneurial orientation includes both organizational and individual level actions and actors. The entrepreneur and staff both show a big commitment and determination to their company and the sport. The entrepreneur's motivation to run the business is more connected to enthusiasm towards the sport itself and to motivation to excel than monetary revenues. The entrepreneur's previous knowledge and innovativeness in decision-making, together with the ability to exploit the opportunities when they exist, are drivers for success. Exploitation of internationalization opportunities with the Kontinental Hockey League (KHL) in Russia were important in achieving financial success. Player sales to KHL played a big role in JYP's development (Ahonen, 2017).

Value creation for stakeholders is one key to success in sport event organizing (Woratschek, Horbel & Popp, 2014) and JYP has exploited this by creating high-quality services for sponsors, spectators and fans. Due to cooperation with the city of Jyväskylä in investing into new facilities, JYP had the opportunity to build new service facilities and gain more income from extended restaurant and VIP-lounge services (Ahonen, 2017). Since the game events are more like platforms where value is created for different stakeholders (Woratschek, *et al.*, 2014), the importance of off-field customer services are very great for such a small sport enterprise. The entrepreneurially driven value creation process is essential for sport SMEs in order for them to be less dependent on uncertain sporting success.

JYP's business success has not been the motivator for its entrepreneur but more a facilitator for future development. The owner-entrepreneur's motivation to be a sport entrepreneur has a lot to do with social entrepreneurship. The company has supported the non-profit youth teams and the possibility to make a social contribution to the junior teams and the community act as a motivator to the entrepreneur (Ahonen, 2017). This co-operation can be seen also as an asset influencing future sporting success in terms of future players.

Conclusion

In small countries, with limited markets for sport events and sport services, the importance of SMEs in the sport sector is growing. The public sector is pulling out from funding sport and sport clubs are becoming service providers and commercialized businesses instead of voluntarily run non-profit organizations. Opportunities exist in multiple sectors in sport business, and entrepreneurs who are capable of recognizing and exploiting these opportunities are widely needed. The challenge for SMEs in sport is the lack of financial returns and profits.

Motivational factors play a big role in establishing sport SMEs. The concept of psychological ownership can explain some of the reasons behind sport business ventures. Emotional ties to a certain sport can act as a motivator to become an entrepreneur and a business owner in the field of sport, despite the small monetary returns. The special nature of sport business, with its variety of feelings and passions, offers returns that cannot be found in many other businesses. The challenge of a fast-changing operating environment requires special individual characteristics in sport entrepreneurs including innovativeness, creativity, the capability to act proactively, the ability to bear big financial risks, an entrepreneurial orientation and resourcefulness.

Sport entrepreneurship research is in its infancy and the aim of this chapter is to give an insight into entrepreneurial aspects in sport SMEs. SME's roles in Finland and in the Scandinavian sport sector are important due to the size of the countries and markets. Volunteer work and public funding are decreasing, sport clubs are commercializing and the number of local and international sport events is growing. Entrepreneurial opportunities exist and possibilities for new business ventures are high. Despite a decrease in public funding for sport in Finland, support for start-ups is available and creates a positive environment for establishing new firms in the sport sector.

References

Ahonen, A. (2017). How did a small-town ice hockey club become a European Trophy winner? The case of Jyväskylä Ice Hockey Club, Finland. In S. Chadwick, D. Arthur & J. Beech, *International Cases in the Business of Sport*. London, New York: Routledge.

Alstete, J. W. (2008). Aspects of entrepreneurial success. *Journal of Small Business and Enterprise Development*, *15*(3), 584–594 <doi: 10.1108/14626000810892364>.

Brockhaus, R. H. (1982). The psychology of the entrepreneur. *Encyclopedia of Entrepreneurship* (pp. 39–71). Englewood Cliffs, NJ: Prentice Hall.

Cilletti, D. (2012). Sports entrepreneurship: A theoretical approach. In D. Cilletti & S. Chadwick, *Sport Entrepreneurship, Theory and Practice* (pp. 1–14). Morgantown, USA: West Virginia University, Fitness Information Technology.

Cilletti, D. & Chadwick, S. (2012). *Sport Entrepreneurship, Theory and Practice*. Morgantown, USA: West Virginia University, Fitness Information Technology.

Cole, A. H. (1959). *Business Enterprise In Its Social Setting*. Cambridge, MA: Harvard University Press.

Covin, J. & Slevin P. (1991). A conceptual model of entrepreneurship as firm behavior. *Entrepreneurship Theory and Practice*, *16*(1), 7–25.

Giannetti, M. & Simonov, A. (2004). On the determinations of entrepreneurial activity: Social norms, economics environment and individual characteristics. *Swedish Economic Policy Review*, *11*, 269–313.

Gibb, A. (2002). In pursuit of a new "enterprise" and "entrepreneurship" paradigm for learning: Creative destruction, new values new ways of doing things and new combination of knowledge. *International Journal of Management Reviews*, *4*(3), 223–269.

Gilmore A., Gallagher D. & O'Dwyer M. (2011). Is social entrepreneurship an untapped marketing resource? A commentary on its potential for small sports clubs. *Journal of Small Business and Entrepreneurship*, *24*(1), 11–15.

Hall, C. M. (2006). Urban entrepreneurship, corporate interests and sports mega-events: The thin policies of competitiveness within the hard outcomes of neoliberalism. *Sociological Review*, *54*(2s), 59–70.

Holmes, O. W. [1881] (1946). *The Common Law*. Reprint. Boston: Little, Brown.

Holt, D., Rutherford, M. & Clohessy, G. (2007). Corporate entrepreneurship: An empirical look at individual characteristics, context, and process. *Journal of Leadership & Organizational Studies*, *13*(4), 40–54.

JYP (2017) – Jyväskylä Ice Hockey Club. Available at <www.jypliiga.fi>. Accessed 15 February 2017.

Kirzner, I. M. (1982). Uncertainty, discovery, and human actions: A study of the entrepreneurial profile in the Misesian system. In I. M. Kirzner (Ed.) *Method Process and Austrian Economics: Essays in Honour of Ludwig von Mises* (pp. 139–159). Lexington, Mass: D.C. Hearth.

Kreiser, P. & Davis J. (2010). Entrepreneurial orientation and firm performance: The unique impact of innovativeness, proactiveness, and risk-taking. *Journal of Small Business and Entrepreneurship*, *23*(1), 39–51.

Kuratko, D. F. & Hodgetts, R. M. (1995). *Entrepreneurship: A Contemporary Approach*. Fort Worth: Dryden Press.

Landström, H. (2006). *Pioneers in Entrepreneurship and Small Business Research*. Institute of Economic Research. Lund, Sweden, New York: Springer.

Leibenstein, H. (1968). Entrepreneurship and development. *American Economic Review*, *58*(2), 72–83.

Lumpkin, G. & Dess, G. (1996). Clarifying the entrepreneurial orientation construct and linking it to performance. *Academy of Management Review*, *21*(1), 135–172.

Mariotti, S. & Glackin C. (2012). *Entrepreneurship and Small Business Management*. New Jersey, USA: Pearson Education.

Meichenbaum D. H. (1977). *Cognitive Behaviour Modification: An Integrative Approach*. New York: Plenum.

Misra S. & Kumar E. S. (2000). Resourcefulness: A Proximal Conceptualization of Entrepreneurial Behaviour. *Journal of Entrepreneurship*, *9*(2), 135–154.

Moore, N. & Levermore, R. (2012). English professional football clubs. Can business parameters of small and medium-sized enterprises be applied? *Sport, Business and Management: An International Journal*, 2(3), 196–209.

Pickle, H. B. & Abrahamson, R. L. (1990). *Small Business Management*. New York: John Wiley & Sons, Inc.

Pierce, J. L., Kostova, T. & Dirks, K. T. (2001). Toward a theory of psychological ownership in organizations. *Academy of Management Review*, 26(2), 298–310.

Ratten, V. (2010). Developing a theory of sport-based entrepreneurship. *Journal of Management & Organization*, 16, 557–565.

Ratten, V. (2011). Social entrepreneurship and innovation in sports. *International Journal of Social Entrepreneurship and Innovation*, 1, 42–54.

Ratten, V. & Ferreira, J. (2016). Sport entrepreneurship and the emergence of opportunities. Towards a future research agenda. In V. Ratten, *Sport Entrepreneurship and Innovation*. London, New York: Routledge.

Ruuska, K. (2013). *Suuria Tunteita 90 Vuotta, Jyväskylän Palloilijat – JYP Jyväskylä 1923–2013* (Big Emotions for 90 years, Jyväskylä Ball Club – JYP Jyväskylä 1923–2013). Jyväskylä, Finland: Kopijyvä.

Scarborough, N. (2011). *Essentials of Entrepreneurship and Small Business Management*. Harlow, England: Pearson Education.

Schumpeter, J. A. (1934). The Theory of Economic Development: An Inquiry into Profits, Capital, Credit, Interest and the Business Cycle (trans. R. Opie) (pp. 65–94). Cambridge, MA: Harvard University Press.

Shane, S. (2003). *A General Theory of Entrepreneurship: The Individual-Opportunity Nexus*. Cheltenham, UK; Northampton, MA, USA: Edward Elgar.

Shane S. & Venkataraman S. (2000). The promise of entrepreneurship as a field of research. *Academy of Management Review*, 25(1), 217–226.

Smith, A. & Stewart, B. (2010). The special features of sport: A critical revisit. *Sport Management Review*, 13, 1–13 <doi: 10.1016/j.smr.2009.07.002>.

Smith, A. & Westerbeek, H. (2007). Sport as a vehicle for deploying corporate social responsibility. *Journal of Corporate Citizenship*, 25, 43–54.

Spender, J.-C. (1989). *Industry Recipes. An Inquiry into the Nature and Sources of Managerial Judgement*. UK: Basil Blackwell.

Timmons, J. A. & Spinelli, S. (2009). *New Venture Creation: Entrepreneurship for the 21st Century*. New York, USA: MacGraw.

Venkatamaran, S. (1997). The distinctive domain of entrepreneurship research: An editor's perspective. In J. Kazt & R. Brockhaus (Eds), *Advances in Entrepreneurship, Firm Emergence, and Growth* (pp. 119–138). Greenwich, CT: JAI Press.

Welter F. & Xheneti M. (2013). Reenacting contextual boundaries – entrepreneurial resourcefulness in challenging environments. In A. C. Corbett & J. A. Katz (Eds), *Entrepreneurial Resourcefulness. Competing with Constraints* (pp. 149–183). Yorkshire, UK: Emerald Group Publishing Limited.

Woratscheck, H., Horbel, C. & Popp, B. (2014). The sport value framework – a new fundamental logic for analyses in sport management. *European Sport Management Quartely*, 14(1), 6–24.

35

PARTNERSHIP BUILDING TO CREATE CHANGE

Kevin Heisey

Introduction

In 2015, the CTC Ten Foundation Safe-Hub by AMANDLA EduFootball soccer pitch and community center in Khayelitsha, Site B, near Cape Town, was resurfaced with a new, updated artificial surface. In the years since the first surface was laid and the lights were installed, a successful sport for development and peace programming model has been built, which is serving as an example to be used elsewhere. While sport for development and peace (SDP) projects are countless, long-term successes are relatively rare. It takes much more than resources and establishment backing to make the most of opportunities. A few kilometers away in the Harare area of Khayelitsha, a FIFA-backed Football for Hope center, planned as a legacy of the 2010 World Cup, has struggled (Qwayi, 2016; Windmann, 2013).

The initial success of the CTC Ten Safe-Hub is rooted in the willingness to collaborate demonstrated by the major partners, the CTC Ten Foundation, AMANDLA EduFootball and the Ikhusi Primary School. Related to the willingness to collaborate is the participatory approach used towards developing the physical facilities, the driving purpose, and the programming conducted there to achieve the purpose. This sort of collaboration, between US, German and South African organizations blending their capacities and strengths, can be a model for coordination and cooperation. To mark the 2016 International Day of Sport for Development and Peace, Mark Probst, the Executive Director of the Swiss Academy for Development, stated that "right now it seems like organizations are interested in positioning themselves", and that they needed to "practice what they preach" regarding collaboration (Sportanddev.org, 2016).

The purpose of this chapter is to examine the CTC Ten Foundation Safe-Hub by AMANDLA EduFootball as a case study demonstrating best practices. The chapter is structured as follows; first, the broad context of SDP is established, followed by a brief scholarly treatment of community-based development and benchmark monitoring and evaluation practices. Then a brief overview of the project is followed by a closer look at the key partners. The background, role and core objective for each partner are examined followed by an assessment of the challenges moving forward and lessons that can be derived from what has been accomplished thus far. While the context and focus of this chapter are on SDP, the example of effective partnership spanning borders and cultures is one that offers insights into any international sport business endeavor.

Sport for development and peace

In recent years, the SDP movement has grown rapidly under the direction of the world's leading multi-national organizations. More than a decade ago, in late 2003, the United Nations General Assembly proclaimed 2005 to be "The International Year of Sport and Physical Education" as a "means to promote education, health, development, and peace" through sport (UN General Assembly Resolution 58/5). The UN Inter-Agency Task Force on Sport for Development and Peace was formed in 2002 and a year later released a report, *Sport for development and peace: Towards achieving the Millenium Development Goals* (2003), which found that sport-based initiatives could be effective tools towards achieving general development and peace objectives. A United Nations Office of Sport for Development and Peace was established as an umbrella organization under which multi-national efforts are encouraged. The concept of a sport role in development and peace is one of the Fundamental Principles of Olympism (International Olympic Committee, 2016) and April 6 has been proclaimed the "International Day of Sport for Development and Peace" by the United Nations General Assembly (UN General Assembly Resolution 67/296). The date offers evidence of the overlap between the United Nations and the Olympic Movement in this area; it was the date of the opening of the first modern Olympic Games in Athens in 1896.

Under the umbrella of this international framework there are thousands of efforts to use sport in the promotion of overall development and/or peace. In nature, objectives, length and duration, these efforts are as diverse and unique as the people they aim to serve. Practitioners are enthusiastic about the possibilities and common sense tells us that sport has the potential to contribute to achieving these wider aims. However, success is challenging and it may be the case that the sport aspect is a detriment to the overall development aims. The success of an effort in achieving its objectives is highly context specific and can be reliant on an array of complex factors.

Community collaboration and monitoring and evaluation as keys

In the SDP arena, there is often a gap between the enthusiasm of practitioners and the skepticism of researchers. The enthusiasts are commonly known as "evangelists" and the skeptics as "critics". Evangelists see SDP efforts as all good and use measurements to justify funding, while critics often see neo-imperial, neo-liberal, neo-colonial projects and a Global North/ Global South dependency relationship between donors and beneficiaries (Sugden, 2010). Sport for development and peace organizations are often seen as well-meaning but commonly insensitive to local contexts.

With the above dynamic in mind, the approach in this chapter is anchored in the work of SDP agnostic scholars grounded in the study of effective SDP monitoring and evaluation (ME) practices and community-based development outcomes. Fred Coalter has researched a variety of SDP programs around the world and has developed a framework for ME of these programs (Coalter, 2013). Coalter sees himself as a healthy skeptic of SDP evangelist claims, grounded in the realism that, given the complexity and intractability of the problems which programs attempt to address through sport, ME that shows universal success should be examined closely (Coalter, 2013). Mansuri and Rao treat the broader development arena with a specific focus on community participation in development projects (2013). Their skepticism is evident in their assertion that, while community-based development projects are common, their popularity is based more on theory than empirical evidence. They set out to closely examine what works best and identify some of the challenges and potential drawbacks of a community-based approach (Mansuri & Rao, 2013).

Several key points are drawn from Coalter (2013) that are relevant to examining the effectiveness of the CTC Ten Foundation Safe-Hub case. First, for a robust and effective approach to ME, there needs to be a broad program theory (Coalter, 2013, p. 10). This means that the practitioners need to have a clear, abstract understanding of what they are trying to do, how they aim to do it and what the expected outcome should be. Research and ME approaches should be framed in specific terms of local programs falling under a wider theoretical development of SDP (Coalter, 2013). Coalter also stresses the importance of evaluating the processes in addition to the outcomes (Coalter, n.d.). Finally, in his research of numerous programs, Coalter found that the ME framework was often based on the assumption that the intervening partners provided staff continuity that sometimes did not exist.

Highlighting the support for community-based participatory development approaches, the World Bank spent over $85 billion in the last decade on such programs, and governments and non-government organizations (NGOs) have likely also spent as much (Mansuri & Rao, 2013, p. 23). The theory behind community-based approaches is that they lead to better-designed development projects, more effective service delivery and better targeting of benefits (Mansuri & Rao, 2013, p. 23). This approach is firmly rooted in the historic notions of participatory governance common in Western tradition and culture. Four potential pitfalls of a participatory, community-based approach were identified by Mosse (2002):

- Participatory exercises are often public events that are open-ended regarding target groups and program activities. Thus, such events are inherently political, and the resulting project design is often shaped by local power and gender relations.
- Outside agendas are often expressed as local knowledge. Project facilitators shape and direct participatory exercises, and the "needs" of beneficiaries are often shaped by perceptions of what the project can deliver.
- Participants may concur in the process of problem definition and planning in order to manipulate the program to serve their own interests. Although their concurrence can benefit both project staff and beneficiaries, it places consensus and action above detailed planning.
- Participatory processes can be used to legitimize a project that has previously established priorities and little real support from the community.

The case is made in this chapter that collaboration and cooperation, with the inclusion and participation of the target community in program development, ownership and decision-making, and AMANDLA EduFootball's (AMANDLA) evidence-based approach, are the foundations of the project's achieved overall success. But those elements are examined within the above framework with a full awareness of potential problems and challenges. Considering the concerns and benchmarks above regarding the quality and rigor of the ME approach and the potential pitfalls of implementing a community-based approach to development, the CTC Ten Foundation and AMANDLA appear to do well.

Project background – CTC Ten Foundation Safe-Hub by AMANDLA EduFootball

Since the grand opening of a synthetic turf soccer pitch in 2009, what is now known as the CTC 10 Foundation Safe-Hub by AMANDLA EduFootball in Khayelitsha has been an example of what can be done through cooperative partnerships oriented towards serving a community. Khayelitsha is an informal settlement in the Cape Flats area to the east of Cape

Town. It was established in the mid-1980s and is a remnant of the apartheid era in response to the Group Areas Act, which forbade black South Africans from living in the cities (Wainwright, 2014). In apartheid lexicon, Khayelitsha is known as a "high density township" (Dixon, 2015). Over 30 years later, it can be described as a shantytown with population estimates ranging from several hundred thousand to several million. It is characterized by the blights of disease (tuberculosis and HIV/AIDS), crime, violence, and lack of economic opportunity (Colford-Schoeniger, 2010). While some areas of Khayelitsha feature structured houses and straight, paved streets, the Site B area, where the Safe-Hub is located, is characterized by a high density of makeshift structures separated by winding, narrow pathways.

In the middle of the Khayelitsha Site B community, next to the Ikhusi Primary School, the soccer pitch has become a hub of community activity. In the years since the soccer pitch and lights were first installed, two physical structures have been added; a clubhouse that includes classrooms for educational programming and related activities, and a building known as the Broccoli House that serves as an access point to the center and is equipped with technology that allows for accurate tracking and measurement of attendance and participation. It also serves as a storage area for sport equipment (CTC Ten Foundation, 2014). In 2015, the pitch was resurfaced.

A comprehensive slate of regular activities take place at the center. It is a flagship safe-hub in a network of facilities supported by AMANDLA and the Oliver Kahn Foundation that serve as "safe, educational, youth friendly centers in communities characterized by poverty, unemployment, and inequality" (AMANDLA EduFootball, 2017b).

In addition to the regular programming and events, special events, like serving as a key venue for 2016's Nike Football X Road to BPL Live Qualifying Tournament conducted by Nike and the Barclay's Premiere League (CTC Ten Foundation, 2016), bring external activity and attention to a community that is often on the outside looking in. Around this activity, the Safe-Hub provides a venue for ongoing leadership programs that aim to "equip young, motivated leaders in the Khayelitsha community with skills and work experience to help them start careers" (CTC Ten Foundation, 2014).

Ten years after the formation of the foundation that led to the financing and construction of the physical space, it appears that the center is becoming a permanent, positive part of the community. The results would not be possible without the cooperation of three key partners brought together by the project. The CTC Ten Foundation began in order to honor Chris Campbell, who tragically passed away as a young man. When he passed away, he was in his final year as a student and captain of the men's soccer team at Franklin & Marshall College, Pennsylvania. The foundation raised funds for the initial pitch and subsequent upgrades and provides support in the form of CTC Ten Foundation "Fellows", who serve one-year internships as part of the team in Khayelitsha.

While the foundation had the means and desire to provide physical facilities in the Khayelitsha community, it lacked programming expertise on the ground. It turned to AMANDLA, who had established an orphan soccer league playing on gravel pitches in Khayelitsha, and engaged it as an implementing partner. Partnering with an organization that already had a presence in the community was a key element in the project's success. The willingness of these two organizations to come together positioned the overall project well from the beginning.

Upon visiting at-risk communities in the sub-Saharan Africa region, it is common to find that the ideas, capability and means to implement positive changes exist, but often things just do not happen. One finds a variety of informal reasons and opinions offered that can be concisely summed up as "local government red tape". It appears that endless arguments, posturing and turf wars often doom well-intentioned efforts before they even begin. In Khayelitsha, the Ikhusi Primary School played a crucial role in clearing a path by providing the authority and physical space on which the facility was built.

As key players any of the organizations might be tempted to exert their influence as either the physical holder to the land rights, the primary financer of the facility or the primary operator of the programming. If any did so, however, the outcome would likely be less than what it is, or even a failed project. The partners' willingness to be oriented toward finding common ground, respecting and valuing others' viewpoints and roles and making progress in achieving objectives provides an example of how an international partnership can work. When such a partnership is working, it can look deceptively simple, but the reality is that it is a difficult task to combine diverse organizations as equal partners and sustain progress and success.

The Partners: CTC Ten Foundation, AMANDLA EduFootball and Ikhusi Primary School

CTC Ten Foundation

The CTC Ten Foundation had its roots in the Franklin & Marshall Soccer Team's Soccer Africa project, a small community service project with humble goals (GoDiplomats.com, 2017). One of the team captains and an enthusiastic supporter of the project, Chris Campbell, died unexpectedly on a training run the day before reporting for the first day of camp during his final year in college (*Lancaster Online*, 2007). In response to the tragedy, Campbell's family, with the support of the Franklin & Marshall soccer team and head coach, Dan Wagner, established the CTC Ten Foundation to honor his memory (ctcten.org., 2017). Campbell's passions were international travel, soccer and children and he had a strong empathy for people less fortunate (Colford-Schoeniger, 2010).

Wagner began to look for a community where the foundation could focus its efforts. He initially sought out Grassroot Soccer founder, Ethan Zohn, for assistance in identifying a location (Colford-Schoeniger, 2010). Zohn identified Cape Town and provided Wagner with the initial connection to Khayelitsha (Godiplomats.com, 2008). In Khayelitsha they connected with AMANDLA, which was organizing a Fair Play soccer league for orphans on gravel pitches, and AMANDLA connected Wagner and the CTC Ten Foundation with the Ikhusi Primary school. Having a site on which to build a soccer pitch, the CTC Ten Foundation quickly raised the USD$350,000 to cover the cost and the pitch opened in early 2009 (fandm.edu, 2009) launching operations that continue to the present day.

The ongoing goals of the CTC Ten Foundation are to (ctcten.org, 2017):

- Generate the necessary funds to continue the legacy of the Chris Campbell Memorial Field through fundraisers, individual contributions and grants.
- Oversee the ongoing maintenance of the Chris Campbell Memorial Field and Clubhouse including turf, lighting, fencing, goal repairs and replacements.
- Support the ongoing development of programs at the Chris Campbell Memorial Field through the CTC Ten Intern Program.

Several aspects of the CTC Ten Foundation's approach are noteworthy. First, they envisioned a "permanent connection" with the community in Khayelitsha (Colford-Schoeniger, 2010). This long-term commitment likely played a role in building trust between the foundation and the other partners and is certainly a major factor in the eight-year history of the center. Second, it employs a narrow focus. According to Campbell's father, the foundation is not trying to accomplish things on a grand scale, but to focus on "one school and one community" without trying to do too much at once (Colford-Schoeniger, 2010). Finally, as the narrative regarding the foundation's initial connection with Khayelitsha and the Ikhusi Primary School demonstrates, it seeks collaboration and cooperation. The CTC Ten Foundation was best positioned to finance and construct the facility and found AMANDLA already active in the community with soccer programming aligned with the foundation's intentions. Partnering with AMANDLA enabled it to connect with the Ikhusi Primary School and find a place to construct the soccer pitch.

AMANDLA EduFootball

In 2007, after working for a year in a Khayelitsha orphanage as part of his German civil service requirement, Florian Zech founded AMANDLA with a team of local and international volunteers (AMANDLA EduFootball, 2017a). During his time as a volunteer, Zech started an orphanage soccer league basing scoring on a system that awards more points for teamwork, respect and anger management than it does for goals. Ten orphanages participated in the initial tournament and after a brief return to Germany, Zech decided to come back to Khayelitsha and build on the initial success (Windmann, 2013). He saw a need to provide programming and support for local children who often lacked adult supervision after school (Windmann, 2013).

AMANDLA's mission is to "create safe spaces that bring together the power of football and learning to empower youth and to change lives" (AMANDLA EduFootball, 2015). Prior to their involvement with the CTC Ten Foundation, AMANDLA was organizing their programming on open gravel pitches in the area. Already having established programming and a presence in the community, AMANDLA was well positioned to be an implementing partner of the CTC Ten Foundation.

In contrast to the CTC Ten Foundation's narrow focus on "one school, one community", AMANDLA sees itself as a catalyst for social change on a global scale (AMANDLA EduFootball, 2017a). In Khayelitsha, it developed a Safe-Hub model that it sees as scalable and aims to replicate globally. Its goal for 2020 is to provide 20,000 at-risk young people access to safe-hubs in ten urban communities characterized by poverty, crime and violence (AMANDLA EduFootball, 2015) in partnership with the Oliver Kahn Foundation and others. The Safe-Hub model is a framework that allows for local adaptation that is based on four prongs (AMANDLA EduFootball, 2015):

1. Safety: a place for physical and emotional safety and well-being.
2. Financial sustainability: funding from diverse and integrated sources.
3. Collaboration: a hub for best-practice NGO, public and private sector collaboration.
4. Support: an integrated center for services, opportunity, and support for young people.

This model was developed at the CTC Ten Foundation Safe-Hub, which AMANDLA considers to be its flagship example.

The core programming implemented by AMANDLA at the Safe-Hub is an integrated menu of Fair Play soccer leagues, life skills training and tutoring for all participants, a leadership program for young adults drawn from the other AMANDLA programs and night crime prevention soccer leagues. The Fair Play soccer leagues are derived from AMANDLA's initial orphanage leagues, where competition points are awarded for playing with respect, teamwork, anger management, practicing a healthy lifestyle and regular attendance. Life skills training consists of formal mentorship from coaches and staff combined with a formal curriculum entitled "Go for it!". AMANDLA provides daily homework assistance and much needed academic support and encouragement through its tutoring program (AMANDLA EduFootball, 2015).

The Youth Leadership program targets youth with leadership potential as demonstrated through participation in AMANDLA programs. Youth leaders are integrated in the day-to-day operation and programming of the Safe-Hub gaining work experience. They also take part in accredited training and academic programs. In Khayelitsha, those who completed the program have had success. AMANDLA reports that 84 percent complete the course and 77 percent of those are employed or engaged in further education and training (AMANDLA EduFootball, 2015).

The Crime Prevention Night League gives young men a safe and positive alternative for weekend night recreation. Crime and violence related to drug and alcohol abuse increase on weekend nights. External measures from the South African Police Force indicate that while crime has increased in Khayelitsha in general, in the community nearest the Safe-Hub crime rates have decreased (AMANDLA EduFootball, 2015).

In addition to developing the Safe-Hub model and its programming, AMANDLA uses an evidence-based approach that focuses on the development and improvement of ME systems based on a simple "Theory of Change" model that guides how activities build toward short-, medium- and long-term impacts. The Safe-Hub is equipped with biometric attendance tracking at the single access point that accurately and efficiently measures attendance and participation. This creates a reliable database of the level of intervention of the project's programming (CTC Ten Foundation, 2014).

Data are gathered over the ten-month annual programming cycle with *ex-ante* baseline data collected at the beginning of the year, on-going monitoring of attendance, individual attitudes and behavior throughout the year, and *ex-post* data gathered at the end of each year (AMANDLA EduFootball, 2016). Research is conducted using a variety of methods including surveys, focus groups, semi-structured interviews and competence assessments (AMANDLA EduFootball, 2016). Aligning with the organization's orientation towards collaboration, AMANDLA also collaborates with a variety of external organizations on its ME efforts, including universities, intergovernmental agencies, governments and individual researchers (AMANDLA EduFootball, 2016).

Although AMANDLA's vision, to replicate its model globally, is distinct from the CTC Ten Foundation's focus on "one community, one school", AMANDLA's strategic orientation towards collaboration and cooperation helped create the environment in which to successfully launch the CTC Ten Foundation Safe-Hub. Noteworthy are AMANDLA's integrated programming approach and its relatively sophisticated ME system.

Ikhusi Primary School

The Ikhusi Primary School serves as the local host for the CTC Ten Foundation and AMANDLA efforts. Without its cooperation, the facility would not be possible. The school's approval is required not only for the land use for the soccer pitch and clubhouse but, in effect, for every activity that occurs. School leaders have the ultimate authority to stop or change whatever is happening as they see fit. As it is, Ikhusi Primary School has been a welcoming and open partner, encouraging activities and sharing resources and access to students.

The school partnered with AMANDLA and the University of Western Cape in order to implement the tutoring program as well as to create a rigorous system to evaluate the process and impact. Direct measurement and comparison of participants and non-participants show a 49.2 percent greater pass rate for English and Mathematics compared to a control group (AMANDLA EduFootball, 2016). Overall, Ikhusi went from a poorly performing school to one that gained recognition for academic achievement. In 2013 it was awarded the "best improved school in the district" and received certificates for excellence in English and Mathematics (CTC Ten Foundation, 2013). While not all of this success can be attributed to the Safe-Hub and its activities, the school's principal recognized the impact when he credited the programming with "significantly raising the profile of a once underperforming school" (CTC Ten Foundation, 2013).

When comparing the success of the CTC Ten Foundation Safe-Hub with the struggles of the Football for Hope center in the nearby Harare section of Khayelitsha, it could be the case that the involvement of the school plays a major factor. There appears to be confusion between what the community expects from the Football for Hope center and what the operations team from Grassroot Soccer expects to provide (Qwayi, 2016). In the terms of Coalter (2007) the community in Harare might expect a sport-plus development model, while the Grassroot Soccer people are focused on a plus-sport model. At Site B, it is clear. The CTC Ten Foundation Safe-Hub does not exist to train teams for successful competition or to become professional athletes. It is there to develop people and the community through sport (plus-sport). The Ikhusi Primary School sees that the center serves its objectives and chooses to work with partners dedicated to the same ends.

Conclusion

There are enormous challenges to building a facility and establishing effective SDP program-ming in a place like Khayelitsha. Once the facility is built, collaboration, cooperation and community engagement at all levels appear to have had a positive impact. Additionally, a systematic ME approach makes it more likely that programming matches needs and achieves outcomes.

The potential pitfalls of taking a community participation approach identified by Mansuri and Rao (2013) pertain to political posturing or miscommunication between community members and practitioners in identifying needs. In the example of Khayelitsha, Site B, the community is engaging with the CTC Ten Foundation and AMANDLA through the Ikhusi Primary School, an equal partner. Among the examples that indicate that the center and programming are meeting the community's needs are the structure and layout of the field. When the facility was built, there was a purposeful decision, based on community input, to make the pitch smaller than regulation size and to enclose it with fencing. The community members felt that a regulation pitch would become a center for sport competition and training rather than youth life skills and educational development. Some US donors questioned the image of a protective fence around what they envisioned as a safe space, open to all. But community partners felt that operating the facility with fencing and tightly organized scheduled programming (that is open to all) would better meet community needs.

The FIFA-sponsored Football for Hope center in the Harare neighborhood of Khayelitsha is not enclosed by a fence and provides evidence to support the community members at Site B. There are holes in the turf at the Football for Hope center and soccer clubs control access to the pitch while critics say the center is being used more for training elite players than creating lasting social benefit (Windmann, 2013).

AMANDLA's ME efforts appear to mirror Coalter's (2013) guidelines. They are based on a simple theoretical model of how change occurs, ME instruments and methodology are tailored specifically to the processes and outcomes in the unique context of the Safe-Hub, and AMANDLA focuses on both the processes and the outcomes and impacts. AMANDLA appears to take an evidence-based approach as indicated by its willingness to engage with and learn from research and assessment undertaken by external partners. It has engaged with researchers from University of Cape Town's Safety and Violence Initiative, the International Committee for the Red Cross and independent academics, reporting the external assessment results in their organizational Monitoring and Evaluation Report (AMANDLA EduFootball, 2016). This is an example of the genuine co-creation of knowledge by stakeholders that some often feel is missing in ME efforts (Nicholls, Giles & Sethna, 2011).

Initiating SDP work in challenging environments can be difficult and frustrating. Examples of long-term, sustainable programming that appears to have a consistent positive impact for more than five years are rare. But the CTC Ten Foundation, AMANDLA EduFootball, and the Ikhusi Primary School in Khayelitsha, Site B, appear to be attaining positive outcomes through collaboration and cooperation, sound ME, and through engagement with community members in identifying community needs and implementing and improving programs designed to meet community objectives.

References

AMANDLA EduFootball (2015). *Annual Report 2013−2014*. Retrieved from <https://issuu.com/amandla/docs/amandla_edufootball_ar11_online_web>. Accessed 20 March 2017.

AMANDLA EduFootball (2016). *Monitoring and Evaluation Report*. Retrieved from <https://issuu.com/amandla/docs/20160914_evaluationreport_>. Accessed 20 March 2017.

AMANDLA EduFootball (2017a). *Amandla −AMANDLA EduFootball*. Retrieved from <www.edufootball.org/en/organisation-en/amandla/>. Accessed 20 March 2017.

AMANDLA EduFootball (2017b). *Welcome − AMANDLA EduFootball* [online]. Retrieved from <www.edufootball.org/en/welcome/>. Accessed 20 March 2017.

CTC Ten Foundation (2013). *Annual Report*. CTC Ten Foundation. Retrieved from <https://ctcten.org/wp-content/uploads/2015/01/CTCTen-Annual-Report-2013.pdf>. Accessed 20 March 2017.

CTC Ten Foundation (2014). *Annual Report*. Retrieved from <https://ctcten.org/wp-content/uploads/2014/12/CTC-Annual-Report.pdf>. Accessed 20 March 2017.

Ctcten.org. (2017). *About Us − CTC Ten Foundation*. Retrieved from <https://ctcten.org/about-ctc-ten/>. Accessed 20 March 2017.

Coalter, F. (2007). *A Wider Social Role for Sport* (1st edn). London: Routledge.

Coalter, F. (2013). *Sport for Development* (1st edn). London: Routledge.

Coalter, F. (n.d.). *Sport in Development: A Monitoring and Evaluation Manual*. Retrieved from <www.sportni.net/sportni/wp-content/uploads/2013/03/Sport_in_Development_A_monitoring_and_Evaluation_Manual.pdf>. Accessed 20 March 2017.

Colford-Schoeniger, J. (2010). "Ukuhamba Kukufunda: traveling is learning". *Franklin & Marshall Magazine*. Retrieved from <www.fandm.edu/magazine/archive/features/2010/06/30/ukuhamba-kukufunda-traveling-is-learning>. Accessed 20 March 2017.

Dixon, B. (2015). Making further inquiries: Policing in context in Brixton and Khayelitsha. *South African Crime Quarterly*, *53*, 5–14.

Fandm.edu (2009). Franklin & Marshall – An Emerald in the Rough. Retrieved from <www.fandm.edu/stories/an-emerald-in-the-rough>. Accessed 20 March 2017.

General Assembly resolution 58/5. Sport as a means to promote education, health, development and peace. A/RES/58/5 (17 November, 2003). Retrieved from <www.un.org/sport2005/resources/un_resolutions/engl_58_5.pdf>. Accessed 20 March 2017.

General Assembly resolution 67/296. International day of sport for development and peace. Retrieved from <www.un.org/en/ga/search/view_doc.asp?symbol=A/RES/67/296>. Accessed 20 March 2017.

Godiplomats.com (2017). Soccer Africa Project – Franklin & Marshall. Retrieved from <www.godiplomats.com/DAC/campaign/soccerafrica>. Accessed 20 March 2017.

Godiplomats.com (2008). Survivor Africa Winner and Fox Soccer Analyst Ethan Zohn Coming to F&M – Franklin & Marshall. Retrieved from <www.godiplomats.com/sports/m-soccer/spec-rel/022908aaa.html>. Accessed 20 March 2017.

International Olympic Committee (2016). *Olympic Charter*. Lausanne, Switzerland: International Olympic Committee.

Lancaster Online (2007). "F&M soccer player, 21, dies". Retrieved from <http://lancasteronline.com/sports/f-m-soccer-player-dies/article_826552fe-0e1e-59de-8530-62b35d68c6ed.html>. Accessed 20 March 2017.

Mansuri, G. and Rao, V. (2013). *Localizing Development* (1st edn). Washington, DC: World Bank.

Mosse, D. (2002). People's knowledge, participation, and patronage: Operations and representations in rural development. In D. Narayan-Parker (Ed.), *Empowerment and Poverty Reduction: A Sourcebook* (1st edn). Washington DC: World Bank.

Nicholls, S., Giles, A. R., & Sethna, C. (2011). Perpetuating the "lack of evidence" discourse in sport for development: Privileged voices, unheard stories and subjugated knowledge. *International Review for the Sociology of Sport, 46*(3), 249–264.

Qwayi, M. (2016). Khayelitsha clubs disappointed with Football for Hope. Workers' World Media Productions. Retrieved from <www.wwmp.org.za/index.php/publications/elitsha/303-khayelitsha-clubs-disappointed-with-football-for-hope>. Accessed 20 March 2017.

Sportanddev.org (2016). A call for greater collaboration | sportanddev.org. Retrieved from <www.sportanddev.org/en/news-views/international-day-sport-development-and-peace/idsdp-2016/call-greater-collaboration>. Accessed 20 March 2017.

Sugden, J. (2010). Critical left-realism and sport interventions in divided societies. *International Review for the Sociology of Sport, 45*, 258–272.

United Nations Inter-Agency Task Force on Sport for Development and Peace (2003). *Sport for development and peace: Towards achieving the Millennium Development Goals*. United Nations. Retrieved from <www.sportanddev.org/sites/default/files/downloads/16__sport_for_dev_towards_millenium_goals.pdf>. Accessed 20 March 2017.

Wainwright, O. (2014). "Apartheid ended 20 years ago, so why is Cape Town still a 'paradise for the few'?" The *Guardian*. Retrieved from <www.theguardian.com/citics/2014/apr/30/cape-town-apartheid-ended-still-paradise-few-south-africa>. Accessed 20 March 2017.

Windmann, A. (2013). "Beating FIFA at its own game in South Africa". *Der Spiegel*. Retrieved from <www.spiegel.de/international/world/amandla-soccer-school-in-cape-town-takes-on-poverty-a-914111.html>. Accessed 20 March 2017.

INDEX

Page numbers followed by "f" refer to figures and followed by "t" refer to tables.

Howard, D. R. 81, 82
Humphreys, B. R. 81, 82

Ikhusi Primary School, Khayelitsha 386, 388–389
image rights, athlete 214–223; *Abdul-Jabbar* v. *General Motors Corp.* (1996) 216; *Bedford* v. *The Number (118 118)* (2004) 219; comparative analysis of US and English law 219–220; *Douglas* v. *Hello!* (2003) 219; in English law 217–219; *Fenty* v. *Arcadia Group Brands Ltd* (2015) 219, 220; *Haelen Laboratories, Inc.* v. *Topps Chewing Gum, Inc.* (1953) 216, 220; *Halliwell* v. *Panini* (1997) 218; *Irvine* v. *Talksport Ltd* (2002) 219, 220; *Michael Jordan and Jump 23, Inc.* v. *Dominick's Finer Foods, LLC* (2015) 217, 220; *Mirage Studios* v. *Counter Feat Clothing* (1991) 218; *Palmer* v. *Schonhorn Enterprises* (1967) 216; passing-off, law tort of 218–219; *Proactive Sports Management Ltd* v. *Rooney & Ors* (2011), 218, 220; right of publicity in US 215–217; *Somerson* v. *World Wrestling Entertainment, Inc.* (2013) 217; suggestions for protecting 220–221; *Taverner Rutledge Ltd* v. *Trexpalm Ltd* (1975) 220; *Tolley* v. *J. S. Fry & Sons Ltd* (1931) 218
India, cricket in *see* cricket in India
Indian Premier League (IPL) 69, 348–349, 350, 352f, 353, 369
infrastructure: legacies of mega-events 58–59, 297; polycentric format and arguments for using existing 31, 33–34
Instagram, EAFL on 265
international circuits 40; ownership and rights 43
international competitions: burden on players, coaches and staff 84–85; export of national sport leagues and 5, 9
International Cricket League (ICL) 348
International Cricketing Council (ICC) 347, 348, 349
international management 69–70
international markets, playing regular season games in 79–86; brand awareness 81–82; burden of international competitions on players, coaches and staff 84–85; effects on domestic fan base 83–84; recent history 80–81; revenue generation 82–83; viable export strategy for global stage 85
international multi-sport games 40
International Olympic Committee (IOC): Agenda 2020 26–27, 57t, 60, 61, 92; athletes' committees 202, 205–206; attempt to reduce costs in bidding for Olympics 56; consumer perceptions of 87; monitoring of Olympic brand 88; reforms to combat corruption 62;

selecting hosts 57, 57t; use of GRI reporting tool 321
International Sport Federations (ISFs) 37–53; analytical model 44–46; commercialization of sports events 38; economic model 42–52; economic models, classification of 46; emerging commonalities 43–44; event ownership 42–43; event portfolio central to strategic and functional model 52; event types 39–40; events as a source of revenue 41, 41t; FIFA – one mega-event model 46–47, 47t; FIH – mixed model 49–50, 50t; financial cycles around events 43; FISA – Olympic-dependence model 50–51, 51t; future research 52; growing number and globalization of sports events 38; lack of research on major events from perspective of 38–39; main sources of revenue 40–42, 41t; Olympic revenue 42; Olympic revenue dependence 43–44; from regulating to commercializing events 37–39; resource strategies through major sport events 39–42; stakeholders and profit redistribution 52; UCI – fee-collector model 47–49, 48t
international trade: comparative advantages, theory of 185–186; contract law 193–194; economics of trade 185–186; enforcement schemes for international treaties 190, 191t; evolution from GATT/WTO to FTA 188–189; intellectual property rights 194; legal aspects of free trade agreements 189–191; non-cooperative equilibrium 186–187, 187t, 189, 189t; prisoner's dilemma 187, 188, 189; regional trade agreements 186–188; spectating sport industry and RTAs/FTAs 194–196; of sporting goods 184–185, 191–193; time-inconsistency problem 188
Iran: athlete endorsement in 100–101; celebrity characteristics 104; endorsement and culture 107; products for endorsement 105–106
Irvine v. *Talksport Ltd* (2002) 219, 220

Japan: baseball 81; golf in 274; hosting of mega-events 294; NBA in 80; tennis 113
Jinta Sport 370–371
Jozsa, F. P. 82
JYP Ice Hockey Club case study 378–379

kabbadi 350, 353
Kazakhstan, tennis in 114
Keller, K. L. 89, 95, 253, 257
Krugman, P. 188–189

Ladies Professional Golf Association (LPGA) Tour 271–276; Asian sponsors for Asian markets 274; decreasing US fan base 272–274;